The United States
in the Twentieth Century

The United
in the

PRENTICE-HALL, INC.
Englewood Cliffs, New Jersey 07632

States
Twentieth Century

MELVYN DUBOFSKY

State Univerity of New York at Binghamton

ATHAN THEOHARIS

Marquette University

DANIEL M. SMITH

Library of Congress Cataloging in Publication Data

DUBOFSKY, MELVYN
  The United States in the twentieth century.

  Bibliography
  Includes index.
    1. United States–History–20th century.
I. Theoharis, Athan G., joint author. II.–Smith,
Daniel Malloy, joint author. III. Title.
E741.D823   973.9   77–13246
ISBN 0–13–938712–9

THE UNITED STATES IN THE TWENTIETH CENTURY
Melvyn Dubofsky, Athan Theoharis, Daniel M. Smith

© 1978 by Prentice-Hall Inc., Englewood Cliffs, New Jersey 07632

Printed in the United States of America

10 9 8 7 6 5 4 3 2 1

PRENTICE-HALL INTERNATIONAL, INC., *London*
PRENTICE-HALL OF AUSTRALIA PTY. LIMITED, *Sydney*
PRENTICE-HALL OF CANADA, LTD., *Toronto*
PRENTICE-HALL OF INDIA PRIVATE LIMITED, *New Dehli*
PRENTICE-HALL OF JAPAN, INC., *Tokyo*
PRENTICE-HALL OF SOUTHEAST ASIA PTE. LTD., *Singapore*
WHITEHALL BOOKS LIMITED, *Wellington, New Zealand*

To the memory

of our distinguished colleague
and co-author, Daniel Smith

Contents

II

III

VI

GLOBAL WAR AND ITS RAMIFICATIONS 1939–1953   **287**

VII

VIII

IX

Preface

Writing confidently about the past is a difficult task at best, and especially writing about the twentieth century since events are too recent to permit thoughtful and objective appraisal. In addition, during this tumultuous century, the United States underwent a radical transformation from a predominantly rural agrarian to an urban industrial society; from a second-rate world power to the most powerful nation in the world; and from a more emotive populistic political stance to one more structured, impersonal, and elitist. Formerly wholly unimagined developments became commonplace—whether the ability to communicate instantaneously across millions of miles or the invention of products of convenience, such as the vacuum cleaner, the computer, and the transistor. Reinterpretations of these recent and profoundly dislocative changes further demonstrate that contemporary historians either have raised new questions about the past or have researched into formerly closed manuscript collections.

In no sense, then, can this volume be considered a comprehensive or definitive account. Until recently women's, black, and labor history and the policies of the intelligence community have not commanded the research interests of American historians writing on the twentieth century. The raising of new questions and different research emphases, in the future, will undoubtedly highlight our omissions. To minimize this possible deficiency, the authors have widely and carefully read the available literature—our effort necessarily reflects the emphases and themes of fellow historians writing about twentieth-century America. In addition, since "national security" and other restrictions have precluded research into relevant manuscript collections, especially for the post-1945 period, we recognize that the current scholarship might prove to be partial.

Nonetheless, we feel this book thoroughly covers the recent American past and is distinctive from other competing texts. Ours is not a traditional text focusing narrowly and in detail on economic, political, and diplomatic developments. While we have described the more important legislative and foreign policy decisions, we have also focused on the broader institutional, cultural, and intellectual forces shaping recent America. Thus, social and economic changes assume as important a place in this book as domestic and international politics. Changes in the status of women, ethnics, and labor; the bureaucratic changes altering the American presidency; and the rise of new more consolidated corporations, as much as legislative and national security strategy, contribute to an understanding of American domestic and foreign policy. Accordingly, we have focused on social change, and have given greater weight to what might be described as "popular fads" rather than to the high culture.

This study is organized around three themes. First, we have emphasized the forces of continuity and change besetting American culture and the economy; that is of fundamental persistence in the face of substantial structural change. Second, we have stressed the institutional character of American politics—the rise of the modern, powerful bureaucratic presidency; the cumulative growth of the intelligence community; and the more enduring congressional and party changes. Third, we have surveyed the emergence of the United States to a dominant world role and the particular interventionist and expansionist nature of that role. We might add that while this has been a collaborative effort, the three coauthors' principal contributions have been confined to their respective areas of expertise. Melvyn Dubofsky, however, served as general editor and wrote the section introductions.

Many debts were incurred in the writing of this text. While we cannot acknowledge personally all those who assisted us, we would like to thank our former students (graduate and undergraduate) whose queries contributed to our developing knowledge of this century, and our colleagues at the University of Colorado, SUNY-Binghamton, Wayne State University, and Marquette University who provided expert counsel and assistance. We express our particular indebtedness to Nina Asher, Paul Baker, John Berens, Peter Carlin, Pat Dolloway, Robert Griffith, Robert Hay, Jeanne Hoeting, Carolyn Aladeen Smith, Shirley Stone, Brian Walker, and Bernard Weisberger.

ATHAN THEOHARIS

I

The Past Is Prologue:
The United States in 1900

On New Year's Day 1900, the *New York Times* proclaimed: "Prosperity left scarcely any of our industries untouched and touched nothing it did not enrich. . . . The story of the Nation's material progress . . . is of a nature to appeal to the most ethereal mind and stir the most sluggish imagination." Its optimism about the future of the United States in the new century flowed from the realities of the American nation's material and human advantages and potentialities.

By 1900 the United States was the most populous of the advanced industrial capitalist nations and also the globe's most productive and richest economic power. It exported its surplus foodstuffs around the world; dominated the international oil trade; and led all other nations in the production of coal, iron, and steel; and its economic might translated into overseas power. The other capitalist and expansionist great powers, especially Great Britain, had come to recognize the United States as a participant in global power politics and in the "new imperialism" through which the western nations exercised their influence around the world. In 1900 the United States clearly dominated the Western Hemisphere and in the aftermath of the 1898 Spanish-American War made its influence manifest in the Pacific Ocean and on the Asian mainland as well.

The wealth and power of the United States in 1900, to be sure, was part of a longer historical process. The American present flowed ineluctably from its past and the social, economic, and political structures of the present presaged the shape of the American future. Understanding the context of American society, politics, and foreign policy in 1900 should enable students to see how the past influenced the present and then how in turn current developments shape future trends.

1

A People Many and Diverse: Society and Culture

History is the study of change in a society, an institution, an individual over time. If we are to understand precisely how American society and culture has changed in the twentieth century, we must begin with a clear comprehension of its structure and character in the year 1900. Not even for an instant, however, do the institutions and individuals that together form a society stand still in time. Thus the portrait of American society etched in the following pages will resemble more closely a single frame in a larger motion picture than an individual, integral snapshot. What we shall see can only be grasped in the perspective of the picture frames that preceded it and those that will follow. For a moment we will stop the camera of American history, focus on one isolated frame, enlarge that particular frame, and examine the fabric of society it exposes and the assets and flaws it reveals.

THE ETHNO-RELIGIOUS MIX

"No other large industrial society," writes David Riesman, noted scholar and social commentator, "has substituted color and ethnicity for social class as the basis of stratification and hence of tension." The United

States in 1900 was preeminently a land of immigrants and their children. By that date two immense waves of European immigration had already deposited millions of newcomers on American shores, and a third wave was just then swelling to tidal proportions. In a total population of roughly 76 million in the continental United States in 1900, 26 million, or more than one out of every three, were foreign born or the children of at least one foreign-born parent. Yet such aggregate figures, if anything, understate the dimensions of ethnicity in many regions of the nation. The South, for example, attracted few immigrants, and the immense region from the Great Plains to the Pacific Coast drew only a few hundred thousand. Some nine million immigrants clustered in the Northeastern and North Central states compared to just over a million in the South and West. Even in the industrial north the foreign born were not scattered among the populace. Immigrants and their children were much more likely to concentrate in cities with populations of over fifty thousand and, in general, were more apt to live in urban areas than in the countryside.

Population statistics drawn from several states and cities reveal a remarkable story. At the opening of the twentieth century, 75 percent of the people in Minnesota, 71 percent of those in Wisconsin, 65 percent in Rhode Island, and 63 percent in Massachusetts had at least one foreign-born parent. Late in the nineteenth century, 87 percent of the population in Chicago, 84 percent in Milwaukee and Detroit, 80 percent in New York City and Cleveland, and 78 percent in St. Louis and San Francisco were foreign born or the children of immigrants. In London, by way of contrast, 94 percent of the city's people came from England and Wales.

More remarkable than the absolute number of immigrants in American society was their diversity. No other nation among the world's several immigrant societies drew its inhabitants from as wide a variety of sources. Argentina, for example, lured 67 percent of its immigrants from Italy and Spain; Canada obtained half its settlers from the United Kingdom and another quarter from the United States; Australia and New Zealand recruited almost all their people from Great Britain. But the United States was to draw 12 percent of its immigrants from Italy; 13 percent from Austria-Hungary; 16 percent from Germany; 10 percent from Russia and Poland; 6 percent from Scandinavia; and about 30 percent from Great Britain and Ireland. In 1900 Americans could begin to discern, perhaps for the first time, the dimensions of that diversity. For in that year the number of immigrants arriving from the Slavic lands of east and central Europe and from southern Italy began to approach the massive levels that they would maintain for the next fourteen years.

Thus it was no wonder that for old-stock Americans and for the more established immigrant families from Ireland, the United Kingdom, and Germany, who composed the bulk of first- and second-generation Americans in 1900, the place of newcomers in national society became a hotly debated issue. Among old-line Americans in 1900 one would find

few advocates of cultural diversity but many promoters of "Americanization" and immigration restriction.

Demographic trends aggravated existing anxieties about the impact
of immigration. The immigrants, as a group, were younger, more male,
and seemingly more virile than the inhabitants in the society to which
they were drawn; statistics indeed indicated that immigrant families
tended to have more children than American-born families.

Never totally welcome in the United States, immigrants had to make
fundamental social adjustments. Most of the newcomers who arrived at
Ellis Island in 1900 had just completed a terrifying journey across the
European continent and three thousand miles of ocean. Now they were
about to make the even more frightening psychological journey from a
preindustrial to an industrial society. Torn by history and their own
volition from a traditional, ordered, and comprehensible way of life, they
had to acclimate to a new society and a different mode of existence. In
Oscar Handlin's words they were "uprooted"; the majority of non-Eng-
lish speaking immigrants were "in the new world but not of it." As one
immigrant later recalled his own experience: "I practically knew nothing
of what was happening in the United States . . . almost none of the
American culture penetrated into our settlement. . . . What we acquired by way of culture was almost completely that of our own. . . . we
were demoralized indeed." And because each group of immigrants
brought different cultural baggage with them to the United States, they
interpreted the American experience and reacted to it in different ways,
thus further diversifying the national culture.

Lest we forget, European immigrants were not the only "aliens" in
United States society. In the year 1900 roughly 12 percent of the
population was nonwhite—the vast majority black, with a substantial
minority of Indians, and a smattering of Chinese and Japanese concentrated on the West Coast and in the Rocky Mountain states. Remarkably
what is today one of the largest nonwhite groups in American society—
the so-called Chicanos, individuals of Mexican origin—was so invisible in
1900 that census officials did not even bother to take separate note of its
existence.

Like European immigrants, nonwhites tended to be concentrated
geographically. Almost eight million of the less than nine million American blacks still resided in the South, where the vast majority of them
worked a white man's land, with a white man's mule and a white man's
credit. Other nonwhites were concentrated in the Mountain West and
Pacific Coast states.

In 1900 blacks and Indians had little reason to be content with their
place in national society. Not only had Indians been defeated, and in
some cases exterminated, during the 1880s and 1890s in the course of
armed conflict, but by 1900 the dominant white man's society had destroyed the Indians' last remaining defense—their tribal society and
heritage. Denied his traditional tribal collective existence, stigmatized by
color, warped by successive defeats and betrayals, condemned to illiteracy

and poverty, the American Indian nevertheless was expected to compete in the economic marketplace. The results were to be expected; with some exceptions, Indians sank ever lower into poverty and despondency.

Blacks in 1900 could also look back on a series of political and social defeats. The gains of Reconstruction had been whittled away in the course of the 1870s and 1880s. Then, the creation of the Jim Crow system with its formal legal exclusion from voting and separation in public facilities replaced illegal and extralegal intimidation. And for those blacks who demanded the minimal legal rights that remained theirs, there always lurked the threat of lynching and assassination.

Blacks, like "new" immigrants, had reason to be "demoralized indeed." Significantly the same institution—the church—flourished among both blacks and immigrants as their first line of defense, and sometimes resistance, against a hostile dominant society. Which brings us to one of the paradoxes of American society and culture in the year 1900.

For almost half a century the Western world had seen organized, institutional religion stagger under the heavy blows delivered by science and secularism. Wherever industries and cities spread, formal religious affiliation and church attendance seemed to decline, especially among working-class men. Yet in the United States over the same time period formal religion prospered. Almost all religious bodies experienced a steady growth in membership, until by 1900 more than one-third of all Americans claimed a church affiliation.

How can this trend be explained? The only logical answer readily at hand is the one suggested above: religion's role in protecting and preserving the culture of immigrants and nonwhites in a hostile social environment. Statistics offer some confirmation for this hypothesis. In 1900 the Roman Catholic Church had more than twice as many members as its largest Protestant competitor, and the Catholic Church was preeminently that of the Irish and southern- and eastern-European immigrants. Among Protestant churches the two largest were those with the most substantial black followings: the Methodists and Southern Baptists.

In a society already marked, if not scarred, by ethnic and racial divisions, religious differences, too, often compounded other aspects of social and cultural conflict. In 1900 not only were Italian immigrants considered less desirable than Germans or Scandinavians, but also they were most likely Catholics, in a society whose dominant values had been molded by the Protestant faith. So, too, did Jewish immigrants bear the double burden of social distinctiveness and non-Christian beliefs. Was it any wonder that Catholics and Protestants, Jews and Christians sometimes fought in the streets and more often divided at the polling booths?

On July 30, 1902, for example, when New York City Jews participated in a mass funeral procession for their deceased chief rabbi through the streets of the lower East Side, an Irish-led mob stoned and attacked the mourners. The Irish were apparently incensed at being pushed out of the neighborhood by Jewish immigrants. Leaders of the Jewish community later charged that the Irish police joined in the rioting and habitually treated newcomers with contempt and even brutality. Recalling life in his own Chicago immigrant community of the 1890s, one Jewish American, Abraham Bisno, remarked: "Our neighbors hated us, and our lives and property were not safe." The comment of an Irish labor organizer who had to recruit members among the heterogeneous work force in the Chicago meatpacking industry illustrated the latent racism characteristic of American society. "However it may go against the grain," he counselled fellow Irish-American unionists, "we must admit that common interests and brotherhood must include the Polack and the Sheeny." How ironical that Polish- and Jewish-Americans would seek brotherhood among those who characterized them as "Hunkies" and "Kikes."

As tumultuously and as often as American immigrant groups clashed among themselves, several factors softened the harshness of ethnic conflict. The relative prosperity of the first decade of the twentieth century acted as a solvent for social and economic anxieties. Thus most immigrants fared better materially in the new world than in the old, and the struggle between ethnic groups lost some of its economic edge. And the more ambitious and talented among the newcomers assimilated most rapidly and easily into the host society, their successes removing them as leaders for potentially destructive forms of ethnic warfare.

THE URBAN PROSPECT

By 1900 more and more of the diverse people who composed the American population, whether they came from Europe or United States farms, were settling in cities. Over thirty million individuals now lived in urban areas, which while still less heavily populated than rural America, were growing much more rapidly in population. Moreover, within urban America, large cities consistently demonstrated the most impressive pattern of growth. The age of the industrial city had arrived and with it, as we shall see, the beginnings of the modern metropolitan area, including the central city and its outlying suburbs.

The American city in 1900, as had been true throughout most of the nineteenth century, remained unconducive to good health and long life. Indeed, in some urban areas, especially immigrant and nonwhite slums, the death rate ran the birth rate a close race, leaving precious little room for indigenous population increase. Thus the masses who swelled the population of urban America came from elsewhere. Between 1880 and 1900, six to seven million Americans deserted the countryside for the city. Most of the nine million immigrants who came to the United States in the same period also ended their journeys in urban areas. Urban America thus proved an enormous sponge soaking up the excess American and European rural populations and, in the process, creating cities characterized by substantial settlements of first-generation urbanites.

Just as technological change in Europe and the United States de-

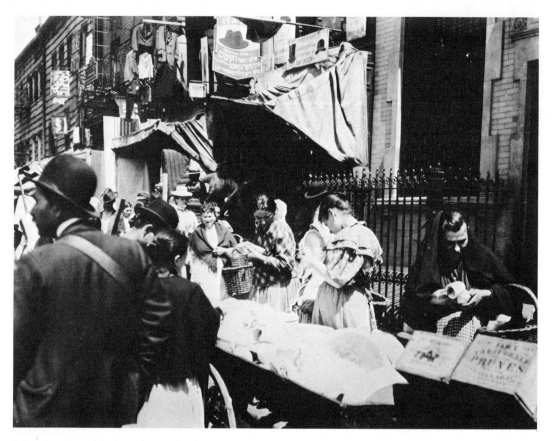

Urban immigrant life, lower East Side of New York,
c. 1890–1914

The Byron Collection/Museum of the City of
New York

populated the countryside, it also transformed urban geography. Throughout history cities had clustered along major waterways, the primary source of transportation in the preindustrial era. In the United States most large cities could be found on the Atlantic and Gulf coasts or along such major internal waterways as the Hudson, Connecticut, Ohio, and Mississippi Rivers. But by 1900, with the railroad age in full growth, urban growth had been liberated from dependence on water transport. Chicago, a railroad center, had far outdistanced St. Louis, the old Queen City of the Mississippi, in all the indicators of urban growth. Railroads had also pushed Cleveland ahead of Cincinnati as Ohio's leading city, while transforming the Pittsburgh-Youngstown district into the nation's iron and steel heartland. Even in the deep South the most rapid urban growth occured in the inland cities of Atlanta and Birmingham.

Transport innovation, however, played an even more critical role in reshaping the internal dimensions of the city. For most of the nineteenth century the distance a man could reasonably walk from home to work controlled the physical and social structure of cities. In such cities, where spatial growth was limited, the vast majority of inhabitants clustered in the center, a district composed of variegated social groups and mixed land uses. There upper-class elites, substantial middle-class residents, respectable working-class citizens, and pockets of the so-called dangerous classes lived in close proximity; banks, mercantile establishments, small shops and factories, churches, theaters, and private residences adjoined each other. But this traditional "walking city" was to suffocate in its own success.

As city populations grew, they packed the old central cities more densely than ever, causing land values to rise substantially and hence the cost of housing and business. More tenants had to be packed into existing structures to meet rising costs, and new buildings had to use every available inch of physical space in order to turn a profit. Consequently residential housing in the core deteriorated and the more substantial elements among the urban populace looked elsewhere for comfortable accommodations. The financial institutions, department stores, theaters, and other basic urban institutions remained in the city center in 1900 but now they were encircled by a ring of filth, disease, and crime. Many an old city downtown was surrounded by rubbish heaps, junk piles, and pools of foul water with rivers, creeks, and streams serving as open sewers. Those few intrepid upper-class people who remained behind in the inner city endured a nightly process of "battening-down the house" to ward off fear and crime.

By 1900 the flight from the center city had been long under way. First horse cars, then cable cars and electric trolleys (1888), and finally elevated railways and subways took people by the millions to new urban sites where land was cheaper and the surroundings more pleasant. Because most cities still retained internal space for expansion the bulk of the population flight from the center still ultimately terminated within city limits; in other words suburbanization was a city phenomenon before it became a metropolitan one.

Perhaps the most remarkable feature of urban development was its uniformity. Everywhere in urban America, despite the absence of planning and zoning codes, thousands of individual decisions led to the same results. New neighborhoods, and neighbors, sorted themselves out on the basis of wealth and occupation rather than nationality and religion, though, as we have seen, ethno-religious affiliation and class position frequently went hand-in-hand. The newly settled regions closest to the city center tended to be packed with respectable white-collar and working-class types who occupied small dwellings of uniformly homely appearance. As the transportation arteries pushed farther out, districts settled by prominent businessmen and professionals developed. These latter neighborhoods more closely approached the suburban ideal of a separate detached house set on a large grassy lot well provided with trees.

Changed patterns of residence brought new styles of life along with new anxieties. As commuting became a common fact of life, the American family assumed its characteristic twentieth-century manifestation. Father left the home daily for work in the office or factory; children departed for school; and mother remained home alone to tend house and care for any preschool children. In the "new suburbs," sprawling districts that lacked a physical center conducive to collective activities, residents withdrew into the security of the tightly-knit nuclear family. Even working-class families, which could not approach the middle-class suburban ideal, found their traditional style of life altered, as this comment by a Cincinnati worker indicates: "When I lived down on Richmond Street in a little house we cooked the corn beef and cabbage in the house and ate it in there, and when we wanted to go to the toilet we went out in the yard; now I live in a fine house, I am made to eat out in the yard, and when I go to the toilet I have to go into the house."

Those who fled to the suburbs in order to find security and comfort grew ever more fearful of the "unrespectable" types left behind. Physical as well as social distance began to separate the upper classes from the lower classes. In the rearranged pattern of urban geography no one could be sure what forces would keep the city poor in their proper place. Thus by 1900 among middle- and upper-class Americans fear of social conflict, mob violence, and senseless crime was a common anxiety. For the remainder of the twentieth century the history of the relationship between upper-class and lower-class Americans would revolve around attempts to create new instruments of social control to replace the mythical old patterns of emulation, neighborly charity, and deference that had allegedly prevailed in the socially heterogeneous traditional "walking city."

COUNTRY LIFE

Although the nature of American life had become considerably more urban by 1900, the majority of individuals still lived in rural areas. What was the style of their lives? If rural Americans were not plagued by foul environments, poor health, and short life expectancies, they had other difficulties and disabilities to ponder.

Just as urban life was becoming marked by sharper lines of class and residential differentiation, rural society was growing more stratified economically. In 1900 fully two-fifths of all farmers were tenants of one type or another, while in the South over half of all farmers were not independent owner-operators. The countryside moreover counted more farm workers than either owners or tenants. The size of the typical farm had grown steadily and so consequently had the costs of farm-making. As a result, it became harder for the rural wage worker to become a tenant and in turn for the tenant to become an owner. Little wonder, then, that the children of less successful farmers together with tenants and farm workers drifted to the cities, especially in prosperous times.

Few aspects of rural life functioned to keep the less successful in the countryside. Indeed the compensations of agrarian existence often proved less than the costs. Hard, drudging physical labor and social isolation characterized life in the countryside. Instead of living in compact rural villages, American farmers were widely scattered across the land and spatially separated from neighbors on their own individual homesteads. The lack of hardtop roads and the slowness of horse-drawn transportation made socializing at best an occasional break in a lonely existence. By 1900 electricity had penetrated even the city slums, but not the countryside. Middle-class urbanites could telephone each other; not so even prosperous farmers. City dwellers had their mail delivered to the door

A rural scene, Black River Falls, Wisc., c. 1890–1914

State Historical Society of Wisconsin

and newspapers available on the streets. Country residents in 1900 had to travel to the nearest town with a post office in order to pick up their mail or purchase a newspaper. Instead of debating whether to attend the latest vaudeville, burlesque, or operetta, the country cousin eagerly awaited his Sears, Roebuck catalogue or the once-a-summer encampment usually featuring a prominent religious evangelist.

Of necessity, fundamental Protestantism and traditional Catholicism remained the rootbed of agrarian culture. All twentieth-century life's salient features seemed to conspire against rural America. Although education was increasing in importance, country schools had shorter years, briefer days, and far fewer resources than their urban counterparts. It was these aspects of rural existence that motivated President Theodore Roosevelt to appoint a Country Life Commission.

WEALTH, INCOME, AND CLASS

Differentiated by nationality, religion, and neighborhood, Americans in the year 1900 were also sharply divided by income, wealth, and class. Whether the United States was ever at any time in its history a land of economic equality has been cast into grave doubt by recent scholarship. That enormous inequalities existed in 1900 is beyond dispute.

What, then, were the realities of social class in turn-of-the-century America? Obviously, position, or status, in society was not directly inherited; that is, fathers could not legally confer their advantages on their children. Room did exist for the emergence of Carnegies—poor immigrant lads whose driving ambition might win them wealth and power—and Rockefellers—American-born boys of modest origins who might turn dreams of industrial empire into reality. But the Carnegies and Rockefellers were patently the grand exceptions to the reality of the American social order. In most cases, family position and the advantages or disadvantages it conferred on its members governed prospects for social advance. Most members of the corporate elite, as well as independent professionals and leading public servants, were drawn from the American-born, Protestant middle and upper classes. The more protracted and more substantial an individual's formal education, the more likely it was that he would achieve superior position and wealth in society. Moreover, the opportunity for secondary and collegiate education depended largely on family status and income; in 1900 postprimary schooling remained a privilege for the minority.

Those individuals fortunate enough to inherit social position or of sufficient cunning to claw their way to the top commanded the major share of society's material resources. The top 1 percent of the population had in excess 10 percent of all income, and the top 5 percent probably possessed more than 25 percent of all income. Disposable income held by the wealthy probably exceeded their proportion of gross income because the existing taxes in 1900 were without exception regressive in impact, hitting the poor relatively harder than the well-to-do. Skewed and unequal as was the distribution of income, the possession of wealth was even more lopsided. Few Americans in 1900 outside the top 10 or 15 percent of the population had any claims to wealth beyond their modest homes and savings bank deposits. And the top 1 percent of Americans owned over 40 percent of the gross national wealth.

Most Americans had to be content with modest incomes and with limited chances for personal or family advancement. Children of day laborers sometimes rose to the ranks of the skilled, and workers' offspring might shed a blue collar for a white one. Sometimes, however, this process worked in reverse with children falling below their parents' rank of the social and occupational ladder. Most workers in 1900 could also look back on a steady, if not spectacular, improvement in wages and living standards. It must be borne in mind, however, that the bulk of the gain in wages came from a falling price level (deflation) and the more rapid growth of employment in high wage industries (iron and steel) than in low wage sectors (textiles), not from any decisive increase in basic wage and earning levels. Even for most of the more fortunate workers, reality was an annual income that allowed little room for personal or family illness, leisure, vacations, and nothing for unexpected unemployment.

If most American wage earners could count on modest improvements in their material circumstances, a substantial percentage in 1900 nevertheless existed at or below the poverty level. Robert Hunter in his classic study of poverty first published in 1904 estimated that in turn-of-the-century Boston and New York nearly 20 percent of the population lived in "distress." Over one-fifth of the people in the nation's industrial states, Hunter asserted, lived in poverty, caused primarily by unemployment, followed at some distance by old age, illness, and youthful dependence.

Income was related to skill, which derived in turn from family background and educational opportunities. This meant that in American society, income and social class could be directly correlated with nationality, race, and religion. The newer immigrants from eastern and southern Europe, mostly Catholic in religion, peasant or preindustrial artisan in occupation, and minimally educated, formed the bulk of a low-paid, unskilled, casual labor force. Frequently in the case of such immigrant families poverty was avoided only at the cost of putting all members to work regardless of age or sex. Low as the newer immigrants' place in the American social order may have been, white American-born workers and nonwhite Americans usually occupied a position several rungs lower on the economic ladder. Since wages tended to be lower in rural than in urban areas and less for workers who migrated from farms, American-born laborers, as the nation's most rural, nonindustrial stratum, often clustered near the bottom of the occupational ladder and wage scale. Yet, invariably, the gap in earnings between the lowest paid white worker and the typical nonwhite exceeded that between more fortunate white laborers and newer immigrants.

Morbidity, morality, and education statistics shed further light on basic class disparities in American society. Unfortunately no statistical series distinguished among white Americans on the basis of class, but we do possess information clearly separating black and white health and life expectancies, and we can make some implicit assumptions about white working-class conditions from the data available. In 1900 white Americans had a life expectancy at birth of 47.6 years; black Americans, 33.0 years. The age-adjusted death rate in that same year was for whites 17.8 per thousand and for blacks 27.8. Aside from those diseases associated with old age, the most common causes of death in 1900 were tuberculosis, influenza, and pneumonia—pulmonary diseases, which especially afflicted the poor. Indeed, at that time, tuberculosis was commonly referred to as the workingman's "white plague," though it claimed its heaviest toll in black lives. In Massachusetts, one of the most industrialized states, tuberculosis was in 1900 by far the greatest single cause of

Lynching the black man in white America
U.S. Information Agency

death, and the disease was most commonly found in such congested mill cities as Lawrence, Lowell, and Lynn.

Those working-class youths fortunate enough to survive childhood could not in 1900 expect wide educational opportunity. Only slightly in excess of 500,000 youths attended secondary school in that year, and 94,883, or 6.4 percent of the seventeen-year-old population graduated from high school. Only 238,000 Americans, or 4.01 percent of the population between the ages of eighteen and twenty-one, attended institutions of higher learning. As usual nonwhite Americans lagged far behind other citizens. Some 20 percent fewer nonwhites were enrolled in school, and in 1900 44.5 percent of nonwhites were illiterate compared to 6.2 percent of white Americans. Obviously, then, in 1900 an American's class and family position determined to a large extent his educational, health, career, and life chances.

CULTURE: POPULAR AND HIGHBROW

In 1900 American culture stood on the threshold of an era of enormous creativity, a time when literary figures would not have to flee the country in the manner of Henry James to escape an environment fostering innocence and simplicity. But in 1900 the United States did not yet possess the self-contained society of intellectuals and bohemians that would become so prominent in the years just before World War I. Such sophisticated writers as Mark Twain and William Dean Howells catered to a genteel society that applauded bourgeois platitudes and homilies.

For the mass of Americans, however, culture began and ended with the daily and Sunday newspapers. In a basically literate society, the newspaper proved an indispensable source of information, entertainment, and gossip. By 1900, as a result of technological innovations, the newspaper had assumed its modern form. The telegraph and telephone provided the foundation for the creation of national wire services, which offered basic national and international news to local newspapers that were unable to employ large reportorial staffs. Improved techniques of printing and photo reproduction made possible the production of cheap Sunday editions with large rotogravure sections and colorful comic strips. Those papers most lavish in their use of photography, comic strips, and color, as well as most willing to add other popular features, won the mass of the reading public. Even foreign-language papers followed the pattern, as the history of the most successful among them—the *Jewish Daily Forward*—illustrates.

For entertainment, Americans thus turned to the "Yellow Kid," "The Katzenjammer Kids," "Happy Hooligan," and "The Toonerville Trolley," comic strips that generally portrayed a society more bucolic and innocent than the one in which most newspaper readers lived. For information about how to behave in an urban society, they turned to the etiquette columns, the women's page, and advice to the lovelorn. "Miss

Lonelyhearts" had arrived in the United States. In its "bintel brief" the Yiddish-language *Forward* offered the same services, including guidance about how traditional parents should deal with Americanized children or how proper Americans blew their noses in public. For hard news there were the dispatches of such intrepid reporters and adventurers as the famous Richard Harding Davis, and for editorial comment the advice of such notable editors as Arthur Brisbane.

More genteel and respectable citizens, however, might prefer such staid newspapers as the *New York Sun* or *Times* and also take a regular weekly or monthly magazine. But even the magazine world had been transformed in 1900 by technological change. Now much cheaper to produce and available at a lower price, magazines could seek a wider audience. Thus the conventional magazines of the Gilded Age—*Nation, Century, Atlantic*—lost popularity to the sprightlier, more entertaining publications of the new century: *Saturday Evening Post, McClure's, World's Work, Ladies' Home Journal.* Just as the newspapers offered working-class readers moral advice, family counseling, and political guidance, the magazines gave their middle-class audiences those services, with a little more polish and refinement.

What Americans chose to read in 1900 was simple, escapist literature, not sophisticated social realism or abstract psychological analysis. As Mark Twain grew more somber and subtle in style and content, his reading public diminished. William Dean Howells never won a mass audience, and Henry James could expect still fewer American readers. Historical adventures, pure romances, and rural tales were the best sellers. Winston Churchill, the popular novelist from New England, was already by 1900 a best-selling author, and he would remain so throughout the pre-World War I years as he produced one simple, morally didactic novel after another.

Cultural and recreational activities also assumed ethnic and class dimensions. Serious drama, symphonic music, and grand opera appealed only to a select audience drawn mostly from among the more highly educated middle and upper classes. Masses of Americans found their entertainment at neighborhood theaters, which they packed for the latest vaudeville and musical comedy sketches. This popular theater reflected quite candidly the character of society. Irish- and German-American dialect comedy teams such as Harrigan and Hart and Weber and Fields indicated the ethnic composition of the vaudeville audiences. And the popularity of the minstrel show with its black-faced white performers personified America's image of the black man. Blacks were to be parodied and laughed at—but only whites were capable of playing the stage roles. The black musician and composer Scott Joplin, who pioneered ragtime melodies and was rediscovered in the 1970s as a result of the musical score for the Academy Award winning film, *The Sting*, wrote his songs and even an opera in relative obscurity during the first years of the twentieth century. Out of such vaudeville theaters and the even more ubiquitous local taverns would come such giants of the popular music world as George M. Cohan and Irving Berlin. Again and again the ethnic strain would enrich popular culture in the United States.

While ethnic influences were readily apparent in popular music and comedy, for some inexplicable reason they seemed negligible in the realm of athletics. No Old World sport or game won more than an ethnic clientele in the United States. At a time when the world of sports was becoming increasingly commercialized and professionalized, all the popular athletic pasttimes were singularly American in origin—baseball, collegiate football, basketball—or not identifiable with any special group or nation—boxing, riding, golf, and tennis. Baseball and boxing, the former on the eve of its establishment as our first mass spectator sport, the latter existing in a shadowy world of middle-class moral disapproval and working-class favor, remained the most popular sports. In those sports poor farm boys and the sons of urban immigrant parents might win fame and fortune.

The upper classes and middle classes, too, had their favorite games. Those with aristocratic pretensions might ride to the hounds in parts of New England and Pennsylvania but especially in Virginia and Maryland. With the increasing popularity of tennis and golf, country clubs sprouted in less crowded city districts and all around the suburban fringes of the nation. And the sons of the equestrian and country club sets could go off to college and gain glory as football players.

Comparatively few Americans, regardless of class, participated in organized or professional sports. For most urban working-class children informal street games, if not outright delinquent activities, formed the core of their play experiences. For their parents, the saloon and the occasional picnic or boat ride sponsored by the local political or ethnic club provided the core of their recreational activities. Respectable middle-class Americans entertained themselves at the church social or at home in the parlor, especially if they lived in more suburban or rural districts. The wealthy, however, could and did take their pleasure at a variety of domestic and foreign vacation resorts—from Newport, Rhode Island, and Saratoga Springs, New York, to Gstaad, Switzerland, and Paris, France.

American society, then, on the eve of the new century was torn by divisions of class, ethnicity, and race. Farmers and workers fought the wealthy business leaders who controlled the United States corporate economy. Their battles shaped the politics of the 1890s. And in the new century no question would be more central to politics than the issue of who ruled the country: the "monopolists" or the "people"? Despite the economic factors often at the root of domestic politics, cultural issues sometimes took precedence. Throughout the South by 1900 the dominant Democrats served as the party of white supremacy, and in the north and west Democrats and Republicans were distinguished more by disputes about immigration, Catholicism, and temperance than by divisions over material or economic questions. Domestic tensions, which intensified during the depression of the 1890s, also influenced United States foreign policy. The nation's emergence as a world power during the Spanish-American War satisfied domestic needs as much as overseas ambitions. Thus the past molded the present and the structure of American society influenced politics and foreign policy.

2

The Structure and Content
of Politics

Throughout the last three decades of the nineteenth century, the forces of political protest struggled against the forces conducive to stability and persistence. Insurgents within the two major parties and genteel middle-class reformers sought to make their political influence felt as third-party advocates, while Republican and Democratic party leaders maneuvered to build more durable and modern structures for politics and government. In the presidential election of 1896 when the Republican party defeated its Democratic-Populist opponents, the forces of stability and persistence seemed to win a substantial victory. A majority of the voters had legitimated the politics of professionalism and modernity. Yet when the new century dawned in 1900, the forces of reform would enter the political arena to win triumphs unexpected during the previous century.

POLITICAL CONSOLIDATION

By 1900, municipal, state, and federal politics had become more impersonal, more professionalized, and less responsive to popular protest. Contributing to this development was a new breed of politicians. The primary commitment of those active in politics—U.S. Senators like Matt Quay of Pennsylvania (1887–1899, 1901–1904), Tom Platt of New York (1881, 1897–1909), Nelson Aldrich of Rhode Island (1881–1911), Arthur Gorman of Maryland (1881–1899, 1903–1906), William Allison of Iowa (1873–1908)—was not principally to implement their vision of a better society. Instead they sought a personally advantageous niche in a successful profession, or as a New York City machine politician contended, "when a man works in politics, he should get something out of it."

The professional's concern was for efficiency and stability. Disorder and disruption must be minimized to insure political success. By astutely using patronage at all political levels, by being sensitive to the needs of an immigrant, lower-class population, and by exploiting power to secure campaign contributions, the professional politicians had forged highly efficient state and local party organizations. Indeed, the years 1860–1880 witnessed the birth of the city machine organized by colorful ward bosses—James McManes (Philadelphia), William Flinn (Pittsburgh), Ed Butler (St. Louis), Martin Lomasney (Boston), and George Plunkitt and William Tweed (New York)—whose power did not necessarily derive from holding elective office. The most notorious machine, the Tweed Ring of New York City, amassed an estimated $200 million during the 1860s through the sale of fraudulent bonds and franchises and through graft collected from corrupt contractors and merchants dealing directly with the city of New York.

Since their basic concern was stability, these new politicians also tended to be nonideological. Political leaders did not seek to assume advanced, controversial stands on social or economic questions, and parties ceased to be structured around issues. In fact, political success largely required defusing issues whenever popular demands intensified and problems grew critical.

These organizational changes meant that a strong two-party system became even less vulnerable to popular protest or third-party politics. At the same time, the two major parties (the Republicans and the Democrats) adopted strikingly similar positions on major issues. That perceptive British commentator, Lord James Bryce, accurately portrayed the American political scene in the 1880s when he wrote:

> neither party has any principle, any distinctive tenets. Both have traditions. Both claim to have tendencies. Both have certainly war cries, organizations, interests enlisted in their support. But their interests are in the main the interests of getting or keeping the patronage of the government.*

The desire for power also enhanced the ability of state party leaders to limit political action and dissident factionalism. The ambitious young man interested in a successful political career usually found it expedient

---

* *The American Commonwealth,* Vol. I (New York: G. P. Putnam's Sons, 1959), p. 151.

to cooperate with the established party leadership. And U.S. senators oftentimes emerged as powerful state party leaders. Senators were then elected by the state legislature and not by the people. Thus, to become senator required that that aspirant's party command a majority in the state legislature. After election, senators retained a close interest in their party's strength and in state and local political developments leading them to support a more disciplined party system. The senator's traditional interest in reelection had thus become transmuted by the new politics into a devotion to party. Although other public officials—including congressmen, state legislators, and governors—were popularly elected, a party system dedicated more to stability than to public service developed similar procedures to curb pressure from below. Before 1900, nomination to these posts was not obtained by popular vote but through state party conventions. Political advancement was the reward for party loyalty. Renomination could be foreclosed regardless of an incumbent's popularity, though the rejected candidate could choose to stand as an independent.

In sum, then, the public's influence on national and state politics had been reduced from what it had been in 1860, and this despite the closeness of election contests between Democrats and Republicans. In the presidential elections of 1876–1892, for example, the successful candidate did not poll a majority of the popular vote and, except in 1892, the winning plurality was less than 1 percent. Electoral campaigns were not, however, the occasion for intensive debate over issues or philosophy of governance. Moreover, while social and economic questions were largely ignored, moral issues such as prohibition and observance of the Sabbath were heatedly debated. An individual's religious, ethnic, or racial characteristics proved the most powerful indicator of party loyalty, and politicians tailored their campaigns around ethno-religious issues.

The structure of state politics also indirectly insured that either party would avoid nominating controversial presidential candidates. The resourceful, dynamic leader would have antagonized too many of the powerful in his party, thereby foreclosing his chances for nomination. Acceptability to the party's various factions virtually assured that presidential candidates would be attractive personalities, but men of limited vision without a well-thought-out legislative program. As a consequence, during the late nineteenth century successful nominees were bland, non-controversial personalities (Ulysses Grant, Rutherford Hayes, James Garfield, Grover Cleveland, Benjamin Harrison, William McKinley). At times the final election was based on nonpolitical issues; salient issues during the 1884 presidential campaign included Grover Cleveland's fathering of an illegitimate child and James Blaine's corruptibility, his earlier efforts to cover-up his questionable relations with railroad lobbyists, and his acceptance of a Protestant clergyman's description of the Democrats as the party of "rum, Romanism, and rebellion." Democrats of this era directed their appeal to white Southerners, Catholic immigrants and their children, while Republicans appealed to American-born Protestants, prohibitionists, and Afro-Americans.

A MORE STRUCTURED CONGRESS

Responding to the same pressures to rationalize state party politics, the House and Senate were transformed during the last decade of the nineteenth century into efficient and centralized bodies. In both federal legislative bodies, a new and numerically small leadership emerged to power by imposing party discipline. Having transformed Congress's institutional structure, this leadership could dominate national politics and shape the formulation of final legislative action.

Given the number of its members, the House of Representatives had always been an unwieldy body. The increase in Congress's legislative responsibilities following post-Civil War territorial and industrial expansion and population growth had made the House even more unwieldy. Long before the Civil War the committee system had evolved and rules of procedure had been adopted delineating how legislation was to be introduced and debated. During the 1890s, these institutional developments were refined and transformed to the influence of those congressmen who were committee chairman or who were members of the rules, appropriations, or ways and means committees. Until then, committee assignments and advancement either to committee chairman or to the powerful rules-making committees of the House had been done through the chaotic and inefficient process of the party caucus. Members of Congress of the same party would caucus to discuss common strategy, including committee assignments and legislative priorities. Decisions were not binding, and seniority did not determine assignment or advancement. There existed, moreover, no formalized means to impose party discipline and to assure the authority of the party leadership over junior or dissident members.

The principal discipline over House members derived from the significant powers of appointment and recognition wielded by the Speaker of the House. Yet the Speaker had not been able to expedite House business. He could not always prevent consideration of bills he opposed or guarantee passage of those he favored. All this changed with the election of the Republican Thomas Reed to the speakership in December 1889. Sensing support within his party for a more efficient system to minimize Democratic obstruction, in February 1890, Reed used Republican control of the House to institute major rules changes. These changes empowered the Speaker to declare certain motions dilatory, thereby reducing floor debate, and to prevent "disappearing quorums" by declaring House members present who were on the floor but who refused to be recognized. Assuming the chairmanship of the Rules Committee with the authority to appoint the other members to that committee, and exercising strategically the Speaker's prerogative of recognizing members during floor debate, Reed imposed a measure of discipline in the House, centralized power, and, thereby, enhanced the leadership's authority. Reed's actions encountered Democratic resistance and the next Democratic Congress did not continue his rules. Reed, however, had created the precedent of strong leadership and discipline. This precedent was not reversed.

Joseph Cannon's election to the speakership in 1903 resulted in even more basic changes in House procedures. Building upon the system Reed had forged and David Henderson (Speaker, 1899–1903) had refurbished, Cannon added a more authoritarian cast. Basically, Cannon employed his prerogative as Speaker to appoint like-minded members to the Rules Committee. Through control of this committee, he manipulated legislative calendars to avert floor action on bills he opposed, to expedite consideration of measures he favored, and to reward those congressmen who supported his leadership. Cannon further acted to control the Ways and Means Committee—important because of this committee's authority to select committee chairmen or to make committee assignments. The Cannon-dominated Ways and Means Committee acted to insure loyalty and discipline, ignoring experience, even seniority, when making committee assignments. As Speaker, with the authority to recognize individual members during debate, to determine the composition of the Rules and the Ways and Means Committees, and to make parliamentary rulings, Cannon significantly shaped the House's legislative actions. He used his power to further conservative policy objectives and thwart dissident congressmen. And Cannon used his control of the Rules Committee to stop any attempt to reform the rules of the House.

The same process, though far less personal and arbitrary, occurred in the Senate. Before the 1890s, senators had been unwilling to institute the House's more regularized procedures for making committee assignments, determining the order of business, and proscribing the duration of debate. Jealous of their power, vain and ambitious, and sensitive to their states' sectional interests, senators guarded their independence and prerogatives. The party caucus alone provided the vehicle for insuring orderly process in the Senate. Lacking the means to effect party discipline and the consideration of legislation, the caucus system precluded neither independent action nor long and dilatory debate. By the late 1880s, then, many influential senators concluded that a more formalized system was needed. At the same time, the vagaries of popular protest posed additional incentives to instill some discipline on the conduct of Senate business.

William Allison's election to the chairmanship of the Republican caucus in March 1897 provided the opportunity for changing the conduct of Senate business. Occurring after the heated 1896 election, which also seemingly highlighted Populism's impact on national politics, his election motivated key Republican senators to instill order and to consolidate their party's electoral gains in the recent presidential and congressional contests. First, as caucus chairman, Allison appointed a small coterie of associates with whom he was socially and philosophically in agreement to the chairmanship and membership of the Republican Steering Committee and of the Committee on Committees, crucial policy-making committees. In conjunction with Nelson Aldrich and James McMillan, Allison then moved to consolidate power in the Senate. Thereafter, seniority determined election to committee chairmanship—and committee assignments were made by the Committee on Committees. An orderly, more efficient system had evolved, one that confirmed the leadership's power and insured that discipline could be enforced. Given the Allison faction's control over key committee chairmanships, notably those of Finance and Appropriations, the enactment of legislative change had been limited. This system also served to minimize (but not eliminate) personal idiosyncrasy: for unlike the House, debate in the Senate could not be tightly limited and the consideration of legislation expedited or prevented. Like the House, however, the power of a numerically small and politically conservative group of Senators had been enhanced.

CONGRESS AND POPULAR DISCONTENT

The process of institutionalizing national politics in turn dictated how the Congress responded to the major social and economic problems besetting American society. The consolidation of economic power with the emergence of large corporations had had a disruptive impact on a formerly agrarian and commercial society. Popular fears that the national economy was tending toward monopoly, if exaggerated, were not totally unfounded. Many individuals now concluded that equality of opportunity could be ensured and abuses of power averted only through some degree of federal intervention. Specifically, they demanded federal action to prevent monopolies, to restrict the rate-making powers of the railroads, and to create a more equitable currency. Similarly, the rather blatant examples of political corruption, most notably during the Credit Mobilier, Star Route, and whiskey ring scandals of the Grant years, and more recently in the 1888 presidential election contest, gave rise to protests over the power and independence of parties and political leaders. In sum, there existed a powerful national sentiment advocating the need to democratize political and economic institutions.

In reaction to the excesses of the Grant Administration, strong support had developed to base federal appointments on competitive examinations and merit rather than on patronage. This effort was led by the literate upper class, the so-called Mugwumps (predominantly college graduates; Eastern editors E. L. Godkin of the *Nation* and George William Curtis of *Harper's Weekly;* pre-Civil War political activists

Lyman Trumball, Carl Schurz, and Charles Francis Adams). The patronage system, the Mugwumps complained, had debased national politics; patronage appointees were often incompetent because they were selected only on the basis of party service and not ability. This patronage system would be rectified by a civil service system, relying on qualifying examinations to determine federal appointment. Responding to the pressure for civil service reform, both major parties adopted planks supporting it at their 1876 and 1880 conventions.

Congress approved a Civil Service Reform Act (also called the Pendleton Act after its legislative sponsor Senator George Pendleton) in January 1883. Instituting a civil service system, this act actually provided for limited reform. A Civil Service Commission was created, composed of three individuals appointed by the president, to administer competitive exams to determine qualifications for future (not incumbent) federal employment. At first only 13,924 of the roughly 120,000 appointive federal employees were subject to the new system and, thus, the President remained, as before, a powerful and partisan dispenser of patronage plums. Subsequently the number of federal positions subject to civil service rules rose slowly but steadily.

The Congress's response to economic issues did not differ substantially. An important and divisive issue since the founding of the republic, federal currency policy assumed even more crucial importance in the post-Civil War years. In the aftermath of the economic crisis of 1873, farmers particularly demanded reissuance of silver coin, which had been withdrawn from circulation, by the Treasury Department in 1873. Responding to this demand, in November 1877, Congressman Richard Bland introduced a bill providing for the "free and unlimited coinage of silver" at the ratio of sixteen to one with gold. The measure overwhelmingly passed the House. In the Senate, however, through the leadership of William Allison, the bill was drastically amended to limit coinage each month to no less than $2 million and no more than $4 million. As amended by the Senate, the bill became law in February, 1878.

The Bland–Allison Act's limits on silver coinage did not abate the demands from the agrarian community and silver mining interests for an increase in the federal treasury's minting of silver. This sustained pressure led the Republicans to introduce and, in 1890, secure passage of the Sherman Silver Purchase Act. That act provided for government purchase of 4.5 million ounces of silver per month to be paid in Treasury notes redeemable either in silver or gold coin. But the act did not produce the monetary inflation desired by heavily indebted agrarians. Farm prices remained low and fell catastrophically with the depression of 1893–1896. Blaming it for the economic crisis of 1893, President Grover Cleveland in 1894 sought and secured the Sherman Act's repeal.

Federal policy toward railroads and industrial consolidation were other important issues of the late nineteenth century. The public service character of railroads and the extent to which their rate policies affected the economic fortunes of those businessmen and farmers dependent on railroads for transportation of their goods had increased demands for federal regulation of the railroads. Most disturbing to shippers were the railroad's discriminatory rate policies: Lower rates were charged for long than for short hauls (it cost less to ship similar goods from Chicago to New York than from Rochester to New York); rates differed between geographic regions (rates from Boston inland were only about half those from New York City); rebates (lower rates) were granted to large users (a New York state investigation of the New York Central's books found that 6,000 special contracts had been offered in a six-month period). Finally, in February 1887, Congress approved the Interstate Commerce Act. That act forbade discrimination in rates among geographic regions, stipulated that all rates be "reasonable and just," prohibited railroads from charging more for a short than a long haul unless approved by the Interstate Commerce Commission, and outlawed pooling and rebates in "substantially similar" circumstances. To administer these provisions, the act created an Interstate Commerce Commission (ICC), composed of five members appointed by the President. Though possessing investigatory powers, the ICC was not empowered to regulate rates. The commission relied on the injunctive powers of the federal district courts, requiring that it prove in court its findings of unreasonable or discriminatory rates. There were, moreover, no clear legislative guidelines for deciding under what conditions differential rates between the long and the short haul would be permitted, what constituted "unreasonable preference," or what were the "substantially similar" circumstances wherein rebates and pooling were prohibited.

Understandably, the vagueness of the Interstate Commerce Act precluded effective regulation of railroad rates. The act also offered distinct advantages to the railroad industry. As Richard Olney in 1892 wrote to the head of a railroad company, "The Commission, as its functions have now been limited by the courts, is, or can be made, of great use to the railroads. It satisfies the public clamor for a government supervision of railroads, at the same time that the supervision is almost entirely nominal."

The Sherman Anti-Trust Act of July 1890 was no more specific or effective as an antimonopoly measure. The act prohibited contracts or combinations "in restraint of trade or commerce" and provided fines of $5,000 or one year imprisonment for "every person who shall monopolize, or attempt to monopolize, or combine or conspire with any other person or persons to monopolize, any part of the trade or commerce." Individuals injured by companies violating the act's provisions were empowered to secure threefold damages. Because its language was vague and because the authorized penalties were limited, the Sherman Anti-Trust Act could hardly serve as an effective deterrent to consolidation. Too much discretion was given the executive office in bringing antitrust suits and to the federal courts in determining their merits. Senator Orville Platt did not exaggerate during Senate debate on the bill when he remarked that the aim of Congress was less to suppress monopolies than "to get some bill headed, 'A Bill to Punish Trusts' with which to go to the country."

THE 1890s

The failures of Congressional reform shaped popular protest in the 1890s. Many discontented Americans had become politicized because of their dissatisfaction with the *status quo,* with the serious economic crisis of 1893–1897, and with the limited effectiveness of legislative reforms. During the 1890s, the nascent, but still weak trade union movement was buffeted by strong rank-and-file pressure for militant action. Indeed, socialists became especially influential in such unions as the United Mine Workers, the United Brewery Workers, the International Association of Machinists, and the Boot and Shoe Workers.

The Populist party demonstrated the disaffection of another substantial sector of American society: small farmers, tenants, and share-croppers. Populists sought to democratize existing institutions and eliminate corporate control of the economy and politics. In the preamble to their 1892 Omaha platform, the Populists charged: "A vast conspiracy against mankind has been organized on two continents, and it is rapidly taking possession of the world. If not met and overthrown at once it forebodes . . . the establishment of an absolute despotism." To return power to its rightful possessors, the "people," the Populists demanded government ownership of railroads and telephone lines, the creation of a postal savings bank system, low interest government loans to farmers, a graduated income tax, free and unlimited coinage of silver, and increasing the amount of currency in circulation to a minimum of $50 per capita. They also demanded the secret ballot, popular initiative, referendum, direct election of Senators, and one-term presidency. And they formed a third party that polled over 10 percent of the popular vote in 1892. If neither socialists nor revolutionaries, the Populists were by the standards of the American 1890s radical enough to frighten more conservative citizens.

Sensing a chance for national victory in the 1896 presidential election, the Populists coalesced with the Democratic party and nominated its candidate, the popular and oratorically flamboyant "boy orator of the Plains," William Jennings Bryan. Bryan and the Democrats endorsed inflation through the free coinage of silver and promised to implement other Populist economic and political reforms. Republicans attacked the devoutly Christian and reformist Bryan as a captive of the radical Populists and hence a candidate of dangerous and even immoral tendencies. As it turned out, the strategy of supporting the Democratic nominee cost the Populists the election as well as their own political independence. Bryan lost the presidency in a hotly contested election. The Republican nominee William McKinley polled 51 percent of the total vote

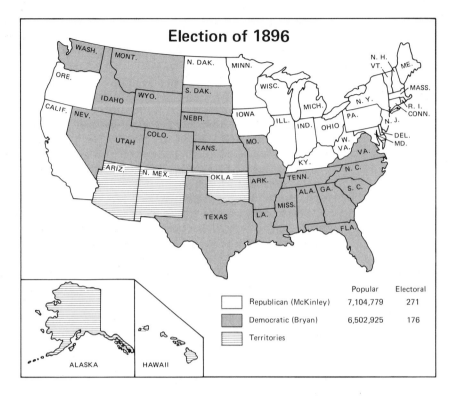

Election of 1896

	Popular	Electoral
Republican (McKinley)	7,104,779	271
Democratic (Bryan)	6,502,925	176
Territories		

(7,104,779) to Bryan's 47 percent (6,502,925), and 271 electoral votes to Bryan's 176, the most decisive result since the Grant years.

Yet despite the defeat of Populism and Bryanite Democracy, conservative politicians had been scared. Hence they hastened to implement the structural changes in Congress that were described earlier in this chapter. Other conservatives, however, now decided that reform was needed to redress popular grievances and eliminate the prospect of future mass uprisings. Theodore Roosevelt, destined to become the president early in the new century, remarked in the 1890s that "we Republicans hold the just balance and set our faces as resolutely against the improper corporate influence on the one hand as against the improper demagogy and mob rule on the other." Roosevelt-style Republicans thus began to advocate political controls over large corporations and corrupt party activities.

Yet another legacy of the Populist movement was its paradoxical and ultimately tragic impact on the racial attitudes and politics of the South. Southern Populists had initially endorsed interracial politics and assaulted the one-party, white-supremacy structure of the post-Reconstruction South. As poor blacks gravitated toward Populism, many southern conservatives sought their disfranchisement. Not coincidentally, the first major efforts of Southern political leaders to disfranchise blacks took place during the 1890s. Beginning with Mississippi (in 1890), followed by South Carolina (1895), Louisiana (1898), North Carolina (1900), Alabama (1901), and Virginia (1901–1902), Southern states adopted a variety of legal devices to disfranchise blacks—including poll tax legislation, literacy requirements for voter eligibility, or amendments to their constitutions. To these were soon added laws segregating such public facilities as schools, public transportation, and public accommodations. An elaborate Jim Crow system was imposed throughout the South. Defeated and frustrated white Populists often blamed their failure on ignorant black voters and joined the ranks of racists. And with the defeat of Populism, southern politics subordinated economic and social issues to racial ones. Conservative control, moreover, was abetted by the new voting laws, which disfranchised poor whites as well as Afro-Americans.

The North as well as the Republican party now also began to tolerate the Jim Crow system. The dominant national sentiment accepted black inferiority. Northern intellectuals and political leaders applauded Booker T. Washington's accommodationist Atlanta Compromise address of 1895, in which he urged blacks to subordinate the desire for equality to the attainment of vocational skills and material progress. The favorable popular response to the Supreme Court's decision in *Plessy* v. *Ferguson* (1896), upholding the constitutionality of a Louisiana statute requiring "separate but equal" railroad coaches for whites and blacks, provided further evidence of racist sentiment.

During the late nineteenth century, American politics had changed significantly. The strains and tensions created by immigration, industrialization, and urbanization had contributed to popular protest and to pressure for corrective action. Farmers, workers, and even more conservative middle-class citizens, had been moved to demand reform. Yet, at the same time, the structure of state and national politics had imposed obstacles to the translation of protest into specific legislative remedies, while serving as a further impetus to reform by accenting the unresponsiveness of political institutions. A structured politics dedicated to stability and a popular discontent that dreamed of change—these were the twin themes as America entered a new century.

3

A New Imperial Power: The United States and the World

In 1900 the United States, flushed with victory in the recent war with Spain and the proud owner of a colonial empire that stretched from the Caribbean to the far Pacific, confidently anticipated the new century that lay ahead. It would be, many predicted, *the American Century*. How had the United States grown from a weak state in 1800, remote from the center of world power, to one of the most powerful nations on the globe by 1900?

THE REVIVAL OF MANIFEST DESTINY

America's rise to great world power resulted from its exceptional growth in population and wealth during the nineteenth century. By 1900 the United States ranked second only to Russia among western nations in population and size of home territory and had become the world's most productive economy. Consequently, businessmen grew more interested in foreign markets, especially as a source of raw materials unavailable at home and as a market for America's goods and capital. The Panic of 1893 and the ensuing severe economic depression that lasted into 1897 hinted what might happen in the absence of overseas markets: cycles of over-production, falling prices, business and farm bankruptcies, mass unemployment, and social unrest. Economic growth and the search for foreign markets thus became important factors in America's imperial expansion as the 1890s drew to an end.

American nationalism also reached a new intensity during the 1880s and 1890s. Memories of the carnage of the Civil War faded and only its tales of glory and daring lived on to thrill a new generation eager for adventure. The process of internal expansion—the advance of the frontier into unsettled regions that had begun at Jamestown and Plymouth—was virtually over by 1890, as the young historian Frederick Jackson Turner pointed out. If the internal frontier had ended, from which presumably derived the American values of democracy, equality, and opportunity, external frontiers must be sought to keep alive those values and provide fresh worlds to conquer for enterprising Americans. A commercial frontier overseas, particularly in the Pacific and Asia, beckoned many. Patriotic organizations such as the Daughters of the American Revolution, founded in 1890, both reflected and fanned this surging feeling of nationalism and expansion, as did the sensationalist yellow press. Many Americans looked enviously upon the great European powers and their colonial empires, and were eager for the United States to emulate them.

Americans had experienced in 1815–1860 a period of intense nationalism and expansionism that historians refer to as the Old Manifest Destiny. Searching for rich virgin land for farmers and good ports on the Pacific, and convinced of their divinely inspired mission to expand the bounds of freedom and democracy, Americans had poured into Texas, Oregon, and California and had cast acquisitive eyes upon Canada, Cuba, Central America, and Hawaii. The watchwords had been the Monroe Doctrine and Manifest Destiny. Both expressed the same basic ideas. The Monroe Doctrine, first proclaimed in 1823, not only declared the separation of the New World from Old Europe, but in effect proclaimed that the Western Hemisphere was reserved for republicanism and United States hegemony. But after annexation of Texas in 1845, acquisition of Oregon in 1846, and the imperialistic war with Mexico that conquered New Mexico and California in 1846–1848, the sharpening sectional rivalry between North and South and the Civil War ended the first wave of Manifest Destiny.

In the 1880s and 1890s a New Manifest Destiny added Darwinist arguments to the older rationalizations for expansionism. Social Darwinists maintained that competition between nations and the struggle for survival of the fittest, comparable to that which took place between species and within human societies, was an inescapable law of natural selection and progress. The law of tooth, fang, and nail prevailed in world affairs as in all other aspects of life. Not to compete, to trust others with one's interests and security, risked decline and death. Moreover, such popularizers of social Darwinism as historian John Fiske and

Congregationalist minister Josiah Strong pointed out that Americans as members of the superior Teutonic or Anglo-Saxon race had a special mission or duty to extend the blessings of civilization to backward peoples. As the British poet, Rudyard Kipling, phrased it:

> Take up the White Man's burden—
> Ye dare not stoop to less—
> Nor call too loud on Freedom
> To cloak your weariness.*

THE OUTWARD THRUST

Signs of the New Manifest Destiny multiplied during the last two decades of the nineteenth century. One involved the growth of the new navy. Traditionally a small naval power, the United States heretofore had regarded itself as geographically protected from the Old World. People believed that wars in Europe could not threaten American security. Hence the United States needed a navy only large enough to show the flag and protect its commercial interests overseas. By 1880 the large Civil War fleet had rusted or rotted away. The United States then had few if any naval warships worthy of the name and ranked about thirtieth among world naval powers. Such ships as the nation possessed were virtually a laughingstock to the world, mostly antique wooden sailing vessels inadequately armed, a veritable floating naval museum in the words of one disgusted American admiral. Meanwhile the world's navies had converted to swift steam-powered steel-hulled vessels carrying rifled cannon firing armor-piercing shells, in contrast to America's smooth bore solid shot or makeshift pieces. As American national pride quickened and interest grew in foreign markets, concerned citizens and persistent lobbyists urged the building of a modern navy equipped to defend the nation's interests and honor. Prophets such as Captain Alfred Thayer Mahan argued that national greatness demanded sea power.

In the early 1880s Congress began appropriating increased funds to construct a new navy. By 1883 the first four modern steel warships had been approved, and in 1890 three first-class battleships were authorized. By 1898 the United States possessed a formidable fleet and had advanced to sixth or seventh among the world's naval powers The new navy was soon to give a most convincing demonstration of its effectiveness in the war with Spain.

A series of foreign crises both reflected and strengthened the surging American nationalism and sense of destiny. In 1891–1892 disagreements with a revolutionary established government in Chile, culminating in the killing of two American sailors in a brawl at the True Blue Saloon in

---

* Reprinted by permission of the executors of the estate of the late Mrs. Bambridge and the Macmillan Co. of London & Basingstoke.

Valparaiso, nearly led to war. The Chilean government yielded to an American ultimatum and offered an apology and indemnity for the incident. Rivalry with Germany and Great Britain in the Samoan Islands threatened hostilities until the issue was settled by a three-power protectorate in 1889. Ten years later Samoa was divided, and the United States obtained a desired naval base and port at Pago Pago, thousands of miles away from North America. American economic interests and missionaries long had dominated Hawaii. Clashes between American residents and the native monarchy caused a "revolution" in 1893. The new republic, controlled by the Americans, promptly signed an annexation treaty with the United States, but domestic politics and the opposition of incoming President Grover Cleveland delayed Hawaiian incorporation until 1898.

In 1895 a long-smouldering boundary controversy between Venezuela and British Guiana precipitated a war crisis between the United States and Great Britain. Alarmed at European economic penetration of Latin America and anxious about American trade and influence there, President Cleveland and Secretary of State Richard Olney invoked the Monroe Doctrine in Venezuela's behalf. In a boastful note to London, Olney proclaimed the United States the sole arbiter of the Western Hemisphere, and when Britain dismissed Olney's presumptuousness, Cleveland in effect threatened war unless England submitted to arbitration. Eager for American goodwill and deeply worried by European developments, the British government capitulated and accepted arbitration. The Venezuelan crisis swiftly passed, but it revealed the newly found sense of American power and the martial mood of many of its citizens. The stage was set for an even greater adventure.

THE WAR WITH SPAIN

Long smouldering popular discontent with Spain's arbitrary rule in Cuba erupted in revolution in 1895. Spain sent thousands of troops and adopted drastic measures to suppress the Cuban revolt without success. The rebels turned to guerrilla warfare, hit-and-run raids, and scorched-earth tactics to defeat the Spanish. The Cuban patriots drew support and recruits from exile colonies within the United States and successfully appealed to American sympathies. Rebel propagandists identified their cause with freedom and democracy, and portrayed Spain as a cruel and rapacious Old World monarchy clinging to the shreds of empire. Spanish methods were ruthless: arbitrary arrests and executions and the *reconcentrado* policy of forcibly removing inhabitants in rebel-infested areas to guarded towns and villages. The yellow press exaggerated these admittedly woeful actions and American readers, unaccustomed to war waged against civilians and their property, reacted with horror to the real or imagined atrocities attributed to Valeriano "Butcher" Weyler, the captain-general of Cuba. The island seemed a veritable charnel house of death and destruction.

President Cleveland handled the Cuban revolution cautiously. Although concerned about the American economic stake in the island, worth about $150 million in trade and investments, he did not feel that intervention could be justified. Cleveland and Olney moreover felt little sympathy toward the rebels whom they thought unfit for orderly self-rule. In their view, the best solution would be local Cuban autonomy under continued Spanish sovereignty. Therefore, Cleveland resisted attempts by Congress to force him to recognize the belligerency of the rebels. In the end, he bequeathed the Cuban problem to his successor, Republican William McKinley of Ohio, winner of the presidential election in 1896.

A kindly and pious man, President McKinley was more sympathetic to the rebels and from the first desired a speedy resolution to the Cuban conflict. Not only did war damage American economic interests in Cuba and disturb the general business climate in the United States, but it violated American concepts of self-rule, decency, and humanitarianism. The demand for intervention to free Cuba swept across the United States and captured the Republican and Democratic parties as well as the short-lived Populist party. Yet McKinley, haunted by memories of bloodshed from the American Civil War, resisted the growing interventionist clamor in Congress as long as any hope remained for a peaceful solution. He responded calmly to events that could have been used as an excuse for war, such as the blowing up of the American battleship *Maine* in Havana harbor on February 15, 1898 from causes that are still not known. He tried without success to persuade Spain to end the strife either by granting the Cubans real autonomy or setting them free.

Spain would not accept American mediation, and the rebels spurned a truce. McKinley decided to act decisively. On April 11, 1898, the President sent his war message to Congress. The results were never in doubt. War was declared on April 21, with the addition of the Teller Amendment disclaiming any intention of annexing Cuba.

Although historians have hotly debated the causes of American intervention, it now seems clear that the war with Spain resulted from the eagerness of influential congressmen and federal officials to flaunt American power on a world stage. The advocates of war, however much they cloaked their motives in pious platitudes and humanitarian rhetoric, wanted the United States to behave like a global economic power. It was time to join the game of imperialism as practiced by England, France, and Germany.

The brief Spanish-American War further stimulated American nationalism and imperialism. A badly out-classed Spain met defeat after defeat. Commodore George Dewey sailed his Far Eastern squadron into Manila Bay, and on the morning of May 1 he leisurely destroyed a decrepit Spanish fleet. American elation knew no bounds, and Dewey became a hero overnight. The Philippines lay open to conquest. Half a world away, an American fleet blockaded a Spanish squadron in

Santiago, Cuba, while the American army, woefully unprepared for war, landed an expedition that besieged Santiago by land. On July 3 the American navy destroyed the Spanish warships when they tried to escape Santiago; the city itself fell on July 16, and an American army seized Puerto Rico. A dispirited Spain sued for peace and an armistice was signed on August 12. In the words of John Hay, McKinley's last secretary of state, it had been "a splendid little war"; Theodore Roosevelt pronounced it "bully for the navy."

THE END OF "FREE SECURITY"

The war with Spain not only dramatized the emergence of the United States as a great world power but made it an imperial state with colonies and dependencies in the Caribbean and the Pacific. A shocked Spain yielded Cuba, Puerto Rico, Guam, and the Philippines and was solaced for its losses by the payment of $20 million. Hawaii also had been annexed during the war, and the United States obtained part of Samoa in 1899.

A war to free Cuba ended as a war for empire. For such influential Republicans as Theodore Roosevelt, Senator Henry Cabot Lodge, John Hay, A. T. Mahan, and Brooks Adams, the war with Spain had provided the opportunity to achieve heretofore frustrated diplomatic objectives. It made the "large policy" of building an American overseas empire a reality, especially as acquisition of the Philippines brought the United States six thousand miles closer to the unsatiable markets of mainland Asia. Influenced by such economic factors and also by the men who demanded a "large policy," President McKinley decided to take the entire Philippine archipelago.

Before long, however, Americans learned the costs of empire. Filipino nationalists, led by Emilio Aguinaldo, who previously had rebelled unsuccessfully against Spanish rule, at first welcomed the Americans as liberators. When they realized that they had merely received a change of masters, however, and that the Philippines would be administered as an American colony, Aguinaldo and his followers again rose in rebellion. The result was a nasty colonial war, 1899–1901, that cost the United States 4,300 American lives before it was suppressed. The white man's burden, it seemed, was more than a mere figure of speech.

In keeping with its principles, the United States began to extend local self-government to its larger possessions. Puerto Ricans were allowed to elect the lower house of the island legislature—the upper house and governor were appointed by the American government—and in 1917 were granted American citizenship. A similar process of local involvement in government also soon began in the Philippines. After a brief occupation, during which various reforms were instituted, the United States recalled its troops from Cuba in 1902. The new republic, however,

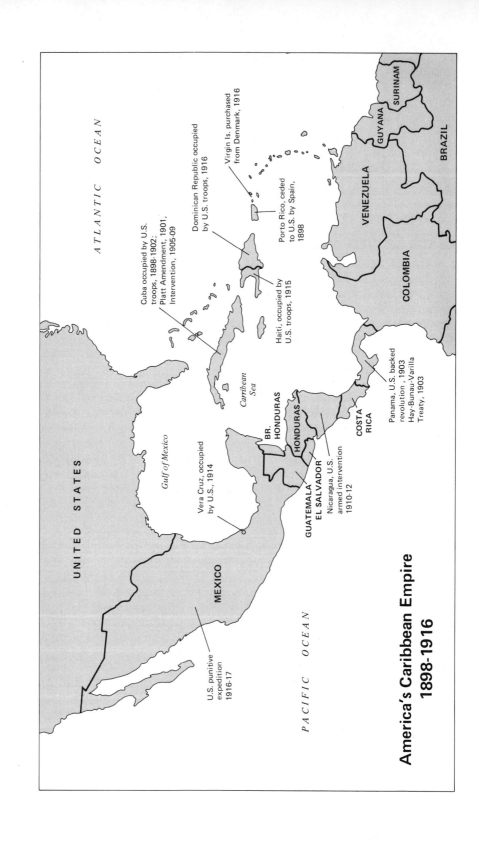

ATLANTIC OCEAN

UNITED STATES

Gulf of Mexico

Caribbean Sea

PACIFIC OCEAN

MEXICO

GUATEMALA

BR. HONDURAS

HONDURAS

EL SALVADOR

COSTA RICA

VENEZUELA

COLOMBIA

SURINAM

GUYANA

BRAZIL

U.S. punitive expedition 1916-17

Vera Cruz, occupied by U.S., 1914

Nicaragua, U.S. armed intervention 1910-12

Cuba occupied by U.S. troops, 1898-1902; Platt Amendment, 1901, Intervention, 1905-09

Haiti, occupied by U.S. troops, 1915

Dominican Republic occupied by U.S. troops, 1916

Virgin Is. purchased from Denmark, 1916

Porto Rico, ceded to U.S. by Spain, 1898

Panama, U.S. backed revolution , 1903 Hay-Bunau-Varilla Treaty, 1903

America's Caribbean Empire 1898-1916

remained an American protectorate. Under the Platt Amendment, incorporated into a treaty with Cuba, the United States could intervene to preserve Cuban independence and restore order and could acquire naval bases in the island, while Cuba was prohibited from alienating territory to any other power or from contracting debts in excess of her ability to repay them.

Acquisition of the Philippines led to a clash with other imperialist powers over the future of China. Policymakers had hoped that possession of the Philippines would help American businessmen to penetrate the China market. Its teeming millions, many Americans believed, offered a vast potential market for surplus American farm and factory goods and for investors. There were dollars to be earned and souls to be saved by Americans in China. Many subscribed to a myth, in fact, that under American guidance China was destined to become modernized and Christianized and to take its place by our side as a westernized nation-state.

Yet China during the 1890s seemed to face imminent dismemberment as the rapacious European powers and Japan sought to carve up the Celestial Kingdom into leased ports, special economic concessions, and spheres of influence. Japan had defeated China in 1894–1895 and won control of Korea and Formosa; Russia was penetrating Manchuria; France was active to the South; and Germany obtained a leasehold in Shantung province. If partition occurred, American businessmen and their products, and American missionaries as well, would face discrimination within the foreign-held spheres of influence. Great Britain, heretofore dominant in the China market, also grew concerned. In 1898 and again early in 1899, Britain sought joint action with the United States to restrain other imperialist powers, but Washington authorities, fearful of foreign entanglements, refused.

After the 1898 war, however, as American interests in China increased, Secretary of State John Hay decided to act alone. On September 6, 1899, he requested of the other major powers assurances that within spheres of interest in China there would be no discrimination against the commerce of others. Hay's Open Door policy thus meant equality of opportunity for all foreign commerce, or fair competition and a free field for all. Although the other powers responded evasively, Hay blandly announced that all had agreed to his proposal.

When an antiforeign outburst occurred in China in 1900, the so-called Boxer Rebellion, the American government again sought to forestall possible partition by stating its position to the powers. In his second Open Door note, Hay declared that the United States aimed at a solution that would preserve China's integrity and commercial equality of opportunity in all parts of the country. He then went well beyond his first note and in effect identified American interest with not only the Open Door but China's territorial integrity as well.

Although his notes were popularly received in the United States—many believed Hay had saved China from dismemberment, but in fact that was due more to the delicate balance among the rival powers—Hay had widened the gap between actual American interests in China and its power to promote them. Despite talk of a potential 400 million customers in China, American commerce with China was always limited and its investments quite small because China was too underdeveloped and poor to offer a market for mass-produced American goods. As for the missionaries' hopes, they predominated in evangelical work in China but were never able to convert more than a tiny fraction of the population. In short, American interests perhaps justified the first Hay note but not the second one in 1900 that vaguely implied American support of China's integrity and independence.

As the Open Door notes signified, the Spanish-American War had immersed the American nation in the swirl of world politics. An age of free security had come to an end. In the past the United States had been relatively secure behind its ocean moats and could safely survive with a small navy and army. After the 1890s that was no longer true. An imperial power, with possessions just off the coasts of Asia and with expanding foreign trade and investments, the United States henceforth would have to pay an ever steeper price for security and the protection of its interests abroad. For better or worse, it now was involved in world affairs, at first in Asia and subsequently in Europe. If most Americans in 1900 failed to perceive these changes and clung stubbornly to the isolationist faith of the past, a perceptive French observer accurately analyzed the meaning for the United States of its new diplomacy. "The United States," André Tardieu noted, "is a world power. . . . A nation of ninety million souls, which sells wheat to the universe, coal, iron, and cotton, cannot isolate itself. . . . The United States intervenes . . . in the affairs of the universe. . . . It is seated at the table where the great game is played and it cannot leave it."

SELECTED BIBLIOGRAPHY FOR SECTION I

Among the most thoughtful studies of immigrants and immigration are the following: OSCAR HANDLIN, *The Uprooted* (1951) *; MARCUS LEE HANSEN, *The Immigrant in American History* (1939) *; DONALD B. COLE, *Immigrant City: Lawrence, Massachusetts, 1845–1921* (1960) ; and MOSES RISCHIN, *The Promised City, New York's Jews, 1870–1914* (1962) .* Poverty in Industrializing America can be seen best in ROBERT BREMNER, *From the Depths: The Discovery of Poverty in the United States* (1956) * and two contemporary accounts, JACOB RIIS, *How the Other Half Lives* (1890) * and ROBERT HUNTER, *Poverty* (1904) .* The story of workers and the labor movement is best summarized in MELVYN DUBOFSKY, *Industrialism and the American Worker, 1865–1920* (1975) .* For the best of the "new" social and labor history see HERBERT G. GUTMAN, *Work, Society*

* Available in paperback.

and Culture in Industrializing America (1976) .* The best accounts of urbanization remain ARTHUR M. SCHLESINGER's classic work, *The Rise of the City* (1933) * and BLAKE McKELVEY's *The Urbanization of America* (1963). A fine brief synthesis is ZANE MILLER, *The Urbanization of Modern America* (1973) .* SAM BASS WARNER, JR., provides an in-depth case study of the process of suburbanization in one local community in *Streetcar Suburbs: The Process of Growth in Boston, 1870–1900* (1962) .* On the changing nature of agriculture see FRED SHANNON's voluminous *The Farmer's Last Frontier: Agriculture, 1860–1897* (1945) .* The plight of black Americans can best be followed in RAYFORD LOGAN, *The Negro in American Life and Thought: The Nadir, 1877–1901* (1954) * and AUGUST MEIER and ELLIOT RUDWICK, *From Plantation to Ghetto: An Interpretive History of American Negroes* (1970) .* Two excellent and recent surveys of women's place in society are ANN OAKLEY, *Woman's Work: The House-wife Past and Present* (1974) * and ROSALYN BAXENDALL et al. *America's Working Women: A Documentary History* (1975) .*

H. WAYNE MORGAN, *From Hayes to McKinley* (1969) and L. D. WHITE, *The Republican Era* (1958) are excellent surveys of presidential politics. DAVID ROTHMAN, *Politics and Power* (1966) * and JOHN DOBSON, *Politics in the Gilded Age* (1972) * survey the change in state party politics and the Senate, while RICHARD BOLLING, *Power in the House* (1968) discusses developments in the House. ROBERT WIEBE, *The Search for Order 1877–1920* (1967) *; JOHN GARRATY, *The New Commonwealth, 1877–1890* (1968) *; and RAY GINGER, *Age of Excess* (1966) * are excellent studies that survey both political and social history. See also the "new political history" of RICHARD JENSEN, *The Winning of the Midwest* (1971) and PAUL KLEPPNER, *The Cross of Culture* (1970) . Solid studies of the political thought of this period include RICHARD HOFSTADTER, *Social Darwinism in American Thought* (1955) *, SIDNEY FINE, *Laissez Faire and the General-Welfare State* (1964) , and R. G. McCLOSKEY, *American Conservatism in the Age of Enterprise* (1951) . The money question, Populism, and the 1896 election are surveyed in IRWIN UNGER, *The Greenback Era* (1964) ; ALLEN WEINSTEIN, *Prelude to Populism* (1970) ; LAWRENCE GOODWYN, *Democratic Promise: The Populist Move-ment in America* (1976) ; S. L. JONES, *The Presidential Election of 1896* (1964) ; R. F. DURDEN, *The Climax of Populism* (1965) ; C. VANN WOOD-WARD, *Origins of the New South* (1951) *; P. W. GLAD, *McKinley, Bryan and the People* (1964) *; and H. WAYNE MORGAN, *William McKinley and His America* (1963) . Immigrant policy and policy toward blacks are discussed in PHILIP TAYLOR, *The Distant Magnet* (1971) *; JOHN HIGHAM, *Strangers in the Land* (1963) *; JACK KIRBY, *Darkness at the Dawning* (1972) *; and C. VANN WOODWARD, *The Strange Career of Jim Crow* (1955) .*

The United States as a new imperial power is perceptively treated in ERNEST R. MAY, *Imperial Democracy: The Emergence of America as a Great Power* (1961) *; WALTER LAFEBER, *The New Empire: An Interpre-tation of American Expansion, 1860–1898* (1963) *; JULIUS W. PRATT,

Expansionists of 1898 (1936) *; Thomas J. McCormick, *China Market: America's Quest for Informal Empire, 1893–1901* (1967) *; Marilyn B. Young, *The Rhetoric of Empire: American China Policy, 1895–1901* (1968) ; and J. A. S. Grenville and G. B. Young, *Politics, Strategy, and American Diplomacy: Studies in Foreign Policy, 1873–1919* (1966) . An in-depth look at the American anti-imperialists is provided by Robert Beisner, *Twelve Against Empire: The Anti-Imperialists, 1898–1900* (1968) .* Also see the same author's *From the Old Diplomacy to the New, 1865–1900* (1975) .* An important contemporary account of the importance of naval power as well as a plea for a larger U.S. role in world affairs is Alfred T. Mahan, *The Influence of Sea Power Upon History, 1660–1783* (1890) .

II

An Age of Reform
1900–1916

From 1873 to 1896 the entire world, especially the leading industrial capitalist nations, had lived through what political economists of that era referred to as the "Great Depression." The economic setbacks of the late nineteenth century produced shock and trauma among capitalist elites everywhere. In the previous generation, the years from 1848 to 1873, which the English historian Eric Hobsbawm characterizes as "The Age of Capital," westerners believed implicitly in *progress*. To quote from Hobsbawm, progress was believed to be "massive, enlightened, sure of itself, self-satisfied but above all inevitable."

Economic depression made many westerners less sure of the inevitability of progress. Those who benefited least during the "Age of Capital" grew especially restless during the late nineteenth century. Across Europe mass socialist movements emerged that challenged the ruling bourgeoisie for power. The United States proved no exception to the rule of popular restlessness in the late nineteenth century. Both discontented urban workers and unhappy agrarians fought the dominant influences in American politics, economics, and society. Workers waged persistent and often violent industrial conflicts against their employers; a small minority even formed independent labor parties and eventually joined the international socialist movement. Farmers built their own political movement, Populism, to challenge the hegemony of industrial capitalism. And during the depression of the 1890s urban and rural discontent combined to threaten the stability of American society and politics. As Populism first emerged as a new third party in 1890–1892 and then appeared to capture the Democratic party in 1896, many conservative citizens feared for their future safety and security. During the crisis of the 1890s many Americans expected their nation to go the way of Europe and collapse into bitter and unending class conflict.

But prosperity returned to the world in 1897 and for the next decade and a half the western capitalist economies once again grew and flourished. By then also, the dominant groups in society had discovered that the discontented masses could be rewarded materially as well as suppressed. In Bismarckian Germany, the nation with the largest mass socialist movement, the country's leaders provided workers with a variety of social welfare benefits ranging from unemployment benefits and pension programs to a form of national health insurance. And in early twentieth-century Britain, the British "New Liberals" sought through government welfare measures to lay a social and economic floor below which no British citizen could fall.

The return of prosperity and the example of European reform induced a new optimism among early twentieth-century American leaders. They, too, believed that progress had once again become inevitable and that mass discontent could be assuaged by welfare reforms. They also believed that the growth of modern science and the triumph of rationality over outmoded traditions had made man the master of his own destiny. In society, economics, politics, and foreign affairs, Americans sought to create more systematic, scientific, and orderly forms of organization and behavior. This effort to "rationalize," or professionalize, basic institutions left scarcely any aspect of United States society untouched. The twin beliefs in the inevitability of progress and human omnipotence through science produced an age of reform in the United States.

Yet in the United States as well as Europe, prosperity and reform did not at first end challenges to the established order. Indeed, almost everywhere from 1900 to 1914 labor and socialist movements grew more rapidly and massively than heretofore. If prosperity and science created optimism among the world's rulers, the spread of militant trade unionism and socialism spread fear and anxiety. On the one hand, then, a sense of security and optimism laid the foundation for an age of reform. On the other hand, the tensions produced by trade unionism and socialism created fears and anxieties that made social reform equally necessary. Whether American reformers in the early twentieth century were motivated by optimism or fear, security or anxiety, they participated in one of the most vibrant eras in United States history, the Progressive Era.

4

The Material Bases of Reform: Economy, Society, and Culture

By 1900 the United States had already been the world's leading industrial power for a full decade. In 1890 both the United States and Imperial Germany had overtaken the initial industrial leader, Great Britain, "the workshop of the world," and both powers continued thereafter to widen their margin of economic supremacy. London's reputation as the world's financial capital in 1914 notwithstanding, the United States had by then become the unsurpassed leader in modern mass production methods and new modes of corporate organization.

The new industrial economies were built on steam and steel, and in that respect the United States was especially fortunate. Few nations, if any, could boast superior soft coal reserves, the primary source of heat for energy and metallurgical refining. From western Pennsylvania to Colorado, Montana, Wyoming, and even Washington state, and from the Great Lakes to northern Alabama, American miners dug coal. In 1900 bituminous coal production surpassed 200 million tons annually, and it nearly doubled over the next ten years, finally reaching in excess of 560 million tons in 1920. Rich lodes of iron ore were uncovered and developed first on the Northern Peninsula of Michigan and later on the fabulously rich Mesabi Range in northern Minnesota. Between 1900 and

1920 iron ore production rose from roughly 27 million tons annually to over 67 million tons. In the Pittsburgh district, around Birmingham and Bessemer, Alabama, in the newly created city of Gary, Indiana, and in Pueblo, Colorado, the coal and iron were combined to build the world's leading iron and steel industry. Between 1900 and 1916, for example, the production of steel increased from just over 10 million tons annually to well over 40 million tons.

Modern means of transportation and communication linked the industrial system together, making it possible to coordinate supply and demand, buying and selling on a scale heretofore inconceivable. Steel rails and copper wire carried goods and messages from one side of the continent to the other, and transoceanic cables and giant steel-plated steamships transported American methods and goods around the globe. At home, entrepreneurs constructed the world's largest railroad network, boasting in 1920 some 400,000 plus miles of useable track and more than two million freight and passenger cars in service. Sitting in their offices in New York, Chicago, Pittsburgh, or San Francisco, business executives, using the telephone, telegraph, and steam transport, managed their far-flung national and even international industrial empires.

Yet even more striking than the speed and vigor with which Americans built their economic machine was the manner in which they did so. For not only did the United States come to lead the world in the production of coal, steel, and copper but it also pioneered in the creation of giant enterprises, the forerunners of today's corporate conglomerates.

THE MERGER MOVEMENT AND ITS RESULTS

In 1904 the financial analyst and Wall Street authority John Moody reported that he found 318 important and active industrial trusts* with a combined capital of over seven billion dollars and representing a consolidation of more than 5,300 previously separate manufacturing plants in nearly every line of industry. Of the 318 industrial trusts, 236 had been incorporated after January 1, 1898, and 170 of those had been organized under the especially lenient New Jersey corporation laws.

These combinations, representing only 1 percent of the nation's business enterprises, by 1904 controlled two-fifths of all the manufacturing capital in the country. By 1910, six interlocking corporate groups controlled 95 percent of the nation's railroad mileage.

Among the most successful and dominant of the new corporate giants was the one associated with John D. Rockefeller. His parent concern, the Standard Oil Company, supplied 84 percent of all domestic oil and controlled over 90 percent of the export market. On a par value of

---

* A term Moody used generically to describe any corporate structure that combined formerly independent operating companies under a single new management, whether through outright merger or the more circuitous holding company technique.

$97.5 million, its net profits early in the century were claimed to exceed $60 million annually of which it paid out over $40 million in dividends. In addition, the Rockefeller interests held a dominant financial stake in the refining of nonferrous metals, associated themselves closely with the handful of companies that controlled the tobacco industry, and also were prominent in public utilities, national railroads, and New York City banks and financial institutions. Of the large business and financial interests that clustered around either the Rockefeller complex or the network of capital woven together by J. P. Morgan, Moody wrote: "These two mammoth groups jointly constitute the heart of the business and commercial life of the nation, the others all being the arteries which permeate in a thousand ways our whole national life, making their influence felt in every home and hamlet, yet all connected and dependent on this great central source, the influence and policy of which dominates them all." Indeed, in 1913, a congressional investigating commission was to report that the House of Morgan and its financial allies alone maintained 341 corporate directorships in 112 banks, railroads, and manufacturing industries valued at more than $22 billion.

How did this system of finance capitalism and industrial oligopoly, i.e., the domination of a given market by a handful of mammoth concerns, come into existence? What factors motivated American businessmen and financiers to build economic empires in which ownership was divorced from everyday management and in which collective authority became more important than individual decision making?

Positive and negative forces, aggressive and defensive influences operated jointly to hasten the movement towards increasing the size of the business firm. The widening of the market in the late nineteenth century as a result of innovations in transport, communications, and production plus the growing urbanization of population opened opportunities for businessmen who could produce consumer goods in greater volume and hence increase their profit margins while maintaining lower unit prices for their products. The same widening of the market increased competition for customers among established firms, caused them to cut prices as a result of excess productive capacity, and compelled them to watch their profit margins fall and often disappear. Rather than risk corporate collapse through unfettered competition, established businessmen began, in the words of one, to realize "that perhaps cooperation . . . was the life of trade and even the law of self-preservation. Competition was a means, not an end; the end of business was profit, and if competition jeopardized that end some better means must be sought. . . . Capital tried to assure profit and then to increase it by limiting or even eliminating competition."

Corporate enterprises eager to garner profits by tapping new customers or restricting competition for old consumers, followed a dual path to expansion and consolidation. Companies producing relatively new items for urban markets tended to expand forward from manufacturing to distribution and sales through the creation of their own marketing organizations. Older industries using a less complex technology and producing staple commodities in excess of existing demand combined horizontally in order to consolidate manufacturing functions and bring production in line with demand. Only later would they, too, move forward into marketing or backward into purchasing. These two paths to corporate expansion were, to be sure, not mutually exclusive.

Developments in the steel and agricultural implements industries were excellent examples of vertical and horizontal combination. McCormick Harvester, which manufactured farm implements of high quality, in sufficient quantity and at attractive prices, met difficulty in marketing them. Unable to sell successfully through jobbers, wholesalers, and commission merchants who had no particular loyalty to the company and who had little knowledge of the technical characteristics of the products (and thus could not service them), the company developed its own marketing organization, which included salaried agents and franchised dealers able to push the product's technical advantages, offer consumer credit, and service the implements. As the McCormick company successfully tapped the agricultural market, other firms became more aggressive in competition and profit margins fell. To deal with this new and threatening economic situation, J. P. Morgan and Company in 1904 arranged a combination, or merger, of previously separate producing firms in the field to be known as the International Harvester Corporation. In this case, then, a corporation that had expanded vertically in the course of the late nineteenth century became, early in the new century, the major element in an horizontal combination.

Steel followed a somewhat similar pattern. Throughout the late nineteenth century as the market for steel products grew and as demand shifted away from steel rails to structural products for the expanding urban markets, iron and steel companies enlarged vertically. The lead here was taken by Andrew Carnegie. This ambitious industrialist not only put together an empire of iron and steel mills but in order to ensure raw materials for his furnaces, he purchased iron mines, coal mines, coke ovens, lake steamers, dock facilities, and railroads. He also developed his own aggressive marketing organization, integrating his empire from mine to marketplace. Other companies followed suit and before long J. P. Morgan and Company established its own colossus in the steel industry—Federal Steel (1898)—to challenge Carnegie. Threatened by Carnegie on one side and Morgan on the other, many previously independent steel companies merged to form the Republic Steel Company, and simultaneously all the industry's large firms struggled to acquire mining properties, transportation facilities, and effective marketing outlets. As a result competition became too intense for some corporate leaders, causing J. P. Morgan to promote a horizontal merger arrangement for the steel industry. In 1901 Morgan brought off his corporate coup by buying out Andrew Carnegie and merging the latter's business interests with his own Federal Steel Company to form the United States Steel Corporation, the nation's first billion dollar enterprise.

What had happened in agricultural implements and steel was indicative of general patterns of development in basic sectors of the national economy. Two of the most rapidly growing consumer industries of the era, both of which pioneered modern advertising and sales methods—meat packing and tobacco products—were dominated by a handful of firms, sometimes referred to as the "big four" or "big five." General Mills and several smaller competitors controlled the processing and marketing of grains and cereals. And a group of large enterprises led by Anaconda dominated the mining and refining of nonferrous metals. Indeed wherever new methods of transportation and merchandising—especially brand-name advertising—opened local markets to national competition, corporate giants threatened to destroy or capture smaller independent local concerns.

Size and success, however, were not necessarily synonymous with efficiency. In many cases, in fact, corporations grew too rapidly for their own good. It was one thing to combine under a single management heretofore independent enterprises; it was quite another matter to coordinate their operations effectively, as United States Steel would unhappily learn. Executives had not yet devised the proper distribution of power and authority between operating officers (line) in charge of production and financial planners (staff) in the central office. Sometimes central staff executives unfamiliar with the basic technology of the industry made decisions that increased production costs; on other occasions the line officers of the operating companies competed with each other for men, materials, and markets to the detriment of the corporation as a whole. In other words, these immense vertically and horizontally integrated corporations too often suffered either from excessive centralization or from management conflicts bordering on corporate anarchy and, like U.S. Steel, found themselves among the least efficient firms in their sector of the economy. But in terms of business stability as distinguished from economic efficiency, size seemed to guarantee success, for the great industrial combinations that emerged in this era remain with us today.

THE MANAGERIAL REVOLUTION

Changes in the structure of the economy inexorably altered the world of business management. With the growing size of the firm and the evolving separation of ownership from actual company management, a professional managerial class emerged in American society. Educated in recently founded schools of business and engineering, trained in corporate law and finance, twentieth-century executives were an extremely specialized and professionalized breed. Drawn from the same social origins as the traditional business elite, the new executives differed in their relationship to the enterprise, their functions, and their aspirations.

In 1900 the typical American business leader was no longer a classical captain of industry. Rather than owning and running his own or his family's company, he now more likely served as the salaried member of a powerful corporate bureaucracy. Mostly American-born (more than 70 percent traced their origins to Colonial families), Protestant, urban, of the middle and upper class, and more highly educated than the mass of Americans, they fit themselves comfortably into well-established bureaucracies with specified channels of authority and clear hierarchies of ascent. Ultimate success was not measured by founding one's own firm; it was calculated on the possibility of a lifetime salaried career that might lead all the way to the top of the corporate hierarchy.

The new structure of management provided especially attractive opportunities for lawyers and technicians. Lawyers, for example, served to guide their corporate masters through political and legal shoals, all the while currying favor with the community on the basis of public relations campaigns. More than 80 percent of the post-1900 business elite never headed an enterprise but remained salaried employees throughout their careers. As a Morgan executive remarked: "I suppose that there is more or less prejudice against me because I wear the Morgan collar, but I am proud of it." After J. P.'s death in 1913, another associate observed: "I took orders from J. P. Morgan. I did as I was told."

The age of daring and domineering business buccaneers was drawing to its end. Respectability and responsibility became the most prized executive virtues. In a business world whose techniques more and more consisted of conference, consultation, and compromise, it was no longer wise to jump about from firm to firm, a trait that only indicated instability or unreliability. The road to the top passed through the established corporate hierarchy to whose orders aspirants on the lower rungs submitted cheerfully. Consultants advised aspiring executives that "ability is likely to be judged by the capacity to be congenial with colleagues, compatible with superiors." Another authority on corporate management observed: "Learning the ropes in most organizations is chiefly learning the who's who, what's what, and why's why of its informal society." Compatability combined with the right measure of specialized training and ambition as well as the requisite social origins made for the ideal corporate executive.

The reorganization of business enterprises brought with it the age of the "organization man." Americans in the early twentieth century continued to worship at the shrine of individualism and free competition, but the dynamics and realities of the business world guaranteed the triumph of collective management and oligopolistic market control.

THE RATIONALIZATION OF AGRICULTURE

The period from 1897 to 1914 is generally considered the golden age of American agriculture. For almost three decades before 1897 American farmers had suffered from falling prices for their products, rising charges for borrowed money, and unfavorable terms of trade between country and city. What had happened was quite simple. Throughout the late nineteenth century, as a result of the opening of virgin land around the world, improved techniques and machines for cultivation, and the spread of rapid, inexpensive forms of transportation, the supply of foodstuffs expanded more rapidly than demand. The production of agricultural products more than kept pace with the fast growing cities and increasing population. The consequence was lower prices for urban consumers and three decades of rural crisis. Thus dawned the era of agrarian protest culminating in the Populist crusade of the 1890s.

After 1897, however, the economic balance between country and city shifted. For a time urban population and demand for foodstuffs increased relatively more rapidly than rises in agricultural productivity. American farmers now had time to adjust to the technological and commercial changes which in the course of the previous century had transformed the basis of agriculture. Not until the 1920s would a second wave of technological and commercial innovations again place agrarians in an unfavorable economic milieu.

All the basic statistics of agricultural economics reflected the farmer's happy situation. Between 1900 and 1914 the acreage devoted to the production of corn and the bushels harvested scarcely increased. As a result the price per bushel of corn rose in that period from 35¢ to 71¢, never falling below the initial figure. Wheat followed a like progression, though in certain years its productivity even declined absolutely. But wheat prices ranged between 62¢ and 97¢ a bushel, also never dropping below the initial figure. Even prices for cotton, a notoriously overproduced and depressed crop, exceeded the fabled 10¢ per pound figure seven times between 1900 and 1914, going as high as 14¢ in 1910.

In a variety of other ways farmers also benefited from the changed terms of trade between country and city. The crisis of the nineteenth century had forced many small, marginal, and inefficient farmers off the land, leaving as survivors those most likely to take advantage of altered conditions and improved opportunities. Staple crop growers always had to contend with the vagaries of a fluctuating international market; hence many more farmers turned to satisfying the needs of urban America. As incomes rose the amount of money expended on primary grains (bread and cereal foods) declined relative to expenditures on other more desired items: vegetables, fruits, dairy products, and fresh meat. Thus farmers who were reasonably close to urban markets diversified their production and switched to crops or products that yielded high financial returns on a per unit basis. In fact such farmers had little choice in the matter, for the closer farm land was to an urban center the higher its value (cost) and the greater the taxes levied on it. Wherever farmers were positioned to respond to changes in demand, they did so.

What farmers had failed to win as a result of political protest and third-party crusades in the late nineteenth century, they now gained as a consequence of economic change and pressure-group tactics. Forming an identifiable bloc in Congress and in state legislatures, farm representatives successfully pushed the demands of their rural constituents. Rural free delivery and parcel post came into operation, extending to farm homes the postal privileges that had long been an urban monopoly. Country roads were improved, widened, and in many instances blacktopped. State agricultural colleges were transformed into elaborate research-oriented institutions that offered a series of innovations for the benefit of successful farmers. Under new federal legislation, farmers obtained funds to support agricultural education programs, special federally guaranteed farm mortgage loans, and federal department of agriculture extension agents who provided farm families with economic and technical advice. As time passed the federal government and the larger state universities became in effect American agriculture's research and development department.

The one glaring exception to the story of prosperity in the "golden age of American agriculture" was the South. Still largely bound to cotton monoculture and producing in the nation's least urban region, Southern farmers failed to benefit as fully as their northern cousins. Although in the years 1900 to 1920 just under half the farms in the United States were located in the South, the region counted more than two-thirds of all the nation's tenants and sharecroppers. Indeed only in the South did the number of farm tenants increase between 1900 and 1920. Nationally the number of tenants increased by about 430,000; in the South there was a rise of almost one million, producing a grand total of 2.1 million southern tenants and croppers. Among blacks, over 70 percent of all farmers were tenants and over 40 percent of the latter were sharecroppers. For the majority of southern farmers who were tenants and croppers, then, there was nothing to look forward to except the crop lien, the merchant's high credit prices, perpetual indebtedness, abysmal poverty, and in some cases outright peonage.

OCCUPATIONS AND INCOMES

The increasing industrialization and concentration of the American economy between 1900 and 1920 is clearly evidenced by the changing structure of the job market and the occupational distribution of workers. Although the size of the total labor force grew by almost 50 percent, there was practically no increase in the number of farm workers and only slightly more than a 10 percent rise in the number of self-employed individuals, including farmers. In fact, the self-employed and the more highly paid and independent strata of the executive class declined from 25.6 percent of the work force to 21.9 percent, while farm workers decreased from 17.7 percent to 11.7 percent. The major increase both absolutely and relatively occurred among manufacturing workers who increased from roughly 5½ million in 1900 to 10.7 million in 1920, or close to 40 percent of the work force. Both in its manpower distribution and growth, the American labor force was concentrated in the primary (extractive industries) and secondary (manufacturing) sectors of the economy, with the tertiary (service and trade) sectors lagging far behind.

Indeed if one focuses on the male labor force, an even heavier concentration of workers in the primary and secondary sectors becomes apparent. Almost 45 percent of all male workers were by 1920 employed in the mining, construction, transportation, or manufacturing sectors of the economy, an increase of some 7 percent since 1900. Females, on the other hand, were already heavily concentrated in the clerical, sales, and service areas. Almost one-quarter of women workers could be found either in the clerical and sales and service field compared to only 9.8 percent of men in the former and 3.7 percent in the latter.

An analysis of the distribution of the labor force also reveals other perhaps unexpected facts. For example, throughout the years 1900–1920, there were always more than twice as many miners and construction workers as iron and steel workers. Moreover not until 1920 did the number of iron and steel employees surpass the size of the cotton textile work force, and then by only ten thousand. Yet more unexpected, perhaps, domestic servants outnumbered all the above categories of workers, rising above the two million level in 1910. Female workers, in particular, were concentrated in domestic service; in both 1900 and 1910 more women found employment as domestics than as manufacturing workers, and they would have to wait another ten years before employment opportunities in the factory surpassed those in the home. Even in manufacturing women had to settle for jobs in the lowest-paying sector of the industrial economy: cotton textiles and the clothing trades.

Skill requirements and levels were also changing for the American workers in the period 1900–1920. The strong back was in the process of becoming less desired than a quick mind or agile hands. Between 1900 and 1920 the proportion of workers described as unskilled fell from 34.9 percent to 28.9 percent, and among male workers alone the unskilled declined from 39.0 percent to 31.5 percent of the labor force. The sharpest increase in the demand for labor came among machine operators who were classified as semiskilled (job training was required but a formal apprenticeship was unnecessary) and who formed the largest proportion of the manual, or blue-collar, labor force.

Wages and incomes, to be sure, correlated closely with level of skill and type of job. The skilled and semiskilled labored more steadily for shorter hours and higher wages than the unskilled. Manufacturing workers generally earned more than twice as much annually as farm workers or domestic servants, both of whom failed to cross the $300 annual earnings threshold until World War I. Within the manufacturing sector employees in the hard-goods industries, especially machinists and skilled steelworkers, earned much more than laborers in textiles, clothing, and other consumer soft goods. Among the traditional skilled and apprenticed trades—printers, carpenters, plumbers, among others—many workers commanded premium wages and developed a life style that could only be considered eminently respectable and comfortable.

Regardless of skill or occupation, life in the years 1900–1920 remained a struggle for most American workers. Business cycles, technological changes, seasonal fluctuations in consumer demand, and even the weather made unemployment a recurrent and serious problem. Between 1900 and 1920 total unemployment ranged from a low of 1.7 percent of the civilian labor force in 1906 to a high of 8.5 percent in 1915, with the figure exceeding the 5 percent level in nine of those years. As a percentage of nonfarm employees, unemployment bulked even larger, ranging from a low of 3.9 percent to a high of 15.6 percent, also exceeding 10 percent for nine years.

Throughout the period annual real wages rose steadily if slowly. Adjusted for likely periods of unemployment as well as changes in the price level, earnings climbed from $445 annually in 1900 to $648 in 1919 at the end of World War I, with the most substantial rise coming during the war years. Yet this substantial increase in real income left the ordinary worker in a less than enviable position. According to estimates made by several independent social workers and government agencies, a minimum health and decency budget in the years 1909–1912 ranged from a yearly income of $800 to $876 for a family of four, to $505 for a single man, and $466 for a working woman. Yet average real earnings during those years fluctuated between $543 and $551, an amount that was scarcely adequate to support a family of four. Moreover, annual earnings for the great mass of workers fell well below the average which was inflated by the incomes of more highly paid workers and even executives. For most working-class families in the Progressive Era a decent standard of living still depended on the existence of multiple breadwinners.

Testimony by a variety of laborers and observers attests to the poverty that was often part of the working-class life. "If our women go to church," said immigrant iron miners on Minnesota's Mesabi Range in 1916, "the priest they say—'What the matter with Austrian women? They stink in church.' If we eat, we can't dress, and if we dress, we don't eat." A woman worker, testifying before a state legislative committee in New York, described her life prior to marriage in these words: "I didn't live, I simply existed. It took me months and months to save up money to buy a dress or a pair of shoes . . . I had the hardest struggle I ever had in my life." Describing the appearance of the children of steelworkers in the Pittsburgh area, a reporter wrote in 1909: "The faces are peculiarly aged in expression, and their eyes gleam with premature knowledge, which is the result of a daily struggle, not for life, but for existence." A Rumanian Jewish immigrant reflecting on his experiences in the new world, said: "This was the boasted American freedom and opportunity—the freedom for respectable citizens to sell cabbages from hideous carts, the opportunity to live in those monstrous, dirty caves that shut out the sunshine."

The American working class thus remained on the margin of poverty at a time when the proportion of income received by the top 5 percent of the population continued to rise and its possession of national wealth increased. In 1910 the richest 1 percent of the population owned about 47 percent of national wealth (property, claims on property, or goods, capital, that is, land, capital, goods, savings, stocks, and bonds which produce income), and in 1916 that same 1 percent earned about 16 percent of national income (money earned as a product of labor, interest payments on savings, dividends from investments—stocks and bonds— and rent derived from land ownership). Furthermore the bulk of the income of the wealthy came not from work but from possession of capital assets, that is, claims on wealth. Dividends, interest, and rent provided the wealthy with their primary sources of income, while steelworkers, for one example, toiled up to eighty-four hours a week merely to survive.

Such disparities in income, wealth, and living conditions produced much of the radicalism and reform politics that set off the Progressive Era from the preceding decades in United States history. The structure of national society and substantial cultural shifts also affected the politics of the opening years of the new century.

THE ETHNO-RELIGIOUS MIX

Features already apparent in the structure of American society in 1900 became even more visible in the succeeding decade and a half. Mass immigration continued to diversify the population; urbanization pro- ceeded apace; and millions of common people regularly moved resi- dences, not only within cities, but also on an intra- and interstate basis.

Until the outbreak of world war in the summer of 1914 European immigrants entered the United States on a scale hitherto inconceivable. In six separate years over one million immigrants arrived, and from 1902 to 1914 the number of newcomers never fell below 648,000 annually. Indeed almost fourteen million immigrants arrived in the United States in a fifteen-year period.

As remarkable as the size of the immigration was the shift in its sources. The bulk of the newcomers were from the lands of central, eastern, and southern Europe, and the vast majority among them were of Slavic or Italian origins with Catholicism and Judaism as their primary religions. Only once in this period did the number of immigrants from Ireland exceed 50,000, and for all of Great Britain the 100,000 level was never approached. As a result by 1910, among the foreign-born residents in the United States, individuals born in central, eastern, and southern Europe outnumbered those from northwestern Europe by almost two to one; by 1920 the differential neared the three to one ratio.

The impact of mass immigration could be seen in almost all aspects and regions of American society. In bituminous coal mining, which was scattered from western Pennsylvania to Wyoming, until 1890 the over- whelming majority of workers had been English-speaking; by 1919 only 5 percent of the workers were of English origin. At the great Carnegie steel plants in Homestead, Pennsylvania, by 1910, 11,694 of 14,349 common laborers were of south or east European extraction. And in the textile town of Lawrence, Massachusetts, in 1911, 74,000 of the 86,000 inhabitants were first- or second-generation Americans with Southeast Europeans (mostly Italian) comprising fully one-third of the population. Even the "wild West" was inundated with immigrant workers. In the same district of Arizona once made famous by gunmen and lawmen—Tombstone—federal investigators surveying conditions among copper miners in 1917 discovered between twenty-six and thirty-two different nationalities at work in the district's mines, with Mexicans, Spaniards, and Italians forming 80 percent of the work force in one-third of the state's copper mining regions. One Chicago garment worker was later to reminisce about his lunchtime coworkers who included two Italians, two Jews, two Croatians, two Swedish girls, a Slavic boy, a Bohemian girl, a French widow, a Lithuanian man, a Russian man, and a Polish girl.

Each of these diverse ethnic groups brought its own traditions to the United States and hence interpreted the American experience in different ways. In many instances the immigrants brought with them long-simmering Old World tensions and hatreds. It did not require the process of immigration and cultural acclimatization to turn Irish Catholics against English or Welsh Protestants, and vice-versa. But it did take the New World experience to cause an Irish worker to observe: "It goes against the grain in an English-speaking man to fetch and carry for a Slovack or a Pole."

Scorned by a dominant society in the grip of racist ideas and divided among themselves, the immigrants sought security through the creation of a tight web of fraternal and religious orders which would both preserve old traditions and ease adjustments to a new society. Wherever they could, newcomers maintained their ethnic heritage. And that heritage shaped their accommodation with American society and determined whether or not their Old World tradition would survive.

East European Jews proved particularly adept at building a variety of ethnic institutions to shield them from the worst shocks of acclimatization. They brought with them to the United States a long history of having to accommodate to alien status in whatever society they happened to live. They also carried along a well-established institutional life based on the synagogue and its educational offshoots, their own self-governing community (Kehillah), and in some cases radical trade unions and political parties (the Polish and Russian bunds).

In the New World, east European Jews proceeded to reestablish their basic communal institutions. First came the synagogues—small and modest initially but increasingly costly and ornate with the passage of time—and then the Yiddish-language newspapers, magazines, and theater followed by East European-style coffee houses and restaurants. The Workmen's Circle developed as a socialist fraternal organization to provide health, death benefits, and also lectures and educational programs to hardworking, poor Jews. For the more militant and secular, there were a myriad of trade unions and the Socialist party of America, which laid down deep roots between 1901 and 1917 in the American-Jewish community. No Jewish immigrant had to bemoan a lack of institutional opportunities.

Not all immigrants, however, were as well prepared as the East European Jews to adapt to American life and society. If Jews represented one pole of the immigrant adaptation, south Italians reflected the other. Singularly oppressed in the Old World and influenced by a superstitious, almost pagan, village and family code, Italian immigrants acclimated more slowly than most. Their basic ties were to the blood family, not to the church, trade union, ethnic society, or political party. Such traditions caused a priest in New York City's Italian immigrant community to lament the fact that "Italian institutions are very few and very poor. . . . I should like to see the eyes of the public open to the fact that very little is done here for Italians by Italian organizations."

Most immigrants experienced a process of adjustment somewhere between that of the Jews and the Italians. Consequently all over urban America in the cities inhabited by new immigrants, Jewtowns, Little Italys, Bohemias, and Hungarys emerged and thrived. Whether in Scranton, Pennsylvania, Binghamton, New York, or Milwaukee, Wisconsin, immigrant neighborhoods could be distinguished immediately, even from the distance, by the golden domes or towering spires of their Eastern Orthodox or Catholic churches.

The Progressive Era was perhaps the golden age of the immigrant ghetto in the United States. Although recent historical research suggests an enormous population turnover in most urban working-class neighborhoods, including immigrant ones, it must be remembered that for most newcomers the ghetto was not a place of residence—it was a state of mind. No matter how many immigrants might enter and leave a particular neighborhood what counted ultimately was the enduring existence of such ethnic institutions as churches, social clubs, coffee houses, and theaters. Regardless of how ethnically diversified communities may appear retrospectively in census statistics, what mattered was whom you prayed with, dined with, drank with, and played with, not whom you lived next door to. After World War I residential mobility and new settlement patterns would undermine the ghetto mentality—but from 1900 to 1917 that was not yet the case.

Although the vast majority of black Americans continued to reside in the South, northern black urban communities assumed clear form in the Progressive Era. In the years before World War I restrictive housing covenants and cunning real estate practices turned a portion of South Side Chicago into a sharply defined black belt. During the same years central Harlem passed from a semisuburban retreat for socially mobile immigrants to a declining community more and more restricted to blacks, for whom there was no escape. In such black settlements the mass of men and women had to content themselves with the most menial jobs. In Chicago, for example, in 1910 over 45 percent of employed black men were porters, waiters, servants, or janitors, while 63 percent of working women were engaged as domestic servants or laundresses. Confined spatially, black Americans, unlike the new immigrants, were becoming by 1917 trapped in the only truly enduring American ghettos.

THE EMERGENCE OF A METROPOLITAN SOCIETY

The Progressive years witnessed a continuation in the drift of population from country to city. Between 1900 and 1910 urban population increased by twelve million compared to a rise of only four million in rural population (approximately forty-two to forty-nine million respectively). The next decade experienced an even greater differential in the comparative urban and rural population growth rates. Between 1910 and 1920 city inhabitants soared by fourteen million while rural people increased in number by less than two million. Thus in 1920, for the first time in the nation's history, urban inhabitants outnumbered rural residents by 54,157,973 to 51,552,647, a differential that would widen vastly in succeeding decades.

Most increases in urban population still occurred within the juridical-political boundaries of established cities. Indeed, in some cases, cities continued to annex adjoining areas or neighboring units themselves sought annexation in order to gain superior city services. In such large cities as New York and Chicago, trolley lines, subways, and elevated railways spread their steel and copper webs around the urban area carrying masses of people to hitherto undeveloped sections. For the first time in over two centuries the population of Manhattan Island actually began to decline, as population spread to the outlying boroughs of Brooklyn and the Bronx. In Chicago residents steadily drifted away from the crowded city center to the far southwest and northwest sides where trolleys carried them to rows of modest one-family bungalows.

In some cities, however, internal space for growth had vanished, or adjoining communities resisted urban imperialism and refused to be annexed. Despite their separate legal existence, towns and villages immediately adjacent to central cities had become an integral part of a larger metropolitan economic and social structure. In 1910 the Census Bureau for the first time recognized the existence of what it labeled as Standard Metropolitan Statistical Areas, districts that ranged from New York (including Newark, New Jersey) with 616,927 acres and 6,500,000 people in the core to Portland, Oregon, with 43,538 acres and 215,048 central city residents. Twenty-five such metropolitan areas in all parts of the nation were identified in 1910. In those twenty-five urban agglomerations, the urbanized areas just outside the central city experienced more population growth than did the core between 1900 and 1910. This process accelerated during the following decade. By 1920 the Census Bureau added fourteen more metropolitan areas and counted seven million residents whom it classified as suburban, composing one-fourth of the total inhabitants of the twenty-nine largest metropolitan districts.

Industry, too, moved with population. Between 1900 and 1920 the industrial suburb became a common feature of American life. By 1920 fifty-seven suburbs housed a larger proportion of wage workers than did the central cities they neighbored.

Within the central cities and their suburban fringes, population continued to spread outward, and residential patterns simultaneously became more marked by social and economic differentiation. Integrated by economics, transportation, and communications, the city remained segregated by community, class, and culture. This was especially true of the larger cities with vast immigrant populations. As soon as income allowed, more fortunate members of the working class would flee the core slums for more sparsely settled neighborhoods. Substantial middle-class and professional individuals would in turn establish residential communities spatially and socially distinct from the neighborhoods of the respectable working class. Thus the residential sections of the old central city were left to those too poor to escape or those sufficiently wealthy to create insulated "silk-stocking" districts. In effect, then, by World War I inhabitants of the same city had become strangers to each other, made alien by differences in income, nationality, race, and religion.

One of the clearest indications of the gulf that had developed between lower-class city dwellers and their social "betters" was the surge of interest in urban America's "Other Half," which might perhaps be dated from Jacob Riis's portraits of New York City slum life in the 1890s. Increasing middle-class concern with slum-dwellers manifested itself in two ways—fear and anxiety and the missionary impulse to carry the gospel of middle-class manners and values to the lower class. Riis's writings and work reflected both impulses. One of the most notable urban reformers of his day, he portrayed slum-dwellers in terms of racial stereotypes and suggested the image of "the man with a dagger," the Progressive Era's counterpart to contemporary America's ubiquitous mugger. More indicative of popular middle-class anxieties were newspaper headlines that, in reaction to the massive Italian immigration of the times, featured the words "Mafia" and "black hand," implying the Italian immigrant's propensity for crime and violence. Fear, however, did not retard the missionary impulse; if anything, it fueled it. The Progressive Era was the heyday of the settlement house movement, that noble effort by middle- and upper-class Americans—largely female it might be noted—to live among the poor, understand them, and ultimately uplift them. Into the settlement houses went such estimable reformers as Jane Addams, Lillian Wald, Florence Kelley, Frances Perkins, and even Eleanor Roosevelt.

Efforts to reform and control the physical growth of the city and its internal social system floundered as a consequence of neighborhood population turnover. In smaller industrial cities within a generation a majority of the working-class inhabitants might pack up and leave. In larger cities and metropolitan districts, working-class residents might well remain within the same city and its suburbs for a lifetime; but it was quite rare for them to stay in the same home for several years or in a neighborhood for a decade or more. Many Americans were beginning to ask how society would hold together in large, impersonal cities where people failed to establish stable residential roots and neighborhoods built on a sense of community. By 1920 the term "urban crisis" was a cliché of social commentators. The University of Chicago urban sociologist, Robert Park, observed that "Cities, and particularly the great cities, are in unstable equilibrium." The result is "that the vast casual and mobile aggregations which constitute our urban population are in a state of perpetual agitation, swept by every new wind of doctrine, subject to constant alarms, and in consequence the community is in a chronic condition of crisis."

THE PROFESSIONALIZATION OF SOCIETY

Not all groups in society existed in a state of perpetual motion and unstable equilibrium. Indeed many citizens occupied positions and practiced professions that provided a foundation for stability and promised to secure social order. Over the course of the Progressive Era these occupational groups sought to become more "professional" by defining themselves more precisely, by adopting stringent formal conditions for membership, and by exercising effective control over admission.

This trend toward professionalization is seen in the field of medicine. During the nineteenth century "quacks" practiced as widely as trained doctors and probably treated more patients. Patent medicines and magical elixirs were a way of life for millions of Americans. Bogus medical schools, willing to offer aspiring "doctors" a diploma for the right price, flourished. No true profession could survive in such a milieu. Even after the founding of the American Medical Association in 1846 doctors had failed to raise significantly the standards of their profession. Then in 1901 the AMA reorganized itself and became a more active force in medicine. Between 1901 and 1910 its membership soared from 8,400 to 70,000. With rising membership came greater social and political influence. In state after state doctors demanded tighter and more scientific standards for admission to practice medicine, and the doctors themselves insisted on setting those standards. With the compliance of state and local governments, medical societies affiliated to the AMA certified and licensed new practitioners, exercised greater control over schools of medicine (reforming the weaker ones and eliminating the bogus ones), and created the medical profession as we know it today.

Public health, too, benefited from the professionalization of medicine. Urban politicians began to shield their public health departments and officers from the pressures of machine politics. Free to act as professionals, not as political hacks, public health officials led vast immunization campaigns and played a major role in the improvement of sewage disposal and the provision of pure water. Their professional status within the field of medicine was recognized in 1912 by the establishment at the Massachusetts Institute of Technology of a school of public health.

In return for allowing doctors to set their own professional standards, Americans appeared to receive improved care and health. The adjusted death rate per thousand fell from 17 to 1900 to 13.2 in 1920 and life expectancy increased from forty-nine to fifty-six years. The falling death rate was especially notable in contagious and epidemic diseases: typhoid deaths fell from 30.8 per 100,000 in 1900 to 5 in 1920, while diphtheria and croup dropped from 44 to 19.6. Moreover, between 1885 and 1915, the infant mortality rate declined by fully a third. In medicine, at least, professionalization seemed to work.

Lawyers did not lag far behind doctors in establishing more professional standards for their occupation. They were as eager to make the self-read and self-taught lawyer of the nineteenth century a relic as doctors had been to remove quacks from medical practice. Throughout the late nineteenth century, after the founding of the American Bar Association in 1878, leaders in the profession struggled to raise the level of legal education and to make graduation from law school a prerequisite for the practice of law. In 1894 they achieved a large measure of success when New York State adopted a central examining board of reputable lawyers to control admission to the profession. New York was the pioneer, not the exception, for by 1916, 48 state and 623 local bar associations functioned as the guardians of the profession and its standards.

Trends in law and medicine foreshadowed the United States drift toward a diploma society. Formal education in state-certified schools replaced apprenticeships-on-the-job in more and more occupations. This trend could be seen in student growth at the secondary school level as well as in the sharp rise in average daily attendance. Between 1900 and 1920 the number of high school students increased four-fold and high school graduates as a percentage of the population seventeen years old rose from 6.4 percent to 16.8 percent. Even more significant perhaps was the growth of public vocational education. By 1910, thirty-four cities provided trade and factory schools, twenty-three technical high schools offered more specialized training, and home economics for girls became the rage. Colleges and universities, too, reflected the tendency, as the number of postsecondary business and engineering schools expanded enormously.

As schools and formal education increased in importance, it became imperative to create professional requirements for teachers. Largely in response to this need public universities in the late nineteenth century began to offer courses and programs in educational theory and practice, and they encouraged the formation of accrediting agencies to certify public school standards.

Teachers, too long exploited by low salaries and victims of minimal public esteem, sought to professionalize their vocation. Eager to increase the prestige of their occupation, improve employment security, and protect themselves from public wrath, teachers successfully insisted on specific, formal, state-sanctioned requirements for professional public school positions. Supported in their struggle by the myriad teachers' colleges and accrediting agencies, the teachers created a new profession with precise licensed standards, established salary scales with built-in increments, tenure of employment, specialized school administrators, and non-partisan school boards. By 1910 the National Eduation Association functioned as the professional educators counterpart to the AMA and ABA.

During the same years social reform and work evolved from a philanthropic to a professional enterprise. The depressions of the late nineteenth century had increased popular demands on private charities and had threatened to bankrupt them. Charity leaders sought to make welfare procedures more systematic, scientific, and hence orderly. In both New York City and Buffalo at the end of the 1890s, local Charity Organization Societies came into existence. These new institutions combined previously autonomous and frequently small charitable societies under one central administration. These institutions sought to establish standards of professionalism and efficiency in the selection of welfare recipients. Linked to the settlement houses and reform institutions such as the Russell Sage Foundation, a new generation of social workers sought to substitute statistics for emotions, facts for feelings, and scientific assistance for chaotic charity.

By 1911 the social workers had become sufficiently conscious of their professional status to form the National Federation of Settlements, and a few years later they took control of the ancient National Conference of Charities and Corrections, which they renamed the National Conference of Social Work. Changes in vocabulary accurately reflected alterations in status. The social workers' primary journal, titled *Charities* (later *Charities and Commons*), was renamed *Survey* in 1909 in tribute to the statistical survey techniques of professional social work. And as a profession, social work needed professional schools, which the University of Chicago and Harvard accordingly provided.

So it went also with architects, journalists, housing reformers, and even city planners. To serve society in progressive America one had to be certified by the right school, the proper professional society, or the requisite state board. Meanwhile, in the universities that catalyzed the professionalization of society and benefited from it, academics perfected such guilds as the American Historical Association and the American Economic Association, which they had inherited from the nineteenth century, or formed new ones to serve such now autonomous disciplines as sociology, political science, and psychology.

WORKING-CLASS LIFE AND INSTITUTIONS

The life of blue-collar Americans remains shrouded in uncertainty. In an era when organization and professionalization assumed overriding importance, workers appeared to be forgotten citizens. Aside from their families, ethnic churches and clubs (if they were first- or second-generation immigrants as the majority were), and perhaps immediate neighbors, blue-collar Americans, then as now, seemed to have little social and institutional life. Professionals, as we have seen, erected their occupational guilds. Nonprofessional middle-class Americans—shopkeepers, realtors, local bankers, among others—swelled the ranks of the plethora American fraternal and service clubs: Masons, Elks, Woodmen, Rotarians, and Kiwanians flourished as never before in progressive America. But the vast majority of workers moved too often to set down firm institutional and community roots. In the words of one scholar, millions of workers seemed "a group of permanent transients, buffeted about from place to place, never quite able to sink roots and to form organizations" and thus appeared "alienated but invisible."

What may have been true for a majority of workers was not representative of a small but significant minority—those involved with working-class efforts at self-organization. Those men and women who actually built and led working-class organizations eagerly sought to make their unions as tightly-knit, efficiently operated, and bureaucratically led as their professional paradigms. And labor leaders achieved some success.

Between 1897 and 1914 the number of union members rose from 440,000 to 2,647,000, and the number of unions affiliated to the American Federation of Labor, the primary national labor center, increased from 58 to 110. In such industries as mining, construction, metals and machinery, and clothing, union growth proved phenomenal, increasing by as much as 2,000 percent in mining (21,000 members in 1897; 380,000 in 1914).

The extent to which the self-image and the behavioral patterns of organized labor were influenced by the professionalization of American society in the Progressive Era can be seen in the rhetoric of the movement's two most prominent leaders: Samuel Gompers, president of the AFL, and John Mitchell, president of the United Mine Workers. Both Gompers and Mitchell in their public speeches and writings frequently compared the trade union to a responsible business corporation, one that provided maximum benefits for its shareholders (union members), dealt fairly with its adversaries (employers), and always considered the public interest (consumers). Union leaders pledged to enforce labor contracts achieved through collective bargaining and to discipline members who broke signed agreements or provoked conflicts with equitable employers. Just as industrialists sought to systematize work processes through scientific management and professionals attempted to control entry to their occupations by certification, labor leaders struggled to enmesh labor-management relations in a tight web of formal rules and procedures binding on both parties.

For those workers enrolled in unions and protected by contracts, bureaucratic labor leaders provided improved job security, higher wages, shorter hours, and better working conditions. But only a minority of blue-collar workers enjoyed such protection, and that minority was not to be found among laborers in the basic mass-production sectors of the economy or among those most exploited.

Not all labor leaders limited themselves to the construction of trade unions patterned on bureaucratic models or to serving the interests of a minority among the nation's workers. A small but idealistic group of trade unionists and radical agitators met in convention in Chicago in the summer of 1905 to found a labor organization better able to serve the mass of workers and to promise them a new, nonexploitative utopian future. To achieve mass organization and a new society, these radicals formed the Industrial Workers of the World, or Wobblies.

During its first five years the Wobblies practically fell apart as a result of internal ideological and personal divisions. But after surviving the difficult years from 1905 to 1909, it became the only organization that offered millions of transient workers "a ready-made dream of a new world where there is a new touch of sweetness and light and where for a while they can escape the torture of forever being indecently kicked about." It offered forgotten workers a sense of self-respect, importance, and power, and consequently from 1909 until it was repressed savagely by public authorities in 1917–1918, some two to three million workers passed through the IWW's ranks and millions more felt its influence. The IWW cadres could be found wherever industrial conflict erupted in progressive America—e.g., Lawrence, Massachusetts, in 1912; Akron, Ohio, in 1913; Wheatland, California, in 1915; Minnesota's Mesabi Range in 1916; or the Washington woods in 1917.

Though the Wobblies failed to survive as a stable organization and to challenge the AFL successfully, they nevertheless raised fundamental questions about American society. The tumultuous history of the IWW revealed lucidly the gap between American ideals of equality and brotherhood and their practice. The IWW pointed out the distance between notions of a society based on law, not men, and one in which those with social and economic power abused the law in order to oppress the weak. How adequate, asked the Wobblies, was political democracy in a nation in which economic power was so unevenly distributed?

CULTURE, THOUGHT, AND RECREATION

During the Progressive Era American culture and thought experienced a renaissance. Every field of creative endeavor enjoyed a dynamic burst of energy and a surge of innovation. This was the age of Theodore Dreiser and Edith Wharton in the novel; William James and John Dewey in philosophy; George Bellows and John Sloan in painting; Louis Sullivan and Frank Lloyd Wright in architecture; Thorstein Veblen in economics; and Charles Beard in history. As one of the bright young intellectuals, Randolph Bourne, was to say in 1913: "It is the glory of the present age that in it one can be young."

A peculiar paradox and dualism of thought gripped intellectuals. Artists and writers saw man (and woman) in the grasp of powerful impersonal forces that irresistibly shaped life and society. Huge corporations and trusts, an anonymous and impersonal urban society, and corrupt political machines dominated individual existence. The novels of Dreiser, as well as those of Frank Norris and Jack London, gloried in revealing man as an aimlessly and carelessly driven mechanism. Norris could be coldly blunt as the following language suggests: "Men were mere nothings, mere animaculae, mere ephermides that fluttered and fell and were forgotten between dawn and dusk. . . . Force only existed—force that brought men into the world—Force that crowded them out of it to make way for the succeeding generation." Yet these same writers called on man to rebel against the forces shaping his life, and typically the heroes of their novels were strong men (in London's case, sometimes supermen) capable, through will and force of personality, of rising above the mass.

Indeed, intellectuals who spoke so glibly about man's impotence in the face of social reality themselves rebelled against inherited and established customs, whether cultural, artistic, or sexual. By 1913 a new spirit seemed to possess artists and intellectuals. That year the Armory art show in New York for the first time introduced an American audience to the impressionistic and cubist techniques then revolutionizing European, especially French, painting. Thrilling to their liberation from the past and to the importation of new ideas from the Old World, young Americans gathered together in small intellectual communities in New York's Greenwich Village, Chicago's near north side, and even in Davenport, Iowa. Bohemia could be found at home now as well as in London, Paris, or Florence. Young rebels freely attacked sexual repression, the institution of marriage, the sanctity of the family, and the existence of a capitalist society (the membership list of Greenwich Village Branch One of the Socialist party read like an honor roll of intellectual and artistic America). In 1911 these cultural innovators had inaugurated publication of *The Masses,* a sprightly edited and attractively designed magazine that combined socialism with wit, serious essays with proletarian poetry, and new art forms with biting political cartoons. Until it fell victim to wartime repression in 1918, *The Masses* effectively carried its message of cultural liberation to its readers, though one wag commented: "They draw nude women for *The Masses.* Thick, fat, ungainly lasses. How does that help the working classes?"

Fresh breezes were also stirring academic America. Unable to hold a steady university post more because of his personal idiosyncracies than his radical ideas, Thorstein Veblen nevertheless transformed the study of academic economics. In his pathbreaking books *The Theory of the Leisure Class* and *The Theory of Business Enterprise,* Veblen turned away from the conventional economist's analysis of the immutable laws of supply and demand to an examination of how the national economy actually functioned in reality. He described a system in which business existed to make profits at the expense of quality and craftmanship and in which businessmen, not engineers, made decisions based on crass material, not technological, considerations. In Veblen's America the leisure class practiced conspicuous consumption, the purchase and display of gaudy, expensive, and unnecessary goods intended to establish one's claim to high status and respect, a custom emulated by the less wealthy who provided the basis for the emergence of the world's first mass consumer society.

In history, Charles Beard's *An Economic Interpretation of the Constitution* (1911) focused the searchlight of scholarship on the founding fathers. Beard's exposure revealed the founding fathers to be men, not demigods, individuals whose personal material interests influenced their political philosophies and practices. That, to be sure, was not an earth-shattering conclusion but in 1911 it approached heresy.

William James and John Dewey were simultaneously revising the meaning and application of philosophy. Challenging immutable philosophic principles, James and Dewey taught that process was more important than conclusion, that the end was implicit in the means used to achieve it. Through observation and experimentation with changing social reality—a method that itself remained constant—philosophers could regularly reinterpret the world and offer society goals that worked in practice as well as in theory. Applying this philosophy of pragmatism, as it came to be known, to the field of education, Dewey sought to bring the real world into the classroom (or take students from the classroom situation to the society around them), a concept that made him indelibly associated with the "progressive education" movement.

By the eve of World War I the intellectual rebels had mounted a devastating attack on the culture and values inherited from the nineteenth century. In thought, scholarship, and life itself, moral certainty fell before the paradoxes of the real world. There was a growing awareness that values might be variable rather than constant, relative rather than absolute. The nineteenth-century belief in inevitable, beneficent progress was also wavering. In the human jungle portrayed by artists, it was the greedy and the cunning, not the ethical and the good, who regularly triumphed. Moreover nineteenth-century forms in the novel, painting, and architecture were strongly challenged by the experimentation of naturalistic novelists, nonrepresentational painters, and functional architects.

Powerful as was the swirl of intellectual currents in Progressive America, the tide of new ideas bypassed the mass of citizens. Most Americans from 1900 to 1917 continued to find their enlightenment and enjoyment in the newspaper, the family magazine, vaudeville, burlesque, and increasingly in that recent innovation, the moving picture. Larger numbers of people were also finding pleasure in attending professional and collegiate sports events.

Baseball, about which Zane Grey wrote, "Every boy likes base-ball, and if he doesn't he's not a boy," assumed its modern dimensions during the Progressive Era. By 1903 the National and American Leagues had both achieved stability, and the victors in the respective leagues inaugurated that great American autumn tradition: the World Series. To satisfy

Jack Johnson, the black
heavyweight fighter
Brown Brothers

the growing spectator interest in professional baseball and also to increase their profits, club owners built a new generation of concrete and
steel ballparks, of which the most famous were the Polo Grounds (Manhattan, the Giants, 1911) and Ebbets Field (Brooklyn, the Dodgers,
1913). Up to 35,000 fans crowded into the ballparks, and team managers
and star ballplayers became front-page newspaper copy and national
culture heroes. Connie Mack and John J. McGraw served as the era's
managerial geniuses and Chicago's Tinker to Evers to Chance double-
play combination, as well as Christy Mathewson, Honus Wagner, and Ty
Cobb, became household names. By 1913 there were not only two major
professional leagues with teams in the nation's largest cities but also forty
minor leagues with clubs in medium-sized and small cities all over the
nation.

Intercollegiate athletics, especially football, also developed a mass spectator appeal. After some years of chaos and physical mayhem, which threatened to end permanently college football, the game was reorganized in 1906 under the control of the newly formed National Collegiate Athletic Association. Rule revisions, which opened up the style of play and made the game more exciting, increased spectator interest so much that by 1914 it was no longer unusual for a major intercollegiate contest to attract a crowd of fifty thousand or more. Off the playing fields of Harvard, Yale, Princeton, Chicago, and Michigan, the football powerhouses of the day, came a generation of sports heroes known as All-Americans.

Intercollegiate football seemed a strange phenomenon indeed. Apparently in the United States amateur athletes had to become as "professional" as doctors and lawyers, and football teams had to function as efficiently as corporations. An elaborate system of recruiting potential stars and training them in preparatory schools and colleges had gone a long way, according to *Nation* Magazine in 1912, "to removing the silly notion that intercollegiate games are played just for the fun of the thing." How could fun exist, wondered the magazine, when autumn practice followed spring practice, schools enlisted an army of expert coaches who drilled their football pupils at protracted blackboard sessions, and coaches dispatched special scouts to discern the secrets and weaknesses of opposing teams?

Professionalization and rationalization seemed to become the leitmotifs of American society and economics in the early twentieth century. The same influences that led to the restructuring of the business corporation, the professional society, academic institutions, and intercollegiate athletics ineluctably impinged on politics and transformed the terms of debate and the implementation of policies in the political arena.

5

Local and State Reform
1900-1917

The progressive movement that had its inception at the state and local level during the late 1880s was most strikingly successful at the federal level during the early years of the 1910s. Increasing numbers of dissatisfied Americans became active in local and state politics, and by 1910, they had secured enactment of an impressive list of political reforms. The variety of these measures revealed both the extent of the dissatisfaction and the conflicting priorities that had moved many Americans to support reform. Among those attracted to progressive politics were feminists, settlement house workers, antitrusters, municipal reformers, advocates of the eight-hour work day and of women's and child labor legislation, consumer advocates, proponents of tax reform, advocates of educational innovation, moral crusaders seeking to eradicate gambling, drinking and prostitution, efficiency experts espousing scientific management and scientific agriculture, and conservationists.

Such diversity led to the founding of a wide variety of organizations including the General Federation of Women's Clubs (1890), the National Municipal League (1894), the National Consumers League (1898), the National Civic Federation (1900), the National Child Labor Committee (1904), the Playground and Recreation Association of America

(1906), the National Association for the Advancement of Colored People (1910), the National Federation of Settlements (1911), the American Birth Control League (1914). This penchant for forming organizations was not confined to reformers; during the early twentieth century the United States Chamber of Commerce (1912), the Rotary International (1905), the Kiwanis International (1915), and the Optimist Club (1911) were also founded.

THE EVOLUTION OF PROGRESSIVISM

As a diffuse, even amorphous movement, progressivism was essentially but not exclusively middle-class and urban in its origins and orientation. Rural areas that had earlier supported populism also provided strong support and many former small-town critics of populism, like the *Emporia* (Kansas) *Gazette* editor, William Allen White, would during the early 1900s become ardent proponents of reform. Progressivism did not emerge suddenly on the national scene in the 1900s. Rather, it evolved gradually and fitfully as demonstrated in the careers of social worker Jane Addams of Hull House and the Republican reformer Robert LaFollette of Wisconsin.

Ms. Addams began as a settlement house worker (forming Hull House in 1888) to relieve the plight and promote the assimilation of the urban poor and recent immigrants. From private charity and assistance, she became active in Chicago politics; she then joined national organizations (like the National Child Labor Committee) to lobby for federal legislation and eventually was a delegate to the founding convention of the Progressive party in 1912. A conventional Republican politician of the 1880s, LaFollette during the 1890s assumed leadership of the reform wing of the Wisconsin Republican party. Securing the Republican gubernatorial nomination in 1900, he won election to that post and thereafter introduced a variety of reforms, the so-called Wisconsin System, that served as a model for other states. In 1906, La Follette entered national politics, soon assuming leadership of the progressive forces in the U.S. Senate and in 1911 helping found the National Progressive Republican League.

An influential group of journalists known contemporaneously as the "muckrakers" articulated the dissatisfaction that contributed to the evolution of progressivism. Writing for popular magazines like *McClure's, The Outlook, American Magazine, Colliers,* and *Arena,* Lincoln Steffens, Ray Stannard Baker, Ida Tarbell, Thomas Lawson, Charles Edward Russell, and others developed a new journalistic style of exposure. They also capitalized on the larger reading market made possible by the higher educational level, leisure time, and professionalism of a developing middle-class society. Emulating the changed format and emphasis that had been instituted with the penny press of the 1890s, they appealed to a

Jane Addams, (left) the famous Hull House director, c. 1931

Wide World Photos

Margaret Sanger, (right) the noted advocate of birth control

Wide World Photos

mass audience. Combining lower cost (about ten to fifteen cents a copy) with a less partisan and specialized editorial policy made these journals successful publishing ventures, and thereby powerful media of opinion formation.

Exposing corruption in the cities and business influence on the Senate while assailing the abuse of power by financiers and industrial magnates, the new journalists wrote in a highly emotional and moralistic style which won for them the label "muckrakers"—a description popularized by President Theodore Roosevelt in 1906 and proudly adopted by these writers. Roosevelt had intended to be derogatory by disparaging exposé-style journalism as sensationalist naysaying. The president had specifically recalled the character in John Bunyan's *Pilgrim's Progress* "who could look no way but downward with the muck rake in his hand; who was offered a celestial crown for his muck rake, but who would neither look up nor regard the crown he was offered, but continued to rake to himself the filth of the floor."

Muckraking journalism varied in its quality and at times seemed to be cynical; nonetheless, its prevailing tone was decidedly optimistic. What made the muckrakers distinctive was not their radicalism—there was little if any of that—but their willingness to investigate either formerly ignored or not extensively publicized issues and the "inside dopester" quality of their writing. Their style had dramatic impact as it brought individual readers inside municipal politics and corporate practice; exposed corrupt deals, covert influence, and abuses of power; and suggested that an outraged public, by reasserting its responsibilities, could readily rectify corruption. The most notable among the many muckraking efforts included Ray Stannard Baker's study of the aftermath of the 1906 Atlanta race riot, "Following the Color Line"; Lincoln Steffens's series of articles on municipal corruption, "The Shame of the Cities"; David Phillips's exposure of corporate influence on the Senate, "The Treason of the Senate"; and the articles by Ida Tarbell, Burton Hendrick, Charles Lawson, and Thomas Lawson detailing how corporate executives had attained unparalleled economic power.

BOSSISM AND CORRUPTION

Muckraking succeeded because it entertained as well as exposed; many Americans purchased and avidly read muckraking magazines because they told an interesting and suspenseful story. The most important articles, however, focused on political corruption and abuses of power. Their appeal reflected less journalistic influence than response; at best, the muckrakers fortified a predominant belief that serious reform was required. By 1900, many middle-class Americans had already become politicized. Increasingly active in local and state politics, they believed that those who made policy were no longer accountable to public opinion and that the consequences were corporate abuse and political corruption. Middle-class adherents of progressivism accordingly demanded a variety of legislative changes to "open up" and thereby democratize politics. Uneasy about mass politics yet appalled by "bossism"—whether on the municipal, state, or federal level—the predominantly middle-class progressives supported proposals that included: municipal reform, initiative, referendum, recall, direct primary, direct election of U.S. Senators, state regulatory commissions, lobbying and corrupt practices legislation, and legislative reference.

Initially those attracted to progressivism had sought only to elect honest mayors—e.g., Hazen Pingree, mayor of Detroit in 1889; Samuel "Golden Rule" Jones, mayor of Toledo in 1897; Tom Johnson, mayor of Cleveland in 1901; or Seth Low, mayor of New York City in 1901. Their basic premise had been that the election of "good" men and the defeat of the bosses would insure more honest politics. The brief tenure and limited impact of many reform mayors, however, soon led some progressives to support more extensive municipal reforms. Advocated in the name of democracy and the public interest, these reforms also had less altruistic purposes.

Significantly, businessmen and professionals (most notably, local chambers of commerce) provided much of the leadership for municipal reform. Capitalizing on middle-class antipathy to the independent power of ward bosses and local machines, influential local leaders advocated a "business system" of government run by experts. Whether in the commission system instituted in 1901 in Galveston, Texas (initiated on the state level until the courts in 1903 required that commission members be popularly elected), or the city manager system instituted in 1908 in Staunton, Virginia, the fundamental change involved substituting appointive (city managers or commissions) for elective officials (strong mayors or aldermanic government based on the ward system). The reformers sought a more rational and efficient government, having concluded that a system based upon ward politics stimulated corruption and precluded the disinterested professionalism necessary in managing the complex modern city.

This antipathy to the power of the ward boss also underlay support for other municipal changes to replace the ward system mode of election to common councils and school boards by one based on a city-wide vote. Reform proposals effectively reduced local control over municipal decisions and enhanced the chances for election of those either having extensive organizational support (machine candidates, ironically) or city-wide reputations that derived either from editorial support of the major newspapers or an established family name. Hence the attack on ward politics proved simultaneously reformist and antidemocratic. Skeptical about the intelligence and values of the masses of working-class and immigrant voters, many municipal reformers had concluded that new institutional arrangements were required to shield the office-holder from popular pressure. Indeed, the Voters League of Pittsburgh, a local reform organization, issued a pamphlet affirming that certain occupations inherently disqualified an individual from public service: "Employment as ordinary laborer and in the lowest class of mill work would naturally lead to the conclusion that such men did not have sufficient education or business training to act as school directors. . . . Objections might also be made to small shopkeepers, clerks, workmen of many trades, who by lack of educational advantages and business training, could not . . . [administer] properly the affairs of an educational system, requiring special knowledge, and where millions are spent each year."

Many political reforms did reduce the power of an increasingly restive immigrant and working-class community. Because their intent was not democratic, it was not unusual, or contradictory, to find that many advocates of municipal reform had little sympathy for broader social and economic reforms. This situation produced curious results. Whereas social reformers and businessmen combined to push through the city manager system and were opposed by urban machine politicians, at other times social reformers and urban bosses supported state regulation of tenement housing and factories and were then opposed by businessmen. Nor did businessmen support measures intended to maximize popular influence in decision making, like the initiative and referendum proposals. Justifying this opposition to popular democracy, one Galveston (Texas) leader commented: "We have in our city a very large number of Negroes employed on the docks; we also have a very large number of unskilled white . . . laborers; . . . Under these circumstances it would be extremely difficult to maintain a satisfactory city government where all ordinances must be submitted back to the voters of the city for their ratification and approval." In contrast, such urban politicians as Martin Lomasney of Boston and Edwin Vare of Philadelphia supported the proposed constitutional amendment to elect U.S. Senators by popular vote. Direct election of Senators, rather than the prevailing system of election by the state legislature, would increase the political influence of urban machine bosses. An electoral system based on popular votes would redound to the advantage of urban bosses who could turn out large urban majorities; it would reduce their need to bargain for the support of rural legislators. Reformers and party bosses thus often times supported change for contradictory reasons. Reformers argued that the commission form of government would reduce popular and party influence on municipal decisions; bosses believed that the direct election of Senators would increase the influence of Tammany Hall in state Democratic politics.

Yet the motivation behind the changes instituted by the progressives was never simply conservative. Central to the typical progressive's reformism was a strong antipathy toward bossism. The direct election of Senators, a measure the Populists advocated and popularized during the 1890s, reflected such antipathy. The intent was to make the Senate more accountable to the popular will by reducing the power of party leaders in the selection of U.S. Senators. The U.S. Constitution had originally provided for the indirect election of senators by state legislatures. The evolution of a strong party system during the post–Civil War years almost inevitably forced elected Senators to consolidate their position within the state party. Men of ability and ambition, U.S. Senators used their control over federal patronage and their presenatorial political alliances to forge a tightly-knit and disciplined state party system. Their resultant power made them vulnerable to the charge of bossism. There had emerged as well a growing conviction that senators were unduly influenced by special interest groups, a view popularized in David Phillip's diatribe, "The Treason of the Senate." Thus by 1912 twenty-six primarily Western states amended their state constitutions providing for the statewide popular vote of Senators with the state legislature simply ratifying the majority choice. Ratification in 1913 then of the seventeenth amendment requiring the direct election of senators simply confirmed what had become standard practice in a majority of the states.

Antiparty boss sentiment also provided support for substituting the direct primary for the system of nomination exclusively by state party convention. The Wisconsin reformer Robert LaFollette made this the central issue of his challenge to the established Republican leadership. In 1904 he succeeded in having the direct primary submitted and approved as a state referendum. The Wisconsin progressive also secured adoption of a legislative reference service. This idea originated from LaFollette's close relationship with the University of Wisconsin faculty and the progressive movement's penchant for fact-finding. The Wisconsin faculty had provided LaFollette with advice and the detailed statistics that he used to develop state policy. This affinity for fact-finding constituted the core of the progressives' reform philosophy: the belief that solutions to problems would be uncovered through scientific study, preferably by professionals. In addition, by providing alternative sources of research and information, legislative reference could reduce the leverage of lobbyists—leverage derived from the lobbyists' ability to provide sympathetic legislators with drafts of speeches or statistics buttressing particular legislative positions.

The initiative and the referendum were also proposed to reduce the party boss's influence on the legislative process. Adopted first by South Dakota in 1898, the initiative and referendum directly involved the electorate in enacting legislation: the referendum by allowing state legislatures or municipal bodies to submit questions for voter approval and the initiative by making it possible for citizens directly to get legislative proposals on the ballot for voter approval. An additional reform was the corrupt practices legislation, enacted by South Dakota in 1907, which prohibited covert attempts to influence legislators by requiring publication of lobbying activities and campaign contributions.

These reforms by Wisconsin and South Dakota progressives were emulated in Arkansas, Oregon, Washington, Arizona, Minnesota, North Dakota, Iowa, Missouri, and California. In addition, other states enacted inheritance, income, and *ad valorem* corporation taxes to reduce the tax burden of the middle class and to insure that the wealthy and large corporations contributed their fair share. Led by Wisconsin, many state legislatures also established transportation, industrial, and public utilities commissions to fix rates and guarantee services, enacted unfair-trade-practices legislation, and instituted a series of state services including low-cost life insurance and assistance to cooperatives.

The most controversial of the progressives' political reforms, however, was the recall proposal whereby a stated percentage of the electorate could petition to have a special election to determine if an elected official should be turned out of office before the completion of the term. Enacted first by Oregon in 1908, the recall principle by 1914 had been adopted by California, Arizona, Idaho, Washington, Colorado, Michigan, Louisiana, North Dakota, and Kansas. The principal controversy over the recall proposal, however, centered on whether it should be extended to judges and to judicial decisions. The judiciary's conservatism had led many reformers to view recall as one means for reducing the court's conservative impact, thereby removing an obstacle to effective regulation of business. Since the late nineteenth century, in a series of rulings involving due process, property rights, and state police powers, federal and state courts either declared unconstitutional or stringently limited state and federal regulation of business. Such decisions included *Wabash* v. *Illinois* (1886) in which the Supreme Court ruled unconstitutional state regulation of interstate railroad rates; *Chicago, Milwaukee and St. Paul Railroad Co.* v. *Minnesota* (1890) and *Smyth* v. *Ames* (1898) in which the Court ruled that state regulatory legislation was unconstitutional because the restrictions imposed upon business were "unreasonable"; *U.S.* v. *E. C. Knight Co.* (1895) in which the Court ruled that sugar refining was manufacturing and not interstate commerce and was therefore outside the regulatory powers of Congress; and *Pollock* v. *Farmers Loan and Trust Co.* (1895) in which the Court challenged the constitutionality of the income tax provision of the Wilson-Gorman Tariff of 1894.

A similar belief, that bossism was responsible for unresponsiveness and corruption, underlay all the structural political reforms proposed for adoption by the states. Progressives shared the common conviction that somehow the public had lost control of the legislative and party system, that the party bosses were irresponsible and arrogant, and that for these reasons corruption and special interest favoritism prevailed. The progressives optimistically reasoned that specified procedural changes would suffice to establish responsive and honest politics. It was only natural then that the progressives would advocate extending these principles to national politics; by the 1910s they demanded presidential preference primaries, federal corrupt practices legislation, and the popular election of the president. By 1912, thirteen states had instituted presidential primaries, and in 1911 a vast grass roots organization, the National Progressive Republican League, was formed with chapters in the more important states and municipalities.

The progressives' optimism flowed from their belief that regardless of social origin or economic interest most individuals shared common values and the desire to create a harmonious order. As a Milwaukee banker commented at the Church and Labor Social Union in 1894, we must build a "new society" where "class privileges will be abolished because all will belong to the human family."

SOCIAL FEMINISM AND WOMEN'S SUFFRAGE

The women's movement was not the least of the components of state and local progressivism. To achieve reform, the women's movement specifically advocated extending the right to vote to women. As with progressivism in general, the women's suffrage movement initially had concentrated its efforts on the state level. Its principal objective had been to obtain the suffrage through state legislation or by amending state constitutions. By 1900, however, only the western states of Wyoming, Utah, Colorado, and Idaho had enacted women's suffrage. Early twentieth-century efforts at the state level had similar limited results: prior to enactment of the federal constitutional amendment in 1920, an additional seven western states had amended their constitutions to permit full women's suffrage, although other states had passed laws providing for partial suffrage, usually for school board elections. Reflecting both frustration over the paucity of state action and the optimistic mood that gave rise to progressivism, in 1912 the suffragettes shifted their focus to the national level. Thereafter, by lobbying Congress and the major party conventions and through mass demonstrations, they demanded a federal constitutional amendment. This proposal's appeal and the feared power of women gradually led ambitious political leaders (like Woodrow Wilson and Theodore Roosevelt) to support women's suffrage openly. In 1919, the amendment (the nineteenth) passed the Congress and in 1920 it was ratified by state legislatures.

The women's movement had not been exclusively concerned with the suffrage, although its more conservative adherents confined their involvement to that issue. Many women were attracted to the suffrage movement because of their earlier efforts to enact social and economic reform legislation. Social feminism, the product of profound dissatisfaction with the quality of life in industrial America, had at first moved many women into settlement house work, then to support of local, state, and federal regulation of business, and then to the women's suffrage movement. The social feminists were motivated by a concern over the plight of child and female labor. Dramatic injustices abounded. To social feminists, the tragedy of the 1911 Triangle Shirtwaist Factory fire in New York City was hardly atypical: 148 women had died during a fire in a loft building that had no safe means for escape. For the social feminist, the suffrage became the means for altering work conditions. The apparent indifference of private employers and public officials to human suffering

Suffragette parade on Pennsylvania Ave.,
Washington D.C., c. 1913

Library of Congress

and to their moral responsibilities toward the helpless convinced social
feminists of the importance of political action by women. Having the
right to vote would enable women both to publicize evil and to enact
legislation. Only then, social feminists concluded, could a humane and
morally just society be attained and the recurrence of injustice averted.

An integral part of the broader progressive movement, social
feminists actively lobbied for state laws prohibiting child labor, regulating hours and working conditions of women workers, and requiring
minimal safety standards for factories and tenements. Their effort
brought results. By 1914, every state but one had enacted minimum wage
laws for child labor, and a majority of the states (less so in the South)
had limited the working day of children. By 1916, moreover, all but eight
states had enacted some kind of industrial insurance and liability legislation, establishing the employer's formal responsibility for industrial
accidents, an all-too-frequent occurrence in many industries where even
minimal safety devices had not been provided. A majority of states had
also enacted minimum wage legislation for women; in addition, by 1913
twenty states had approved pensions for widows with dependent children.

Significantly, the basic impetus to social feminism and to this broad range of regulatory legislation had been humanitarian rather than economic. Like the progressives, the social feminists were primarily concerned about the condition of the weak and the powerless. Their protest was directed principally at the dissolution of the family and the social problems of an uneducated and physically exploited youth; most did not view these conditions as the consequence of the established values and interests of industrial capitalism. Although the reformers advocated minimum wage and maximum hour legislation, pensions for widows with dependent children, and regulations to insure safe working conditions, they did not generally advocate unemployment compensation and old age pensions. Nor did they affirm state responsibility either to alleviate social and economic inequities or to promote trade union organization.

Legislative measures covering these latter issues would not be enacted until the New Deal era and were the product more of the political-economic crisis of the Great Depression than the fulfillment of the progressives' reform efforts. To the progressives of the 1900s, such proposals smacked either of socialism or special interest legislation. They wanted to create a more rational and efficient system but not to institute far-reaching institutional changes. Remaining committed to a negative view of state responsibilities, progressives (even when advocating state action) held to a belief that the state should prohibit unfair practices but not positively assist economically disadvantaged groups. Moreover, the progressives' commitment to "good" politics made them suspicious of the ethnics' and trade unionists' style of political reform.

A similar split between the desire merely to clean up government and to use state power as a positive force to shape the society and economy, between a desire to democratize politics and to professionalize public service, also characterized national politics in the era of reform. The presidencies of Theodore Roosevelt, William Howard Taft, and Woodrow Wilson would bring progressivism into the national political arena.

6

Toward a More Active Federal Government: From Roosevelt to Wilson

The dislocating changes of the late nineteenth century—the rise of large business corporations, the institutionalization of state parties and of congressional politics, the greater complexity and impersonality of life in an increasingly more urban industrial society—contributed to the emergence of reform politics during the early twentieth century. Historians, as did contemporaries, often describe the politics of the early twentieth century as progressivism. The motivating principle of progressivism was expressed pointedly by Woodrow Wilson in his book *The New Freedom,* published in 1913: "Anything that depresses, anything that makes the organization greater than the man, anything that blocks, discourages, dismays the humble man is against all the principles of progress."

What, then, is progressivism? A simple answer cannot be given to this question for a number of reasons. First, the movement that shaped the politics of the early twentieth century was characterized by inconsistency and contradictions; there were no well-defined, internally consistent principles governing progressive politics. Indeed, some of the programs sought by contemporary reformers were based on principles contrary to other programs. Moreover, not all reformers supported or advocated all the measures enacted into law in the first two decades of the twentieth century. Second, many who were active in reform politics were themselves ambivalent about the desirability of reform and sought to contain change. Third, the effect of progressivism on national values and institutions, despite the enactment of a significant number of legislative measures and constitutional amendments, was limited. That astute political commentator Finley Peter Dunne succinctly conveyed the impact of progressivism when he commented: "Th' noise ye hear is not th' first gun iv a rivolution. It's on'y th' people iv the United States batin' a carpet."

A fear of bigness, a sense of optimism that conditions could be improved, an ambivalence about change, a concern based equally on a sense of injustice and a fear of radicalism—these were the sources of progressivism. The concern that provided whatever unity there was to early twentieth century politics was a fear of bigness and the abuses of power deriving therefrom—whether the large impersonal business corporation or the equally impersonal and powerful political machine. Woodrow Wilson best articulated this sentiment when he noted that "If there are men in this country big enough to own the government of the United States, they are going to own it." The progressives had also concluded that bigness was the cause of periodic economic crises (the depression of 1893–1897, the recessions of 1901 and 1903, the Panic of 1907). Bigness also was held responsible for recent inflationary trends (between 1897 and 1913, the very years of a sharp increase in trust formation, the cost of living increased about 35 percent).

Yet the progressives did not demand institutional reforms based on principles of "participatory democracy." Rather they advocated reforms based on the principles of professionalism and of exposure. To insure against abuse of power by large corporations, they favored appointive regulatory commissions, such as the Civil Service and Interstate Commerce Commissions created during the 1880s. Such commissions, staffed by nonpartisan experts, could develop the facts necessary for a rational policy as well as provide the leadership essential for channeling popular protest along responsible lines. To insure against abuses they further advocated subjecting decisions to public scrutiny. Woodrow Wilson pointedly affirmed that "There ought to be no place where anything can be done that everybody does not know about." The threat of exposure would insure that powerful men would act responsibly. "More important than any legislation," Theodore Roosevelt counselled, "is the gradual growth of a feeling of responsibility among capitalists and wage workers alike."

Progressive leaders were not necessarily Democrats. They sought simply to reform glaring abuses and to discriminate between wrongdoing and the responsible use of power. In 1902, President Theodore Roosevelt admonished his fellow citizens that "the line of demarcation we draw must always be on conduct, not on wealth; our objection to any corporation must be, not that it is big, but that it behaves badly." In 1903, Roosevelt counselled the need to use "power fearlessly, but with moderation. Let me say again—with moderation, with sanity, with self-restraint."

Nor was this ambivalence peculiar to Roosevelt. Woodrow Wilson, another progressive president, shared these sentiments when affirming "I am for big business and I am against the trusts."

At bottom, then, this commitment to professionalism was intended to insure that decisions governed by intelligence, not mass passions, would determine when the line between "big" business and "bad" business was overstepped. For if the progressives were motivated by a sense of injustice, they were also alarmed by the militancy and growth of the trade-union movement and the steady increase in votes and membership of the Socialist party. The specter of radicalism haunted many progressives, who viewed themselves, and justified their proposals, as providing a buffer between radicalism and reaction. Progressive lawyer and theorist Louis Brandeis described progressive goals as to provide "a position of independence between the wealthy and the people, prepared to curb the excesses of either." Theodore Roosevelt supporter George Perkins more pointedly articulated this concern in 1910, expressing alarm over the growth of the socialist vote and the "rapidly approaching crisis in this country on the question of the relationship between capital and labor and business and the state."

If the student, then, finds progressivism to be confusing, that confusion stems from the ambivalence and conflicting concerns of the movement itself. If motivated by an impulse to reform American society, if lamenting recent developments and speaking to the need to democratize political and economic institutions, the progressives nonetheless preferred those measures that rationalized decision making to those that would have increased popular control and entailed institutional reform.

THE PRESIDENCY OF THEODORE ROOSEVELT

Progressivism differed from earlier reform politics in its tactics and in its efforts to forge a more rational and humane system. The progressives did not, however, totally repudiate the conservative assumptions underlying late nineteenth-century politics. The contrast with Gilded Age politics was more striking than substantive; one factor contributing to progressivism's distinctiveness was the style of its most prominent leader, Theodore Roosevelt.

Acceding to the presidency in September 1901 because of the assassination of William McKinley, Roosevelt viewed that office as a "bully pulpit" from which to instruct the public and the Congress on required changes and how specific problems could be intelligently resolved. In contrast to late nineteenth-century presidents, Roosevelt was an active and dynamic chief executive. His activism made national politics exciting and indirectly legitimated the reformist efforts of many who had formerly been active in state and federal politics.

To his contemporaries, Theodore Roosevelt embodied the reformer in politics; his national reputation was that of a trust-buster. The trust-buster reputation, however, owed more to one widely heralded antitrust suit against the Northern Securities Company than to Roosevelt's own priorities or to the number of suits (only forty-four) instituted during his two-term presidency.

Organized in 1901 to reduce railroad competition in the Northwest, Northern Securities was a holding company composed of competing railroad corporations headed by J. P. Morgan and James Hill on the one hand and E. H. Harriman on the other. The Roosevelt Administration responded to the obvious attempt to reduce competition by bringing suit against Northern Securities in 1902 under the Sherman Anti-Trust Act. Having challenged a firm headed by J. P. Morgan, the symbol of Wall Street, Roosevelt thereby acquired his image as a bold reformer and opponent of the trusts—an image distinctly popular at the time. The dramatic quality of Roosevelt's action was captured in Morgan's arrogant response to the impending suit. Securing an interview with the president, he suggested: "If we have done anything wrong, why don't I send my man to your man [i.e., the attorney general] and we can fix it up." Roosevelt rejected Morgan's proposal. Subsequently, the Supreme Court in a five to four decision of 1904 upheld the government's claim that the holding company was in restraint of trade.

Roosevelt's action contrasted strikingly with those of his predecessors Cleveland and McKinley; however, his real views on the anti-trust question scarcely matched his trust-buster image. The Roosevelt administration subsequently used the Sherman Act to pressure Congress either to enact regulatory legislation or to establish the president's publicly pronounced distinction between "good" and "bad" trusts and "artificial" and "natural" monopolies. Beyond these political efforts, Roosevelt's corporate policy was distinctly conservative. For Roosevelt viewed the Sherman Anti-Trust Act as archaic and harmful. The trend toward bigness was not economically harmful, the president argued: "It is not true that as the rich have grown richer the poor have grown poorer. . . . The captains of industry who have driven the railway systems across this continent, who have built up our commerce, who have developed our manufactures, have on the whole done great good to our people." Legislation could not avert this trend and, in fact, might increase public disrespect for the law. What was needed, Roosevelt affirmed in his annual message to Congress in 1905, was "not sweeping prohibition of every arrangement, good or bad, which may tend to restrict competition, but more adequate supervision and regulation as will prevent any restriction on competition from being to the detriment of the public. . . . Publicity is the only sure remedy which we can now evoke."

To ensure this objective, in 1903 Roosevelt had advocated legislation to create a Bureau of Corporations within the Department of Commerce and Labor. Then, in 1907, the president proposed additional legislation requiring licensing by the Bureau of Corporations of all corporations doing interstate business.

Congress never enacted Roosevelt's federal licensing proposal. Lacking legislative sanction, Roosevelt nonetheless devised an elaborate, but covert, détente system whereby the Bureau of Corporations cooperated with major corporate firms (U.S. Steel, International Harvester, J. P. Morgan) to avert their prosecution under existing antitrust laws. In effect, the bureau condoned the efforts of these corporations to extend control over competing firms (the acquisition of Tennessee Coal and Iron by U.S. Steel in 1907, for example).

In 1907, Moore & Schley, a Wall Street investment firm then in deep financial trouble, approached U.S. Steel for a loan of $6 million. As collateral, it offered to sell stock in a number of companies including the Tennessee Coal and Iron Company, the major steel producer in the South. Since this acquisition would extend U.S. Steel's control of the market in possible violation of the Sherman Anti-Trust Act, U.S. Steel executives Elbert Gary and Henry Frick sought President Roosevelt's prior approval. Not identifying Moore & Schley, Gary and Frick intimated that unless this unnamed investment firm received support it would collapse and possibly cause a serious crisis on Wall Street. Disclaiming any interest in acquiring the Tennessee company, Gary and Frick said that they would agree to do so as their public duty. Accepting their word at face value, Roosevelt promised not to prosecute should U.S. Steel acquire this southern firm. (Significantly, Roosevelt was not told by Gary and Frick that Moore & Schley had alternative collateral, other than Tennessee Coal, and that the firm needed only a $6 million loan and not as much as the $45 million of the southern company's total stock.)

Roosevelt's reformist reputation also derived from his advocacy of legislation to regulate business practices. Capitalizing on public discontent over conditions in the meat-packing industry, in 1906 the president released excerpts from a private study of this industry's unsanitary methods prepared by James B. Reynolds and Charles P. Neill. Roosevelt's action succeeded in forcing House Agriculture Committee Chairman James Wadsworth to report the Administration-supported meat inspection bill and thereby to insure congressional enactment of the Pure Food and Drug Act of 1906. To protect against adulteration of products or unsanitary processes, this measure authorized federal inspection of the meat, food, and drug industries. The cost of inspection would be borne by the federal government.

Roosevelt also championed another popular issue—legislation to regulate railroad rate practices. Farmers, and shippers in general, demanded legislation outlawing what they believed were arbitrary and unfair railroad rates. Their ire centered on the railroads' high rates and rebates to large corporations. Although rebates ostensibly had been prohibited by the Interstate Commerce Act of 1887, that act's vague language and limited scope had rendered this prohibition ineffectual. To overcome this deficiency, which even the railroads opposed, Congress in 1903 enacted the Elkins Act to increase penalties for rebating, provide for more stringent enforcement, and extend the ICC's rate-regulating authority.

The Elkins Act did not abate popular sentiment for rate-setting legislation. Responding to this pressure, Congress in 1906 passed the Hepburn Act. As drafted in committee and amended during floor debate, this measure so limited the ICC's rate-setting powers that congressional reformers like Senator Robert LaFollette opposed its passage, fearing that enactment would only undercut pressure for effective legislation. Railroad companies were prohibited from transporting in interstate commerce materials in which the company or its subsidiaries had direct interest. Rebate provisions were further tightened. In addition, the ICC's membership was increased to seven and its supervision extended to express and sleeping car companies and to spurs and shopyards. Although empowering the ICC to set reasonable rates, the Hepburn Act did not authorize commission access to the books of the railroad companies as the basis for making this evaluation. Furthermore, the ICC's role was strictly limited: it could act only on complaints from shippers and its rate decisions were subject to court review.

Philosophical conservatism and not political necessity or a disinterest in power also determined Roosevelt's policies toward the Republican Old Guard. Highly sensitive to the importance of patronage, as president, Theodore Roosevelt made federal appointments to further personal political ambitions: (1) in 1902–1904 to insure that delegations from the South to the Republican National Convention were loyal to his candidacy for the Republican presidential nomination and (2) in 1906–1908 to effect the nomination of his hand-picked successor, William Howard Taft. Moreover, Roosevelt tolerated the power of the Republican Old Guard—Speaker Joseph Cannon in the House and Nelson Aldrich in the Senate—out of preference. Responding to a letter from William Howard Taft, chiding him for his close relationship with the Old Guard congressional leadership, Roosevelt wrote: "You are unjust to Senator Aldrich. My experience . . . has made me feel respect and regard for Aldrich as one of that group of Senators, including Allison, Hanna, Spooner, Platt of Connecticut, Lodge, and one or two others, who together with men like the next Speaker of the House, Joe Cannon, are the most powerful factors in Congress." As Roosevelt viewed matters, Aldrich and Cannon were not only powerful men but more responsible and realistic than such reformers as Robert LaFollette and George Norris. Given Roosevelt's preferences and his aversion to public debate that could become demagogic, the discipline exercised by the Old Guard had positive advantages.

THE WILLIAM HOWARD TAFT ADMINISTRATION

Roosevelt's successor as president, William Howard Taft, inherited this ambiguous legacy: bold reformist promise yet temporizing, qualified change. Unlike Roosevelt, however, Taft did not have the inclination or the opportunity to sustain the initiative by promising reform. The Panic of 1907 and the proven limited results of the Roosevelt reform program had created a political situation that determined the problems associated with Taft's one-term presidency.

Unlike Roosevelt, Taft never acquired the image of a trust-buster even though he instituted sixty-five antitrust suits during his four-year tenure compared to the forty-four of Roosevelt's eight years. He failed to support antitrust legislation, a passivity that proved inadequate to deal with the pressures created following the 1907 Panic and two U.S. Supreme Court decisions of 1911. A series of economic crises precipitated by actions of large corporations—those of 1901 and 1903 and the more serious Panic of 1907—had dramatically raised the specter of corporate irresponsibility. The recurrence of such crises, congressional reformers pointedly charged, was inevitable as long as powerful corporations remained unchecked. Then in 1911, the Supreme Court declared the Standard Oil and the American Tobacco companies in violation of the Sherman Anti-Trust Act, at the same time enunciating a "rule of reason." By this ruling the Court had arrogated to itself the prerogative of ascertaining when combinations "unreasonably," as opposed to "reasonably," restrained trade. The Court's decisions intensified an already strong progressive distrust of the judiciary's conservatism (a distrust that underlay the reformers' advocacy of the recall of judicial decisions).

Popular sentiment also insisted on tariff reform, so Taft did not have the luxury of ignoring this demand (as had his popular predecessor). By 1908, the Republicans had abandoned their opposition to tariff reform and in their platform pledged to support revision. Accordingly, in 1909 the recently inaugurated Taft called Congress into special session to consider tariff reform. A low tariff bill eventually was approved by the House. When the bill came to the Senate, however, over eight hundred amendments were added during consideration by the Senate Finance Committee, under Senator Aldrich's direction, virtually eliminating from the free list the products of every major industry seeking protection and even increasing the average rates of certain items over the protectionist Dingley Tariff of 1897. Because such products as jalap, alazarin, nux vomica, and works of art over twenty years old were placed on the free list, political commentator Finley Peter Dunne sarcastically noted: "Pr-r-ractically iverything necessary to existence comes in free."

Led by Senator Robert LaFollette, Senate progressives sought to defeat the Aldrich amendments by demonstrating their protectionist character. Failing in this effort, and without President Taft's intercession to pressure the Senate leadership to make concessions, the progressives reacted bitterly to the president's later defense of the tariff bill as a positive improvement. The tariff measure further harmed Taft's reputation, as in 1909 in return for Speaker Cannon's agreement to report a tariff bill he had agreed not to support the effort of House reformers to reduce the powers of the Speaker.

By the end of the first decade of the twentieth century, Joseph Cannon's arbitrary direction of the House had made "Cannonism" a powerful issue commanding widespread support. In 1908, many Republicans and Democrats won election to the House by assailing Cannonism. In 1910, the Democrats gained control of the House for the first time since 1892 by adopting the mantle of progressivism and particularly the issue of Cannonism, while forty incumbent Republicans were defeated for renomination by announced progressive Republicans.

The first attempt to curb the speaker's powers occurred in 1909. Dissident Republicans then joined the minority Democrats in an attempt to reform the rules of the House. This effort failed when in return for certain favors Tammany Hall Democrats defected from this coalition and supported Cannon. Frustrated in 1909, in March 1910 the Insurgents (as they were then known) successfully amended House rules during a heated long-drawn-out session to deny the speaker the right to appoint members of the Rules Committee. In 1911, the Democrats enacted further rules changes, having gained control of the House. To replace Cannon's highly arbitrary and centralized rule, the Democrats introduced a system whereby the Ways and Means Committee made committee assignments, subject to the approval of each party's caucus, with committee chairmen selected on the basis of seniority. While it was an improvement over the old system whereby the speaker selected the membership of both the Rules and the Way and Means Committees and indirectly the chairmen of other committees, seniority is now recognized as a principal obstacle to legislative reform. A system of appointment and advancement based on seniority, moreover, in no way insured that Congress's business would be determined by issues debated in recent congressional or presidential campaigns. (The only other congressional change enacted during the Progressive Era was a constitutional amendment in 1912 requiring the popular election of U.S. Senators.)

The limitations imposed by the Elkins and Hepburn Acts on the ICC's authority—the requirement for court review, the absence of subpoena powers, and the stipulation that the ICC could not initiate rate review but act only on complaints from shippers—moreover, had sustained demands for additional, more effective rate-regulation legislation. Eventually in 1910, Congress enacted the Mann-Elkins Act. Introduced in Congress with the support of the Taft administration, the original bill would have empowered the ICC (1) to set rates though subject to review by a specially created Court of Commerce and (2) to supervise railroad stocks and bonds. The bill also would have permitted railroads to acquire competing lines (known as pooling, one of the railroad companies' major legislative goals since the 1890s). Congressional progressives (whose numerical strength had increased since 1906) immediately denounced this bill and insisted upon a series of amendments—the most important one called for physical evaluation of railroad property (requiring access to the companies' books) to determine whether the rates charged by the railroads were reasonable and fair. By supporting statehood for Arizona and New Mexico, the Taft Administration won over the basically conservative Democratic leadership to its more limited proposal. As finally passed, then, Mann-Elkins empowered the ICC to initiate rate-making proceedings rather than to respond to complaints by shippers. These ICC rate decisions were subject to review by a special Commerce Court. Rate rulings would not be based upon physical evaluation, as the progressive congressmen advocated; the bill's pooling provision, however, was defeated.

The inaction and political ineptness of the Taft Administration, and not the president's conservative political philosophy, shaped the politics of the 1912 campaign. By 1911, Taft had come to be popularly identified with the Republican Old Guard. Congressional progressives no longer looked to the president for leadership or direction. Both to develop popular support for a reformist legislative program and to deny William Howard Taft renomination, in 1911 a number of progressive Republicans (led by Robert LaFollette, Jonathan Bourne, and Gifford Pinchot) formed the National Progressive Republican League. Intended to build up state and local progressive organizations, the league sought to develop support for specific goals, which included the direct election of U.S. senators, the direct election of delegates to national conventions, corrupt practices legislation, and more stringent antitrust and banking legislation.

THE 1912 CAMPAIGN AND THE
WOODROW WILSON ADMINISTRATION

LaFollette had expected to command the unified support of progressive Republicans in his bid for the Republican presidential nomination, but his expectation proved unwarranted. In February 1912, Theodore Roosevelt announced his candidacy for the Republican nomination—adopting the mantle of progressivism and accusing Taft of having betrayed reform. Roosevelt's announcement almost immediately transformed the Republican contest into a two-man race—the former president's greater popularity and the support he commanded from established party bosses (like Pittsburgh's William Flinn) led many progressives who had cooperated with LaFollette in the National Progressive Republican League to rally behind Roosevelt's candidacy.

Roosevelt successfully demonstrated his greater popularity and Taft's unpopularity in that year's thirteen primaries, winning 278 delegate votes to Taft's 48 and LaFollette's 36. Yet, the crucial contest between Taft and Roosevelt centered in the South. Traditionally, Republican presidents had controlled delegations from the southern states through their power of patronage (and in 1902–1904 and again in 1906–1908 Roosevelt had so acted to insure pro-Roosevelt southern delegations to the 1904 and 1908 conventions). Challenging this system in 1912, Roosevelt's southern appeal led many former independents to become involved in Republican politics; in some states and counties counter-conventions were held to those of the established party leadership. As a result, two delegations (involving 254 delegates to the Republican National Convention) were elected from most southern states.

Controlling the National Committee, the Taft forces dominated the credentials committee (which ruled on the seating of delegations) and organized the convention. This power was then used to seat 235 of the Taft-supported delegates from the South, thereby insuring Taft's nomination on the first ballot. Embittered by the methods by which the contests were resolved and convention affairs ordered many of Roosevelt's supporters walked out of the convention agreeing to meet again in Chicago in August 1912.

At Chicago, these disaffected Republicans joined other independents to form a third party, and Roosevelt accepted that party's presidential nomination. Yet the Progressive party did not then possess a grass-roots organization; its supporters also were not firmly convinced that a permanent third party was needed. Only after the 1912 election was a half-hearted effort made to forge a permanent party. And even then, differences among liberal and conservative supporters of Roosevelt's candidacy resulted in acrimonious debate, and an effective organization was never created. Liberals had deep suspicions about Roosevelt's conservative advisers Frank Munsey and George Perkins. The liberal Emporia, Kansas, newspaper editor, William Allen White, articulated this distrust in a later obituary when he pointedly characterized Munsey as having "the talents of a meat-packer, the morals of a money-changer and the manners of an undertaker. May he rest in trust."

Yet the third-party movement had not dissolved because of internal divisions alone. In large measure, these early twentieth-century reformers were moved by a sense of moral outrage, and moral outrage could not be sustained. Not coincidentally, the atmosphere of the 1912 Progressive National Convention had resembled a religious revival with its campaign songs of "Battle Hymn of the Republic" and "Onward Christian Soldiers."

In 1912, however, progressive reform apparently triumphed. A third party was formed and the Democrats nominated the progressive New Jersey governor Woodrow Wilson. In the presidential election, Roosevelt polled 4,118,571 (27.4 percent) popular and 88 electoral votes to Republican nominee William Taft's 3,486,720 popular (23.2 percent) and 8 electoral votes. The division in formerly Republican ranks contributed to Democratic candidate Woodrow Wilson's election as he received only 41.9 percent of the popular vote (6,296,547) but 435 electoral votes. Combined, the two reform candidates polled roughly 69 percent of the popular vote (with the Socialist Eugene V. Debs receiving 6 percent).

Since 1908, the Democrats had sought to insure political success by championing antitrust, low tariff, banking and currency reform, and by condemning Cannonism. Yet the progressives had not won control of the Democratic party. Indeed Wilson had won the Democratic nomination in 1912 only on the forty-sixth ballot. His success derived from a combination of unusual factors: a series of deals by his floor leaders with im-

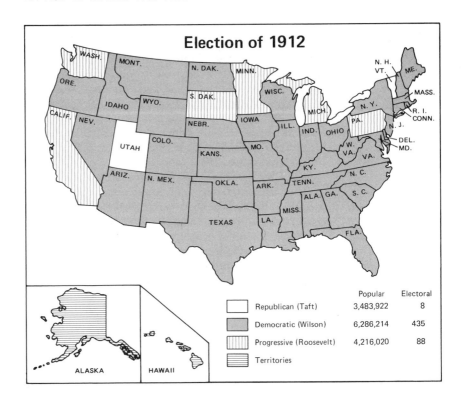

Election of 1912

		Popular	Electoral
☐	Republican (Taft)	3,483,922	8
▨	Democratic (Wilson)	6,286,214	435
▥	Progressive (Roosevelt)	4,216,020	88
▤	Territories		

ALASKA   HAWAII

portant party leaders, including offering the vice-presidential nomination to the conservative Thomas R. Marshall of Indiana (famous for suggesting that what the nation needed was not reform but a "good five-cent cigar") ; the convention's two-thirds rule (not changed until the 1936 convention), which required that the nominee receive the vote of two-thirds of the delegates and thereby denied the nomination to the front-runner, Speaker of the House James Beauchamp (Champ) Clark; and the attractiveness of Wilson's candidacy—his nomination could insure the support of dissatisfied Republican progressives as well as of disgruntled Democratic progressives, who might have bolted if a more conventional candidate had been selected.

As president, then, Woodrow Wilson had the opportunity to push for effective legislative change and, through his control over patronage, advance the influence of progressives within the Democratic party. For of the 290 Democrats elected to the House of Representatives in 1912, 114 were newly elected, having won in formerly Republican districts by espousing progressivism. President Wilson did not use patronage, however, to assist Democratic progressives. Instead, bowing to the advice of his conservative appointee as postmaster general, Omar Burleson, Wilson sought cooperation with the conservative congressional leadership. In this action, Wilson underscored his Administration's willingness to limit the impact of legislative change.

Increasingly after 1907, the Democrats had sought to capitalize on antitrust sentiment and in 1912 specifically adopted a strong antitrust platform plank. During the 1912 presidential campaign, moreover, the Democratic presidential candidate had called for "regulated competition" and condemned "an extraordinary and very sinister concentration in . . . business." Since the 1912 elections had resulted in Democratic control of the presidency and of both houses of Congress, enactment of a new antitrust bill seemed insured.

Acting on this reality, in December 1913 Congressman Henry Clayton initiated hearings on the entire problem of trust legislation and in January 1914 introduced four bills to amend the Sherman Act. As originally drafted, these bills would have prohibited (1) interlocking directorates among large banks, competing railroads, and corporations; (2) price-cutting to destroy competition or the acquisition of stock of other corporations when the effect would lessen competition; and (3) exclusive contracts between large firms. In addition, the Clayton bills would have made owners or directors of corporations criminally responsible for civil violations of the antitrust laws.

The original Clayton bills never became law. Instead, an omnibus bill incorporating these provisions emerged from the hearings and floor deliberations; pressures from President Wilson and from conservatives, however, had resulted in the enactment of a number of far-reaching amendments. Thus, the resultant Clayton Anti-Trust Act of October 1914 exempted banks with resources of less than $5 million from the prohibition against interlocking directorates and prohibited interlocking directorates and unfair trade practices only "when the effect may be to substantially lessen competition . . . or tend to create a monopoly in any line of commerce." Having failed to specify these conditions, the Clayton Act's qualified prohibition meant that once again the courts would determine what constituted "unreasonableness" and further that the initiation of suits would be determined by the priorities of appointive personnel in the Department of Justice or the recently-created Federal Trade Commission. Not inappropriately then, one of the bill's critics aptly described the measure as "a tabby cat with soft gums, a plaintive mew, and an anemic appearance."

By 1914, President Wilson had shifted from basing corporate regulatory policy on more stringently defined antitrust legislation. Wilson's corporate policy then centered on Congressman Raymond Stevens' bill, introduced in April 1914, to create a Federal Trade Commission (FTC). After considerable debate centering on its vagueness and court-review provisions, the Stevens Bill passed Congress in September 1914. The act created a five-member commission, to be appointed by the President and confirmed by the Congress, empowered after conducting hearings to issue "cease and desist" orders against "unfair methods of competition." No clear standards were provided to determine commission action. And although authorized to subpoena witnesses and information, the commission did not have final power: its decisions would be subject to court review. Wilson's original appointments to the FTC almost immediately negated whatever regulatory impact this measure might have had. They included Edward Hurley (a manufacturer and president of the Illinois Manufacturers Association), William Harris (a Georgia businessman), Will Parry (a newspaperman and former shipbuilder), and Joseph Davies (then head of the Bureau of Corporations). Furthermore, applicants for even routine jobs with the commission were asked to submit "letters of endorsement from some good, sound businessmen."

Popular demand had also increased pressure on the Congress to regulate the banks and insure an adequate federal currency. As the Panic of 1907 had demonstrated, existing federal currency policy, combined with the lack of coordination among private banks preceding and during financial crises, precluded the resolution or prevention of periodic economic crises. Even bankers advocated legislative remedies; the larger banking firms supported a bill introduced by Senator Aldrich. Then, the startling revelations of the so-called Pujo Committee, a special subcommittee of the House Banking Committee chaired by Arsene Pujo of Louisiana, further strengthened this legislative demand. In hearings conducted in 1912 and 1913, the Pujo Committee disclosed that five Wall Street banking firms held 341 directorates in 112 corporations with aggregate capital of about $22 billion, seemingly confirming Wall Street domination and the interlocking relationship between investment banks and corporate consolidation. The committee's findings, moreover, were popularized by Louis Brandeis (a leading progressive lawyer who viewed the "curse of bigness" as the principal national problem) in *Other People's Money,* published in 1913. The Money Trust and its interlocking relations with industrial combinations, Brandeis argued, were the sources of the twin problems of corporate bigness and financial instability. The resultant trend toward large business units was particularly dangerous, he warned, insuring "many unfair and unlawful practices, . . . [and] inefficiency by imposing their unwieldy business structure on the productive process."

By 1913, the Pujo Committee's work, the popular impact of Brandeis's book, and the Democrats' consistent pledge to enact banking and currency legislation assured some form of federal legislation. Controlling both the Congress and the White House, the Democrats were in an excellent position to enact reform. The result was the Federal Reserve Act of December 1913, requiring all national banks to join a federal reserve system (state banks were permitted to join) and creating twelve federal reserve districts. Each district would be headed by nine directors, six elected by the member banks and the other three appointed by the Federal Reserve Board. The system's supervisory authority, the Federal Reserve Board, was to be a seven-member board composed of the secretary of the treasury, the comptroller of the currency, and five others appointed by the president and subject to Senate confirmation.

Instead of having currency issued based on the national banks' holdings of federal bonds, this act permitted regional districts to issue Federal Reserve Notes to member banks in exchange for ninety-day commercial and six-month agricultural notes and on 40 percent gold reserves. In essence, the Federal Reserve Act created a more centralized banking system, though one controlled by the banking community. A more flexible currency was insured although this act did not meet the inflationists' objectives of using currency policy to reform the economy and significantly limit the economic power of those possessing capital. As with the FTC, the act's regulatory effect was greatly reduced by President Wilson's original appointments to the Federal Reserve Board: including Paul Warburg (of the Wall Street banking firm Kuhn, Loeb and Company) and W. P. G. Harding (the president of the largest Alabama bank). Wilson had also hoped to appoint Harry Wheeler, former chairman of the United States Chamber of Commerce, Richard Olney, Cleveland's conservative attorney general, and Thomas Jones, a director of International Harvester. Wheeler and Olney declined appointment, however, and the Senate rejected Jones's nomination.

Throughout the twentieth century the Democrats had championed the low tariff issue. Seeking to capitalize specifically on the unpopularity of the Payne-Aldrich Tariff of 1909, in 1911 and 1912 the Democratic-controlled House passed a series of bills reducing rates on particular commodities (all of which Taft vetoed). Democratic presidential and congressional election victories of 1912 thus practically assured a low tariff. The House immediately passed such a measure, introduced by Congressman Oscar Underwood. During Senate consideration, however, the Underwood Bill seemed destined to be substantively amended by senators responsive to the interests of regional industries. Successfully defeating this effort, Senator Robert LaFollette challenged each senator to disclose his personal holdings in protected industries. By identifying the amending of the Underwood Bill with the dual evils of lobbying and self-interest, LaFollette helped insure passage of a bill reducing average tariff rates from the 44 percent *ad valorem* level of the Payne-Aldrich Act to 28 percent. In addition, to offset the expected loss of federal revenue resulting from reduced tariff rates and to exploit the opportunity provided by the recently enacted federal income tax amendment, a proviso was appended to the tariff bill imposing a 1 percent tax on all personal or corporate income over $4,000 and a graduated surtax reaching 6 percent on incomes over $500,000

Much like other progressive measures, however, the Underwood Act had limited consequences. Tariff rates had been lowered; the protectionist principle was nonetheless sustained. And the objective of the income tax was to sustain federal revenue but not to redistribute income (which LaFollette and George Norris had sought through amendments to increase the maximum tax on individual incomes to 10 percent and on inheritance to 75 percent) nor to obtain additional revenue to cope with the social and economic problems of slums, poverty, and unemployment.

IMMIGRATION, CIVIL LIBERTIES, AND RACIAL POLICY

An aversion to traditional values and principles, because they were chaotic and unscientific, also led to advocacy by progressives of immigration proposals that repudiated the tolerant, open-ended policy dating from colonial times. Joining conservative trade unionists and congressmen, many progressives lobbied for immigration legislation to exclude individuals who possessed what they considered undesirable political and social traits. The ethnic character of immigrants changed after the 1880s, and progressive support for immigration restriction stemmed partly from the racialist belief identifying late nineteenth-century social and economic radicalism with "new" immigrants. The progressives also correlated the upsurge of crime and municipal corruption with the arrival of the predominantly Slavic and Catholic immigrants. The public release in 1911 of the voluminous reports of the Dillingham Commission (created by Congress in 1907 to study the problem of immigration) popularized these themes. In brief, the commission recommended immigration restriction for "economic, moral and social considerations." Classifying immigrant groups by ethnic stereotypes, the commission distinguished between the motivation for emigration to the United States of the "old" and "new" immigrant: the latter came for economic and materialistic reasons, the former from a desire for political and religious freedom. Progressive immigration policy accordingly assumed two forms. The first effort sought to exclude radicals; the second, through the literacy test, to limit unwanted immigration by certain ethnic groups.

In his first annual message to Congress of December 3, 1901, Theodore Roosevelt urged enactment of antiradical and intelligence restrictions. Having acceded to the presidency through Leon Czolgosz's assassination of William McKinley (Czolgosz was a native-born anarchist with a foreign-sounding name), Roosevelt urged a "war with relentless efficiency . . . against anarchists . . . [and their] active and passive sympathizers." The president proposed to exclude "all [immigrants] who are known to be believers in anarchistic principles or members of anarchistic societies. The second object of a proper immigration law ought to be to secure by a careful and not merely perfunctory educational test some intelligent capacity to appreciate American institutions and act sanely as American citizens."

In 1903, Congress enacted legislation meeting Roosevelt's first objective by making ineligible for entry those individuals who either were anarchists or were affiliated with anarchistic organizations. An anarchist who secured entrance illegally was deportable if arrested three years after entry. By the Nationalization Act of 1906, the Congress further changed the citizenship test. From the simple loyalty oath to the Constitution required since 1798, after 1906 aliens seeking citizenship would have to affirm that they were not anarchists and were not affiliated with anarchistic organizations. An applicant for citizenship also would have to produce as character witnesses two citizens to attest that for the five preceding years "he had behaved as a man of good moral character" and had been loyal to the principles of the Constitution.

With the principal leadership assumed by the Immigration Restriction League (IRL), progressives joined conservatives like Henry Lodge to seek congressional approval for a literacy exclusion test. The immigrant's illiteracy, the IRL argued, frustrated assimilation and insured manipulation by urban bosses. Attributing the virtual absence of poverty and corruption in an earlier America and the formation of constitutional government to the Puritan and Anglo-Saxon character of the colonial and early national population, the IRL offered a pseudoscientific, but racial, explanation for the social and economic ills besetting America during the late nineteenth and early twentieth centuries.

Until 1917, the League's efforts were unsuccessful. Presidents Taft (in 1913) and Wilson (in 1915) vetoed immigration bills that included both literacy test and antiradical provisions. In February 1917, however, Congress enacted such a measure over Wilson's veto. Thereafter, immigrants were excluded or made liable to deportation if they could not read or if "any time after entry [they] shall be found advocating or teaching the unlawful destruction of property, or advocating or teaching anarchy or the overthrow by force or violence of the Government of the United States."

Racial prejudices underlay the literacy test standard and all such efforts to reduce immigration from eastern and southern European countries. Progressive racial prejudices more clearly evidenced themselves in their support for or failure to oppose southern efforts to maintain a racially segregated society.

Consistent with their party's traditional principles, the Republicans at their 1904 and 1908 conventions had pledged to support the enforcement of the 13th, 14th, and 15th Amendments. Republican presidents Roosevelt and Taft, however, never used federal power to challenge the various racially discriminatory laws enacted by southern legislatures (poll tax and literacy tests for voting, and segregation of restaurants, schools, courtrooms, theatres, and hotels), laws advocated by many southern progressives. (Roosevelt lobbied against even inclusion of an enforcement pledge in the 1908 Republican platform.) The 1912 Republican platform, moreover, did not contain a plank supporting the post-Civil War amendments, and Progressive party nominee Theodore Roosevelt conducted a "lily white" campaign in the South extolling segregation and the exclusion of blacks from any role in politics. Defending his action, Roosevelt argued that "by appealing to the best white men of the

South . . . and by frankly putting the movement into their hands . . . we shall create a situation by which the colored man of the South will ultimately get justice."

Northern progressives also shared the paternalistic view that the better class of whites could more effectively advance the rights of blacks than blacks themselves and that disfranchisement was reformist because it removed the race question from politics. Consequently, more progressives supported Booker T. Washington's accommodationist philosophy than the egalitarian opposition to discrimination, which in 1910 had led to the formation of the National Association for the Advancement of Colored People (NAACP). Not surprisingly, then, the newly-elected Wilson Administration would in 1913 institute segregation in the federal bureaucracy. By the end of the Progressive Era, a politics of race had relegated blacks to second-class citizenship and segregation had been accepted as an enlightened and scientific response to racial divisions.

This conservative aversion to disorder, and the tendency to attribute national tension and unrest to "outside agitators," explained why the Federal Bureau of Investigation (FBI) would be created during the Progressive Era. Established in 1908 by executive order as an investigative division within the Department of Justice, the Bureau of Investigation (in 1934 named the FBI) was initially opposed on libertarian and traditional grounds by many conservatives and liberals. Until the early twentieth century, the concept of a federal investigative agency was viewed as threatening individual liberty, violating states' rights, and as emulating the methods of the Czarist secret police. This view soon changed. At first Roosevelt and later Woodrow Wilson, in the more emotional setting precipitated by World War I, successfully undercut opposition to a federal investigative agency by identifying such opposition with criminality or disloyalty. Both presidents, moreover, depicted the bureau as a logical and progressive response to the serious problems of internal subversion and crime. Was it not a professional organization that provided the investigative techniques necessary for meeting the problems of a complex industrial society?

Their attitudes toward the bureau symbolized the progressives' priorities: a preference for order and professionalism over the dissent and disorder intrinsic to a more inefficient if more democratic politics. As one historian, William O'Neill, has concluded, the Progressive Era was more "an age of modernization than of reform," whose predominant changes insured an efficient and rational government, which laid the basis for "the bureaucratized, business-dominated, limited welfare state we live in now."

7

The Foreign Policy
of Emergent Globalism

The Spanish-American War, the failure of the antiimperialists to block ratification of the Treaty of Paris, and the enunciation of the Open Door notes did not insure an expansionist foreign policy. There remained strong popular and congressional opposition to increased United States involvement overseas. The United States' pursuit of expansionist foreign policies during the early twentieth century, then, was an indirect by-product of the impact of progressivism.

If we define *progressive* as support for principles of democracy, territorial and political integrity, humanitarianism, and egalitarianism, then United States foreign policy in the early twentieth century was nonprogressive. The Roosevelt, Taft, and Wilson administrations intervened in the internal affairs of weaker states in Latin America and Asia. And economic and strategic interest led the United States to oppose European and Japanese expansion.

Just as domestic progressivism was a product of a desire for efficiency and order, so, too, was foreign policy. The foreign policy of the Progressive Era presidents and diplomats was based on the belief that experts should lead public opinion, on elitist and racialist conceptions of Latin American and Asian inferiority, and on the conviction that federal activism, not laissez faire, would best advance the nation's economic and strategic interests. The Progressive conception of expert leadership, combined with an underlying moralistic conception of reform, led to an evolving globalist foreign policy conducted by strong-minded presidents.

THEODORE ROOSEVELT AND LATIN AMERICA

An ardent expansionist before acceding to the presidency, Theodore Roosevelt chafed under the restrictions within which United States foreign policy was conducted. He also believed that the United States should increase its military strength, act as a great power, and promote international order and stability. Unable always to convince the public and the Congress that his foreign policy was proper and not reckless, Roosevelt sometimes acted unilaterally. His penchant for executive action was best revealed in his policies concerning the Panama Canal and the Roosevelt Corollary to the Monroe Doctrine.

Roosevelt desired an isthmian canal on economic and strategic grounds: it would promote trade and also enable a one-ocean American fleet to operate in both the Atlantic and the Pacific oceans. American interest in such a canal dated from the Clayton-Bulwer Treaty of 1850, by which the United States and Great Britain agreed that construction of a canal would be a joint project and that neither would seek exclusive control or fortification. By 1901, Britain recognized United States dominance in the Western Hemisphere, and that year's Hay-Pauncefote Treaty granted the United States the exclusive right to build, operate, and fortify an isthmian canal.

A year later Congress in the Spooner Act (1902) directed the administration to begin negotiations with the Columbian government to secure rights to construct, operate, and fortify a canal. If Columbia refused, the administration was directed to open negotiations with the Nicaraguan government. On January 22, 1903, Secretary of State John Hay negotiated a treaty with the Columbian ambassador to Washington, Tomas Herran. The Hay-Herran Treaty granted the United States perpetual rights to a canal zone six miles wide in return for payment to Columbia of $10 million and an annual rental of $250,000. The Columbian Senate, however, rejected the treaty, demanding instead a higher payment of $20 million and the right to maintain a Columbian peace force in the canal zone.

Rather than negotiating with the Nicaraguan Government, President Roosevelt instead sought to compel the Columbian government to relent. When Columbia remained intransigent, Roosevelt confided to individuals interested in the Panamanian route that he wished Panama would become an independent state and also that the U.S. warship *Tennessee* would arrive on November 2, 1903 just off the Columbian port of Colon. Accordingly, officials of the French-chartered Panamanian Company (which had gone bankrupt but hoped partially to recoup its losses by selling its construction rights to the United States for $40 million) started a "revolution" on November 3 to secure Panamanian independence. The *Tennessee* arrived in time to prevent the Columbian government from sending troops to suppress the insurrection. Then, acting quickly, the administration negotiated a treaty with the minister of the Panamanian revolutionary government in Washington, Philippe Bunau Varilla (an agent of the Panamanian Company who had lobbied actively in Washington to obtain Senate preference for the Panamanian rather than the Nicaraguan route in the Spooner Act). The new treaty reaffirmed the provisions of the Hay-Herran Treaty with the addition that the United States had officially recognized the independence of Panama and specifically pledged to guarantee her independence. Roosevelt's later boast of 1911 that "I took Panama!" was not wholly unfounded. The president had acted unilaterally to extend American interests at the expense of the territorial integrity of Columbia.

The Roosevelt administration responded similarly to internal instability in the Dominican Republic in order to avert European intervention. A revolution in 1903 that toppled a corrupt dictatorship worsened financial chaos in that Republic, and created the likelihood that the French, German, and Italian governments might intervene to assist investors who held Dominican bonds. Concerned over this prospect and convinced that action was necessary to avert future crises, Roosevelt, in his annual message to Congress in December 1904, proclaimed the Roosevelt Corollary to the Monroe Doctrine:

> Chronic wrongdoing, . . . may in America, as elsewhere, ultimately require intervention by some civilized nation, and in the Western Hemisphere the adherence of the United States to the Monroe Doctrine may force the United States, however reluctantly, in flagrant cases of such wrongdoing or impotence, to the exercise of an international police power.

Roosevelt thus unilaterally proclaimed a more expansive view of United States' hemispheric responsibilities. He sought stability and order in the Caribbean, and hence signed an agreement with the Dominican government authorizing the United States to appoint an American as collector of Dominican customs and director of its finance. American revenue management would enable the Dominican government to meet its debt obligations, thereby averting the need for European intervention and increase Dominican dependence on the United States. Based on *Realpolitik* conceptions of power and interests, the Roosevelt Corollary was couched in moralistic terms and made consistent with traditional American goals in order to mollify domestic critics of expansionist foreign policy.

Nor was the Dominican crisis the only occasion for Roosevelt's expansionist hemispheric policy. In January 1902, he unsuccessfully sought to purchase the Virgin Islands from Denmark. And in 1903, the president responded to a Venezuelan request to arbitrate her differences with the British, German, and Italian governments—who had collaborated to blockade five Venezuelan ports to force payment of Venezuelan debt obligations to their citizens. Earlier, in March 1901, Congress had adopted the Platt Amendment, which stipulated that Cuba could not make any treaty with any foreign power that should "impair its independence" and must not contract any debts beyond her capacity to pay, and authorized the United States "to intervene for the preservation of Cuban independence [and] the maintenance of a government adequate for the protection of life, property, and individual liberty." Reluctant at first, the Cubans in May 1903 adopted the Platt Amendment as an "annex" to their constitution, on the assurance that the purpose was to avert European intervention and not to give the United States the right to determine Cuban affairs.

ROOSEVELT AND THE FAR EAST

Roosevelt also promoted a more expansionist Far Eastern policy. Concerned over Russian expansionism in Manchuria, Roosevelt welcomed the Anglo-Japanese alliance of 1902 as a check on Russia. Then, when war erupted between Russia and Japan in 1905, the president favored Japan as a counterweight to Russia. The extent of the Japanese military success, however, disturbed Roosevelt, for it might disrupt the balance of power in Asia and threaten the Open Door. Accordingly, the president confidentially offered to mediate the war. Roosevelt's persistence and the costly military stalemate eventually led Japan and Russia to accept the president's mediation offer in the summer of 1905.

Convening in Portsmouth, New Hampshire, in August 1905, the conference ended the war. Pressuring the Japanese government to make concessions, Roosevelt helped negotiate a treaty in which the Russians recognized Japanese predominance in Korea, ceded South Sakhalin to Japan, and turned over the Chinese port of Port Arthur and the Russian-controlled railroads in South Manchuria to Japan.

For his role in ending the Russo-Japanese war, Roosevelt in 1906 received the Nobel Peace Prize. His objective, however, had been less to obtain peace than to protect a balance of power. In Roosevelt's conception of a rational foreign policy, the Great Powers had the responsibility to preserve order and stability, even if that might entail encroachments on the rights of less powerful states (in the case of the Portsmouth Treaty, the territorial and political sovereignty of China).

ROOSEVELT AND GLOBAL PEACE

Similar considerations underlay Roosevelt's mediation role at the Algeciras Conference of 1906, his advocacy of arbitration treaties, and his support for the Second Hague Conference of 1907.

Conflict between Germany and France in Europe and Africa had reached the point in 1905 where war seemed likely. Roosevelt again promptly acted as peacemaker and used his influence with the German Kaiser to bring the French and the Germans together in a conference in Algeciras, North Africa. There, statesmen arranged a Franco-German compromise, which ended what European diplomatic historians have described as the First Moroccan Crisis.

Roosevelt's conviction that wars between "civilized" nations would destroy civilization underlay his mediation at Algeciras as well as his support for arbitration agreements with other nations permitting American presidents to open arbitration without the Senate's consent. At the Second Hague Conference, the American delegation (carefully selected by Roosevelt to insure that no pacifists were members and that the focus would be on arms limitations, not disarmament) worked hard for a general arbitration agreement, the creation of an international court of justice, and the freezing of navies at their existing size and strength. The conferees failed to win all their points.

Roosevelt's actions reflected his own conception of a proper foreign policy and tended to be unilateral because Congress did not share his views. If not always opposed to the purposes of the president's policies, the Congress was not reconciled to Roosevelt's conception of presidential power. Accordingly the Senate refused to yield its power to consent in arbitration matters and insisted on a voice to insure that national interests were indeed sufficiently safeguarded. Roosevelt thereafter had to be sensitive both to the interests of foreign nations and the Senate. Democratic senators, moreover, denounced Roosevelt's mediation role at Algeciras for involving the United States in European affairs.

ROOSEVELT AND JAPAN

Conflict between the Congress and the president surfaced again over Roosevelt's decision in 1907 to send the entire American battleship fleet around the world. Roosevelt desired to impress the Japanese with American military strength. American-Japanese relations had deteriorated following Roosevelt's mediation role at Portsmouth—his pressures on the Japanese to moderate their treaty demands had precipitated anti-American rioting in Tokyo and other Japnese cities. Concurrently, anti-Oriental sentiment in California—especially the San Francisco School Board's decision to assign all Oriental children to segregated schools—led the Japanese Government to protest this racial insult. Expressing concern over such "outrageous action against the Japanese," Roosevelt promised to remedy the situation. Yet, because school policy was not a federal matter, the president could do little. He did finally secure a Gentleman's Agreement with Japan—there could be no treaty with Japan, as provisions fell outside the president's powers—whereby San Francisco authorities promised to rescind their policy of school segregation in return for a Japanese promise to deny passports to Japanese laborers seeking to emigrate to the United States.

Roosevelt's decision in 1907 to send the fleet around the world thus raised grave concerns. Members of Congress and newspapers condemned it as dangerous (it left the United States coastline unguarded) and provocative. Roosevelt simply dared the Congress not to support his policy. Using contingency funds, he sent the fleet to the Pacific. However, the contingency funds were sufficient only to pay the costs of transporting the fleet to the Pacific; Roosevelt thereby forced the Congress to vote additional funds to bring the fleet home. The crisis envisioned by the president's critics never materialized: the Japanese Government invited the fleet to visit Tokyo. And, on November 30, 1908, the Japanese ambassador in Washington negotiated an executive agreement with the American secretary of state, the Root-Takahira Agreement, whereby both nations agreed to recognize each other's territorial possessions in the Pacific, to preserve the Open Door, and to respect Chinese territorial integrity.

Roosevelt's *Realpolitik* conceptions also led him to support necessary military reforms. Under the leadership of Secretary of War Elihu Root, the authorized strength of U.S. armed forces was increased and reforms were instituted to modernize military training—including creation of an Army War College and establishment of a general staff corps. Its increased overseas role also led the administration to secure an increase in naval appropriations and in the size of the American fleet.

Although resorting to moralistic rhetoric to justify particular actions, Roosevelt's foreign policy was based on distinctly realistic conceptions and was intended to advance American economic and strategic interests. Committed to preserving a balance of power internationally, Roosevelt believed that developments that contributed to disorder and instability threatened world peace and undermined efforts to expand American trade, investments, and political influence. Pursuing an expansionist foreign policy at a time of relative United States military weakness, Roosevelt succeeded in advancing American interests because competing European states and worldwide European involvement minimized the risks of such a policy. The international setting, combined with Roosevelt's willingness to act boldly and to define policy in terms that insured popular support, underlay the striking achievements of the Roosevelt years. In a real sense, the president had altered fundamentally the direction and nature of the nation's foreign policy role.

TAFT AND DOLLAR DIPLOMACY

William Howard Taft inherited the role and problems Roosevelt's approach posed for American diplomats. An astute student of international relations (his prepresidential experiences included service as governor general of the Philippines and then secretary of war in Roosevelt's cabinet), Taft shared Roosevelt's conception of the need for an expansionist foreign policy. Unlike Roosevelt, however, Taft failed to shape effectively the nation's foreign policy. In part, Taft's failure derived from opposition by a more assertive Congress, one more jealous of its prerogatives and one that challenged the priorities basic to the administration's policies. More important, Taft's failure stemmed from his style of leadership: his was a more passive conception of the presidency, as executor of the laws and not as a "bully pulpit" from which to rally public opinion. Taft also enunciated policy in more direct and forthright terms.

In striking contrast to Roosevelt's moralistic rhetoric, which emphasized the American mission in traditional "manifest destiny" terms, Taft defined his objectives as "dollar diplomacy." By this term, the president emphasized, the United States proposed to "substitu[te] dollars for bullets" to advance American interests and influence. This characterization, however, rendered the Taft administration more vulnerable to the charges of such progressive congressmen as Senator Robert LaFollette of Wisconsin, who claimed in 1912 that the State Department was "a trading post for Wall Street interests" and who condemned the administration's policies as imperialistic.

LaFollette's criticisms derived their substance from the Taft Administration's own explanation of its efforts to promote peace and stability through American trade and investments. Indeed, when testifying in May 1911 before the Senate Foreign Relations Committee in support of a treaty that the administration had negotiated with the Nicaraguan government (the Senate refused to accept the treaty), Secretary of State Philander Knox forcefully articulated Taft's foreign policy position. The administration's purpose, the American secretary emphasized, was "to make American capital the instrumentality to secure financial stability, and hence prosperity and peace, to the more backward Republics in the neighborhood of the Panama Canal."

Knox referred specifically to the Taft administration's general policy of seeking to insure stability in Latin America by financially reorganizing the area's more unstable and unpopular governments. To remove the danger of foreign intervention, Taft sought to have Latin American debts renegotiated through loans floated by American banks. Since this plan required reliance on private bankers, the administration had to provide assurances that would lead American bankers to invest in countries with histories of internal unrest and instability.

Hence the administration adopted a more interventionist approach. When revolution erupted in Nicaragua in 1909 and again in 1912, Taft sent marines and sailors to preserve order and stability. The 1911 assassination of the president of the Dominican Republic, resulting in a situation bordering on anarchy, led the administration to resort to economic pressure to force a change in Dominican leadership. Then, following the overthrow of the Mexican dictator Porfirio Diaz in 1911 and the start of the Mexican Revolution, the Taft administration refused to recognize the new provisional government headed by Victoriano Huerta. Taft insisted on withholding recognition until the U.S. was assured that the new government would respect American interests and investments in Mexico. Taft never formally established diplomatic relations before leaving office.

Consistent with his Latin American policy, President Taft also pursued an activist policy in China. Concerned about Japanese expansion in Manchuria, the administration sought to protect American interests by involving private bankers in China. In 1910 and 1911, Taft and Secretary of State Knox entered into arrangements insuring that American bankers would be included in a consortium planning to lend $125 million to China to build railroads in south and central China. Knox also proposed that Manchuria be neutralized (i.e., that Japanese influence be curtailed) through the floating of a multinational loan to China to repurchase the Manchurian railroads. These efforts failed. The British, Russians, and Japanese would not abandon their spheres of influence in Manchuria. American bankers, moreover, hesitated to invest in China, owing to Chinese political instability.

The Taft administration's foreign policy, then, differed from Roosevelt's in tactics and rhetoric, not in its aims. These differences nonetheless proved crucial in limiting the administration's ability to command the support necessary for an expansionist foreign policy.

WILSON AND MISSIONARY DIPLOMACY

Woodrow Wilson did not agree with Taft's practical foreign policy approach. A moralist, Wilson believed that the nation's foreign policy should be governed by principle, not by crass self-interest or material gain. Yet Wilson was not indifferent to economic or strategic considerations; he advocated a well-defined foreign policy intended to advance the national interest. Like Roosevelt and Taft, he was committed to preserving the balance of power and to advancing trade and commerce. Equally important to this son of a Presbyterian minister was the need to replace Taft's "dollar diplomacy" with "a system more in harmony with our nation's traditions and ideals." That the Wilson administration would not ignore economic considerations was revealed in a 1914 speech of Secretary of State William Jennings Bryan to the American Export Association. Assuring these businessmen of the administration's keen interest in promoting foreign trade, the American secretary affirmed: "my Department is your department; the ambassadors, the ministers, and the consuls are all yours. It is their business to look after your interests and to guard your rights." Bryan, however, was not enunciating a policy that merely identified the national interest with foreign trade expansion. He was affirming the administration's intent to service the legitimate needs of Americans engaged in foreign trade and commerce and to create stable conditions in which peaceful commerce flourished.

Accordingly, the Wilson administration reversed Taft's finance policies concerning China: first, by pressuring American bankers to withdraw from the international consortium to finance Chinese raiload construction and second, by extending diplomatic representation to the new Chinese republican government. Wilson's China policy was clearly based on the objective of promoting internal stability and order and certainly was not indifferent to power politics. It also pleased those Wall Street bankers who saw investment risks in China as greater than potential gains.

Wilson's essential conservatism was dramatized by the apparently contradictory course the administration pursued toward the Mexican Revolution. Taft had bequeathed his successor no Mexican policy. On March 11, 1913, Wilson denounced those who had seized power "to advance their own personal interests or ambitions" and refused to recognize the new Mexican government (which he labeled "a government of butchers" because it came to power through murder). For Wilson, nonrecognition was a conscious and moral policy. Its purpose was to base policy on the principle that the United States should not recognize any government coming to power by force or in violation of its national constitution. Yet Wilson's unprecedented doctrine of nonrecognition was both elitist and interventionist; the administration reserved to itself the right to judge whether a foreign government reflected the interests of its people, and it encouraged resistance within Mexico to Huerta's government.

Wilson's attitudes toward the Huerta government hardened, and he soon concluded that Huerta must be removed. The president attempted first to negotiate with the Mexican leader in order to secure democratic elections for a new government. Concluding that Huerta could not be trusted, the president drafted a sharp note to other European powers requesting that they end diplomatic recognition and financial aid for Huerta. Succeeding in isolating Huerta diplomatically, Wilson in February 1914 lifted an American embargo on arms sales to Mexico—an action that indirectly assisted the forces led by Venustiano Carranza, who were seeking to overthrow Huerta and restore constitutional government.

The dynamics of the Mexican Revolution stymied the administration. In a series of confusing and seemingly contradictory actions, the administration first imposed a blockade on the Mexican ports of Tampico and Veracruz, then ordered the military occupation of Veracruz, and finally accepted the offer of Argentina, Brazil, and Chile to mediate America's dispute with Mexico.

When Carranza's forces occupied Mexico City on August 20 and defeated Huerta, Wilson found Carranza as difficult to deal with as Huerta. The new Mexican president refused to accept Wilson's conditions for recognition: immediate restoration of constitutional procedures and respect for the rights of foreign investors. Thus when the bandit leader Francisco (Pancho) Villa broke with Carranza and civil war resumed, the American president at first supported Villa. Wilson soon changed course again and in October 1915 recognized Carranza's government as the "de facto" government of Mexico. "De jure" recognition was formally extended on August 31, 1917. It was not respect for Mexican integrity but, rather, the outbreak of the European war in 1914 and Wilson's desire to restore stability south of the border that led to toleration of Carranza—but not before the United States and Mexico almost went to war in 1916.

The objective of promoting stability and order, not respect for the independence and integrity of weaker states, explained Wilsonian diplomacy. Not surprisingly, then, the Wilson administration did not hesitate to order military intervention in Latin America. In July 1915, the president authorized the marines to intervene in Haiti to quell fighting between competing armed factions. Then, in September 1915 the Haitian government signed a treaty with the United States establishing a protectorate similar to that in Cuba under the Platt Amendment. Similarly, in April 1916, the president sent the marines to the Dominican Republic to preserve order and prevent a revolution. American troops remained in Haiti until 1934 and in the Dominican Republic until 1924. Then Assistant Secretary of the Navy Franklin D. Roosevelt actually drafted the constitution of Haiti. The Wilson administration also acted to qualify what had been a consistent Democratic platform pledge since 1900—to grant independence to the Philippines. Instead, the Jones Act of 1916 granted legislative autonomy and a large measure of administrative control, but not independence, to the Filipinos. The rationale was that additional time and American tutelage were necessary to prepare Philippine leaders for self-government and to create conditions essential to independence.

Nor did the Wilson administration abandon Roosevelt's and Taft's economic diplomacy. During Wilson's tenure, Latin American economic dependence on the United States increased, and by 1914 the United States commanded roughly 50 percent of all Latin American foreign trade. After World War I the total value of U.S. exports from and imports to Latin America increased from $798 million in 1914 to $3,393 billion by 1920. And in 1918 Wilson abandoned his earlier opposition to American investment in the Far East and supported a four-power consortium to aid Chinese economic rehabilitation. He did so because the administration feared that World War I had disrupted the balance of power in Asia to Japan's advantage and thus threatened the Open Door. Earlier, through an exchange of notes on November 2, 1917 (the so-called Lansing-Ishii agreement), the Wilson administration secured Japanese respect for the independence and territorial integrity of China and an open door for trade and investment. In return for Japanese concessions, the administration recognized Japan's "special interests in China, particularly in the part [Manchuria] to which her possessions are contiguous."

During the Progressive Era, then, a number of far-reaching changes had altered the conduct of American foreign policy. The era witnessed the rise of presidential power in foreign affairs despite congressional resistance. And gradually changing were the ideas that there should be

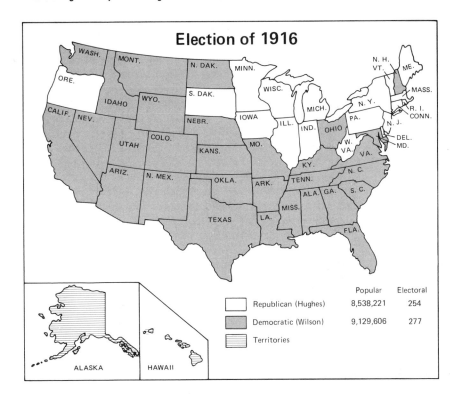

Election of 1916

	Popular	Electoral
Republican (Hughes)	8,538,221	254
Democratic (Wilson)	9,129,606	277
Territories		

ALASKA   HAWAII

limits to U.S. power, that foreign involvement should be minimized, and that military intervention should be avoided. Policymakers increasingly acted on the belief that the United States had worldwide interests, that a more activist approach was needed to safeguard the national interest, and that American leaders had the moral responsibility to direct the internal affairs of less powerful and inferior peoples. The Progressive Era thus marked the dawn not only of a new century, an American Century, but also of a foreign policy conceived in righteousness and motivated by a heady sense of unlimited power. The actions of American policymakers were motivated by a sense of American omnipotence and omniscience, beliefs that would inevitably involve the United States in World War I.

SELECTED BIBLIOGRAPHY FOR SECTION II

The growth of the national economy and industry is fully surveyed in the old but still revealing work by THOMAS C. COCHRAN and WILLIAM MILLER, *The Age of Enterprise: A Social History of Industrial America* (1942).* Other valuable studies of American industrial development are

* Available in paperback.

GLENN PORTER, *The Rise of Big Business, 1865–1910* (1975) *; and
ALFRED D. CHANDLER, JR., *Strategy and Structure: Chapters in the History
of Industrial Enterprise* (1969).* Also see the still valuable work by
HAROLD U. FAULKNER, *The Decline of Laissez-Faire* (1951). A classic
multivolume study which covers the social history of the period is MARK
SULLIVAN's *Our Times* (6 vols., 1926–1935). Equally useful but shorter is
another old account, HAROLD U. FAULKNER, *The Quest for Social Justice,
1898–1914* (1931). On immigrants and ethnic groups during this era see
JOHN HIGHAM, *Strangers in the Land: Patterns of American Nativism*
(1963) *; and DAVID REIMERS and LEONARD DINNERSTEIN, *Ethnic Americans* (1975).* For a brief treatment of workers and the labor movement
see MELVYN DUBOFSKY, *Industrialism and the American Worker, 1865–
1920* (1975),* and for the relationship between one industry and its
workers read DAVID BRODY, *Steelworkers in America: The Nonunion Era*
(1960).* The situation of black Americans in an age of reform can be
seen in C. VANN WOODWARD, *The Strange Career of Jim Crow* (1955) *;
RICHARD B. SHERMAN, *The Republican Party and Black America: From
McKinley to Hoover, 1896–1933* (1973); and DAVID SOUTHERN, *The
Malignant Heritage: Yankee Progressives and the Negro Question, 1901–
1909* (1968). An excellent survey of women during the period is ROBERT
SMUTS, *Women and Work in America* (1959).* Special aspects of society
and reform in the progressive era can be followed in JAMES H. TIMBER-
LAKE, *Prohibition and the Progressive Movement, 1900–1920* (1963) *;
WILLIAM L. O'NEILL, *Divorce in the Progressive Era* (1968) *; and DON-
ALD K. PICKENS, *Eugenics and Progressives* (1968). The world of ideas,
literature, and culture is examined in MORTON G. WHITE, *Social Thought
in America: The Revolt against Formalism* (1957); CHARLES B. FORCEY,
*The Crossroads of Liberalism: Croly, Weyl, Lippmann and the Progres-
sive Era, 1900–1925* (1961) *; CHRISTOPHER LASCH, *The New Radicalism
in America, 1888–1963* (1965) *; C. C. REGIER, *The Era of the Muckrakers*
(1932); and HENRY F. MAY, *The End of American Innocence* (1960).*
   There is a rich history of political progressivism. The best studies
include RICHARD HOFSTADTER, *The Age of Reform* (1955) *; ERIC GOLD-
MAN, *Rendezvous with Destiny* (1952) *; GEORGE MOWRY, *The Era of
Theodore Roosevelt* (1952) *; ARTHUR LINK, *Woodrow Wilson and the
Progressive Era* (1954) *; and SAMUEL P. HAYS, *The Response to Indus-
trialism* (1957).* Among the more recent studies critical of the political
reform tradition are GABRIEL KOLKO, *The Triumph of Conservatism*
(1963)*; ROBERT WIEBE, *Businessmen and Reform* (1962)*; JAMES WEIN-
STEIN, *The Corporate Ideal in the Liberal State* (1969) *; DAVID THELEN,
The New Citizenship (1972); and WILLIAM L. O'NEILL, *The Progressive
Years* (1975).* For more radical aspects of national politics read DAVID
SHANNON, *The Socialist Party of America* (1960) *; JOHN H. M. LASLETT,
Labor and the Left (1970); and MELVYN DUBOFSKY, *We Shall Be All:
A History of the IWW* (1969).* On efforts to curb dissent and radicalism
see WILLIAM PRESTON, JR., *Aliens and Dissenters* (1963) *; PAT WATTERS
and STEPHEN GILLERS, eds., *Investigating the FBI* (1973) *; SANFORD

UNGER, *FBI* (1975); and JEROLD AUERBACH, *Unequal Justice* (1976). The best accounts of state and local reform movements are GEORGE MOWRY, *The California Progressives* (1951) *; A. D. KIRWAN, *Revolt of the Rednecks* (1951) *; JACK T. KIRBY, *Darkness at Dawning: Race and Reform in the Progressive South* (1972) *; EARL S. POMEROY, *The Pacific Slope* (1965) *; HOYT L. WARNER, *Progressivism in Ohio, 1897–1917* (1964); MELVIN G. HOLLI, *Reform in Detroit: Hazen S. Pingree and Urban Politics* (1969) *; ZANE L. MILLER, *Boss Cox's Cincinnati: Urban Politics in the Progressive Era* (1968) *; and JAMES CROOKS, *Politics and Progress: The Rise of Urban Progressivism in Baltimore* (1968). More specialized reform movements, such as feminism and city welfare, are treated in ELEANOR FLEXNER, *Century of Struggle* (1959) *; WILLIAM L. O'NEILL, *Everyone Was Brave* (1969) *; AILEEN KRADITOR, *The Ideas of the Woman Suffrage Movement* (1965) *; ROY LUBOVE, *The Professional Altruist* (1965); and ALLEN DAVIS, *Spearheads for Reform* (1967).*

Several thoughtful interpretations of American foreign policy during this period are HOWARD K. BEALE, *Theodore Roosevelt and the Rise of America to World Power* (1956) *; RICHARD W. LEOPOLD, *The Growth of American Foreign Policy* (1962); ARTHUR S. LINK, *Wilson: The Diplomatist* (1957) *; and GEORGE F. KENNAN's classic study, *American Diplomacy, 1900–1950* (1951).* Two fine studies of American policy in the Carribean are DAVID F. HEALY, *The United States in Cuba, 1898–1902* (1963) and DANA G. MUNRO, *Intervention and Dollar Diplomacy in the Carribean, 1900–1921* (1964). Latin America is surveyed in J. L. MECHAM, *The United States and Inter-American Security, 1889–1960* (1961) and SAMUEL F. BEMIS, *The Latin American Policy of the United States* (1943).* The Far East is discussed in RAYMOND A. ESTHUS, *An Uncertain Friendship: Theodore Roosevelt and Japan* (1966) and JOHN K. FAIRBANKS, *The United States and China* (1958).*

III

The World at War 1914–1920

For a century—from the signing of diplomatic agreements that ended the era of Napoleonic wars in 1815 to the outbreak of world war in the late summer of 1914—the Western world had seemed to rule the globe without challenge. Its economic wealth and technological virtuosity made western military power dominant and enabled such nations as Great Britain, France, Germany, and later the United States to control much of Asia, Africa, and the Near East. But the eruption of general war in 1914 among the western nations shattered the illusion of western superiority.

World War I not only ended a century of relative peace but also rearranged the structure of world power. It unleashed a new wave of revolution precipitated by the success of Bolshevism in Russia, weakened the power of such nations as Britain and France, and validated Japan as a major Asian power. Four years of war, especially costly in terms of human life, bled France, Germany, and Britain white; it also crippled their economies. Soviet Russia emerged from the war stripped of much of its prewar territory in the West, and its Bolshevik leaders faced the challenge of achieving their revolutionary goals in the face of counterrevolutionary armed forces supplied by the western powers. The Austro-Hungarian Empire collapsed in the ashes of war and was replaced by a congeries of small successor states in Central Europe, none of which were large enough or strong enough alone to preserve their independence and national security. Only the United States, a late and somewhat reluctant entrant into World War I, emerged from the conflict relatively unscathed. Indeed, in 1919 the United States was the only nation that deserved to be characterized as a great power, and it was the only western state economically and materially capable of replacing Britain as a global policeman. But the United States in 1919–1920 neither desired nor accepted a new role as the world's dominant power.

8

The Grand Illusion: American Neutrality 1914-1917

The Great War that erupted in Europe in August 1914 began a cycle of destructive wars and social upheavals that tore apart the fabric of Western civilization. Although most American and European observers reacted with shocked disbelief, the outbreak of a general war was the logical fruit of decades of frustrated nationalism and, even more, of the costly arms race between the rival alliance systems of the Old World. Industrial growth and economic competition led the great powers to struggle for domination of markets and acquisition of colonies. Insecurities bred competing alliances, which merely enhanced the power struggle and deepened national anxieties.

Blundering diplomats, impatient militarists, extreme nationalists, and ardent imperialists plunged Europe into over four years of bloody warfare that eventually involved most of the world and that cost an estimated *fifteen million lives* and billions of dollars. When it was over, the old order had been smashed. Russia had experienced a titanic social revolution, Austria-Hungary had dissolved, and a once proud Germany lay humbled in defeat. The victors were scarcely more fortunate. France had been ravaged by the war, Italy hovered on the brink of social chaos, and Great Britain had lost much of her wealth and trade. And all the

European belligerents sacrificed a generation of young men on the battlefields, history's "lost generation." Only the United States, among the great powers, emerged relatively unscarred as the world's foremost economic and potentially military power. How did such shattering developments occur after a century of relative world peace and prosperity?

TOWARD THE ABYSS

Perhaps the key underlying factors were the rapid industrialization of Germany and the decline of the once dominant French power on the continent of Europe. Anxious to isolate a revenge-minded France, defeated in the 1870 Franco-Prussian War, Germany formed the Triple Alliance with Austria and Italy in 1882. Subsequently, in 1893, France and Russia countered with the Dual Alliance. Great Britain, fearful of German economic and naval competition, in 1904 and 1907 reached colonial understandings or ententes with France and Russia respectively. The Triple Alliance now faced the Triple Entente. Britain also cultivated a rapprochement or improved relations with the United States and in 1902 signed a defensive alliance with Japan to shore up her Asian flank. Any chance spark threatened to involve these rival alliance systems in a major general war.

A chance spark ignited general war in 1914. A young Serbian terrorist shot and killed Archduke Franz Ferdinand, heir to the Austro-Hungarian throne, and his wife at Sarajevo on June 28. Determined to humble Serbia and remove its threat to the Slavic peoples under Austrian rule, and encouraged in its obduracy by Germany, the Viennese government declared war against Serbia in late July. But the war could not be localized. Russia came to Serbia's aid and Germany, fearful of losing the advantage if it did not strike first, declared war on Russia and invaded France through neutral Belgium—an act that prompted British intervention. By August 4 the Central Powers of Germany and Austria, subsequently joined by Bulgaria and Turkey, were at war with the Entente or Allied Powers of Russia, France, and Great Britain. Japan also entered on the Allied side and in 1915 Italy, bribed with promises of Austrian territory, joined against the Central Powers.

AMERICA THE NEUTRAL

The great majority of Americans rejoiced in August 1914 that the wide Atlantic separated them from the slaughter on the European battlefields. They cheered their president when he not only proclaimed official neutrality but also urged his fellow citizens to seek impartiality in thought and speech. Yet as the war continued, most Americans simply could not avoid sympathizing with one belligerent side or the other. Because of their English origins and historic cultural and economic ties, and the traditional Franco-American friendship, the greater number of Americans were drawn toward the Entente or Allied cause. That was particularly true of "elite" intellectuals, academicians, and important newspaper editors and journalists. Great Britain and France seemed to be fighting in self-defense against a brutal and autocratic German military power that had raped Belgium and invaded France. Moreover, German-American relations had deteriorated in recent years, as the Samoan controversy and suspicions of German intentions in the Philippines during the Spanish-American War had illustrated. Yet, millions of German-Americans looked favorably upon the Fatherland, joined by many British-hating Irish-Americans and anti-Russian Jewish-Americans (because of virulent anti-Semitism within the czarist empire).

Belligerent propaganda strengthened these various sentiments but only to a secondary degree. Even before propaganda could have much effect, the majority of Americans already favored the Allies. German propaganda in America sought to portray the Reich as a center of culture and civilization fighting in self-defense against French revengists and Russian imperialists. But propaganda could not compensate for her violation of Belgian neutrality or invasion of France; moreover, the Germans used such disturbing weapons as poison gas, aerial bombing of cities, and the submarine; and few prominent Americans could be found to defend the German cause.

British propaganda soon eclipsed the enemy in efficiency and scope. Shaping their appeals to specific American groups and classes, British propagandists skillfully presented the Allies as fighting for democracy and morality against a cruel and militaristic autocracy. Germany, they charged, was the modern regimented Sparta. The famed Bryce Report in 1915 also tried to prove that Germany deliberately committed war crimes and atrocities in occupied Belgium and France. Finally Britain controlled the seas and the cables between America and Europe, enabling her to censor and direct the flow of war information.

A small minority of influential Americans from the first regarded an Allied victory as essential to American interests, whether on moral, ideological, economic or security grounds. A German triumph, they feared, would weaken democracy everywhere, damage international law and morality, threaten American economic bonds with western Europe, and potentially pose a menace to the security of the United States itself. Former President Theodore Roosevelt held such views, as did the journalist Walter Lippmann and many other influential easterners. High administration officials also shared pro-Entente sentiments: Colonel Edward M. House, Wilson's friend and advisor; Robert Lansing, legal counselor and Secretary of State after William Jennings Bryan's resignation in mid-1915; and most members of Wilson's cabinet and his ambassadors in London and Berlin. Only Bryan inclined toward a strict neutrality and impartiality. Even President Wilson was pro-Ally and shared to some degree the views of his advisers that a German victory was not desirable. Yet he saw neutrality as the wisest course for the United States and clung to it as long as he thought American interests permitted.

A SILENT PARTNER OF THE ALLIES

In keeping with the past and its own economic interests, the United States opened its markets to the belligerents. Since Britain ruled the seas, that meant that only the Allies had access to American markets, and they began to purchase vast quantities of foodstuffs, raw materials, and war goods. By early 1917, over a billion dollars worth of munitions alone had been sold to Britain and France. That one-sided trade brought booming prosperity to the United States and also in effect made the country a "silent partner" of the Allies. Yet when the Central Powers complained, the American government blandly defended the war traffic as neutral and consistent with international law and neutrality—true in theory but not in practice.

Financial ties followed closely upon the growing war trade. At first the administration via the so-called Bryan loan ban had discouraged private loans to the belligerents as unwise and likely merely to feed the flames of the war. But as the Allies began to exhaust their finances in America, the administration realized that either loans and credits had to be permitted or the prosperity-inducing flow of purchases would evaporate. Consequently the ban was scrapped and the green light given to bankers and investors. By early 1917, nearly $2⅓ billion had been privately loaned to the allies to finance war purchases, one more indication that American neutrality in fact worked heavily in favor of the Anglo-French side.

Some historians and critics later tried to argue that these economic and financial ties with the Allies finally dragged the United States into the war against Germany. According to their several versions, the United States finally went to war to save its stake in an Allied victory—or an enraged Germany struck at America and its war trade with the submarine. Both arguments are unsound. Most Americans, including Wilson, expected the Allies to win without our intervention. When Wilson did decide in favor of intervention, it was to protect American security as defined by the president, not to save Wall Street bankers. Indeed, the original loans were intended, in the administration's view, to bolster the Allied cause and thus serve American national aims. Finally, whatever the United States did, Germany would have continued U-boat warfare, as she was determined to gain total victory. From the first, then, Wilson regarded the Allied cause as vital to American security and encouraged aid to Britain and France as consistent with national interests; ultimately, as a last resort, he turned to intervention.

BLOCKADE AND THE U-BOAT

From the start the British government waged economic war against Germany. She expanded greatly the list of contraband goods (war materials) subject to seizure if shipped to the enemy, and her navy shut off direct neutral sea commerce with the Central Powers. Then in March 1915 the British proclaimed in effect a blockade of Germany and bordering neutrals and began to seize cargoes shipped from the United States to Holland, for example, on the grounds that the goods were destined ultimately for Germany or her allies.

The American government naturally protested such interference with American trade. Yet though its protests often were sharply phrased, the American government never threatened Great Britain with dire consequences if she continued her practices. For Wilson and his advisers sympathized with the British and trusted their leaders to do only what was necessary for victory. Until 1916, Sir Edward Grey, the able British foreign secretary, managed to strengthen Wilson's trust and to make concessions to the United States when necessary.

Washington reacted much less tolerantly when Germany turned to submarine warfare. Its surface fleet thwarted by the British, Germany struck back early in 1915 by proclaiming a submarine blockade of the British Isles. Within that zone Allied shipping would be subject to destruction, and neutral ships were warned to stay away lest they be attacked accidentally. In practice, U-boats would torpedo all ships without warning and without giving crews and passengers time to escape in safety. President Wilson and Robert Lansing—Bryan was away from the capital—viewed the submarine blockade as contrary to international law and morality. It was an inhumane form of warfare against noncombatants and neutrals. In their view, neutrals had the right to travel the high seas freely and in safety. Also, the two American officials apparently interpreted the German use of the U-boat as an affront to the national honor and a threat to legitimate trade.

Consequently President Wilson solemnly condemned underseas warfare and warned Germany, in a note on February 10, 1915, that the United States would hold her to a "strict accountability" for any violations of American lives and property. By refusing to accept submarine warfare, he thereby placed the United States squarely in opposition to what Germany saw as one of its most promising weapons.

LUSITANIA AND *SUSSEX* CRISES

On May 7, 1915, a German U-boat off the Irish coast fired one torpedo into the great British passenger liner *Lusitania*. The ship sank in eighteen minutes, with the loss of 1,198 lives including 128 Americans. Virtually all Americans reacted with shock and horror to what seemed like pointless destruction, but war sentiment was confined largely to the eastern states. The press described the sinking as "assassination," "wholesale murder," and "piracy," and demanded a firm stand.

President Wilson reflected majority sentiment in his resolve to uphold American rights and interests without war. On May 13 he sent a note to Berlin condemning the attack as contrary to international law, and he requested that Germany disavow the act and make reparations. The German response proved evasive. Bryan, fearful of war and opposed to Wilson's firm position, chose to resign as Secretary of State rather than sign a harsher note to Berlin. In his view, Americans should be warned to avoid belligerent ships and the war zone, and the issue with Germany should be postponed for postwar settlement (as were issues with Britain). Lansing, Bryan's successor, signed the second *Lusitania* note repeating American demands. Most of the press rallied to Wilson's side, and Bryan was widely criticized for deserting his post in an hour of crisis. Clearly, many citizens agreed with the president that the nation's honor and interests were intolerably challenged by the submarine. Once again, however, the German response was unsatisfactory. Since both Berlin and Washington preferred to avoid a showdown, Wilson's third note merely warned that any repetition of submarine outrages would be seen as "deliberately unfriendly."

The lull ended on August 19 when another U-boat torpedoed the British liner *Arabic* with the loss of two American lives. Fearful of war, German Chancellor Theobald von Bethmann-Hollweg persuaded the kaiser and his military advisers that concessions must be made. In the *Arabic* pledge Germany promised not to sink passenger ships without warning and without making safety provisions for those on board. Room for diplomatic maneuver had narrowed greatly as Wilson fully committed American honor and prestige against ruthless submarine warfare.

These repeated crises with Germany touched off a great "preparedness" debate in the United States. Should the nation not take immediate measures to improve its defenses against possible enemies? Reluctantly acceding, Wilson in late 1915 and early 1916 demanded vastly increased expenditures for the army and the navy. The ensuing public controversy over preparedness aroused the opposition of pacifists and peace advocates and divided Wilson's progressive supporters, but Wilson obtained much of what he wanted. Congress authorized increases in the army and national guard and greatly accelerated naval construction.

The *Sussex* crisis occurred during the preparedness debate. On March 24, 1916, a U-boat torpedoed the unarmed French channel steamer *Sussex*. Viewing the attack as a violation of the *Arabic* pledge, Wilson on April 8 sent Germany an ultimatum: cease such warfare immediately or the United States would break diplomatic relations. Once again the German chancellor managed to restrain his more bellicose colleagues. He feared that a break would lead to war, thereby dooming

Germany to defeat as the United States brought its vast economic strength and manpower to bear. Consequently, he promised on May 4 not to attack without warning unresisting enemy passenger and merchant shipping. Significantly, however, Germany's *Sussex* pledge reserved freedom to act in the future if the United States failed to persuade the Allies to abide by international law on the high seas ("freedom of the seas").

In 1916 Wilson sought reelection under the banners of peace and progressivism. The Democratic convention coined the slogan, "He kept us out of war," and Democratic leaders charged that a Republican victory would mean war with both Mexico and Germany. Wilson also won progressive support by endorsing more advanced legislation than he had been willing to seek in the past. Even so, Wilson barely won reelection. (Election map 1916, see p. 105)

WAR COMES TO AMERICA

The end of neutrality followed closely upon the 1916 election. Aware that Germany might soon renew underseas warfare, and long eager to mediate the war, President Wilson made two peace moves after reelection. On December 18, 1916, he requested the belligerents to state their war aims, in hopes for a peace opening. Neither side responded positively. Then on January 22, 1917, the president addressed the Senate and urged a "peace without victory," a lasting peace based upon justice and reason rather than conquests and spoils. Again his effort failed. Both Germany and the Allies had sacrificed too much blood and money and had aroused too many popular hatreds to admit the possiblity of a peace without conquests, a mere return to the prewar status quo. Each side still hoped to defeat the other and to win empire and security on the battlefield. And, finally, neither wanted the American president to play a role in the eventual peacemaking, as long as the United States remained neutral.

Events within Germany meanwhile ended American neutrality. The German high command—Field Marshal Paul von Hindenburg and General Erich Ludendorff—agreed with the navalists that unrestricted use of the submarine promised to produce a decisive victory by starving Great Britain into submission. Influential elements within Germany, embittered at the American war trade with the Allies, also called for full U-boat warfare. The military brushed aside arguments that the United States would enter the war, convinced that it already aided the Allies as much as it could and confident of knocking Britain out before many American troops could arrive in Europe. Since Kaiser Wilhelm II also agreed, the apprehensive German chancellor had to give way. On January 31, 1917, the German government notified the United States that after February 1 all ships, neutral as well as belligerent, would be destroyed within the war zone around the British Isles.

President Wilson in view of his past declarations had no choice but

A German skeleton lies unburied on a battlefield,
one of the nearly fifteen million men and women killed
during World War I

Imperial War Museum, London

to break diplomatic relations, which he did on February 3. He still
hoped, however, that Berlin would not carry out its threat of unrestricted
submarine warfare. That hope vanished as German U-boats sank American ships. The Zimmermann Telegram further revealed Germany's hostile intentions. That telegram from the German Foreign Office to its
representative in Mexico City invited Mexico, in case of war between
Germany and the United States, to join Germany's side and to seek the
recovery of territory lost to the Americans in the 1846–1848 Mexican-
American War. The telegram was intercepted by the British and published in the American press. Most Americans now readily agreed with
Wilson that Germany indeed was an enemy.

On April 2, Wilson went before Congress and asked it to recognize a
state of war with Germany. Because of her hostile acts, he declared,
neutrality was no longer possible. He then proclaimed the goals for
which America would fight. We did not seek territory or other selfish

gains, but only to defeat an autocratic militarism that threatened the liberties of all free nations: "The world must be made safe for democracy." The president thus transformed a war in defense of the nation's rights and interests into an ideological crusade for democracy and a new world order. Congress approved a war declaration by a vote of 82 to 6 in the Senate and 373 to 50 in the House. The opposition came largely from parts of the Midwest where there were many German-Americans and where a type of agricultural progressivism and pacifism was strongest. The country as a whole agreed with the president that there was no alternative to the war imposed by Germany.

In the years since 1917, many scholars, politicians, and ordinary citizens have asked why the nation abandoned its traditional neutrality to intervene in the war. During the disillusioned 1920s and 1930s, so-called revisionists denied the official explanations of the war entry and charged that it had been unwise and unnecessary. Then why had we become involved? Because, they answered, wily British propagandists played upon American sympathies, and profit-seeking munitions makers and bankers entangled us with the Allies. The submarine was a mere excuse. But their critics argued that the United States had been genuinely neutral during 1914–1917 and entered the conflict only when forced by repeated German outrages and provocations. Recently, more radical scholars, such as William A. Williams, N. Gordon Levin, and Lloyd Gardner, have explained American intervention as a quest for an "open-door empire" that the United States could exploit and dominate, a world safe from German imperialism and safe for American economic preeminence.

All such explanations are incomplete though the analysis of the more radical historians comes closest to reality. Most American historians now agree that American neutrality had worked in favor of the Allies and to Germany's harm. Closely tied by sentiment, economics, and security to Britain and France, the United States had tolerated their infractions on the high seas while firmly opposing those of Germany. And clearly war did not result merely from the submarine alone—other courses, after all, could have been adopted by the United States, as Bryan had urged. Yet without the submarine issue the United States probably would have remained at peace. The U-boat provided the necessary point of contact and hence of conflict between the two nations. It revealed how sharply divergent were their interests—the United States satisfied with the existing balance of power and British control of the seas, and Germany seeking to change that balance by force. President Wilson and most Americans saw no reason to adjust to submarine warfare. Instead they opposed it as inhumane, illegal, and an intolerable affront to American honor, rights, sentiment, and interests. Finally, by early 1917, Wilson and many of his fellow citizens viewed Germany as the chief threat to the world's peace. And an Allied victory would thwart Germany's imperialistic ambitions and leave the world economy in control of the "open-door" capitalist nations among whom the United States would reign *primus inter pares.*

9

The United States
as Combatant and Peacemaker
1917-1920

War, observed Karl von Clausewitz, the famed nineteenth-century commentator, is merely the continuation of policy by other than diplomatic means. Force supplements the diplomat in pursuit of political goals. Though the United States often has been criticized for missing this connection, especially in the First and Second World Wars, American leaders in both great struggles in fact sought more than mere military victory. Woodrow Wilson formulated American ideals and interests during World War I, and his successors have continued to pursue his goal of a stable and peaceful world. Wilson sought a "liberal capitalist world order." He envisioned a world of democratic states with free trade and security for all under a league of nations. There would be cooperation among the great powers in exploiting and developing backward areas of the world. This new system, he proclaimed in his War Address in 1917, must be made safe from Prussianism or the older type of militarism and imperialism. And after the Bolshevik Revolution in Russia, Wilson concluded that his new order also must suppress radical social revolutions and communism. Thus, while Americans thought of their nation alone as selfless in the Great Crusade, in fact they were fighting for what may be termed an enlightened self-interest: a stable capitalist world within which the United States, as well as others, could prosper and grow. It is essentially the same goal that the United States pursues half a century later, for the Cold War emphasis upon containing Communist expansionism traces back to the Wilsonian era.

OVER THERE

Most Americans and their leaders had assumed in April 1917 that the Allies were winning a war of attrition against the Central Powers. Therefore, there would be no need to send more than a token army to Europe. America's contribution presumably would be primarily economic and financial, with naval assistance against the U-boat campaign. Allied war missions to the United States soon dispelled that illusion. The slaughter on the Western Front, where first one side and then the other launched costly and futile offensives against heavily defended trenches, had so wasted Allied manpower and sapped their morale that large numbers of American troops would be necessary to achieve victory.

As the United States entered the war, the French army experienced a large-scale mutiny at the senseless blood-letting incurred by the offensives launched by its generals. The high command of both sides seemed to learn little and persisted in repeated frontal attacks against heavily defended trenches. The French army mutiny left the road open to Paris if the Germans only had realized it. Fortunately it was hushed up. Moreover, Russia collapsed during the year, giving the Germans for the first time a military manpower edge and the opportunity to shift troops from the east to the Western Front. As the new French commander, General Henri Pétain, remarked, France would have to "wait for the Americans" to swing the tide. Yet at first very little could be done. It took time to raise, equip, train, and transport sizeable American forces to Europe. As a symbol of that promise of relief, the War Department hastily sent the First Division to France where it paraded through Paris on July 4, 1917 to the cheers of Parisian multitudes.

General John J. ("Black-Jack") Pershing commanded the American Expeditionary Force sent to France. He concluded that Allied manpower and morale were so weakened by years of bloody fighting that the burden of winning the war would necessarily fall upon the fresh and undaunted American "doughboys." For that reason as well as for national pride, he insisted that Americans must fight as a unit in France rather than be dispersed among the more experienced Allied troops as the Allied military leaders wished. American troops arrived in France only in a trickle at first, so that with Pershing's insistence upon lengthy training before battle it looked as if 1918 would be over before many got into action. Gradually the flow increased, approaching 150,000–200,000 per month by early 1918 and 300,000 monthly by summer.

It was none too soon. Germany's General Ludendorff, in a race against time and the flood of American arrivals, opened a massive offensive on March 21, 1918, on the Western Front. Over six thousand guns heralded the mighty offensive. Striking first the British and then the French, Ludendorff scored great gains and threatened Paris. The Allies were compelled by their desperate plight at last to unify their military effort. They established the Supreme War Council to coordinate military activities and finally named Marshal Ferdinand Foch generalissimo of all Allied armies. Foch called Pershing's men into action, checked the German drives, and then launched a tattoo of counterblows that soon had the enemy reeling.

The A.E.F. got its first large taste of battle at Chateau-Thierry and Belleau Woods, where the Germans nicknamed U.S. marines the "devil dogs" (*Teufelhunden*). At St. Mihiel, Pershing took the offensive against a well-fortified German salient and his troops also were involved in the Meuse-Argonne offensive. In the St. Mihiel drive, 550,000 American troops, 3,000 cannon, and 1,500 planes saw action. By the Armistice, Pershing commanded 1 million men in the battle zones and held about one-fourth of the Western Front. American casualties tended to be rather high, reflecting both inexperience and aggressiveness in combat. Even so, total American battle losses were much smaller than those of the Allies— 50,000 combat deaths versus almost 1 million Britishers, $1\frac{1}{3}$ million Frenchmen, and nearly 2 million Russians. Yet it seems clear that the fresh American manpower helped swing the balance decisively against the Germans and opened the way to the Armistice.

Even prior to American belligerency, President Wilson began to conceive of a peace program that he felt should shape the postwar world. After American intervention, he continued to develop his plans. The United States, he believed, with its political democracy and free enterprise, represented the future for all mankind. It must spread its ideals and values as an antidote to the autocracy (statism) and militarism of the old order and to social revolutions such as Russia was to experience late in 1917. The key to the new order Wilson sought lay in a league of nations, a universal organization of states pledged to respect each other's sovereignty and territory and to cooperate against aggressors. None of these ideas originated solely with Wilson, but he proclaimed them in such lofty and moving phrases that he became the umistakable leader of the world liberal peace movement.

Wilsonian rhetoric mobilized liberal opinion in America and the Allied countries and, to a large degree, everywhere including even the enemy nations. Similar to the later crusade against totalitarianism in the Nazi-Fascist era, Wilson proclaimed a historic showdown between authoritarianism, whether of the Right or Left, and the forces of democracy. The president drew a sharp distinction between the unfortunate people of Germany and their "military masters" who must be eliminated from power and their plans for world conquest defeated in order to make the world safe for democracy. There could be no peace, he replied to Pope Benedict XV's appeal in August 1917, until the world had been freed

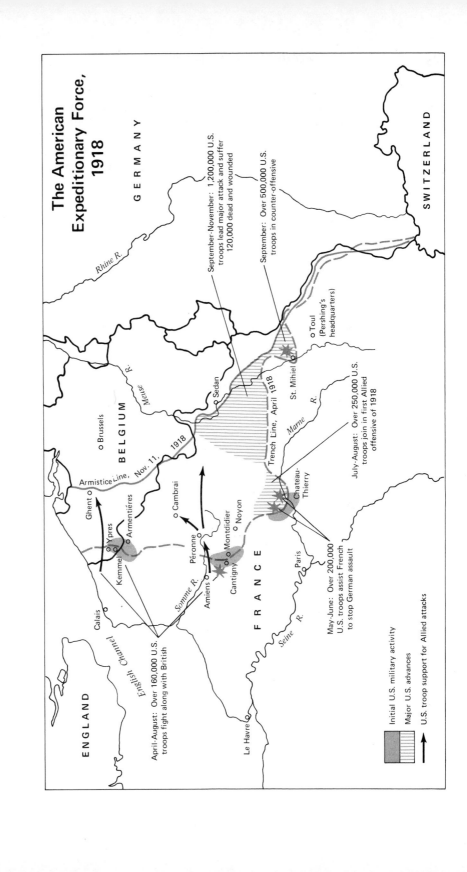

The American Expeditionary Force, 1918

GERMANY

SWITZERLAND

September–November: 1,200,000 U.S. troops lead major attack and suffer 120,000 dead and wounded

September: Over 500,000 U.S. troops in counter-offensive

Rhine R.

Toul (Pershing's headquarters)

Meuse R.

Sedan

St. Mihiel

Trench Line, April 1918

Marne R.

July–August: Over 250,000 U.S. troops join in first Allied offensive of 1918

BELGIUM

Brussels

Armistice Line, Nov. 11, 1918

Ghent

Ypres

Armentiéres

Cambrai

Chateau-Thierry

Kemmel

Péronne

Noyon

Montdidier

Calais

Somme R.

Amiens

Cantigny

Paris

FRANCE

Seine R.

May–June: Over 200,000 U.S. troops assist French to stop German assault

ENGLAND

English Channel

April–August: Over 160,000 U.S. troops fight along with British

Le Havre

Initial U.S. military activity

Major U.S. advances

U.S. troop support for Allied attacks

"from the menace and the actual power of a vast military establishment controlled by an irresponsible government which . . . planned to dominate the world." Eventually the president and his advisers enlarged the concept of an evil authoritarianism to embrace militarist Japan (privately, for she was an "ally") and especially the revolutionary Bolshevik regime in Russia, which openly proclaimed world revolution and class war.

In his famed Fourteen Points address to Congress on January 8, 1918, President Wilson aimed at rallying liberal support in America and the Allied countries behind his cause, splitting liberal elements within the Central Powers from support of their own governments, and appealing to the Russian masses over the heads of their Bolshevik leaders. Stating the essentials of a just peace, Wilson called for the enemy to evacuate all occupied territory and to restore Alsace-Lorraine to France; an independent Poland should have access to the Baltic Sea; and the nationalities living under Austro-Hungarian and Turkish rule should be permitted autonomy. Certain principles should guide the peacemaking: open diplomacy (an end to secret treaties) ; freedom of the seas; a reduction of armaments; and the settlement of colonial claims with due consideration of the interests of the colonial peoples. The fourteenth and, to Wilson, most important point, called for creation of a "general association of nations" to ensure all states mutual guarantees of territorial integrity and independence.

Because Wilson defined American war aims so idealistically, he had no choice but to expound equally grandiose peace terms—especially since he knew that secret treaties among the Allies called for carving up German and Austrian territory as well as all of Germany's overseas empire. Italy, Russia, and France were to receive large chunks of prewar enemy territory on the Continent and England the bulk of Germany's colonies. Such secret treaties lent credence to Socialist and pacifist charges that the war sacrificed workingmen's blood to gain capitalist and imperialist objectives. Wilson promised a generous peace based on free seas, national self-determination, and open diplomacy to prove that the war was *not* a sordid struggle for markets or empire. Wilson's peace program not only repudiated the secret treaties of his nation's allies; it soon brought the United States into direct conflict with Lenin and the Russian Bolsheviks.

RIVAL PROPHETS: WILSON VERSUS LENIN

If Wilson by his exalted phrases and concepts made himself the moral leader of the liberal Western world, he found his principles sorely tried and his leadership challenged by the Bolshevik Revolution in Russia. In a real sense the Communist leader V. I. Lenin became Wilson's chief rival. Wilson, the prophet of liberal democracy and limited change, faced Lenin the prophet of social revolution and radical change. Although Wilson remained convinced that ultimately the Russian people would accept his Fourteen Points despite Bolshevik opposition, he now saw his new order threatened not only by the older imperialism but also by a newer radicalism demanding universal class war and global revolution.

When the United States entered the war in April 1917, Russia had seemed, in Wilson's words, "a fit partner for a league of honor." For in the March Revolution the Russians had toppled the absolutist czarist regime and installed a democratic republic, which the American government promptly recognized. Former Secretary of State Elihu Root led a special mission to Russia in mid-1917 and the Wilson administration loaned the provisional regime a total of $325 million for war purposes. Both the United States and the other Allies insisted, of course, that Russia must continue to play its part in the great crusade against Prussianism. They thereby failed to consider the immense losses Russia already had experienced in the war, the collapse of Russian industry and transport, and the war-weariness of the masses. Americans particularly, both officials and the public, were ignorant of the seething discontent and radicalism within Russia and too optimistically assumed that Russia would continue to evolve along democratic lines and remain in the war on the Allied side.

The Bolshevik Revolution in November 1917 (October by the old calendar) therefore came as a stunning surprise. On the eve of the coup, the State Department had received an optimistic report from its ill-informed ambassador in Russia that the provisional authorities were ready to crush the Bolsheviks. Led by Lenin and Leon Trotsky, the Communists, or Bolsheviks, seized power and took prompt steps to withdraw from the war. They concluded an armistice with the Central Powers in December and in March 1918 signed drastic peace terms at Brest-Litovsk. The Allies feared that masses of German troops would be transferred to the Western Front in a final bid for victory before the Americans could arrive in strength. London and Paris denounced the Bolsheviks as perfidious and as tools of the Germans. Bolshevik publication of the secret Allied treaties dividing the hoped-for spoils of war did nothing to allay Anglo-French hostility.

President Wilson felt most concerned about the undemocratic nature of the Red regime and its willingness to hold power by force if necessary. Secretary of State Robert Lansing furthermore pointed out the revolutionary nature of Communist ideology and its call for worldwide class war and proletarian revolutions against all existing governments. The Wilson administration consequently decided not to recognize the new government. It hoped perhaps that nonrecognition of a government lacking control in much of Russia would speed that government's demise.

The Allies, fearing a major German breakthrough on the Western Front, desperately urged Wilson to support an armed intervention that might restore Russia to the war. The president refused on the grounds of both principle—the Russian people must be allowed to determine their own form of government—and the impracticability of restoring an eastern front. It became increasingly more difficult to rebuff one's associates, however, especially as the German offensive made great gains in France. Japan, eager to extend her sway in East Asia, also urged armed action. Worn down by incessant pleas, and alarmed at grossly exaggerated reports that Germany was taking control of virtually all Russia, Wilson weakened. The Germans seemed to threaten the military supplies that the West had shipped to Russia earlier in the war and that had accumulated at Murmansk in north Russia and Vladivostok in maritime Siberia. Moreover, around sixty-five-thousand Czechoslovakian troops, allowed by the provisional government to form and fight on Russian soil against the Central Powers, were trapped by the Bolshevik coup and withdrawal from the war. While the Czech legion tried to evacuate across Siberia, clashes occurred with local Soviet authorities. Many Americans as well as Britishers and Frenchmen felt anxious about the plight of the brave Czechs and demanded action to protect them against the "bloodthirsty" Reds. Republican party spokesmen in the United States particularly attacked Wilson for inaction.

For essentially military and sentimental reasons, President Wilson in mid-1918 reluctantly consented to armed intervention in north Russia and Siberia. The interventions, he insisted, must be limited to protecting the endangered supplies and rescuing the Czechs. There must be no interference in Russia's internal political affairs. If anti-Bolshevik motives played only a secondary role in Wilson's decision to intervene, the actual American intervention lent support to the Russian counter-revolutionaries.

Wilson detested the Communists and confidently hoped their regime would soon collapse of its own weaknesses. He also hoped that the mere presence of American and Allied troops in Russia would encourage the emergence of a non-Communist government. His principles, however, saved him from supporting anything more, and he would not have consented to even that much intervention except for what he viewed as the overriding military reasons of curbing German advances and saving the Czech legion.

American troops sent to northern Russia and Siberia followed strict orders not to intervene in Russia's civil strife between the Reds and the various "White," or anti-Communist movements. The British and French, still dreaming of a restored eastern front, openly backed the anti-Bolsheviks in northern Russia while Japan aggressively extended her control deep into Siberia. Wilson objected strenuously and after the Armistice withdrew American forces from northern Russia in 1919 and from Siberia early in 1920. Unquestionably these interventions left a legacy of hatred and distrust among the Russian Bolsheviks and fueled charges of a capitalist plot led by the United States to smother the

War poster—The war on the home front

Huntington Hartford Collection

Communist regime in its infancy. Yet Wilson deserves much credit for resisting pressures for an even larger, more costly, and probably futile all-out intervention.

THE ARMISTICE

The Central Alliance began to collapse during the summer and early fall of 1918. The ramshackle Austro-Hungarian Empire sued for peace, and Turkey and Bulgaria succumbed to Allied blows. Ludendorff's great offensives along the Western Front had failed, and bolstered by a flood of American troops, Foch launched a counter-offensive that broke the Hindenburg Line and threatened to hurl the enemy back to the Rhine. Fearing disaster and hoping at least for a lull to regroup their forces, Hindenburg and Ludendorff compelled the Berlin government to request an immediate armistice. Consequently the new chancellor, Prince Max, on October 4 requested of Wilson a peace based upon the Fourteen Points.

Despite Allied fears that the Germans would deceive the president into granting unwise terms, Wilson handled the diplomatic exchanges skillfully and successfully. Nationalists and conservatives in England and France, and the Republicans in America, urged completely crushing Germany and imposing on her a harsh peace while more liberal elements here and in Europe looked to the president to achieve the just and lasting peace of which he had spoken so often and so eloquently. In his reply to the German note, Wilson asked if Germany unequivocally accepted the Fourteen Points. She also must evacuate Belgian and French territory, and the president indicated his wish to deal only with a truly representative German government. When Prince Max responded favorably but asked for a joint commission to arrange the details of an evacuation, the Allied powers feared that Berlin sought a gradual and orderly withdrawal of her armies to a defensive position that would permit her to continue the war. Wilson avoided that trap, making it clear that the Allied military leaders would frame the armistice terms and again indicating his preference for a democratic Germany.

By this stage Ludendorff had recovered confidence and preferred to prolong the war rather than accept Wilson's terms. It was too late. News of the peace bid had discredited the war among the German public. The people of Germany were wearied of war and its bloody toll, and they were beginning to feel hunger as the Allied blockade tightened. Germany seethed with unrest that led to a brief revolution and the abdication of the kaiser. Early in November a republic was proclaimed that accepted Wilson's terms. No doubt many Germans hoped that the creation of a republic would insure easier peace terms, and when such terms were not forthcoming, many charged a betrayal. Perhaps it would have been wiser to have left the kaiser or his son on the throne and to have compelled the monarchy to assume full responsibility for waging and losing the war. But in light of the ideological overtones of the war and the war passions of the Allied and American publics, such foresight was not possible.

After Germany had accepted Wilson's terms, the Allies remained to be convinced. The president sent Colonel House to Europe to persuade them to agree to give Germany a peace based upon the Fourteen Points. House found the Allied leaders singularly unenthusiastic. Obviously they had in mind the several secret treaties dividing the spoils, which might be nullified by the Fourteen Points. Wilson and House became so exasperated that they threatened the possibility of making a separate peace with Germany. Finally the premiers consented to the Fourteen Points as the basis of peace with two qualifications, one relating to freedom of the seas and the other requiring Germany to pay damages for destruction caused by the war. This was the so-called Pre-Armistice Agreement. Armistice terms were made so severe that Germany would not be able to renew the war if she objected to the peace terms. German armies must quickly evacuate occupied territories and surrender to the Allies vast numbers of cannon, machine guns, warplanes, and war supplies; 160 submarines also were to be yielded and the surface fleet interned.

Peace came at last to a war-weary world. On November 8, a German delegation journeyed to a railway carriage in Compiegne Forest to be icily received by the victorious Foch and his staff (Adolf Hitler humbled the French in a similar ceremony at the same spot in 1940). The terms were more severe than Germany had expected, but the new government had no choice but to sign the Armistice. On November 11 at 11 A.M. the guns on the Western Front at last fell silent. Dazed troops crawled from the trenches and burst into tears and cheers at the end of so cruel a war. Yanks and Germans met between the trenches in shell-pitted no man's land to talk and trade souvenirs. As the news reached Paris, London, Rome, and the United States, great crowds joyously abandoned work and took to the streets in celebration. Cars blared their horns, girls kissed every serviceman in sight, and mobs repeatedly hanged or burned effigies of the ex-kaiser. The Great Crusade was over. President Wilson, armed with Allied and German acceptance of the Fourteen Points, confidently looked forward to the peace conference, where he expected to guide the writing of a just and lasting peace settlement.

President Wilson prepared to sail for Europe and the greatest peace conference since the Congress of Vienna in 1815. He envisioned his mission as the supreme opportunity to create a progressive and liberal world order—one capable of promoting social progress within each nation and peace and stability in international relations. Germany, the other defeated countries, and Russia, whenever bolshevism had been repudiated or purged of its radicalism, should be reintegrated into world society. Yet, what one historian has called the "forces of order"—conservative and nationalist influences—sought to use the peacemaking to defeat or curb the "forces of movement"—i.e., reformist and socialist groups. Conservatives in Britain, France, and Italy, and Republicans in the United States, played upon the passions of the masses by calling for drastic treatment of Germany and the defeat of radicalism (bolshevism) everywhere. Because of these conservative pressures and his own wavering between a moderate and a more punitive treatment of Germany, Wilson at Paris was to compromise and to agree to a harsher peace than he and other liberals had thought desirable. Such compromising was virtually inevitable; the ideal can rarely, if ever, be fully achieved in a world inhabited by imperfect human beings.

BLUNDERS ON THE EVE OF THE PEACE CONFERENCE

Wilson understandably felt anxious about the outcome of the congressional elections of 1918, coming on the eve of the forthcoming peace conference. A Democratic victory would strengthen his hand at Paris while a Democratic defeat would leave him in a weakened position. Hence he yielded to the pleas of the politicians and publicly urged the electorate to vote Democratic: "The return of a Republican majority . . . would . . . be interpreted on the other side of the water as a repudiation of my leadership." His Republican opponents shrilly charged him with repudiating his own wartime slogan, "Politics is Adjourned," and accused him of attacking the patriotism of Republicans who had loyally supported the war effort. When the votes were counted, the Republicans had won control of both houses of Congress. Wilson unwisely had called for a vote of confidence and seemingly had lost.

Wilson's critics received fresh ammunition when the president announced the membership of the peace commission. Wilson would personally attend the conference, accompanied by four other commissioners: Secretary of State Lansing, Colonel House, General Tasker H. Bliss, and Henry White, a minor Republican and a diplomat. The president had failed to name a single senator or prominent Republican, in contrast to President McKinley's appointments in making peace with Spain in 1898. He refused to do so, it seems, because he was unwilling to have in Paris any strong-minded and independent commissioners who might challenge his leadership or plans. Consequently, he had ruled out Senator Henry Cabot Lodge of Massachusetts, his hated opponent, who was to head the Senate Committee on Foreign Relations in the next Congress, and other Republican leaders such as former President Taft, Elihu Root, or Charles Evans Hughes. In naming himself to head the commission, Wilson broke precedent—never before had a president left the country while in office.

Angry Republicans charged that Wilson had revealed a messianic complex and had packed the delegation with yes-men. In a way they were right. The moralistic president felt highly confident of his own rectitude and vision. Once he had committed himself thoroughly to a course, he tended to view any criticism as either disloyal or stupid. He felt that he had a sacred mission to rebuild the world and, increasingly inflexible, was determined to dominate the peacemaking. He was in no mood for dissent from within his own delegation, remarking to one listener "I tell you frankly, I am descended from Scottish Presbyterians and am therefore somewhat stubborn." He compounded these errors, for so they seem except for his decision to attend the conference personally, by failing to consult the Senate on the terms to be framed at Paris. Yet the Senate ultimately would have to pass on any treaty framed there. Thus he helped insure that the peace treaty would become a partisan issue and that the Republicans would challenge his leadership in foreign affairs.

THE NEW WORLD PROPHET IN EUROPE

President Wilson and his party sailed for France on December 4, 1918. The president stood at the pinnacle of his fame as the prophet of a liberal peace and a new world order. On December 13, to the salutes of ships in the harbor, Wilson landed at Brest. Europeans went wild with joy at his arrival, confident that he would usher in the millennium. Parisians gave him a reception unequaled since the days of Napoleon's triumphal entries. One huge banner proclaimed "Honor to Wilson the Just." Because the peace conference was not ready to begin, the president visited England, where he dined with King George V and Queen Elizabeth at Buckingham Palace. He then journeyed to Italy where crowds in Rome roared "Viva Wilson, god of peace." Everywhere he was acclaimed as the deliverer of mankind from the ravages of war, the symbol of hope for a bright future. But he refused to tour the battlefields in France, fearing that the sight of German destructiveness would inflame his emotions and prevent dispassionate peacemaking.

The Paris Peace Conference got underway early in January 1919. Thirty-two governments sent delegates to the conference. Since the defeated enemy was not invited to send representatives until May, to receive a nearly completed treaty, the first phase, strictly speaking, was a preliminary conference among the victors. The Big Four—Britain, France, Italy, and the United States—dominated the work of the conference. Lesser nations found themselves relegated to minor roles or stood around pleading for their share of the spoils. A variety of commissions handled specialized work, but the final decisions lay in the hands of the Big Four. Throngs of disgusted newspapermen complained of the secrecy of the conference, but Wilson had never meant "open diplomacy" to mean more than that the final results should be made public.

President Wilson dominated the proceedings. He frequently encountered formidable opposition from others among the Big Four: David Lloyd George, the clever and opportunistic British prime minister; Premier Georges Clemenceau, the aged (nearly eighty) "Tiger" of France; and Premier Vittorio Orlando of Italy. Wilson was probably the best informed statesman at the conference. Earlier, in 1917, he had established a group of American scholars known as the "Inquiry" to help him prepare for the work of peacemaking. He took members of the Inquiry with him to Paris, and he devoted long hours to intensive study of the various problems that arose at the conference. Lloyd George and the British delegation generally cooperated with the American diplomats. A broad Anglo-American community of outlook thus existed on most issues, save those relating to colonial territories and reparations. Clemenceau tirelessly advocated French interests, which demanded a harsh peace to provide reparations for rebuilding a badly damaged France and to insure future French security by keeping Germany humbled and powerless. The cynical Clemenceau watched the idealistic Wilson with a mixture of puzzlement and sceptical amusement. About the Fourteen Points he once remarked, "God gave us the Ten Commandments, and we broke them. Wilson gives us the Fourteen Points. We shall see." He also commented that talking to the American president "is something like talking to Jesus Christ."

DRAFTING THE LEAGUE OF NATIONS

Wilson viewed the creation of a new international organization, the League of Nations, as the absolute prerequisite of a just and lasting settlement. Various American, English, and French groups had given much thought to the nature of the world organization. The chief differences at Paris centered around the Anglo-American plan for a truly universal association of nations to keep the peace and French desires for a great power alliance to insure Germany's subordination. The Anglo-Americans essentially won. The Covenant (charter) of the League, embodied within the peace treaty, provided for an assembly of all members and a smaller council composed of the great powers as permanent members and several elected members. Article X, the heart of the covenant in Wilson's view, pledged members to respect and uphold the territorial integrity and independence of all members of the League—in short, a mutual guarantee of collective security. In case of aggression, the council by unanimous vote could recommend moral, economic, or military sanctions against the aggressor. The League through its Secretary-General also would coordinate and facilitate humanitarian activities of various kinds, much like those the present United Nations organization undertakes.

After the covenant had been presented to a plenary session of the conference on February 14, Wilson returned briefly to the United States. He particularly wanted to explain the covenant to the people and to dispel the many false rumors circulating about it. Republican and other critics had begun to charge that the League was a superstate that would dilute American sovereignty. Landing in Boston, the bailiwick of Senator Lodge, a major critic of the covenant, the president defended his handiwork and denounced opponents as selfish and provincial. "I have fighting blood in me," he exclaimed as he challenged his critics. Subsequently he did try to conciliate them but without much success. He invited members of the congressional committees on foreign affairs to the White House for dinner and patiently responded to their questions and doubts.

Senator Lodge was not won over. Lodge, a Harvard trained historian and Ph.D., had basked in the limelight as the "scholar in politics" until overshadowed by the even more impressive credentials of Woodrow Wilson, former president of Princeton, a distinguished historian, and now chief executive of the United States. A cold and bitingly sarcastic man, Lodge viewed Wilson as his intellectual and cultural inferior. Wilson reciprocated his dislike. By 1919 neither man could tolerate the other. In addition, as a major Republican leader in Congress, Lodge undoubtedly felt that he must win some advantage for his party from the peacemaking. He apparently determined to humiliate Wilson and advance Republican interests by attacking the League of Nations. He remarked about the covenant that "as an English production it does not rank high. It might get by at Princeton but certainly not at Harvard."

But the Massachusetts senator also objected to the treaty for reasons of principle. Scarcely an isolationist or a noninterventionist, Lodge nevertheless believed that the treaty's inclusion of a League and Article X would involve the United States in endless foreign wars. He believed that the United States should make its own decisions concerning overseas intervention and not be *bound* by the action of others to defend the claims of the British Empire or the territorial integrity of various European states. Hence Lodge publicly urged that the covenant be separated from the Treaty of Peace and declared that the covenant must be changed to prevent possible League interference in America's internal affairs. A Republican "round robin," signed by six more senators than necessary to block approval of the treaty, branded the covenant in its present form as unacceptable.

Wilson viewed such criticisms as unfair and misleading. Nevertheless, when he returned to Paris in mid-March Wilson sought and obtained changes in the covenant in order to satisfy his congressional critics. These alterations permitted members to decline mandates for former enemy colonies or dependent territories, exempted domestic issues from League jurisdiction, recognized the Monroe Doctrine as a type of regional "understanding" permitted by the League, and allowed members the right of withdrawal upon two years notice.

THE RED MENACE

The problem of Bolshevik Russia loomed as a specter frightening the peacemakers at Paris. Civil war continued to rage in Russia during the peace deliberations, and communism also threatened to infect the defeated Central Powers and perhaps sweep into western Europe. Conservatives, eager to discredit progressivism and reform, exploited the "red scare." President Wilson himself saw violent social revolution and Communist states as threats to the new world order he preferred. And the dangers seemed real in 1919. In Hungary a short-lived Communist regime of Bela Kun came to power in 1919; Bavaria briefly experienced a "soviet republic," while the new German government fought left-wing Spartacist rebels in the streets of Berlin; and Austria also teetered on the brink of revolution. The Bolsheviks in Russia moreover encouraged revolutionary movements in all the capitalist countries and created the Comintern (Communist International) in 1919 to promote world revolution. Small Communist groups split from the Socialists and founded Communist parties even in the United States and intoxicated themselves with the rhetoric of revolution. As World War II would do three decades later, the Great War had shattered older institutions and ushered in a period of chaos and change. And also like that later conflict, it fed anti-Communist hysteria and witch hunts.

Although the Armistice had removed the military excuses for armed intervention in Russia, President Wilson faced insistent demands for even larger involvement in Russia's civil war. Clemenceau wanted to destroy the Soviet regime by economic blockade, and he favored a scheme advanced by Winston Churchill, British war minister, to send volunteer troops to aid the anti-Bolsheviks. In Wilson's view, however, "The real thing with which to stop bolshevism is food." He did not oppose socialistic governments, Wilson claimed, as long as they were democratic. In any case, as he had learned from his earlier experience in Mexico, large-scale intervention would probably merely strengthen the Bolshevik appeal to the Russian masses. Lloyd George agreed for he realized that most Americans and Englishmen did not want to fight in Russia. Liberals in America and Britain already had begun to criticize intervention and to defend Lenin's government as an experiment in human improvement that ought to be allowed its chance.

With a larger intervention ruled out, the great powers sought to arrange a truce between the Red and White factions in Russia. The effort failed because the anti-Communists refused to participate. A second attempt at a truce and food relief also collapsed because of Bolshevik objections. Wilson then reluctantly agreed with the French plan to support Admiral Alexander Kolchak's anti-Communist government at Omsk. But Kolchak depended too heavily on reactionary army officers and landlords. Unable to appeal to the masses, his movement collapsed in complete defeat at the hands of the Red Army by early 1920. Wilson thereupon recalled the American troops in Siberia.

Washington, however, clung to its policy of nonrecognition of the Soviet government. As Secretary of State Bainbridge Colby declared in August 1920, the United States would not deal with an undemocratic regime that had come to power by violence, repudiated its debts and other obligations, and carried on espionage and subversive activities aimed at undermining all other forms of government. Nonrecognition not only reflected moral and ideological aversion but at first also reflected reality, as in 1919–1920 the survival of the Bolshevik regime remained in doubt. Later, when the Soviets held undisputed control of Russia, the American policy of course became completely unrealistic. Wilson's use of nonrecognition for moral and idealistic reasons, first toward Mexico and then Russia, set an unfortunate precedent for American nonrecognition of the People's Republic of China during the later Cold War. And Wilson's reaction to the Bolsheviks set an historical precedent that would produce bitter fruit during the post-World War II Cold War.

A PEACE OF JUSTICE?

In general, despite compromises he felt compelled to accept, Wilson at Paris sought to achieve his goals of a reasonable and just peace. The resultant terms for Germany, while severe, were not nearly as harsh as they might otherwise have been. The president, supported by Lloyd George, firmly resisted French schemes to partition Germany into several states, annex the Saar Valley, and create a Rhineland buffer state under French control. At one stage the conference almost collapsed in bitter conflict between the stubborn president and the equally stubborn Clemenceau. Finally a compromise arranged for French security without partitioning Germany. The Big Three agreed to demilitarize the Rhineland and to permit French troops to occupy strategic bridgeheads within it for fifteen years. The Saar and its valuable coal mines came under French occupation, with the agreement that a plebiscite at the end of fifteen years was to decide its future. As a stop-gap security device until the League could come fully into operation, Britain and the United States signed treaties promising to assist France in the event of a future German attack. These pacts never became effective because the American Senate refused to act upon the Franco-American pact. The military terms imposed upon Germany also were intended to protect France. Germany could have an army no larger than 100,000 men, the general staff was dissolved, possession of warplanes and poison gas prohibited, and the navy sharply limited.

The peace treaty stripped Germany of her colonies and awarded parts of her previous territory to France, Belgium, and the new state of Poland. Other peace terms, especially the reparations clause, further reduced German power. The Allies, despite Wilson's objections, determined to shift as much of the cost of the war as possible to the defeated enemy. Wilson managed to eliminate imposition of total war costs but he conceded to Allied pressure to include veterans' pensions in the category of civilian damages to be assessed to Germany, thereby more than doubling the reparations bill. Finally the president also abandoned his effort to fix a definite sum in the peace treaty. Instead, the Allies compelled Germany to sign a blank check. A reparations commission, without

American participation because of the Senate's failure to approve the Versailles Treaty, ultimately set reparations at $33 billion plus interest, payable over forty-two years. Disillusioned liberals in America and Britain attacked these provisions as a form of economic slavery that would embitter Germans and enable demagogues to exploit mass discontent, which is precisely what Adolph Hitler would do. World War I was a graphic demonstration that in modern war, even for the victors losses exceed their gains.

The other terms agreed to at Paris generally conformed to Wilsonian principles. Poland received German-inhabited territory in order to have access to the sea—the Polish Corridor that Hitler used as an excuse for war in 1939—but Wilson and Lloyd George modified Polish territorial demands and placed the German port city of Danzig under League supervision. Czechoslovakia obtained former Austrian territory in order to have defensible borders, the so-called Sudetenland that Hitler also exploited later. Italy received Austrian-inhabited territory and Slavic areas to the north and east, but Wilson refused to concede her the city of Fiume, which he thought should be reserved as a port for the new Yugoslavia. But Wilson could not compel Japan to relinquish former German holdings in Shantung, China, seized in 1914–1915. When Japan threatened to walk out of the peace conference and the League, Wilson surrendered. He had no choice. For Japan actually held Shantung and could be evicted only by force, an act that was unthinkable under the circumstances. Subsequently Japan kept her oral pledge to restore the area to China.

In an ironic footnote to the conference, Russia, one of the original Allies, also lost prewar territory. Russia lost immense and valuable areas of land that went to the restored Baltic States (Latvia, Lithuania, and Estonia), Poland, and Rumania. And Russia, like Germany, refused to forget her treatment at Versailles, an experience that led her two decades later to sign a diplomatic pact with Hitler that precipitated World War II.

These were the main provisions of the Treaty of Versailles that German delegates were forced to sign on June 28, 1919, the fifth anniversary of Sarajevo. Although disillusioned liberals in England and America attacked the treaty as a betrayal of the Fourteen Points, a victor's peace that probably insured a future war, it seems clear that it was a much better peace because of Wilson's efforts than otherwise would have been the case. In general, far more of Wilson's liberal program was achieved than could reasonably have been expected, granted over four years of bloody warfare, the collapse of great empires and social upheaval, and embittered popular passions. The principles of self-determination and boundaries along nationality lines had been followed more than they had been violated when due weight is given to security requirements and intermixtures of nationalities, and Germany had not been dismembered. Above all, Wilson hoped that the League of Nations, after passions had cooled, would be able to correct defects in the settlement. Given United States participation, his hopes were not unrealistic. Versailles could have

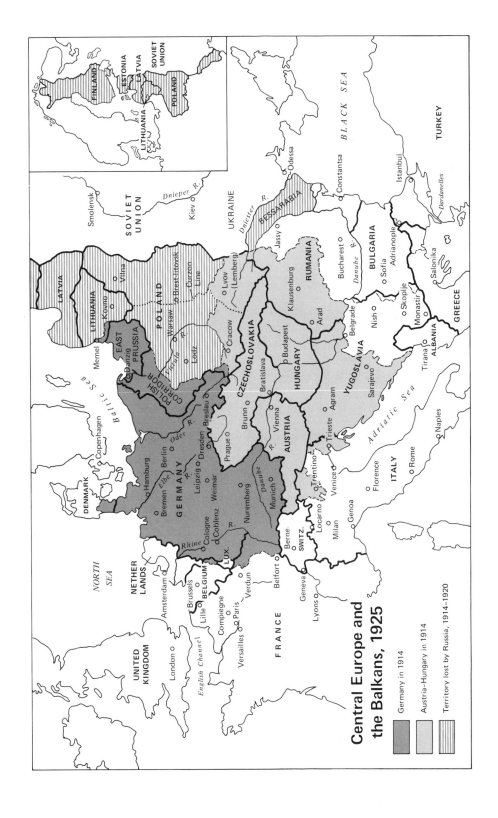

Central Europe and the Balkans, 1925

Germany in 1914

Austria–Hungary in 1914

Territory lost by Russia, 1914–1920

SOVIET UNION

FINLAND

ESTONIA

LATVIA

LITHUANIA

POLAND

BLACK SEA

TURKEY

Smolensk

Dnieper R.

Kiev

UKRAINE

Dniester R.

BESSARABIA

Odessa

Constantsa

Istanbul

Dardanelles

LATVIA

LITHUANIA

Vilna

Curzon Line

Brest-Litovsk

Lvov (Lemberg)

Jassy

RUMANIA

Bucharest

Danube R.

BULGARIA

Sofia

Adrianople

Salonika

Memel

EAST PRUSSIA

Danzig

POLAND

Warsaw

Lodz

Vistula R.

Cracow

Klausenburg

Arad

Belgrade

Nish

Skoplje

Monastir

GREECE

Baltic Sea

Copenhagen

POLISH CORRIDOR

CZECHOSLOVAKIA

Breslau

Oder R.

Brunn

Bratislava

Budapest

HUNGARY

Agram

Sarajevo

YUGOSLAVIA

Tirana

ALBANIA

DENMARK

Hamburg

Bremen

Berlin

Leipzig

Dresden

Elbe R.

Prague

Weimar

GERMANY

Nuremberg

Munich

Vienna

AUSTRIA

Danube R.

Trieste

Trentino

Venice

Adriatic Sea

Naples

Rome

ITALY

Florence

Genoa

Milan

Locarno

Berne

SWITZ.

Geneva

NORTH SEA

NETHER-LANDS

Amsterdam

Rhine R.

Cologne

Coblenz

LUX.

BELGIUM

Brussels

Lille

Verdun

Belfort

Compiegne

Paris

Versailles

FRANCE

Lyons

English Channel

UNITED KINGDOM

London

Kovno

Hamburg

preserved peace and evolved into a more progressive and stable world order if dissatisfied nations had accepted what was basically an American, English, and French definition of global relations, or if the United States had exerted itself more vigorously on the world stage. Instead of making the world safe for democracy, western-style, Versailles sowed the seeds of a subsequent world war—seeds that spread socialism around the globe.

THE SENATE AND THE TREATY

Americans traditionally have tended to ignore foreign affairs, except during crises, and they revealed a strong tendency after the Armistice to concentrate once more on personal interests. After incessant wartime propaganda about the great crusade for democracy and peace, people seemed weary of idealistic appeals. Many citizens also saw the League as a danger to American sovereignty and membership in it as a departure from the solemn advice of Washington's Farewell Address against entangling alliances. Some feared that the League would interfere with American tariffs and would prevent restriction of immigration. A ditty chanted by returning "doughboys" from France summed up the feelings of many Americans:

> We drove the Boche across the Rhine,
> The Kaiser from his throne,
> Oh, Lafayette, we've paid our debt,
> For Christ's sake, send us home.

Moreover, many German-Americans, Irish-Americans, and Italian-Americans criticized the Versailles Treaty for its harshness or its failure to satisfy the interests of their former homelands. Finally, as we have seen, a number of liberals who had supported President Wilson and the war to end wars had been alienated by his failure to achieve a more liberal peace program.

Although newspaper polls and editorials indicated that the majority of Americans still approved membership in the League, popular support seemed to lack depth and faded away as debate over the treaty intensified. A substantial number of congressmen and probably most citizens preferred to limit postwar American commitments, in contrast to the Wilsonian "strong internationalists" who favored a wholehearted involvement in world responsibilities. Probably Wilson would have been well advised to have discussed League membership publicly primarily in terms of enlightened self-interest, emphasizing its advantages in curbing costly armaments races and promoting a peaceful and prosperous world. But the president, who had already transformed a sordid war into a glorious crusade, had to portray his peace plan as an agency of deliverance for all humanity.

The president laid the 264-page treaty before the Senate on July 10, 1919. As the result of the 1918 election, the Republicans by a narrow majority (49 to 47) held control of the Senate and its influential Committee on Foreign Relations. Republican leaders, anticipating recapturing the White House in 1920, understandably wanted to reap maximum gain from the treaty issue. Wilson and the Democrats must not be permitted to claim sole credit for waging war and making peace. A small group of noninterventionists or "irreconcilables," including such men as Senators William E. Borah of Idaho and Hiram Johnson of California, firmly opposed involvement in any kind of league. Republican "mild reservationists" advocated membership with only a few changes in the covenant and "strong reservationists," led by Senator Lodge of the Foreign Relations Committee, proposed more sweeping alterations to make the League safe for American membership. Lodge favored a League based primarily upon arbitration and a world court, versus Wilson's insistence on one founded upon collective security to maintain peace. In addition to doubts about the covenant's meaning, a number of senators in both parties deeply resented Wilson's autocratic approach and apparently saw the debate on the treaty as a chance to reassert congressional influence in foreign affairs.

Lodge adopted a brilliantly conceived strategy in the treaty fight. He drafted a number of reservations that would unify Republicans and embarrass Democrats. If Wilson accepted them, Republicans could claim that they had repaired defects in the League and made it safe for America; if the president rejected the reservations, he and his party would bear the responsibility for defeat of the treaty. From his knowledge of Wilson's personality, Lodge confidently expected the president to play into his hands by spurning his changes.

Lodge deliberately stalled for time, taking two weeks to read aloud the entire treaty before a nearly empty committee room. He consumed an additional six weeks in hearings with much of the testimony not only bitterly hostile to the League but often irrelevant. He finally reported to the Senate a treaty burdened with numerous amendments and reservations. Most of the fourteen Lodge reservations were designed primarily to curb the executive's control over foreign policy. The most important reservation concerned Article X of the covenant and provided that the United States would assume no obligation to defend the integrity of other states or to use its armed forces at the request of the League without the specific approval of Congress in each case. Two reservations claimed for the U.S. sole authority to define domestic matters beyond the League's power and the right to interpret and apply the Monroe Doctrine unilaterally. Lodge's last reservation freed the United States from any League decision in which a member had cast more than one vote (the British empire and commonwealth had six seats in the League Assembly). This was a crass bid to lingering anti-British sentiment in the United States and an attempt to appeal to Anglophobe Irish-Americans.

A frustrated Wilson decided to appeal his case directly to the people.

Hoping to arouse enough popular support to force the Senate to approve the treaty with little or no change, the president in September began a speaking tour through the midwestern and far western states. His health, never robust, had been further weakened by the toils and tensions of Paris. Although warned by his personal physician, Wilson decided that his duty came first. He delivered more than thirty major addresses in defense of the Versailles Treaty before he collapsed at Pueblo, Colorado. Exhausted and suffering blinding headaches, the president reluctantly had to cancel the remainder of the tour.

After his return to Washington, Wilson on October 2 suffered a cerebral thrombosis that left him bedridden and partially paralyzed. For several weeks he lay near death, unconscious for a while, and for a much longer period he was unable to perform vital presidential duties. Wilson's wife and close advisers, however, would not request the vice president to assume the executive duties. A virtual conspiracy of silence was thrown around the president's sickroom, while members of his cabinet carried on the government as best they could. This problem of presidential disability was not to be solved until President John F. Kennedy arranged a workable solution with his vice president in the early 1960s.

As Wilson began to recover, slowly and never completely, he refused to compromise with Senator Lodge. Physically weaker but as stubborn as ever, Wilson preferred defeat by the Senate to membership in the League with the Lodge reservations. When the treaty came up for a vote on November 19, 1919, and again on March 19, 1920, the President advised loyal Democrats to vote against it with the Lodge reservations. Since the Democrats could not muster enough votes to approve the treaty without changes, Wilson had insured its defeat. The final vote on the treaty with the reservations fell seven votes short of the necessary two-thirds for approval, forty-nine for to thirty-five against. The Senate then returned the rejected instrument to the White House.

But the fight was not yet over. Wilson determined to convert the 1920 presidential contest into a national referendum on the League. As Wilson should have been aware, presidential contests provide no mandate on a single issue. Traditional political loyalties, personalities, and a variety of issues and grievances eclipsed the League as an issue in 1920. The result was a Democratic debacle. Harding overwhelmed his opponent.

Although the election in fact was not a mandate on the League, Wilson by his insistence on a "Solemn Referendum" had helped insure that the Republicans would interpret their victory as a decisive popular rejection of membership in the League. The Republicans in office treated the issue as dead, and the United States joined outcast Russia and defeated Germany among other lesser states in staying out of the League. Political and personal partisanship, isolationist sentiment, and genuine doubts by many citizens who viewed themselves as at least mild internationalists, combined to defeat the treaty and the covenant. Above all, Wilson by his insistence on all or nothing insured the final outcome. The

United States thus betrayed Wilsonian ideals and perhaps its national interests. Having entered a war largely the result of rival European imperialisms and power struggles, the United States had sought to turn the conflict into a struggle for a just peace and a stable postwar world, only to abandon the field when the war was over. A weakened France and a declining Britain were left to uphold the new settlement, a task at which they ultimately failed. Yet while the Wilsonian internationalists had lost, it proved impossible in the 1920s to ignore the legacy of American intervention and victory in World War I, or to return fully to the nineteenth-century pattern of geographical isolation. World War I marked the beginning of a great departure for the United States from the isolationism of the past to the global responsibilities of the future. Its results also laid the foundation for a greater war two decades later that again would involve the United States and make another Democratic president—Franklin Delano Roosevelt—the symbol of global brotherhood and peace.

10

The War at Home: Domestic Reform and Repression

When European war erupted in late summer of 1914 many statesmen, politicians, and even common people breathed a sigh of relief. Perhaps they sensed that the domestic turmoil, class struggles, and militant radicalism that threatened the stability of European society might instead be dissolved in the euphoria of national unity and patriotism. Still other Europeans, especially the Fabians in England, perceived national crisis as the opportunity, indeed the occasion, to implement social reforms unimaginable under conventional peacetime conditions. Either because of anxiety about the social order or a belief that a national emergency would improve the chances for significant domestic reform, war came as a blessing in disguise to millions of Europeans.

War, too, offered significant benefits to the United States. If not as deeply rocked by class struggles as Old World countries nor as troubled by radical politics, the United States also had its domestic problems early in 1914. Woodrow Wilson's New Freedom had apparently run its reform course and had terminated late in 1913 in a severe economic recession that threatened to worsen into a major depression. The years 1911 and 1912 had seen a series of local Socialist electoral victories, a sharp rise in the Socialist party's national vote, and a surge of working-class struggles.

Lawrence, Massachusetts, in 1912 and Paterson, New Jersey, in 1913 had been wracked by tumultuous strikes under IWW leadership. And in 1913–1914 industrial warfare culminated in the bloody Colorado coal miners' strike against the Rockefeller interests, leading to the infamous Ludlow Massacre.

To a nation uncertain of its goals, European war came first as a surprise and then as an opportunity to achieve the national unity and spiritual élan that had been absent in peacetime. The savage struggles on Old World battlefields distracted the American people's attention from the lesser conflicts being waged at home. More important, after the initial shock caused to international trading relations by the eruption of war, the United States economy began to pulsate healthily in response to rising European war orders. By 1915 American bankers, manufacturers, farmers, and workers waxed rich from the sufferings of Europe. Soon Americans themselves would share directly in the satisfactions of the martial spirit and climb economic heights never before scaled. If, from 1914 to 1916, European war cured many of the United States' economic ills, after April 1917 it brought many Americans even more ample fulfillment. Yet, as we will see, beneath the tangible material gains that war brought to the American people lurked more sinister and, in the end, more triumphant forces.

WAR, SOCIETY, AND THE ECONOMY

It is by now a truism to observe that modern wars are won as often on the home front as on the battlefield. World War I proved no exception to this rule. For most Americans participation in the conflict meant exactions and expenditures previously undreamed and unimagined. Most citizens willingly made the sacrifices required because they received a full measure of compensation. After some early bumbling in 1917, Americans by 1918 were intent on achieving victory through "war socialism," a primitive forerunner of the welfare-warfare state.

Most difficult and cumbersome of all the wartime problems was the organization of manpower. Not only did vast numbers of young men have to be recruited for the military services, but millions more had to be allocated properly and efficiently for labor in the war industries and on the nation's farms. In many cases a skilled worker or a farmer's son was more valuable at home than overseas. Labor had to be relocated from surplus regions, primarily the Deep South, to deficit areas, largely the North Central industrial heartland and the Pacific Coast. This was a particularly acute problem as the war had effectively terminated mass immigration, the major source of the nation's unskilled labor army. Here, then, was an opportunity for advancement by many Americans hitherto excluded from the economy: blacks, Mexican-Americans, and women.

Beginning in 1917 and with increasing frequency in 1918, blacks and Mexican-Americans found jobs in the meatpacking and steel plants of the Chicago–Gary area, and in the metal working and heavy industries of such cities as Pittsburgh, Cleveland, Akron, and Detroit. Women, too, entered industry in new capacities. More than 100,000 females worked in munitions plants, and the number of women in the iron and steel industry tripled. Other females drove streetcars, ran elevators, stoked furnaces, and laid bricks. Such gains notwithstanding, only 5 percent of women war workers had taken paid jobs for the first time, and old prejudices against female labor ran strong. Male trade unionists urged women workers to leave the labor force after the war as rapidly as they had entered it during the emergency, and the federal government preferred to train female workers for such traditional occupations as sewing and embroidery. (It also discriminated against them in the hiring of civil service workers.) And, then, when the war ended, observed reformer Mary Van Kleeck, "The prejudices came to life once more."

But the wartime-inspired redistribution of the labor force never stirred the controversy caused by mass conscription. In past wars, except for the Civil War, the nation had relied on voluntary enlistments. The rudimentary draft of 1863–1865 caused large-scale resistance and severe rioting in New York in 1863. Remarkably, conscription during World War I engendered relatively little overt resistance. Many socialists and a number of anarchists and pacifists campaigned openly against conscription and even refused to register and serve; the Greencorn Rebellion of 1917 sputtered and stalled among angry, poverty-wracked Oklahoma tenants and sharecroppers; nevertheless under the terms of the 1917 Selective Service Act over 40 million Americans registered for the draft and more than 2 million were conscripted.

Money was as vital to the war effort as manpower. Suddenly public officials accustomed to pinching pennies had to consider spending billions. Indeed the war occasioned a remarkable transformation in the size and substance of federal finance. Washington war administrators forgot about the imperative of a balanced budget, which they subordinated to the urge for military victory. In the words of one official, Charles Dawes: "Hell and Maria, we weren't trying to keep a set of books, we were trying to win the war." The government in 1916 collected less than $1 billion in revenues and ran a surplus of almost $50 million (gross federal debt in that year stood at just over $1 billion). The following year the government broke the $1 billion barrier in collections, expended almost $2 billion, and more than doubled the national debt. By 1918 receipts surpassed the $3.5 billion level, expenditures soared to over $12.5 billion, and the national debt approached the latter figure. A year later expenditures climbed to over $18 billion and the federal debt peaked at over $25 billion.

Where did the government obtain the funds to pay for the war? As the statistics for the national debt indicate, most of the money came from loans which charged the costs of war to future generations. Extravagant

Liberty Loan campaigns promoted by stage and sports celebrities promoted Liberty Bonds sales among the mass of Americans. But the bulk of the borrowed funds came from banks and large investors, who commanded the major share of society's savings.

Although the greater part of war costs was paid by borrowing, federal taxes also rose appreciably and signaled a temporary internal revenue revolution. The War Revenue Act of 1917 imposed 74 percent of the increased tax burden on large corporate and individual earnings, and the Revenue Act of 1918 increased the total tax load another 250 percent, with large incomes, corporate profits, and estates bearing 80 percent of the new burden. In 1916 federal income from alcohol and tobacco excise taxes had exceeded that from individual and corporate earnings. By 1918 alcohol and tobacco taxes accounted for only one-sixth of federal income. The remaining bulk was derived from personal and corporate income taxes. Between 1916 and 1919 the number of individual income tax returns soared from roughly 437,000 to well over 5,000,000. And income taxes affected only those Americans earning over $3,000 annually, with the heaviest burden borne by those earning more than $15,000. This meant that the mass of the population escaped the payment of federal income taxes. As a result the proportion of total national income received by the top 5 percent of the population declined between 1917 and 1919 by more than 2 percent. War at least served to effect a marginal redistribution in national income.

Money and manpower were useless unless they could be effectively allocated and efficiently used. To overcome the inefficiencies that had weakened the initial war-production effort, the Wilson administration invited the nation's industrial leaders to direct the planning process. The noted Wall Street financier, Bernard Baruch, was appointed in December 1917 as director of the War Industries Board. This board was granted enormous authority to set economic priorities and to allocate resources. The Board could order manufacturers to produce particular items at federally set prices in certain quantities. But to make federal planning palatable to private businessmen, Baruch generally enlisted the executives dominant in various sectors of the economy to manage precisely those sectors. Thus John D. Ryan, chief executive officer of the Amalgamated Copper Company (Anaconda), was placed in charge of the production of copper. And so it went. The federal government in effect vested private businessmen with vast amounts of public power to manage the domestic economy in the interest of national security. Such were the beginnings of the twentieth-century's military-industrial complex.

Almost every sector of the domestic economy felt the heavy hand of public authority, usually exercised by dollar-a-year recruits from the national business elite. Harry A. Garfield, director of the Fuel Administration, rationed coal supplies, instituted daylight savings time, on occasion closed nonessential industries, and made profitable the opening of marginal coal mines. An Emergency Fleet Corporation provided a cornucopia of federal funds for the expansion of the merchant marine. At the end of December 1917, President Wilson created the United States Railroad Administration. This administration, headed by his son-in-law and also secretary of the treasury, William G. McAdoo, was to create order out of the nation's chaotic and competitive rail system. Under McAdoo's supervision, the country for the first time in its history operated a unified national transportation and communications system— one that in time included telephone and telegraph lines as well as railroads. And Herbert Hoover, world-famous mining engineer and financial genius, returned from abroad to direct the Food Administration. As food administrator, Hoover encouraged wheatless and meatless days, the consumption of whale and shark steak, and federal price supports for raisers of wheat, hogs, and cattle. He envisioned a complete domestic war effort and enlisted children in that effort, encouraging them not to waste food, including apples, for "nowadays even children must be taught to be patriotic to the core."

The war effort illustrated the possibilities inherent in government-corporation cooperation and the efficacy of a planned economy. War confirmed the triumph of large-scale business enterprise, for Washington propaganda agencies taught the public that big business made an essential contribution to victory. No more, then, would Americans worship at the shrine of antitrust legislation; instead they would walk contentedly through the doorway of the 1920s into an era of unprecedented corporate consolidations and mergers.

LABOR: A POWER IN THE LAND

Big business was not alone in benefiting from the war effort. Unemployment which had stood at 9.7 percent of the civilian labor force in 1915 declined to 1.4 percent in 1918. Along with reduced unemployment went steadier work and higher wages and annual earnings. Hourly wage rates went up by almost 80 percent between 1916 and 1919, and annual earnings, excluding farm labor, rose in the same years from $765 to $1,272. But wage rates and annual earnings ran a close race with inflation. Workers in many cases had to run harder than ever to stay where they had been at the start of the sprint. This economic squeeze, combined with disappearance of the usual reserve labor army, induced working-class militancy, a surge in union ranks, and the threat of walkouts in vital war industries.

Even before the United States entered the war in April 1917, President Wilson had been cultivating the support of prominent labor leaders. Endorsement by Samuel Gompers and the railroad brotherhoods had certainly aided Wilson's reelection in 1916, and he was not about to be ungrateful. He invited Gompers and other union officials to sit on various councils of national defense and war preparation agencies. And when war came the president maintained his administration's liaison with trade unionists. Gompers had easy access to the White House and the War and Labor Departments. Moreover, numerous friends and sympathizers of the AFL served during the war as second-line officials in the War and Labor department bureaucracies. In such essential industries as shipbuilding, airplane production, and cantonment construction, Wilson established tripartite boards representing business, organized labor, and the "public." These wartime boards mediated labor-management conflicts, instituted a uniform eight-hour work day, set prevailing basic wage rates on government work, and created an environment favorable for the expansion of AFL unions. For the duration of the war, at least, many employers halted their own private struggle against those unions approved by Washington.

Government concessions to Gompers and the AFL notwithstanding, total industrial harmony could not be insured. Much to the chagrin of the administration, in the spring and summer of 1917 industrial conflict erupted in the copper mines of the Rocky Mountain states and the forests of the Pacific Northwest. Both of these industries were vital to the war effort. Worse yet, from Washington's perspective, the strikes in copper and lumber were the work of the radical, irresponsible IWW.

Eager to end the troublesome walkouts, equally anxious to purge the Wobbly influence, but also committed to retaining the wartime cooperation of the AFL, the Wilson administration sought to placate the strikers and substitute "legitimate" AFL unions for the IWW. Wilson sought to accomplish his aims by the appointment of a special presidential mediation commission charged with the investigation of labor conflict in essential war industries. This commission, chaired by Secretary of Labor William B. Wilson and guided by Felix Frankfurter, made its findings and recommendations public in January 1918. The commission called on employers to recognize and bargain collectively with responsible AFL trade unions, institute the eight-hour day, and establish effective machinery for the amelioration of their workers' legitimate grievances. In return for bargaining with "responsible" unions and implementing other job reforms, employers were promised by federal authorities that Wobblies and other radical agitators would be eliminated and that a stable supply of labor would be made available.

Shortly after the Mediation Commission completed its assignment, President Wilson formalized its recommendations by the creation in March 1918 of a National War Labor Board chaired jointly by former president William Howard Taft and Frank P. Walsh, a radical Democratic attorney and noted advocate of organized labor. Consisting of an equal number of representatives from industry, the AFL, and the public, the War Labor Board conferred federal sanction on labor's right to organize and bargain collectively; it also endorsed the eight-hour day, wage rates set in accordance with prevailing local standards, and equal pay for women. In return for the federal promise to maintain labor-management harmony, employers promised not to lock out their employees and the AFL vowed not to strike during the war.

The AFL prospered under federal guardianship. Total union membership rose from 2,772,000 in 1916 to 3,368,000 in 1918 and peaked at 5,034,000 in 1919. The NWLB in particular assisted labor in organizing the Chicago packinghouses in 1918 and helped lay the foundation for an organizing campaign of nationwide proportions among steelworkers.

Never before had organized labor in the United States seemed in such a secure position. Not only did Gompers offer valued advice to a president and his cabinet officials, but President Wilson also chose Gompers and other labor leaders to serve on American diplomatic missions abroad. Gompers represented the government in England, France, and Italy where he even dined with the king in an effort to dampen antiwar sentiment among Allied workers. Other AFL officials served on a mission to Russia which aimed to convince the Bolsheviks to remain in the war on the Allied side. War had indeed brought many blessings to the AFL and its members.

But as the AFL and its affiliates advanced, socialists, labor radicals, and Wobblies suffered irretrievable losses. Collaboration with the ruling groups carried rewards; conflict brought retribution.

THE AMERICANIZATION OF IMMIGRANTS AND THE URBANIZATION OF BLACKS

As significant as the rise in influence of organized labor was the war's transforming impact on immigrants and blacks. Before 1914 many of the newer immigrants thought of themselves as temporary inhabitants in the "promised land." They were here only long enough to earn sufficient funds to purchase land in the old country. But with the outbreak of war in 1914 a return to Europe became impossible and also less desirable.

As immigrant workers established firmer roots in the United States between 1914 and 1917, employers and government officials stimulated the process of Americanization, especially after the United States entered the war. Public officials desired to ensure absolute loyalty among immigrants who were encouraged to learn English, American history, and the mores of their adopted land. The federal government funded state and local propaganda programs among immigrants and made the foreign born a particular target of Liberty Loan drives. Employers, who once had perceived immigrant laborers as a transient, easily replaceable workforce, now sought to transform immigrants into more content and stable employees. Where government-funded Americanization programs failed to reach immigrant workers, plans developed by such large employers as United States Steel and International Harvester filled the vacuum.

More important perhaps than formal attempts to Americanize immigrants was the war's impact on their occupational fortunes. As part of management's strategy for stabilizing the immigrant labor force, foreign-born workers experienced an upgrading in wage rates and job classifications. Skilled positions and supervisory posts, previously reserved for American-born workers, became available to immigrants. Masses of new immigrants for the first time climbed up the occupation ladder in steel and underground mining.

Regardless of their reason, millions of immigrants came to consider themselves Americans. Visions of landed status in the old country paled before the reality of economic opportunity in the New World. These new citizens became more conscious of the need to struggle politically and economically in order to better their status. This new spirit would soon manifest itself in the Great Steel Strike of 1919 and later revive with the presidential candidacy of Al Smith and the political coalition constructed by Franklin D. Roosevelt.

While immigrants developed a new consciousness, Afro-Americans accelerated a pattern of migration that was to continue for the remainder of the century. From the border states and the Deep South, black Americans moved north in response to industry's insatiable demand for labor. Employment once denied blacks suddenly opened—in steel, machine shops, and shipyards. Several hundred thousand Negroes went north in 1917–1918, opening a trail millions more would later follow to New York, Philadelphia, Cleveland, Pittsburgh, and Chicago. Between 1910 and 1920, the black population of Chicago increased by 148 percent, Detroit by 611 percent; Cleveland by 308 percent; New York City by 66 percent; and Philadelphia by 59 percent.

Race relations, which had been a singularly southern "problem," now assumed national dimensions. Prior to the war Afro-Americans had endured residential segregation in most larger northern cities, but with war-induced increases in nonwhite urban population, patterns of segregation hardened. Areas such as Harlem in New York and the South Side in Chicago became large and recognizable black subcommunities within the city. With firmer residential segregation there also appeared for the first time in many northern cities a refusal by hotel and restaurant proprietors to serve Afro-Americans. Although segregation in the North developed without legal sanction, indeed often in violation of the law, its effect scarcely differed from the legally mandated Jim Crow system in the South. In 1917 race riots erupted in Philadelphia and Chester, Pennsylvania. Even more brutal rioting occurred in East St. Louis, Illinois, a grimy industrial suburb of St. Louis. Here, competition for jobs and scarce housing cost the lives of thirty-nine Negroes—the heaviest toll in any twentieth-century "race riot." Northern crises in race relations in 1917–1918 only foreshadowed what was to occur in 1919 and subsequent decades.

THE DARK SIDE OF WAR

If war benefited workers and their labor movement, hastened the Americanization of immigrants, and redistributed the Afro-American population, it also had a perceptibly less beneficial impact on American society. Government efforts to inculcate loyalty in a time of crisis easily passed beyond the limits of patriotic propaganda campaigns. Indeed the inculcation of loyalty implied the suppression of disloyalty—a concept with a singularly elastic meaning.

Such propaganda techniques as renaming sauerkraut "liberty cabbage," German measles "liberty measles," and dachshunds "liberty hounds" had their comic aspects. But when the German language was banned by statute from public and even parochial schools and German-Americans were threatened with violence if they refused to buy Liberty Bonds, loyalty crusades assumed a less healthy aspect.

Official and unofficial loyalty crusades combined to crush dissent. In June 1917, Congress enacted an espionage act that included vocal opposition to conscription as a form of espionage, and in May 1918 it passed a sedition act that categorized nearly all criticism of the federal government's wartime policies as a crime The Justice Department received regular reports from its regional attorneys concerning violations of the wartime statutes and its Bureau of Investigation agents fanned out across the nation in an aggressive hunt for suspected "traitors." Because the government's resources were in fact limited, the Justice Department encouraged private citizens to combine and form their own federally-sanctioned, antispy network known as the American Protective League. With government approval thousands of ordinary citizens spread wartime vigilantism to every section of the nation.

The impact of government and citizen surveillance of "radicals" was immediate and severe. Under the terms of the 1918 sedition act over fifteen hundred Americans were arrested. Postal authorities, using the espionage act as a pretext, denied mailing privileges to such radical and antiwar publications as the *New York Call, Milwaukee Leader,* the *Masses,* and *Tom Watson's Magazine.* Socialist leader Eugene V. Debs was arrested for a mild antiwar speech delivered in Canton, Ohio, in 1918. He was charged under the sedition act and was convicted and sentenced to the federal penitentiary in Atlanta. Hundreds of lesser-known socialists and antiwar advocates, especially those with foreign-sounding names or who came from foreign countries, suffered fates similar to Debs's. Vigilante tactics, postal restrictions, and arrests decimated the Socialist party in such rural strongholds of socialism as Oklahoma. What could socialists expect when the president of Columbia University remarked of the antiwar senator from Wisconsin, Robert LaFollette: "You might as well put poison in the food of every American boy that goes to his transport as to permit that man to talk as he does."

Domestic repression in wartime, Bisbee, Arizona
National Archives

Not only did the wartime hysteria paralyze socialists and ostracize reformers as prominent as LaFollette, but it also led to the repression of the nation's most troublesome labor radicals—the Wobblies. Not only did IWW members refuse to endorse the war but their actions tied up vital war industries. Because they threatened national goals, in practice as well as in rhetoric, the Wobblies felt the full wrath of government action and citizen vigilantism. In July 1917 over twelve hundred workers, alleged to be IWW members, were forcibly deported in cattle cars from the copper-mining town of Bisbee, Arizona, and dumped in the New Mexico desert; the following month, vigilantes in Butte, Montana, lynched the IWW militant, Frank Little. And in September 1917 the Justice Department raided IWW headquarters everywhere in the nation because, as one United States attorney observed, it was time "to put the wretches out of business." Afterwards the government arrested the entire leadership cadre of the IWW and indicted them on a wide variety of espionage and sedition charges.

In the spring of 1918 the federal government held a showcase trial of 113 Wobblies in Chicago. After a trial of almost four months, during which the defendants were charged with having committed more than ten thousand separate crimes, the jury deliberated less than an hour before finding all the defendants guilty on each and every count. Later the Justice Department conducted similar courtroom charades against less prominent Wobblies in Wichita, Kansas, and Sacramento, California, and also secured convictions. More fortunate were a group of sixty-four Wobblies who sat in an Omaha jail for eighteen months before the government dismissed the charges against them owing to a lack of evidence.

The IWW never recovered from wartime repression. After 1918 it functioned more as a legal defense agency than as a labor organization fighting to protect its members on the job. The experience of the Wobblies lent weight to the observation of the progressive Republican senator from California Hiram Johnson: "The war has set back the people for a generation. They have bowed to a hundred repressive acts. They have become slaves to the government. . . . They are docile; and they will never recover from being so for many years."

1919: ANNUS MIRABILIS

In 1919, however, Hiram Johnson's prophesy seemed absolutely mistaken. Everywhere one looked that year—whether in Russia, Germany, Hungary, Italy, France, England, and even the United States—turbulence, not stability, plagued society.

"The world," in the words of an immigrant American labor leader, "is in the midst of a new social era." The signs were abundant. The Bolsheviks by 1919 had secured their revolution in Russia and through the formation of the Communist International (Comintern) seemed ready to spread revolution worldwide. Hungary experienced its own Bolshevik revolution under Bela Kun; Communists seized power in Bavaria and took to the streets in Berlin; Italian workers sat-in and occupied industrial plants; Turkey and China erupted in left-wing nationalist revolts; in staid England, the British Labour Party adopted an avowedly Socialist program for the reconstruction of postwar British society; and in the United States not one, but two Communist parties were formed in the spring of 1919.

Liberated from the restrictions of war and eager to make up ground lost to price inflation, labor exploded in militancy. In January 1919 workers in Seattle declared a general strike and for four days closed tight the city's commercial and industrial life. The disciplined strikers maintained public order and provided essential services. That summer Boston's police, unable to win recognition for an AFL union they had formed, walked off the job. The public rallied against the police strike. Harvard students served as volunteer officers, Massachusetts Governor Calvin Coolidge vowed to smash the strike, and an antilabor crusade fueled the local press; Boston's police lost their struggle. Throughout the summer and fall of 1919 more than 400,000 coal miners waged an on and off struggle against mine owners and the federal government. This conflict was ended only by President Wilson's intervention and the issuance of unusually broad federal antistrike injunctions. These industrial conflicts served as a prelude to the year's climactic battle: the national steel strike which began on September 22. Led by the ex-Wobbly and soon-to-be Communist William Z. Foster, and sanctioned by the AFL, 350,000 steelworkers fought their bosses, local police, state militia, federal troops, strikebreakers, the judiciary, and a well-financed antiunion propaganda campaign. Against such odds, the steelworkers cracked and surrendered in January 1920. All in all, the year 1919 witnessed over thirty-six-hundred strikes involving more than four million workers.

Other ominous signs appeared. In the spring of 1919 a series of events reminiscent of nineteenth-century anarchist plots emerged. Bombs were sent to the mayor of Seattle and a former governor of Georgia; and a New York postal clerk discovered over thirty similar packages addressed to such notable enemies of organized labor as John D. Rockefeller, Postmaster General Burleson, and Judge Kenesaw Mountain Landis (the judge in the Chicago IWW trial). But the list of bomb targets also included such eminent reformers as Frederick C. Howe and Secretary of Labor William B. Wilson. On June 2 bombs exploded in several cities, including one at the doorstep of Attorney General A. Mitchell Palmer.

Beset by labor militancy on the one hand and alleged anarchist conspiracies on the other, the nation suddenly found itself confronted with savage racial conflicts. During the war, housing, schooling, and employment problems had worsened in cities with rapidly growing black populations. With the return of veterans at the war's end, whites and blacks competed intensely for jobs and apartments; also, Negro soldiers who had fought for freedom in France were less likely to accept second-class citizenship at home. As a result of white anxieties and black desires, race relations deteriorated. 1919 saw ten Negro veterans lynched, including several public burnings. In July a riot occurred in Longview, Texas, and on July 27 Chicago exploded. For thirteen days, whites and blacks fought and rioted on Chicago's streets with the Black Belt suffering the greatest violence and destruction. When it was all over, 15 whites and 23 blacks had died, 172 whites and 342 blacks had been injured, and over one thousand families, mostly black, had been made homeless. During the next two months race riots spread to Knoxville, Tennessee, Omaha, Nebraska, and Elaine, Arkansas.

Fear of revolution and anxiety about the social order became common among public officials and molders of opinion. The guardians of public order acted decisively. Federal intervention had already turned the tide against labor militancy. Now it would be used to extirpate radicalism.

Under the direction of A. Mitchell Palmer and his loyal servant, J. Edgar Hoover, the Justice Department initiated a nationwide "red" hunt. On November 17, 1919, the department arrested 249 Russian immigrants, a large number of whom were held for deportation. On December 21 federal agents arrested still more alleged foreign-born subversives, including the anarchist Emma Goldman, and prepared to deport them to Soviet Russia. General of the Army Leonard Wood gloated that the alleged Bolsheviks should be deported "in ships of stone with sails of lead, with the wrath of God for a breeze and with hell for their first port." Palmer next obtained warrants for the arrest of over three thousand alien members of the Communist parties, and on the night of January 2, 1920, his agents raided homes and headquarters in thirty-three cities and arrested over four thousand suspects. Hundreds were held incommunicado and many were arrested for no apparent reason, including three hundred suspects in Detroit who were held in jail for a week, denied food for twenty-four hours, made to sleep on the floor, and in the end found innocent. The Justice Department held citizens for eventual trial and turned aliens over to the Immigration and Naturalization Service for deportation.

State governments and local authorities conducted their own red hunts. They also used wartime techniques. New York City instituted a Who's Red and Who's True Blue campaign among its schoolteachers, while the state legislature appointed a special committee to investigate revolutionary radicalism. To cap matters, the New York legislature in 1920 refused to seat five socialist assemblymen elected and then reelected by their constituents.

Such repressive tactics served their purpose. Most labor conflicts ended in union defeat or destruction; a decimated Communist movement went underground; Socialists seemed either organizationally impotent or paralyzed; and racial conflict abated. Overseas in Europe, Bolsheviks outside Russia had been crushed, and the Comintern proved to be a largely paper organization. Prewar conservatives again exercised the upper hand and apparently assured the maintenance of social stability. With Warren G. Harding about to enter the White House in March 1921, Americans looked forward to economic prosperity, world peace, and domestic order.

SELECTED BIBLIOGRAPHY FOR SECTION III

The period preceding American intervention in World War I is covered in: ERNEST R. MAY, *The World War and American Isolation, 1914–1917* (1959) *; ARTHUR S. LINK's two volumes, *Wilson: The Struggle for Neutrality* (1960) and *Wilson: Confusions and Crises, 1915–1916* (1964) ; N. GORDON LEVIN, *Woodrow Wilson and World Politics: America's Response to War and Revolution* (1968) *; H. C. PETERSON, *Propaganda for War: The Campaign against American Neutrality, 1914–1917* (1939) ; CHARLES SEYMOUR's classic work, *American Neutrality, 1914–1917* (1935) ; and CHARLES C. TANSILL's revisionist anti-Wilson study, *America Goes to War* (1938) .

The historical scholarship on U.S. involvement in World War I offers many different interpretations. Wartime diplomacy is perceptively analyzed in CHARLES SEYMOUR, *American Diplomacy during the World War* (1934) ; WARREN I. COHEN, ed., *Intervention, 1917: Why America Fought*

* Available in paperback.

(1966) *; DANIEL M. SMITH, *The Great Departure: The United States and World War I, 1914–1920* (1955) *; ARNO J. MAYER, *Politics and Diplomacy of Peacemaking* (1967) *; and SEWARD LIVERMORE, *Politics Is Adjourned: Woodrow Wilson and the War Congress, 1916–1918* (1966) .*

Peace negotiations are surveyed in THOMAS A. BAILEY, *Woodrow Wilson and the Lost Peace* (1944) and *Woodrow Wilson and the Great Betrayal* (1945) *; ARTHUR S. LINK, *Campaigns for Progressivism and Peace, 1916–1917* (1965) *; and SELIG ADLER, *The Isolationist Impulse: Its Twentieth Century Reaction* (1961) .* American policy toward the Bolshevik Revolution and the Soviet Union is studied in JOHN M. THOMPSON, *Russia, Bolshevism, and the Versailles Peace* (1966) and in GEORGE F. KENNAN's *Soviet-American Relations, 1917–1920* (1956) .*

The domestic effect of World War I is analyzed in SAMUEL HABER, *Efficiency and Uplift* (1964) *; JESSE D. CLARKSON and THOMAS C. COCHRAN, eds., *War as a Social Institution* (1941) ; and EDWARD M. COFFMAN, *The War To End All Wars: The American Military Experience in World War I* (1968) . Excellent analyses of wartime economic developments appear in GEORGE SOULÉ, *Prosperity Decade: From War to Depression, 1917–1929* (1947) *; ROBERT D. CUFF, *The War Industries Board: Business-Government Relations during World War I* (1973) ; and MELVIN I. UROFSKY, *Big Steel and the Wilson Administration: A Study in Business-Government Relations* (1969) . The mobilization of public opinion through propaganda can be followed in JAMES R. MOCK and CEDRIC LARSON, *Words that Won the War: The Story of the Committee on Public Information* (1939) and in a book by the Committee's chairman, GEORGE CREEL, *How We Advertised America* (1920) .

The following are studies critical of the federal government's handling of pacifists, dissenters, and radicals during the war: H. C. PERTERSON and GILBERT FITE, *Opponents of War, 1917–1918* (1957) *; HARRY N. SCHEIBER, *The Wilson Administration and Civil Liberties, 1917–1921* (1960) ; WILLIAM PRESTON, JR., *Aliens and Dissenters: Federal Suppression of Radicals, 1903–1933* (1963) *; DONALD O. JOHNSON, *The Challenge to American Freedoms: World War I and the Rise of the American Civil Liberties Union* (1963) ; and MELVYN DUBOFSKY, *We Shall Be All: A History of the IWW* (1969) .* Developments among workers and the labor movement can be followed in MELVYN DUBOFSKY, *Industrialism and the American Workers, 1865–1920* (1975) *; FRANK L. GRUBBS, JR., *The Struggle for Labor Loyalty: Gompers, the A.F. of L. and the Pacifists, 1917–1920* (1968) ; and RONALD RADOSH, *American Labor and United States Foreign Policy* (1969). Pacifism is thoughtfully studied in C. ROLAND MARCHAND, *The American Peace Movement* (1972) and in CHARLES CHATFIELD, *For Peace and Justice: Pacifism in America, 1914–1941* (1971) .*

Labor disturbances and the "Red Scare" are covered in STANLEY COBEN, *A. Mitchell Palmer: Politician* (1963) ; ROBERT K. MURRAY, *Red Scare: A Study in National Hysteria, 1919–1920* (1955) *; DAVID BRODY,

Labor in Crisis: The Steel Strike of 1919 (1965) *; and ROBERT L. FRIED-
HEIM, *The Seattle General Strike* (1964). Changes among black Ameri-
cans during World War I can be followed in WILLIAM M. TUTTLE, JR.,
Race Riot: Chicago in the Red Summer of 1919 (1970) *; ALLAN H.
SPEAR, *Black Chicago* (1967); and FLORETTE HENRI, *Black Migration*
(1975).*

IV

A New Era Dawns:
The Prosperous Twenties

During the 1920s the United States benefited in numerous ways from its global economic hegemony. Wall Street replaced Lombard Street as the center of world banking and the United States surpassed Great Britain as the globe's banker and principal exporter of surplus capital.

More so even than in the preceding Progressive Era, American leaders during the 1920s believed that science and knowledge guaranteed mankind full control of its fate and insured a good life for all. Enlightened businessmen and astute government administrators, it was believed, could now build a new form of cooperative capitalism that would supersede the competitive, often destructive capitalism inherited from the nineteenth century. Businessmen and government leaders perceived science and bureaucracy as institutions in the service of mankind; they believed implicitly that experts, freed from irrational popular pressures, could create and then manage a contented, prosperous, stable, and secure society. The road to utopia lay through voluntary business-government planning and scientific management, not through popular participation and open democratic practices in government and business. The New Era, the decade in which every citizen would eat chicken and drive a car, would come as a gift to the nation from its scientists, engineers, managers, and bureaucrats. The Republicans who dominated the politics of the 1920s and set the tone for much of the nation's life felt that they had found an effective alternative to socialist and other visionary views of a harmonious, cooperative society.

Yet the men who exercised economic and political power at home and abroad during the 1920s did so with minimal responsibility for their actions. They gloried and gloated in their successes, all the time paying little or no attention to the victims of their policies whether in the United States or overseas. And when their grand new system collapsed in 1929, the scientists, engineers, and managers who built it found themselves at sea without a compass to guide them to a safe harbor during a gale-force storm. The builders of the New Era were forced to watch almost impotently as their system gave way first to a Great Depression and then to a New Deal.

11

Hedonism, Babbittry, and Grim Reality: Economics, Society, and Culture in the New Era

Jazz, flappers, prohibition, speakeasies, "bathtub gin," "monkey trial," "normalcy" are words suggestive of the years between the end of World War I and the onset of the Great Depression. It was a time when young men and women danced the "black bottom"; a time when undergraduates swallowed goldfish and wore raccoon coats; a time when women bobbed their hair, raised their skirts, and rolled down their stockings; a time when sex fled the bedroom for the "silver screen" and the backseat of autos; a time when the business of America was business. The 1920s meant liberation, hedonism, prosperity; it was a decade that presaged the creation of an affluent, consumer-based, mass society.

Not all Americans, however, were equally prosperous, sexually emancipated, or carefreely hedonistic. Like all historical decades, the 1920s encompassed contradictory realities and tendencies. If some citizens waxed wealthy, others endured poverty. If some Americans experimented with sex, marriage, and family patterns, many others preferred traditional modes of life. If some openly violated prohibition, still others worked all the harder to secure a healthier, cleaner, more moral society. If some warred against inherited traditions and orthodox values, a majority cherished the old, the established, the comfortable.

159

PROSPERITY IN THE NEW ERA

The 1920s were known as a "prosperity decade" for a good reason. All the basic economic indicators heralded good times. The gross national product soared from $78.9 billion to $104.4. billion by 1929, a per capita increase of $755 to $857 (over 16 percent for every man, woman, and child).

The wages and earnings of American workers bore further witness to the decade's prosperity. Adjusted for changes in the price level, average real earnings rose from $619 in 1920 to $793 in 1929; the increase for nonfarm employees, a larger proportion of the work force than ever, proved still greater: from $672 to $855. Wages and earnings rose most rapidly in those economic sectors—personal, professional, trade, and public services—that foreshadowed the emerging mass consumer society.

Throughout the decade the national economy shifted away from the production of heavy capital goods and toward the manufacture of household durables and soft consumer items. Having built its economic infrastructure and a strong foundation of heavy industry in the years between the end of the Civil War and World War I, the United States economy in the 1920s inaugurated what Walt W. Rostow characterized as the "age of high mass consumption."

Most representative of the consumerism of American society was the automobile. Previously a luxury available only to the wealthy, the motor car was transformed by Henry Ford into a mass-produced, moderately priced commodity, which in the 1920s became an essential artifact of family life. At his massive River Rouge plant just outside Detroit, Ford introduced the perpetual-motion assembly-line principle, which by 1925 produced standardized Model Ts and then Model As at a rate of one every ten seconds. Ford aimed his cars at a mass market and offered so standardized a product that it was said that the consumer could have his Model T in any color provided he chose black!

Ford's methods brought quick results. In 1919 Americans purchased almost 2 million cars, and by 1929 that figure would reach almost 4½ million. Between 1923 and 1929 annual sales of autos only once fell below the 3 million mark. As a result of such phenomenal sales, motor vehicle registrations soared from 7.5 million in 1919 to 26.7 million in 1929, or one vehicle for every 4.5 Americans. No wonder cars sold so well, when some of the families that the sociologists Robert and Helen Lynd met in Middletown, Indiana, in 1925 sacrificed better housing, sanitary plumbing, and even food to meet the payments on their auto.

The car stimulated the economy and created prosperity in myriad ways. Millions of new car owners provided the highway lobby with the political muscle it hitherto lacked. Between 1919 and 1929 the mileage of surfaced roads almost doubled and the nation's drivers could also hazard some 3 million miles of unpaved rural roads. By 1929 the federal govern-

The auto age arrives
Michigan Dept. of State/State Archives

ment had expended $199 million on 8,500 miles of highway and desig-
nated some 190,000 miles as part of a growing federal highway system.
From 1919 to 1929, moreover, annual state highway expenditures never
dropped below the $80 million level. Also necessary for the motorist were
gasoline, lubricants, and spare parts. Before long the gas station became
as ubiquitous an artifact of American life as the car itself, so commonplace an institution that it provided the inspiration for the popular
comic strip, "Gasoline Alley." The great oil companies meanwhile waxed
fat and powerful, wielding enormous power in national politics and
international affairs. Well they should when crude petroleum production
jumped from 380 million barrels in 1919 to over one billion barrels by
1929.

As the car made Americans more mobile than ever, the electric power
and appliance industries lit the home better and made it more comfortable. The production of electricity increased from 56 million kilowatt
hours in 1920 to 117 million kilowatt hours in 1929, and the number of
homes with electric service climbed from 34.7 percent to 67.9 percent. By
the end of the decade it was rare to find a city dwelling without elec-

tricity, though only 9.2 percent of farm homes had such service. Household appliances became hot-selling items, and by 1926 more than 80 percent of the homes with electric service had electric irons; 37 percent had vacuum cleaners; and 25 percent had clothes washers, fans, and toasters. By 1929 the refrigerator was replacing the ice-box, rendering the iceman as superfluous as the harness-maker.

Mass consumption was stimulated by advertising and fueled by installment-buying methods. Then, as now, advertisers implied that their products would assure sexual triumphs, or if more expensive than their competitor's product, would confer greater status. The weight-conscious learned to substitute a cigarette for a sweet, and husbands and lovers to "say it with flowers," a slogan that purportedly doubled the flower business between 1921 and 1924. Pioneering in popular psychology and the creation of status and sexual anxieties, American advertisers by 1927 were spending over $1.5 billion on promotional campaigns conducted through newspapers, magazines, mails, billboards, and, for the first time, the radio. Readily available consumer credit enabled citizens to satisfy their freshly stimulated desires. By 1927, 15 percent of all goods were purchased on installment contracts at a retail value of nearly $6 billion. Over 85 percent of furniture, 80 percent of washing machines, 75 percent of phonographs, and the bulk of most new consumer items were purchased on time. A prime reason General Motors pulled far ahead of Ford in car sales was that GM pioneered in financing the sale of its products through the General Motors Acceptance Corporation (GMAC), a consumer-credit company. Americans increasingly followed the seller's advice to "enjoy now, pay later."

Prosperity seemed permanent; the 1920s indeed seemed to be a new era. Calvin Coolidge assured Americans that "we are reaching and maintaining the position where the propertied and employed class are not separate, but identical." And Lincoln Steffens, who had once glimpsed the future in Soviet Russia, now proclaimed that big business "is producing what the socialists held up as their goal: food, clothing, and shelter for all." At his presidential inauguration Herbert Hoover boasted that "we in America are nearer the final triumph over poverty than ever before in the history of any land . . . we shall soon with the help of God be in sight of the day when poverty will be vanished from this nation."

THE GRIM REALITIES

The rhetoric of Coolidge, Steffens, and Hoover cloaked the grim realities of life experienced by millions of Americans. Prosperity was as unequally distributed as ever, perhaps even worse. The share of national income held by the top 1 percent of the population rose between 1919 and 1929 from 12.96 percent to 14.5 percent. The share possessed by the top 5 percent also rose from 23 percent to 26 percent. More remarkable still, after taxes were paid, the top 5 percent received over 33 percent of national income. A similar maldistribution of income occurred among business enterprises. The top 5 percent of business corporations in 1929 earned over 84 percent of business income—up from 76 percent in 1919. Meanwhile, the share of the smallest 75 percent of businesses shrank from 7 percent to 3.9 percent.

Not surprisingly, then, in 1929 71 percent of American families earned incomes of under $2,500 annually, the level that the Bureau of Labor Statistics considered minimal for an adequate health and decency budget for a family of four. The wealthiest thirty-six thousand families, however, received as much income as the twelve million families (42 percent) with incomes of $1,500 or less.

Despite a general increase in real wages some workers suffered considerable decreases in their earning power. This was especially true for bituminous coal miners and railroad workers who, as a result of changing consumer preferences and new technology, experienced extensive unemployment. In the South, where women and children continued to toil in textile mills from fifty-four to seventy hours per week, the average hourly wage for a male weaver was twenty-five cents and, for a female spinner, seventeen cents. Unemployment remained a persistent working-class problem. During the brief postwar depression, unemployment (computed as a percentage of nonfarm workers) hit 19.5 percent in 1921 and 11.4 percent in 1922. In 1924, it climbed from 4.1 percent to 8.3 percent, dropped to 2.9 percent in 1926, and was back up to 6.9 percent in 1928.

If some workers experienced occasional unemployment, two regions of the country slid into permanent economic depression. New England textile and shoe towns declined in the face of southern competition. And from western Pennsylvania to southern Illinois, as well as in hundreds of isolated Appalachian hollows, unemployed coal miners passed the time in frustration and defeat. Knowing no other occupation and dwelling in regions that offered no alternative jobs, the miners were trapped in poverty.

One reason workers failed to share fully in the decade's prosperity was the paralysis of the labor movement. The membership of trade unions fell from a high of over 5 million in 1920 to 3.6 million members in 1929. The nation's largest and most powerful union in 1919, the United Mine Workers of America, was by 1929 bankrupt, debilitated, and impotent. Only the aristocratic crafts in the construction trades thrived and grew. As too often had been the case in the past, those workers most in need of union protection were least likely to gain it. If they were fortunate, unorganized workers received the benefits that employers granted under "welfare capitalism"—i.e., Christmas bonuses, profit-sharing, stock purchases, retirement funds, clean cafeterias, and company picnics. However, these benefits scarcely covered more workers than the labor movement and thus left the mass of employees unprotected by unions or paternalistic employers.

Farmers, too, failed to share in the prosperity. The favorable terms of trade between country and city that had existed between 1900 and 1919 reversed themselves. The replacement of horses and mules by Ford tractors was one factor among many that caused agricultural production to increase more rapidly than demand for foodstuffs. As a consequence, between 1919 and 1929 net farm income dropped by a third, the value of farm land and buildings fell by over 10 percent and total indebtedness soared. As had happened from 1873 to 1897, once again in the 1920s marginal farmers fled the countryside for the city while others declined from owners to tenants. By 1930 only 57 percent of farmers owned the land that they worked, the lowest percentage ever in American history. Agricultural America, like textile New England and coal-mining Appalachia, suffered economic decline in a time of prosperity.

A DEMOGRAPHIC PORTRAIT

During the 1920s the American people on the average grew older, healthier, more urban, and more educated. Population increased at a slower rate than it had previously, a trend initiated during the previous decade. Men still outnumbered women (a residual impact of unrestricted immigration) and the nonwhite population held fast at under 10 percent of the total. The median age of Americans continued to inch up, while the median age at first marriage maintained its slow decline, falling by 1930 to 24.3 years of age for men and 21.3 years of age for women. Between 1920 and 1930 urban population climbed by over 15 million whereas rural population increased by less than 3 million. Because of the restrictive 1921 and 1924 immigration laws, the percentage of the foreign born began to shrink though they remained concentrated in the cities of the Northeast and North Central states. During the 1920s the black population in those states passed one million as its size stabilized in the South. Overall the states of the Old South, northern New England, the nonindustrial Midwest, and the Rocky Mountains lost people to the most prosperous northern industrial states, especially New York, New Jersey, Illinois, and Michigan. California, to be sure, led all states in receiving internal migrants, and Florida was already breaking away from the southern pattern by attracting its share of newcomers.

For the first time sharp declines were registered in the birth rate for all classes of women, with foreign-born and nonwhite females achieving the sharpest reductions. The birth rate for native white women between fifteen and forty-four fell from 109 to 86 per thousand, while for all white women it dropped from 115.4 to 87.1 per thousand, and for all women from 117.9 to 89.2 per thousand. Since men and women married at a younger age and more often than ever, one can only assume that Americans practiced contraception regularly and effectively. Otherwise one is hard pressed to explain Freud's American triumph, the decline of the double standard in sex, and women's claim to enjoy sex as much as men.

Given the falling birth rate, a steadily declining death rate accounted for the decade's substantial population growth. Further medical advances caused respiratory and contagious diseases to fall markedly as the causes of death. But illnesses associated with age, such as cardiovascular diseases and malignancies, became the greatest killers. Yet significant differences remained between the life chances of whites and nonwhites. At the start of the decade nonwhites had a life expectancy almost ten years less than their white cohorts, and by 1930 that gap had widened to over fourteen years for nonwhite females and over twelve years for males. The nonwhite infant mortality rate per thousand live births in 1930 was 99.9 compared to 60.1 for whites, and the maternal mortality rate per 10,000 live births was 117.4 for nonwhites to 60.9 for whites. Finally, the nonwhite death rate was over 50 percent higher than the white rate. No solider evidence substantiated the United States' color based caste system.

American women, liberated from customary household responsibilities by contraception and electric appliances, failed to find great opportunity in the job and career market. Indeed the more likely a woman was to have a small family, a full panoply of appliances, and even domestic help, the less likely was she to work or have a career. In their investigation of Middletown, the Lynds discovered only one business-class wife who worked regularly. Middle-class wives were supposed to exercise their new freedom in bridge groups, women's clubs, and charity societies.

Working-class women and wives, however, worked out of necessity—the unmarried to support themselves and the married to earn the additional family income requisite to keep up with the Joneses in the consumption race. Although the total number of female workers did not rise appreciably in the 1920s, the percentage of working wives did. Unfortunately, most of the working women remained in the lowest paid lines of work: domestic service, textiles, clothing, sales and clerical help. In fact, whenever women entered a trade in large numbers, men fled, reinforcing the belief that woman's work was inferior and hence worth less, a "reality" confirmed by the substantial differentials in male and female wage rates. It should also be noted that black women, including married ones, worked more often than white women, and clustered at the lowest paid jobs, especially domestic service.

The American occupational universe meantime assumed a new dimension in the 1920s. Among the established blue-collar, manual occupations only construction labor increased in size; the labor force in manufacturing stabilized, and the number of workers in transportation and mining declined. Most of the labor force growth occurred in the tertiary service and trade sectors. The number of workers in retail trade rose by over 50 percent; in finance by over 66 percent; in civilian government service by about 45 percent; and in the service trades by over 10 percent. Labor in the United States was fast becoming "postindustrial" in composition, as the proportion of blue-collar manual workers began to decline in comparison to the number of service, sales, and clerical workers.

As demand for manual labor declined, the importance of education intensified. In response the average school term grew longer, regular attendance improved, and the secondary school population doubled as did the number of high school graduates, which climbed from 16.8 percent of the seventeen-year-olds in 1920 to 29 percent by 1930. College enrollments underwent a similar expansion, almost doubling in the course of the decade and reaching over 12 percent of the eighteen to twenty-one age group by 1930. As the latter figure suggests, collegiate education remained very much an elite privilege.

THE METROPOLITAN AGE

Cars, highways, and electric power all played a part in reshaping urban America. Motor transport and cheap electricity severed the relationship between city growth and internal waterways and railroads. As industries decentralized in order to locate closer either to their supplies or markets, large metropolitan districts emerged in new parts of the nation. Meat-packing, for example, deserted Chicago for new plants in such places as Omaha, Kansas City, and Denver. Though still concentrated in the Detroit–Toledo region, auto production, too, spread regionally, with Atlanta and Kansas City, among other cities, becoming major assembly centers. In the Southwest, Houston achieved metropolitan status as a result of the Texas oil boom, and on the West Coast, a combination of oil, films, and sun created the city of the future: Los Angeles.

From its origins as a major metropolis in the first decade and a half of the century, Los Angeles heralded the new style in American city-building: low densities of population scattered in large tracts of single-family homes in an area without a precisely demarcated central core. As the city's population passed one million in the 1920s, density of settlement remained low as the automobile liberated real estate developers from dependence on streetcar lines. Wherever land could be graded, streets paved, and water provided, subdevelopments of single-family homes grew. By 1929 Los Angeles was that new phenomenon, the noncity city: an agglomeration of suburban districts linked only by high-speed roads and streets. Los Angeles offered the ultimate in personal choice and mobility, for motor transport allowed all but the poor to select their place of work and area of residence. It also sanctified privacy since most residents owned their own homes, supplied their own transport, and lacked ties to a city center or common culture. (For caustic impressions of the emerging Los Angeles lifestyle one should scan the hardboiled detective stories of Raymond Chandler or the surrealistic novels of Nathanael West.)

The Los Angeles pattern of city-building was common to the 1920s. Everywhere millions of former urban residents now preferred the suburbs. Already the established central cities of the Northeast and North Central states were losing their more affluent residents to the suburbs. Indeed for those citizens able to afford cars and the cost of commutation, the dream of the "garden city" became a reality. The affluent fled the congested, dirty inner city for suburban retreats where bucolic old villages spread out from their core around the commuter railroad station and new residential streets were developed in patterns that blended with the landscape. Such carefully planned communities as Garden City, Long Island, and Riverside, Illinois, retained their physical centers and their separate identities from the central city.

For the great mass of metropolitan residents, however, there were no garden cities. The more fortunate moved into the commodious residencies vacated by the refugees to suburbia. But most of the working and lower-middle class, still dependent on public transit, spread outward from the city core along linear patterns determined by the transit lines. With land at a premium, the gridiron plan of development proved most economical, causing outlying city districts to share the architectural uniformity and gracelessness so characteristic of the first-generation streetcar suburbs of the 1880s. For most urbanites, then, the flight from the core was more an escape from city tensions than a retreat to Arcadia. In their case, the real suburban ideal had to await the end of World War II and the availability of liberal mortgage loan policies.

THE MANAGED ECONOMY

The national economy also progressed along well-worn paths. With the death of antitrust sentiment, American businessmen participated in an unprecedented consolidation movement. The 1920s saw some eight thousand hitherto independent mining and manufacturing enterprises disappear into combinations, and by 1928 five thousand public utilities had been swallowed by a few immense holding companies. Large banks displaced smaller ones; in 1929 1 percent of the nation's banks controlled 46 percent of all banking resources. Ten holding companies in 1930 dominated 70 percent of the electric power supply, and four firms controlled 94 percent of the tobacco trade. Furthermore the assets of large enterprises increased three times as rapidly as small ones; by 1920 the two hundred largest corporations owned nearly half of all corporate wealth and 22 percent of all national wealth.

Even smaller businesses joined the consolidation movement, as the government benevolently approved businessmen's attempts to evade price competition. With economic stability as its aim, the government encouraged the organization of private trade associations that fixed prices on an industry-wide basis, allocated markets, and set the terms for limited competition. Secretary of Commerce Herbert Hoover promoted this movement among smaller businessmen in the hope that they would use technology and scientific management to become as "efficient" as large enterprises.

By 1929 American businessmen had achieved concentration without pure monopoly. Scarcely an industry was dominated by a single firm. But unfettered competition never existed. Instead, in the basic industries a few large firms (usually four or five) competed with each other in an oligopolistic economic universe that bore little resemblance to the cherished American ideal of free enterprise. Indeed, the corporate economy of the 1920s resembled more the world of monopoly capitalism as described by Karl Marx than that of competitive enterprise as extolled by Adam Smith.

Perhaps more important for the future of the economy were certain fundamental changes in the structure of business enterprise. The development of a mass market and the automobile revolutionized retail trade. Mail-order houses, village general stores, and neighborhood merchants fell victim to merchandizing innovations. Robert Wood, president of Sears, Roebuck, explained the change. "When the automobile reached the masses," he said, "it made shopping mobile. In the great cities Sears located its stores well outside the main shopping district, on cheap land, usually on arterial highways, with ample parking space." Hence the origins of the suburban shopping plaza. Wood also explained the implications of a mass market. "The volume of Sears . . . gave opportunity for mass buying, the linking up of mass production and mass distribution. This produced even greater values to the consumer and increased volume."

Manufacturing, too, reacted to the stimulus of a mass urban market. In the course of building a substantial base of heavy industry, the great firms had accumulated an excess of capital technological know-how, and managerial talent. Now they had to adjust their resources to a dominant consumer market. Techniques had to be developed to produce goods and sell them to myriad millions of individual consumers rather than to a handful of familiar manufacturers who traditionally purchased a standard line of capital goods (machinery and materials). Dupont, for example, branched out from the production of munitions to the manufacture of chemicals and synthetics. Oil companies also entered the chemical and synthetics field. Similarly, General Electric and Westinghouse added mass-produced household appliances to their basic line of industrial generators and dynamos. Wherever companies possessed unused financial, managerial, and technical resources in declining production fields, they shifted them to new manufacturing lines. The result was the creation of conglomerate corporations that manufactured goods for totally unrelated markets.

By the 1920s corporate executives had also learned new managerial techniques. Alfred P. Sloan of General Motors and the Massachusetts Institute of Technology pioneered a technique to decentralize management. At G. M., Sloan established separate, autonomous production divisions for each of the firm's numerous car models. Each division retained responsibility for meeting its own production goals and target profits. At the top a central staff engaged in long-range planning that determined the allocation of the firm's basic economic resources. Once the resources were allocated, however, the production or line executives were free to make their own decisions. In practice this seemed to be the only method for inducing efficiency in giant corporations, some of which had annual budgets larger than those of American states or foreign nations. In time the decentralized General Motors pattern became the basic model for American corporate organization.

CULTURE: THE ALIENATED AND THE POPULAR
EMIGRÉS, BABBITTRY, AND MENCKENISM

As we have seen in an earlier chapter, the moral and cultural certainties that Americans inherited from the Victorian age had begun to crumble in the prewar years, a time one historian described as "An End to Innocence." But if innocence ended in these prewar years, optimism remained strong and intellectuals believed that art could liberate humanity. World War I, however, destroyed optimism, if not the trend to experimentation in cultural, artistic, and sexual behavior. Ezra Pound summed up postwar attitudes in two brief lines of poetry: "For an old bitch gone in the teeth,/for a botched civilization." And his equally innovative associate in poetry, T. S. Eliot, gave two of his most famous compositions titles that caught the postwar malaise: "The Hollow Men," and "The Wasteland."

Unable to find spiritual sustenance at home, many young Americans turned to Europe. The old student and bohemian quarters on the Left Bank in Paris became a home away from home for scores of creative Americans. It was in Paris that Ernest Hemingway blossomed as a novelist; one of his finest works, *The Sun Also Rises,* describes life among the expatriates. There Gertrude Stein cultivated her taste in experimental modern fiction, poetry, and art and labored to elevate the artistic sensibility of numerous young Americans.

The intellectuals who remained at home leveled a withering blast of criticism at the society that nurtured them. The sage of Baltimore, H. L. Mencken, left no aspect of America uncriticized. Democracy, marriage, the family, public education, even the clergy felt his scorn. He advised his peculiar American species, the *homo boobiens,* that husbands, instead of courting, should allow themselves to be matched with wives by the common hangman. To citizens who suggested that more gentlemen in politics would cure corruption, Mencken responded that such counsel was comparable to alleging that the cure for prostitution was to send more virgins into brothels. In the privacy of his study, however, Mencken labored to complete his justly famous history of the American language.

With less bite and many more words, Sinclair Lewis described middle-class urban life in the American Midwest. His novels—most notably *Main Street*—demonstrated that commonplace people act in a commonplace manner. And just as Mencken gave the nation the word "booboisie" to type the respectable middle class, Lewis made the name "Babbitt" synonymous with the unthinking real estate and business booster. Sherwood Anderson in *Winesburg, Ohio,* and Edward Arlington Robinson in his *Spoon River Anthology* showed idealized small-town America to be envious, avaricious, unneighborly, and culturally repressive.

NEW LIFESTYLES

The attack on Victorian lifestyles, limited to a small group of bohemians and intellectuals in the prewar years, took hold among the masses in the 1920s. Possibly because of fundamental changes in the American economic structure, orthodox ideals concerning family structure and male–female relations weakened. The sanctity of marriage, the parental dominance of the father, insistence on reflexive obedience by children to their parents, and the attitude that sex was functional, not pleasurable, all lost some of their traditional grip on human behavior.

The achievement of woman's suffrage after World War I seemed to signify a new era for females. Now free to vote at last, some women demanded the right to shape their own lives. No longer content with a middle-class world, where marriage was a condition of female existence, militant women shouted: "Come out of the kitchen, never darn a sock."

The damage done to traditional family structure and functions by the imperatives of urban-industrial life provided additional reasons for women to desert the hearth. Public schools increasingly replaced the home as the daytime custodian of the child; commercial bakeries, laundries, and eating places lessened the home's role as a center of domestic industry; the dance hall, the cinema, and the ballpark substituted as sources of amusement; the availability of cars pulled members away from the parlor; and smaller families lightened woman's customary household responsibilities. As families lost their age-old functions, mutual affection remained the sole link. This led some authorities on family life to suggest an arrangement that they labeled "companionate marriage," a relationship that could be severed by divorce in the absence of children whenever the affectionate bonds snapped. The pleasures of marriage became as important as the duties. As might be expected the number of divorces, usually instituted at the woman's behest, rose steadily, if not spectacularly.

But the American economy failed to offer adequate opportunities for women. Working-class females could readily obtain employment—as long as they were willing to accept either low wages or inferior positions. Middle-class women, however, found themselves frustrated; never a significant proportion in professional and business ranks, they now became even less likely to achieve professional or business careers—this at a time when their reasons and opportunities for doing so had grown.

Denied opportunity, American females organized a militant feminist movement, one that included a National Woman's Party. But the coalition of middle- and working-class women, radicals, moderates, and conservatives, which had achieved success with the ratification of the women's suffrage amendment, collapsed as the terms of battle changed. The more militant middle-class women demanded full legal equality; however, working-class women and their middle-class reform allies supported the numerous welfare laws that gave women special legal protection. Having achieved suffrage, radical females desired to use it to change the entire basis of male–female relationships; conservative women, however, had in many cases supported suffrage for precisely the opposite reasons: in their minds, female voters would preserve the sanctity of marriage and the family from dissolute, drunken, lower-class immigrant men. Beset by severe factionalism, the women's movement grew moribund.

Whether it was caused by women's economical and social frustration, the Freudian fad, or the sensuality promoted in movies and advertisements, a sexual revolution occurred in the 1920s. At a time when Americans learned that sexual repression in infancy was the root of adult neuroses and when advertisers transformed soap from a cleansing agent to an aphrodisiac, it was little wonder that sexual mores changed. Technology, too, did its share to change sexual mores. Sex in the backseat of a car was harder to control than on the living room sofa; and cheaper, more effective means of contraception lessened the risks of "illicit" sex. The subsequent findings of such investigators of sexual behavior as Alfred Kinsey indicated that the generation of women who came of age in the 1920s were more likely to have experienced premarital and extramarital sex than their ancestors. Supporting evidence could be found in the relative disappearance of brothels and streetwalkers from city streets. For, as women's sexual behavior changed, so, too, did men's. Though it was probably true, as the Englishman Lord Birkenhead observed, that "the proportion of frail to virtuous women is probably constant throughout the ages in any civilization," it was clear during the 1920s that the definition of virtue had changed somewhat.

The twenties also sanctified youth. Lionized by their elders, counseled by adults who behaved like adolescents, provided with cars, teased by advertisers, and stimulated by the movies, boys and girls created their own culture. Was it any wonder that parents, such as the ones the Lynds met in Middletown, felt that they had lost control over their offspring?

As what Edmund Wilson called "the spirit of hedonism" appeared to sweep all before it, a cultural clash erupted between the avant-garde and the orthodox. The reborn Ku Klux Klan acted as the spearhead in the traditionalist's struggle against innovation. The post-World War I Klan grew in the North as well as the South, the city as well as the country. And it directed its hostility more against Jews, Catholics, "new" immigrants, and "wets" (antiprohibitionists) than against blacks. It was also as concerned with maintaining prohibition, sexual purity, and traditional social and religious values as with defending white supremacy, the primary achievement of the original Klan.

Yet the cultural warfare that afflicted the 1920s was more than a struggle between city and country; it was fought out in the city as well as the countryside, and many urban KKK'ers, prohibitionists, and antifeminists proved more militant than their country cousins. Those who preferred the traditional truths crusaded aggressively against dirty books, filthy films, alcohol, gambling, dancing, sexual immorality, and even evolution. In the state of Tennessee, a high school biology teacher, one John Scopes, was accused of teaching Darwinian evolution to his students in violation of a state law; he was convicted in the now famous "monkey trial" in which William Jennings Bryan led the prosecution and Clarence Darrow the defense. Only because the countervailing forces were stronger in urban America and the innovators ultimately defeated the traditionalists has the cultural struggle of the 1920s seemed in retrospect largely a war between the city and the country.

TOWARD A MASS SOCIETY

Hard as the orthodox fought they could not stay the tide of change. The Klan was no match for the radio; Billy Sunday could not compete equally with Douglas Fairbanks, Al Jolson, Charlie Chaplin, Theda Bara, and Clara Bow. By the end of the 1920s radio and the movies had become the two most popular forms of entertainment.

By 1925 movies were the nation's fourth largest business enterprise with a capital investment of over $1½ billion. In 1927 some twenty thousand movie houses with a seating capacity of 18 million entertained almost one hundred million Americans weekly. Theaters were built to resemble palaces and temples, suggesting that they had become the real shrines at which twentieth-century Americans worshipped.

Across the nation the movie audiences glimpsed the same images and learned the same lessons. And, after 1927, when Al Jolson's "The Jazz Singer" proved that movies could be made to talk, Americans, regardless of their region, began to hear a uniform Hollywood dialect.

Radio had a similar impact on American life and culture. The first station to broadcast on a regular basis was KDKA in Pittsburgh, which began operations on Election Day 1920. By March 1927 the nation had 732 stations and Congress had established the Federal Radio Commission to allocate the limited number of wavelengths equitably. A year later at least ten million radio sets were in use reaching an audience estimated at

FLAMING YOUTH

featuring

COLLEEN MOORE

First National Pictures

An accomplished necker

A seasoned vamp

Learning to flirt

Her first red kiss

Her first Cocktail

Her first Cigarette

Hollywood in the twenties

Wisconsin Center for Film and Theater Research

fifty million or more. In 1926 two broadcast companies introduced the network system on a two-city basis; before long national networks produced radio shows heard over affiliates in every part of the nation. So effective was the network system in reaching a mass audience that in 1928 Henry Ford decided to spend a thousand dollars a minute to advertise his new model on radio.

THE HEYDAY OF SPORTS

The 1920s were the heyday of organized, competitive sports. Such names as George Herman "Babe" Ruth, Walter "Big Train" Johnson, Red Grange, Bronco Nagurski, Jack Dempsey, and Gene Tunney were familiar to Americans wherever they lived. Live and re-created radio broadcasts and sports newsreels brought millions of Americans a new breed of heroes. From mid-April to early October baseball fans jammed major and minor league ballparks to watch their favorite baseball players in action. No politician could hope to match the publicity and newspaper coverage that George Herman "Babe" Ruth achieved as first he smashed fifty-nine home runs in 1921 and then sixty in 1927. As a result of the "Babe's" popularity, the New York club in 1923 built and opened the cavernous Yankee Stadium, "the house that Ruth built."

When autumn came sports excitement did not abate. College football teams took up the slack, as each Saturday they waged their wars on countless athletic fields. Between late September and Thanksgiving of 1927, some thirty million fans paid over $50 million to watch college football. To accommodate the crowds eager to see the performances of such collegiate celebrities as Red Grange of Illinois and Bronco Nagurski of Minnesota, American universities built stadiums, sometimes derided as "lunar craters," that held between 70,000 and 100,000 spectators.

Boxing, however, remained the most popular working-class spectator sport, and blessed in the 1920s with such popular fighters as Jack Dempsey and Gene Tunney, the million-dollar gate became common. Golf also boomed as every Zenith City built its country club and the invincible Bobby Jones played the hero to the country-club set. Tennis, too, surged to popularity among the affluent as "Big Bill" Tilden dominated the best players France, England, and Germany turned out. Not until the 1960s would sports enjoy a boom of comparable proportions.

Now that Americans shopped at A&Ps and Sears stores, drove Fords and Chevys, brushed with Pepsodent, gargled with Listerine, smoked Luckies, read the *Reader's Digest* or *Saturday Evening Post,* watched the same movies, and listened to similar radio programs, a mass society came into being. Economic change as well as social and cultural innovations joined to weaken regional and sectional distinctions, and these new forces were reshaping the American nation in untold ways.

Babe Ruth
Wide World Photos

Red Grange, carrying the ball
Wide World Photos

12

The Politics of Prosperity
1921-1929

The New Era—this descriptive phrase seemingly distinguished the conservative politics of the 1920s from the preceding Progressive Era. The newness of the 1920s, however, derived from distinctive emphases and priorities, and not from an outright repudiation of progressive principles. In common with their predecessors, the political and business leaders of the 1920s shared a commitment to efficiency and order and a confident optimism that society could be improved. But they did not share the progressives' moralistic commitment and their dissatisfaction with the status quo.

Nor was the decade of the 1920s altogether a benign, confident period. The specific economic and social policies advanced by the nation's conservative leaders were also motivated by a nagging insecurity and a distinct fear of change. What ensued was, on the one hand, a close cooperative relationship between the business community and the federal government and, on the other, far-reaching restrictions on the rights of minorities and dissenters.

NEW ERA BUSINESS POLICIES

Their experiences during World War I had convinced many articulate Americans of the importance of positive federal action. The federal government justified its wartime spending and economic policies, which had stimulated national productivity and prosperity, as necessary but temporary expedients. In 1919–1920, moreover, the Wilson administration quickly dismantled the bureaucracy created to mobilize the nation for war. No demobilization and conversion plan was instituted to alleviate the declines in European war orders and federal spending. Yet most businessmen and political leaders drew two conclusions from their experiences with wartime economic planning: first, that federal policy should minimize industrial competition and promote national prosperity by reducing wasteful competition; second, that it should foster a more rationalized economy conducive to long-term management planning. These conclusions determined New Era economic policies.

In this sense, President Calvin Coolidge's statement that "the business of America is business" exemplified New Era priorities. Under the leadership of Secretary of Commerce Herbert Hoover, a Bureau of Standards and a Bureau of Domestic and Foreign Commerce were established. By compiling detailed statistical information—the Bureau of Standards on prices, production levels, and product lines within various industries and the Bureau of Domestic and Foreign Commerce on foreign trade and investment opportunities—both bureaus enabled businessmen to base production and investment decisions on the basis of solid information concerning domestic and foreign markets. At the same time the Department of Justice enforced antitrust laws more leniently. Instead of prosecuting companies, the Department relied on out-of-court consent decrees whereby, in return for nonprosecution, an accused corporation agreed to cease certain practices believed to be in restraint of trade. In addition, the Federal Trade Commission acted as if its principal responsibility was not the regulation but the protection of business. Thus, the commission, particularly under Coolidge's appointee as chairman, William E. Humphrey, often advised businessmen on how to avert antitrust prosecution. The FTC advocated greater cooperation among competing firms by urging them to adopt codes of business practice and ethics, which involved exchanging information on sales, costs, and production in order to avert "unfair" competition. The FTC, Humphrey believed, should cease being "an instrument of oppression and disturbance and injury instead of a help to business" or a "publicity bureau to spread socialistic propaganda."

The Rogers Act of 1924 further expressed New Era priorities. The consular and diplomatic services were merged into a single Foreign Service, merit provisions for entrance into the foreign service through examination were strengthened, and the salaries of Foreign Service officers were increased. The basic purpose was to professionalize the consular service by reducing patronage appointments. A more efficient and expert service, it was believed, would provide the assistance and information essential to extending private export and investment opportunities.

A similar conviction underlay the Budget and Accounting Act of June 10, 1921, creating two separate agencies—a Bureau of the Budget to assist in the development of a comprehensive federal budget and a General Accounting Office to review how appropriations were spent. Until 1921, the budgetary requests of the various federal departments and agencies had not been incorporated into a single federal budget. Inevitably, then, federal expenditures were not correlated with anticipated federal revenues. Instead, each department (for example, agriculture) submitted its appropriation requests to the respective congressional committee. Given the self-interest this fostered, this procedure only encouraged parochialism and obstructed budgetary planning. The sharp increase in federal spending during World War I dramatically confirmed this system's inefficiency and led the Congress and President Wilson to advocate a central budgetary bureau to coordinate revenue with spending. President Wilson's insistence on his right to control the proposed bureau, however, created an impasse and prevented passage of the budget bill. Harding's less abrasive relations with Congress and his willingness to compromise by insisting only on the president's right to appoint the director of the bureau led to enactment of the law instituting more businesslike and efficient federal budgeting and accounting procedures.

A CONSERVATIVE POLITICS

The decidedly conservative character of New Era politics—if masked by the term new—indirectly dramatizes the limits of the Progressive Era political reforms. Despite the sound and fury of the progressives' political dissent, the so-called Old Guard's influence within the Congress and the major parties had not been substantially affected. Accordingly, conservatives during the 1920s effectively utilized their institutional base to retain the legislative initiative and to determine the selection of candidates and the party platform. In addition, adopting advertising techniques increasingly employed by private business, American politics became more packaged and American politicians more image conscious.

The ablest practitioners of this public relations politics were Presidents Warren Harding and Calvin Coolidge. Whatever their limitations as statesmen and political thinkers—neither had a vision of a just society or an appreciation of fundamental problems—both Harding and Coolidge were masterful politicians. Nor were they merely accidental presidents. Both men attained the presidency and commanded popular support by astutely using rhetoric to cultivate and project an image of sound, responsive leadership. Harding's speeches, as pompous and meaningless in content as they often were, were impressive political performances. His now-infamous August 1920 speech in which he popularized the phrase "normalcy" best reflects his image politics. In this speech, Harding maintained that "America's present need is not heroism but healing, not agitation but adjustment, not surgery but serenity, not the dramatic but the dispassionate, not experiment but equipose, not submergence in internationality but sustainment in triumphant nationality."

This studied use of alliteration to create a balanced effect, to appear as a moderate statesman averse to extremes but committed to unspecified positive action and leadership, exemplified the essence of Harding's political strategy. Harding's strength at the deadlocked Republican convention of 1920—deadlocked because neither General Leonard Wood nor Illinois governor, Frank Lowden, the two front-running candidates, could obtain the nomination—and the bitterness of their preconvention contest stemmed from his ability to appear moderate and noncontroversial. Acceptable to supporters of both front-runners, Harding also appealed to a party leadership committed to nominating a sufficiently conservative, but noncontroversial candidate. Harding cultivated an image of accessibility and responsiveness—by opening the White House to tourists, by joining lodges and playing golf, and by holding regular press conferences. Harding indirectly exploited Woodrow Wilson's image of secrecy and unilateralism, first to win the presidency and later to retain the initiative for his policies.

This cultivated image of responsiveness and moderation masked Harding's conservative politics. Having pledged during the 1920 campaign to bring the "best brains" to Washington, Harding appointed several highly intelligent principled conservatives to the Cabinet—Herbert Hoover as secretary of commerce, Andrew Mellon as secretary of the treasury, and Charles Evans Hughes as secretary of state. Other appointees such as Albert Fall as secretary of the interior, and Harry Daugherty as attorney general were neither intelligent nor principled. Sharing a narrow conception of the public interest, these men differed in abilities and conceptions of their responsibilities. Their principal differences were that Hoover, Mellon, and Hughes did not seek to enrich themselves through federal office, while Fall and Daugherty did. The glaring corruption, which surfaced with the series of scandals involving Teapot Dome, the administration of the Veterans Bureau, and the office of Alien Property Custodian, was not, however, fundamentally inconsistent with the administration's more general special interest politics.

Nor did Coolidge's political style differ. Far less the politician than Harding, Coolidge also projected an image of sound moderation to undercut pressure for legislative reform and to commend conservative economic principles. Inheriting the scandals of Harding's administration, Coolidge finessed the corruption issue by firing Harding's tainted attorney general, Harry Daugherty. Quickly dissociating his presidency from the Harding scandals, Coolidge succeeded in making the revelations of 1923 and 1924 involving Teapot Dome, the Alien Property Custodian, the Veterans Bureau, and the Federal Prison Administration appear simply as the independent and irresponsible actions of individuals who had exploited Harding's trust and naïveté. Thus Coolidge restored faith in the integrity of the administration and the Republican party and revealed an astute political sense. The slogans associated with his 1924 campaign and his presidential style further express his image-consciousness: "Silent Cal," "Keep Cool with Coolidge," "Coolidge or Chaos."

Ironically, Herbert Hoover, the ablest and most sophisticated of the New Era presidents, was ultimately the least popular. Hoover came to the presidency having a reputation as the "Great Engineer" and the "Great Humanitarian," images based not on press agentry but on positive actions and a long distinguished public and private career. In contrast to Harding and Coolidge, Hoover had a definite vision of a better America; he intended through the presidency to implement that vision and chart the direction of American politics. He failed in that effort, though not for want of trying. His failure derived principally from intellectual rigidity, disdain for democratic politics, and the narrow political options that followed the economic crisis of 1929.

NEW ERA PRIORITIES

Given the basic conservatism of New Era presidents and their conviction that the society was fundamentally sound, it is not surprising that little effort was made to confront basic social and economic problems. Confronted by an economic recession—dating from 1920—and a serious problem of unemployment, the Harding administration and congressional leaders, most notably Congressman Albert Johnson of Washington, supported immigration restriction legislation. Immigration from Europe, which had temporarily been cut off by World War I, in 1920 mounted to about 900,000. A combination of groups thereafter lobbied for stricter legislation to limit immigration. These groups included nativists who since the 1880s had actively sought to curb immigration; returning veterans who were dissatisfied with the postwar unemployment problem and were distressed that many immigrants who had not fought had been able to retain employment; and conservatives who believed that immigrants were the principal cause of the flurry of strikes that beset the nation (there were approximately thirty-six-hundred involving four million workers in 1919 alone).

Responding to these pressures, Congress in 1920 passed an emergency immigration bill. President Wilson vetoed this bill, but Warren Harding's election and the Republican platform pledge removed this obstacle to a restrictionist immigration policy. The resultant Emergency Quota Act of May 1921 limited the annual number of immigrants admitted to

350,000. It also set ethnic quotas for those to be admitted from each European country equal to 3 percent of the foreign-born population native to that country residing in the United States as determined by the 1910 census. An emergency experimental measure, the act was to last only one year. Congress, however, extended it until enacting a modified version in 1924.

The 1921 act significantly reduced immigration. Subsequent immigration trends resulting in higher numbers of immigrants from southern and eastern European countries moved restrictionists to demand additional legislation. In 1922, for example, 50 percent of the quota for northern European countries had been unfilled, while 95 percent of the quota allotted for Italy, the Balkans, and Russia had been filled. Such statistics inspired the more stringent and racialist National Origins Act of May 1924. The Act further limited the number of immigrants admitted annually to 150,000 and retained with significantly altered allotment procedures the principle of ethnic quotas. Until 1927, quotas were to be based on 2 percent of the *foreign-born* population in the United States as determined by the 1890 census. After 1927, quota allotments would be based on 2 percent of the *national origins* of the U.S. population as determined by the 1920 census. Shifting the basis for quota allotments would reduce the admissible number of eastern and southern Europeans and thereby preserve the Anglo-Saxon character of the American population. Immigration from eastern and southern Europe had not become significant until after the 1880s; by basing quotas on "national origins" the English quota would be increased since descendants of English immigrants constituted a larger percentage of the native-born population.

The respectability of racialist beliefs (a quota system directed against Jews and Catholics was also introduced by many Ivy League colleges during the 1920s to determine eligibility for admission) also determined the national response toward blacks. Intense racial prejudices gave rise to a rebirth of the Ku Klux Klan and fanned the popularity of a film eulogizing the Klan, *The Birth of a Nation*.

Initially reorganized as a social and fraternal organization, the Klan espoused antiblack, anti-Semitic, anti-Catholic, and antiimmigrant prejudices. Its membership steadily increased, reaching over two million by 1924 (some sources estimate membership at five million). The reorganized Klan actively entered state politics and soon commanded nationwide influence (particularly in the states of Indiana and Oregon). The Klan's political clout was further reflected in the 1924 presidential contest and conventions.

Appalled by the Klan's crude violence, overt anti-Semitism, and anti-Catholicism, northern Democrats introduced a resolution at the 1924 Democratic National Convention specifically condemning the Klan. Led by William Jennings Bryan, southerners and rural Democrats defeated this resolution by one vote. The Republicans temporized on the Klan issue at their convention, commending Klan principles but not its methods. During the campaign, Coolidge remained silent on the Klan issue while his vice-presidential running mate, Charles Dawes, indirectly sought Klan support. Moreover, when in 1925 the Klan announced a parade in Washington, D.C. to demonstrate its strength, Coolidge absented himself from the city so that he would neither be required to review the parade nor publicly condemn the Klan.

The major parties' response to the lynching issue during the New Era scarcely befitted a democratic nation. Although the Republicans adopted specific platform planks at their 1920, 1924, and 1928 conventions supporting antilynching legislation, and although Presidents Harding and Coolidge formally expressed support for such a measure, Republican congressmen and presidents did not press for such legislation. The House passed an antilynching bill in 1922 and again in 1924. Both times the bill was killed in the Senate as the result of a southern-led filibuster.

Not surprisingly, then, no challenge was raised to the system of segregation that had been institutionalized in the South. Indeed, at the 1928 Democratic National Convention held in Houston, Texas, when northern forces in the party successfully overcame southern and rural opposition to the nomination of urban Irish Catholic Al Smith, the few black delegates who attended were physically separated from the other delegates by a chicken-wire fence.

This antipathy towards blacks and immigrants reflected not only strong racial prejudices but a basic aversion to change. The conviction that American institutions were under alien and radical attack persisted throughout the 1920s. The dramatic wartime and immediate postwar violations of civil liberties were not repeated; nonetheless, restrictions on the political activities of radicals continued. Thus during the 1920s, thirty-nine state legislatures either enacted or extended anarchist or criminal syndicalist laws. Although the atmosphere was less tense and the prospect of revolutionary change more distant, the U.S. Supreme Court in *Gitlow* v. *New York* (1925) and *Whitney* v. *California* (1927) upheld the constitutionality of such laws. Free speech was not absolute, the Court reasoned; states had the right to restrict forms of speech which might incite unlawful acts, even though the danger of the commission of such acts was not imminent.

The Supreme Court's aversion to radicalism followed from its changed personnel—indeed, during his brief presidency Warren Harding appointed four conservatives to the court, including William Howard Taft as chief justice. The predilections resulting in these appointments also determined federal surveillance policy. During the early 1920s the FBI continued its surveillance of domestic radical organizations despite the absence of specific statutory authority—radical politics constituted no federal crime, and the Espionage and Sedition Acts (the latter repealed by Congress in 1921) applied only during wartime. Unable to use the information it gained for federal prosecution, the FBI turned the results of its investigations over to state authorities or private employers. The extralegality of this move created a cause célèbre in 1924 when, coincident with disclosures that FBI agents had instituted mail checks and illegally entered the offices of congressmen investigating the Teapot Dome scandal, the question of the FBI's abuses of power assumed dramatic impact. Attorney General Harry Daugherty's forced resignation in late March 1924 (owing to his refusal to testify in a congressional investigation relating to a scandal involving the Justice Department) and Coolidge's nomination of Harlan Fiske Stone as attorney general on April 2, 1924, led to a wholesale revamping of the Department of Justice. Stone's first actions were to terminate the FBI's extralegal actions and to professionalize the bureau. To accomplish these objectives he appointed J. Edgar Hoover to head the bureau, abolished the wartime-created General Intelligence Division, prohibited wiretapping, and limited FBI investigations to cases involving violations of federal laws.

NEW ERA ECONOMIC POLICIES

New Era economic policies were also based on a belief in an essentially harmonious society. There were, however, conflicting views of the proper responsibilities of Congress and the president. But this conflict was more a dispute over methods of determining policy than a disagreement over fundamental principles. In 1922, for example, Congress formally stipulated the terms by which the European war debts were to be renegotiated, conditions that negated the Harding Administration's desire for flexibility. Congress's sensitivity to its prerogatives to define the nation's foreign policy was but one legacy of the abrasive legislative-executive relations stemming from President Wilson's unilateral conduct of foreign policy.

There was, nonetheless, a broad legislative-executive consensus on the major economic issues of New Era politics—i.e., the tariff, agricultural relief, and tax questions. Tariff policy was the central political issue of the early 1920s. In contrast to the low tariff principles of the Progressive Era, New Era tariff policy sought to satisfy businessmen and not consumers. This shift in sentiment flowed from a decline in exports following the war, the increasing foreign competition with the restoration of European peacetime production, and the postwar economic recession of 1920 to 1922.

In 1921 Congress enacted an Emergency Tariff Act, a temporary measure to alleviate wartime-created pressures by raising tariff rates. In September 1922 the trend toward high tariffs was made permanent. Responding to continued lobbying efforts by industrial and agricultural interests, Congress enacted the Fordney-McCumber Act raising U.S. tariff rates to an average ad valorem level of 33 percent. Agrarian congressmen had concluded that high tariffs would increase domestic agricultural prices. Agricultural prices did not rise, however. American farmers sold on a world market and their commodities did not face competition at home from foreign food imports.

The organized farmers' basic conservatism during the 1920s, specifically that of the Farm Bureau, also shaped their general legislative objectives. Concerned over falling farm prices throughout the 1920s, farm representatives nonetheless believed this to be principally a marketing problem—a perception that determined their specific legislative strategy. Congressional enactment of such legislation as the Packers and Stockyards Act of 1921, the Grain Futures Act of 1921—which provided for government regulation of stockyards and grain exchanges—or the Capper-Volstead Act of 1921—which exempted agricultural cooperatives from antitrust prosecution—neither alleviated the serious economic plight nor responded to the interests of the voiceless small farmers. The Capper-Volstead Act, a central legislative objective of organized farmers, only assisted those whose principal economic difficulties stemmed from high overhead costs; cooperatives could purchase materials at wholesale prices and then more efficiently market and distribute farm commodities.

These measures ultimately failed to insure agrarian prosperity. American farmers continued to experience economic distress—distress caused by falling commodity prices at the same time as the prices of the products they purchased stabilized or increased. This dilemma eventually led the organized farm community to support a bill introduced in 1924 by Congressman Gilbert Haugen of Iowa and Senator Charles McNary of Oregon, and drafted by George Peek and Hugh Johnson, president and general counsel respectively of the Moline Plow Company. The McNary-Haugen Bill proposed a complicated two-price system to increase domestic prices of selected agricultural commodities. A federal export corporation, the Federal Farm Board, would be created to purchase agricultural commodities on the domestic market when they fell below a parity point. (The parity point was arrived at by balancing purchasing power and income based on the years 1905–1914.) The corporation in turn would sell these commodities at the lower world market prices. The losses involved would be covered by an equalization fee imposed on the domestic processor of that commodity. In the case of wheat, this meant that millers would pay the fee. Attractive because it promised to increase agricultural prices without controlling production, the McNary-Haugen plan would be the farmer's equivalent of the protective tariff for industry, a safeguard from the effects of world competition.

The bill did not pass when first proposed in 1924. Redrafted in 1926 to make it more acceptable to southern Congressmen by incorporating tobacco and cotton as special commodities, the revised bill passed Congress in 1927 and again in 1928. President Coolidge vetoed the bill both times, objecting to the principle of federal protection and its special interest nature.

Coolidge's opposition to McNary-Haugen did not end agricultural protest about what had become the intertwined issue of federal tariff policy. Following his election to the presidency in 1928, Herbert Hoover inherited this legacy. Opposed to McNary-Haugen, Hoover nonetheless supported some form of federal relief to farmers. Calling Congress into special session, the president proposed to revise tariff policy and assist farmers. Rather than pass a combined bill, the Congress instead considered the tariff and agricultural relief questions separately and in June 1929 approved the basic outlines of Hoover's agricultural relief policy. The Agricultural Marketing Act of 1929 created a Federal Farm Board having control over a revolving fund of $500 million from which to make loans to cooperatives, associations, and certain stabilization corporations. The board was empowered to use these funds to buy, store, or sell commodities to avert a surplus. The measure's purpose was to aid and stimulate cooperative marketing and to control seasonal surpluses. As such, it reflected the optimistic conviction of New Era policymakers that a serious agricultural problem did not exist.

The Congress went well beyond Hoover's tariff recommendations. Extensive lobbying by interested manufacturing groups combined with the economic decline following the October 1929 Stock Market Crash led to enactment of the highly protective Hawley-Smoot Tariff Act of June 1930. This act raised the average ad valorem rate to 48 percent (from the 33 percent level of Fordney-McCumber) and specifically raised tariff levels on 890 different products. This tariff bill, however, did little to stem the nation's economic decline, served to worsen international trade, and complicated the president's attempts to promote economic development through international cooperation.

A limited conception of national responsibility also underlay federal tax policy. Prewar income and corporation taxes, which had increased with the sharpened need for revenue to finance World War I, came under review during the New Era. Secretary of the Treasury Andrew Mellon, supported by Presidents Harding and Coolidge, advocated reducing both federal expenditures and the high wartime tax levels. Operating on the premise that lower taxes would encourage businessmen to invest and that the economy would thereby benefit, Mellon eventually secured congressional approval for significant reductions in federal taxes on the wealthy. At first, Congress responded cautiously and by the Revenue Act of 1921 reduced the maximum surtax to 50 percent and repealed the excess profits tax. Then, by the Revenue Acts of 1926 and 1928, Mellon secured congressional elimination of the gift tax and further reductions in the inheritance and the surtax levels of wealthy individuals and corporations. The consequent tax reductions were such that by 1928 a millionaire paid only one-third the taxes he had paid in 1921.

DISSENT DURING THE 1920s

Neither the limited conception of the national interest in general nor the social and economic policies of New Era presidents in particular went wholly unchallenged during the 1920s. Voices of dissent, however, were muted. The Socialist party, for example, virtually disappeared during the 1920s. Moreover, in contrast to the 1912 and 1916 campaigns, the influence of reformers at the major party conventions and the ensuing presidential campaigns was minimal. Nomination and election turned on personality, not issues. Thus, in 1920 both parties nominated safe and conventional candidates, the Republicans Warren G. Harding and the Democrats James M. Cox. Moreover, Cox ran a lackluster campaign, distinguished principally by the Democratic nominee's unsuccessful efforts to establish an identity separate from the Wilson administration. Instead, Harding and the Republicans conducted an effective nonissue campaign, capitalizing on often-contradictory but widespread hostility to Wilson's leadership. Republican strategy successfully appealed to elements that could coalesce only in their opposition to Wilson. By 1920 there were many embittered segments of the population: many German-, Italian-, and Irish-Americans were embittered by Wilson's wartime and peace policies; civil libertarians by the administration's wartime suppression of individual liberties; internationalists by the compromises of international principles of the Treaty of Versailles; nationalists by the treaty's undue compromises of national sovereignty; and conservatives by government controls and regulation of the economy. This strategy succeeded as Harding polled over 60 percent of the popular vote. At the same time, Republican control in the House increased to 303-131 and in the Senate to 59-37.

Harding and the Republicans had won on a national tide of protest. The 1920 election, however, was no mandate for "normalcy," whatever Harding meant by that term. Nor did it constitute popular affirmation for the basically conservative policies pursued by the Republican administration and Congress. The persistence of economic distress and the unpopularity of many of the measures enacted during the subsequent term of Congress, led disaffected reformers, labor leaders, and agrarians to attempt to combine forces. In February 1922, reform groups formed the Conference on Progressive Political Action (CPPA). Antipathetic to third party politics, the CPPA also lacked a specific reform program except the desire to alter the Administration's conservative priorities. In addition, these groups' principles diverged widely: organized labor sought an end to court injunctions against strikes while farmers desired direct governmental assistance. Not surprisingly, then, the reformers could not agree to form a third party and instead worked within the two major parties. This strategy appeared to offer potential for success. In the 1922 elections, twelve of the sixteen gubernatorial candidates endorsed by the CPPA were elected, progressive Republicans won resounding victories (LaFollette winning by 300,000 votes in Wisconsin), and the Democrats cut sharply into the Republican majorities gaining 7 seats in the Senate and 76 in the House. Thus, the new Senate was composed of 51 Republicans, 43 Democrats, and 2 Farmer-Laborites; the new House seated 225 Republicans and 205 Democrats.

The 1924 conventions, however, demonstrated the naïveté of the

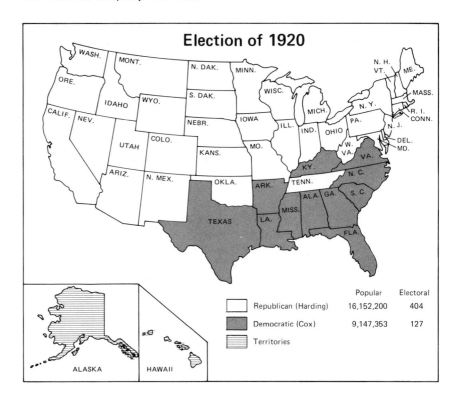

Election of 1920

	Popular	Electoral
Republican (Harding)	16,152,200	404
Democratic (Cox)	9,147,353	127
Territories		

ALASKA   HAWAII

reformers' hope to influence the decisions of the two major parties. The Republicans nominated the conservative Calvin Coolidge, who had acceded to the presidency following Harding's death on August 2, 1923. Efforts by labor leaders at the Republican Convention to secure a plank decrying the extensive use of court injunctions in labor strikes, and by other reformers to obtain agricultural relief, low tariff, and antitrust policy planks, failed as the Republicans adopted a safely conservative platform.

Nor were the reformers more effective at the deadlocked Democratic Convention of 1924. The Democrats divided sharply over whether to condemn the Klan, but adopted a vaguely worded but decidedly conservative platform that contained planks hinting at social and economic reform. The 1924 Democratic Convention was distinguished by the bitter division between the supporters of Wilson's former Secretary of the Treasury William McAdoo and then New York Governor Al Smith. These divisions, however, derived not from conflict over economic and social reform but from social policy questions—focusing specifically on Al Smith's Catholicism, opposition to prohibition, and urbanism. For a time, it appeared that these divisions would destroy the Democratic party. Only on the 103rd ballot was the deadlock broken with a compromise candidate, John Davis, a conservative corporation counsel.

Having been rebuffed by both major parties, only then did the progressive adherents of the CPPA decide to form a third party, the Progressive party. Nominating Robert LaFollette as their presidential candidate at their July convention in Cleveland, the Progressives adopted a platform that rehashed the antimonopoly and democracy battle themes of the Progressive Era. Its planks included more stringent antitrust laws, tariff reduction, nationalization of railroads, popular election of the president and judges, national referenda, and curbs on the Supreme Court. Hampered by a lack of funds, by internal divisions, and by an effective Republican campaign strategy identifying LaFollette with radicalism and suggesting that the alternative to a vote for Coolidge was chaos, LaFollette and the Progressives suffered defeat in 1924. Coolidge polled 15,718,211 (54 percent) popular and 382 electoral votes to Davis' 8,385,283 (28.8 percent) popular and 136 electoral votes and LaFollette's 4,831,289 (16.6 percent) popular and 13 electoral votes. (LaFollette carried only his own state of Wisconsin.)

Their lateness in organizing a third party and their failure to develop an effective grass roots organization earlier did not mean that the prospects for third party reform were untenable. LaFollette received fewer votes than Theodore Roosevelt had in 1912; nonetheless, in 1924 he outpolled Democratic candidate Davis in thirteen states. His Wisconsin victory confirmed the importance of an effective organization and

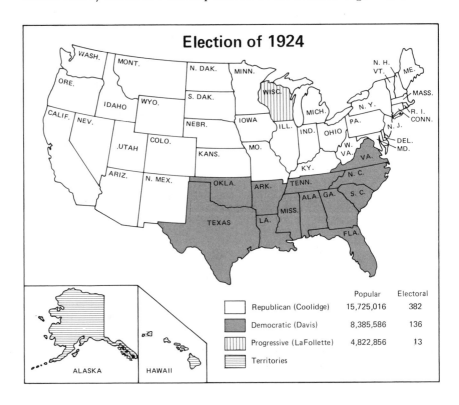

Election of 1924

	Popular	Electoral
Republican (Coolidge)	15,725,016	382
Democratic (Davis)	8,385,586	136
Progressive (LaFollette)	4,822,856	13
Territories		

ALASKA   HAWAII

a positive identity. Ultimately, the Progressive party's demise stemmed from its adherents' ambivalent commitment to permanent third party politics. No attempt was made before, during, or after the campaign to develop a structured party organization. Indeed, in February 1925, when the Progressives reconvened in Chicago, they failed to decide on future strategy and adjourned *sine die*.

HERBERT HOOVER AND THE NEW ERA

The conservatism of New Era politics derived from the relative prosperity of the 1920s, intense social and racial concerns, and the ambivalence and hesitancy of reformist and dissident groups. And it was only confirmed by Herbert Hoover's triumphant election in 1928. The new Republican president's victory confirmed the values of old-stock, rural, Protestant Americans. In contrast to the Democratic candidate, Al Smith, who personified the sidewalks of New York and their teeming "new immigrant" masses, extolled Roman Catholicism, and demanded the repeal of prohibition, Hoover symbolized the rolling prairie of his native Iowa, the Protestant ethic, and the virtue of prohibition. Much more consonant with the dominant cultural values and symbols, Hoover not only swept the North and the West; he also dented the hitherto solid, one-party, Democratic South.

The new president not only symbolized the most cherished traditional American myths and symbols, but he also personified the New Era's highest political and economic values. A successful international engineer, multimillionaire, famous overseas famine relief administrator, and experienced public official, Hoover endlessly extolled the necessity for government-business cooperation. The federal government, he believed, should assist private businessmen to build an economic system in which an exploitative, cutthroat nineteenth-century capitalism would be replaced by a public-spirited, service oriented, cooperative twentieth-century capitalism. In Hoover's conception, government would encourage, not coerce, business; it would release, not restrain, private accumulative capitalism for the benefit of mankind.

Hoover, moreover, believed implicitly in the confident optimism expressed by President Coolidge in a December 1925 message to Congress in which the president observed that "the general condition is one of progress and prosperity. Here and there are comparatively small and temporary difficulties . . . but . . . the results demonstrate that we are going in the right direction." And Hoover reaffirmed that belief in his acceptance speech at the 1928 Republican Convention, stressing that "We in America are nearer to the final triumph over poverty than ever before in the history of any land." Hoover intended to dedicate his presidency to the achievement of that ultimate victory over human want. Instead, as we will see in the next section, he was to preside over the worst economic catastrophe in United States history.

13

Economic Hegemony and Foreign Policy 1921-1929

Despite their victories over Wilson and the Democrats in the fight over the Versailles Treaty, Republican leaders in the 1920s found it impossible to return to the comfortable and undemanding foreign policies of the prewar era. The First World War had wrought too many changes to permit the United States to ignore the rest of the world in ostrich-like fashion. The war left tangled questions of war debts and reparations, and the nation faced a potentially dangerous and costly naval arms race with Great Britain and Japan. Above all, as the world's foremost economic power and creditor, the United States necessarily had a vital interest in international peace, stability, and prosperity. If the nation chose not to embrace Wilsonian internationalism and could not revert to a nineteenth-century form of Continentalism, some new course had to be charted.

Historians have disagreed sharply about the character of American foreign policy during the 1920s. Liberal scholars branded Republican policies as isolationist, in contrast to the internationalism of the preceding Wilson era and that of the subsequent New Deal period. Conversely, radical writers, always conscious of economic factors, have seen the 1920s, not as isolationist, but as a decade of vigorous overseas economic expansion by the United States in an effort to create an open-door world dominated by efficient American businesses. Perhaps the most accurate description of the diplomacy of the decade, however, is that it was neither isolationist nor vigorously internationalist. Republican foreign policies reflected a cautious internationalism that sought to serve American interests by promoting a peaceful and stable world order without assuming any binding political responsibilities or treaty obligations.

STATESMEN OF THE TWENTIES

Charles Evans Hughes served first Harding and then Coolidge as secretary of state from 1921 to 1925. A brilliant and impressive-appearing man but a narrow legalist, the former Supreme Court justice acted cautiously to obtain practical objectives. Both Harding and Coolidge deferred to him in foreign affairs. By no means an isolationist, for he had favored membership in the League of Nations with reservations, Hughes believed that he must avoid divisive fights with the Senate over foreign policy. Consequently he dropped the League issue and sought by other means to serve the national interest. Perhaps he could have attempted more, but the climate seemed most unfavorable.

Frank B. Kellogg, secretary of state from 1925 to 1929, was a pedestrian chief of the State Department. A former senator from Minnesota, Kellogg was a cautious and sometimes naïve man. Dubbed a "nervous Nellie" by reporters, he constantly looked over his shoulder to avoid affronting the powerful isolationists in the Senate. In any case, President Coolidge, who had little interest in foreign affairs, probably would not have supported him in any really daring moves entailing binding diplomatic obligations by the United States.

Kellogg's successor, Henry L. Stimson, secretary of state from 1929 to 1933, came from a sterner mold. He believed that the United States must act vigorously to uphold the new international moral and legal order established at the end of the First World War. However, he found himself restrained by his pacifistically inclined chief, President Hoover.

Senator William E. Borah, the maverick "Lion of Idaho," led the isolationists in Congress. In many ways he was naïve and ignorant about foreign affairs. He viewed the League of Nations as a "traitorous scheme" and a supporter of it as one who "no longer wants an American Republic, no longer believes in nationalism, and no longer desires to see the American flag a little higher than that of any other nation." Borah felt convinced that the true course for the United States lay in remaining fully independent and unentangled in foreign affairs while setting a moral example to the rest of the world. He and his followers saw most State Department moves toward cooperation with other nations as snares and traps. From 1924 on, as chairman of the powerful Senate Committee on Foreign Relations, Borah presented a key roadblock to the State Department. The department found him baffling and unpredictable, intensely suspicious, and boastful that his private sources of information were superior to its intelligence gathering.

THE WASHINGTON CONFERENCE AND NAVAL ARMS LIMITATIONS

World War I left the world on the verge of a great naval arms race. The war had eliminated the German and Russian navies as major factors in world power and had left France weakened. Great Britain, the United States, and Japan ranked in that order as the three naval giants. Each had plans for large-scale naval construction but each also faced insistent demands at home for economy. The United States during the war had embarked on an ambitious construction program, one which if not matched by its rivals would give it naval hegemony. Neither Britain nor Japan could permit that, and although they were poorer economically, they felt compelled to match American expenditures.

But American naval supremacy was more potential than actual, for the American public and Congress felt disinclined to tax and spend for military ends. Peace groups especially questioned the need for a huge navy, following upon a war to end wars, and urged that an international conference be called to solve the problem by arms limitations. Senator Borah enthusiastically endorsed naval limitations and introduced a resolution in Congress for a 50 percent reduction in naval building and the convening of a conference of the major naval powers.

Although resentful of Senate intrusion into foreign policy making and apparently eager to continue naval expansion until parity had been achieved with the British, the Harding administration gave way before the growing public clamor. Secretary Hughes invited the major naval powers to meet in Washington at a conference that had been broadened to consider Far Eastern problems as well. Hughes then carefully culti- vated the Senate and included Republicans and Democrats in the dele- gation to the conference in order to ensure subsequent approval of any agreements that might be made.

The Washington Conference opened on November 12, 1921, the day after solemn Armistice Day ceremonies interring America's Unknown Soldier at Arlington National Cemetery. Hughes boldly seized the initia- tive in his opening address: "the way to disarm is to disarm." He stunned the delegates by proposing specific reductions, rather than merely utter- ing the expected pious generalities. Capital warship construction, except for replacements, should be suspended and the United States should scrap twenty-eight vessels for a total of 845,740 tons; Britain twenty-four ships for 583,000 tons; and Japan sixteen craft for 435,328 tons. Naval experts listened in stunned silence but the press in America and abroad hailed the speech as one of the most notable in human annals. At last, it seemed, a means had been offered to lift the arms burden and to insure peace.

Because Britain, the United States, and Japan all preferred to avoid a costly arms race, Hughes obtained his goal. The Five Power Pact signed at the conference proclaimed a ten-year hiatus in capital ship construction and established a 5:5:3 ratio in battleships and aircraft carriers for the United States, Great Britain, and Japan in that order. France and Italy obtained 1.75 ratios each. Japan received compensation for its smaller tonnage allocation by Anglo-American pledges not to fortify further advanced bases west of Hawaii, east of Singapore, and north of Australia. Japan thereby was left virtually unchallengeable in the waters around its home islands.

Other agreements at the Washington Conference sought to stabilize the Pacific area and to preserve the Open Door policy in China. Americans for some time had opposed renewal of the Anglo-Japanese Alliance since there was apprehension about its significance in case of a Japanese-American war. The British dominions, Canada and Australia, opposed continuation of the alliance for similar reasons. Consequently the British and the Japanese, the latter reluctantly, agreed to scrap the alliance and to replace it with a loose consultative agreement. The Four Power Pact also signed at the conference pledged Britain, the United States, Japan, and France to respect each other's rights in the Pacific and to consult about problems endangering the peace and stability of the area. This innocuous pact had no enforcement provisions and committed no power to do more than to talk about Pacific problems. In the Nine Power Pact, the signatories agreed to respect the independence and integrity of China and to observe the principles of the Open Door. In connected settlements, Japan restored Shantung to China and promised withdrawal from Siberia. Japan also agreed to grant the United States cable rights on Yap, one of the small Pacific islands it had seized from Germany.

Although the Senate approved these treaties, it attached a reservation to the Four Power Pact disavowing any obligations upon the United States to uphold the agreements by force or alliance. It was precisely that attitude, of course, that made these and other treaties concluded in the 1920s worthless when challenged by aggressors. Americans wrongly assumed that it was enough merely to state ideals and principles, and that peace and stability could be insured without any real sacrifices or obligations on their part. Although Republicans hailed the Washington pacts as the "greatest peace document[s] ever drawn"—it was the first major international conference to be held in the United States—the settlement did not compensate for nonmembership in the League of Nations and full participation in its work for peace.

Yet within the perspective of the times, the Washington Conference represented a notable success. The United States had not really surrendered anything of value, for its naval superiority was potential rather than actual and the public and Congress in any case probably would not have authorized the sums required by existing construction plans. Moreover, England and Japan would have been compelled to counter-build. The conference, therefore, merely ratified the existing naval balance of power and benefited all with some reductions in expenditures. From a larger viewpoint, therefore, the Washington settlement ended a costly capital ship arms race, stabilized the Pacific for a decade, and strengthened the Open Door in China. For those interested in arms limitations it also offered a lesson that progress is achievable only when a favorable balance of power exists and all sides find an agreement beneficial.

The Five Power Pact only limited capital warships. A race in lesser craft, such as cruisers, destroyers, and submarines, loomed unless agreements could be reached for those categories. A conference called at Geneva in 1927 failed primarily because of different British and American needs. Britain desired more light cruisers in order to guard its overseas empire; America needed fewer but heavier cruisers with longer sailing range to compensate for its inadequate bases overseas. The deadlock was broken by both a threatened construction race in cruisers and Hoover's skillful diplomacy. President Hoover spoke of a "naval yardstick" to equate different needs and sizes of vessels—no satisfactory formula ever really emerged—and he invited the British prime minister, Ramsay MacDonald, to the United States for discussions in the fall of 1929. They agreed upon a new effort. At the London Naval Arms Conference in 1930, the delegates approved a 10:10:7 ratio and tonnage limitations for the United States, Great Britain, and Japan in lesser naval vessels. Japan also obtained parity in submarines.

The entire Pacific treaty system collapsed in the early 1930s when Japan embarked on an aggressive expansionist course. Since during the intervening years a pinch-penny Congress had failed to build the navy up to treaty limits, the United States was to find itself in a much weakened position. The nation had become lulled into a false sense of security and continuing peace. Even so, that cannot be attributed solely or even primarily to the architects of the naval agreements. They had coped reasonably well with complex problems in the twenties and erected a system that with better fortune and more American realism might have preserved peace and stability indefinitely in the Pacific.

ECONOMIC FOREIGN POLICY

The World War had seen the United States emerge as the leading economic power of the world. At home its productive capacity grew prodigiously, so that by the late 1920s the country's industry produced 46 percent of the world's total output. A vast export of private capital reversed America's historic position as a debtor to Europe and made it the world's creditor. New York City supplanted London as the center of global finance, and investments poured into Canada, Latin America, the Far East, and even into Europe. To escape foreign trade barriers, American industry also began to establish subsidiaries abroad. American firms, with government encouragement or acquiescence, reached agreements with foreign competitors to stabilize prices and divide markets. The State Department tried to guide private investments abroad in such a way as to stabilize various areas of the world and to discourage arms races or unwise enterprises, but with only limited success. Europe by 1929 owed the United States, on the governmental and private levels, an estimated $21 billion.

The self-centered economic foreign policies followed by Washington proved short-sighted and unwise. The United States, with an immense stake in world stability and prosperity, should have been more conscious of the need to aid Europe in postwar recovery and to open channels of trade. Instead, it at first acted narrowly, and only belatedly shifted toward a more responsible policy. In 1920, European states owed the United States government about $10⅓ billion for wartime and postwar loans, an immense sum by the standards of the times. The Allies asserted that these debts had been incurred as part of a joint war effort, America's contribution to match Allied sacrifices in manpower and lives, but the United States insisted that the loans were straightforward financial arrangements that should be repaid in full with interest. The United States had asked nothing from the war, many said, so why should it have to shoulder most of the financial costs? As Coolidge reportedly remarked, "They hired the money, didn't they?" Only a few liberals and bankers advocated sharp reductions or cancellations, perceiving that the debts would be very difficult to collect and would hinder postwar economic recovery.

Congress authorized the World War Foreign Debt Commission to negotiate with the debtors for repayment over a period of twenty-five years at 4.25 percent interest rates. The commission departed from those guidelines only in reductions of interest and extensions of the time period to sixty-two years. The debtor nations very reluctantly came to terms, France most reluctantly of all. The American government had to embargo private loans to France to bring her to terms in 1926 for her debt of nearly $3½ billion. The result was mutual ill will in Europe and America as their respective presses exchanged bitter insults about "Uncle Shylock" and ingrates.

If the United States insisted upon repayment of the war debts, it should have opened its ports freely to European trade. Debtors must be allowed some means of discharging their obligations, and payment in gold was impractical. Yet Republicans retained a "debtor complex" and instituted high protective tariffs. Although Europeans complained and threatened retaliation, the effects of the high rates in drying up trade were cushioned by the outflow of American investment capital to Europe. In effect, the United States financed continued European purchases from America. When the Great Depression began, Congress further raised tariff rates, from the previous average of 25.9 percent to 50.2 percent, the highest in American history. It was sheer economic idiocy, critics felt. European countries, already running trade deficits with the United States, struck back with tariff walls and trade barriers of their own. By

1932 world trade was fast drying up and American commerce declined to
the level of 1905.

American economic policy retarded Europe's postwar recovery and
later intensified the world economic depression. Yet Washington did seek
to promote world prosperity. The European debtor nations argued that
their ability to repay war debts depended on German payment of reparations. Germany had been assessed $33 billion plus interest for World War
I civilian damages. Although the State Department officially refused to
see any connection between the debts and reparations, in practice it did.
In 1922 Secretary of State Hughes admitted that the United States could
not ignore Europe's postwar economic distress, and he suggested that
private American representatives investigate the reparations problem. In
1924 Charles G. Dawes, a Chicago banker, helped formulate the Dawes
Plan, which ended the French-Belgian occupation of the Ruhr, reorganized German finances with a private loan (much of it from the United
States), and arranged for Germany to begin reparations payments.
Again, in 1930, private Americans took part in the Young Plan, which
scaled Germany's reparations debt to about $9 billion. In 1931, President
Hoover tried to salvage the world financial system by proclaiming a one-
year moratorium, or suspension of payments, on all intergovernmental
debts. It was a statesmanlike act that in fact conceded some connection
between war debts and reparations.

Encouraged by Hoover's proposal, the European powers met at
Lausanne and offered in effect virtually to cancel Germany's remaining
reparations if the United States would similarly cancel the war debts. In
the midst of a worsening depression, the Americans reacted adversely to
such an idea and nothing was done. The only practical result of Hoover's
moratorium was the virtual cessation of Allied payments on the war
debts. Within a short time all the debtors except Finland defaulted,
much to the disgust of the American people. Americans railed against an
"ungrateful" Europe, and some offered novel proposals that Britain or
France liquidate their debts by turning over their colonies in the
Western Hemisphere or parts of their navies to the United States.
Ironically, the United States had received war debts payments about
equal to the actual reparations paid to the Allies by Germany and
approximating the amount of American private capital invested in Germany during the 1920s.

RELATIONS WITH THE LEAGUE OF NATIONS

The first year of American relations with the League of Nations can only
be described as petty and shameful. The Republicans interpreted the
results of the 1920 elections as a decisive popular mandate against the
League. Moreover, they apparently assumed that the League was still-
born since the United States would not join. Consequently the State

Department ignored all League communications, while President Harding assured Congress the nation would have no part in that world organization with its "super powers." The State Department concluded a separate peace with Germany, retaining all of the benefits of the Versailles Treaty but none of its obligations. When it became publicly known that the government was not even responding to routine League Secretariat communications, a public outcry compelled the State Department to make a rather ungracious reply. As the *New York Times* editorialized, some Americans, for partisan or other motives, resented the fact that the League was functioning and clearly hoped for its failure.

By 1923, the official American attitude toward the League shifted from hostility to tolerance. At least, many now admitted, the League was helping the Old World to preserve peace. Moreover, it carried on certain nonpolitical functions, dealing with such issues of common world interest as suppression of the opium traffic, radio communications, copyrights, and world health that were of concern to the United States. Therefore the United States began to send "consultative observers" to nonpolitical humanitarian conferences sponsored by the League. These unofficial delegates did not vote, however, lest supersensitive isolationists in America perceive this involvement as a move to enter the world organization via the back door. As President Coolidge phrased it, the United States would not join the League, but it was happy to cooperate with other nations for humanitarian purposes.

Gradually the American government leaned toward more direct relations with the League's nonpolitical work. It began to send official delegates, who participated fully in the proceedings, to various special conferences. By 1928 the Republican platform boasted of that kind of cooperation, although it reassured voters that there was no intention of joining the League. Except for complaints from a few die-hard isolationists, most Americans accepted that kind of limited cooperation. In effect, the United States would cooperate with the League for humanitarian purposes but not in its labors to preserve peace. Under President Hoover, cooperation became more pronounced, and the United States even sat in at sessions of the League Council when it debated Japanese aggression in Manchuria. America had turned nearly full circle from initial hostility to cooperation with the League, illustrating the American course of limited internationalism during the 1920s.

Limited internationalism, without binding political obligations, was also revealed in the American approach to the World Court. The World Court had been authorized by the Covenant of the League of Nations but was a separate body. Since the United States long had prided itself on leadership in arbitration and the peaceful settlement of international disputes, many Americans argued that the least the nation could do was to join what in a sense was its own creation. Peace groups endorsed the World Court, some as a means of eventually entering the League and others as an end in itself. Most Americans favored membership, although intransigent isolationists remained opposed to what they viewed as an indirect move to enter the League. Both major political parties approved membership, and a treaty was negotiated to enter the Court. The die-hards managed to block it in 1926, however, by attaching unacceptable reservations to membership. Again, in 1935, after compromises had been worked out painfully with other World Court members, the isolationists mustered enough strength to prevent entry—the treaty failed to obtain the necessary two-thirds majority by seven votes in the Senate. Supporters of the Court clearly had won a majority of Americans to membership but could not overcome a substantial Senate minority.

OUTLAWRY OF WAR

Many Americans were attracted to an even simpler scheme to solve world problems. Why not outlaw war? Peace thereby would be assured without any entanglements or obligations by the United States. The movement to ban aggressive war was supported by many internationalists, who viewed it as a means of linking the United States to the League and collective security, and by an even larger number of moralists, pacifists, and isola-tionists, who were attracted by the simplicity of the scheme and its lack of obligations. In the view of the latter, such a ban would depend for enforcement not upon force but upon enlightened world moral opinion and international law.

The movement for outlawry began with the propaganda work of a Chicago lawyer, Salmon O. Levinson. Senator Borah, the arch isola-tionist, was won to the cause, and various peace groups endorsed it. They persuaded Aristide Briand, France's foreign minister, to propose early in 1927 a Franco-American pact embodying the concept. Briand did so through a press announcement on the tenth anniversary of America's entry into World War I. President Coolidge and Secretary of State Kellogg reacted coolly to such unorthodox diplomacy, whereas Briand saw a pact as a sort of negative alliance that would strengthen French security. But public opinion rallied to the idea, and Briand soon formally pre-sented the American government with a bilateral treaty pledging the two nations to rely upon peaceful measures to resolve all future disputes. Kellogg then turned the tables on Briand, proposing instead a multilateral treaty to prohibit war. Briand reluctantly consented.

Sixty-four nations eventually ratified the Kellogg-Briand Pact, or Pact of Paris, signed in August 1928. The treaty solemnly pledged signatories to "condemn recourse to war for the solution of international controversies, and [to] renounce it as an instrument of national policy in their relations with one another." All disputes should be settled by pacific means. The pact contained no provisions for enforcement, and signers in effect reserved their rights to self-defense. The American Senate granted its approval by a vote of eighty-five to one, reserving the right of self-defense and preservation of the Monroe Doctrine and foreswearing any obligation to enforce the pact. Hailed by millions here and abroad as a signal achievement for a world without war, the Pact of Paris, as its critics noted, was merely an innocuous international kiss of peace. In a sense it was disastrous, because it encouraged the false but comforting assumption that peace and security could be obtained without risks and without costs. And ironically, it did make neutrality in future wars more difficult by labeling in advance "aggressive" war as immoral and illegal. Whether fortunately or not, it also pointed the way to the Nuremburg and Tokyo war crimes trials that were to follow World War II.

The Pact of Paris could scarcely have been more ill-timed. For roughly a decade, American economic prosperity and the export of America's surplus capital had kept the world that had been patched together at Versailles in 1919 in rough equilibrium. An American foreign policy that used economic power rather than military might or binding treaties seemed to work well for the United States and the remainder of the world. But when world depression struck only a year after the ratification of the Kellogg-Briand Pact, American economic diplomacy collapsed. Depression fostered international economic warfare, the rise of dictatorships, military aggression, and the failure of arms limitation and peace treaties. When the delicate global equilibrium of the 1920s shattered during the 1930s, the United States would be compelled to choose between collective security based on military power or withdrawal into a continental Fortress America.

SELECTED BIBLIOGRAPHY FOR SECTION IV

The standard economic history of the 1920s is GEORGE SOULÉ, *Prosperity Decade* (1947),* but other equally valuable studies are BROADUS MITCHELL, *Depression Decade: From New Era to New Deal* (1947),* ALFRED D. CHANDLER, *Strategy and Structure* (1962),* and JAMES PROTHRO, *The Dollar Decade* (1954).* A detailed contemporary study of society and culture, PRESTON SLOSSON's *The Great Crusade and After* (1930)* can be augmented by two highly informative and also contemporary accounts: The President's Research Committee on Social Trends, *Recent Social Trends in the United States* (1933) and *Recent Economic Changes in the United States: Report of the Committee on Recent Economic Changes of the President's Conference on Unemployment* (2 vols., 1929). The classic examination of American society and culture in a typical industrial city remains HELEN and ROBERT LYND's *Middletown* (1929).* Three other excellent surveys of the period are JOHN BRAEMAN et al., *Change and Continuity in Twentieth Century America: The 1920s* (1968); OTIS L. GRAHAM, *The Great Campaigns: Reform and War, 1900–*

* Available in paperback.

1928 (1971) *; and ELIZABETH STEVENSON, *The American 1920s: Babbitts and Bohemians* (1970).*

Besides the standard survey of American labor in the 1920s, IRVING BERNSTEIN's *The Lean Years* (1960),* one might read ROBERT H. ZIEGER, *Republicans and Labor, 1919–1929* (1969). Two studies critical of conventional accounts of the 1920s are CLARKE A. CHAMBERS, *Seedtime of Reform: American Social Service and Social Action, 1918–1933* (1963) * and DONALD C. SWAIN, *Federal Conservation Policy, 1921–1933* (1963). The KKK is surveyed in DAVID CHALMERS, *Hooded Americanism: The First Century of the Ku Klux Klan, 1865–1965* (1965),* while religious issues are studied in NORMAN F. FURNISS, *The Fundamentalist-Controversy, 1918–1931* (1954); ROBERT M. MILLER, *American Protestantism and Social Issues, 1919–1939* (1958); and PAUL CARTER, *The Decline and Revival of the Social Gospel: Social and Political Liberalism in American Protestant Churches, 1920–1940* (1960).

The political left is discussed in THEODORE DRAPER, *The Roots of American Communism* (1963) *; JAMES WEINSTEIN, *The Decline of Socialism in America, 1912–1925* (1969) *; and LEWIS COSER and IRVING HOWE, *The American Communist Party: A Critical History* (1962).* Women during the 1920s are reviewed in GERDA LERNER, *The Woman in American History* (1971) *; WILLIAM H. CHAFE, *The American Woman: Her Changing Social, Economic, and Political Roles, 1920–1970* (1972) *; and J. STANLEY LEMONS, *The Woman Citizen: Social Feminism in the 1920s* (1973).* The struggle of black Americans is well treated in E. DAVID CRONON, *Black Moses: The Story of Marcus Garvey and the Universal Negro Improvement Association* (1962) *; THEODORE VINCENT, *Black Power and the Garvey Movement* (1970); and the classic study by ABRAM L. HARRIS and STERLING SPERO, *The Black Worker: The Negro and the Labor Movement* (1931).* Two important studies of the literature and high culture of the decade are MALCOLM COWLEY, *Exiles Return: A Literary Odyssey of the 1920s* (1934) * and FREDERICK J. HOFFMAN, *The Twenties* (1955).

Good surveys of the national politics of the "New Era" include WILLIAM LEUCHTENBERG, *The Perils of Prosperity* (1958) *; ARTHUR SCHLESINGER, JR., *The Crisis of the Old Order* (1957) *; SAMUEL LUBELL, *The Future of American Politics* (1952) *; DON KIRSCHNER, *City and Country* (1970); and DAVID BURNER, *The Politics of Provincialism* (1968).* For detailed studies of presidential politics see ROBERT K. MURRAY, *The Harding Era* (1969) and DONALD MCCOY, *Calvin Coolidge* (1967). The social tensions of the 1920s—including policies involving immigration, civil liberties, the Klan, and prohibition—are discussed in JOHN HIGHAM, *Strangers in the Land* (1963) *; KENNETH JACKSON, *The Ku Klux Klan in the Cities* (1967) *; A. S. RICE, *The Ku Klux Klan in American Politics* (1962); ANDREW SINCLAIR, *Era of Excess* (1962) *; RUTH SILVA, *Rum, Religion, and Votes* (1962); JOAN HOFF WILSON, ed., *The Twenties* (1972) *; PAT WATTERS and STEPHEN GILLERS, eds., *Investi-*

gating the FBI (1973) *; SANFORD UNGAR, *FBI* (1975) ; and RAY GINGER, *Six Days or Forever* (1958) .

Most of the best accounts of American foreign policy during the 1920s have been written recently. The standard works include HERBERT FEIS, *The Diplomacy of the Dollar: First Era, 1919–1932* (1950) * and ROBERT H. FERRELL, *Peace in their Time: The Origins of the Kellogg-Briand Pact* (1952) .* Two other solid but conventional studies are L. ETHAN ELLIS, *Republican Foreign Policy, 1921–1932* (1968) and THOMAS H. BUCKLEY, *United States and the Washington Conference, 1921–1922* (1970). More critical accounts of U.S. foreign policy can be found in JOAN HOFF WILSON, *American Business and Foreign Policy, 1920–1933* (1971) *; WILLIAM A. WILLIAMS, *The Tragedy of American Diplomacy* (1962) *; CARL P. PARRINI, *Heir to Empire: United States Economic Diplomacy, 1916–1923* (1969) ; and JOSEPH TULCHIN, *The Aftermath of War: World War I and United States Policy toward Latin America* (1971) .

V

A Great Depression and a New Deal 1929–1939

The Great Depression, which perhaps struck the United States more severely than any other industrial nation and which lingered longer there, was in fact an international phenomenon. All the nation-states that were part of the capitalist world system's trading network experienced falling prices, decreasing production, and rising unemployment. Whether they were developed industrial states or underdeveloped colonial societies, the world's nation-states paid a heavy toll in human costs for the economic losses induced by depression.

Economic depression not only left the capitalist economies in ruins, but also placed the Western liberal democracies on the defensive and sowed doubt about their future survival. Only the nondemocratic, totalitarian states of Italy, Germany, Soviet Russia, and Japan seemed to escape the depression relatively unscathed. The Italian Fascist government of Benito Mussolini, it was said, not only drained Rome's malarial swamps but also made the trains run on time. Hitler and his Nazi movement not only restored the pride of the German people in their nation but also eliminated unemployment. Stalin's Russia, too, eagerly recruited new industrial workers, as the Soviet dictator sought, at whatever human cost, to transform his backward agrarian nation into an advanced industrial society. And in Asia an increasingly militarized Japanese nation sought to become the region's dominant power. During the mid-1930s, then, the future of the globe seemed to be in the hands of the antiliberal, antidemocratic forces.

Yet one beacon of light shone through the general gloominess of liberal democracy in the early 1930s: Franklin D. Roosevelt and his New Deal. Not only did liberal capitalists in the Western world look to Roosevelt and the United States to show them a path out of the Great Depression, but also the followers of socialist Leon Blum, who came to power in France in 1936 with his Popular Front government, and members of the British Labour party looked to the New Deal as a reform movement that might preserve Western civilization's most cherished human values. Democrats around the globe were convinced that the future of liberal capitalism depended on the success of Roosevelt.

Such beliefs were reinforced by the diplomatic realities of the 1930s. The apparent collapse of democratic liberalism led the totalitarian states to seek to satisfy territorial, economic, and imperial desires that had been frustrated during and after World War I. Mussolini's Italy went to war in Africa to recapture the imperial glories of that nation's Roman past; Hitler's Germany aggressively sought first European and then global hegemony; and Japan invaded first Manchuria and then China itself to establish its dominance in the western Pacific and on the Asian mainland. The Great Depression thus tied together the domestic and global fortunes of liberal capitalism and left their destiny in doubt.

14

The Great Crash
1929-1933

In the early autumn of 1929 most Americans thought their land the best of all worlds. The middle and upper classes basked in the golden glow of prosperity. The business of America was to promote business and to allow entrepreneurs the freedom to pursue profits. This was a course that seemed to guarantee economic growth, prosperity, and, as the new president promised, the abolition of poverty. *Time* magazine in its issue for the third week of October featured a triple-page advertisement promoting a new magazine, *Fortune,* which was to be dedicated to the commonplace that "America's great achievement has been Business."

Then something strange happened. On Wednesday, October 23, speculators began to sell overpriced stocks on Wall Street. The next day, "Black Thursday," hysteria swept the street as investors hurried to sell before stock prices tumbled even lower, and shareholders who had purchased their stocks on credit sold hastily to cover their debts. By October 29, over sixteen million shares had changed hands, and by the month's end over $15 billion in stock value had been wiped out; two months later the paper loss represented $40 billion. In the piquant words of a *Variety* headline: "Wall Street Lays an Egg."

Thus began the Great Depression. Initially most citizens had little reason to panic. Although in 1929 more Americans than ever before owned stock, the large majority of the population remained unaffected by declining Wall Street values. President Hoover had correctly assured the nation that, despite stock market vagaries, its fundamental economic foundation—the production and distribution of real goods—was sound. Why panic when pieces of paper rather than industrial plants collapsed, or when a few impecunious speculators suffered paper losses?

Much to the distress of most citizens, however, after the stock market crashed the wheels of industry slowed down. As production fell, so too did working hours, wages, and total employment. Good reason for anxiety now existed, and Hoover's assurances concerning the soundness of the economy began to sound hollow.

THE STATISTICAL TOLL

The Great Depression (1929–39) was an experience few Americans who endured it could forget, but it was a phenomenon whose reality is hard to comprehend for later generations that have known only prosperity. Students who read about the depression must naturally wonder why, if conditions were indeed as grim as those portrayed by most historians, Americans failed to rebel. Students may suspect that depression survivors have exaggerated the material and mental anguish wrought by the "Crash" in order to magnify the accomplishment of their own survival. Skepticism about accounts of history is always in order, but there is scant reason to doubt the reality of the economic catastrophe known as the Great Depression.

Statistics explain one aspect of the depression's impact. Between 1929 and 1932 the gross national product dropped from $149.3 to $107.6 billion (almost a 30 percent decline); personal consumption expenditures fell $20 billion; gross private investment declined from $26.8 to $3.3 billion; nonfarm housing construction fell five-fold; the index of manufacturing production (1929 equals 100) plummeted to 57; wholesale prices declined a third; and corporate profits vanished: firms that had earned $9.6 billion in 1929 lost $3 billion in 1932. In this era before governments were expected to take up the slack in spending and investment from the private sector during an economic slump, total government expenditures increased by only a little over $1 billion, and the federal debt rose by only $2.5 billion.

The drying up of private investment and the budget-balancing practices of local, state, and national governments spelled disaster for the American worker. By 1930, in what Elmer Davis sarcastically called "the second year of the abolition of poverty," over four million workers, or 14.2 percent of the nonfarm labor force, were unemployed. A year later the number unemployed had doubled and represented 25.2 percent of the labor force. Worse was to come. By the end of 1932 and in early 1933, over twelve million men and women, between 36 percent and 38 percent of the nonfarm labor force, were without jobs. And these estimates were conservative, since they excluded those still fortunate enough to labor part-time and those too transient or too dejected to be counted as job seekers.

Sometimes the impact of the depression proved more severe in a particular locality than in the nation as a whole. Residents of the industrial city of Donora, Pennsylvania watched helplessly as unemployment approached the 90 percent mark. Coal-mining communities, which somehow had survived the 1920s, died economically during the depression, leaving the entire local working-class populations without a source of income. Large metropolitan areas were not spared. Chicago counted almost half a million unemployed workers, and the city was so short of 'unds that it stopped paying its teachers, 750 of whom consequently lost eir homes. Even Babe Ruth had to accept a salary cut, and Fifth enue shops advertised sales on everything from French perfumes to 'k coats.

Small vignettes testified to the impact of depression on individual In New York City thousands of unemployed adults took to the to sell apples and shine shoes. "Shining shoes," one jobless but still ¹us worker told a reporter, "is more profitable than selling apples. when you get a shoeshine kit, it's a permanent investment, and t cost as much as a box of apples." Other unemployed men t any straw, some one hundred thousand applying in 1931 for ¹d skilled jobs in Russia advertised by Amtorg, the Soviet trade re dispirited men escaped from winter weather by sleeping in 's (or if they could not afford the five-cent fare, resting in des), and they considered arrest a stroke of luck since it ¹ free meals and shelter. Rural folk also suffered. "The roads and the Southwest," the radical journalist and humorist ger told a congressional committee in 1932, "teem with ikers. The camp fires of the homeless are seen along every I saw men, women, and children walking over the hard icked up a family. The woman was hugging a dead ¹ ragged coat. When I had asked her where she had ¹l, first she told me that she had found it dead in the lded in grim humor, 'They promised me a chicken in ¹ I got mine.'" Such experiences explained why in ary 1931, hungry crowds rioted and raided food stores Minneapolis, St. Paul, and elsewhere.

sity hit middle-class and professional citizens perhaps han workers. Workers, at least, had had long experi- ith seasonal, technological, and cyclical unemploy- f pay due to sickness. They knew what to do when how to survive on minimal incomes or relief. But ass Americans were simply lost. Discharged by their em- like common laborers or unpaid by their clients and patients,

The faces of depression
Frederic Lewis/American Stock Photos

respectable citizens were too proud to apply for relief or to retrench on their accustomed standard of living.

Already suffering economically in the 1920s, American agriculture went from bad to worse. As crop prices fell to new lows, gross farm income declined from $12 billion to $5 billion. In 1930 and 1931, moreover, drought struck the Plains States denying farmers crops to sell even at low prices. Ironically for the first time in decades the number of farm tenants declined because landlords simply tractored them off the soil, as happened to the Joads and the other Oklahoma families in John Steinbeck's *The Grapes of Wrath*. Misery and hunger stalked rural as well as urban America, causing hundreds of thousands of dispossessed farm folk, like the Joads, to seek rainbows in California.

By 1930–1931 breadlines dotted American cities, men supported themselves by selling apples on streetcorners, and a popular song asked: "Brother, can you spare a dime?" Never had public relief agencies and private charities had to cope with an economic tragedy of such dimensions. Structured to manage temporary, minor local problems, these agencies could not ameliorate a national economic crisis. In Detroit, for example, the mayor borrowed funds from large banks and auto companies to meet relief payments, but private financiers supplied the money only on condition that the city reduce welfare support per family and eliminate one-third of the families then on relief. In order to balance their books many cities denied relief to blacks and other minorities. Last hired and first fired by the private sector, nonwhites were also often the last group assisted by public agencies.

With relief organizations in a state of collapse, Americans desperately struggled to sustain themselves. Hundreds of thousands of young men and women (perhaps millions) took to the road in a vain search for employment or sustenance. Armies of women and children plundered local dumps and restaurant scrap cans. The landscape of urban America became pockmarked with shantytowns constructed of tarpaper, waste lumber, and tin, and derisively labeled as "Hoovervilles."

What had happened? Why had the economy failed so abysmally?

THE ROOTS OF DEPRESSION

The causes of the Great Depression were deeply embedded in the prosperous twenties. Indeed the prosperity of the "New Era" had been built on a shaky foundation. Dependent to a greater extent than ever before on mass consumption, the economy failed to sustain the conditions necessary for the maintenance of a mass buying public. Nor did public policy compensate for inadequacies in the private sector; in fact, it aggravated them.

Hindsight later perceived numerous harbingers of depression in the 1920s. Farmers, a substantial segment of the consumer market, suffered economically throughout the decade, and their reduced incomes undermined sales in the agricultural implements and supplies industries. The plight of the unemployed coal miners and the forgotten New England textile hands revealed another flaw in an economy geared to mass consumption. Less evident at the time but more important was the maldistribution of national income. Between 1923 and 1929 as corporate profits increased by 62 percent and dividends by 65 percent, workers' wages rose by only 11 percent. Spiraling profits supplied substantial sums of money for savings and investment but lagging wage rates curtailed the potential consumer market for American industry's cornucopia of new products.

As a result of the widening gap between the economy's productive capacity and the public's ability to consume, investment in the basic consumer industries began to diminish after 1925. The auto and construction industries, which had spearheaded the economic boom, peaked in 1925 and declined afterwards. For a time, however, high profits and higher stock values liberated corporations from the usual credit restraints set by the capital markets. Because unusually large profit margins enabled corporations to amass their own investment funds internally, plant expansion proceeded heedless of declining consumer demand.

Public economic policy during the Coolidge years encouraged the worst faults in the private sector. Instead of using fiscal and monetary policy to bolster agricultural and working-class incomes, federal measures made additional funds available for savings and investment. Treasury Secretary Andrew Mellon solved the budget surplus by sharply reducing private and corporate income taxes. When he completed his fiscal reforms, the mass of Americans bore a heavier proportionate tax burden than the wealthy. Mellon, however, argued that the great wealth of the few, invested productively, would trickle down to the masses. Trickle it did—in a small stream never ample enough to sustain a mass consumer market. Monetary policy led to the same result. Low interest rates and a loose money policy, as practiced by federal reserve officials, stimulated private investment and stock market speculation. As long as profits remained high and stock prices soared, economic seers and public officials overlooked deficiencies in consumption.

International economic policy and government attitudes toward domestic business also distorted the economy. Federal tariff and trade policies aggressively promoted American exports and investments abroad but decisively shut the domestic market to foreign producers. As long as American investment funds flowed overseas, our businessmen literally subsidized their own exports. And from 1919 to 1930 private United States investment abroad climbed from $7 billion to $17.2 billion. But what would happen when the return to American capital exceeded annual new investment, that is, when the interest earned by overseas investments was more than the amount spent or sent abroad annually and foreigners could no longer afford American products? Or when economic failure overseas threatened not only export markets but also investment capital? The Great Depression provided the answers. Meantime, at home, federal agencies pursued practices that limited the potential consumer market. The Federal Trade Commission, created in 1914 to regulate business in the public interest, served throughout the 1920s as private enterprise's most effective voice in Washington. In the words of the commissioners in 1927: "The legitimate interests of business are in perfect harmony with the true interests of the public." The FTC thus encouraged businessmen to cooperate rather than compete; it watched benignly as hitherto competing firms merged into single units and scores of small companies allied in trade associations. The result was a price structure less sensitive to changes in demand, one under which prices remained artificially high.

A variety of factors, then, hinted at economic trouble even before the stock market collapsed. The failure of wage rates to rise as rapidly as productivity and profits and the resulting maldistribution of income denied masses of consumers adequate purchasing power. Business decline in such traditional industries as textiles, coal, and railroads added hundreds of thousands of workers to the ranks of the unemployed, wrecked the economy of entire cities and regions, and further diminished consumer purchasing power. Stagnation in agriculture, falling farm incomes, and the flight from the countryside cut into another sector of consumer demand for manufactured goods. Finally, the inability of foreign nations to increase, or even to maintain, the amount of United States goods that they purchased also reduced aggregate demand for American industrial products. In short, the failure of consumers to absorb the full product of American industry could have but one result: excess inventory that caused businessmen to cut production, discharge workers, and reject new investment. Wall Street's collapse was only the curtain-raiser to a protracted depression that flowed inexorably from the flawed economy of the New Era.

The stock market crash in October 1929 suddenly revealed the economic rot underlying the prosperous twenties. Overnight the optimism of the New Era turned to pessimism. Just as optimism stimulated investment and stock purchases, regardless of economic realities, pessimism had the reverse effect. Retrenchment became the order of the day; in the callous words of Andrew Mellon: "Liquidate labor, liquidate stocks, liquidate the farmers, liquidate real estate." As investors unloaded their stocks, manufacturers reduced production, farmers lost their land, and workers their jobs, the nation sank deeper into the pit of depression and the depths of despondency.

THE SHOCKED SOCIETY

Initially many Americans refused to accept the reality or persistence of depression. Public rhetoric belied private anxieties. Newspapers and businessmen spokesmen advised citizens that the economy was undergoing a temporary adjustment—a natural feature of the business cycle—and that good times would quickly return. Some even suggested that the depression had been inflicted by God to punish Americans for their profligacy and hedonism during the Jazz Age. Once Americans purified their souls through hard labor and temperate behavior the economic skies would brighten. Madison Avenue techniques were used in an attempt to belie the economic reality. Business groups distributed buttons proclaiming: "I'm sold on America. I won't talk depression." Henry Ford assured his fellow citizens in November 1929 that "things are better today than they were yesterday." And the president of the National Association of Manufacturers added: "I can view little on the horizon today to give us undue or great concern." Month after month economists and financiers issued forecasts predicting the imminence of business revival, while politicians promised that prosperity was just around the corner. Yet the depression worsened.

Reality could not long be ignored. When prosperity failed to appear round the next corner, the nation's business and political elites acted in an unprecedented manner. In previous depressions in American history federal officials had refused to intervene in the economy and employers had cut wages with a vengeance. This time President Hoover moved decisively to combat depression and the business elite joined his war to save the economy.

Committed to a voluntary, noncoercive approach to economic planning, Hoover invited corporation executives and labor leaders to the White House to obtain their cooperation. From businessmen he received the promise that there would be no precipitate price cuts and that they would voluntarily maintain existing wage rates. Labor leaders agreed not to demand wage increases nor to threaten strikes against cooperative employers. Such promises, while honored, protected employed workers, temporarily stabilized big business, and supported purchasing power. But they provided no assistance to the unemployed—by then well over four million—nor to farmers who had to pay high prices for industrial goods while prices received for farm products plummeted.

To aid those not covered by voluntary agreements, Hoover stepped up federal construction and urged states, municipalities, and private utilities to do likewise. But presidential pleas to invest public and private funds conflicted with economic realities. As long as private demand declined, business investors had no cause to increase their productive capacity. Bound by constitutional clauses that forbade unbalanced budgets, states and municipalities could not increase their spending when tax revenues declined. Absolutely opposed to deficit spending, Hoover could never pump sufficient federal funds into the economy to boost it back to prosperity.

Federal efforts to assist farmers also proved frustrating. Acting under the Agricultural Marketing Act of 1930, Hoover purchased surplus crops in order to maintain price levels. But the funds appropriated under the act were too small to diminish farm surpluses significantly. As their incomes continued to fall, more and more farmers faced mortgage foreclosure.

Neither voluntary economic agreements nor federal actions taken in 1930 and 1931 proved sufficient to combat depression. Unemployment rose and prices fell. As demand sagged further, industrialists led by United States Steel responded logically; they cut wages across the board. But demand and prices continued to fall, leading in 1932 to a second round of across-the-board wage cuts. Lowered wages further diminished purchasing power, causing employers to cut production and discharge yet more workers. By mid-1932 there seemed to be no escape from the vicious economic circle, nor did there appear to be a limit to the extent of unemployment.

As Hoover began his fourth year in office, the nation's economy was in shambles. There was no question about Hoover being the world's greatest engineer, quipped his critics, for "in a little more than two years he has drained, ditched and damned the United States." Not only had the economy collapsed, but public and private relief agencies could no longer serve their multiplying clientele. The survival of capitalism itself seemed in question.

The president acted swiftly to save capitalism, less decisively to succor the unemployed and the hungry. Two immediate problems confronted Hoover: the collapse of the nation's corporate structure and the bankruptcy of relief agencies. In December 1931 the President proposed to Congress the creation of a federal agency to assist corporate enterprises —the Reconstruction Finance Corporation (RFC)—and in January 1932 Congress passed the enabling legislation. The RFC, as administered by Hoover, preserved the framework of capitalism by extending billions of dollars in federal loans, especially to large banks on the brink of failure. The largest financial institutions received the greatest share of RFC funds, a windfall that allowed them to survive but not to make new investments. If capitalism was perhaps saved by federal action, the unemployed and the hungry remained damned. Early in the depression, Hoover had promised that "should federal aid be the only alternative to starvation, then federal aid we must have; but I have faith that such a day shall not come." In this instance presidential faith proved unflagging. On the one hand, Hoover insisted that hunger did not exist in depression America, and, on the other hand, he warned that federal relief (which he derisively labeled the dole) would undermine the moral character of its recipients, transforming them into useless drones. So, despite continuous pleas from state, local, and private charity society officials for financial aid, Hoover refused to release federal funds for such use. As a Harvard economist noted, the president had a split vision on the issue of public relief: the recipients of the dole were not the hungry supplicants to charity societies but the great industries that fed gluttonously at the public trough.

The paradox of the times is not that Hoover denied the existence of hunger nor that the federal government treated corporation executives more generously than common citizens. It is rather that so little popular protest flared between 1929 and 1932.

THE RESPONSE OF FARMERS AND WORKERS

In the face of declining employment, reduced wages, and spreading economic misery, American workers appeared quiescent. The first three full years of depression—1930 through 1932—witnessed fewer strikes and industrial disputes than the last year of prosperity, 1929. Indeed the prosperous years from 1923 through 1926 experienced 50 percent more industrial conflict than did the early depression years. If one excluded from the statistics the mass strikes involving Southern textile workers and a sporadic series of strikes by desperate coal miners, American labor in the years 1930 through 1932 slept. Why?

At first, of course, economic depression did not represent as rude a shock to workers as it did to other citizens. Unemployment of one sort or another had long been a part of working-class life. Having had much past experience adjusting to seasonal layoffs, technological unemployment, and income losses caused by illness, workers simply tightened their belts while their families pursued time-honored expedients of survival. However, when the immensity of the Great Depression sank in and workers began to realize that it was an experience without precedent, they had few places to turn for guidance.

The American labor movement had come out of the prosperity decade whipped and humbled. Smaller in numbers and weaker in economic muscle in 1929 than in 1919, the labor movement suffered further blows during the depression. Such stalwart, progressive unions as the United Mine Workers, the Ladies' Garment Workers, and the Brewery Workers (victims of prohibition as well) were moribund by 1932. The remaining power centers in the labor movement represented the most satisfied and the least imaginative sectors of trade unionism.

Consequently the AFL and its spokesmen offered old bromides. They petitioned federal officials to gather statistics on unemployment and then to provide public works and relief. They asked employers to establish a thirty-hour week, a request well within employers' ability to meet if it included proportionate wage cuts. Quite often, in fact, workers shared jobs at reduced hours for existing hourly wage rates. Having failed to spread unionism during the prosperous twenties, the AFL was not likely to gamble on organizing during the depression. Retrenchment was the order of the day for labor as well as for government and business. Labor leaders, moreover, shared Hoover's commitment to voluntarism. Until 1932 the executive council of the AFL opposed minimum wages, unemployment insurance, and old-age and survivors' benefits. Not until 1932, when unemployment reached the 15 million level, did the council approve unemployment compensation, and even then only by the barest majority. Such a labor movement was unlikely to encourage working-class militancy and popular protest.

Unable to turn to the official labor movement for aid, unemployed workers had few avenues of recourse. Sympathetic intellectuals and socialists who had done so much in the past for the labor movement were now impotent or nonexistent. Only Communists, subsidized partially by a Soviet state unaffected by the Great Depression, rushed to assist the oppressed and the unemployed. For good reason, then, the southern textile strikes, the violent conflicts in the coal fields, and the increasingly frequent unemployment demonstrations in urban America were led by dedicated Communists.

Farmers, like workers, needed time to realize that the depression represented a qualitative change in their existence. They, too, had been adjusting since 1921 to an unfavorable economic environment marked by falling prices and incomes. Depression only meant a little more of the same. For those agrarians totally wiped out by the crash—mostly white tenants and black sharecroppers—powerlessness guaranteed invisibility. Typically they responded to adversity in individualistic fashion either by migrating to California like Steinbeck's Joads or aimlessly taking to the road. In 1930 and 1931 agrarian America, traditionally a milieu for popular protest movements, seemed as placid as urban America.

The popular quietude of 1930 and 1931 cloaked a deep despair and a swelling tide of anger. As realization mounted that the Great Depression was indeed unprecedented and that Washington provided alms for the mighty but not the needy, subsurface anger began to flare into public protest and direct action. Organized by Communists into councils and leagues, the urban unemployed marched in New York, Detroit, Cleveland, and elsewhere to demand jobs, food, and assistance. As 1930 passed into 1931 and 1931 into 1932, clashes between the unemployed and the police became more common and so bitter that deaths frequently resulted.

Local manifestations of discontent assumed national dimension with the creation of the Bonus Expeditionary Force (BEF), an organization of unemployed World War I veterans committed to obtaining early payment of their federal war bonuses by marching on Washington. In the spring of 1932 veterans and their families descended on the nation's capital to petition Congress for relief. Unable to gain aid from Congress or the president, many of the BEF members returned home. Others, however, set up camp in the mosquito-infested Anacostia Flats district and vowed to stay until they obtained federal assistance. Congress, however, rebuffed them and the president sent the army instead of relief. Fearful that Communists were plotting a rebellion among the restless veterans, Hoover ordered then General Douglas MacArthur to evict the veterans from their tent colony on the Flats. With tear gas, torches, and drawn sabres, the real army routed the Bonus Army, leaving behind among the wreckage, according to a favorite apocryphal story of the time, a dead three-month old infant for whose epitaph the following was proposed: "Here lies Bernard Myers, aged three months, gassed to death by order of President Hoover."

Restlessness was also spreading across rural America. Farmers questioned why they were being asked to restrict acreage and to plant less when so many citizens seemed in real need. So absurd did the situation seem that a Wisconsin farmer told a congressional committee: "I honestly believe that if some of them [fellow farmers] could buy airplanes, they would come down here to Washington to blow you fellows all up." And the racist congressman from Mississippi, Theodore Bilbo, observed: "Folks are restless. Right here in Mississippi some people are about ready to lead a mob. In fact, I'm getting a little pink myself." Out in the Midwest, meanwhile, a local farm leader named Milo Reno was doing something tangible to assist farmers. Founder of the Farm Holiday Association, Reno led its members in western Iowa, Nebraska, and the Dakotas in a movement to keep produce from the markets in order to raise prices. Association supporters blocked roads, seized and spilled milk headed for market, and threatened noncooperating farmers. Boycotts and other forms of direct action spread rapidly to Minnesota, Wisconsin, and Illinois. Other farmers organized local vigilante groups to buy foreclosed property for token bids at public auctions and then restore the land to the foreclosed farmer. Unrest and sometimes violence surged relentlessly across the corn and wheat belts.

Yet the spread of discontent and the upsurge of protest brought no relief to the millions of unemployed or to the long-suffering farmers. Instead the depression seemed to worsen as the economy rolled further downhill. As the winter of 1932–1933 approached, the American nation entered the worst year of the Great Depression.

THE VALLEY OF DESPAIR

The winter of 1932–1933 was a dark period indeed. Unemployment had soared well above the twelve million mark, and some statisticians estimated it at more than fifteen million, with another thirty to forty million family members dependent on the jobless breadwinners. Conservative estimates placed the jobless at between 36 percent and 38 percent of nonfarm employees. For those still with jobs times were scarcely better. Real wage levels had fallen to their lowest level in a quarter of a century; only once in the years since 1905—during the recession of 1908—had wages fallen lower than they did in 1933.

Though prices also fell—bread tumbling from 8.8¢ a pound in 1929 to 7¢ in 1932, bacon from 43.9¢ to 22¢ a pound, and milk from 14.4¢ to 10.7¢ a quart—wages, including the cost of unemployment, fell even more rapidly. Only the fully employed worker, a rare specimen in the year 1932, benefited substantially from falling prices. In this depression, falling prices relieved the plight of only a small minority of the working class.

Beset by plummeting incomes, farmers and workers had to repay substantial debts incurred during the prosperous twenties. With national income in 1933 only half what it had been in 1929, how could people meet the mortgage payments on their homes and farms? There was no way. Banks and mortgage companies hounded their mortgagees—but to no avail. Foreclosure provided no relief, as no market existed for the sale of farms and homes. Lenders, in short, were in as dire a predicament as borrowers. As bankers proved unable to collect their loans, depositors grew anxious about the safety of their savings. This concern sparked bank runs that often caused bank failure. When increasing numbers of banks closed their doors or passed into insolvency, panic spread. It was bad enough that homes had been lost, but now savings disappeared also. What would remain? To insure that something in fact might be left, individual states began to declare bank holidays that, in effect, shut down banks; by Roosevelt's inauguration in March 1933, scarcely a bank remained open. By the end of the month, emergency federal legislation set a national bank holiday. So close to collapse did American capitalism now seem that Roosevelt conceded in his inaugural address: "Only a foolish optimist can deny the dark realities of the moment."

Dark as the moment was for millions of Americans, rebellion lacked a stimulus. The Bonus Army had already met its terrible defeat. Milo Reno's Midwestern farmers may have spilled some milk, less blood, and blocked several farm-to-market roads, but they scarcely relieved depressed farmers, nor did they endanger public authority. Sporadic and spontaneous demonstrations and marches by the unemployed continued to flare in the cities, but they changed nothing.

It was as if the nation awaited divine deliverance. The secular apostles of socialism and communism, as the 1932 election proved, had failed to win an army of converts. The labor movement lost followers instead of attracting them. It seemed sometimes as if Mussolini and Italian fascism had more sympathizers in the United States than any other social movement. Even more dismaying in this dark depression winter was the rise to power in Germany of Hitler and naziism as one response to the imminent collapse of capitalism. Most Americans seemed to be awaiting a bolt of lighting or deliverance from the political right. In March 1933 the present seemed grim, the future foreboding.

15

The Roosevelt Revolution: Reality or Legend?

The Great Depression recast American politics. Many of the most significant changes will be forever associated with the name Franklin Delano Roosevelt. Roosevelt, the only president to serve more than two terms (1933–1945), made his name and policies synonymous with the politics of an entire decade. His New Deal, the most famous reform movement in American history, led his admirers to praise and his critics to damn what became known as the "Roosevelt Revolution."

As president, Roosevelt transformed popular values and national politics, acting as the catalyst for three far-reaching political changes: 1) the emergence to dominance of a realigned Democratic party; 2) the undermining of traditional state rights and of laissez-faire attitudes; and 3) the acceptance of federal responsibility to alleviate economic and social inequities. Yet it remains problematic as to how far the New Deal's political reforms altered economic and social realities for most Americans. Perhaps the real "Roosevelt Revolution" consisted not of a movement that transformed basic structures but of a psychological triumph that turned a dispirited people into a hopeful one, that replaced apathy with activism.

THE 1932 PRESIDENTIAL CAMPAIGN

1932 promised to be a Democratic year. The incumbent Republican administration had become firmly identified with the Great Depression, and Hoover's decision to seek renomination especially favored a Democratic victory. Any Democratic nominee conceivably could win by espousing reform and denouncing Hoover. And to further strengthen the Democrats' chances, the party had an attractive candidate in Franklin D. Roosevelt. The efficient behind-the-scenes efforts of Roosevelt campaign aides Louis Howe and James Farley had built up Roosevelt's delegate support in the South and the West. Also, by 1932 he had acquired a national reputation as a man of action and a leader of great promise.

An exciting personality, the patrician reformer from Hyde Park, New York, had emerged to national prominence as the result of both his successful recovery from polio during the 1920s and his record as governor of New York (1928–1932). Roosevelt was able to convey a sense of concern, an empathy with the suffering, and an open-mindedness toward new ideas. His speeches and his breezy manner helped restore American confidence. Ever attuned to political realities, his speeches expressed the hopes and aspirations of the nation. His final national address of the 1940 presidential campaign exemplifies this: "We Americans of today—all of us—we are characters in the living book of democracy. . . . But we are also its author. It falls upon us now to say whether the chapters that are to come will tell a story of retreat or a story of continued advance." Roosevelt never defined how victory over the depression could be achieved. Indeed, the core of his vaguely expressed reform program could be summarized as experimentation and abandonment of tradition: "We must lay hold of the fact that economic laws are not made by nature. They are made by man." In another speech Roosevelt counseled: "The country needs and . . . demands bold, persistent experimentation. It is common sense to take a method and try it. If it fails, admit it frankly and try another. But above all, try something."

The acknowledged Democratic front-runner, Roosevelt overcame all major obstacles to securing the Democratic presidential nomination in 1932. First, he projected the image of a reformer who was not too reformist. The exigencies of the convention's two-thirds rule specifically necessitated such a strategy. Thus, candidate Roosevelt appealed to common voters with populist rhetoric while simultaneously courting Southern conservatives, big-city bosses, and disaffected reformers. He could do so effectively, for in 1932 he had few convictions that he intended to translate into policy. Roosevelt's preconvention effort, then, was dictated by the lack of ideology, sheer political necessity, and a willingness to innovate.

Although he was the unquestioned front-runner, Roosevelt had to wait until the fourth ballot to win the nomination. Unable to win a first-ballot triumph and fearful that their delegate strength might dwindle, the Roosevelt forces politicked feverishly and eventually won over conservative delegates supporting Speaker of the House John Nance Garner, who gained the vice presidential nomination. Equally important, many delegates and political leaders refused to waste a golden opportunity for victory over the Republicans. The memory of their stalemated 1924 convention and the bitterness it had engendered among Democrats was a silent factor in Roosevelt's fourth-ballot nomination.

Having won, Roosevelt electrified the convention and the country by dramatically breaking tradition and flying to Chicago to accept in person the nomination of the Democratic party. (Since the 1830s it had been accepted tradition that the convention appoint a delegation to inform the nominee of his selection.) Roosevelt's decision was actually more dramatic than substantive. It conveyed a sense of bold and purposeful action but involved no basic changes in how party decisions were made.

Characteristically, Roosevelt did not use his national campaign to articulate principles and develop support for a program to end the depression. For the most part, he ignored Hoover's call to debate. Roosevelt instead concentrated on the Hoover administration's failures. He realized that most voters reacted more strongly to the sins of the incumbent rather than the virtues of the contender. Hence, he suggested redistributing wealth and also advocated a balanced budget. He appealed to a broad spectrum of interest groups, offering something for everyone. In the midst of a major crisis, at a time in the nation's life when action was required as never before, Roosevelt intentionally left unchallenged many outmoded assumptions and principles. His strategy worked.

Roosevelt won the election indebted to no section or interest group and possessing only a mandate for action. And what a mandate it was! The Democratic nominee captured 57.4 percent (22,809,638) of the popular vote and 472 electoral votes to Hoover's 39.7 percent (15,758,901) and 59 electoral votes. But the overwhelming repudiation of Hooverian conservatism hardly added up to radicalism. That the public's radicalism of 1932 was more emotional than ideological was clearly revealed by the vote totals of the candidates of the Socialist (881,951) and Communist (102,785) parties.

Roosevelt's strategy, and popular disaffection with Hoover's leadership, also contributed to Democratic control of Congress. The resulting distribution in Congress was that 313 Democrats, 117 Republicans, and 5 Farmer-Laborites or Progressives were elected to the House and 59 Democrats, 36 Republicans, and 1 Farmer-Laborite to the Senate. Even these impressive figures do not fully reveal how responsive this new Congress would be to proposals for federal action. Many Republican congressmen, most notably Robert LaFollette, Jr., and George Norris, were progressives. Moreover, fully 131 of the freshmen Democrats were elected from formerly Republican districts.

BUILDING AN ADMINISTRATION

Because he was committed to no specific course or proposal, Roosevelt had maximized his options. There remained only one immediate political problem for the newly-elected president: the formal transfer of the office and the power would not occur until March 4. (Before 1936, the Constitution would be amended to make January 20 the inaugural date.) The discredited Hoover was to continue in office for nearly four months after his repudiation at the polls. All the while the economic crisis worsened.

Hoover tried to use the interregnum to convince Roosevelt to adopt the discredited Republican administrator's domestic and foreign economic programs. The newly-elected president rejected Hoover's advice.

Roosevelt, however, did not use the interregnum to formulate a clear course of action, to draft a specific program distinct from Hoover's, or to select a cabinet committed to extensive change. For the most part, his cabinet appointees were conservative and conventional. Cabinet officials included Cordell Hull (a Tennessee Senator) as secretary of state, businessman William Woodin as treasury secretary, and James Farley (Roosevelt's campaign manager) as postmaster general. But three new appointees hinted that the administration might move in more adventurous directions. Secretary of Agriculture Henry Wallace and Secretary of the Interior Harold Ickes both came from progressive Republican backgrounds and were known for their rectitude and faith in reform. Even more startling was the president's selection of Frances Perkins as secretary of labor. Not only would she be the first woman ever to serve in the cabinet but she occupied a post customarily reserved for a male trade unionist.

In his inaugural address, moreover, Roosevelt did not even hint at the principles that would shape his soon-to-be-enacted New Deal. He simply called for action and promised to innovate. Roosevelt exhorted the nation to a renewed sense of purpose and self-confidence affirming that "the only thing we have to fear is fear itself. . . . This Nation asks for action and action now. . . . [if necessary I shall ask Congress to cede] broad Executive powers to wage a war against emergency, as great as the powers that would be given to me if we were in fact invaded by a foreign foe." Concluding, Roosevelt emphasized that the 1932 election was a mandate for "discipline and direction under leadership." Roosevelt sought to convey the impression of a popularly mandated administration, one committed to such programs as were clearly necessitated by the magnitude of the depression. The new president affirmed that the measures he would propose constituted no departure from tradition and stressed the parallel with the Wilson administration's wartime emergency responses.

Action for the sake of action characterized the early Roosevelt New Deal. Roosevelt was a pragmatist, if by that term one means an affinity for results, innovative methods, and an undefined philosophy or consistent set of principles. Initially convinced that the magnitude of the depression derived from Hoover's intellectual rigidity and standpattism, Roosevelt intended to provide bold presidential leadership. He intended to use power to effect economic recovery.

Reflecting his disdain for theory, the president relied on such diverse advisers as Raymond Moley, Rexford Tugwell, and Felix Frankfurter. Following their conflicting recommendations, Roosevelt moved in many different directions. At times, the president seemed to believe that economic revival required business-government cooperation. At other times, he preferred national economic planning. At still other times, Roosevelt favored antitrust and stringent federal regulation of business, only to reverse himself and instead implement manipulation of the currency and an inflationary monetary policy. Naturally, as policies were discarded, confusion resulted.

THE ONE-HUNDRED DAYS

Acceding to the presidency on March 4, 1933, Roosevelt had a mandate to act. The public seemed restive and was insistent upon action. The conservative congressional leadership lacked an alternative program; moreover, it lacked even the will to challenge the fifteen legislative measures that the president eventually introduced, which would be enacted into law between March 5 and June 15, 1933. This period, the now-famous 100-Days, was so-called because of the scope and drama of this heretofore unprecedented presidential legislative initiative.

The first order of business confronting the president was a serious banking crisis: by March, 1933 commercial banks either had closed or were operating under severe restrictions and, to prevent further bank failures, twenty-two states had declared banking holidays. The public had either lost confidence in the soundness of banks or were compelled by the decline in personal income to withdraw their savings from banks. Because many banks had invested heavily in the inflated stock market of the late 1930s, and had thereby lost heavily with the crash, the loss both of deposits and public confidence aggravated an already serious money crisis.

Immediate action was required, the president believed. Accordingly, relying on provisions of the Trading with the Enemy Act of 1917, Roosevelt on March 6 declared a four-day banking holiday suspending all banking operations. Simultaneously, the president called Congress into a special session on March 9 to pass an emergency banking bill that provided ex post facto legalization of the President's declaration of a banking holiday, authorized the reopening of all banks except those in a hopeless condition, and funded distressed banks. The bill charged the RFC, the Federal Reserve Board, and the comptroller of currency with providing private banks with the resources to reopen. The bill passed the House and Senate in less than eight hours, without formal hearings or even the printing of the text of the measure. The sense of desperation that led Congress to enact this measure so rapidly was clearly evidenced when efforts by some House members merely to have the text of the bill read were shouted down.

The drama of Roosevelt's sudden action masked the limited character of bank reform. At a time when nationalization of the banks commanded widespread support, the Emergency Banking Act provided federal assistance to the private banking system. Senator Bronson Cutting of New Mexico later wrote, "I think back to the events of March 4, 1933 with a sick heart. For then . . . the nationalization of banks by President Roosevelt could have been accomplished without a word of protest." The act stimulated the reopening of the banks, reinstituted traditional banking policies, and reversed the psychology of fear that had threatened to close additional banks.

More significantly, the two most important legislative measures enacted during the 100 Days—agrarian relief and industrial recovery—reflected congressional pressure as much as presidential initiative. The bills also disclosed Roosevelt's desire to assuage the fears of businessmen and plot a moderate course of reform.

In the aftermath of the campaign, key administration leaders (including Secretary of Agriculture Henry A. Wallace and Undersecretary of Agriculture Rexford G. Tugwell) joined George Peek and leaders of the organized farm community to draft legislation to combat the agrarian crisis. Yet, as was true generally with the Roosevelt administration's policies, the participants in this drafting session diverged widely on how best to effect recovery. Their theories ranged all the way from economic planning and production controls advocated by such men as Jerome Frank to the more conservative demands of those like Peek who advocated assisting farmers simply by promoting export marketing. No well-defined integrated program was formulated. Instead, the specific bill drafted under Wallace's leadership was sufficiently vague and comprehensive to satisfy at least minimally all the divergent groups.

Submitted by the administration to the Congress on March 16 as a temporary measure—the statutory authority requested would last only two years—the Emergency Farm Relief Bill nonetheless established the precedent from an enduring agricultural policy. Basically the administration proposal combined two alternatives: marketing agreements and production controls. Its objective was to raise commodity prices to the same exchange value ("parity") of the years 1910–1914, thereby increasing the farmers' purchasing power. As George Peek and other conservatives saw the matter, imposing marketing quotas and providing marketing loans would allow farm commodities to be marketed more orderly with the minimum of governmental controls. In contrast, liberal advisers such as Wallace and the proponents of public planning such as Tugwell supported a program that would raise prices by reducing production by stipulated amounts—a program that would require more extensive and continuous governmental intervention.

A compromise between these divergent views, the Farm Emergency Relief Act of May 12, 1933, was based on a voluntary method of production control—the domestic allotment concept. Farmers would be paid not to produce and would be subsidized through a tax on the primary processor (for example, the miller of grain into flour) . This tax would be passed on to the consumer as a part of the cost of the commodity. An Agricultural Adjustment Administration (AAA) was created to implement the program with authority to provide low interest loans to farmers, remove surpluses from the market, administer acreage controls, make payments, and collect the processing tax. An elaborate licensing system was established to enforce the law's crop restrictions. Basing this authority on the interstate commerce provisions of the Constitution, the drafters of the bill also sought to extend coverage to commodities grown and marketed wholly within one state by stipulating that all products would be covered if they should "in any way affect interstate . . . commerce." To supplement the market agreement and production control provisions, a Commodity Credit Corporation was established. The corporation was empowered to lend money to farmers on the security of their crops; the CCC would also assume all interest on these loans. Funded through the RFC, this system would enable producers of nonperishable commodities to play the market at minimum risk and cost.

Congress debated none of the AAA's obvious deficiencies. Committed to combating agricultural distress as one means to effect economic recovery, congressmen did not consider whether the institution of production controls would create economic hardship for farm laborers, tenants, and sharecroppers. What limited debate there was centered on the method of paying farmers. James Simpson, the president of the small-farmer-dominated Farmers Union, lobbied for a provision whereby payments would be determined by the cost of production, i.e., what it cost a farmer to produce a commodity as opposed to how much land was taken out of production. Given the small farmer's lower margin of profit, reducing acreage in production would not alleviate his plight or insure prosperity. The House ignored Simpson's proposal as the administration's bill sailed through after only two days' debate and six days after being introduced. Debate was lengthier and more pointed in the Senate, although Secretary of Agriculture Henry Wallace successfully dissuaded senators from adopting the cost-of-production principle by emphasizing its negative features.

The farm bill exemplified the administration's initial short-range approach. Its specific objective was narrowly confined: not to reform society but to end the immediate crisis. Thus the word "emergency" in the title of the bill reflected both a perception of the gravity of the immediate crisis and the belief in its temporary duration. The program was to expire in two years, though it could be renewed; in this sense it was experimental.

An increasingly worsening industrial crisis simultaneously provided the specific impetus to congressional efforts to promote industrial recovery. In December 1932 Democratic Senator Hugo Black of Alabama introduced a bill prohibiting the interstate shipment of goods produced by labor working more than thirty hours per week. Intended to relieve economic distress by sharing work and thereby increasing consumer purchasing power, Black's bill expressed a sense of frustration and an urgent belief in action.

But in March 1933, the Roosevelt administration had developed no legislative program to deal with the industrial crisis. Accordingly, on April 6, 1933, the Senate passed the Black bill. House approval also seemed likely. Yet, Roosevelt opposed the Black bill, deeming its provisions inflexible and possibly unconstitutional. To avert passage of the Black bill became the administration's main goal. First, Secretary of Labor Frances Perkins lobbied with key leaders of the House to have the bill amended. Then, during House hearings, the secretary proposed specific amendments to the Black bill to set a floor on wages and to impose government controls over production; decisions on wages and production, moreover, would be subject to review by specially created industrial boards.

Simultaneously, a group of progressive senators, led by Robert Wagner and Robert LaFollette, Jr., advocated a huge public works program to stimulate recovery. Congress thus confronted a plethora of industrial recovery programs that encompassed sharing work, stimulating investment, undercutting monopolistic power, increasing public spending, and adopting a policy of national economic planning. And, the administration found itself unable to resolve the confusion in its industrial recovery policy.

To maximize support from diverse and powerful interest groups for an acceptable recovery program, Raymond Moley (a key Roosevelt adviser) conferred with representatives from the administration, Congress, labor unions, and industry. Moley's meetings produced a hastily drafted and vaguely worded National Industrial Recovery Bill, which the president submitted to Congress on May 17 and which legislators formally approved on June 16, 1933.

A compromise measure, the bill contained provisions tailored to the demands of the major pressure groups. Title I, welcomed by the leaders of the corporate business community, created a National Recovery Administration (NRA) with responsibility for developing codes of fair competition, minimum wages, and maximum hours, to be drafted by specially created authorities on an industry by industry basis and subject to presidential approval. To insure compliance with their regulations, the code authorities were accorded licensing powers, and their decisions were exempted from antitrust prosecution. Section 7a of this title, demanded by organized labor, guaranteed to individuals the right to form unions and to bargain collectively through representatives of their own choosing. Title II, welcomed by proponents of public spending, created a Public Works Administration (PWA) with appropriations of $3.3 billion.

Still, the act provided no clear legislative guidelines for future policy. In approving the measure, Congress had ceded discretionary authority to the president, having defined neither the purpose nor the standards by which the licensing or code provisions of this act were to be administered.

Given Congress's willingness to defer to the executive when approving agricultural and industrial relief legislation, in 1933 Roosevelt had the opportunity to chart whatever course he thought most feasible to promote recovery. Not political necessity but his own preferences determined the results of his policy. Indeed, Roosevelt's appointees to head the NRA, PWA, and AAA revealed the president's extreme sensitivity in 1933 to the concerns of conservative congressmen and businessmen. Thus, to maximize support from commercial farmers and Mississippi Senator Pat Harrison, Roosevelt appointed George Peek to head the AAA. Peek viewed his function as administrator narrowly: to achieve agricultural recovery, not agrarian reform. Opposed to production controls, the head of the AAA emphasized the program's marketing and export functions. To disarm possible charges of waste and inefficiency in the administration of public works projects, Roosevelt appointed Secretary of Interior Ickes to head the PWA. And, to insure maximum support from the business community for the industrial recovery program, the president appointed the bumptious businessman Hugh Johnson to head the NRA.

As head of the NRA, Johnson recognized that the industrial recovery program would inevitably be delayed until the specific codes could be implemented. To provide an interim policy, in July, 1933 Johnson mandated the president's Reemployment Agreement as a "blanket code" for minimum wages and maximum hours and urged businesses to comply with these standards. Because compliance was voluntary, Johnson resorted to the kind of propaganda that had made the Liberty Bond drives of the World War I years successful. Through a concerted public relations effort and considerable ballyhoo including a massive New York City parade of support, the head of the NRA sought to insure business compliance. Specifically, he stipulated that those businesses that were in compliance with the agreement display the symbol of the Blue Eagle. As a consequence, two million employers agreed to abide by the blanket code.

Eventually, 557 code authorities covered large and small businesses. Larger corporations assumed leadership in drafting and enforcing the various codes: labor was represented on only fifty-one (less than 10 percent). Moreover, the majority of "public" members of the code authorities were businessmen who formerly had been engaged in the specific industries being licensed and who were convinced that business leaders could be counted on to do "the right thing." A conservative industrial recovery program, one clearly responsive to the interests of the more powerful and organized business interests, had been established.

Rounding out the administration's legislative actions during the 100 Days were a variety of measures. On April 18, by an executive order based on provisions of the Trading-with-the-Enemy Act of 1917, Roosevelt prohibited exports of gold bullion. This action essentially took the nation off the gold standard. Three weeks later Congress ratified this action. It aimed at freeing American economic recovery from the plight of other depressed nations and exemplified how the Great Depression stimulated economic nationalism everywhere.

Of greater consequence and potentially the most far-reaching measure enacted during the 1930s, was the Tennessee Valley Authority (TVA), created by Congress on May 18, 1933. Initiative for the TVA derived from the efforts of Senator George Norris, who during the 1920s had prevented the sale of the federally-owned Muscle Shoals nitrate plant to private industry and had demanded a federal corporation to operate the nitrate plants and construct additional dams. Authorized to construct dams for water control and to generate electricity to sell, in turn, to cooperatives, the TVA constituted a vast regional development program under public control and planning. Those supporting the TVA had differing objectives—to curb periodic flooding, which had devastated the region surrounding the Tennessee River, to manufacture cheap fertilizer for sale to farmers, to provide cheap electricity to benefit both industry and farmers in that region, or to establish a yardstick by which to judge the rates of private utilities.

On May 12, 1933, Congress approved the Federal Emergency Relief Act, creating an administration (FERA) with authority to provide grants-in-aid to states for relief purposes. Headed by Harry Hopkins, the FERA distributed $500 million in funds to construct roads, hospitals, schools, and municipal buildings, stressing the principle of work relief and not cash handouts. The act established no guideline for determining wage rates, and Hopkins established no uniform wage standard. Instead, he tolerated regional and skill wage-differentials, often offering lower wages than those of private industry.

In June, Congress passed the Banking Act of 1933 (the Glass-Steagall Act) creating a Federal Deposit Insurance Corporation (FDIC) to insure savings and deposits up to $2,500, divorce investment affiliates from commercial banks, impose controls over member banks, and permit the substitution of government securities for gold.

In an effort to provide relief and stimulate economic recovery, Congress passed the Home Owners Loan Act, which refinanced home mortgages, and the Emergency Farm Mortgage Act and created the Civilian Conservation Corps (CCC). In return for renegotiating mortgages over longer periods, banks and other lending institutions received government bonds, which could either be converted to cash or retained for regular interest payments. The CCC, an innovative social experiment, recruited youths aged eighteen through twenty-five to protect and develop reservoirs, watersheds, forests, and parks. The CCC not only provided employ-ments to youths but its appeal to youthful idealism provided the prece-dent for later programs such as the Peace Corps. The CCC's activities in the conservation field had lasting societal benefits, and this type of work experience contributed to changing the attitudes of many toward federal responsibility and authority.

The fifteen legislative measures enacted during the 100 Days neither exhausted the legislative innovations of the Roosevelt New Deal nor established a precedent for subsequent legislation. During the 100 Days, the administration had not sought to reform the national economy. Its primary objective had been to promote economic recovery by stimulating prices, production, and investment. Consequently, little thought had been given to the effect of the agricultural relief program on marginal farmers or farm workers. Nor at first did presidential advisers consider the consequences for small business of a program tailored to the specifica-tions of large corporations, or whether the labor provisions of NRA served the interests of most workers. Nor did federal relief programs eliminate hard-core poverty. And securities and banking legislation left financial power largely in private hands. Finally, the Roosevelt adminis-tration had yet to consider tax reform as a potential means to redis-tribute wealth and income.

Clearly, then, the initial Roosevelt program—what some historians have labeled the "First New Deal"—was scarcely radical. If a few po-tentially radical measures such as the TVA—a precursor for public planning—and Section 7a of NIRA—a mandate for trade unionism—slipped into the program, the First New Deal largely addressed the needs of larger farmers and the great corporations. It aimed at promoting economic recovery through harmonious relations between federal officials and the nation's dominant economic interests. In other words, in return for federal aid and encouragement, Roosevelt expected businessmen to increase investment, raise production, and reemploy labor. Until private recovery occurred, Roosevelt favored emergency federal relief programs that put labor to work on necessary public projects, rescued teenagers from delinquency, averted starvation, and saved small private home-owners from the mortgage hammer.

CRITICS OF THE FIRST NEW DEAL

The reforms of the first 100-Days proved a mixed blessing. Agricultural prices increased (net farm income doubled between 1933 and 1935), and the downward spiral of wages and employment reversed itself (by 1935, four million more workers were employed than in 1933). But the greatest beneficiaries had been large commercial farmers and giant corporations. Marginal farmers, tenants, and sharecroppers fared worse than ever, and more than nine million Americans remained unemployed.

As 1933 drew to an end, popular and congressional dissatisfaction with the limited achievements of the New Deal became manifest. A diverse group of dissidents—including Senators Robert Wagner, Bronson Cutting, Edward Costigan, Huey Long, Robert LaFollette, and George Norris and public figures like Francis Townsend and Father Charles Coughlin—capitalized on popular frustrations to demand reforms considerably to the left of those already enacted under the New Deal. They also criticized the actual impact of the agricultural and industrial reforms instituted under the first AAA and NIRA.

The conflicts involving the NRA dramatized the president's political problems. As administered by Hugh Johnson, the NRA promoted business-government cooperation. Although opposition to business domination of the code authorities came principally from within the administration, Roosevelt at first supported Johnson in every conflict. Roosevelt even overruled the objections of the president's Special Industrial Recovery Board and Secretary of Interior Ickes to the NRA's price policies and production controls. He proved as eager as Johnson to secure business sanction for the New Deal.

By 1934, however, opposition to NRA became public. Congressional liberals and consumer groups, led by Senators William Borah and Gerald Nye, specifically demanded that the members of the code authorities reveal their business associations. They also charged that NRA price policies encouraged monopolization and higher prices without significantly improving wages or promoting economic recovery.

The administration could not ignore such protests. Accordingly, in March, 1934 the president created a special committee headed by the famous criminal lawyer Clarence Darrow to investigate the operation of the NRA. After studying eight code authorities, the Darrow Committee released its report on May 20, 1934. It concluded that small business had been penalized and a trend toward monopoly stimulated. The committee thus called for substantial reforms in the composition of the code authorities and their policies.

The Darrow Committee report fortified critics of NRA. By mid-1934, radicals and liberals branded NRA as a failure and a hoax, and conservatives condemned it as socialistic and unconstitutional. Yet the president, in February 1935, requested that Congress extend NRA for another two years with more stringent controls over monopolistic price-fixing (and not, as Tugwell had earlier recommended, with general government price-fixing authority).

Before Congress could act, however, the Supreme Court, in *Schechter Poultry Corp.* v. *U.S.* (May 27, 1935), unanimously ruled that the National Industrial Recovery Act was unconstitutional. In its decision, the Court held that Congress had unconstitutionally delegated its powers to the executive branch when it stipulated that guidelines for the code and licensing provisions should be determined by the president. The Court also ruled that the authority to license businesses by regulating hours and production fell outside the scope of the interstate commerce clause and that the claimants had been deprived of liberty and property without due process of law. The Supreme Court's decision left the administration temporarily without an industrial recovery program.

Just as NRA failed to achieve industrial recovery, the enactment of the Farm Emergency Relief Act of 1933 did not resolve the serious agrarian crisis. A complex of problems almost immediately confronted the AAA and its beleaguered administrator, George Peek. Specifically, prior to the act's passage, farmers had already planted their crops. Faced with the prospect of bumper crops which would further depress agricultural prices, the AAA paid farmers to plow under crops and slaughter livestock. The deliberate elimination of ten million acres of cotton and six million baby pigs poignantly exemplified the economic contradictions of the depression: to waste abundance amidst widespread poverty.

More long-term farm production policies also exacted a heavy toll of human suffering. By making landowners alone eligible for production payments, the AAA penalized tenants and sharecroppers and made them more dependent than ever. As landowners cut production and discharged tenants and sharecroppers, relief rolls in the South rose. Indeed, in the first year of the program's operation fully 15 to 20 percent of tenants and sharecroppers were displaced from the land and forced to seek relief assistance.

Subsequent 1934 amendments in agricultural policy that substituted mandatory production controls for voluntary compliance (the Bankhead Cotton Control Act and the Kerr-Smith Tobacco Control Act) failed to resolve the conflict between the interests of landowners and tenants. The more conservative leaders, such as Cully Cobb, then head of the Cotton Division, maintained that the AAA's sole responsibility was to raise agricultural prices without tampering with traditional landowner-tenant relations. The more radical leaders, such as Jerome Frank, head of the Legal Division, viewed the economic crisis as an opportunity to transform fundamentally the traditional landlord-tenant relationship of southern agriculture.

Chester Davis, George Peek's successor at the AAA, sought to resolve the conflict. If sympathetic to the plight of the hapless tenant, Davis nonetheless viewed his responsibilities narrowly. The purpose of the AAA, he once stated, was to deal with an immediate agricultural crisis and not solve "a deep-seated social problem." But the two could not be separated, and poor southern whites and blacks formed an interracial farm workers' union in 1934, the Southern Tenant Farmers Union (STFU), that militantly pressed their interests.

STFU efforts to organize tenant farmers became intertwined with the question of how the AAA should enforce the provision of the Bankhead Act that required landowners to keep the same number of tenants on the land. Did this section mean merely the same number of tenants or the same individual tenants? In an effort to resolve this question, the Legal Division in January, 1935 ruled that farmers would be in violation of their contractual obligations if they did not retain the same tenants.

This was neither a disinterested nor purely legalistic ruling: in effect it would have favored STFU organizational efforts by removing tenants' fear of discharge and served the objectives of reformers within the Legal Division.

The Legal Division's ruling, however, was never implemented. First Chester Davis and, then, Henry Wallace and Roosevelt repudiated it. As a consequence, during the life of the AAA landowners received 90 percent of total payments. Not only did sharecroppers receive one-ninth of the payments made during 1934–1935, but more particularly, black sharecroppers received an average of $295 and white sharecroppers an average of $417.

Nevertheless, the AAA, like the NRA, soon came into conflict with more conservative opponents. On January 6, 1936, in response to a suit instituted by the receivers of a cotton processing firm, Hoosac Mills, the Supreme Court in *U.S.* v. *Butler* ruled in a 6–3 decision that the AAA's processing tax was unconstitutional. This levy was not a legitimate use of federal taxing powers, Justice Owen Roberts declared in the majority opinion; rather, it was "the expropriation of money from one group for the benefit of another" and an encroachment upon the powers of the states.

THE SECOND NEW DEAL

The early 1930s produced a new and more radical breed of political leaders—Louisiana Senator Huey Long, the novelist-radical Upton Sinclair, retired physician Francis Townsend, and the Catholic priest Charles Coughlin. Before his election to the U.S. Senate in 1932, Huey Long had been a popular and colorful governor of Louisiana. Styling himself as the candidate of the back country and the foe of the established political and business leadership, Long successfully rose to political dominance in the state. Indifferent to constitutional requirements for his actions as governor, Long improved the quality of schools, roads, and hospitals. The Louisiana senator began as a Roosevelt supporter; at the 1932 Democratic National Convention he sustained support for the presidential aspirant within the wavering Mississippi delegation. The flamboyant senator, however, soon broke openly with Roosevelt. Although projecting the image of simplicity (Long wore loud suits, had a boylike appearance, and preferred sarcasm to reasoned analysis), the Louisiana senator possessed a shrewd intelligence and a quick mind. In 1934, he advocated a radical plan to redistribute income and fund advanced social and economic programs through confiscatory taxes on the wealthy and soon claimed a nationwide membership of 7.5 million in 27,000 Share Our Wealth clubs.

Long's transition from Roosevelt supporter to Roosevelt critic paralleled that of the Royal Oak, Michigan, radio priest, Charles Cough-

Father Coughlin
Brown Brothers

Huey Long
Wide World Photos

John L. Lewis
Wide World Photos

FDR
Wide World Photos

Dr. Townsend
Wide World Photos

lin. An eloquent and compelling speaker, since 1930 Father Coughlin had a nationwide weekly radio program on CBS—the Golden Hour of the Little Flower—which reached an estimated thirty to forty-five million listeners. An avowed critic of "capitalism" and particularly international bankers, Coughlin at first welcomed and effusively praised the Roosevelt New Deal. The president's failure to support nationalization of banks and utilities, redistributive taxes, and monetary inflation (including "free silver") soon led the Royal Oak priest to criticize the New Deal. On November 11, 1934, Coughlin announced the formation of the National Union for Social Justice. To further the aims of this organization Coughlin in 1936 founded a weekly tabloid newspaper, *Social Justice*. Thereafter, he bitterly denounced the New Deal.

In contrast, neither Upton Sinclair nor Francis Townsend began as ardent Roosevelt supporters. A retired Long Beach, California, physician, Townsend became concerned over the dire economic plight of the elderly. In January 1934 he founded the Old Age Revolving Pensions organization, which he claimed had 1,200 clubs by the end of that year. Townsend proposed that every person over sixty should receive a monthly pension of $200, on the conditions that this money be spent within the month and that the individual retire from all gainful work. Sinclair's objectives were more far-reaching and less consistent with New Deal reformism. In 1933, the novelist publicly announced a plan, End Poverty in California (EPIC), which he used to mount a campaign for the California Democratic gubernatorial nomination. Sinclair proposed to end poverty by having the state government assume the responsibility to provide work (and not relief) to the unemployed. His plan called for the state to buy or lease land on which the jobless could grow food and to rent unused factories at which the unemployed could manufacture clothing and furniture. Those employed in these state-financed enterprises would be paid in scrip that could be redeemed only to purchase the essential commodities (food, clothing, furniture) produced under this state system. The attractiveness of this proposal enabled Sinclair in 1934 to win the Democratic gubernatorial nomination, snowing under his closest competitor, George Creel, 436,000 to 288,000 and polling more votes than the incumbent conservative Republican governor, Frank Merriam, did in the Republican primary. Liberal fears about Sinclair's program resulted, however, in the reelection of this Republican arch-conservative, who trounced Sinclair 1,139,000 to 880,000.

As mass unemployment persisted and the economy limped along, despite the Roosevelt reforms, pressure continued to build on the president from the left. The cries of Long, Townsend, and Coughlin resonated among the restive American people, and a new wave of militancy washed across America in the late spring and early summer of 1934. As industrial workers fought armed battles in the streets of Toledo, Minneapolis, and San Francisco, radical congressmen, heedless of the administration's advice to go slow, introduced wide-ranging legislation. And in the November 1934 off-year elections, Democrats, progressive Republicans, and independent radicals swept the polls, forming one of the most radical congresses in history.

Encountering criticism on his left, Roosevelt responded both opportunistically and vigorously. Turning away from businessmen ungrateful for New Deal measures that had benefited them economically, Roosevelt moved to the left. By the time Congress reconvened in 1935, the president was preparing to place himself at the vanguard of a second reform movement, dubbed the "Second New Deal." If Congress enacted fewer major bills in 1935 than it had done during the 100 Days, the bills it did pass proved more significant in their implications. Four laws—the Wagner Labor Relations Act, the Social Security Act, the Revenue Act of 1935, and the Public Utility Holding Company Act—that Congress passed in 1935 exemplified the Second New Deal.

Far more than the president, Senator Robert Wagner of New York provided the leadership in securing federal legislation that helped bring about a strong labor union movement. Well known as a reformer since his early days in the New York state senate (1911–1915), the senator from the Empire State during the 1930s proved to be one of the labor movement's best friends in Congress.

Originally appointed by President Roosevelt to head the NRA's Labor Review Board, Wagner soon became frustrated with that board's lack of enforcement authority and by that act's failure to preclude company unions, to foster independent unions, and to stabilize industrial relations. Hence, in 1934 Wagner introduced legislation to create a permanent national labor board with statutory enforcement authority. Roosevelt and certain key advisers, however, feared that Wagner's proposed labor legislation would sustain labor militancy and precipitate strikes, thereby delaying economic recovery. Administration pressure postponed congressional action on the bill in 1934. By 1935, as his political options narrowed, the president agreed not to oppose Wagner's proposed legislation, though he still refused publicly to endorse it. On May 6, 1935, the bill passed the Senate by an overwhelming margin (63–12). Roosevelt consequently came out publicly in its support on May 24. After limited hearings the House approved it on June 27, and the president signed it into law on July 5.

Wagner's proposal, the National Labor Relations Bill, created an independent National Labor Relations Board (NLRB) empowered to supervise and enforce stipulated labor-management provisions. These provisions included the prohibition of company unions and of management's interference with labor's efforts to organize by discriminatory hiring and firing of union organizers. The NLRB was empowered to supervise elections between organizations seeking to represent labor to determine which commanded majority support, thereby incorporating the principle of majority rule. More tightly worded than the National Industrial Recovery Act, the Wagner Act also based its constitutional authority on the interstate commerce clause, asserting that it was intended to avert industrial disputes that injured interstate commerce.

Almost immediately, employers fought the Wagner Act. Buoyed by the recent Supreme Court ruling in the Schechter case, lawyers of the conservative American Liberty League denounced the act as unconstitutional. The resultant challenges to its rulings and its authority crippled the NLRB for a time. Only when the Supreme Court in April, 1937 upheld the constitutionality of the Wagner Act in *N.L.R.B.* v. *Jones and Laughlin* did the NLRB become fully effective. A further obstacle was removed when the Court, in a January 1938 ruling, prohibited federal district courts from enjoining NLRB proceedings on the grounds that since the act had provided for circuit court enforcement, employers could not claim damages until a board decision had been made.

The passage and legitimation of the Wagner Act set the stage for the emergence of a mass labor movement and incorporated organized labor into the Roosevelt Democratic coalition. No other piece of New Deal legislation so drastically affected the distribution of economic power or engendered such heated opposition from the business class.

By 1934, unemployment compensation and old age assistance were ideas whose time had come. If critics of federal action still condemned the effect of public welfare on individual initiative and private property, their voices were heard less often. The persistence of mass unemployment and the suffering of the aged had spelled the death of conventional beliefs concerning charity, public relief, and self-help. The issue now was not whether a social security program would be adopted but what form it would take.

The impetus for what became the Social Security Act of 1935 again came from outside the Roosevelt administration. For over a year, Francis Townsend, Huey Long, and Upton Sinclair had been promoting a variety of plans to succor the aged, abolish poverty, and redistribute wealth. And in Congress in 1934 Senator Wagner introduced an unemployment compensation bill. Roosevelt could not resist reacting to such pressures, however contradictory and ill-defined the suggested programs were. On June 29, 1934, the president appointed a cabinet-level study group, the Committee on Economic Security.

The committee consisted of cabinet members and an advisory board composed of prominent businessmen, reformers, and labor leaders. The character of the appointees insured that a compromise measure would be drafted. The committee recommended that both unemployment compensation and old age pensions be funded through a payroll tax on both employers and employees paid directly to the federal government. The states, moreover, retained the authority to administer unemployment compensation. Initially unemployment benefits averaged $15 to $18 per month and lasted only twenty weeks in a program subject to minimal federal supervision. Resistance from Congressional conservatives produced a compromise measure that excluded from coverage about one-half of the labor force, including farm workers, retail clerks, service employees, and state and municipal employees. The original social security system also provided only the most minimal pension benefits (initially ranging between $10 and $85 a month), based them on personal earnings rather than need, and made no provision for sickness assistance.

Yet, however deficient were the 1935 bill's provisions, it did establish for the first time in United States history the principle that the federal government bore responsibility for insuring the welfare of unemployed and indigent citizens—no mean accomplishment.

By 1935 popular sentiment and many congressional radicals demanded that the concentration of wealth in the hands of a few individuals and corporations be eliminated. No one better exploited this widespread sentiment than Senator Huey Long, whose "Share Our Wealth" program proposed to restrict the wealth and power of the rich through confiscatory taxes and then to use the increased federal revenue to provide social benefits for the majority of Americans.

The Roosevelt administration reacted immediately to Long's popularity. First, it denied federal patronage to the senator's Louisiana political machine and had federal agents check the income tax returns of Long and his followers. More important, on June 19, 1935, the administration introduced a major revenue bill. Labeled by its critics a "soak the rich" measure, the Wealth Tax of 1935 included a graduated corporate income tax, an increase in inheritance and gift taxes, and a graduated income tax on "very great individual incomes."

Having submitted the bill, the president did not intensively lobby Congress to insure passage. In the ensuing hearings and floor debate, the administration's revenue bill was considerably amended. Congressional conservatives succeeded in diluting the proposed steep graduated corporate income tax (instead Congress passed an excess profits tax), reducing gift tax levies, and eliminating the proposed increase in the inheritance tax.

The Wealth Tax Act of 1935 hardly merited the alarmist fears of its conservative critics (publisher William Randolph Hearst described it as "soak the successful") much less the praise of Senator Long (who upon conclusion of the reading of the bill announced "I just wish to say Amen"). Taxes on the wealthy were increased, but only an additional $250 million in revenue was produced. The Revenue Act of 1936 imposed a modest graduated tax on undistributed corporate profits, thereby pressuring corporation executives to distribute profits in the form of higher dividends to their stockholders. Significantly, neither the 1935 nor the 1936 acts redistributed income, reduced the economic power of large corporations over the economy or their advantages over smaller competitors, or provided substantial revenue for social welfare programs.

Yet again, the New Deal had established an important precedent, the principle that the federal government could use its fiscal power to redistribute wealth and finance welfare measures.

Similar political pressures prompted Roosevelt to favor more extensive reform of the financial community, and in 1935 Congress again responded positively. It enacted two bills—the Public Utilities Holding Company Act and the Banking Act of 1935—to make power companies and private banks subject to greater public control.

The ineffectiveness of state regulation and large capital investment needs had enabled holding companies to acquire local electrical companies and to form them into large interstate systems. This structure effectively averted price competition and permitted essentially monopolistic pricing practices. Believing in the need to break up these complexes, the president, in March 1935, proposed legislation that included a "death sentence" provision empowering the SEC to dissolve (after January 1, 1940) any utility holding company that could not justify its existence. Roosevelt's proposal encountered intensive opposition from the utilities industry, leading to House defeat of the "death sentence" in July 1935. Despite counter-lobbying by the administration and well-publicized congressional hearings revealing the extent of the industry's lobbying efforts, the president was forced to modify his proposal. The resultant measure did prohibit all utility holding companies more than twice removed from the operating companies but required that the SEC (and not the companies as the original bill had provided) justify a dissolution order. The act also required all utility companies to register with the SEC and authorized the commission to supervise these companies' financial transactions.

To assist rural dwellers whom the private power companies refused to serve, owing to the poor profit potentialities of selling electricity in the countryside, the administration created the Rural Electrification Authority in May 1935. The REA did not construct electrical power units; it authorized low interest loans to nonprofit cooperatives to construct power lines in rural areas. By 1941, these loans had enabled four out of ten American farms to have electricity (in contrast to the 1935 ratio of one in ten). Silently, the REA revolutionized living conditions in rural America, making feasible the purchase of electrical appliances (notably the radio) and encouraging economic diversification through light industry.

The Banking Act of 1935 constituted a major departure from both the Federal Reserve Act of 1913 and the Glass Steagall Act of 1933. Again Roosevelt's support for bank reform developed slowly, partly because the bill faced considerable opposition from banking interests and congressional conservatives, led by Senator Carter Glass of Virginia, who objected to its proposed extension of public control over banking and currency policy. Through Glass's efforts the bill was watered down, though the principle of public control remained intact. The revised bill empowered the president to appoint the seven members of the newly named Board of Governors of the Federal Reserve System. Congress ceded to the new board unprecedented power over the basic operations of private member banks. The board now determined basic interest rates, the availability of credit, and the actual supply of money—three factors essential for the effective operation of a modern capitalist economy. Here public and private power mixed in an effort to make capitalism less subject to periodic collapse.

As the Second New Deal took form in 1935, Roosevelt and his advisers paid greater attention to those Americans previously neglected. An executive order of April 1935 established the Resettlement Administration (RA) to benefit marginal farmers and tenants. Funded through appropriations authorized under the Emergency Relief Act of 1935, RA provided loans to individuals to purchase land or establish cooperatives. Penurious appropriations, however, limited the program's impact. In one use of this authority, the newly appointed head of RA, Rexford Tugwell, funded the construction of three "greenbelt" towns (near Washington, D.C., Cincinnati, and Milwaukee) located close to urban employment and girdled by green countryside. More significantly, roughly forty-five-hundred families were resettled to more fertile land.

Resettlement continued to command congressional support although the concept of community planning did not. To extend these resettlement efforts, Senator John Bankhead of Alabama introduced what became the Bankhead-Jones Farm Tenancy Act of July 1937. The act created a Farm Security Administration to replace the RA, with authority to provide rehabilitation loans to enable landowners to convert marshy land into productive farms, low-interest long-term loans to selected farmers to buy family farms, cash to purchase supplies, and camps and other forms of assistance (including medical care) to migratory farm workers. The funding for this program was also limited. Congress appropriated only $10 million for its operation during 1938, increasing this to $25 million for 1939. Loans could not exceed $50 million in any given year. Limited already, the program was abruptly cut in 1943, and eventually phased out by 1946.

In 1935, the administration also increased public works spending to alleviate unemployment and extended its various relief programs for the indigent. Because New Deal measures had not resolved the economic crisis and liberal congressmen insisted on a vast new public works program, Roosevelt moved opportunistically. He could do so because Congress in April 1935 passed the Emergency Relief Appropriations Act authorizing $4.8 billion for federal relief, to be spent at the discretion of the president. Unencumbered by congressional guidelines, the administrator of the Works Project Administration (WPA), the redoubtable Harry Hopkins, initiated a wide-ranging series of programs that encompassed a Federal Theater Project, a Federal Writers Project, a Federal Artists Project, and the Resettlement Administration.

The National Youth Administration (NYA) was also funded through this act. Created in June 1935, the NYA gave part-time employment to those aged eighteen to twenty-five who either had left school or were attending high school or college. Intended to keep youths off the job market and to enable them to continue their education, the NYA enabled heretofore excluded students to attend college.

The central component of the 1935 relief act, however, was an extensive public works program. By 1941 over 8 million different individuals (one-fifth of the total labor force) had been employed under it. Thousands of school buildings, hospitals, playgrounds, and airport landing fields had been constructed and parks and waterways improved. Attacked by conservatives and radicals for its alleged boondoggling and make-work, the WPA sought to provide employment, not a relief dole. Under WPA, wages were higher than relief payments but lower than wages in private industry. Total WPA expenditures (through July 1941), moreover, reached almost $11.4 billion of which 78 percent was spent on construction projects and the remaining 22 percent on community service projects (education, culture, public health, school lunches).

The administration limited potential opposition to its vast public works program in several ways. It required that wage levels not harm private industry, that eligibility be terminated if an individual was offered private employment, and that wages correspond to the wage levels of the various geographic regions. The requirement of public usefulness minimized potential competition with the private construction industry; a requirement of local sponsorship minimized the potential challenge to the power of established local and state political leaders. Roosevelt also minimized the WPA's long-term impact by pointing out that it was an immediate response to a grave emergency and claiming that the federal government had a responsibility to alleviate unemployment or poverty when the private sector proved inadequate to the task. Moreover, the funds spent on public works were very limited: total public works expenditures during the 1930s were less than defense spending during the same period—a period of strong antimilitary sentiment. In contrast to the $11.4 billion for the WPA, by July 1940 Congress had authorized $12 billion in defense expenditures. Within the next nine months, total defense expenditures would increase dramatically to $35 billion. It was not mere happenstance, then, that full economic recovery occurred during the 1940–1942 period and not the New Deal years. Yet again, once the federal government had set the precedent for relieving unemployment, it could not in the future sit back passively if the private sector collapsed.

The reform measures associated with the "Second New Deal" showed a distinct shift in Roosevelt's priorities. Now he evinced more concern for workers than for employers and for the poor than for the wealthy and more interest in consumption than in production. But, ever the adept politician and eager to put together an unbeatable coalition for the 1936 presidential election, Roosevelt still favored economic measures beneficial to important industrial and agricultural interests.

Although Roosevelt developed no full-blown alternative to the discredited and rejected NIRA, he still pursued government-business cooperation. A series of legislation in 1935—the Guffey-Snyder Act, the Connally Act, and the Motor Carrier Act—sought to stabilize the coal, oil, and trucking industries by reducing excessive production and eliminating unnecessary competition. Each of the three affected industries, then, obtained for itself a miniature NIRA. Subsequent legislation—the Robinson-Patman Act of 1936 and the Miller-Tydings Act of 1937—succored small businesses. Through "fair trade" restrictions on the pricing practices of chain stores, this legislation sought to shelter small high-overhead businesses from the price-cutting competition of retail giants. Thereafter, for the remainder of its life, New Deal business policy would shift back and forth between an antitrust impulse and the stimulation of economic planning, free competition, and controlled cooperation.

Finally, to assist farmers satisfied with the operation of the first AAA and to save them from the impact of the Supreme Court decision invalidating it, Congress in February 1936 passed the Soil Conservation and Domestic Allotment Act. Seeking to raise prices by reducing production, the 1936 Act authorized government payments to farmers who diverted production from such soil depletion crops as cotton and wheat, to soil conservation crops such as grasses and legumes. To circumvent the Court's prohibition, these payments were to be subsidized out of tax revenues. Yet, because the 1936 act relied on voluntary compliance, it was a poor substitute for the original AAA. A measure that could meet the Court's prohibition and yet impose mandatory production controls still was needed and commanded support from the organized farm community.

The so-called Second AAA of February 1938 met the test. Controls were justified on the basis of the general welfare clause of the Constitution and the soil conservation principle basic to the 1936 act, and not on federal taxing or interstate commerce authority. Production controls were to be imposed for five basic commodities—wheat, corn, rice, cotton, and tobacco—when over two-thirds of farmers consented; payments would be subsidized out of general tax revenues. The act further authorized the secretary of agriculture to assign national acreage allotments, provided penalties for noncompliance, and introduced a parity system. The concept was that farmers should be as prosperous relative to the remainder of the population as they had been from 1909 to 1914. Nonrepayable commodity credit loans were provided to farmers through the Commodity Credit Corporation. Farmers could use these funds to pay for storage of commodities until sold, a system that, in effect, enabled farmers to play the market. Only if the farmer sold the stored commodity need he repay the loan. In operation, this amounted to direct grants to farmers. In essence, a system of direct price supports that relied on a dual system of production controls and storage loans/grants was established. Although the Second AAA failed to resolve the problem to rescue the small family farm, it did stabilize prices through direct government purchase of wheat and an export subsidy to cotton growers. The Second AAA also introduced the "ever normal granary" concept; nonperishable commodities would be stored as surpluses during bumper crop years to provide insurance against future crop failures or to provide a reserve for a food stamp program to assist the needy.

A NEW POLITICS: THE ELECTION OF 1936

The first and more so the second New Deal resulted in a significant and enduring realignment of national politics. By the time Roosevelt ran for reelection in 1936, he had reshaped the Democratic party's constituency and effectively ended four decades of Republican national political supremacy. New groups acquired for the first time a voice in national politics, as increasing numbers of city dwellers, Catholics, ethnics, and blacks shifted to the Democratic column. In 1932, the Democratic presidential vote in heavily industrial and urban New York, New Jersey, and Pennsylvania increased by roughly 1.8 million over 1928. Roosevelt failed to carry only a dozen cities that had a population of over 100,000. Not only did Roosevelt carry 104 cities with populations of over 100,000 in 1936, but he also won the twelve cities that he had not won in 1932, one by a margin of 74 percent. Moreover, in 1936 Roosevelt undermined traditional black support for Republicans, winning two out of every three black votes in many cities owing to New Deal relief and recovery measures. In addition, in certain regions of the country, Roosevelt appointed the first Catholic federal judges. He also appointed the first Italian-American and the first black ever to sit on the federal bench.

Catholics particularly were grateful both for the New Deal's legislative assistance and increasing recognition of Catholics in the form of federal appointments. (For example, of the 207 federal judges Harding, Coolidge, and Hoover had appointed, only 8 were Catholics; of the 197 appointed by Roosevelt, 52 were Catholics. In addition, one out of twenty-five of all Roosevelt's appointments went to a Catholic.)

The Committee on Industrial Organization (which became the Congress on Industrial Organization [CIO] in 1938) also helped align organized labor closely with the Roosevelt Democratic party as it actively entered partisan politics. In 1936, CIO unions contributed $770,000 to the Roosevelt campaign and organized a special committee, Labor's Non-Partisan League, to work for the reelection of Roosevelt and New Deal congressmen. After 1936, the CIO formalized this effort, creating a permanent committee, the Political Action Committee, to turn out the labor vote and influence national elections. By the 1940s, the CIO's counterpart within the labor movement, the AFL, also dramatically abandoned its hitherto ambiguous politics and formed a special subdivision, the Labor League for Political Education.

His broadened constituency, coupled with the popularity of the New Deal, insured Roosevelt's renomination and reelection in 1936. Overwhelming his Republican opponent, Alf Landon of Kansas, and minor

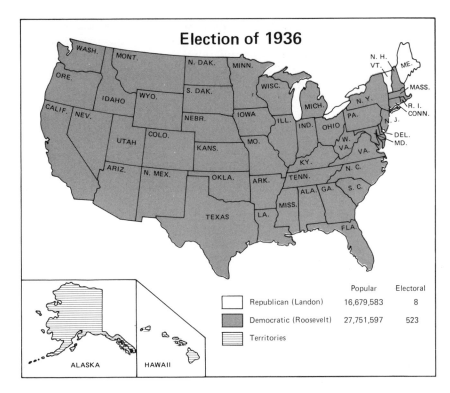

Election of 1936

	Popular	Electoral
Republican (Landon)	16,679,583	8
Democratic (Roosevelt)	27,751,597	523
Territories		

party candidates William Lemke of the Union party, Norman Thomas of the Socialist party, and Earl Browder of the Communist party, Roosevelt polled 27,752,869 popular votes (over 60 percent) to Landon's 16,674,665, Lemke's 882,479, Thomas' 187,000, and Browder's 80,000. Equally important, Roosevelt won 523 electoral votes to Landon's 8, winning all the states of the union except Maine and Vermont. Nor was it merely a personal triumph of Roosevelt: the Democratic party's victory in the congressional elections exceeded the size and scope of the president's. The House seated 331 Democrats, 89 Republicans, and 13 Progressives of various stripes, and 76 Democrats, 16 Republicans, and 2 Farmer-Laborites and Progressives were elected to the Senate.

THE WANING OF THE NEW DEAL

By 1936, then, the Republicans had been reduced to an insignificant and ineffectual minority. Apparently, the New Deal's finest hour was at hand. Ironically, after 1936 Roosevelt failed to secure the enactment of his major legislative measures. Why? An informal conservative coalition in Congress emerged in 1937–1938, led principally by certain southern Democrats who controlled its major committees. As the Roosevelt New Deal moved left after 1934, many leading southern Democrats began to question the president's policies. Federal assistance to dispossessed groups, the New Deal's repudiation of states' rights, and the broadened constituency of the Democratic Party soon caused many southern congressmen to question the principles and consequences of the Roosevelt New Deal. The specific catalysts to this reassessment were the sit-down strikes in the rubber and automobile industries of 1935 and 1936 and the efforts by northern liberal congressmen, led by Senator Wagner, to enact antilynching legislation in 1934 and again in 1937. (Roosevelt, as usual the political opportunist, respected southern power in Congress and never openly supported antilynching legislation; indeed, his silence helped frustrate the efforts of liberal congressmen to override southern-led Senate filibusters of 1934 and 1937.)

A confrontation between the congressional leadership and the administration surfaced publicly when Roosevelt suddenly announced in February 1937 his intention to "reform" the Supreme Court. The president intended to eliminate the Court as an obstacle to New Deal legislation. He proposed to reform the Court by increasing the Court's membership from nine to fifteen by adding new members when judges who had served on the Court for ten years did not retire upon reaching the age of seventy. Roosevelt's plan was denounced by many liberals and conservatives who opposed this assault on the independence of the judiciary.

Roosevelt ultimately abandoned this specific measure, for he had indeed succeeded in altering the character of the Court. In May 1937, the conservative Justice Willis Van Devanter retired; and a chastened Court, in a series of 5–4 decisions during 1937, reversed the impact of its earlier rulings. Earlier decisions had ruled the NRA and AAA unconstitutional, but the Court now upheld the constitutionality of the Wagner Act, the Social Security Act, and the Farm Mortgage Act of 1935. The main consequence of the Supreme Court fight, however, was that it enabled the congressional leadership to seize the initiative. Attacking the exercise of presidential authority (but not openly opposing the New Deal), conservative congressmen emphasized Congress's responsibility to examine the wisdom of presidential policy. Not only were they now less deferential toward the executive branch but they effectively used their institutional power as chairmen of committees to delay legislation. Dilatory hearings, Senate filibusters, and rulings by the House Rules Committee either averted floor consideration of the president's legislative recommendations or forced significant amendments that watered down the original proposal.

Seeking to regain control over Congress and his party, Roosevelt in the summer and fall of 1938 called for the defeat during party primaries of anti-New Deal Democrats. But his attempted purge failed; prominent southern conservatives such as Millard Tydings of Maryland, Ed Smith of South Carolina, and Walter George of Georgia won primary victories. Of those anti-New Dealers singled out by name by Roosevelt, only Tammany Hall Democrat John O'Connor (the chairman of the House

Rules Committee) was defeated. Roosevelt's failure to purge conservative Democrats carried over to the fall elections, in which the Republicans increased their membership in the House by 80 seats (with the new ratio being 251 Democrats to 169 Republicans) and in the Senate by 7 (68 Democrats and 24 Republicans).

Aside from the Miller-Tydings Act of 1937, the Bankhead-Jones Farm Tenancy Act of 1937, the Second AAA of 1938, and the refunding of WPA in 1938, the president failed to secure congressional approval of his programs to extend the New Deal. The president's only other major legislative successes included enactment of the Wagner-Steagall Housing Act of 1937 and the Fair Labor Standards Act of 1938.

The Wagner-Steagall Housing Act created a public corporation, the United States Housing Authority housed within the Department of the Interior, with authority to loan $500 million to local public housing agencies for the construction of low-cost housing. No bold attack on urban slums (only 180,000 units were constructed under this measure), Wagner-Steagall's importance was principally symbolic of the federal government's acceptance of the responsibility to relieve urban poverty. The Fair Labor Standards Act prohibited child labor and established a minimum wage of forty cents per hour and a maximum forty-four hour work week; but employers were granted eight years before those standards would be imposed and the minimum wage would begin at twenty-five cents per hour. These and other provisions led one conservative critic, Congressman Martin Dies, to comment sarcastically that the new administrator of this program should be required to report back to the Congress ninety days after appointment "whether anyone is subject to this bill." Dies's comment was not without merit: under this bill the wages of only about 500,000 workers were raised although nearly 12 million workers in interstate commerce were earning under forty cents per hour.

The Wagner-Steagall and Fair Labor Standards acts were the dying gasps of an administration becoming more involved in foreign affairs than the precursors of a third New Deal. It was overseas events, not the incompleteness of his New Deal, that led Roosevelt in 1940 to break the most sanctified American political tradition by seeking a third term in office. And the campaign itself grew most heated and bitter in the arena of foreign affairs. Republican nominee Wendell Willkie initially refrained from criticizing foreign policy decisions as potentially controversial as the destroyer-bases deal. However, by the concluding weeks of the campaign, Willkie, who had not succeeded in exploiting the third-term issue or the failure of the New Deal to bring about recovery, adopted the peace issue, portraying Roosevelt as a war monger and a man not to be trusted. In one of his sharper speeches, on October 22, 1940, the Republican candidate questioned "If [Roosevelt's] promise to keep our boys out of foreign wars is no better than the promise [of 1932] to balance the budget, they're already almost on the transports."

In 1940, Roosevelt played it coy. Never formally announcing his candidacy for the Democratic nomination, he sought to appear as responding only to the will of the Democratic Convention. In fact, Roosevelt employed his prestige and influence to insure both his nomination and, over the opposition of the conservative wing of the Democratic party, the nomination of Henry Wallace as vice president. Roosevelt did not campaign actively, but he kept his name in the newspapers as president by making well-publicized tours of military installations. The momentum of Willkie's peace campaign, however, forced Roosevelt to alter this strategy. He appealed to reformist sentiments by stressing the opposition of Republican conservatives to New Deal programs. And, in an election eve speech in Boston, he affirmed "While I am talking to you mothers and fathers, I give you one more assurance. I have said this before, but I shall say it again and again and again: Your boys are not going to be sent into any foreign wars." His strategy succeeded. In 1940, Roosevelt won an unprecedented third term, receiving 449 electoral votes and polling roughly 55 percent of the popular vote (27,307,819). Republican nominee Willkie received 22,321,018 popular votes and 82 electoral votes.

The 1940 election confirmed the Democrats as the new majority party. Now, large numbers of blacks, farmers, small businessmen, and laborers, hitherto Republicans, again voted Democratic. As a consequence, Roosevelt was able to forge a far more liberal and urban national Democratic party. The constituent members of the new coalition, more militant and powerful because they were organized, shaped the subsequent internal conflicts within the Congress and the widening executive-legislative confrontation over presidential authority and congressional prerogatives that continued in sharpened form into the Truman years.

Even before World War II magnified enormously the economic and social role of the federal government—rendering forever dead the distinction between private and public power, national and state's rights—the New Deal had set one precedent after another in extending the powers and prerogatives of the federal government. "Dr. Win-the-War," who in Roosevelt's terminology moved into the White House in 1942, would only finish the job started by "Dr. New Deal."

16

Legacies of the New Deal

In retrospect, the Roosevelt New Deal was neither as radical nor as innovative as it had been portrayed by its contemporary liberal supporters and conservative critics. It did not fundamentally redistribute wealth and power—though it did extend the power of newly organized groups, especially trade unions, at the expense of established elites. A broker state had been created, though not one where competing interest groups vied on equal terms for power and influence. At best, Roosevelt's New Deal redefined national politics and instituted innovative programs that shattered tradition. Capitalism remained intact—but financiers and industrialists now had to share power with labor leaders and federal officials.

THE MODERN PRESIDENCY

The most substantive change of the New Deal years was the transformation of the office of the presidency. Roosevelt extended presidential powers by exploiting national crises—whether the Great Depression or World War II. Roosevelt's increased power derived as well from an expanded bureaucracy, created in efforts to promote national economic recovery and respond to the international tensions that culminated in World War II.

During the 1930s, a number of new federal agencies were formed to alleviate poverty and stimulate economic recovery. Some temporary, others permanent, these agencies encroached upon what had formerly been an exclusively private domain. Moreover, these agencies administered programs involving the expenditure of large sums of money. The rapidity with which these agencies had been created, the distinctly new role played by the federal government, the deference of Congress and the private sector to the executive branch did not centralize power in the presidency. The scope and variety of these programs in fact meant that no one individual, no matter how purposeful or visionary, could control the federal bureaucracy. In short, the New Deal had created a bureaucratic monster, a system seemingly unmanageable and not easily adaptable to presidential control and initiative.

Bureaucratic growth impelled Roosevelt to reorganize the executive branch. Confronting, however, a Congress that was increasingly jealous over its prerogatives and a congressional leadership that was convinced by 1937 that Congress had been unduly subservient to the president, Roosevelt had to modify his efforts to reorganize the executive branch. Nonetheless, Roosevelt fully exploited what legislative authorization he already had and on September 8, 1939, by Executive Order 8248, established the Executive Office of the Presidency.

This order formally enhanced presidential authority, extended the executive's control over the federal bureaucracy, and shaped the development of national policy in two important respects. First, a White House staff was established, manned by six presidential assistants responsible and loyal to the President alone (the White House staff would mushroom to the thousands by the 1970s). This relatively minor change itself had two important consequences for the presidency: the president's independent sources of information were maximized, thereby lessening his dependence on the cabinet, and the president's ability to shape legislation was enhanced because he now had the personnel and information essential to influencing Congress on key votes. Second, the order transferred the Bureau of the Budget from the Treasury Department to the White House. This supervisory control, with the bureau's direct accountability to the president, centralized budgetary and accounting procedures and provided Roosevelt with a mechanism for establishing clear policy priorities.

These institutional changes accompanied an equally important development involving presidential exploitation of the communications media. Although Roosevelt's use of the media was at first the consequence of his own singular style of leadership, it created a powerful precedent that was subsequently followed by later presidents. Roosevelt held regular twice-a-week press conferences at which his own initiative and actions created news. Infrequently, Roosevelt also went on radio to deliver major policy statements on crucial domestic and international developments (the now famous fireside chats). These fireside chats were direct attempts to shape public opinion. Both the press conferences and the radio messages involved conscious efforts to elicit public support for Roosevelt's program and definition of the national interest, thereby reducing his dependence on Congress and the press. In addition, the president often employed these forums to focus public attention on the Congress.

In combination, the increase in executive personnel, the extension of presidential control over the cabinet and the budget, and the public influence that came with exploiting communications opportunities, forged the "modern presidency." Thereafter, Congress's legislative program was shaped by the priorities outlined in the president's State of the Union address. Less the personal priorities of one man or a review of national trends and problems, the State of the Union address had become a guideline for Congressional action—or reaction. And, while a president may not always have secured the enactment of his legislative program, even in failure he defined how Congress responded and what constituted responsible action.

The requirements of efficiency leading to the extension of presidential authority also involved important changes in the relationship between the executive and judicial branches. Despite Supreme Court decisions in the Schechter and Butler cases, the New Deal continued to encroach upon the powers of private enterprise. And, while the Supreme Court during the early 1930s interpreted the interstate commerce clause narrowly, in the aftermath of Roosevelt's Supreme Court "packing" plan of 1937, the Court adopted a less rigid position and, as in decisions involving the Wagner Act and the Social Security Act, conceded the constitutionality of extensive federal control over the private sector. In addition, the Schechter case was the last time the Supreme Court struck down legislation on the premise that Congress had unconstitutionally delegated its authority to the executive branch. During the Cold War years, this deference to the executive increased as the Court sought to avoid addressing issues such as the establishment of an extensive classification system and the creation of a federal employee loyalty program, both instituted unilaterally by the executive branch.

THE ORIGINS OF THE WELFARE STATE

A further institutional change involved the relationship of the federal and state governments. Many New Deal programs—notably public works and unemployment compensation—were administered by local and state governments. The guidelines were established at the federal level, but they were not clearly formulated, and there was no conscious effort to institute a system based upon public planning. The most enduring change—introduced almost inadvertently by the New Deal—was the principle of federal responsibility to address crucial social and economic problems. The motivation behind this approach was humanitarian and reflected an interest in the need for action. Roosevelt expressed this conviction when justifying federal aid to artists not as a cultural but as a relief program: "Why not? They are human beings. They have to live. I guess the only thing they can do is paint and surely there must be some place where paintings are wanted." In time, experimentalism gave way to permanency, as the New Deal created a number of programs and agencies—for example, the Rural Electrification Administration, the Federal Deposit Insurance Corporation, the National Labor Relations Board, and an enlarged Federal Reserve Board.

Increased during the early 1930s, and extended still further during World War II, spending also evolved as a permanent feature of federal policy to promote growth and recovery. During the New Deal years of 1933–1939, domestic spending programs, to be sure, did not bring recovery, and Roosevelt only reluctantly unbalanced the budget. But federal spending increased more dramatically during World War II, demonstrating the crucial role the federal government could play to effect recovery and avert recessions. Thus, whereas in 1939 federal expenditures had constituted only 9 percent of a gross national product of $88.6 billion, by 1944 it increased to 45 percent of a GNP totalling $199.2 billion. Federal expenditures during 1941–1945 (roughly $320 billion) were almost twice as large as the total expended by the federal government between 1789 and 1941. A sharp economic upturn ensued: the index of industrial production, which had averaged 87 over the period 1930–1939, reached 112 by April 1940 and 174 by 1942.

Such developments redefined federal power and paved the way for the so-called welfare state. Unfortunately the welfare state, as it actually functioned, assisted the most indigent least of all. It was not the poor who benefited most from New Deal public works, agricultural relief, banking, or mortgage assistance policies but rather skilled workers, commercial farmers, depositors and bankers, and homeowners and lending institutions. As is usually the case, power flowed from organization, and the unorganized remained voiceless and powerless.

In addition, the New Deal amalgam of private and state capitalism, benefits for the wealthy, and welfare for organized groups, significantly altered the American political world. It prepared the way for public acceptance of a dominant federal government and strong executive direction of domestic and international affairs. As a consequence, Roosevelt's adept politics silenced rightist libertarian criticism and defused leftist demands for redistributive policies.

THE REALIGNED DEMOCRATIC PARTY

Despite Roosevelt's political ingenuity, Republicans bitterly assailed New Deal programs. Yet none of the relentless conservative criticism stopped the Democrats from replacing the Republicans as the dominant national party. The enactment of specific relief and recovery programs and the administration's responsiveness to their needs led a variety of conflicting groups and interests—ethnics, urbanites, Catholics, small businessmen, farmers, blacks—to identify with the New Deal Democratic party. No longer the party of Tammany Hall politicians and the unreconstructed South, the Democratic party had developed a strong, urban, northern, liberal base.

One legacy of this development was an intense conflict within the Democratic party. As new groups commanded influence and power they came into conflict with a congressional leadership unreconciled to a new politics. Because of their numbers, the influence of these new groups would increase at the Democratic National Convention and in the selection of presidential candidates, as dramatically revealed in the Democratic party's shift on the civil rights issue. As northern blacks shifted to the Democratic column during the 1930s and black migration from the rural South to the urban North soared during the wartime and postwar years, Democrats took a new interest in Afro-Americans. The 1940 Democratic platform for the first time used the word "Negro," boasted of the party's friendship for the black man, and noted that "Our Negro citizens have participated actively in the economic and social advances launched by this administration."

Similarly, after the formation of the CIO, the labor movement became an arm of the Democratic party. In the 1936 presidential campaign, organized labor contributed funds and personnel to elect New Deal Democrats, a policy that was later formalized with the CIO's formation of the Political Action Committee. At the same time, the labor movement employed its resources to influence the policy decisions of the Roosevelt administration and the national Democratic party. Thus while the Democratic party remained a coalition party, during the 1930s its constituent groups had been broadened.

THE INSTITUTIONALIZATION OF RED-BAITING

New Deal challenges to the power and prerogatives of traditional interest groups also contributed to a further legacy: an intensified politics of red-baiting. Consistently, since the Alien and Sedition Acts controversy of the 1790s, conservatives had often responded emotionally and bitterly to reformist demands for socioeconomic change. Blindly associating dissent with disloyalty or disorder, conservative antireformism had been somewhat altered in the aftermath of the Bolshevik Revolution of 1917. Then, antiradicalism became anticommunism, and this refinement led to an effort to identify demands for social and economic reform with foreign-directed subversion.

The impact of the Great Depression and the New Deal had sharpened many conservatives' obsession with security. By the late 1930s conservatives (whether in Congress or organizations such as the American

Liberty League or newspaper publisher Frank Gannett's National Committee to Uphold Constitutional Government, which had originally denounced the constitutionality of New Deal legislation) were challenging the loyalty and associations of New Deal personnel more than they were the philosophy and policies of the New Deal.

Capturing this shift in focus, in May 1938 southern Democratic congressman Martin Dies of Texas reintroduced a resolution to create a special committee to investigate "subversive and un-American" activities. (Dies had first introduced this resolution in July 1937 with the encouragement of leading Southern conservatives, including Vice President John Garner of Texas, Speaker of the House William Bankhead of Alabama, and House Majority Leader Sam Rayburn of Texas.) Exploiting then-prevalent anti-Fascist and anti-Communist sentiments, these conservatives secured House approval for the Dies resolution. When establishing the temporary House Committee on Un-American Activities (HUAC), Congress had limited its scope and influence both by restricting its funds and confining its existence to a seven-month period.

Under Dies's leadership, HUAC's investigations did not focus on foreign threats to the national security so much as on domestic radicalism. For example, the German-American Bund was never thoroughly investigated. But the CIO and federal employees, most notably those engaged in the Federal Theatre Project, were investigated. This temporary committee's authority was subsequently renewed annually (until formally made a permanent committee in 1945), and its appropriations were increased. For the conservative leadership of Congress, HUAC fulfilled the notable function of identifying radicalism (and indirectly the New Deal) with disloyalty.

The creation of HUAC transformed the political debate by providing an instrument for proscribing certain ideas and activities as un-American. HUAC was far more effective in this regard than similar efforts by conservative interest groups. For, in contrast to the privately funded American Liberty League, which was specifically identified with the corporate business community, HUAC was funded by Congress, and its reports had the aura of a more impartial, public investigation. An instrument of congressional conservatives, HUAC symbolized one component of the executive-legislative conflict that continued into the Cold War years and that helped determine the politics of that later period.

HUAC, however, was not so much the initiator as the instrument of conservative attempts to discredit the New Deal. Nowhere was this more dramatically revealed than in the enactment of the Alien Registration Act of July 1940—the so-called Smith Act. HUAC had not drafted or pushed for this legislation, though the title of the bill might have suggested a committee interest and concern. The origins of the bill reflected a narrow concern on the part of individuals in the administration over external threats to the national security. The specific catalyst was the desire to prevent within the United States the so-called fifth column activities that had imperiled the security of European states during the 1930s. (The term "fifth column" started in Spain, where Fascist and Communist groups had acted in ways to subvert the independence of their nation—the Spanish Fascist General Francisco Franco boasting after the successful seige of Madrid during the Spanish Civil War that his four columns attacking the city had been assisted by a fifth column within the city.) The fears of internal subversion had been heightened following the outbreak of war in Europe in 1939 and led the Roosevelt administration to seek ways to meet a potential internal security threat. The original bill expressed these limited objectives by requiring the fingerprinting and registration of alien residents. The conservative Virginia congressman, Howard Smith, however, immediately exploited this legislative opportunity and the crisis, introducing during floor debate a far-reaching amendment to the bill. His amendment extended the 1917 Espionage Act's prohibition against any written or spoken efforts that "in any manner cause insubordination, disloyalty, mutiny or refusal of duty by any member of the military or naval forces" to include any teaching or advocacy to "overthrow or destruction of any government in the United States by force or violence; or to become a member of, or affiliate with, any such society, group, or assembly of persons." By 1940, political tests that defined the mere holding or advocacy of certain beliefs as grounds for denial of federal employment or prosecution for subversive activities became accepted.

Accompanying the extension and legitimization of HUAC's often crudely partisan attacks on the New Deal was a similar change in the role and influence of the FBI. Between 1933 and 1944, FBI personnel increased from 326 to 13,317 as a consequence of the extension of the definition of federal crimes. In 1933, Congress enacted a series of bills making it a federal crime to assault or kill a federal officer, rob a federal bank, flee from one state to another to avoid prosecution, kidnap across state lines, or use interstate communications in extortion attempts. In July 1935, the bureau established a national police academy to train law enforcement officials, an action further extending its respectability and personnel.

In time, moreover, the focus of FBI investigations shifted to involve surveillance of domestic radicals and alien residents. Domestic surveillance derived from the European crisis of 1939 and fears that Nazi and Communist agents might weaken American resistance to totalitarianism.

Executive orders provided the formal authority for the FBI's role. In 1940, President Roosevelt authorized the FBI to wiretap in national security cases; in 1939 he had directed citizens and police officials throughout the country to forward to the FBI any information of suspected espionage activities. In 1936, moreover, Roosevelt had directed the FBI to investigate fascist and communist activities throughout the country. While the intent behind Roosevelt's 1936 order had been limited, the authority it had ceded was extensive and led to FBI involvement in domestic political surveillance. Not simply foreign agents but citizens engaged in radical politics came under FBI surveillance, and particularly employees within the federal bureaucracy who were active in radical politics or who had associations with radical causes.

The investigative files compiled by the FBI were not used to prosecute citizens who had violated no federal law. Nonetheless, the information gained through such surveillance detailing membership in radical organizations, personal meetings with foreign embassy personnel or with known radicals, was retained. The files would have importance only later during the 1940s. At that time they were used by conservatives in Congress and the press to lend credence to claims that many federal employees were disloyal and that, accordingly, an extensive loyalty program was required to purge the federal bureaucracy and more stringent antisubversive legislation was needed. Domestic political surveillance that began on a limited scale in the late 1930s would grow during World War II and become uncontrollable during the World War years.

NOT RADICALISM, BUT A NEW DEAL

How red was the so-called red decade? Ironically, conservative fears of New Deal radicalism were as unfounded as were their fears that most New Dealers were disloyal, even subversive. If the New Deal thoroughly repudiated the governing political assumptions of the 1920s, it did *not* transform the basic social and economic system. Much as during the Progressive Era, glaring abuses were rectified and a more humane and responsive order created.

Roosevelt's reforms failed to ameliorate the lot of America's most dispossessed citizens. The poorest of the agrarian poor, tenants and sharecroppers, were tractored off the land. Blacks especially suffered as they were even excluded from participating in the selection of nominees to local AAA committees and thereby denied a direct voice in allotment decisions that determined their economic livelihood.

The race question emerged as a national issue during the 1930s, but only inadvertently. Although the stated intent of New Deal programs had been to relieve the distress of all Americans, segregation had not been confronted so much as sustained. The Civilian Conservation Corps discriminated against black applicants and often segregated them in camps; employment and housing arrangements during the construction of the Tennessee Valley Authority were based on segregation. The housing programs of the 1930s, involving grants to construct public housing units and federal guarantees for mortgage relief, enforced segregation patterns in northern urban communities. Of the forty-nine low income housing units built by the Public Works Administration during the 1930s, fourteen were constructed for blacks alone and eighteen for whites alone. In the North almost all the housing projects that blacks occupied were built in all-black neighborhoods. The consequence of these housing decisions was more congested housing in black ghettos, which combined with the increased black migration to the North during the 1940s, contributed to the explosive housing and educational crises of the 1960s.

Nor was the impact of public works spending equitable. The poor benefited from this program, but the provision for skill and geographic differentials sustained earlier wage and employment inequities. Again the experiences of blacks demonstrate this most graphically. On the one hand, black unemployment in Cleveland was reduced from about 50 percent to 30 percent by the mid-1930s, as the federal government became the largest employer of blacks. Yet, blacks generally were assigned only the lower-paying unskilled jobs. Thus, in a 1937 survey of WPA jobs in Cleveland, of those employed in public works jobs, 16.7 percent had formerly been employed in skilled jobs but only .6 percent held such jobs in emergency work projects. Not a single black held a job on the city's WPA staff, not even as one of the hundreds of clerks, and not one was on the executive staff of the county WPA. NRA labor codes also operated to the disadvantage of blacks through devices such as occupational and geographical job classifications, wage loopholes, and simple lack of enforcement.

Popular attitudes concerning the proper role of the federal government were altered during the New Deal years, but national politics had not been radicalized. The seriousness of the Great Depression and the New Deal's failure to restore prosperity (by 1939 roughly ten million Americans remained unemployed) did not reinvigorate the American left. Throughout the 1930s, the Socialist and Communist parties remained weak and indeed suffered a steady decline in their popular influence. Never a major political force, the Communists polled scarcely .25 percent of the total popular vote in 1932 and even less in 1936 and 1940. The Socialists were no more successful, polling only a little more than 2 percent in 1932, thereafter suffering a catastrophic decline.

In part, the decline of radicalism flowed from the political strategy of the New Deal Democratic party. Within that party, the voice of formerly excluded groups—organized labor, ethnics, Catholics, urbanites —increased as established elites were forced to share power. Southern Democrats and northern urban bosses no longer controlled the selection of the party's presidential candidate or platform. Democratic National Convention procedures became open. For a time, at least, the Roosevelt Democratic party appeared to be in the process of becoming a liberal-labor organization, the American counterpart of the British Labor party and Continental Social Democratic parties.

Yet despite the New Deal and the Roosevelt coalition, Southern conservatives remained entrenched in Congress, and their power (based on seniority and control of key committee posts) went unchallenged. Some interest groups thus remained more powerful than others and a genuinely pluralistic politics of *equally* competing groups had not evolved. All in all, the New Deal had not transformed the nation so much as it had revitalized and realigned interest groups. In a real sense, then, the term "new deal" captures the limits of Roosevelt's reformism: he reshuffled the cards, but did not introduce a new game with new rules.

17

A World in Ruins: Depression Foreign Policy

The Great Depression because of its global character shattered international stability as well as domestic tranquillity. The international order established at Versailles in 1919 and precariously balanced during the 1920s collapsed with the Great Crash. Nations, never eager to act collectively in the best of times, in the worst of times rushed pell mell to salvage their national economies through extreme nationalistic policies. And some nations, especially Germany and Japan, sought to use the economic crisis to gain foreign policy goals denied previously by Anglo-American power. As nations scrambled to save what they could from the economic debacle, the globe became torn by rebellion, aggression, and war.

The postwar order began to disintegrate in 1931. The Great Depression tipped the balance toward extreme nationalism and militarism in the Far East and Europe, while it paralyzed the western democracies' will to resist. The comforting assumptions of the twenties that security could be purchased cheaply by pious international platitudes and innocuous treaties were swept into the dustbins of history before the whirlwind of violence unleashed by the economic and political collapse of the old order. Japan plunged its sword into Manchuria and China, while spellbinding demagogues in Italy and Germany diverted mass anxieties into tyranny at home and military adventures abroad. In the United States the shattering effects of the Great Depression and the specter of foreign war initially increased the popular mood of isolationism from world affairs.

JAPAN CHALLENGES THE POSTWAR ORDER

The initial explosion, opening a decade of mounting tensions and crises that culminated in the Second World War, took place in Manchuria in the fall of 1931. Chiang Kai-shek's Nationalist movement had unified China and began a campaign to eliminate foreign special privileges and to evict the Japanese from their sphere in Manchuria. Most Japanese regarded Manchuria as vital, economically and strategically, to their island empire and were deeply disturbed by Nationalist tactics—boycotts of Japanese merchants and goods, building of competing rail lines, and other forms of harassment. Moreover, Japan experienced internal social tensions resulting from rapid industrialization and urbanization. A group of Japanese supernationalists and militarists, unhappy with Japanese parliamentary government, distressed at the rise of big business interests, and alarmed at developments in Manchuria, resolved to restore Japan to its ancient virtues. They also called for an end of the policy of cooperation with the western powers and a unilateral Japanese policy to achieve dominance in the Far East. Western signs of discrimination against Orientals, such as the 1924 immigration act in the United States barring Japanese immigrants, trade discriminations, and the inferior naval ratio accorded Japan, aided the extremists in undermining more moderate elements in Japan.

The Japanese army, largely independent from civilian governmental control, struck suddenly in Manchuria on the night of September 18, 1931. After rigging a small explosion on the lines of the Japanese-owned South Manchurian Railway and charging Chinese provocation, Japanese troops moved out of their leased areas and began to seize the major cities. By early 1932 all Manchuria had fallen to the Japanese, and Chiang Kai-shek's officials and troops had been evicted. The puppet state of Manchukuo was established as a front for Japanese control.

The Japanese government at first apologized and promised to recall the army, but it could not assert authority over the military. Gradually, through propaganda and the assassination of opponents, the extremists took control of the Japanese government and committed the nation to an expansionist course. Japan withdrew from the League of Nations in 1933, denounced the naval arms treaties in 1934, steadily encroached into north China, and finally, in 1937, began an undeclared war to subdue all China to her will.

The American government reacted to Japanese aggression in Man-

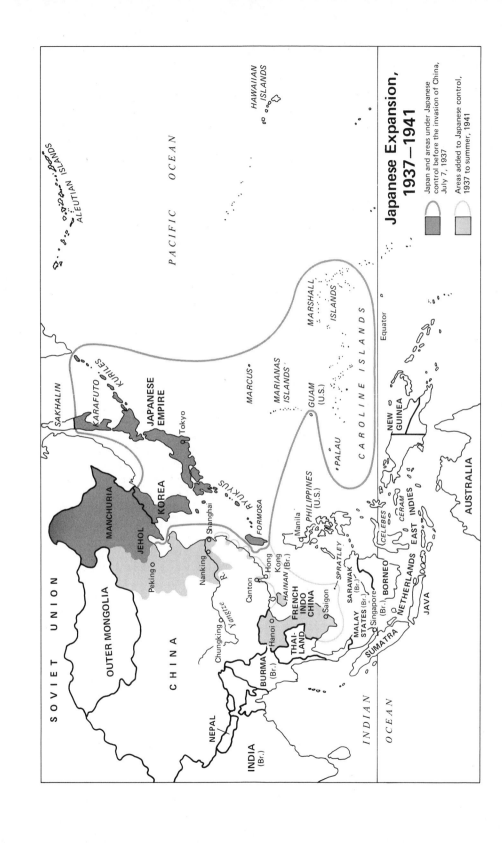

Japanese Expansion, 1937–1941

Japan and areas under Japanese control before the invasion of China, July 7, 1937

Areas added to Japanese control, 1937 to summer, 1941

SOVIET UNION

OUTER MONGOLIA

CHINA

MANCHURIA

JEHOL

KOREA

JAPANESE EMPIRE

SAKHALIN

KARAFUTO

KURILES

Tokyo

RYUKYUS

FORMOSA

Peking

Nanking

Shanghai

Yangtze

Chungking

Canton

Hong Kong

HAINAN (Br.)

Hanoi

FRENCH INDO CHINA

THAI-LAND

Saigon

BURMA (Br.)

NEPAL

INDIA (Br.)

MALAY STATES (Br.)

Singapore

SUMATRA

SARAWAK (Br.)

SPRATLEY

BORNEO

NETHERLANDS EAST INDIES

JAVA

CELEBES

CERAM

PHILIPPINES (U.S.)

Manila

GUAM (U.S.)

PALAU

MARIANAS ISLANDS

MARCUS

MARSHALL ISLANDS

CAROLINE ISLANDS

Equator

NEW GUINEA

AUSTRALIA

INDIAN OCEAN

PACIFIC OCEAN

ALEUTIAN ISLANDS

HAWAIIAN ISLANDS

churia with a policy of moral resistance only. As a major Pacific power and the self-appointed spokesman for the Open Door in China, the United States felt greatly distressed by the Japanese conquest. Secretary of State Stimson, with President Hoover's approval, sent a representative to the League Council when it debated invoking the Pact of Paris. A few days after the League acted, the State Department also reminded the belligerents of their obligations under that treaty. Subsequently, the American government warned both Japan and China, on January 7, 1932, that it would not recognize any changes in China achieved by force and in violation of the Pact of Paris and other treaties. This was the famed Stimson Non-Recognition Doctrine.

At the time not too disturbed as Japan "disciplined" the Chinese, Britain and France similarly failed to act although later they fell into line. Great Britain was inclined to let the Americans bear the responsibility of checking Japan. Consequently, after the bloody Japanese "rape" of Shanghai, Stimson in a public letter to Senator Borah of the Foreign Relations Committee reaffirmed the Open Door in China, invited other powers to join in his nonrecognition policy, and warned Japan by implication that since she had violated the Nine Power Pact the United States might feel free to expand its navy beyond the levels of the limitations treaties.

Stimson was a firm moralist who believed that aggressors must be curbed and the international legal order upheld. He wanted, therefore, to back diplomatic rebukes with more forcible action. Aware of Japan's economic vulnerability, for she depended upon the United States for much of her oil and steel, Stimson sought to remind her of American naval power and, at least, to threaten trade restrictions or embargoes. President Hoover, however, was more pacifistically inclined; he feared that economic threats might lead to war rather than to peace. Moreover, he was preoccupied with the problems of the depression within the United States. Consequently Hoover refused to move beyond mere moral condemnation of Japan's course.

Hoover was more in step with American public opinion on this question than was Stimson, for while most Americans sympathized with China, they did not want to risk war. From a practical standpoint moreover, the United States had a far larger trade with Japan than it had with China. American attachments to China, therefore, were largely sentimental and moral—a reflection of missionary nurtured myths and old but forlorn hopes of a vast market in that huge country. Yet if the United States insisted upon morally condemning Japan's course, it probably should have been ready to back words with actions. Moral gestures merely enrage others without restraining them. Hoover and Stimson had rebuked Japan, and thereby fueled the extremists' propaganda about American hostility, but they left her free to pursue her course. Not surprisingly many Japanese began to regard America with contempt, convinced that expansion would meet only verbal opposition.

NEW DEAL DIPLOMACY

The first term of Franklin D. Roosevelt failed to reveal a clear or consistent pattern in foreign relations. On the one hand, as an old Wilsonian, FDR had a strong interest in international relations. He closely observed ominous developments in Europe and the Far East and perceived a second world war in the making. Yet he too was affected by the nationalist currents of the times, and he necessarily devoted most of his attention to devising plans to overcome the depression in the United States. Consequently until 1937 he continued in general along the same middle-of-the-road course as his Republican predecessors. He too insisted upon repayment of the war debts, although by 1933 that seemed a forlorn hope, and he made no effort to reopen the question of membership in the League or to cooperate with it politically.

When the World Economic Conference convened at London in 1933 to consult about broad international measures against the depression, Roosevelt clearly placed his domestic recovery program first. He refused to discuss the war debts issue, which he felt would be unpopular with the American public. Roosevelt also ruled out tariff reductions for the moment and declined to accept a temporary international monetary stabilization agreement. These changes might interfere with experiments to raise domestic prices and production by barring entry to competing foreign goods and by devaluing the gold backing of the dollar.

Yet the following year FDR agreed to the low tariff plans of Cordell Hull, the secretary of state. Hull, also an old Wilsonian and a devout believer in freer trade as a cure-all for world depression and war, obtained from Congress the Reciprocal Trades Agreement Act of 1934, authorizing bilateral tariff reductions with foreign governments. By 1940 Hull had negotiated twenty-two reciprocal agreements, the bulk with Latin America. Although these had some effects in quickening commerce, they fell far short of the secretary's hopes. The world depression was too deep and the dictator states relied too much upon state controlled economies for Hull's simple solution to work.

Recognition of the Soviet Union, a long overdue and realistic step, also proved to be of little immediate significance in promoting a more peaceful world. The Republicans during the twenties had continued Wilson's policy of nonrecognition of the Communist government in Russia. Yet with the passing of time American opposition gradually lessened. When Lenin died in 1924, many Americans were pleased that he was replaced by the obscure Joseph Stalin instead of Leon Trotsky, the well-known advocate of continuous world revolution. Moreover, the Great Depression increased the attractions of trade with the Soviet Union. By 1933 several American firms, such as General Electric, Ford, and International Harvester, were active in the Russian market. Business leaders and politicians urged that recognition would greatly expand Soviet-American trade. Of course, many remained opposed to recognition on moral and religious grounds; the more outspoken of these critics included patriotic groups such as the American Legion and the Daughters of the American Revolution, members of Protestant and Roman Catholic churches, the AFL, and the National Chambers of Commerce. As long as Hoover, an arch anti-Communist, occupied the White House, anti-Soviet views prevailed.

FDR's election cleared the way for recognition. The new administration opted for formal diplomatic relations—first, on the realistic grounds that the Soviet regime had existed for sixteen years despite America's attitude, and second, in the hope that a restoration of official relations would bolster the status-quo in the Pacific against Japan and thus strengthen nonaggressive forces in Europe. Soviet Foreign Commissar Maxim Litvinov came to Washington for the negotiations. Completed on November 16, 1933, the accord established diplomatic relations, provided freedom of religious worship for Americans in Russia, and promised to halt Russian propaganda and subversion in America. Russian claims for compensation for damages during the American intervention in North Russia and Siberia were dropped, while further negotiations on the questions of debts were promised. These involved loans made to the provisional government and the expropriation of American owned property in Russia.

Although widely approved by the American people, recognition of the Soviets failed to alter the course of international affairs. Trade remained small, primarily because Russia lacked the necessary funds and long-term credits were either unavailable or deemed too risky. The hoped-for political benefits also proved illusory, for no notable collaboration was achieved either in regard to Japan or Europe. Disillusionment speedily ensued when the debt negotiations also ended in disagreement and the American Communist party continued to accept direction from Soviet officials.

THE GOOD NEIGHBOR POLICY

The genesis of the Good Neighbor Policy toward Latin America long antedated Franklin Roosevelt's arrival at the White House. Republican administrations in the twenties became aware of the intensity of Latin American resentment of the United States and adopted measures to reduce it. American businessmen, eagerly seeking new markets and resources, urged a less militaristic course on the State Department. Other Americans joined them, disturbed by the often exaggerated accounts of harsh military rule by the marines in Haiti and Santo Domingo. Consequently, since the United States no longer felt insecure about the

Panama Canal after 1918, the government began to modify its imperialistic policies.

Washington withdrew its marines from Santo Domingo in 1924, although it retained financial controls until 1941. A treaty with Colombia in 1921 paid her $25 million for the 1903 Panama affair, and cleared the way for eager American oil firms to operate in that country. American forces left Nicaragua in 1925, only to return the following year when revolutionary disturbances broke out; they remained there until 1933, and the financial controls lasted until 1944.

Mexico presented a difficult problem, but there too relations improved during the Republican era. Acute controversy had resulted from Article 27 of the 1917 Mexican Constitution, providing for national ownership of all subsurface oil and mineral deposits. Did these provisions apply retroactively to American and other foreign concessions in Mexico? Moreover, the anticlerical policies of the Carranza regime aroused much ill-will among Roman Catholics in the United States. President Venustiano Carranza had interpreted Article 27 retroactively, though he did not enforce it. After Carranza's fall, Hughes negotiated the Bucareli settlement with his successor, Alvaro Obregon, in 1923. Article 27 was not to apply retroactively and compensation was to be paid to foreign owners of land expropriated for Mexico's agrarian reforms.

The next Mexican administration, however, under Plutarco Elias Calles, returned to the Carranza position and imposed severe restrictions on foreign oil properties. The largest American oil companies resisted and appealed to the State Department for protection. President Coolidge and Secretary of State Kellogg at first reacted sharply, alleging Communist Russian influence in Mexico. The two quickly adopted a more conciliatory approach, however, when Calles indicated a willingness to arbitrate, and a U.S. Senate resolution endorsed a peaceful solution. Coolidge sent his old friend, Dwight Morrow, on a special conciliatory mission to Mexico City. Morrow speedily established rapport with Calles and the Mexican people. He arranged a goodwill visit by humorist Will Rogers and a special flight to Mexico City by America's air idol, Charles A. Lindbergh. These handsome gestures helped ease the way to a face-saving arrangement reviving the Bucareli agreement. It proved to be only a temporary solution to the oil problem, but at least talk of war ended and a degree of harmony returned to Mexican-American relations.

President Hoover particularly made notable contributions to Pan Americanism. While president-elect, Hoover undertook a goodwill tour of Latin America in 1928. As president he refrained from further interventions, removed American troops from Nicaragua in 1933, and promised withdrawal in Haiti (this was done in 1934). He also abandoned the moralistic recognition policy of Wilson and returned to the traditional practice of recognizing de facto regimes in Latin America regardless of how they came to power. Yet Hoover refused to foreswear possible armed intervention in the future. Treaty arrangements with several Caribbean states sanctioned that right and the United States could not be certain that interventionism to protect foreign lives and property might not again be necessary.

In his inaugural address in 1933, President Roosevelt pledged a policy of "the good neighbor" toward all the world, but the phrase became the exclusive catch-phrase for his Latin American policy. Aided by Secretary Hull and others devoted to the cause, Roosevelt hoped to deepen Pan American harmony and solidarity. Not only was this desirable in itself but it also served as a means to quicken American commerce during the depression. Later, with the threat of war from the Fascist and Nazi powers in Europe and their meddling in Latin America, the Good Neighbor policy proved invaluable in promoting the security and unity of the Western Hemisphere.

The Good Neighbor policy can be summed up as an effort to demilitarize the Latin-American policy of the United States. Roosevelt and his advisers decided that direct United States armed intervention and heavy-handed imperialism south of the border produced more liabilities than benefits. Instead of asserting a unilateral right of the United States to intervene in the southern half of the hemisphere, Roosevelt sought to involve Latin American nations in a common front under North American leadership. Unlike the Republican Roosevelt who threatened to compel Latin-Americans to behave properly (the Roosevelt Corollary to the Monroe Doctrine), the Democratic Roosevelt preferred voluntary cooperation by his neighbors to the south. However much their diplomatic efforts differed, the two Roosevelts sought a similar aim: to insure that Latin America remained within the United States' sphere of influence.

Economic diplomacy sought to accomplish by indirect means what military imperialism achieved by force. By granting tariff preferences in the American market for Latin American raw materials, Cordell Hull's reciprocal trade pacts sought to open Latin American markets to United States manufactured goods. Under Hull's form of "open-door" imperialism, the United States would serve as the Western Hemisphere's industrial capitalist metropolis; the Latin American nations would remain its economic colonies, providing North Americans with cheap coffee, sugar, bananas, copper, nitrates, and oil. To achieve these larger, long-term economic advantages, Roosevelt and Hull sometimes sacrificed lesser, short-term American business interests.

As early as 1933, Roosevelt and Hull began to implement their modified Latin American policy. At the Seventh Pan American Conference at Montevideo in 1933, Hull pledged noninterventionism by armed force in the internal affairs of any Western Hemisphere state. He reiterated that pledge in more categorical terms at the special Pan American conference convened at Buenos Aires in 1936, held at the request of and personally opened by President Roosevelt. Meanwhile, the administration withdrew the marines from Haiti in 1934 and that same year abrogated the Platt Amendment with Cuba. It also lowered trade barriers under the Reciprocal Trade Agreement Act and established an Import-Export Bank to lend money and stimulate trade with Latin America.

Two Latin American nations—Argentina and Mexico—posed a threat to United States dominance of the region, and the administration acted to resist them. During the 1930s, Argentina, the most economically advanced, prosperous, and Westernized Latin American nation, drifted toward fascism and became subject to Nazi German influence. Argentina thus appeared to United States policymakers as a potential wedge for German penetration of a United States sphere of influence, especially as it persistently blocked United States efforts to persuade American nations to accept a binding commitment for mutual measures to repel outside aggression. The best that Hull could do was to obtain a loose declaration at the Eighth Pan American Conference at Lima in 1938. The Declaration of Lima proclaimed the solidarity of the Western Hemisphere and promised consultation and cooperation against subversion or external threats to the peace of the hemisphere.

Mexico posed a more direct and immediate threat to United States economic interests. Its president, Lazaro Cardenas, thought of himself as the leader of the underdeveloped world's antiimperialist bloc, and he determined to expel foreign-owned business enterprises from Mexico and reassert his nation's ownership of its own land and natural resources. Finally, in 1938, he expropriated foreign-owned land and Anglo-American oil properties. Rather than risk a direct confrontation, exacerbate anti-imperialist sentiments, and perhaps threaten American business interests elsewhere in Latin America, the Roosevelt administration compromised with Mexico. Cardenas promised to pay compensation to the expropriated American oil companies ($24 million for holdings the companies valued at $500 million). And later the administration arranged an Import-Export Bank loan to enable Cardenas's successor to pay the agreed compensation. While acquiescing in the expropriation of United States oil companies in Mexico, the administration simultaneously promoted the interests of oil companies in Venezuela and Peru and mining companies in Chile and Bolivia.

If the Good Neighbor now spoke more quietly than ever and usually hid its big stick, it nevertheless continued to dominate the Western Hemisphere, whose southern half remained within the United States' sphere of influence.

THE ILLUSION OF NEUTRALITY

As events abroad increasingly pointed toward a new cycle of wars, a mood of withdrawal gripped Americans with increasing strength. More and more citizens viewed intervention in the First World War as a mistake and resolved that it must not be repeated. America must shun any entanglements that might lead to war. These sentiments existed across the nation but seemed particularly strong in the midwestern states, physically remote from either coast, where large numbers of German-Americans resided who held memories of 1917 and where a type of agricultural populism, that was suspicious of eastern bankers and munitions makers, was widespread. Antiwar novels, movies, and histories, with their messages about the inhumanity and futility of all wars and particularly the recent "war to end war," enjoyed wide acceptance almost everywhere. Best selling books, such as *Merchants of Death* by H. C. Englebrecht and *Iron, Blood and Profits* by George Seldes, persuaded the public that the common man fought and died to enrich bankers and munitions manufacturers. Peace groups paraded against war and young college students demanded the removal of R.O.T.C. units from campuses. The great majority of intellectuals and scholars supported isolationism and joined church and peace groups in pouring out a flood of antiwar literature, unequalled until the later antiwar movement of the 1960s. The Nye Committee hearings, presided over by Senator Gerald P. Nye of North Dakota during 1934 and 1935, supplied the public with garish headlines about war profiteers in 1914–1917 and created the impression that profit-hungry capitalists had dragged the United States into the Great War.

The threat of war between Italy and Ethiopia set the stage for passage of the First Neutrality Act in 1935. President Roosevelt, apparently hoping to free his hands of troublesome neutrality issues in case of war, suggested that American citizens be barred from travel on belligerent ships. Instead Congress presented him with a measure for a mandatory embargo on arms shipments to belligerents; the President also could warn citizens against taking passage aboard belligerent vessels. FDR signed the measure because it was temporary, hoping to obtain a more satisfactory one later.

Europe once more stood on the threshold of war. Benito Mussolini and his black-shirted Fascists had come to power in Italy in the early 1920s with their promises of reform and efficiency. On the whole Mussolini did not adopt an adventurist foreign policy until emboldened in the 1930s by Japan's successful challenge of the League and by the rise of Hitler in Germany. Adolf Hitler's National Socialists (Nazis) exploited German unhappiness with the Versailles settlement and the economic misery of the depression to take power in 1933. Rapidly consolidating his brutal dictatorship, Hitler began to rearm Germany in defiance of Versailles. The Fuehrer also horrified much of the world by his violent anti-Jewish persecutions and laws.

In this climate, dreaming of a new Roman empire, Mussolini invaded Ethiopia in the fall of 1935. Backward Ethiopia, some of whose troops went into battle armed with spears against warplanes, tanks, and poison gas, proved an easy conquest for the Duce's legions. The League revealed its powerlessness to help the victims. Britain and France, virtually paralyzed by memories of World War I bloodletting and still struggling with the depression, feared that strong measures would drive Mussolini and Hitler into alliance. Consequently the League invoked only mild sanctions against Mussolini, leaving untouched his vital oil supply.

Although Italy had not formally declared war against Ethiopia, Roosevelt invoked the neutrality law in hopes that it would aid the victim of aggression. He then moved beyond the mild League sanctions by declaring a moral embargo against oil shipments to Italy. The embargo was hard to enforce, however, and it failed to encourage Britain and France to stronger measures. Encouraged by the supineness of the major League powers, in 1936 Hitler violated Versailles by reoccupying and fortifying the Rhineland. The Rome-Berlin "Axis," also concluded in that same year, and supplemented by German and Italian anti-Comintern pacts with Japan, put the finishing touches on the new alignment of militaristic and fascist powers against the democratic West.

The Second Neutrality Act, enacted in 1936, prohibited private loans as well as arms sales to belligerents. When the Spanish Civil War broke out in the summer, pitting the democratic government of the "Loyalists" against the fascist-backed rebels of General Francisco Franco, Congress extended the neutrality acts to apply to civil wars. Many Americans sympathized deeply with the Loyalists and saw the issue as between democracy and dictatorship ("totalitarianism"), but most citizens supported the cautious neutrality of the administration. Because Britain and France had obtained a nonintervention agreement in Europe, FDR cooperated by invoking a moral embargo against arms sales to both sides in the Spanish conflict until the neutrality act was extended to cover that war. Yet, Germany and Italy openly aided Franco with war goods and "volunteer" troops; Soviet Russia helped the Loyalists. Later Roosevelt did contemplate raising the embargo but did not act because of domestic opposition and the hopelessness of the Loyalist cause.

The Neutrality Act of 1937 represented the cresting of the antiinterventionist movement in America. That act renewed the ban against loans and arms sales to belligerents and prohibited private travel on belligerent ships. President Roosevelt had wanted a measure that would allow him to discriminate between aggressors and their victims, but he gave way to isolationist demands for an airtight ban. The President's freedom of maneuver was curtailed and the United States in effect announced to the world that it would treat aggressors and defensive states alike. Traditional neutral rights were abandoned as the United States, in the words of several commentators, tried to legislate itself post facto out of World War I.

Antiinterventionism, of course, fell far short of a viable foreign policy. A great power necessarily influences events, whatever its role; time also revealed that most Americans deep-down were pro-British and pro-French, and that the majority of citizens could not avoid reacting morally to events abroad.

THE SHADOW OF GLOBAL WAR

Events moved swiftly toward the Second World War. Japan, determined to break or bend Nationalist China to her will, launched the "China Incident" in July 1937. Hitler seized Austria in March 1938 and by the summer threatened war if the German-inhabited Sudetenland of Czechoslovakia was not turned over to his Third Reich. British Prime Minister Neville Chamberlain, determined to appease the hungry dictators, joined the French premier at Munich in the fall of 1938 where "peace in our time" was purchased at Czechoslovakia's expense. Hitler promised that he had no more territorial demands in Europe. He soon broke his word by swallowing the remainder of Czechoslovakia and then turning his attention to those Germans living within the Polish Corridor. Eager not to be entirely surpassed by his fellow dictator, Mussolini seized tiny Albania in April 1939. Only then, as Hitler revealed an insatiable appetite for territory and complete untrustworthiness, did the British and French governments abandon appeasement and draw a firm line in Poland against further aggression.

After his reelection in 1936, President Roosevelt clearly moved toward a policy opposing aggression and favoring collective security. He saw that war was imminent and that it would have a tremendous impact upon American ideals and security. After Japan attacked China in 1937, FDR sounded the alarm in his famed Quarantine Speech at Chicago on October 5, 1937. There was no way of ensuring, Roosevelt warned, that war would not touch the United States or that it would not be attacked. Roosevelt declared that the peace-loving peoples of the world, the overwhelming majority of mankind, ought to quarantine aggressors as society quarantines the carriers of contagious diseases. Apparently Roosevelt had no definite plans in mind, however, and when opponents criticized him as a warmonger, he beat a hasty retreat from the implications of his address.

A conference of the Nine Power Pact states and the Soviet Union convened at Brussels in 1937 to consider Japan's invasion of China. Shortly before it met, however, FDR clearly indicated that the United States would not take any forceful measures. Japan declined to attend and only Russia advocated strong action. Britain and France left responsibility to Roosevelt, while he and Hull drew back from economic sanctions. Consequently Brussels achieved nothing positive. In fact, it was a most unfortunate failure, for the meeting encouraged China to resist in hopes of aid while the lack of action emboldened Japan. The *Panay* incident a few weeks after the conference revealed the reluctance of America to become embroiled with Japan. When Japanese planes sank the American gunboat in Chinese waters, most Americans merely wanted to get out of China and welcomed Japan's apology for the affair.

As Japan continued to drive deeper into China, American policy

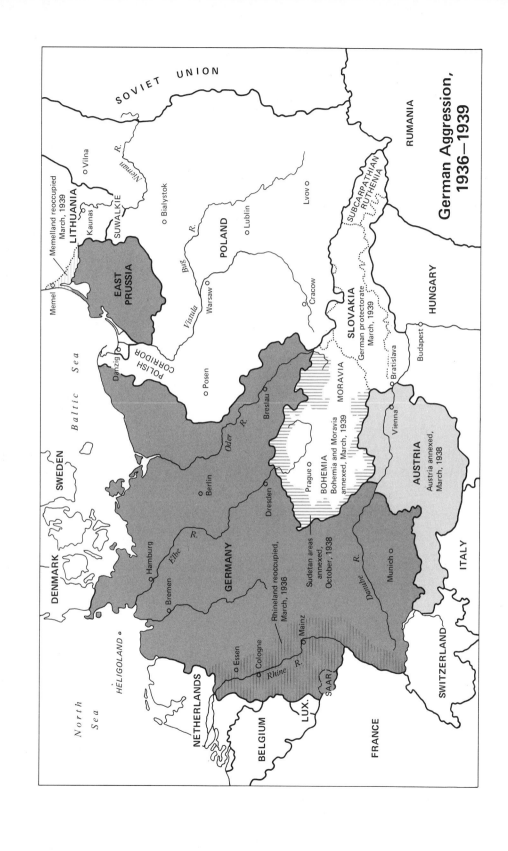

German Aggression, 1936–1939

toughened. Congress in 1938 authorized vast increases in naval construction, a graphic reminder to Japan of American naval power. Secretary Hull rejected Japanese attempts to proclaim a "New Order" in the Far East and reaffirmed the principles of the Open Door. Chiang Kai-shek received a money loan to bolster his currency in 1938, and the administration declared a moral embargo against airplane sales to Japan. Finally, in 1939, the United States placed Japan on notice by terminating its commercial treaty with her, thereby opening the way for trade embargoes to curb her aggressions. Increasingly, Washington saw economic pressure as the only hope to halt Japan without war.

The United States had virtually no part in the Czechoslovakian crisis. FDR did cable Hitler in behalf of peace, and he approved Chamberlain's effort to enlist Mussolini in a peaceful settlement. Most Americans, like most Europeans, reacted with relief when the Munich Agreement averted war. That mood swiftly passed as Hitler continued his aggressive course. Americans particularly were appalled at the anti-Jewish persecution in Germany, and the administration dramatized its condemnation by recalling the American ambassador from Berlin—Hitler reciprocated.

As the depression decade drew to a close, the United States looked out upon an anarchic world. Hitler was about to plunge Europe into a catastrophic war, and Japanese armies marched ahead on the Asian mainland. And soon the three major powers that had lost the most in the aftermath of World War I—Germany, Japan, and Russia—would be bound together by mutual defense and nonaggression pacts. Sheltered from foreign war by its two ocean frontiers and weak neighbors to the north and south, the United States would soon have to decide whether to draw more tightly into its own hemispheric fortress or foster national security by more active intervention overseas.

18

An Uncertain Future: Depression and the American People

How does one evaluate the impact of economic catastrophe on a society? Some effects of the Great Depression are easily measured. During the depression decade, for example, unemployment never dipped below the high 1930 level. Indeed only once during the New Deal years, in 1937, did unemployment fall below 25 percent of the nonfarm civilian labor force. Real earnings suffered equally. As late as 1940 average earnings for all employed workers remained, in real dollars, $40 beneath 1929 levels ($793 to $754). At the decade's lowest point, in 1933, real wages had fallen 25 percent below 1929 levels, and only once before 1940 did average earnings rise above $700 annually ($704 in 1937).

It seems only logical to assume that protracted economic collapse plus the reforms and turbulence associated with the New Deal would fundamentally alter society and culture. Yet when one examines more closely the structure of national society in the 1930s, a host of paradoxes emerge. Despite apparent economic and social innovations, society experienced fewer substantial structural transformations than in any other decade of the century. Despite the rise of militant mass movements, people by and large were no more rebellious in 1940 than in 1930.

Paradoxically, social continuities persisted despite extensive reforms, apathy endured in the face of militancy.

CONTINUITIES: THE BROAD PICTURE

Demographic trends during the depression decade are exceedingly difficult to separate from basic long-term population changes. Variations in the rates of population growth, births, and family size are evident; so, too, is an apparent trend to aging in the population. How much these changes resulted from the Great Depression, however, is hard to discern. Population grew during the 1930s but at only half the rate of increase for the previous decade. But statistics explode the common belief that depression reduced the number of marriages and caused men and women to wed at a later age. Except for 1932, when the number of marriages dropped precipitously, there was no discernible downward trend. By 1934 marriages had surpassed their 1929 level and remained high for the remainder of the decade. In 1940, in fact, the percentage of married and single Americans remained precisely the same as it had been ten years previously. In 1930 men first wed at a median age of 24.3; ten years later men first married at the same age, though women delayed perhaps a month longer. The median size of a household further declined—from 3.4 to 3.28 members—but the rate of decline did not deviate from the longer-term trend. The birth rate also fell, but, except for sharper than normal declines in 1934 and 1936, it basically followed a trajectory set in previous decades. (During the prosperous 1920s the birth rate fell by 21 percent compared to only 9 percent for the depressed thirties.)

As population growth slowed, life expectancy maintained its steady rise. A man born in 1940 could expect to live sixty-one years compared to fifty-eight years for a man ten years his senior; for women life expectancy rose from sixty-two to sixty-five years. The death rate continued a slow but steady decline, as the age-old scourges of infant and maternal mortality, respiratory diseases, and childhood illnesses became less common killers than diseases associated with aging or the deaths inflicted by motor vehicles.

Also persisting throughout the depression decade was the traditional demographic disparity between white and nonwhite Americans. In 1940 the life expectancy of a nonwhite male was nine years less than that of his white cohort, and of nonwhite females twelve years less. Nonwhite infant mortality also remained much higher than for whites (73.8 per thousand births compared to 43.2 per thousand births), and the disparity in maternal mortality proved greater still (32.0 per ten thousand for whites to 77.3 per thousand for nonwhites). It should be noted, however, that in both absolute and relative terms average life expectancy rose more rapidly for nonwhites than for whites and infant and maternal mortality rates fell more sharply for nonwhites than whites.

If demographic statistics belie the notion that the depression caused extraordinary social changes, some qualitative changes in values nevertheless occurred. During the 1930s the Sears, Roebuck Catalogue for the first time listed contraceptives, and public opinion polls revealed a growing majority of adults in favor of family planning through contraception, with women more pro than men. This, too, reflected a trend that had begun in the prewar years, accelerated in the 1920s, and would likely have expanded in the 1930s even without a depression.

Just as the depression failed to cause fundamental shifts in the size and structure of the population, it had little impact on the distribution of workers among jobs and occupations. The growth rate in white-collar retail and service employment declined as the consumer market shrank, and blue-collar workers remained the dominant sector of the labor force. As a result of economic retrenchment, American industry introduced few technological innovations, and skill levels and types scarcely changed.

If employees tended to have much the same kind of jobs in 1940 as in 1930, there was, however, a significant alteration in the kind of person likely to work. The surplus labor market drove teenagers, aged workers, and nonwhites out of the work force. Those three groups bore a disproportionate share of the unemployment burden. Women also suffered occupationally. Though the total number of female workers rose from 10.7 million in 1930 to 12.6 million in 1940, the rate of increase was lower than for the three preceding decades.

The internal distribution of the population also underwent few basic alterations. For the first time in over a century urban population grew less rapidly than rural (in the first depression years unemployed city workers returned to the family farm), and in the countryside the decline in farmer-owners reversed itself. Out of the total decennial decrease of 670,000 farmers, 510,000 were tenants and sharecroppers. Indeed during the depression decade the percentage of owners compared to renters rose from 57 percent to 61 percent of the farm population. The foreign-born proportion of the population maintained a decrease initiated by the restrictive immigration laws of 1921 and 1924 and compounded by the depression. The 1930s also witnessed a hiatus in black migration out of the South, and natural increase accounted for most of the minimal growth in black population in the North and West. No region of the country, other than the Pacific Coast, experienced an unusual growth or decline in population. (The Pacific Coast states experienced unusual growth; California alone increased its population by 1,230,000, a rise of about 18 percent.)

If the depression failed to alter substantially the demographic composition of the American people, did it perhaps have a greater impact on values and beliefs? Evidence subjects even this natural assumption to grave doubt. In Middletown, Indiana, to which sociologists Helen and Robert Lynd returned in 1935 to investigate what changes, if any, had occurred since their initial survey of local society in 1925, the dominant social values of the 1920s seemed alive and well. The local newspapers still railed against relief and asserted that those men who refused public assistance personified "the original spirit that is America." A local union official informed the Lynds, in almost the same words that they had heard ten years before, that so long as local workers "have a car and can borrow or steal a gallon of gas, they'll ride around and pay no attention to labor organization; and if they can't get gas, they're busy trying to figure out some way to get it." Another Middletown informant observed that "most of the families I know are after the same things today that they were after before the depression, and they'll get them in the same way—on credit."

Similar tendencies were discovered by a Yale University sociologist who examined behavior among the unemployed in New Haven.* Instead of transforming working-class neighborhood and political patterns, depression intensified them. Normally isolated from their neighbors socially, unemployed New Haven workers became more socially separated as lack of income reduced their self-esteem and made visiting and entertaining both uneconomical and unpleasurable. Most of the workers he interviewed still thought of government as an alien institution, one from which they took orders but to which they never gave them. Yet most of the city's unemployed adjusted to depression without experiencing personal or family breakdown because as a brassworker noted: "The poor are used to being poor."

CHANGES: THE BROAD PICTURE

Ironically the Great Depression, unlike the prosperity decade, marginally redistributed national income. Between 1929 and 1941 the proportion of families receiving under $2000 annually fell by 22 percent (from 25.6 percent of all families to 19.9 percent). The share of income received by the bottom two-fifths of the population also rose slightly, while the share obtained by the top fifth declined 10 percent (54.4 percent to 48.8 percent) and the share of income of the top 5 percent fell 20 percent (30.0 percent to 24.0 percent). Similar trends could be discerned in the percentage share of disposable (after tax) income received by both the top 1 percent and the top 5 percent of the population between 1930 and 1940; the top 1 percent's share fell from 15 percent to 11 percent, and the top 5 percent's share from 31 percent to 25 percent. Such income redistribution as occurred resulted however from what might best be characterized as the economics of misery. If the wealthy now earned marginally less in the form of dividends, interest, and rent, they still lived privileged, comfortable lives. But most workers struggled simply to maintain a decent existence.

* E. Wright Bakke, *Citizens Without Work: A Study of the Effects of Unemployment upon the Workers' Social Relations and Practices* (1940; reprinted ed., Hamden, Conn.: Shoe String Press, 1969).

The persistent gap between wealthy and poor Americans combined with a decade of high unemployment and minimal economic opportunity to stimulate class consciousness. New Deal rhetoric, especially the speeches of President Roosevelt, and the frenzied opposition to New Deal reforms by Liberty Leaguers and leading Republicans reinforced the sense of class that was emerging among millions of workers. As one worker in New Haven, Connecticut, put it: "It's funny how some guys feel they are working class and some don't. But I guess we all recognize it." Another worker in the same city explained more fully the realities of life: "Hell, brother, you don't have to look far to know that there's a working class. We may not say so. But look at what we do. Work. Look at who we run around with and bull with. Workers. Look at where we live. If you can find anyone but workers in any block, I'll eat 'em. Look at how we get along. Just like every other damned worker. Hell's bells, of course there's a workin' class, and its gettin' more so every day."*

What workers actually did during the depression decade was well worth watching. From 1933 to 1940 the number of annual strikes never dipped below 1,700 and the total rose as high as 4,740 in 1937. Over the same period, organized labor marched from the periphery of the national economy directly into its core. The number of union members soared from 2.85 million in 1933 to 8.94 million by 1940, an increase of over 300 percent. Organized labor expanded from 10 percent of the nonagricultural labor force to 27.2 percent. More important, trade unionism now penetrated such basic mass-production industries as autos, steel, rubber, and electrical goods.

This labor upsurge sparked savage struggle and much bloodshed. Two great waves of labor discontent marked the 1930s. In 1934 working-class militancy first rocked the nation. That year, strikers in Toledo fought militia in the city streets; teamsters in Minneapolis-St. Paul, led by avowed radical socialists, tied up the city and waged a pitched, bloody battle with local police; and San Francisco longshoremen precipitated a citywide general strike, one that caused the governor of California to dispatch to the strike scene national guard troops armed with tanks and machine guns. But the 1934 strike wave, however illustrative of working-class militancy, failed to bring lasting gains to the labor movement, largely because of the hesitancy and bumbling of the American Federation of Labor.

Where workers wanted action, the AFL offered advice. Where laborers desired to battle their bosses, the federation suggested collaboration. And where workers in the mass-production industries demanded industrial unions which encompassed all workers in a plant regardless of skill or job classification, the AFL provided craft unions which separated workers by skill.

Between 1934 and the next labor upsurge in 1937 several ambitious, militant labor leaders allied to transform the national labor movement.

* Bakke, *Citizens Without Work.*

John L. Lewis, president of the United Mine Workers, Sidney Hillman, leader of the men's clothing workers, and five other labor leaders in 1935 formed the Committee on Industrial Organization as their response to the AFL's failure to organize workers in the mass-production industries on an industrial rather than craft basis.

Traditional craft unions of the type that dominated the AFL in 1935 preferred to organize workers by skill, placing machinists, carpenters, teamsters, electricians and other craftsmen in distinct unions of their own. This left the enormous residue of semiskilled and unskilled workers in the basic industries in second-class unions or as second-class members of existing craft unions. Industrial unionists intended to organize all workers in such mass-production industries as autos, steel, and rubber into integrated unions that encompassed all employees in an industry regardless of skill or job. Actually the real struggle between the craft unionists and the industrial unionists was not over structure but about whether mass-production workers could in fact be organized. Most AFL leaders agreed with Teamsters president, Dan Tobin, that the labor movement could do "without the rubbish [mass-production workers] at its door."

Daring where AFL officials were cautious, militant where federation men were moderate, the CIO leaders, especially Lewis, enthusiastically supported rebellious workers in 1937.

The 1937 labor rebellion began just before New Year's eve when General Motors workers in Flint, Michigan, literally occupied a Chevrolet plant. For almost two months the Flint auto workers maintained their occupation of General Motors property, sitting-in until the corporation in February 1937 recognized the United Auto Workers, thus breaching the industry's traditional barrier to trade unionism. In the aftermath of union success in Flint, hospital workers, pencil makers, dogcatchers, sailors, Woolworth girls, and garbage collectors sat down on the job. In January there were 25 sit-down strikes, in February, 47, and in March, 170. "Sitting down," observed *Time* magazine hyperbolically, "has replaced baseball as a national pastime."

United States Steel executives did not require a sit-down strike to convince them that the time had come to bargain with labor. In March 1937 steel executive Myron Taylor and John L. Lewis signed an agreement that opened another basic industry to trade union penetration. Before the year was out, rubber, electrical goods, and the merchant marine would also fall before the CIO onslaught.

The rewards of unionization immediately became clear to workers. Wage rates rose more rapidly in the union than the nonunion sectors of the economy and union members received protection unavailable to the unorganized against arbitrary action by foremen and supervisors. As a formerly antiunion auto worker in Flint noted: "We now have a voice, and have slowed up the speed of the line. We are now treated as human beings, and not as part of the machinery. . . . It proves clearly that united we stand, divided or alone we fall." Even the wives of the new unionists had their consciousness transformed, as they joined in their husband's strikes or the ladies' auxiliary of the union. "I'm living for the first time," observed one striker's wife, "with a definite goal. . . . Just being a woman isn't enough any more. I want to be a human being with the right to think for myself."

Voting behavior further illustrated the heightened class consciousness of American workers. Already attracted to the Democratic party by Roosevelt's first term reforms, workers were pushed further in the same direction by the policies of the CIO and the president's own class-laden rhetoric. In 1936 the CIO unions formed a labor political committee (Labor's Nonpartisan League) amply supplied with funds to campaign for the reelection of Roosevelt and Democratic congressmen. That same election year saw socialists in the clothing trades unions break with tradition and endorse a Democratic presidential candidate, albeit on a third-party ticket. (FDR was the nominee of the American Labor party.) Thereafter working-class voters would remain the single most loyal group of constituents of the Democratic party.

Heightened feelings of class consciousness and the successes of the labor movement could not but affect black Americans. No social group was more working class in composition or suffered more from the depression. Black workers, moreover, were concentrated in precisely those industries penetrated by the CIO: autos, steel, coal mining, and meatpacking. CIO unions cultivated black membership, frequently establishing special civil rights branches to fight for the rights of Negro-Americans and often symbolically reserving union offices for black members.

During the 1930s Communists also labored assiduously to attract a black following, and they, like the CIO, achieved success. The NAACP, long the primary institutional defender of black Americans, found itself with a more militant and aggressive competitor in the National Negro Congress, a new organization with firm links to CIO unions and left-wing political groups, including the Communist party. A. Philip Randolph was the founder and president of the all-black Brotherhood of Sleeping Car Porters, which became more militant, aggressive, and politically effective as the 1930s wore on. "The New Negro" of the World War II and postwar years had clearly emerged by the end of the Great Depression.

As black Americans grew more assertive during the 1930s, the "new woman" retreated. As pointed out earlier, the rate of female entry into the labor market diminished not because women chose to stay at home but because prevailing values demanded that when jobs were in short supply men (primary breadwinners) must have preference. Many states consequently adopted antinepotism statutes, laws directed at eliminating working wives from public service, especially schoolteaching. The Great Depression confirmed man's role as economic provider and woman's as homemaker and mother. Necessity might still compel females to work but society insisted that they had more important functions, and in the 1930s, unlike the 1920s, few women or influential women's organizations rebelled against this definition of woman's role.

CULTURE IN A TIME OF CRISIS

If the literature of the prosperity decade stressed the absurd, deprecated the masses, and considered social reform a chimera, culture during the depression addressed itself vigorously to the amelioration of social problems. Indeed some writers preferred revolution to reform, as evidenced by the number of novelists, dramatists, and critics who in 1932 endorsed William Z. Foster, the Communist party's candidate for president. Many creative artists and intellectuals remained Communists or party sympathizers until later in the decade when news of either Stalin's purges or the signing of the Nazi-Soviet Nonaggression Pact disillusioned them. Until that time, however, American literature was unabashedly proletarian in theme and style.

Although the cult of the proletarian produced much mawkish and maudlin literature, it also resulted in several classical novels of social and economic change. No work captured the nation's fall from the peaks of prosperity to the depths of depression better than John Dos Passos' fictional trilogy—*U.S.A.* (1936). Using innovative literary techniques that wove the artifacts of popular culture into the novel, Dos Passos glorified the working-class radical and rebel and denigrated the barons of business and politics. The trilogy incorporated dazzingly sympathetic biographical sketches of William D. Haywood, Eugene V. Debs, and Joe Hill. Although no other work of fiction reached the level achieved by Dos Passos in *U.S.A.*, several other novelists also used proletarian themes successfully. James T. Farrell's *Studs Lonigan* series, for example, portrayed with clarity and empathy the passage of the urban Irish in Chicago from working-class to insecure middle-class status. John Steinbeck, the most successful of the decade's "problem" novelists, treated sympathetically the plight of California's migrant farm workers, first in *In Dubious Battle* (1935)—the tale of a bloody fruit pickers' strike—and then in the more famous and popular Pulitzer Prize winner, *The Grapes of Wrath* (1939). The black proletariat, too, appeared in fiction, most notably in Richard Wright's brilliant evocation of ghetto life in Chicago's "black belt," *Native Son* (1940). Even Sinclair Lewis devoted himself to the elucidation of social problems, writing a fictional warning of the Fascist threat to America, *It Can't Happen Here* (1935).

The stage also vibrated to the beat of class conflict. Labor struggle entered center stage in Clifford Odets's drama of a New York City taxi drivers strike, *Waiting for Lefty* (1935), and in Marc Blitzstein's folk opera about the CIO's attack against the steel industry, *The Cradle Will Rock* (1937). Less popular at the time but more faithful and truthful as description of life among the urban Jewish-American families of socialist inclinations were Odets's *Awake and Sing* (1935) and *Paradise Lost* (1937). More didactic and more applauded was the International Ladies'

Garment Workers' Union's own musical production, *Pins and Needles,* which achieved Broadway success and gave a special White House performance.

Despite the ubiquity of proletarian literature during the depression era, the decade's bestsellers were escapist fiction. Hervey Allen's *Anthony Adverse,* a historical romance set in the Napoleonic era and characterized by one critic as "a mountain of trash" was a runaway bestseller in 1933. Yet it could not compare in popularity or sales with the bestseller of 1936, Margaret Mitchell's *Gone With the Wind,* a novel that glorified antebellum southern life on the large plantation (Tara). This paean to plantation masters and their ladies, loyal sambos, and Uncle Toms, won a Pulitzer Prize and sold more than eight million copies in thirty languages by the time of Mitchell's death in 1949.

However much the serious literature of the 1930s stressed radical social themes, most Americans received their culture from the movies, radio, comics, and advertising. By the end of the decade the radio had become an indispensable source of entertainment, news, and knowledge. For a single, initial expenditure, the whole family obtained nearly cost-free entertainment—no mean achievement during the depression. By 1940, three and a half times as many radios were in use as in 1929, and by then a total of 86 percent of the population owned 44 million sets, to which they listened an average of four and a half hours daily.

Radio became increasingly concentrated economically and homogenized culturally. By 1940 at least a third of the nation's commercial stations were controlled by newspapers, and three networks—the National Broadcasting Company, Columbia Broadcasting System, and Mutual—dominated the airwaves transmitting slickly produced and packaged programs that originated in New York or Hollywood. "Soap Operas," so labeled because their primary function was to advertise soap products to housewives, dominated the morning and early afternoon hours. After school and before dinner such serialized adventures as "Jack Armstrong," "Captain Midnight," and "Little Orphan Annie" enthralled youngsters. Evening hours featured such escapist family programs as "Amos and Andy," in which two white men played the roles of comical blacks who were to be laughed at as much as with; "The Lone Ranger," introduced in 1933, which substituted a loyal Indian, Tonto, for the more common Sambo type, such as Jack Benny's Rochester, played by Eddie Anderson; and "The Quiz Kids," illustrative of society's worship of precocious children. Squeezed in between escapist fare produced primarily to advertise consumer goods (by 1940 radio was the dominant advertising medium) were programs of public service news analysis and serious music. Most notable of the music programs were the Saturday matinee performances of the Metropolitan Opera (which are still broadcast live and still sponsored by the Texaco Oil Company) the Sunday afternoon concerts of the New York Philharmonic, and, the performances of the NBC Symphony Orchestra. The latter orchestra was made up of virtuoso musicians especially selected by the network to play under the direction of the eminent Italian conductor, Arturo Toscanini. Maestro Toscanini was considered by many to be the outstanding musical genius of his time.

Movies, however, remained the preeminent form of popular entertainment. After declining slightly as a result of the depression, films rebounded with vigor. Aided by the complete triumph of talkies and the introduction of technicolor, the movie industry by 1939 grossed box-office receipts of nearly $700 million, which represented an average annual family expenditure of $25. For their money most moviegoers saw a steady stream of formula Westerns, lavish musicals, and sophisticated comedies. The decade was not without its problem films—e.g., "I Was a Fugitive with a China Gang," "Dead End," "Our Daily Bread," and Charlie Chaplin's bitter critiques of contemporary industrial society, "Modern Times" and "The Great Dictator." But Hollywood existed to make profits, and escapism, not social realism, made the turnstiles whirl. Even most of the more serious films adhered to the Hollywood convention of happy endings and virtuous heroes or heroines.

Two of Hollywood's more notable ventures into social realism illustrated the grip of convention. *Dead End* (1936), adapted from the Pulitzer Prize–winning play of the same title by Sidney Kingsley and starring Humphrey Bogart, Joel McCrea, Sylvia Sidney, and a group of juveniles soon to become famous as the "Bowery Boys," starkly contrasted wealth and poverty in New York City. The film intended to show that poverty produces crime. Bogart, as a ruthless criminal, returns to the slum streets that spawned him and is lionized by the neighborhood children. The film almost collapses into a conventional love story. Joel McCrea plays the slumdweller who, by virtue of his character and thirst for knowledge, rises above his environment. He courts a Sutton Place debutante, yet remains loyal to his working-class girl and, in the end, wins the admiration of the neighborhood boys after gunning down Bogart following a dramatic rooftop chase. Goodness thus repels evil; the handsome actor subdues the more homely one; and the poor girl wins the hero. Simply stated, virtue and beauty are their own rewards! In the original Broadway play, by contrast, the male lead was an envious, embittered cripple (a hunchback) who "does in" the famed criminal by tipping off federal agents. The play ends with the street gang mourning the criminal's death and reviling the informer. Poverty, in this case, creates its own values.

Black Legion (1937), also starring Bogart, suffered from the same distorted vision. Its opening moments capture the rhythm of life among skilled workers in a large machine plant, both on the job and at home. It also probes the workers' desire to rise inside the plant and the intensity of ethnic conflict. An embittered American-born worker, played by Bogart, is passed over for a foremanship in favor of a Polish-American. He then joins the "Black Legion," a secret anti-Catholic, antiimmigrant order, to seek revenge. Thereafter the movie degenerates into a conventional violent murder story in which Bogart causes the death of his best friend

*A product of Hollywood's dream machine portrayed
by Edward G. Robinson*
Culver Pictures, Inc.

and finally, out of remorse, exposes the "Black Legion" at the cost of his
own freedom and probably his life.

If depression and political reform influenced the movies at all, it was
in the fact that in most films produced during the 1930s, little guys
triumphed over big guys; the good defeated the evil; and the Jeffersonian

yeoman bettered the metropolitan wheeler-dealer. Indeed Gary Cooper and James Stewart rose to Hollywood fame and fortune playing honest men from small-town or rural America who in the end always preferred virtue to riches and won heroine Jean Arthur's lovely hand.

Movies were only one aspect of the triumph of the visual arts in popular culture. During the 1930s, tabloid newspapers, which featured pictures and comics, outsold their bulkier and more traditional competitors. (The most successful of the tabloids was the New York *Daily News*.) Over a billion and a half cartoon strips circulated weekly. Avid readers of all ages eagerly awaited Clark Kent's next adventure in "Superman"; Terry's coming clash with inscrutable Orientals in "Terry and the Pirates"; "Smiling Jack's" new airplane exploit; and "Little Orphan Annie's" homilies to social Darwinism as delivered by Daddy Warbucks, the American comic strip's Andrew Carnegie. From the newspaper pages America's comic strip heroes galloped off into the comic books, which by the war years sold some eighteen million copies each month.

Sports, too, by the middle of the 1930s regained the popularity and cash crowds associated with the prosperity decade. Baseball held its place as the preeminent professional sport and its World Series remained the single most important athletic event. The New York Yankees, who began the decade with baseball greats Babe Ruth and Lou Gehrig and closed it with Joe DiMaggio, dominated the American League, though they were challenged often by the Detroit Tigers, who were led by baseball's first great Jewish-American star, Hank Greenberg. In the National League Dizzy Dean and his "Gas-House Gang" teammates in St. Louis reigned during the first half of the decade. By the end of the 1930s those zany ballplayers, "dem Bums," the Brooklyn Dodgers, had become the new comic heroes of baseball culture.

Important as victory was to American athletics—recall Dodger manager Leo Durocher's comment that "nice guys finish last"—professional team owners, coaches, and players refused to breach the color barrier in order to recruit the best talent available. With one exception, professional sports remained closed to blacks, who had to form teams and play in their own Negro professional baseball and basketball leagues. The lone exception, boxing, produced the single most prominent professional athlete of the decade, "the Brown Bomber," Joe Louis, who would dominate heavyweight boxing into the 1950s and attract the million-dollar gates once associated with such white heroes as Jack Dempsey and Gene Tunney.

College sports, especially football, remained as much a "big business" and mass spectator sport as it had been during the 1920s. On Saturday afternoons, crowds of between 50,000 and 100,000 continued to jam football stadiums in such "Big Ten" cities as Ann Arbor, Columbus, Madison, and Urbana. And on New Year's Day, equally large crowds packed the Rose Bowl in Pasadena, California, to watch the bowl game, which ostensibly matched the nation's two best college elevens. Intercollegiate sports, especially in midwestern public universities, also provided

some breathing space for nonwhite athletes. Indeed the depression decade's most famous amateur athlete, Jesse Owens, first starred on the
track team at the University of Illinois. He went on to win three gold
medals in the 1936 Berlin Olympics, thus shattering Hitler's and the
Nazi's visions of Aryan superiority. But even in college sports the black
athlete on the white campus remained a rare and usually lonely figure.

THE AMERICAN PEOPLE ON THE EVE OF THE WAR

The American people had not yet recovered fully from a decade of
depression when the fragile international order established at Versailles
after World War I collapsed under the assaults of Germany and Japan
and threatened to involve the United States in another bloody world
struggle. As we have seen, by 1940 many of the predepression era social
patterns had firmly reasserted themselves. Americans, as a people, continued to live longer, marry young, bear fewer children, grow healthier,
and stay in school longer. Society still supported a caste system that
excluded nonwhites from basic sectors of the economy and assigned them
a hereditary inferior status. White ethnics, however, as a result of the
decline of immigration and also of their incorporation into the political
and economic order through the Roosevelt New Deal coalition lost some
of their social distinctiveness. Those Irish-Americans who had risen
economically, admittedly a small minority, seemed largely assimilated by
the WASP hierarchy. Other ethnics, such as Jews and Italians, by changing their names and mores, also could assimilate into the dominant
society.

Despite the persistence of older social trends and the increasing
solidarity of white Americans, the American people remained less than
confident in 1940. Roosevelt's two terms had produced many necessary
social and economic reforms, but the New Deal had conquered neither
depression nor its most insidious effect: mass unemployment. As in 1930,
Americans in 1940 were a mature society with a stagnant economy, a
nation that had now seen its economic frontiers disappear as its land
frontier had once vanished. With no new frontiers available for exploitation, some citizens thought that perhaps the nation had reached a state of
chronic economic malaise. For most citizens in the year 1940 the future
seemed problematic, and the world a frightening war-torn landscape.

SELECTED BIBLIOGRAPHY FOR SECTION V

The Great Depression is critically analyzed in JOHN K. GALBRAITH,
The Great Crash, 1929 (1955) *; ROBERT SOBEL, *The Great Bull Market:
Wall Street in the 1920s* (1968) *; and PAUL A. BARAN and PAUL M.

* Available in paperback.

Sweezy's Marxist analysis, *Monopoly Capital: An Essay on the American Economic and Social Order* (1966).* Excellent contemporary accounts of the plight of the unemployed can be found in E. Wright Bakke's two volumes, *Citizens without Work* (1940) and *The Unemployed Worker* (1940); Eli Ginzberg, *The Unemployed* (1943); and in Robert and Helen Lynd, *Middletown in Transition* (1937).* The persistence of poverty and hard times for millions of Americans is discussed in Dixon Wecter, *Age of the Great Depression, 1929–1941* (1948).*

The New Deal has precipitated a voluminous body of scholarship, generally sympathetic to Franklin D. Roosevelt, although more recent and radical scholars have become increasingly skeptical about the efficacy of New Deal reforms. Those studies providing a good overview of national politics include William Leuchtenberg, *Franklin D. Roosevelt and the New Deal* (1963)*; James Burns, *Roosevelt: The Lion and the Fox* (1956)*; Paul Conkin, *The New Deal* (2nd ed., 1975)*; Barton Bernstein, "The New Deal: The Conservative Achievements of Liberal Reform," in Barton Bernstein, ed., *Towards a New Past* (1968)*; Broadus Mitchell, *Depression Decade* (1947)*; and Carl Degler, *Out of Our Past* (1959).* Politics, dissent, the major legislative changes, civil rights, and civil liberties are examined in James Patterson, *Congressional Conservatism and the New Deal* (1967); Donald McCoy, *Angry Voices* (1958); George Wolfskill, *The Revolt of the Conservatives* (1962); T. Harry Williams, *Huey Long* (1969)*; Charles Tull, *Father Coughlin and the New Deal* (1965); J. Joseph Huthmacher, *Senator Robert F. Wagner and the Rise of Urban Liberalism* (1969)*; David Conrad, *The Forgotten Farmers* (1966); Jerold Auerbach, *Labor and Liberty* (1967); Sandford Ungar, *FBI* (1975); Jerold Auerbach, *Unequal Justice* (1976); and Richard Polenberg, *Reorganizing Roosevelt's Government* (1966). The New Deal origins of the "broker state" and modern liberalism are best seen in John K. Galbraith, *American Capitalism* (1952)*; Grant McConnell, *Private Power and American Democracy* (1966); and Theodore Lowi, *The End of Liberalism* (1969).*

Important studies that shed light on the New Deal's impact on different parts of the country and different groups in society include Bernard Sternsher, ed., *Hitting Home* (1970)*; Irving Bernstein, *Turbulent Years: A History of the American Worker, 1933–1941* (1970); Sidney Fine, *Sit-Down: The General Motors Strike of 1936–1937* (1969); David Brody, "The Emergence of Mass-Production Unionism" in John Braeman et al., *Change and Continuity in Twentieth Century America* (1968); James O. Morris, *Conflict within the AFL: A Study of Craft versus Industrial Unionism, 1900–1938* (1958); Bernard Sternsher, ed., *The Negro in Depression and War* (1969)*; Dan T. Carter, *Scottsboro* (1969)*; and Raymond Wolters, *Negroes and the Great Depression: The Problem of Economic Recovery* (1970). Radicalism during the depression and New Deal can be followed in John Shover, *Cornbelt Rebellion* (1965); Frank A. Warren, *Liberals and Communism* (1966) and *Alternative Vision: The Socialist Party in the 1930s* (1975); James Wein-

STEIN, *Ambiguous Legacy: The Left in American Politics* (1975) *; and JAMES B. GILBERT, *Writers and Partisans: A History of Literary Radicalism in America* (1968). The arts and culture during the 1930s are discussed in MAXWELL GEISMAR, *Writers in Crisis* (1947) *; DANIEL AARON, *Writers on the Left* (1961) *; HARVEY SWADOS, ed., *The American Writers and the Great Depression* (1966) *; JANE D. MATTHEWS, *The Federal Theatre, 1935–1939* (1967); and RICHARD H. PELLS, *Radical Visions and American Dreams* (1973).*

The best studies of New Deal foreign policy during the 1930s include JOHN E. WILTZ, *From Isolation to War, 1933–1941* (1968) *; SELIG ADLER, *The Uncertain Giant, 1929–1941: American Foreign Policy between the Wars* (1965) *; LLOYD C. GARDNER, *Economic Aspects of New Deal Diplomacy* (1964) *; ROBERT A. DIVINE, *The Illusion of Neutrality: Franklin D. Roosevelt and the Struggle over the Arms Embargo* (1962) *; WILLIAM LANGER and S. EVERETT GLEASON, *The Challenge to Isolation, 1937–1940* (1953) *; ROBERT SMITH, *The United States and Cuba* (1960) *; and BRYCE WOOD, *The Making of the Good Neighbor Policy* (1961) * and *The United States and Latin American Wars, 1932–1942* (1960).

VI

Global War and Its Ramifications, 1939–1953

World War II presented the greatest challenge ever faced by Western liberal capitalism and Open Door diplomacy. It also produced one of the stranger diplomatic alliances in world history. As the Axis powers—Germany, Japan, and Italy—threatened to overrun the globe in the early years of the war, the two primary liberal capitalist powers—the United States and Great Britain—had no alternative but to seek out an alliance with the world's most committed anticapitalist nation-state, Soviet Russia.

This strange alliance between the leading capitalist societies and the only existing Communist power succeeded in defeating Fascist and Nazi aggression. World War II, moreover, destroyed the old world order, in which the leading Western capitalist powers tended to dominate the globe, and replaced it with a new alignment of power. The United States and Soviet Russia emerged as the two dominant superpowers, representing the global interests of capitalism and communism respectively.

But in 1945, the United States gladly assumed the global burdens and responsibilities it had refused in 1919, after World War I. As the only power to survive the Second World War with its domestic economy unscathed and its military might unmatched and, for several years, the possessor of an atomic monopoly, the United States willingly served as liberal capitalism's global policeman. Its leaders actively sought to restrain what they perceived as Soviet Russia's aggressive designs on weaker nations and also to thwart anticapitalist and anticolonial revolutions in the so-called emerging Third World. The United States' assumption of global responsibilities set the stage for the era of the Cold War during which the forces of capitalism and communism clashed globally.

The Cold War, however, also had grave domestic ramifications. As chief executives and secretaries of state described the clash between capitalism and communism as vital to American national security, domestic affairs increasingly were shaped by Cold War images. Full employment was considered important if the United States were to thwart communism abroad, and the military expenditures necessary to play the role of global policeman in turn stimulated industrial productivity and hence employment. Civil rights for nonwhite Americans and the repression of domestic radicals also reflected Cold War priorities. Harry S. Truman's "Fair Deal," the emergence of a civil rights movement, and the era of Joseph McCarthy were all partially or wholly products of the conflict between the United States and Soviet Russia.

19

The Road to War: FDR and the Axis, 1939-1941

Ironically, the collapse of global stability and the aggressiveness of Germany, Japan, and Italy during the Great Depression did more to combat the economic doldrums in the United States than any of the New Deal's domestic reforms. By the end of the 1930s, as Franklin D. Roosevelt grew more concerned with foreign than domestic affairs and conceived of substituting "Dr. Win-the-War" for "Dr. New Deal," he pursued policies fated to stimulate the American economy, reduce unemployment, and stimulate mass prosperity. International disaster from 1939 through 1945 would once again prove to be a blessing in disguise.

By 1939 FDR believed that noninterventionism and neutrality did not serve the nation's vital interests. More and more Americans, unable to avoid moral judgments about foreign events and fearful of spreading totalitarianism, agreed. Yet the noninterventionists still were strong, especially in rural areas and thus in Congress where rural areas tended to be overrepresented. In April, Roosevelt appealed to Hitler and Mussolini for reassurances that they would not attack thirty-one nations that he listed; his gesture earned only their derision. In early 1939 the president also tried unsuccessfully to persuade influential members of Congress that the neutrality acts should be amended or repealed in order to permit him

289

to exempt peaceful states from the arms embargo if they were attacked. The opponents of intervention refused to relent, and Senator Borah stated that his information was more accurate than that of the State Department. The senator, moreover, confidently predicted that there would be no war in Europe in 1939.

THE UNDECLARED WAR IN THE ATLANTIC

Contrary to Senator Borah's beliefs, Hitler even then planned to unleash his powerful war machine upon Poland. On August 23, 1939, a startled world learned of the Nazi-Soviet nonaggression pact. For years Soviet Russia had called for a "Popular Front" of non-Fascist states against the Nazi menace and even then was discussing defensive military arrangements with the British and the French. Apparently Stalin decided that the western democracies could not be trusted, and in August 1939 he chose to safeguard Russia by a deal with Hitler. Subsequently it became clear that Stalin also had agreed to divide Poland with Germany. With his flank secured, Hitler on September 1, 1939, unleashed his attack upon the hapless Poles. Britain and France declared war against Germany but could do little to aid their ally. Poland fell before the onslaught. The Second World War had begun.

Neutralist sentiment in America began to diminish after the opening shots of the war. Polls revealed that most Americans regarded Germany as morally wrong; 84 percent desired an Allied victory and 76 percent, if hoping to remain at peace, expected the United States eventually to be drawn into the war. President Roosevelt believed that if given access to America's markets Britain and France might win a battle of attrition against the Nazis. Consequently he requested revision of the neutrality act to permit arms sales to belligerents, rationalizing that his purpose was to perfect American neutrality. Despite strong opposition to such legislation, Congress passed the Fourth Neutrality Act and FDR signed it into law on November 4, 1939. The measure repealed the arms embargo, required that belligerents pay cash for all purchases in America and carry them away in their own ships ("cash and carry"), and prohibited American ships from entering the war zones. Clearly a majority of Americans, while still hopeful of avoiding entanglement, wanted to give the Allies at least this much help in overcoming forces that they, too, regarded as evil.

Hitler's *blitzkrieg* (lightning war) in the spring of 1940 had a shattering effect upon American opinion. Ending the winter's so-called phony war, the Nazi panzers occupied Denmark and overran Norway in April, and in May knocked out Holland and Luxembourg, crushed Belgium, and smashed France into submission. On June 22, 1940, France signed an armistice in a humiliating ceremony at Compiegne. Britain came under intensive aerial bombing and seemed likely to succumb to an imminent invasion. More and more Americans realized that neutrality could not protect the nation's security and its democratic institutions. If Britain fell, the United States would be isolated between a voracious Fuehrer in Europe and the Japanese in Asia. If alarmists overstated the Nazi menace—Hitler would not have been able to attack the United States directly even if he so desired, and probably the United States could have held this hemisphere against all challenges—there could be little doubt that a Nazified Europe threatened the Wilsonian conception of a liberal world order and basic human values. The United States would be isolated economically and psychologically, its beliefs under attack everywhere, and it would have had to arm heavily in self-defense. Hitler had no plans to invade the United States, but he did not trouble to conceal his contempt for what he viewed as this mongrel and crassly materialistic democracy; privately he talked of eventually regenerating a degenerate Yankeedom.

Roosevelt sounded the full alarm to his fellow citizens. At Charlottesville, on June 10, 1940, he pledged aid to those resisting aggression and called for "full speed ahead" in defensive preparations. The crisis also apparently persuaded him to seek an unprecedented third term in office. Congress responded by passing huge appropriations for the army and navy and by adopting the first peacetime conscription in American history. In the destroyers-bases deal in September 1940 the United States moved from so-called neutrality to the status of a nonbelligerent who openly aided one side in the war. British Prime Minister Winston Churchill pleaded for some over-aged American destroyers to use against the U-boat offensive as he girded his island for the threatened invasion. FDR's advisers found a legal way to dispose of the ships without Congressional authorization by exchanging fifty destroyers for a chain of British bases from Newfoundland to the Caribbean. By the agreement, the United States received leases to six bases; Churchill added two more as gifts and informally pledged that the British navy would never fall into Hitler's hands. FDR made sure that his Republican opponent in the presidential election, Wendell L. Willkie, would not attack the deal, and he justified it to the American people as the most important reinforcement to defense since the Louisiana Purchase. Although the President had acted solely upon his own executive authority and clearly violated international law and neutrality, neither Congress nor the voters repudiated his action.

In May 1940 the supporters of the administration's policy of aiding Hitler's opponents by all means short of war formed the Committee to Defend America by Aiding the Allies. Known as the White Committee, after its national chairman Kansas Republican newspaperman William Allen White, this group established local organizations across the country and carried on a massive educational and propaganda campaign. In September a rival organization, the America First Committee, emerged to oppose any involvement in the war. The America Firsters mobilized such prominent citizens as Henry Ford, General Hugh Johnson, and Charles A. Lindbergh, in an attempt to persuade the public that the war in Europe had no bearing on American security and that FDR's policies risked a needless involvement. Although Communists, labor leaders such as John L. Lewis, and such Socialist pacifists as Norman Thomas associated themselves with America First, it increasingly became identified as a conservative anti-New Deal movement.

In the 1940 presidential campaign, Wendell Willkie, the Republican nominee, fearing that he was falling behind, accused his opponent of plotting war and pledged that he would not send American boys to fight in a European war. Stung, FDR repeated his party's platform pledge that the nation would not engage in war unless attacked. During a speech in Boston on October 30, however, the president unreservedly affirmed: "I have said this before, but I shall say it again and again and again: Your boys are not going to be sent into any foreign wars." The president's tendency during the campaign to pledge that American boys would never fight in a foreign war led critics to charge him with deceiving the American people. Indeed, the Democrats' 1940 campaign resembled Woodrow Wilson's 1916 race, in which the slogan—"He kept us out of war"—was associated with the Democratic candidate. And the 1940 election would bring a similar foreign policy result.

After he had won reelection in November, Roosevelt recognized that such aid as he had managed to offer the British barely sufficed to ensure their survival, much less the victory over the Nazis that he believed American interests required. Effective aid, his advisers urged, required him to seek formal congressional authorization. Churchill wrote him that Britain needed vast quantities of arms and lacked the funds to buy them. At last persuaded, Roosevelt, on December 29, 1940, spoke to the American people and asserted that America's own interests demanded a massive program to lend arms and war goods to those resisting aggression, the Lend-Lease Act of 1941. In that way America could stay at peace and yet protect itself by becoming "the great arsenal of democracy." Realizing that most citizens favored the British cause but also preferred American noninvolvement, Roosevelt rationalized that material aid to Britain would restrain the Nazi war machine, though he knew better.

The Lend-Lease Act became law on March 11, 1941. Despite furious opposition, the administration had successfully steered the measure through both houses of Congress by emphasing its defensive character—indeed Lend-Lease was cited as "An Act to Promote the Defense of the United States." Clearly most Americans, including most congressmen, agreed that Britain must survive. Yet the administration evaded questions of whether convoying aid shipments would not soon follow and, with it, armed clashes with German submarines. The Lend-Lease Act, a politically expedient, but obviously unneutral policy, openly made the United States a nonbelligerent fully committed to the Allied cause. It also marked in fact the death knell of noninterventionism.

From this point, the United States, by executive actions, gradually slid into an undeclared naval war with Germany in the Atlantic. Roosevelt acted without seeking congressional or popular approval. In January 1941, for example, the administration opened military and naval discussions with British representatives. Apparently, by mid-1941 the president had decided that even lend-lease was inadequate and that the United States probably would have to enter the war to insure a Nazi defeat. Because he feared to risk political repudiation by a Congress and a people unready for actual war, Roosevelt increasingly acted on his own in foreign affairs. If he was less than candid in explaining his actions to those unfamiliar with world events, he scarcely deceived most congressmen or knowledgeable citizens. Yet his actions represented a substantial growth in executive powers and set precedents for the precipitous behavior of later chief executives during the Cold War era.

In 1941 Roosevelt ordered the seizure of Axis shipping in American ports and froze their assets. In April, he directed that Greenland, a dependency of Nazi-seized Denmark, be occupied. In July, Iceland also was occupied, to prevent a possible German takeover. Patrolling and convoying of American and other ships transporting lend-lease also began in July and August. Roosevelt met Churchill off Newfoundland in August to discuss military problems, and the two issued the Atlantic Charter, a Wilsonian-type statement of liberal war goals.

Armed clashes, as critics had predicted, soon occurred between American naval vessels and German U-boats. In September 1941 the destroyer *Greer* was fired upon; in October the *Kearney* was attacked and the *Reuben James* was sunk. When announcing these sinkings to the public, Roosevelt uncandidly labeled them unprovoked attacks by Germany and said that he had issued shoot-on-sight orders against Nazi submarines. In fact, the *Greer* had been trailing a U-boat and the *Kearney* and *Reuben James* had been engaged in hostile antisubmarine actions. Hitler chose not to rise to the bait. Now fighting both the British and the Russians—he had invaded his erstwhile Soviet ally in June 1941—the Fuehrer preferred to postpone dealing with the United States. Meanwhile, acting in response to German U-boat attacks, Congress in November approved a virtual repeal of the remaining restrictions of the neutrality laws.

WAR VIA THE PACIFIC

Emboldened by Hitler's dazzling victories in Europe during the spring of 1940, Japan's militarists determined to exploit the opportunity to carve out their much talked of "Greater East Asia Co-Prosperity Sphere." A new ministry, headed by Prince Konoye, included General Hideki Tojo as War Minister and the strongly anti-American Yosuke Matsuoka as Foreign Minister. In September 1940 Japan forced the weak French Vichy regime to permit its armed forces to occupy northern Indo-China. Shortly thereafter Japan signed the Tripartite Alliance with Germany and Italy. The pact obviously aimed at neutralizing the United States by threatening it with war in both oceans. In April 1941 Japan and Russia concluded a neutrality pact, further freeing Japan for a southern lunge.

Washington refused to be frightened into retreat by these moves. American opinion hardened against Japan, now seen as a fit partner for an evil league of totalitarian dictatorships preying upon weaker states. Roosevelt and his advisers agreed that economic pressure offered the only hope of curbing Japanese expansionism short of war. Consequently, the administration began a gradual process of clamping down on exports to Japan, reserving the vital oil weapon until the last. Roosevelt's advisers assumed that a Japan that was heavily dependent upon the United States for steel and oil—over 80 percent of Japanese petroleum supplies came from the United States and its friends—would surely see the wisdom of moderation. Export of aviation gasoline was banned in July, and scrap iron in October 1940. When Japan occupied southern Indo-China in July 1941, an obvious launching platform for further military thrusts, Roosevelt froze Japanese assets and embargoed all oil exports to Japan.

Japan's leaders now faced a dilemma: either come to terms with the United States before their oil reserves ran out or strike at the Netherlands East Indies for an independent supply. Neither government wanted war but neither would abandon its course. The United States viewed Hitler as the main danger and preferred to concentrate on Europe, yet it was unwilling to allow Japan a free hand in China and elsewhere. Japanese leaders, especially the militarists, refused to allow the United States to define Japan's China policy. Moreover, they determined to end what they regarded as Japan's humiliating economic dependence upon the United States for oil supplies. Consequently an almost endless round of diplomatic conversations between the two governments in 1941 failed to resolve the deadlock. In effect, Japan demanded that the United States restore trade and cease to bolster Chinese resistance. In return, Japan would pull her troops back into northern Indo-China. The American government viewed those terms as unacceptable. Public opinion, especially among liberals, objected strenuously to any such arrangement, for in effect it would have conceded Japan a virtually free hand in China. Moreover, Japan would not denounce the Axis alliance and there was no assurance that she would not resume an expansionist course.

Japan decided to fight. Prime Minister Konoye's August 1941 proposal of a summit conference meeting in the Pacific failed to come off, because Secretary of State Hull convinced FDR that it would be unwise without advance assurances that an acceptable agreement could be reached. The Japanese navy began to practice a surprise attack on Pearl Harbor, which would tie up the American fleet while Japanese forces seized the vital oil and rubber of Southeast Asia. Japanese navalists, if less optimistic about war prospects than army commanders, also saw the crisis of the West as a propitious moment to secure hegemony in the Pacific. The Japanese government resolved to strike if last minute negotiations in Washington failed.

In November, 1941, Japan presented her last two offers. The first was totally unsatisfactory. The second, Plan B, presented on November 20, called for the raising of the United States embargo and cessation of United States support of Chiang Kai-shek, in exchange for Japanese troop withdrawals into northern Indo-China and assurances against new military drives. Roosevelt and Hull viewed Plan B unacceptable but, because the Americans had broken the Japanese diplomatic code and knew the general outline of Japanese intentions, they considered and then rejected proposing a temporary arrangement. Even a truce would undermine Chinese resistance, they feared, and would seem like appeasement of the militarists. Consequently Hull's reply, on November 26, rejected the Japanese proposal and fully restated the American demand for Japanese withdrawal from Indo-China and China. Though critics have charged that Hull sent Japan an ultimatum, his note in fact merely summarized the American position for the historical record, a position that offered no alternative but war.

Japan responded with a surprise carrier raid upon Pearl Harbor on December 7, 1941, but its main blows fell upon Southeast Asia. In the daring attack on Pearl Harbor, Japanese planes sank or damaged five battleships, three cruisers, and other warships, and destroyed large numbers of aircraft. Japan suffered a loss of only twenty-nine aircraft and three submarines in the attack. Although fortunately the American aircraft carriers were not in port when the attack came, Japan had severely weakened American naval power in the Pacific and gained time for her offensives to overrun Malaya, the Dutch East Indies, and the Philippines. Although some writers later charged that FDR deliberately had provoked Japan into war, and even had dangled the fleet at Pearl Harbor as tempting bait, the evidence merely indicates that the American government, military, and public were unprepared for war. Only in hindsight does it seem that Washington should have been more alert to an attack upon Pearl Harbor. At the time, however, such an attack seemed highly improbable to most military and naval analysts, who expected that the major Japanese blow would fall in Southeast Asia. As for war with Japan, the record makes it clear that the administration did not want it, preferred to use economic pressure to thwart Japan, but was prepared to fight if Japan rejected United States terms.

And so war came to America at last and via the Pacific. Pearl Harbor galvanized the American people into a resolute war spirit and silenced the American Firsters. Congress recognized a state of war with Japan on December 8. Three days later, Germany and Italy declared war upon the United States. The Second World War had become a global struggle.

20

Waging War and Planning Peace 1941-1945

World War II was for the United States a truly global conflict. American military forces waged war in the Atlantic and Pacific oceans, the hot desert sands of North Africa, the European continent, and the Asian mainland. In World War II, unlike in World War I, the United States was clearly the preeminent combatant among the Western allies; by the time America entered the war, Britain was a declining island empire and France a defeated, occupied nation. Moreover, in World War II the Western allies desperately needed the military might of the nation that they had done much to weaken from 1917 through 1919: Soviet Russia. A global conflict without precedent produced strange allies and stranger results.

American policy in World War II was aimed not merely at victory over the enemy but at establishing the foundations for a better postwar world. President Roosevelt and his advisers viewed the unity of the Big Three—the United States, Great Britain, and the Soviet Union—as absolutely essential both to win the war and to win the peace. Russia, understandably suspicious of its liberal capitalist allies, presented a major problem, but American policymakers hoped that a policy of conciliation and generosity would win Soviet cooperation. There seemed to be no other choice if the postwar world were to be significantly different from the nightmare that preceded it.

THE STRANGE ALLIANCE

But first it was necessary to reduce or eliminate the suspicions and hostility with which many Americans had viewed the Soviets since the Bolshevik Revolution. The Nazi-Soviet nonaggression pact of August 1939 and Russia's subsequent attack on Finland during the winter of 1939–1940 intensified American suspicions. When Russia reincorporated into its own domain the Baltic states of Latvia, Lithuania, and Estonia, created as independent states at the conclusion of World War I, many Americans equated Stalin with Hitler. And the Japanese-Soviet neutrality pact in April 1941 led other Americans to compare the Soviets to the Nazis and the Japanese, an ally of the Fascists, equally committed to aggression against the democratic states. Some Americans even urged that diplomatic relations be broken with Moscow. Although the State Department used economic pressure against Russia, Roosevelt and Hull viewed the Nazi-Soviet embrace as an uneasy one and anticipated that it would soon be broken.

One of the dramatic turning points of the war occurred on June 22, 1941. On that day, and without warning, Hitler attacked Russia, which he now referred to as a nation of "Mongol half-wits." British Prime Minister Winston Churchill, long a staunch anti-Communist, welcomed Russia as an ally. As the doughty old war leader remarked privately: "If Hitler invaded Hell, I would make at least a favorable reference to the Devil in the House of Commons."

Churchill urged FDR to extend aid to Soviet Russia though Roosevelt needed little persuasion, for he too appreciated the importance of her addition to the anti-Nazi camp. Although the State Department proved less receptive, the President in November 1941 formally extended lend-lease aid to the Soviets, declaring then that "the defense of the [Soviet Union] is vital to the defense of the United States." At first the flow of aid was small, but ultimately the United States provided the Soviets with war materials and supplies valued at $10 billion. FDR attached no strings to the aid because he wanted to win Russian goodwill and cooperation, he understood the enormity of Russia's sacrifices, and he probably realized that any promises obtained by coercion would prove worthless.

Most Americans also speedily forgot the past and welcomed their new ally, especially after Pearl Harbor plunged the nation fully into the war. The government and the communications media launched a campaign to "sell" America's new ally. The Russians fought bravely, and the grim events of 1942, as Japan inundated Southeast Asia and Germany held most of Europe in its iron grasp, demonstrated the need of allies of whatever ideology. Moreover, the Russians seemed to be changing for the better. The Soviet government signed the Declaration of the United Nations in January 1942 (pledging to support the ideals of the Atlantic Charter and mutual cooperation), concluded an alliance with Great Britain, stressed Russian nationalism rather than communism, and in 1943 disbanded the Comintern. Consequently, most Americans shared their government's view that friendship with the Soviets was both possible and necessary.

MOBILIZATION

The United States in December 1941 found itself better prepared for war in many ways than it had been in World War I. Prior to Pearl Harbor, Congress had authorized large increases in the army and navy and had adopted military conscription. Of course, it had proved difficult to equip these new forces adequately until the Japanese attack caused a dramatic shift from a peacetime consumer-oriented economy to one geared primarily for war. By mid-1941 the American army had increased to 1,400,000 men; by the end of the war it had grown to 8,300,000. During the same period the navy went from 131,485 to 3,400,000 personnel. Numerous women enlisted in military auxiliaries—the Wacs (army), Waves (navy), Spars (coast guard), and Marines—to release men for combat duty and to perform other tasks essential to a great military machine.

The Army Air Force achieved virtual autonomy from the regular army. It successfully argued that airpower not only was important as tactical support for land forces but had a strategic function in directly attacking the enemy's economy. Thus, for example, the Eighth Air Force in England cooperated with the Royal Air Force in raids deep into Nazi-held Europe. The British relied upon night attacks, in part because they were safer, and sent their air fleets to pulverize German cities in mass indiscriminate bombing aimed at breaking enemy civilian morale. The Americans preferred high-altitude daylight bombing pinpointed against war industries and transportation centers. By 1943, accompanied by long-range fighters for protection, fleets of western bombers ranged deep into Europe. In 1944, Berlin became a major target of mass bombing.

Science and technology contributed immensely to the allied military effort. Expecting a short war, Hitler failed to mobilize his scientists until 1943, too late to catch up with the Anglo-Americans. In Great Britain and the United States, close relations were established between university scientists and the military. Dr. Vannevar Bush directed the Office of Scientific Research coordinating research in such areas as radar, rockets, torpedoes, navigation systems, and improved medicine (penicillin, sulfa drugs). Many of the scientists who contributed so importantly to the eventual victory were refugees from Nazi Germany and Fascist Italy. Thus Albert Einstein and Enrico Fermi helped initiate the decision to develop the atomic bomb. President Roosevelt created an advisory committee on the bomb, headed by Dr. Bush, and the code name of Manhattan Project was selected. The chief problems involved obtaining sufficient refined uranium (U-235) and plutonium and devising a triggering device. A number of British and Canadian physicists were involved and $2 billion was expended before a successful test was conducted at Alamagordo, New Mexico, in July 1945. Although the scientists had feared that German physicists might beat them to the weapon, for nuclear fission was not a secret, they learned after the war how far behind the enemy had been.

THE INVASIONS OF NORTH AFRICA, SICILY, AND ITALY

While the United States prepared to mobilize fully for war, Russia was reeling under the Nazi onslaught. The Soviets did not collapse, despite Hitler's confident predictions, but they were forced to trade territory for time to rally their forces. By November 1941, Nazi panzers had overrun the Baltic provinces; they laid siege to Leningrad and Moscow and drove deep into the Ukraine and to the Black Sea. Renewing the offensive in the spring of 1942, the Nazis captured Sevastopol and smashed into the Caucasus before the Soviets rallied. Early in 1943, in perhaps the most crucial battle in the European theater of operations, Soviet forces concentrated at Stalingrad inflicted a decisive defeat on Hitler's legions. The defeat presaged an important turn in the course of the war, reversing the steady advances the Nazis had made since the war began in September 1939. Russian losses in that great battle alone exceeded American losses in the entire war. And by the time the conflict ended, Soviet casualties would surpass those of all the other combatants combined.

During these hectic months, Stalin desperately pleaded for a second front in Western Europe that would relieve Nazi pressure in the east. Moreover, he and other Soviet leaders apparently still feared that the western democracies might make a sudden deal with Germany or at the least watch calmly as the Soviet and German armies bled each other to death on the plains of Russia. Such fears were fed by publicly voiced American congressional sentiment that suggested that the United States pursue precisely that policy. (Indeed, following the German attack on the Soviet Union in 1941, then Senator Harry Truman recommended that "If we see that Germany is winning the war we ought to help Russia, and if Russia is winning we ought to help Germany and in that way kill as many as possible.") But FDR appreciated Soviet anxieties and was eager to help. Consequently he informed Foreign Minister Vyacheslav Molotov, early in 1942, that he hoped to launch a second front in Europe before the year was over. Stalin took that as a definite promise and felt betrayed when the invasion of the continent was postponed first to 1943 and ultimately to 1944. Soviet suspicions were heightened and the seeds of the Cold War planted by such delays.

The American military chiefs were also eager to launch a second front, but Churchill and his advisers persuaded Roosevelt that the Western allies were not ready. Until the buildup of invasion forces in England could be completed and Hitler's Fortress Europa softened by heavy aerial bombing, the British urged peripheral operations in the Mediterranean. The frustrated American military felt that Britain was still shell-shocked from World War I. With German armies occupied primarily in Russia, the American military saw little reason to delay a cross-channel invasion of the continent. If denied the cross-channel invasion for political reasons, they were prepared to shift American military emphasis to the Pacific and Japan. The president, however, overruled them and hewed firmly to a Europe-first strategy. He agreed with Churchill that limited operations were better than nothing until the time came for the direct invasion of the continent.

Instead of attacking Germany on the continent and relieving the Soviets, the Anglo-Americans chose to engage the enemy on a peripheral front in North Africa. General Bernard Law Montgomery had defeated General Erwin Rommel, the "Desert Fox," and his famed Afrika Korps at El Alamein and drove them back into Tunisia. A successful landing to the west would catch Rommel in a great pincers movement. The Anglo-Americans hoped that the Vichy French regime, headed by the aged Marshall Henri Phillipe Pétain, would not resist. The invasion forces landed November 8, 1942, at Oran, Algiers, and Casablanca. French resistance ceased when Admiral Jean Darlan, a high-ranking Vichyite official, in return for American recognition of his political authority over French North Africa, collaborated with the Anglo-American invaders, whose initial landings thus went uncontested. Bitterly denounced by the American press, the Darlan "deal" ultimately was not implemented, as the Vichyite official was assassinated on December 24, 1942. American forces received their first real baptism by fire at Kasserine Pass, where Rommel inflicted a sharp defeat, but they rallied and with the more experienced British troops forced the remaining Axis troops in North Africa to surrender on May 12, 1943.

The invasion of Sicily followed victory in North Africa. Although his advisers objected to more diversions that postponed a cross-channel invasion, FDR agreed with Churchill that a great opportunity existed to knock Italy out of the war and to tie up large numbers of German divisions in southern Europe. American and British forces, led by Generals George S. Patton and Montgomery, each a colorful and controversial leader, and under the overall command of General Dwight D. Eisenhower, landed in Sicily on July 9, 1943. Sicily fell after five weeks of hard fighting. Mussolini, the once bombastic *Duce*, was forced from power, and a new government under Marshall Pietro Badoglio sued for peace and eventually changed sides in the war. The British and Americans ignored Russia during the armistice proceedings, a lesson Stalin did not forget when Soviet armies occupied Eastern Europe. Nazi troops poured into Italy to fight the Allies and rescued Mussolini and established him as head of a puppet republic. Meanwhile, Allied forces early in September invaded mainland Italy, where they encountered fierce resistance and difficult terrain. Rome did not fall until June 4, 1944, and as late as April, 1945, Allied troops still were south of Bologna.

CASABLANCA AND TEHRAN CONFERENCES

In mid-January 1943, as the North African campaign continued, Roosevelt and Churchill met at Casablanca to confer on future military operations. They agreed upon an invasion of Sicily, as noted before, and subsequently decided to follow it up with an attack upon Italy. During a press conference at Casablanca, with Churchill by his side, FDR stated the "unconditional surrender" policy. The Allies, in contrast to World War I, this time would continue the war until the enemy had laid down its arms without condition.

Although Roosevelt gave the impression that the idea of unconditional surrender had just occurred to him, he and his advisers had given it much thought. FDR long had viewed the Armistice in 1918 as a mistake, for it had left the German people with the impression that they had not been defeated on the field of battle. Most Americans and Britishers shared his conviction that Germany this time must be physically occupied and its people compelled to realize the full extent of their defeat. Moreover, it seemed morally inconceivable that the Allies should negotiate or deal with Hitler or his successors, and that applied as well to Japan. Finally, and probably most important, unconditional surrender offered a way to reassure Russia, still clamoring for a second front in Europe, that the war would be fought to the final end and without any deals with the enemy (a concern raised indirectly by the Darlan deal of 1942). It also postponed discussion of postwar boundaries and settlements until the enemy had laid down its arms.

Some writers have charged that unconditional surrender undercut potential resistance within Germany to Hitler and thereby prolonged the war. The evidence fails to bear them out. No sign of popular discontent, let alone uprisings, emerged, and the only real possibility of a successful rebellion against Hitler lay among the higher officer ranks of the German army. As long as victory seemed possible, they subordinated themselves to the Nazi warlord, and in fact, most served him to the bitter end. A small group did try to assassinate the Fuehrer in mid-1944 but failed and paid with their lives. Unconditional surrender, to be sure, enabled Nazi Propaganda Minister Joseph Goebbels to charge that the allies planned to enslave Germany. Probably he would have done so in any case. Finally, it must be noted that unconditional surrender applied primarily to Germany, for ultimately Italy received better terms and Japan was allowed to retain its emperor.

The first meeting of the Big Three took place at Tehran, the Iranian capital, December 2–7, 1943. Previously, Cordell Hull had attended a

Mass graves at the Belson Concentration Camp,
c. 1945

(U.S. Office of War Information/National Archives)

conference of foreign ministers at Moscow that reiterated the unconditional surrender policy, established an advisory commission to discuss
plans for occupation of enemy states, and called for creation of a new
international peace-keeping body, the future United Nations Organization. At Tehran, Roosevelt at last had a chance to apply his personal
charm to the Soviet dictator. Stalin, reassured that there would be a cross-
channel invasion in 1944, promised that Russia would enter the war
against Japan after Germany had been beaten. He also began to sketch to
a sympathetic Roosevelt and Churchill the nature of his postwar territorial aims. These included the Baltic states, Poland east of the Curzon
Line, and in the Far East an ice-free port in Manchuria, as well as the
return of southern Sakhalin and the Kurile islands. The three chiefs
reached no firm decision about dismembering Germany, but they concurred that it would be occupied by the three powers with an interallied
zone in Berlin. Tehran clearly foreshadowed the agreements to be
reached subsequently at Yalta, as Roosevelt, then in good health, and
Churchill indicated a willingness to meet Stalin's desires. FDR was
greatly pleased with the conference and concluded that Stalin was a
realist with whom one could deal successfully. He reported optimistically

to the American people that Great-Power collaboration had been achieved and would continue.

YALTA

On June 6, 1944 the final phase of the war in Europe began. In January 1944 Soviet armies had crossed the old Polish boundary driving the Nazis further back in the east; in June the Anglo-Americans launched the long-postponed cross-channel invasion of France. General Eisenhower served as supreme commander of the Allied Expeditionary Force that landed 176,000 troops on the beaches of Normandy. It was the most audacious amphibious operation in history, involving 4,000 landing craft supported by a vast armada of 600 warships, 4,000 other craft, and 11,000 warplanes. Allied forces rapidly increased, totalling one million by early July and two million by early August. After savage fighting, the AEF broke out of the beachheads and began a rapid advance across France. Paris was liberated on August 25 and by autumn allied armies had fought their way to the German frontier. In December, Hitler ordered a last desperate counter-offensive, but the allies rallied and won the Battle of the Bulge. That battle cost the United States its heaviest casualties of the war (77,000) but opened the way to invading the heart of Germany. Hitler's doom was sealed between the advancing allied and Soviet armies.

The Big Three met at Yalta in February 1945 to plan the final military drives and the occupation of the defeated countries. Prior to that conference, in October 1944, Churchill had met with Stalin at Moscow, and the two leaders had concluded a "spheres of influence" agreement recognizing their predominant role in the Balkans. Roosevelt had given his tacit consent to this agreement. Although he had recently lost much weight and was sixty-two years old, FDR seemed as alert as ever at Yalta. Once more he plied his personal charm on Stalin in an attempt to win him to an enduring cooperation. The president never had taken ideology too seriously and hoped that the Americans and Russians could transcend their real differences. Moreover Roosevelt realized that whatever the United States did, Russia necessarily would reap enormous gains in power and influence as a result of Germany's defeat. He made a supreme effort, therefore, to allay Stalin's suspicions and to promote a lasting peace. And, ever the realist, Roosevelt saw that Russian armies already had overrun most of Poland and the Balkans, while the Anglo-Americans were recovering from the Battle of the Bulge and were still halted along the Rhine. In the Far East, American military advisers urged Russia's entry into the war, saying that it would greatly speed Japan's collapse and save thousands of lives. Far from acting naively at Yalta, FDR simply conceded to Russia that which she could not be denied.

Germany presented the most urgent problem to the three conferees gathered at the old tsarist resort on the Black Sea. No one questioned that Germany must be demilitarized and purged of nazism. But should she be dismembered into several independent states? And how much reparations should be exacted for the destruction wrought by the Nazis? Some American officials advocated drastic treatment of the hated enemy. Treasury Secretary Henry Morgenthau, Jr., fearful of a soft peace, urged what became known as the Morgenthau Plan: a partition of Germany and reduction of her economy to a near-agricultural basis. Only in that way, he thought, could Germany be made safe for the world. Russia also favored a harsh peace. State and War Department planners, however, asserted that the allies could not reduce some sixty or more millions of people to a semistarvation level and that a degree of German industrial revival was essential to Europe's postwar reconstruction and prosperity. Consequently, while recommending a stringent occupation and other safeguards, these officials urged that reparations must be reasonable and that Germany must be left enough industry to sustain itself. Roosevelt, distrustful of the Germans, whom he thought irreparably militarist, inclined strongly toward Morgenthau's position. All Germans, and not just the Nais, he said in 1944, must be treated toughly, and he even thought it might be well if the German people had to be fed from army soup kitchens after the war. He and Churchill in the fall of 1944 had initialed a draft of the Morgenthau Plan. Their other advisers, however, protested sharply and won them away from that approach.

At Yalta, Stalin advocated drastic treatment of Germany. The Soviet premier particularly wanted heavy reparations from the defeated enemy with which to rebuild his war-ravished country. Stalin spoke of $20 billions in reparations, half to go to Russia in view of her greater losses. Roosevelt and Churchill agreed that reparations must be paid and that Russia deserved the larger share, but they doubted if so huge a sum could be extracted from the wreckage of the Third Reich without starvation resulting. The Big Three finally agreed to leave the amount of reparations to be fixed to a special commission, and to refer the question of dismemberment to their foreign ministers for further discussion. Meanwhile they decided to divide Germany into four occupation zones; France receiving one carved from the Anglo-American areas. Berlin was to be jointly occupied; and a four-power control commission would set economic and other policies for Germany as a whole. The conference did not fix definite routes for the western powers to gain access to their zones in Berlin, which was to be deep within the Soviet zone. If that proved a mistake, Russia also was to regret ever having agreed to joint occupation of the German capital. Obviously neither side foresaw the Cold War and the controversies over Berlin.

Poland presented a potentially disruptive issue at Yalta. Britain had gone to war over Poland in 1939, and it sheltered the Polish exile government in London. As for the United States, Roosevelt could not overlook Wilson's role in Poland's rebirth during World War I or the influence of millions of Polish-American voters. Yet Soviet armies had liberated Poland and Stalin could impose any solution that he wished.

The princes of war at Yalta—Churchill, FDR, Stalin
(Wide World Photos)

The crux of the problem, at least outwardly, involved Poland's eastern boundary. Although the Paris Peace Conference in 1919–1920 had set the so-called Curzon Line as the proper eastern boundary for ethnic Poland, the new state had soon conquered territory far beyond it from the weak Soviet government in 1920. Stalin had regained the area in his 1939 deal with Hitler, and he demanded that the western allies accept the Curzon Line as the proper boundary. Prior to Yalta he had broken diplomatic relations with the exile government and in January 1945 had recognized the Lublin Committee of Polish communists and sympathizers as the legitimate provisional government of that liberated nation.

At Yalta, Churchill and Roosevelt viewed sympathetically Stalin's demand for the Curzon Line, although they hoped for some modifications in Poland's favor. Their main concern, however, focused upon the nature of the Polish government. Stalin refused to discard the Lublin regime, and he rejected the proposals that postwar elections be supervised by the three Great Powers. After days of discussion, the western leaders accepted a compromise rather than disrupt the conference. The Lublin government would be reorganized to include other Polish leaders, and free elections would be held as soon as possible. Poland would be compensated for its losses east of the Curzon Line by the annexation of parts of Germany, but no precise western boundary was fixed. FDR realized that the settlement was ambiguous, but he hoped that continued Soviet cooperation would ensure a democratic and autonomous Poland. In any case, it was either this kind of agreement or none, with Russia thereby retaining a free hand to act as she chose.

Concerning the Far East, Stalin asked for and obtained at Yalta the return of southern Sakhalin and the Kurile Islands, the status quo in Outer Mongolia (a Soviet puppet), a naval base at Port Arthur, a port at Darien in Manchuria, and joint Sino-Soviet management of the Manchurian railways. In return, he pledged to enter the war against Japan within two to three months after Germany had surrendered and eventually to conclude a treaty of defense and friendship with the Chinese Nationalist Government. Roosevelt conducted these negotiations with Stalin, although Churchill concurred. Because Russia needed time to prepare for war in the Far East and Nationalist China was a sieve of information to the Japanese, Chiang Kai-shek was not informed of these agreements.

Despite subsequent charges that he had weakned or betrayed China, FDR's motives were the realistic ones of protecting China and insuring a quick end to the war in the Far East. As noted before, his military advisers deemed Soviet aid highly desirable in finishing off Japan with minimum costs in lives and money. Moreover, by obtaining Stalin's cooperation, Roosevelt hoped to protect Nationalist China against possible loss of Manchuria to the Soviets or a sudden Soviet recognition of the Chinese Communists. Obviously Russia could enter the war whenever she chose; the problem was to insure that she did it at a time and in a way to convey the maximum benefit. Finally, except possibly for the Kuriles, Roosevelt had given Stalin nothing that he could not have taken in any case.

The Yalta Conference reiterated previous pledges to create a new international organization to keep the postwar peace. The British and American people, the latter eager to make amends for the sins of 1919 and 1920, attached an enormous and, as time proved, unrealistic importance to this task. Roosevelt personally favored a world run by the "Four Policemen"—Great Britain, the United States, the Soviet Union, and China—but he had to give way to the clamor for a new Wilsonian league based on the theories of the sovereign equality of all members and collective security. The United Nations Charter, framed at Dumbarton Oaks in 1944 and adopted at the San Francisco conference in the spring of 1945, established a General Assembly of all member states, a Security Council where the five permanent members (America, Britain, France, China, and Russia) possessed an absolute veto power over substantive actions, and a Secretariat plus other organs. Americans fondly believed that with their participation and that of the Russians, peace could be preserved this time. On July 28, 1945, the Senate granted its approval to the Charter by a vote of eighty-nine to two.

THE FALL OF GERMANY AND
THE POTSDAM CONFERENCE

In the weeks after Yalta, Germany rapidly succumbed to the advancing Anglo-American and Soviet armies. British and American air armadas rained death and destruction upon the cities and industries of the Reich. The German *Luftwaffe's* fighter protection was destroyed in a decisive week of aerial battles in late February. Thereafter allied air fleets roamed the German skies at will. One thousand bombers killed 25,000 people in Berlin on February 3. This was followed by fourteen hours of continuous bombing of Dresden that destroyed the heart of the city and killed around 135,000 people. Meanwhile the Russian armies drove upon Berlin, and Eisenhower's forces crossed the Rhine and pushed eastward against crumbling opposition. The last great Russian offensive opened only thirty-five miles from Berlin. Churchill and his advisers wanted to try to beat the Soviets to that capital but Eisenhower objected and Roosevelt upheld him. Eisenhower's armies then were around two hundred miles from Berlin and he viewed nearby objectives as more imperative. Although some writers have criticized the Americans for failing to appreciate the psychological and political advantages of taking Berlin before the Russians could, the city lay well within the Soviet zone of operations, and a lightning drive might have failed in any case. As it was, the Soviets paid for the honor with over 100,000 casualties. A similar caution motivated American decisions not to try to capture Vienna and Prague.

Hitler conducted a last-ditch defense from his underground bunker in Berlin. As the Third Reich collapsed around him, and Russian armies fought their way into the doomed city street by street and house by house, the Fuehrer and his bride committed suicide, their bodies cremated by loyal adherents. On May 7, the German government under Hitler's successor, Admiral Karl Doenitz, surrendered to the Anglo-Americans at Reims, followed by a similar ceremony in Berlin on May 8. Europe's most bloody war in modern history had come to an end, leaving behind a stench of death and destruction in the heart of western civilization.

Already a rift had begun to emerge among the victorious Big Three. Prior to his death, on April 12, Roosevelt became alarmed at signs that Soviet cooperation would not outlast the war. He and Churchill were distressed at indications of continued Soviet suspiciousness; both were dismayed that the Yalta agreements had not ushered in allied cooperation and harmony. Indeed, through their respective roles as occupying powers (the Anglo-Americans in Italy and France and the Soviet Union in

Assault on the Germans in Europe

Rumania, Bulgaria, and Hungary), all three powers had tacitly rejected the princple of joint participation and a coequal voice in their respective spheres.

Harry S. Truman, FDR's vice president and successor, was clearly less eager to cooperate with the Russians and more blunt in indicating his displeasure at Soviet tactics. The British and the Americans interpreted Yalta to provide for a broadly based reconstituted Polish government, representing fairly all nonfascist elements. The Soviets, however, merely added a few noncommunists to the Lublin regime. When Molotov passed through Washington in late April 1945, Truman sharply berated him for the Soviet failure to observe the Yalta agreements. On May 11, after the German surrender, the president, as part of a pattern of acts intended to modify Soviet behavior, cut back sharply on lend-lease aid to Russia. Overzealous officials, moreover, exceeded Truman's intentions and even recalled loaded ships enroute to Russian ports.

Critics of Truman's foreign policy view the lend-lease episode as part of a pattern in which the president shifted from conciliation to toughness and attempted to coerce the Soviet Union. Truman's defenders, in contrast, asserted that the president acted awkwardly to place lend-lease to

Russia on the same footing as aid to other countries. They added that because Russia was not yet at war with Japan and, under the requirements of the Lend-Lease Act, Truman was reducing aid to all countries, including Britain, the Soviets must be treated the same. Yet no doubt the episode deeply offended Stalin.

The new Truman administration clearly shifted away from FDR's balanced policy toward Russia and instead sought to thwart Soviet aims. Nevertheless, the American government still expected cooperation. Consequently Truman rejected Churchill's advice to insure bargaining leverage by leaving American troops deep inside the designated Soviet zone, where they had driven in the closing days of the war. Truman feared that would lead to bitter disputes, and besides he wanted to shift troops as rapidly as possible to the Pacific, against Japan. Instead in May 1945 he sent Harry Hopkins, FDR's close adviser, to Moscow to try to clear the atmosphere. Hopkins spoke frankly to Stalin of western unhappiness at recent Soviet actions, particularly in Poland, and listened to Stalin's complaint about the cut-off in lend-lease. Mutual reassurances followed, including the resumption of lend-lease shipments, and the way was cleared for the final Big Three wartime leaders' conference.

Truman and Churchill met Stalin at Potsdam, near Berlin, to deal with occupation problems in Europe. The conference, which began on July 17 and lasted to August 2, 1945, was noticeably less cordial than Tehran and Yalta. In part that reflected Truman's replacement of FDR, and Churchill's departure midway in the conference after losing the general elections in Britain—Laborite Clement Attlee succeeded him— but in part also the obvious fact that with Germany prostrate, less reason existed for submerging allied differences. Stalin, recovering from a recent heart attack, treated Truman courteously, but he was scoffing toward Churchill. Sharp controversy ensued over German reparations and Poland. Stalin insisted that the figure of $20 billion in reparations had been agreed at Yalta, while the Anglo-Americans, fearful of having to feed starving Germans and desiring a minimum liveable economic level, objected that such an amount was excessive and unrealistic. A compromise emerged whereby each power would extract reparations from its own occupation zone. The western powers would provide Russia with 15 percent of the capital equipment within their zones in exchange for food and raw materials from the Soviet zone and would make a free gift of another 10 percent in recognition of Russia's greater suffering in the war. As for Poland, Churchill objected sharply to a Soviet fait accompli, the turning over to the Poles of that part of Germany east of the Oder-Neisse line. Although disguised as a merely temporary arrangement pending the peace conference, the Polish government treated the area as part of the new Poland and a mass flight of German inhabitants took place. The British and Americans also expressed acute unhappiness that the Polish government had not been reconstituted. The Soviets finally agreed to include a few more non-Communists in the Polish ministry but that government remained Communist-controlled. Free elections were also promised within a short time but they were not to be held until 1946 and were not to be free in the western sense.

Truman reported to the American people that cooperation among the Big Three had continued at Potsdam. Privately, however, he and his advisers felt deeply disturbed at what they viewed as signs of Russia's intransigence and a determination to organize eastern Europe as its exclusive sphere. Stalin, for his part, believed that Russia was merely implementing the Yalta agreements in eastern Europe. Moreover, the cursory manner in which Truman had informed Stalin at Potsdam of the United States' successful development of the atomic bomb introduced a further complicating factor in U.S.-Soviet relations. While American possession of an atomic monopoly would not insure tensions or diplomatic conflict, it introduced another dimension, raising thereby the issue of international control or independent action. As Yalta had represented the high tide of Big Three cooperation and harmony, Patsdam represented its ebb.

THE COLLAPSE OF JAPAN

Japanese expansionism had reached its high water mark in 1942. By the middle of that year, she had conquered Guam, Wake, the Philippines, Hong Kong, Singapore, Malaya, and the Dutch East Indies. Large supplies of oil, lead, rubber, tin, and other vital materials lay in her grasp. But her vaunted New Order was vastly overextended and vulnerable to American counter-attacks. Compared to the United States, Japan was markedly inferior in manpower and industry. Although the United States gave priority to the war against Hitler, it could spare more than enough power to begin to crush Japan. After American forces had checked Japan's advance in the battles of the Coral Sea, Guadalcanal, and Midway, a twofold strategy was adopted to achieve victory. General Douglas MacArthur directed an island-hopping thrust northward from Australia that ultimately carried him back to the Philippines by the fall of 1944. Meanwhile, under Admiral Chester Nimitz's general command, powerful aircraft carrier naval task forces began to smash through Japan's Central Pacific island screen directly toward her homeland. By the spring of 1945, carrier planes were attacking Japan itself, and island bases had been captured in the Marshall Islands, Carolines, Marianas, and Okinawa. Earlier, in the greatest naval battles in history, the first and second battles of the Philippine Sea, the back of the Japanese navy had been broken. Long-range B-29 bombers began to rain destruction upon Japan. By mid-1945, Japan was a shambles, largely beréft of a navy and merchant marine, her cities subjected to daily aerial pounding, her industry smashed or running out of fuel and raw materials. An estimated eight million people were homeless.

For some time Japanese moderates had realized that the war was

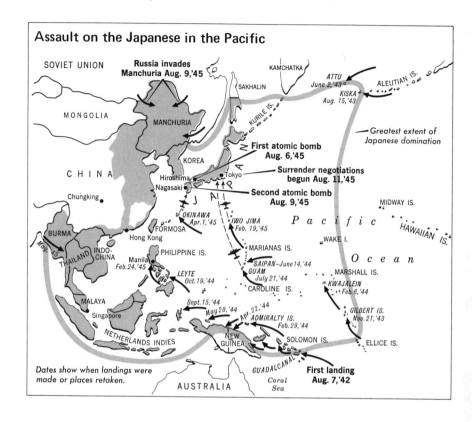

Assault on the Japanese in the Pacific

Dates show when landings were made or places retaken.

lost. For a while they hoped to obtain Russian mediation and thus perhaps save some of the gains of war, or at least to escape unconditional surrender and occupation. Those efforts failed because Russia secretly planned to enter the war against Japan. Consequently, the moderates advised seeking terms from the Allies but the military refused to give up. Japan still had about one and one-half million troops in the home islands and over five thousand aircraft that could be used in Kamikaze or suicide attacks against American naval vessels. Army leaders spoke optimistically, if unrealistically, of meeting the invaders on the beaches of Japan and hurling them back into the sea. Japan thus could win better terms than surrender.

American officials and the military concluded, in the light of Japanese suicidal defense of such island bases as Iwo Jima and Okinawa, that it would be necessary to invade the Japanese home islands to terminate (successfully) the war. Some navalists thought Japan could be starved into submission but went along with the army planners. Consequently, Truman approved an invasion of Kyushu scheduled for late 1945, and then of Honshu, the main island, early in 1946. Meanwhile, the State Department and Secretary of War Stimson thought Japan might be induced to capitulate if promised retention of the imperial system, but that approach was not tried early enough to preclude what followed. In part that was because Truman and others saw no reason to offer Japan anything, and in part it was because the emperor was viewed as the center of the feudal system responsible for Japan's wayward course.

The third American approach to bringing Japan to her knees involved use of the atomic bomb. After considering exploding an atomic bomb over an uninhabited area as a warning of more to come, Truman decided to drop it on an unwarned live target. The United States had materials for only a few bombs, the triggering mechanism might malfunction, and the greatest political effect would come from shock use. On August 6, 1945, a B-29 dropped the first A-bomb on Hiroshima. An estimated eighty thousand people perished in the fireball that enveloped the doomed city. On August 8, Russia entered the war and on August 9 the second atomic bomb fell this time on Nagasaki.

Japanese generals tried to minimize the new weapon and still spoke of continuing the war, but Emperor Hirohito overruled them at a special conference and ordered a surrender. Japan asked only that she be allowed to retain the imperial system, and on August 14 the allies agreed to that condition. The formal surrender ceremony took place on September 2 aboard the battleship *Missouri* in Tokyo Bay.

Although most Americans at the time approved of the dropping of the atomic bombs, later some questioned the necessity and the morality of their use. Was not Japan already beaten, they asked. They deplored America's moral burden as the first to employ the dreaded new weapon. Still others wondered whether racial bias were involved, the A-bombs being deemed fit for Orientals but presumably not for Europeans. Several historians even charge that the nuclear weapons were used as much to influence Russian behavior and moderate its demands as to defeat Japan.

One must keep a sense of historical perspective in evaluating these views. Dreadful though it later appeared, use of atomic weapons seemed rational granted wartime attitudes. The allied fire-bombing of Dresden and Tokyo more than matched Hiroshima and Nagasaki in destructive impact and human cost and suggested that the allies might have used atomic weapons against Germany had she not collapsed before their availability. Moreover, not even the scientists at first appreciated the magnitude of the A-bomb or its long-term harmful side effects. And it seemed logical to believe that American possession of a weapon of such magnitude might indeed modify Soviet behavior. Finally, use of the weapons did hasten Japan's surrender, thereby saving untold numbers of American and Japanese lives that would have been lost by the planned invasions.

The mushroom clouds that rose over Hiroshima and Nagasaki not only dramatized to all the world that mankind had entered a new and more terrible age of potential mass destruction, but also they presaged man's inability to build as well for peace as for war. The defeat of Germany and then of Japan, instead of ushering in an age of peace,

A new age dawns
(Official U.S. Airforce Photo)

precipitated a new form of international conflict, soon to be known as the Cold War. For the post–World War II generations not only lacked a peaceful globe but endured under the perpetual shadow of nuclear extinction. Peace was to become as perilous as war for the duration of the Cold War.

21

A People's War: The Home Front

World War II, like World War I, was waged as vigorously on the home front as on the battlefields, and its domestic impact, owing to its global scope, proved even more substantial. Surface similarities, to be sure, existed in the domestic response to war, but Americans of the 1940s had learned much from the experience of the first war. Citizens and public officials acted with more self-assurance than they had in 1918; indeed, as they reordered priorities and reshaped society, they gave every indication of having accepted Henry Luce's challenge to make the future "the American Century."

ORGANIZING A WAR ECONOMY

In 1941 Americans had had a decade of unsuccessful experience in combating economic stagnation and unemployment. Hard as they had tried, New Dealers had failed to resolve the paradox of poverty in the midst of plenty. War, however, changed everything: shortages of labor and supplies replaced surpluses; production had to be stimulated, not regulated; workers had to be recruited for industry, not eliminated on the basis of age, race, or sex; businessmen, who acted cautiously, had to be encouraged to behave daringly. How would the Roosevelt administration shift from its crusade to salvage a depressed economy to organizing a war economy?

Answers came quickly. Instead of criticizing economic royalists, Roosevelt flattered them. Hard-headed and tough-fisted industrialists replaced idealistic New Dealers in key federal agencies. When Roosevelt established an Office of Production Management late in 1940 to prepare for the eventuality of American intervention, he appointed Sidney Hillman of the CIO and William Knudsen of General Motors as codirectors, with the latter essentially in command of industrial planning. When war came in December 1941 Congress no longer balked at presidential power, and it granted Roosevelt unprecedented authority to regulate the domestic economy. Acting decisively, the president in January 1942 established the War Production Board under the direction of Donald Nelson, a former Sears, Roebuck executive.

At first, Nelson and the WPB proceeded cautiously. Still troubled by the trauma of depression, most businessmen were unsure of how to respond to the imperatives of war. They realized that production must be increased and also that a profitable market had developed, yet they feared that fresh investments would result in postwar excess capacity reminiscent of the 1930s, and an ensuing economic collapse. Nelson and Roosevelt reassured businessmen through various tactics. To build business confidence in federal wartime policy, the administration invited the nation's leading industrialists to supervise the production effort. Scores of dollar-a-year men—unpaid federal officials who retained their private executive incomes—flocked to Washington to serve the nation. To increase capital investment, the federal government sometimes played the role of investor. New industrial plants, especially in the synthetic rubber and aluminum industries, were built with federal funds and then turned over to private corporations to operate. The companies that managed the government plants did so, moreover, with the implicit promise that they could purchase the properties at reduced prices after the war. Washington also assured businessmen that profits would be protected. In cases where the cost of new products could not be calculated in advance, the government signed cost-plus contracts—agreements that allowed industrialists to charge the full cost of production plus a negotiated rate of profit. As Secretary of War Henry L. Stimson remarked: "If you are going to try to go to war, or prepare for war, in a capitalist country, you have to let business make money out of the process or business won't work." And business made money. After-tax profits soared from $6.4 billion in 1940 to $10.8 billion in 1944. Finally, government agencies shelved antitrust regulations for the duration of the war and granted the most profitable contracts to the largest corporations.

Thus reassured, American businessmen endorsed government wartime economic regulations. By the spring of 1942, the WPB had its plans running smoothly, and by June it had reduced the production of durable consumer goods by almost a third. As the board allocated scarce resources to military production and denied them to nonessential activities, tanks, jeeps, and airplanes instead of Fords and Chevys rolled off the assembly lines in Detroit. WPB Chairman Nelson commented: "It was not so much industrial conversion as industrial revolution, with months and years condensed into days."

Labor, as essential to the war effort as capital, proved less tractable—and for good reason. Unemployment vanished, and its disappearance liberated workers to seek the gains that had eluded them through two decades of prosperity and depression. Needed as never before—the number of blue-collar manufacturing workers rose by seven million or 60 percent during the war—workers switched jobs in search of higher wages. As employers chased workers and laborers pursued the best-paying jobs, annual real earnings almost doubled between 1940 and 1944, rising from $754 to $1289. In such a milieu unions as well as individual workers flexed their economic muscles, posing no mean problem for Washington officials.

Although workers had fewer friends than businessmen in wartime Washington, they were not without their advocates. Much as some government officials, occasionally the president himself, desired to treat civilian labor like military men, they never succeeded. A "work or fight" order issued by a federal administrator in 1943, who wanted to coerce workers into jobs in essential industries, was thwarted by political opponents and labor lobbyists. At best the administration obtained cooperation from local draft boards, which denied exemptions to workers in nonessential categories, and voluntary cooperation from individual laborers and trade unions in meeting government employment targets. Although many workers undoubtedly won draft deferments for nonessential jobs, the combination of minimal federal coercion and voluntarism worked well enough to turn the United States into what President Roosevelt called the "arsenal of democracy."

For organized labor the wartime payoff was immediate and full. Even before the Japanese attack on Pearl Harbor, CIO unions cracked the last two major antiunion basic industries: Ford and Little Steel.* On the eve of the war, John L. Lewis's mine workers, defying federal power, presidential wrath, and public opinion, wrested a union shop contract from the recalcitrant steel industry's captive coal mines.† A month after Pearl Harbor, in January 1942, Roosevelt appointed a National War Labor Board, composed equally of management, labor, and public members, to supervise wartime labor relations. Under the NWLB's guardianship, trade unions flourished. CIO affiliates, in particular, benefited from the board's establishment of the "maintenance of membership" principle, which provided a form of compulsory union membership for the dura-

---

* The so-called independent steel companies not a part of United States Steel that had defeated CIO-SWOC in the bitter 1937 Little Steel strike.

† Mines owned directly by the steel companies and which did not sell their metallurgical coal on the open market.

tion of a contract and covered almost four million workers by 1945. Under the principle, workers who had joined a union voluntarily could not leave the union during the term of the existing contract. "Maintenance of membership" thus provided a form of union security midway between the open shop and the union or closed shop. Total union membership climbed from 8,944,000 in 1940 to 14,796,000 in 1945, or 35 percent of nonagricultural civilian employment. Perhaps more important, employers grew accustomed to living and dealing with unions on an everyday basis.

Labor's power, which flowed from its scarcity, caused spontaneous militancy. Between 1941 and 1944 more strikes involving more workers occurred annually than in any single depression year. These wartime strikes, however, resulted in minimal loss of time and seldom involved the explosive issues of union organization and recognition. The one strike that proved an exception to the wartime rule of short spontaneous walkouts, was the long, costly, and bitter 1943 bituminous coal strike. Again defying mine owners, Congress, the president, the military, and the public—which "damned his coal black soul"—John L. Lewis led his miners to a remarkable victory. As a result of the 1943 strike settlement, coal miners became the nation's highest paid industrial workers. But trade unionism in general paid a high price for Lewis's triumph. What seemed to many as Lewis's cavalier disregard for "national security" resulted in a swelling tide of popular antiunionism, which applauded Congress's overriding of a presidential veto in June 1943 to pass the antilabor Smith-Connolly Act. The bill, also known as the War Labor Disputes Act, required unions involved in war production to issue public notices before ordering strikes and mandated a thirty-day "cooling off" period and a National Labor Relations Board supervised vote before a walkout could begin. It also authorized the president to seize any struck facility and forbade political contributions by unions in federal elections.

Despite rank-and-file militancy, numerous spontaneous walkouts, and John L. Lewis's defiance of the president, workers wrote an excellent production record. Less time was lost to labor disputes in the United States than in England, and the chairman of the NWLB observed: "It is the best this nation or any other nation has ever done in wartime or peacetime."

As important as organizing industry and labor was the need to raise revenue and to control prices. The cost of modern warfare made the New Deal's antidepression expenditures seem small change. Between 1940 and 1945 federal government expenditures soared from just over $9 billion annually to well over $98 billion, the deficit from $3.9 billion to $53.9 billion, and the total national debt from $43 billion in 1940 to $257 billion in 1945. To pay its bills the government lowered the minimum income subject to federal income tax and raised rates at all levels. Internal revenue receipts rose from $5.3 billion in 1940 to $43.9 billion in 1945, and individual income taxes from $982 million to $19 billion. In 1940 the government received only 14.6 million income tax returns of which almost half were nontaxable. Five years later income tax returns were filed by 50 million Americans of whom 42.6 million owed taxes. Although Congress refused to make wartime taxes as heavy and progressive as the president wished, the Revenue Act of 1942 brought almost all citizens into the system, and the 1943 act established the basis for an efficient federal income tax system by introducing regular withholding of taxes from the paycheck. Again, despite Roosevelt's desire to place a $25,000 limit on annual earnings and an actual mandated increase in the top tax rate from 60 percent to 90 percent, the highest effective rate of income tax increase occurred at the lowest income levels, especially beginning at under $6,000.

Taxes covered almost half the costs of war, a far better record then during World War I, but the remainder had to be borrowed. Just as in 1917 and 1918, the government enlisted celebrities, athletic heroes, and Madison Avenue hucksters in a nationwide campaign to sell war bonds. School children each week purchased war stamps with their nickels and dimes, and their working parents allowed the payroll office to deduct the cost of small denomination bonds from their paychecks. Seven war bond drives netted almost $135 billion; still, the bulk, sold in denominations from $10,000 to $100,000, was purchased by banks, insurance companies, and corporations—the financial institutions in command of most of the nation's wealth and income.

Taxes and bond sales proved insufficient to control inflation. The scarcity of labor and consumer goods necessitated direct controls on wages and prices. Roosevelt charged the NWLB with holding the line on wage increases, a task it performed exceedingly well, except for the 1943 coal miners' award, because most workers, after a decade of depression, were content with full employment and the opportunity to earn overtime wages. Workers, however, would not have tolerated wage restraints if prices had soared out of control. Here the Office of Price Administration (established in April 1941) entered the scene. Not only did the OPA seek to restrain wholesale and retail prices; it also instituted rationing of such scarce items as beef, coffee, sugar, and gasoline. It allocated rationing stamps to individuals and families on the basis of need and size and allowed retailers scarce commodities only in proportion to the total ration coupons they accumulated. Generally, most merchants and consumers voluntarily cooperated with the program, though black markets did develop for beef, gasoline, and other products in short supply. By and large, OPA restrained inflation, holding the total rise in the consumer price index between 1940 and 1945 to 28 percent, most of which occurred before 1943.

For most Americans the wartime economic system worked well. A small minority of affluent citizens may have suffered restrictions on their freedom of choice and their standard of living, but the vast majority of Americans, liberated from unemployment and low wages, earned more, ate better, and grew healthier than ever.

A militarized society thus brought abundant social payoffs. All the

New Deal's peacetime welfare expenditures had failed to restore prosperity; in 1945, when out of a total federal budget of over $98 billion, over $86 billion went to "defense" related items and only a little over $1 billion to labor and welfare (cut to one-third of its 1940 level) the nation flourished. Giant corporations fattened at the federal trough, trade unions won respectability and a slice of the corporate fat, and common citizens achieved a real "social security." What would later become known as the "military-industrial complex" was in 1945 a successful American institution.

WAR AND DOMESTIC LIBERTY

However beneficial war may be to a society's economic well-being, it ordinarily circumscribes or even eliminates basic civil liberties. World War I, for example, had witnessed savage attacks on German-Americans, stringent restrictions on speech and the press, and mass repression of socialists and labor radicals. World War II, despite its length and severity, resulted (with one notable exception to be discussed below) in fewer restrictions on personal liberty. Why? Not, apparently, because Americans had grown more tolerant or sophisticated. Prominent left-wing liberals, among others, favored censorship. One left intellectual, Freda Kirchwey, editor of the *Nation,* suggested that "treasonous" newspapers "should be exterminated exactly as if they were enemy machine gun nests in the Bataan jungle." Another prewar civil libertarian, Arthur Garfield Hays, suddenly found the FBI miraculously transformed into a "clean-cut, intelligent, college-educated crowd." And a third liberal, Aubrey Williams, advised the president that "The *right* of free speech carries with it the obligation not to use it to aid the enemy." But repression nevertheless proved the exception not the rule. Why?

Two factors explain the relative toleration for civil liberties exhibited by public officials and private citizens. First, World War II was considered by most Americans to be a just cause, a war necessary for moral, political, and strategic reasons. After Pearl Harbor there was scarcely any domestic opposition—political, ethnic, or religious—to United States involvement. Second, unlike in World War I, domestic radicals and leftwingers now proved to be the most ardent advocates of a total war effort. Whether they were Communists anxious about the safety of Soviet Russia, Jewish-American socialists eager to destroy naziism, or union militants crusading against fascism, domestic radicals became superpatriots. Only a few domestic Fascists and German sympathizers with minimal political influence threatened domestic unity. For the most part they could be restrained informally, as Roosevelt showed by intervening with the Roman Catholic hierarchy to silence the increasingly pro-Fascist Detroit radio priest, Father Charles E. Coughlin.

Conscientious objectors, too, benefited from the overwhelming unity of the American people regarding the war. With organized opposition to conscription nearly absent, men opposed to the war for reasons of religion or conscience could obtain noncombatant status, or, if they objected to military service in any form, engage in work of national importance under civilian direction. The first Selective Service director, Dr. Clarence Dykstra, former president of the University of Wisconsin, defined conscience broadly, although when General Lewis Hershey became director in 1942 he defined objection solely in religious terms, excluding all conscientious objectors who objected on the basis of moral conscience.

Most American objectors who belonged to the traditional pacifist churches—Quaker, Mennonite, Church of the Brethren—participated in the Selective Service system, either entering the military without restriction or accepting noncombatant service, usually in the medical corps. About 12,000 religious objectors who refused to wear uniforms labored without pay in civilian public service camps improving national forests and irrigating dry land. The most committed objectors—those who refused even to register for the draft and those who could not prove religious objection to war—suffered imprisonment. Of the 5,500 men who went to jail, three-fourths were Jehovah's Witnesses, members of a religious sect that traditionally presented the American judiciary with its toughest civil liberties cases.

For one group of Americans, political intolerance and racism joined to produce a major social tragedy and the most glaring violation of civil liberties in American history. However much citizens were united in their hostility to the Axis powers, popular hatred of the Japanese exceeded that of the Germans, "who at least were white men." Japanese-Americans were concentrated on the Pacific Coast, especially in California, where fear about an impending invasion ran rampant. Customary victims of racial prejudice, despised by many white Californians because they had proved successful economically, and now considered potential saboteurs as well, the Japanese-Americans found themselves in a dire predicament after Pearl Harbor.

Feared by military authorities as agents of the Japanese military, Japanese-Americans were rounded up and forcibly removed from their homes and businesses on the West Coast. In early 1942 the War Department, acting under what it defined as the needs of military security, began the evacuation of more than 110,000 people of Japanese ancestry to relocation centers in interior desert states. Two-thirds of those moved were American citizens. Crowded into one-room barracks, denied all but the most minimal personal possessions, encircled by barbed wire, and patrolled by armed guards, the Japanese-Americans roasted away in the desert sun for almost three years. Individual camp residents, mostly young Nisei, many of whom joined the armed forces, were allowed to leave the camps. But the bulk of the occupants of America's "concentration camps" had to wait until January 20, 1945, to be liberated. While they waited, President Roosevelt refused to rescind the War Department's original evacuation order, and the Supreme Court, despite a blistering dissent by Jusice Frank Murphy, upheld the constitutionality of relocation as a war emergency measure. The experience of the Japanese-Americans as contrasted to that of the German-Americans, who as a group were unscathed by anti-Nazi sentiments, illustrated the enormous weight of popular racialist emotions on American culture.

THE SOCIAL IMPACT

War stimulated the social processes that depression had retarded. Beginning in 1940 Americans resumed their customary pattern of internal migrations. Now, however, a large component of coercion was introduced into the process, as almost twelve million men entered military service. Civilians, too, moved freely in response to the demands of a war economy. Americans tended to leave agrarian states for industrial ones, declining manufacturing regions for booming ones. Most states in the South, the upper Midwest, the Great Plains, and New England lost net population, while Michigan, with its war-converted auto industry, and California, with airplane and shipbuilding firms, experienced enormous in-migrations. Only Connecticut among New England states, a traditional manufacturer of arms and munitions, gained population.

Within the general pattern of migration, important subpatterns emerged. White Americans tended to move from the Northeast and Midwest to the Southwest and especially the West Coast. Blacks, however, migrated to the Northeast and Midwest, as well as to California. Between 1940 and 1950 every northern and midwestern state except Maine gained black population, with New York, Ohio, Illinois, and Michigan setting the pace. Meanwhile every former Confederate state, except Florida, lost blacks (the net loss running to almost 1.3 million people, the largest number of whom migrated from Alabama and Mississippi). Despite agriculture's wartime importance, more families left farms between 1942 and 1945 than moved to them. In three war years, 1942–44, nearly six million people deserted farms, peaking at about three million in 1943. Those who remained behind, however, increased agricultural productivity by 25 percent. Finally, owing to conscription and a consequent disparity in the civilian sex ratio, three of every five civilian migrants were female.

The extent and rapidity of population movement caused increasing concern about family stability. How, it was asked, could families hold together when fathers left home for military service, mothers migrated either to follow their husbands or find better jobs, and children attended a series of different schools? How could even united families maintain customary social standards when they migrated to war-boom communities that lacked the elementary amenities of life? Yet statistics fail to indicate any substantial deterioration in family life. Divorce rates remained constant and, more important, birth rates reversed a decades-long decline and in 1943 reached the highest level since 1927 (the famous postwar baby boom actually began during the war). Only an increase in the reported incidence of juvenile delinquency, especially evident in war-boom communities, suggested the tensions afflicting separated and uprooted families.

The decision by millions of women, most notably married ones, to take jobs was equally as important in its effect on the family as was migration. During the war the rate of female participation in the labor force increased by 24 percent, reaching in 1944 a peak of 19,370,000 women workers. Not only did women move into jobs customarily allocated to them, but now, as a result of the extraordinary labor shortage, they began to occupy positions hitherto reserved for men. By 1943 women composed about 10 percent of the labor force in the coke plants, blast furnaces, and rolling mills of the steel industry. They filled the same proportion of jobs in the shipyards and an even more significant percentage in the airplane industry. Women also operated diesel trains, buses, and taxis, and generally demonstrated that they could perform in these tasks as well as men.

Owing to overcrowded schools and the unavailability of daycare centers, however, work for married women brought added burdens to them and their children. Women not only had to work a full day but also retained responsibility for the customary domestic chores, which were made more onerous by wartime rationing and long food lines. The working mother who lacked older offspring able to tend younger siblings or who had preschool children might become a nervous wreck trying to find adequate supervision for her family while she worked. The impact of crowded schools, inadequate daycare centers, and a lack of adult supervision, though difficult to measure precisely, undoubtedly had social and psychological effect on children. Fear for the future of the American family induced by wartime demographic patterns may have been an important factor in the postwar sanctification of the family as an institution.

Wartime tensions not only affected family relationships but also exacerbated racial relations. By 1941, as we have seen, more militant black spokesmen, as demonstrated by membership in the National Negro Congress or in CIO unions, had emerged. War stimulated black militancy. In 1940 and 1941 black leaders and newspapers advised their followers not to leap to preserve democracy abroad if they could not obtain civil rights at home. A. Philip Randolph, ex-Socialist, president of the Brotherhood of Sleeping Car Porters, and gadfly to the AFL, demanded that blacks have full and equal access to all defense employment opportunities. To gain his goals Randolph planned a mass march on Washington set for the late spring of 1941. President Roosevelt, eager for political and national unity at a time of crisis, feared the impact a mass march might have on racial relations. To avert a possible calamity, the president offered Randolph a compromise: Executive Order 8802. This presidential proclamation, in return for which Randolph canceled the march, forbade discrimination in employment on all government-related defense contracts and established a Fair Employment Practices Commission (FEPC) to investigate complaints and enforce rulings. Because Randolph's pressure tactics worked, some black spokesmen concluded: "We get more when we yell than we do when we plead."

Still, it proved more difficult to upgrade black employment opportunities than to get presidential proclamations. Some firms, such as North American Aviation, bluntly stated: "The Negro will be considered only as janitors and in other similar capacities." Such attitudes led Randolph to plan public demonstrations for twenty-six cities in the summer of 1943, because in his words, "If we don't demand now, when are we to demand?" More important than planned protests in improving employment prospects for blacks were economic realities. By mid-1943 employers, in order to meet production targets, had to hire workers regardless of race or sex. By 1943 the number of skilled black workers had doubled, and the proportion of semiskilled had risen even more steeply. Nearly two-thirds of the one million blacks who took war jobs were women. But despite real improvements and continuing federal pressure on employers to cease discrimination, the bulk of nonwhite workers remained unskilled and employers reserved managerial and white-collar positions for whites.

As blacks moved north to already crowded industrial cities, racial frictions festered. In such places as Detroit, where black and white migrants from the South competed for scarce housing, schools, and recreational facilities, the smallest spark could set off a racial explosion. Not surprisingly, on a hot Sunday afternoon in June 1943, racial conflict between teenagers erupted at a Detroit recreation spot, setting off a chain of rumors and a bloody riot. Not until twenty-five blacks and nine whites were killed did federal troops restore order to Detroit. Two months later, in August, Harlem ignited. There, a rumor that a white policeman had killed a black soldier sent thousands of residents into the streets where they hurled rocks, broke store windows, and looted. Before the violence subsided, six blacks had been killed and three hundred had been injured. Harlem and Detroit illustrated the tensions that boiled beneath the surface in a black America that felt oppressed and excluded.

Brown Americans, too, experienced racial violence in the summer of 1943. In South California, especially Los Angeles, where Mexican-Americans occupied the inferior social role held by blacks elsewhere, wartime tensions caused conflict. Mexican-American teenagers who sought security against oppression through gangs originated a singular style of dress, known as the "zoot suit"—a form of attire marked by a suit jacket with exaggerated shoulders, narrow waist, and great length; trousers flared at the knees and tightly tapered (pegged) at the shoetops; narrow pointed shoes, broad-rimmed felt hats; and long key chains, which the wearers ostentatiously twirled around their index fingers. These gangs with their distinctive costumes (which also appealed to black and white working-class youths) made Mexican-Americans in the Los Angeles area the objects of fear and derision. In June, uniformed sailors stationed in the area

*Victim of prejudice—a Chicano zoot-suiter in Los
Angeles, c. 1943*

(Wide World Photos)

attacked Mexican-American youths on the streets and stripped them of
their clothes while Los Angeles police looked the other way. Not as
bloody or as deadly as the black ghetto conflicts, the "zoot suit" riots also
aimed to keep nonwhites in their place by teaching Mexican-American
youths not to challenge WASP sartorial customs.

If nonwhite Americans, too, benefited economically from the imperatives of war, they remained in a much more vulnerable social position.
The 1943 riots in fact signified that explosive racial relations were present,
even in the midst of a national emergency.

National crisis, however, did seem to diminish ethnicity among citizens of white immigrant origin. Aside from Hollywood war movies that featured stock platoons including a Brooklyn Irishman, a bespectacled urban Jew, a brawny Pole, a comic Italian, and American farmboy-cowboy types, ethnic distinctions and tensions seemed minimal. War set the social foundation for the type of nation some postwar scholars would perceive as tripartite in character: Protestant, Catholic, and Jew.

POLITICS AS USUAL

One of the more remarkable features of the war was the continuation of partisan politics. Though Roosevelt invited prominent Republicans Henry L. Stimson and Frank Knox into his wartime cabinet to imply the creation of a government of national unity, Republicans, as a party, criticized the administration and benefited from the anti-New Deal tide that had begun to build in the elections of 1938. The 1942 off-year elections saw Republicans increase their strength in Congress and, together with conservative southern congressmen, amass a working majority. Against this effective congressional conservative majority, Roosevelt beat a hasty retreat from his prewar demands for ambitious social welfare programs. Indeed, as war prosperity eliminated the need for welfare and Congress abolished New Deal agencies, the president, recognizing political reality, declared that Dr. Win-the War had replaced Dr. New Deal.

Elated by six years of relative political success, Republicans looked with optimism to the presidential election of 1944. Their nominee, Governor Thomas E. Dewey of New York, campaigned with enthusiasm and poured scorn on Roosevelt. In the midst of global war, presidential politics followed its customary course of stressing personalities over principles, rhetoric over issues, slander over truth. In the event, however, the Roosevelt coalition proved invincible. Though the Democrats lost considerable support among farm voters, rural folk, and middle-class urbanites, especially in smaller cities, Democratic support held firm in the larger cities among union members, Catholics, Jews, and most ethnics, as well as in the "solid South." In 1944 Roosevelt's party remained the home for non-Protestant urban working-class Americans linked in a singular alliance with rural, white southern Protestants. More ironical still, the political party that harbored the core of organized resistance to Negro rights had become by war's end the choice of most blacks who voted.

THE PROSPECT AHEAD

Just as the depression left much unchanged in American society, so, too, did five years of war leave much of the nation the way it had found it. If most Americans bettered their material circumstances, the distribution of

wealth and income remained as unequal as ever. In 1946 the top fifth of
the population still received 46.1 percent of personal income compared
to the 5.0 percent received by the bottom fifth. And the top 5 percent of
the population, which commanded over 18 percent of basic income in
1945, derived most of its earnings from capital (wealth) not labor, although a senatorial committee had reported in January 1944 that twenty
million Americans "dwell constantly in a borderland between subsistence
and privation, where even the utmost thrift and caution do not suffice to
make ends meet."

The fear of depression also hung heavily over the land as the war in
1945 relentlessly drew to its end. Conversion from a war to a peace
economy resurrected anxieties about unemployment and economic
collapse. When twelve million men were discharged from military duty,
how would the economy absorb them? With factories no longer producing tanks, planes, jeeps, guns, and munitions, how would workers find
jobs? How would an economy and a society that for five years had tolerated govenment-set prices and wages, the planned allocation of materials
and men, and the commanding presence of national authority adjust to
the elimination of wartime controls and the dimunition of federal
power?

Some of the answers were not long forthcoming. Despite the rapid
reconversion from war to peace, the prompt discharge of servicemen, and
the quick elimination of mandatory wage-price controls, the economy
prospered. Wartime savings and the government's decision to rebuild war
torn Europe fueled an industrial boom. More important, perhaps, federal
power did not shrink back to prewar levels. Congress in 1946 passed a
law—the Employment Act—that mandated that the federal government
accept responsibility for guaranteeing national prosperity. By 1946 Americans, moreover, seemed to have implicitly accepted the image of their
society that John K. Galbraith would make famous in his 1952 book,
American Capitalism. In that volume Galbraith argued that the United
States had achieved economic prosperity with a system in which three
primary power centers—big business, big labor, and big government—
checked and countervailed each other to the benefit of the consumer. The
massive strike wave of 1945–46, which saw the major industrial unions
challenge corporate giants, offered support for Galbraith's description of
social reality. Not able to defeat each other, nor free to override federal
desire for industrial peace, labor and management avoided violent confrontations and brought the strikes to a peaceful, compromise conclusion.
What might happen, however, when big business, big labor, and big
government cooperated with each other instead of countervailing each
other, few citizens asked in 1946. They simply enjoyed postwar prosperity
and expended their energies in consumption.

22

Neither War Nor Peace: Truman and the Origins of the Cold War 1945-1952

The cracks in the Grand Alliance that opened at the Potsdam conference of July 1945 presaged the tenor of relations among the victorious allies in the postwar world. With Germany and Japan defeated, the two surviving world powers—the United States and Soviet Russia—eyed each other warily. Their cooperation during World War II had broken a tradition of Russo-American antipathy dating back to the 1917 Bolshevik Revolution. No longer compelled by wartime needs to collaborate, United States and Soviet policymakers soon began to combat each other's postwar aims. United States officials saw Soviet efforts to secure Russia's western flank by control of the Baltic, east European, and Balkan nations as part of a Communist plot to topple capitalism everywhere. Soviets viewed the emergence of the United States as the world's preeminent power and some of its postwar demands as a threat to Russian security. Such mutual suspicions made Russo-American conflict inevitable.

From our present perspective it can be seen that neither side alone bears the onus for the Cold War. Stalin pursued traditional Russian national security goals in Eastern and Southern Europe while solidifying his personal power domestically. To Truman and Churchill, however, the Soviet ruler seemed to be breaking his promises by seizing control of

Poland and other Eastern European countries and rendering them Communist satellites. Churchill and Roosevelt heretofore willingly had conceded Russia's need for "friendly governments" along her frontiers but Truman now balked at what he characterized as enforced sovietization. Although it might have been difficult for the United States to accept Soviet policy in Eastern Europe without protest, a milder opposition than occurred might have moderated Soviet behavior and thus lessened the intensity of the Cold War. The United States, to be sure, had its own, if more benevolent "spheres," in Western Europe and Latin America. Russia expected a comparable role in Eastern Europe.

Yet American officials feared that Soviet influence and power might spread into the heart of Western Europe. The war had damaged badly the economic and social systems of Western Europe. Truman's advisers suggested that communism, feeding on disorder and decay, could make serious inroads in such countries as Italy and France and might even come to power by parliamentary means. The American government understandably felt greatly concerned at the possible westward thrust of communism and in 1947 began to adopt measures to contain it and hold Western Europe for democracy and liberal capitalism. The danger, we now see, was primarily economic and political, but the United States from 1946 on in fact feared Soviet military power. Although the United States, despite demobilization, possessed the world's second largest army, its largest navy, and an atomic monopoly, its leaders worried that numerically superior Russian armies might suddenly overrun all Europe.

Each side felt threatened as fears fed upon fears, insecurities upon insecurities. The postwar period thus shattered the false wartime hopes of most Americans for a peaceful and largely democratic and free trade world, based upon great power cooperation and the United Nations. Once again, as had happened in 1918 and 1919, American hopes for a democratic and liberal capitalistic world order reflecting traditional American ideals and values about the mission of the United States and the blessings of freedom and trade to all mankind seemed threatened by communism. Soviet power, as radical historians have observed, also potentially blocked American global economic hegemony. Consequently when Russia proceeded to organize Eastern Europe as a Soviet sphere, American policymakers reacted with shock, horror, and moral condemnation. And stimulated by their leaders, Americans overreacted and soon became almost hysterically anti-Communist and anti-Russian.

THE BREAKDOWN OF BIG THREE COOPERATION

Even as World War II ended, Big Three amity came to an end. A foreign ministers' conference in London, in September 1945, ended in deadlock when Russia rejected western complaints about the governments it had imposed upon Rumania and Bulgaria. Poland as before remained the

Division of Europe, 1945–1955

Areas annexed by USSR
Areas controlled by Poland
Allies of U.S., 1955
Allies of USSR, 1955
Independent communist states, 1955

greatest stumbling block to amity between the Soviets and the west. In the Middle East, Russian troops continued to occupy northern Iran, despite a wartime agreement for prompt withdrawal of British and Soviet forces, but Stalin eventually in 1946 retreated under western pressure.

Russia also menaced Turkey, demanding a new treaty that would permit her to establish bases within the strategic Dardanelles. Since 1946 a civil war raged in Greece between the western-backed legal and conservative government and Communist rebels.

Simultaneously the Russian press denounced the West and renewed its emphasis on the ideological theme of a hostile capitalist versus Communist worlds. Stalin, in an address in February 1946, reaffirmed the validity of the Marxist-Leninist thesis of rivalry between the two competing systems. He launched a new five-year plan to prepare Russia for possible attack by the moribund but still powerful and hostile capitalist powers.

Strangely, Stalin's militant language was in striking contrast to his moderate behavior. He neither supported the Greek rebels nor assisted French and Italian Communists to seize power. Whatever his reasons, Stalin recognized Western spheres of influence, as he expected the Anglo-Americans to tolerate Soviet spheres.

Yet Winston Churchill, now out of office, in a speech at Fulton, Missouri, on March 5, 1946, denounced Soviet policy and called for an Anglo-American alliance to lift the "iron curtain" Stalin had dropped across the center of Europe. His speech proved prophetic as American sentiment against Russia hardened with Germany providing the turning point.

Contrary to the Yalta and Potsdam agreements, it proved impossible to manage Germany as whole via the Four Power Control Commission. Russia, eager for compensation and understandably unconcerned about German feelings, stripped her zone of industrial equipment and even current production. She also failed to ship food and raw materials to the western zones as agreed upon in exchange for reparations. The British and the Americans—France initially was uncooperative as she had her own designs upon Germany—feared that food exports to their zones would be required indefinitely to prevent mass starvation. Moreover, they were convinced that Germany must be allowed more industry than previously planned in order to play a necessary role in the economic revival of the rest of Western Europe. Consequently, early in 1946 Great Britain and the United States halted the dismantling and shipping of industrial equipment in their zones to the Soviets. Meanwhile Russia treated her zone as virtually a closed area, placing German Communists or subservient Germans in positions of power and prohibiting independent political parties. The West tolerated but discouraged the Communist party in its zones but allowed all other political parties (except Nazis) to operate freely. The Soviets confiscated all large estates in eastern Germany, closed all banks and accounts, and nationalized most industries in their domination of their area.

President Harry S. Truman, inexperienced in statecraft but resolute, decisive, and loyal to his advisers, soon tired of what he called "babying the Soviets." Yet he and Secretary of State James F. Byrnes sought partially to allay Soviet fear of a German military revival. In April 1946,

Byrnes offered Russia a four-power treaty guarantee for twenty-five years against German rearmament. And when the Soviets proved unreceptive, Byrnes at Stuttgart, on September 6, 1946, made clearer the administration's "policy of firmness and patience." The United States, he declared, would not retreat from Germany but would keep its troops there as long as necessary. Germany should not be allowed to become a pawn between East and West, its living standard should not be reduced further, and there would be no more reparations until it became economically self-sufficient. Subsequently, the British and Americans merged their zones into Bizonia for economic purposes; France joined later, thus laying the basis for the West German Republic. Russia responded with a Communist-ruled government in East Germany.

The administration's move toward a firmer approach did not please all Americans. Some still believed that collaboration with the Soviets was possible. Henry A. Wallace, formerly FDR's secretary of agriculture and vice president, and currently serving as secretary of commerce, regarded himself as the heir to New Deal policies at home and abroad. In an address in New York City on September 12, 1946, six days after Byrnes's Stuttgart speech, Wallace pointed out that Russia naturally would socialize her sphere of influence as the West democratized its spheres. Still she did not threaten Western Europe. A tough attitude on our part, he warned, would merely sharpen world tensions: "The tougher we get, the tougher the Russians will get." He called, therefore, for mutual trust and cooperation. Byrnes, still in Europe, was greatly disturbed by Wallace's address and in effect threatened to resign unless President Truman repudiated the commerce secretary. Thereupon Truman dismissed Wallace. When Wallace later led a new political group, the Progressives, against Truman in the 1948 presidential election, however, liberals and intellectuals solidly supported Truman's program of anticommunism abroad and a Fair Deal at home.

THE TRUMAN DOCTRINE AND CONTAINMENT

The Truman Doctrine signaled the final abandonment of official hopes for cooperation with the Soviets and the formal resort to measures to contain potential communist expansion in Europe. The British government in February 1947 warned Washington that it no longer could bear the burden of underwriting Greek and Turkish resistance to Communist threats. Truman and his advisers welcomed the opportunity to launch a new policy aimed at containing Russia. Moreover, they feared that Russia might break into the Mediterranean area and endanger the southern flank of Western Europe. Heeding the advice of the Republican leader, Senator Arthur H. Vandenberg of Michigan, to "scare hell out of the country," Truman went before Congress on March 12, 1947 and requested $400 million for military and economic aid to bolster Greece and Turkey. After describing the Communist threat to Greece and Turkey, the president warned the American people that their goal of a peaceful and free world was endangered: "We shall not realize our objective . . . unless we are willing to help free people to maintain their free institutions and their national integrity against aggressive movements that seek to impose upon them totalitarian regimes." The United States heretofore had protested violations of the Yalta Agreements that imposed communism on Poland, Rumania, and Bulgaria, and it must now stand ready to aid others to resist similar impositions: "I believe that it must be the policy of the United States to support free peoples who are resisting attempted subversion by armed minorities or by outside pressures."

Most Americans responded positively to the president's address. A few conservatives expressed fear that the United States might bankrupt itself by an open-ended commitment to containment; some liberals expressed concern that the administration was weakening the United Nations by bypassing it. Still others, such as columnist Walter Lippmann, warned against an ideological holy crusade against communism. A Republican-controlled Congress, however, in a display of bipartisanship under Senator Vandenberg's guidance, approved the Greek and Turkish aid bill in July. It was an epochal step. The Truman Doctrine signified the United States's assumption in a time of nominal peace of long-range commitments and obligations to contain communism. It focused upon Europe initially, but later was to be extended to East Asia and the Middle East, until containment became in fact a global policy. Finally, despite the ideological overtone of Truman's references to "free peoples," containment did not represent a doctrinaire support of democracy. American aid became available to all who resisted Moscow, whatever the character of their governments, as exemplified by support of the communist regime of Tito in Yugoslavia and of Syngman Rhee in Korea, Chiang Kai-Shek in Taiwan, Franco in Spain, and Salazar in Portugal.

The philosophy of containment, enunciated by State Department adviser George F. Kennan in *Foreign Affairs* in July 1947, placed the Truman Doctrine in a broadened global setting. Carefully analyzing Communist ideology and the nature of the Soviet state, Kennan concluded that Russian leaders were impervious to argument. Relying upon the Marxist "science" of history, the Soviets continuously pressed forward probing for weak spots, confident that ultimately their system would triumph everywhere. Lasting cooperation and amity therefore were impossible. Only counterforce could make any impression upon these opponents with ideological blinders: "The main element of any United States policy toward Soviet Russia must be that of a long-term, patient but firm and vigilant containment of Russian expansionist tendencies." Kennan saw the contest as a test of American maturity as a great power, and he predicted that if a containment policy were followed, ultimately Russia would either collapse under the pressure and its own internal weaknesses or gradually mellow as a regime. Although Kennan later wrote, in his memoirs, that the administration misconceived the Soviet threat as primarily military, in fact it viewed it also as political and adopted both economic and military measures to shore up Western Europe.

THE MARSHALL PLAN

The Marshall Plan underscored the fact that containment was economic and political as well as military. Early in 1947, General George C. Marshall, the retired wartime chief of staff whom Truman had appointed secretary of state in January 1947 to succeed Byrnes, returned from a futile foreign ministers' conference in Moscow. At that conference Molotov had refused to cooperate in an economic policy for all Germany unless Russia obtained a share in control of the Ruhr; Marshall ended that gambit by proposing also a western role in controlling Upper Silesia, which the Soviets had turned over to Poland. Molotov then charged that the Anglo-American Bizonia violated the Potsdam Agreement, though he was silent about Russian violations in seizing current production as reparations and in isolating East Germany from the west. But Marshall felt less distress at these disagreements than he did at multiplying signs that Communist parties were exploiting successfully growing economic and social disorder all across Europe.

Despite the outlay of around $14 billion by the United States in loans, gifts, and aid to Western Europe and Japan since the end of the war, Europe seemed on the verge of collapse by 1947. Although Great Britain had received a loan of $3.7 billion and France $1.4 billion, it was to little avail in repairing the damages of war and in restoring their accustomed trading role. Germany, of course, still lay in ruins and its people lived on a semistarvation diet. The unbelievably severe winter of 1946–47, with its freezing weather followed by disastrous spring floods, dealt Europe another blow. Mines flooded, factories closed for lack of fuel, and homes went heatless for days. Production fell by 50 percent in Great Britain and other countries also suffered severely. In this climate of unemployment and misery, it seemed that communism might triumph by democratic means. Indeed, the Communists polled around one-fourth the popular vote in France and one-third in Italy.

Marshall requested his advisers in the State Department to come up with some well-designed plan to cope with this crisis. As these advisers saw the problem, the crisis reflected not communism per se but the misery upon which it fed. They decided that the best means of attacking social rot lay in a cooperative approach whereby Europe would plan its needs collectively and the United States would promise to underwrite a long-term recovery program. Russia also would be invited to participate, though it was expected that she would refuse to join in a plan intended to promote capitalism. Thus European unity would be encouraged and the United States would avoid charges of mere anticommunism or of trying to dominate Europe.

Secretary Marshall announced the new policy in a commencement address at Harvard on June 5, 1947. The European response was immediate and favorable. Britain and France invited Russia to a meeting in Paris to draft a reply to Marshall. Apparently Stalin at first viewed the offer as another welcome lend-lease handout, for he sent Molotov with a large delegation to the Paris meeting. Subsequently, however, Molotov denounced the whole affair as a scheme of Yankee imperialism to dominate Europe and walked out of the conference. Several reasons probably explain the Soviet rejection. First, Russia wanted individual aid and opposed any cooperative planning or controls, reflecting Soviet suspicions of capitalism. Second, Stalin apparently became apprehensive when Czechoslovakia wanted to participate. The Marshall Plan might weaken his control over Eastern Europe. Finally, Stalin understandably feared anything that increased American power and influence in Europe or kept her involved in the affairs of that continent.

By July 1947 sixteen nations had met to establish the Committee on European Economic Cooperation and to draw up plans for a systematic recovery over the next four years. Franco Spain, tainted with fascism and former Axis ties, was excluded, while Russia and the eastern bloc absented themselves. Although some American conservatives criticized the Marshall Plan as a global give-away that would bankrupt the United States, most citizens agreed that it was a wise measure to shore up Western Europe against communism and to prevent American isolation within its hemisphere. Senator Vandenberg again led in a bipartisan effort to obtain congressional approval.

An unexpected Communist campaign in Czechoslovakia in February 1948 also helped to overcome opposition to an expensive aid program. With a coalition cabinet containing nine Communists, Czechoslovakia had tried to serve as a half Socialist–half capitalist bridge between East and West, retaining democratic institutions and ties with the Western world while existing within the Soviet sphere of influence. Stalin tolerated a more ambiguous status for Czechoslovakia than for any other Soviet satellite until the Western powers began to integrate West Germany more firmly into the liberal capitalist order. In response to Anglo-American actions in Germany, Stalin precipitated a Communist coup in Prague. The West especially reacted with horror at the murder (alleged suicide) of Jan Masaryk, the Czech foreign minister and son of the founder of the republic.

In April 1948, Congress appropriated $5.3 billion to implement the Marshall Plan. By 1952 the United States had expended $13.6 billion for European economic recovery. It was an immense success on the whole, increasing Western Europe's industrial production by 200 percent in four years and laying the basis for its subsequent affluence. Communist political gains diminished in the West and Communists were excluded from the ministries governing France and Italy. The aid worked so effectively because of its planned long-term approach and because Western Europe, unlike many other recipients of American aid, possessed the basic industries, skills, and resources to utilize it effectively. Although Churchill hailed the Marshall Plan as the most unselfish act in history, clearly it served the enlightened self-interest of the United States. The recovery program strengthened an area vital to the United States strategically, economically, and culturally and, equally important, stimulated the American economy.

THE COLD WAR HEATS UP

Stalin responded to the Marshall Plan by tightening his rule over Eastern Europe and launching a series of counter moves intended to discredit the United States and perhaps force it off the continent. In September 1947 the Soviets created the Cominform (Communist Information Agency) to perfect their control over the countries within the eastern sphere. The Czech coup followed early in 1948, and Communist agitators and labor unions precipitated a wave of strikes and protests against American imperialism across Europe. The pro-Communist artist Pablo Picasso even designed a "peace dove" for this massive anti-American campaign. Russian propaganda revealed an almost hysterical fear that the United States might wage a so-called preventive war while it still possessed a monopoly of atomic weapons.

In June 1948, the Berlin blockade further aroused widespread fear of war in Europe and America. In part the blockade of Western access routes to their zones in Berlin reflected Soviet fear of Western attempts to revive the German economy. In 1946 the Anglo-Americans had fused their zones into Bizonia, and by the end of 1947 France agreed to join what became Trizonia. Early in 1948, the British and the Americans established a transitional government for Bizonia and launched a currency reform, foreshadowing creation of the West German state. Consequently, the Russians stalked out of the Four Power Control Commission for good and imposed a blockade of Berlin. The Soviets intended the blockade either to drive the western powers from Berlin, thereby strengthening Russian control of East Germany, or to wreck their attempts to revive the western zones economically and politically. In a larger sense, the blockade perhaps would reveal American weaknesses and discredit the western alliance that was beginning to take shape.

The Russian interruption of the road, rail and water routes linking the western zones in Germany with their zones over a hundred miles away in Berlin posed a crucial challenge for American leadership and power. Washington reacted to the blockade with great anguish. Some of President Truman's advisers saw no choice but to abandon Berlin, since they believed that the United States faced vastly superior Russian armies in Europe and the atomic bomb seemed inappropriate to the crisis.

Others felt that the Russians were bluffing and advised running an armed convoy through East Germany to Berlin. The Truman administration chose a middle way between capitulation and force. An airlift was begun to feed the western garrisons and the two and a half million people in West Berlin. Russia, also recoiling from the prospects of war, dared not thwart the airlift. By flying in planes around the clock, the airlift brought in thirteen thousand tons of supplies, including coal, to Berlin daily. (This far exceeded the estimated daily minimum requirements of four thousand tons.) West Berliners not only survived but enjoyed a higher living standard than before and far higher than that of East Berlin. After 324 days of blockade, Russia finally, in effect, acknowledged failure and called it off in May 1949.

The Berlin blockade also inadvertently boosted President Truman's political fortunes; it silenced Republican critics, promoted Truman's standing with the electorate, and probably assisted his election to the presidency in 1948.

THE NORTH ATLANTIC TREATY

The severed atmosphere in Europe culminated in another transformation in American foreign policy: the first peacetime alliance in our history. Western Europe, apprehensive of Soviet intentions, paved the way by concluding the Brussels Pact in March 1948. Sentiment mounted within the United States to join such an alliance. Two years of Cold War had transformed American sentiment and overcome the lingering tradition against foreign entanglements. The American and the West European overreaction to an alleged Soviet menace, in effect, furthered West European unity.

The North Atlantic Treaty was signed by twelve nations on April 4, 1949. The United States and Canada joined Great Britain, France, Holland, Belgium, Luxemburg, Italy, Portugal, Iceland, Norway, and Denmark in a defense alliance, subject to renunciation or alteration after twenty years. The key clauses defined an attack upon one member as an attack upon all and pledged mutual cooperation in planning the common defense. Unlike in the thirties, would-be aggressors were forewarned that an attack anywhere in Western Europe or North America would trigger a general war.

The overwhelming majority of Americans approved of the alliance as a painful necessity. Even its few critics did not deny that a United States commitment to Western Europe was necessary but only wanted to safeguard America's constitutional procedures against an automatic war or to guard against open-ended defense expenditures. The Senate granted its approval by a vote of eighty-two to thirteen on July 21, 1949. Russian fears of encirclement, which had led Soviet leaders to intensify their control over Eastern Europe in 1947 and 1948, thus unwittingly stimulated the encirclement the Soviets dreaded. The Soviets rightly, of course, claimed that the pact was aimed solely at them and charged that it violated the spirit and letter of the United Nations Charter. It did, to be sure, reflect western disillusionment with the veto-ridden UN as a peace-preserving agency. Although apparently necessary, granted the fears of 1949, the North Atlantic Treaty froze east-west differences into a permanent mold and led to a counteralliance, the Warsaw Pact.

Initially the western allies had not planned to supplement the North Atlantic Treaty with an actual in-field European military. Russia's successful testing of an atomic device in September 1949, obviously ending the American nuclear monopoly, caused a change in plans. Western Europeans feared that henceforth they would be vulnerable to Soviet nuclear blackmail. In January 1950 President Truman announced that the United States would develop the hydrogen fusion or "super-bomb," and plans were made to supplement the North Atlantic Treaty Organization. By early 1950, NATO had been established with a council and secretariat, a supreme headquarters, and regional commands of military, aerial, and naval forces. General Eisenhower left retirement to serve as NATO's first supreme commander. NATO forces would provide a "Trip-wire" in case of a Soviet armed aggression anywhere in Europe, unleashing America's Strategic Air Command to strike directly at Russia with nuclear bombs. Later, as tactical nuclear weapons became available, the Americans turned to a new strategy, "flexible response," that presumably allowed a choice ranging from conventional to tactical weapons in case of Russian overt attacks.

Thus as 1949 drew to an end, Soviet-American relations had reached a bitter and frightening denouement. Dreams of a stable postwar world made peaceful through Great Power cooperation had dissolved even before the final defeat of the Axis powers. The early verbal protests against Soviet aims in Eastern Europe and the Middle East gave way to stronger action: Truman and his advisers acted to shore up Western defenses on Russia's frontiers. The Truman Doctrine converted containment into a global policy. With the implementation of NATO, the United States had encircled Russia with enemy forces and bases. And now with Russia's rupture of the American atomic monopoly, the accelerating militarization of the Cold War threatened global annihilation. The bright dreams of 1945 had thus turned into a dreadful nightmare.

DEBACLE IN THE FAR EAST

The American government and people had met the crises of the early postwar years without a resort to force. It seemed that at last the United States had truly acted as a great world power. But events in 1949 and 1950 shook the self-confidence of the American people and revealed that realism did not always guide foreign policy. The final collapse of Nationalist China in 1949, the frustrations of the Korean War, which began in June 1950, and domestic spy exposés of 1948–1950 and conservative charges of extensive Communist infiltration of government, led to an exaggerated fear of communism at home and abroad and touched off the "great debates" of 1950–1951 about the soundness of American foreign policy. These debates were public reexaminations of the nation's basic policies, conducted in an atmosphere of shrill hysteria and reckless charges of blundering or even treason in high places. As had been so often true in American history, many sought scapegoats to blame for national disappointments and reverses in foreign affairs.

Pearl Harbor occurred because the United States would not abandon Nationalist China to Japan's "New Order" for East Asia. During the Second World War, consequently, the American government sought to aid China to fight Japan and to strengthen her so that after the war China would be able to join the United States in stabilizing the Pacific area. At first Washington authorities thought of focusing the Pacific war effort upon China, a strategy that Chiang Kai-shek, the Nationalist leader, for obvious reasons strongly favored. That plan was abandoned in the face of harsh realities. Japan's control of most of the Pacific throughout 1942 allowed only a trickle of military supplies to Chiang's armies. Japanese forces held China's seacoast and drove the Nationalists into the remote interior of China. In China itself, the Nationalists and the Chinese Communists, led by Mao Tse-tung, were at each other's throats. Chiang tied down huge forces in guarding against the Chinese Communists, rather than in fighting the Japanese. Moreover, his regime was thoroughly corrupt and inefficient. Finally, the later success of General Douglas MacArthur's island-hopping drive from the South Pacific and Admiral Chester Nimitz's naval aircraft carrier raids westward into the Japanese ring of island bases promised the most direct and speediest means of terminating the war. China, therefore, was pushed into the background as a theater of war.

Nevertheless, the United States sent several military and political missions to China to strengthen Chiang's war effort against Japan and to prevent a flare-up between the Nationalists and the Communists that could only weaken China. In short, American policy favored a unified China strong enough to protect her own interests and to play a constructive role in the postwar world—hence President Roosevelt's frequent, if not accurate, references to China as one of the great powers, much to the annoyance of British Prime Minister Churchill, who saw full well that she did not yet merit so exalted a rank.

General Joseph W. "Vinegar Joe" Stilwell went to China in 1942 to control American aid to China and to serve as Chiang's chief of staff. He found his mission a series of frustrations. Chiang refused to overhaul his army to eliminate corrupt and inefficient officers, and he was reluctant to commit sizeable forces to any large-scale and risky campaigns against the Japanese. The crux of the difficulty lay in the American desire to concentrate all forces to defeat the Japanese in the shortest possible time versus Chiang's interest in maintaining the basis of his own power within Nationalist China and his determination to curb and eventually crush the Chinese Communists. From his point of view, the United States should take care of Japan, so that he could concentrate upon the internal balance of power within China.

Such divergent interests insured that American attempts to patch up a truce between the Nationalists and the Communist Chinese would fail. The Chinese Communists originally had comprised the left wing within the Nationalist movement of Sun Yat-sen, but the latter's death and his succession by Chiang Kai-shek had led to civil war between the right and left wings in the 1920s and 1930s. In the Long Trek of 1934–1935, the Chinese Communists had retreated to remote North China, where they dug in and emphasized peasant reforms. A Nationalist-Communist truce in 1937 against the Japanese invaders soon broke down and both factions warily watched and maneuvered against each other. The Chinese Communists steadily enlarged the areas under their control and strengthened their army, until by 1945 they controlled an estimated 116 million people, or one-fourth of China's population, and had over a million troops under arms.

From the American point of view, only compromise offered any hope of averting a ruinous Chinese civil war. Yet all efforts, such as Vice-President Henry A. Wallace's trip to China in 1944, failed. Neither the Nationalists nor the Communists trusted each other; both felt confident of ultimate victory, and so refused to make the compromises essential to forging a workable coalition. The Americans persisted in their efforts to mediate this internal conflict, however, while the Yalta Agreement, as noted before, attempted to protect China against either a Russian seizure of Manchuria or Russian recognition and aid to the Communists. At Yalta Stalin agreed that Manchuria belonged to China, though he obtained railroad concessions and a naval base therein, and he continued to deal only with the Nationalist government. Apparently Stalin had no great affection for Mao Tse-tung and his followers,* perhaps because they were too independent for his taste, and he overrated the strength of Chiang's regime.

The Pacific War ended in August 1945 before the United States could do much to build up the Nationalists' power via newly opened sea routes to China. More important, as became evident, Chiang's regime was morally bankrupt and had alienated vast numbers of Chinese. During the war, driven inland by the Japanese, Chiang had been compelled to rely upon the conservative landlord class. Consequently, it proved impossible to undertake needed rural reforms, as his Communist rivals were doing. Runaway wartime inflation, heavy taxation, discriminatory military conscription (often exempting sons of the wealthy), and corrupt officials further alienated the peasant class from the Nationalists. After

---

* Stalinist policy and advice had been partly responsible for setbacks during the 1920s to Communists in China.

the war, the Nationalists lost support of the intellectuals and students, who were repelled by the corrupt and undemocratic nature of the regime, while business and financial groups were irked by inflation and the nepotism of the ruling Chiang Kai-shek family and friends. Drastic police control and looting and raping by the "liberating" Nationalist armies completed the process. Communist behavior, in contrast, seemed a model of reform, moderation, and fair government. Under these circumstances the Nationalists lost the "Mandate of Heaven," or popular consensus to govern, as more and more Chinese became apathetic or defected to the Communists. Nonetheless, in 1945 and 1946 the Americans gave what aid they could to Chiang, supplying and helping the Nationalists to move their armies to key areas where they could disarm the Japanese and take control before the Communists could arrive. General George C. Marshall also served as a special envoy in 1946 to try to achieve a truce and some form of coalition government. He failed.

In 1947 a confident Chiang Kai-shek launched a major campaign to crush his enemies. He commanded nearly three million troops against slightly over a million Communist regulars and guerrillas. Ignoring American advice, Chiang used his forces not to pursue the Communists but to capture and hold cities. He thereby spread his forces thin and left them virtually besieged in cities while the Communists controlled the countryside. With growing strength and confidence, the Chinese Communist forces began to attack the Nationalist armies. Chiang met a series of disasters. By November 1948 he had lost Manchuria and 400,000 troops; by early 1949, Peking and North China fell; in May, Shanghai; and in October, Canton and the south. Chiang's armies simply lost the will to fight, and 75 to 80 percent of the arms and military goods supplied by the Americans—over $2 billion worth—fell into Communist hands. By the end of 1949 the Chinese Communists reigned supreme on the mainland, while Chiang and a remnant of the Nationalists sought refuge on the island of Taiwan (Formosa).

Washington publicly cut loose from the Nationalist cause only in the famed China White Paper of August 1949. As the State Department contended in this public document, the United States could do no more to save the Nationalists. It had supplied generous aid and sound military and political advice, which had been wasted or ignored. Certainly the United States lacked the necessary troops to intervene on the China mainland in 1948–1949, and most Americans probably would have opposed any such entanglement so soon after the end of the bloody Second World War. The chief mistake of the Truman administration, it would seem, lay not in failing to rescue Chiang, but in a failure to face Congress and the public squarely with the painful alternatives in China. Congress if compelled to debate the issue no doubt would have agreed with the administration that American armed involvement in the mainland civil war was unwise. Unfortunately, President Truman's failure to be frank with Congress left his administration open to later political charges that it had betrayed Chiang Kai-shek and abandoned China to Communist rule. The collapse of Nationalist China, which most Americans long had regarded as their friendly ally and the principal hope for a stable Far East, and its replacement by a hostile and alien Communist regime, was a traumatic shock to the American public. And many Americans simply refused to realize that China was not theirs to lose.

THE FRUSTRATING KOREAN WAR

Korea had been jointly occupied by Soviet and American forces after Japan's surrender in 1945. Russian troops disarmed Japanese forces north of the 38th parallel, Americans south of that line. The United States favored the uniting of Korea and persuaded the United Nations to supervise elections in 1948. The Russians refused to permit the UN elections to be held in the north. Consequently, the United States recognized the Republic of Korea in the south and withdrew its occupying forces in 1949, leaving behind a revanchist, authoritarian government headed by Syngman Rhee. The Russians had withdrawn from the north the year before, after installing a Communist regime in power. The Americans supplied the South Koreans with economic and military aid, the latter essentially of a defensive nature to discourage Rhee from a forcible attempt at unifying his country. Washington regarded South Korea as its protégè but, as Secretary of State Dean Acheson's famous press statement in January 1950 made clear, not of strategic importance to the American position in the Pacific.

Suddenly, on June 25, 1950, a heavily armed North Korean army invaded the south and threatened to overrun the ill-prepared South Koreans. The cause of the attack remains obscure, but at the time, American leaders believed that North Korea acted at Stalin's orders in order to encourage neutralism in Japan, undercut the American position in East Asia, and weaken the western alliance system. Stalin's role in the invasion scarcely seems primary, considering that the Soviet delegate to the Security Council had recently "walked out" over the western refusal to admit Communist China to the UN.

The Truman administration found itself in a painful dilemma. If it abandoned Korea, it feared catastrophic effects upon the containment system everywhere, yet America was not prepared to fight a ground war in Asia. The American army was not combat ready, as the nation relied upon its atomic weapons and air power to deter what it deemed the most likely Soviet threat, a military attack against Western Europe. In keeping with that deterrent strategy, the defense budget had neglected to provide for substantial contingents of ground troops. Nevertheless, President Truman decided that the Korean aggression must be resisted. The UN Security Council, at America's behest and with Russia absent, demanded a North Korean withdrawal and then requested members to aid South Korea in resisting the invasion. Asserting his executive authority to

RUSSIA

MONGOLIA

Amur R.

Sungari R.

CHINA

o Vladivostok

Farthest penetration
by UN northward,
Nov. 24, 1950

Peking o

Yalu

o Pyongyang   *Sea of Japan*

38th
Parallel

KOREA

o
Seoul

JAPAN

o Tokyo

Yellow R.

Armistice Line,
July 27, 1953

*East
China
Sea*

R.

Yangtze

Shanghai o

Pusan perimeter,
farthest penetration
by North Korea
Sept. 15, 1950

PACIFIC OCEAN

**The Korean War
1950–1953**

protect American occupation forces in Japan and uphold treaty commitments (the UN Charter), the President on June 27 unilaterally ordered
naval and air forces to aid South Korea. On June 30 he ordered American ground forces into Korea and directed the Seventh Fleet to neutralize
the Formosa Straits. Without Congressional authorization or clear constitutional authority, a Cold War President had for the first, but not the
last, time involved the United States in a foreign war.

The Korean War oscillated wildly in 1950. Appointed UN supreme
commander in Korea—fifteen other nations sent troops to serve under the
UN flag, but the overwhelming burden fell upon the United States and of
course South Korea itself—General MacArthur rallied allied forces
around Pusan at the southern end of the peninsula. Adopting bold
tactics, he coordinated a break-out offensive from Pusan with an
amphibious landing behind North Korean lines at Inchon in September.
Caught in a nutcracker, North Korean armies were almost annihilated,

and the remnants fled north of the 38th parallel. Despite Communist Chinese warnings, in October the United States decided with UN Assembly backing to drive north of the border and unify all Korea into one republic. At an October 14 conference on Wake Island, General MacArthur assured President Truman that there was little danger of Chinese intervention; if China intervened, he declared confidently, American air power would prevail.

MacArthur's forces drove northward, capturing the North Korean capital at Pyongyang on October 19. Although by November it was known that Chinese troops, so-called volunteers, had entered Korea, MacArthur grossly underestimated their number. On November 24 he ordered a final offensive to liberate all Korea and end the war before Christmas. With his troops approaching the Yalu River, the border between Korea and Manchuria, and spread thin along a three hundred mile front, MacArthur was caught by surprise by a massive Communist Chinese counter-offensive. His forces extricated themselves from the trap with great difficulty and fell back in rapid retreat. The Communists drove once more into South Korea and recaptured Seoul before the allies rallied and retook that battered capital. By spring 1951, the UN forces had fought their way back to approximately the old 38th parallel line. Heavy casualties were inflicted upon the Communists in an operation known as "Meat-Grinder," which utilized American air supremacy and superiority in artillery and mechanized warfare.

THE GREAT DEBATES

Shrill public debates in the United States followed in the wake of the reverses in Korea. The public already had been shocked by the fall of Nationalist China in 1949 and Washington's announcement in September of that year that the Soviet Union had exploded an atomic bomb. The era of American nuclear monopoly, so reassuring during the early years of the Cold War, had passed. Now came the frustrating and costly Korean War, a novel struggle to most Americans accustomed to think only in terms of decisive military victory. In addition, congressional investigations and trials such as that of Alger Hiss, a former high State Department official who was convicted and sentenced to prison in January 1950 for perjury when denying charges of having transmitted confidential State Department documents to a Communist agent in 1938, convinced many Americans that a major cause of Cold War difficulties came from extensive Communist infiltration of our government. One Republican senator raged, "How much more are we going to have to take? Fuchs and Acheson [a frequent target of the witch-hunters] and Hiss and hydrogen bombs threatening outside and New Dealism eating away the vitals of the nation. In the name of heaven, is this the best the nation can do?" It was this outlook that plunged the United States into that period of hysteria and frantic search for domestic Communists and traitors known as "McCarthyism." The State Department, headed by the suave and highly intelligent Dean Acheson, became the symbol of unwanted responsibilities and foreign frustrations.

The first of the great public debates was ignited when former President Hoover in late 1950 in effect criticized America's allies as unreliable and called for a defensive strategy to make the Western Hemisphere an impervious Gibraltar. Others followed and the opposition crystallized around the Republican leader, Senator Robert A. Taft of Ohio. The debate about postwar foreign policies received new vigor when President Truman in late 1950, claiming executive authority, ordered four divisions of troops to Europe to strengthen NATO against a possible Russian attack while the country was distracted by the Korean War. In 1951, Congressional opponents railed against this presidential "usurpation." Senator Taft, especially, felt that the executive branch of our government was becoming too strong and was overcommitting the United States. He genuinely feared that expensive foreign aid projects and defense involvements, plus extensions of the New Deal at home, would lead to bankruptcy and socialism. Hence he advocated what critics called "bargain-basement" containment—reliance upon less costly sea and air power to deter the Communists and avoidance of expensive foreign aid projects.

The last and most important of the great debates grew directly out of American frustrations in Korea, the "Asia First versus Europe" debate touched off by Truman's removal of General MacArthur from Far Eastern command in April 1951. MacArthur, an able but histrionic general who found reverses difficult to tolerate, thirsted for revenge against Communist China. Moreover, his concept of the international Communist threat caused him to advocate striking China's "privileged sanctuary" in Manchuria and other bold measures to win complete victory in Korea. It seemed to him that world communism now focused upon Asia rather than Europe and that time was on the communists' side. Therefore, Manchuria should be bombed to cut off supplies and troop movements to Korea, China's coast should be blockaded, Chiang should be unleashed to threaten a diversionary invasion of the mainland, and the bombing of China proper should be considered.

After a brief discussion, and in response to British and other allied pressures, the administration decided against such bold measures. In its view, the chief danger of Communist expansion still lay in Europe. The administration further feared that MacArthur's strategy might culminate in Soviet intervention and World War III, or at least would bog down American forces in an interminable struggle with China's masses on the mainland of Asia. A prolonged war in Asia would "bleed us dry," Truman and his advisers concluded, and divert attention from the main task of shoring up Western Europe, while leaving Russia free to strike. In short, in contrast to MacArthur's "Asia First" approach, the administration adhered to its Europe-first strategy for the Cold War and decided to keep the Korean War limited until it could be ended by negotiations.

Although MacArthur may have been correct that Russia would not have dared to intervene directly in a major Sino-American war, the administration probably was behaving wisely in its general assessment of the situation and its option for limited war.

But General MacArthur refused to accept the decision of his superiors. He tried to force Truman's hand by appealing to the American public and prominent Republicans in Congress. Contrary to military discipline and in violation of direct orders, MacArthur wrote letters and sent telegrams to various Americans pleading for an Asia-first policy. The final straw, as far as the administration was concerned, came when the general's letter to Republican House minority leader Joseph W. Martin, Jr. was read on the floor of the House of Representatives: "if we lose the war to communism in Asia the fall of Europe is inevitable; win it and Europe most probably would avoid war and yet preserve freedom. There is no substitute for victory." MacArthur's criticism of the administration's policies in Asia met enthusiastic reception among many Republicans searching for political issues against the Democrats, and it also appealed to many Americans accustomed to simplistic thinking about victory in war, and weary of the Korean stalemate. President Truman, fully aware of the storm that would result, decided that he had no alternative but to remove his insubordinate commander. The constitutional role of the president as commander-in-chief and the principle of military subordination to civilian authority must be upheld. On April 11, 1951, Truman announced that MacArthur had been recalled from his Far Eastern command. The great war hero of the Pacific had been fired by the ex-haberdasher in the White House.

The storm broke upon the administration with unbelievable fury. Condemnatory letters and telegrams flooded the White House, Truman was publicly booed, and several Republicans in Congress muttered darkly about impeachment. Republican Senator William Jenner of Indiana claimed that "this country today is in the hands of a secret inner coterie which is directed by the agents of the Soviet Union. We must cut this whole cancerous conspiracy out of our Government at once. Our only choice is to impeach President Truman. . . ." A Gallup poll revealed that 69 percent of those contacted supported MacArthur versus only 29 percent in Truman's favor. MacArthur returned to the United States to receive a hero's welcome and to address a joint session of Congress. Everywhere, speaking in behalf of his views, MacArthur seemed to nurture presidential ambitions. Gradually, however, he faded away into the background, his presidential candidacy did not meet with success in 1952, and he would accept a post with the Remington Rand Corporation.

Meanwhile, the last of the great debates raged amidst shrill charges of blundering and betrayals. Critics of the administration apparently supported all-out war for victory in Korea regardless of the consequences. Congress conducted hearings from May 3 to June 25, 1951, during which charges were aired that China had been lost by blunders or worse and that now the same processes were at work in Korea. Even conservative

Senator Taft once remarked, "The Korean War and the problems which arise from it are the final result of the continuous sympathy toward communism which inspired American policy." Obviously, many Americans were frustrated and angry. Unable to understand why the most powerful nation in the world could not always achieve its ends, they were in the mood to search for convenient devils to flay, for conspiracy theories to explain the inexplicable.

THE FREEZING OF AMERICA'S CHINA POLICY

The great debates and the shrill anti-Communist hysteria did not change American policy toward Korea. The war remained limited despite the onslaught of critics. Upon sober second thought, many Americans apparently were persuaded by General Omar Bradley's testimony to Congress that MacArthur's approach would lead to "the wrong war at the wrong place, at the wrong time, and with the wrong enemy." Soviet Russia, not China, posed the principal threat to western security and Europe still remained the focal point of the Cold War struggle. In July 1951, the Communists agreed to truce negotiations at Panmunjom in Korea. The talks dragged on for two years of small-scale fighting until the armistice at last was signed in July 1953. Total American casualties numbered 33,629 dead and another 115,000 wounded. Expenses mounted to $22 billion. But at least Korea represented a "victory" for the concept of limited war, and it helped mark out the delicate boundaries of Communist-western conflict in a nuclear age in which both sides increasingly feared mutual destruction.

The war and the hysterical domestic debates left American Far Eastern policy in a straitjacket. Prior to Korea, the Truman administration apparently had been feeling its way toward eventual recognition of the People's Republic of China. Taiwan had not seemed vital to American security in the Pacific, and its fall to the Chinese Communists appeared to be only a matter of time. Then came the fateful Korean War, Truman's order to the Seventh Fleet to patrol the Formosa Straits, and China's intervention in Korea. The People's Republic of China had become an enemy of the United States and waged war against it. The feverish American reactions to the Korean War and China's role, therefore, had the effect of freezing American policy into rigid nonrecognition and hostility toward the Mao government. For the next two decades nonrecognition and containment of the People's Republic became fixed dogmas in American foreign relations. A defensive alliance was concluded with the Nationalist regime on Taiwan in 1954; a peace treaty was negotiated unilaterally with Japan in 1951; and SEATO (Southeast Asia Treaty Organization) was formed in 1954 to bar Communist expansion southward. Twice—in the off-shore islands clashes in 1954–1955 and again in 1958—American entanglement with Taiwan threatened to involve the nation in large-scale war with China. Long after China had begun to drift apart from Soviet Russia, American policy thinking still regarded the People's Republic as an expansionist menace to our interests in Southeast Asia and the Pacific. It awaited the Nixon administration in 1971–72 to take the first important steps toward dissolving this rigid and increasingly unrealistic policy in East Asia.

In the fevered climate precipitated by the Korean War and Communist China's intervention, it was probably only the existence of nuclear weapons that prevented a titantic armed struggle between east and west. Ironically, the mutual deterrence of these dreaded new weapons imposed a measure of rationality on both antagonists. The "balance of terror" thereby perhaps saved the world from a third major world war for a quarter of a century and eventually created a new balance of power that in time promoted détente between east and west.

23

The Cold War at Home: Truman, National Security, and the Fair Deal 1946-1952

Postwar domestic politics proved as perilous as foreign affairs—and for similar reasons. Although no depression afflicted peacetime America, as many citizens feared would happen, the Cold War struck home and infected domestic affairs. Worse, during the troubled early postwar years, 1945–1948, the nation functioned with an accidental president, and one ill prepared to implement the policies of his predecessor. Yet the new chief executive soon proved himself more than willing to exercise executive authority and to inflate the power of an office that had been expanding ever since the New Deal and even more since World War II.

The sudden death of President Roosevelt on April 12, 1945 thrust Vice President Harry S. Truman to the pinnacle of power. Selected as Roosevelt's running mate in 1944, the new president had limited knowledge of his predecessor's basic policies, having met him personally only five times during the campaign and three times after the inaugural. Rather abruptly, then, the newly inaugurated president was forced to redress his ignorance, to project an image of bold leadership, and to assure the American public and world leaders of the continuity of United States policy.

Surely these difficulties were more than enough for any conventional politician. Further complicating Truman's problems were the intense partisanship and rabid anticommunism of national politics following the deterioration of U.S.-Soviet relations with the development of the Cold War. The postwar obsession with the Soviet threat to national security spilled over to the domestic political arena and shifted American politics rightward. Victory in the Cold War, perhaps even national existence, it came to be believed, required a stringent internal security program. Policies and principles came to be judged by new norms: the degree to which they conformed to anti-Communist goals.

THE TRANSFORMATION OF THE PRESIDENCY

Franklin Roosevelt's domination of national politics—particularly his extension of federal and executive powers—had significantly altered the national political debate. One byproduct of this domination was the evolution of a radically different conservative politics, one that focused on the perils of strong executive leadership. The conservatives' suspicions of Roosevelt's leadership were but one of the legacies Truman had inherited.

During the Cold War years, power within the executive branch became more centralized and decisions were made more secretively. The National Security Act of 1947 centralized executive control over foreign policy by creating institutions (the National Security Council and the Central Intelligence Agency) for planning foreign policy, correlating policy needs with resources and capabilities, and increasing the president's sources of information. Because the personnel staffing these committees were not confirmed by Congress, they were not required to testify before congressional committees (as were the secretaries of state and defense and lower echelon State and Defense Department officials). The mania for secrecy soon led Truman to establish by executive order an elaborate classification system restricting congressional and public access to intelligence information, planning papers, and policy decisions.

Of equal consequence, the presidency evolved into an inflated bureaucracy, with executive office staff employees expanding from 600 to 1200. The Bureau of the Budget no longer simply prepared the federal budget but acted as the clearing house for departmental legislative proposals. The bureau's legislative reference service and the requirement that all departmental recommendations receive budget clearance permitted the president to exercise continuous control over the budgetary and legislative requests of the various federal agencies. Simultaneously, Truman reorganized the White House staff. The legal counsel to the president (Clark Clifford until 1949, thereafter Charles Murphy) assumed responsibility for coordinating the staff's activities, and met daily with the president and weekly with key White House personnel. Further administrative innovations created a hierarchically stratified and specialized White House staff with precise areas of responsibility (civil liberties, economic policy, congressional liaison). Specialization enabled staff members to utilize their knowledge best and to concentrate their lobbying efforts. Administrative expansion and reorganization enabled Truman more effectively to shape national policy. These changes did not insure that Truman could achieve his total legislative program. But they did magnify the president's power.

ANTICOMMUNISM AND THE POLITICS OF 1945–1948

In one area, however, the president reacted to congressional initiatives. Continually throughout Truman's tenure, leaders of the conservative political and journalistic communities accused his administration of "softness toward communism" and of being infiltrated by Communists. Although Senator Joseph R. McCarthy may have ridden charges of "Communists in Government" to national prominence during the early 1950s, the senator did not invent the tactic nor was he its sole practitioner. Although the phenomenon of anti-Communist politics came to be described as "McCarthyism," the senator from Wisconsin's role was more dramatic than innovative.

Since the 1930s, conservative critics of the New Deal had attempted to exploit the subversion issue. Anti-New Dealism coupled with fears of internal threats had led to the formation of the House Committee on Un-American Activities (HUAC) as a special committee in 1938 and to the subsequent annual extension of its authority and appropriations until it was made a permanent committee in 1945. For such House conservatives as John Rankin of Mississippi and J. Parnell Thomas of New Jersey, HUAC served a useful function in challenging the loyalty and principles of New Deal personnel.

HUAC became a serious threat to the administration only in 1949 in the aftermath of the Alger Hiss–Whittaker Chambers confrontation. A professed ex-Communist, Chambers was senior editor of *Time* magazine in 1948. In testimony before HUAC in August 1948, he accused Hiss, then president of the Carnegie Endowment for International Peace and a former employee of the AAA and the State Department, of having been a member of a Communist cell during the 1930s. At first denying that Hiss or other members of his alleged cell had engaged in espionage, Chambers on December 2, 1948, dramatically changed his accusations. Leading HUAC staff members to a pumpkin patch on his Westminster, Maryland, farm, Chambers produced three roles of microfilm of classified State Department documents (dated 1938), the so-called Pumpkin Papers. Thereafter the ex-Communist accused Hiss of having transmitted to Chambers classified documents, which he turned over to Soviet agents.

Chambers's testimony led HUAC to focus more narrowly on internal security issues. Thereafter, HUAC and its Senate counterpart, the Internal Security Subcommittee of the Committee on the Judiciary, publicized the gravity of the Communist threat to national security. In 1949, HUAC initiated an investigation into espionage in the atomic bomb project. In July, 1951, the Internal Security Subcommittee investigated the role of Communists and fellow travelers in the Institute for Pacific Relations, an academic institute specializing in the study of Far Eastern history. The institute, the committee concluded, had helped shape U.S. policy toward China and thereby had contributed to the defeat of the Chinese Nationalists.

While the communization of China in 1949 and the outbreak of the Korean War in 1950 precipitated McCarthyite anti-Communist politics during the 1950s, earlier events presaged the new domestic "red scare." As early as June 6, 1945, the FBI had raided the offices and private residences of the editors of an obscure Far Eastern periodical, *Amerasia*, and in the spring of 1946 a Canadian Royal Commission released a report detailing wartime Soviet espionage.

The 1945 FBI raid, using illegal entries and surveillances, uncovered 1,700 classified State and Navy Department documents. More important, the Canadian Royal Commission's investigation established that members of the Canadian Communist party in collaboration with military and scientific personnel had sought to transmit secrets involving wartime military installations and technology to the Soviet Union. Combined, the *Amerasia* raid and the Canadian report seemingly confirmed a serious internal security problem.

Seeking to capitalize on these developments, in the spring of 1946, a special House subcommittee, chaired by conservative southern Democrat Sam Hobbs of Alabama, uncovered examples of lax State Department security procedures. A subcommittee of the House Committee on Civil Service in the summer of 1946 initiated an investigation of federal employee loyalty and in July, 1946 recommended the enactment of legislation requiring that all federal employees be fingerprinted and the establishment of a special committee to ascertain whether additional internal security legislation was needed. In a companion action, on July 5, 1946, conservative Democratic Senator Pat McCarran of Nevada introduced a rider to a State Department appropriations bill authorizing the secretary of state to dismiss summarily all individuals whose continued employment he deemed dangerous to the national security. This rider was approved on August 16, 1946.

During the 1946 congressional campaign, moreover, Republican candidates seized on the loyalty issue. The choice facing the electorate, Republican National Committee Chairman B. Carroll Reece maintained, was "between communism and republicanism. . . . no taint of communism attaches to the Republican party. The same cannot be said of our opposition." Republican candidates also criticized continuance of federal wartime controls, housing and food shortages, postwar inflation, and labor unions following the upsurge of strikes during late 1945 and 1946. (One and one-half million man hours were lost in April 1945 owing to strikes and this figure increased to four million in September 1945 and twenty-three million by February 1946.) Republican campaign slogans suggested: "Had Enough? Vote Republican," "To Err is Truman," and "Under Truman: Two Families in Every Garage." So unpopular was Truman that pundits affirmed that the president's smartest move was not to campaign for Democratic candidates; in an effort to capture the magic of Truman's predecessor the demoralized Democrats played recordings of Roosevelt's voice.

This strategy paid off handsomely for Republicans, who won twenty-five governorships and for the first time since 1930 gained control of both houses of Congress: 245–188 in the House (with 1 American Laborite) and 51–45 in the Senate. The new Congress would be dominated by conservatives: newly elected Senators included Joseph McCarthy, William Jenner, and Zales Ecton; Republicans who had survived the lean years of the 1930s as consistent critics of New Deal policies would assume the chairmanships of important congressional committees. For these Republicans, the 1946 election results and their party's steady gains since 1938 were a mandate to repudiate the New Deal. And their control of committees like HUAC, Judiciary, and Appropriations insured that their assault on the New Deal would involve investigations into federal employee loyalty and administration security procedures.

The 1946 election results were not lost on a Truman administration already concerned about internal security matters. An earlier recommendation by the House civil service subcommittee that Congress tighten loyalty procedures had led Attorney General Tom Clark, for one, in July 1946 to urge Truman to institute a federal loyalty program. Expressing sympathy for the idea, Truman at first did nothing to implement it, simply keeping the proposal under study. The president developed a keen interest in this recommendation, however, following the congressional election.

In late November 1946, President Truman appointed the Temporary Commission on Employee Loyalty to study existing loyalty procedures and to recommend whether any action needed to be taken. Eager to retain the initiative, Truman directed the commission to report back to him by February 1, 1947. Political realities virtually insured that a formal loyalty program would be recommended. And on March 22, 1947, the president issued an executive order (9835) formally establishing the Federal Employee Loyalty Program. The objective of this program was the impossible standard of absolute security: the president asserting that the existence of "even one" disloyal employee would constitute a serious threat to national security.

All incumbent and prospective federal employees were required to undergo an intensive loyalty investigation administered by specially created departmental loyalty boards. These investigations covered all federal employees, janitors as well as atomic scientists. Federal employees would be dismissed if it were proven that "reasonable grounds exist for the belief that the individual is disloyal to the Government of the United

States." "Reasonable grounds" included past or present membership in alleged subversive organizations, and the accused employee, despite having the right to appeal his dismissal, was not guaranteed the right to question directly those who challenged his loyalty. And, although initially intended only for internal use in the conduct of the loyalty program, the attorney general's list of alleged subversive organizations was publicly released in December 1947. Private, state, and local employers soon used the list to judge the loyalty of their employees.

The administration's haste to undercut congressional conservatives had led it to create a poorly conceived yet far-reaching loyalty program. Even this program did not disarm congressional conservatives. Almost immediately they challenged the adequacy of the president's program. Responding again to pressure, the administration in time revised the program in ways that further undermined individual liberties and legitimized anti-Communist politics. Truman's appointees to administer the loyalty program were invariably individuals holding strongly conservative anti-Communist views. Moreover, in 1951 the president revised the standard for dismissal from proof of "disloyalty" to "reasonable doubt as to . . . loyalty." Not accidentally, then, the administration of the program was often unfair, and some employees were denied clearance simply because they opposed racial segregation or subscribed to liberal periodicals such as *The Nation* or the *New Republic*.

The compiling of loyalty files on federal employees, moreover, soon led to a confrontation between HUAC and the executive branch. In response to a March 1948 HUAC request for the loyalty file of the director of the Bureau of Standards, Edward Condon, President Truman issued an executive order prohibiting department heads from turning loyalty files over to congressional committees unless specifically authorized by the president. Truman's 1948 order changed the emerging congressional-executive debate from one centering on the adequacy of the administration's loyalty program to one involving congressional prerogatives and the executive's refusal to cooperate with ongoing congressional investigations. In 1948 and thereafter, Truman's bold assertion of the claim to executive privilege engendered considerable congressional protest and laid the basis for the charge that the motivation behind his order was a desire to "cover up."

LEGISLATIVE-EXECUTIVE CONFLICT

A conflict between the president and the Congress had been building over executive powers and the wisdom of New Deal policies. Indeed, HUAC's hearings of 1947 and 1948 coincided with a broader congressional effort to reverse New Deal programs. Congressional conservatives attempted to undercut federal policies instituted during the 1930s by reducing appropriations for rural electrification, public power, school lunches, and crop storage, by sharply reducing corporate and individual income taxes, and by enacting antilabor legislation (Taft-Hartley Act). In 1947, Congress also approved what in 1951 became the Twenty-Second Amendment, limiting the president to two terms, an indirect slap at Roosevelt's four-term presidency.

The flurry of labor strikes in 1945 and 1946 had increased popular support for legislation to curb the powers of labor unions. Responding to this sentiment and convinced that the Wagner Act of 1935 favored unionization, congressional conservatives secured passage of a measure, the Taft-Hartley Act, to outlaw "unfair labor practices." This bill specifically prohibited secondary boycotts, jurisdictional strikes, the closed shop, and union political contributions; made unions liable for breach of contracts with management; authorized employers to petition the NLRB for new representational elections when they concluded that a recognized union no longer commanded majority support; denied NLRB rights to unions having Communist officers; and (through the controversial section 14b) permitted individual states to enact laws banning the closed shop (the so-called "right-to-work" laws). Responding to the serious European crisis created by the existence of nearly one million displaced persons living in Germany, Austria, and Italy, and 600,000 in U.S. camps, the conservative 80th Congress enacted the Displaced Persons Act of 1948, guided by nativist sentiments and replete with discriminatory provisions. Relaxing existing immigration laws to permit the admission of only 200,000 displaced persons over a two-year period, the Congress further adopted specific provisions to govern eligibility: 30 percent of those admitted must have been agricultural workers and 40 percent former residents of the Protestant Baltic states (thereby discriminating against Catholics and Jews), and only those could be admitted who had entered Western-occupied zones before December 22, 1945 (eliminating approximately 100,000 Jews).

Condemning the Displaced Persons Bill's "callous discrimination" against Catholics and Jews, Truman nonetheless signed the measure into law on June 25, 1948. On June 20, 1947 he vetoed the Taft-Hartley Bill, denouncing it as a "slave labor bill" and as insuring an increase in labor strife. Although his veto was overridden, Truman's action enabled the president to lay claim to being a friend of the workingman. The veto also undercut union hostility to his administration that had resulted from his 1946 efforts to break the railroad workers' strike. Unable to shape congressional policy, Truman frequently resorted to the veto—which enabled him to acquire a liberal image and to identify the Republican Congress with reaction. In 1947, the President successfully vetoed a tax-reduction bill, claiming that it granted savings of only $30 to those having annual incomes under $2,000 but $5,000 to those in the $50,000 bracket. (In 1948 Congress passed a modified version of this measure over the president's veto.) Truman also vetoed a protectionist wool bill (he claimed that it undercut administration efforts to negotiate reciprocal trade agreements), pocket-vetoed a bill establishing the National Science

Foundation (he claimed that placing the proposed foundation outside presidential control negated the president's administrative responsibility), pocket-vetoed a bill that would have excluded newspaper vendors from social security coverage (Congress overrode Truman's veto of this bill in 1948), and unsuccessfully vetoed a measure exempting motor carrier associations from antitrust prosecutions.

At first, Truman sought to cooperate with Congress, in part out of a desire to insure congressional approval for his major foreign policy recommendations (the Truman Doctrine and the Marshall Plan) and in part out of personal belief. By late 1947 (on the advice of White House counsel Clark Clifford, among others), Truman reversed this strategy of accommodation.

To insure renomination and then reelection, Clifford advised Truman, the president would have to acquire a more liberal image and thereby undercut former Vice President Henry A. Wallace's appeal to many New Deal liberals who had become disenchanted with Truman's foreign and domestic policies. In 1948, the obstacles to Truman's renomination and reelection appeared overwhelming. The Roosevelt Democratic coalition was on the verge of collapsing, as the radical wing of the party rallied behind Wallace, and many conservative southern Democrats threatened to defect over the administration's civil rights program. In addition, many labor leaders, particularly in the left-wing CIO unions, were disturbed by the administration's belligerent foreign policy, its support for a loyalty program, and its actions in 1946 against railroad and coal miners' unions.

In early 1948, Truman, acting on Clifford's advice, sought to retain the support of liberals, labor, and southerners by exploiting their fears of the Republican-controlled 80th Congress. Appealing to labor, he vetoed the Taft-Hartley Bill and pointedly denounced this "slave labor" measure. Truman also appealed to liberals by extending diplomatic recognition to Israel on May 14, 1948, the same day the independent state was created and, more specifically, to Afro-Americans by proposing a bold civil rights program. More generally, the president and his supporters appealed to liberal fears of the 80th Congress and sought to "red-bait" the Wallace campaign.

Truman's revival of a domestic New Deal as a Fair Deal, however, complicated the president's relationship with the conservative southern wing of the Democratic party. When more liberal party members led by Minneapolis mayor, Hubert Humphrey (a candidate for the U. S. Senate), compelled the Democratic National Convention, meeting in Philadelphia in July, to adopt a strong civil rights plank by a narrow vote, 300 infuriated southern delegates walked out of the convention. One week later, on July 17, delegates from thirteen southern states convened in Birmingham, Alabama and nominated a States Right (Dixiecrat) party ticket of Governor Strom Thurmond (South Carolina) and Fielding Wright (Mississippi). (That same month, Truman issued two executive orders desegregating the federal civil service and the armed services.)

Confronted by these divisions, by the reluctant support even of the party faithful, Truman adopted an aggressive campaign strategy; its essence was revealed in an electrifying acceptance speech he delivered at the convention. He announced that he was calling Congress back into special session on July 26 to vote on a series of needed measures. Truman pointedly emphasized that in their 1948 platform the Republicans had pledged to enact these proposals. In this effort, Truman sought both to dramatize Republican duplicity and, more important, to make the "reactionary" record of the 80th Congress (Truman's specific phrasing) *the* issue of the ensuing campaign. The 80th Congress, Truman subsequently charged, had passed a labor bill that could "enslave totally the workingman," had "stuck a pitchfork in the backs of farmers," and had passed an "anti-Semitic, anti-Catholic" immigration bill. If the Republicans came to power, he warned the voters, America would become "an economic colony of Wall Street."

The Republicans had held their convention earlier in July. Their proceedings were characterized by a minimum of recrimination, as the Republicans caucused with full confidence that they were selecting the next president of the United States. New York Governor Thomas Dewey's efficient organization and skillful efforts at projecting an image of statesmanship secured him the nomination on the third ballot. His subsequent campaign emphasized the need for unity and amounted to an indirect assault on the divisiveness of Truman's appeals to diverse interest groups—whether blacks, ethnics, Catholics, organized labor, or farmers. In the ensuing months, Dewey acted as if he had already won the presidency. His campaign statements consisted of glittering generalities, and he sought to concentrate his efforts in a way that would insure Republican victories in closely contested senatorial and gubernatorial races.

Dewey's conviction that his election was assured was based on a split Democratic party, Truman's unpopularity, and the predictions of professional pollsters and commentators. In 1948, Dewey received not only the editorial support of 65 percent of the nation's dailies to Truman's 15 percent but their confident predictions of his inevitable victory. In its election eve coverage the *New York Times,* for example, estimated that Dewey would win 345 electoral votes to Truman's 105 and Thurmond's 38. And a *Chicago Tribune* banner headline in an early edition that went to press before the election results were in reflected the overwhelming judgment of the professional pollsters and columnists: DEWEY DEFEATS TRUMAN.

Voter turn-out in 1948 was surprisingly low—less than 55 percent of eligible voters. Nonetheless, Truman won, polling 24,179,349 popular votes (49.5 percent) and winning twenty-eight states with 303 electoral votes to Dewey's 21,991,291 popular votes (45.1 percent) and 189 electoral votes (carrying only sixteen states). Thurmond received only 1,176,125 popular and 39 electoral votes, carrying the Deep South states of South Carolina, Mississippi, Alabama, and Louisiana. Wallace's can-

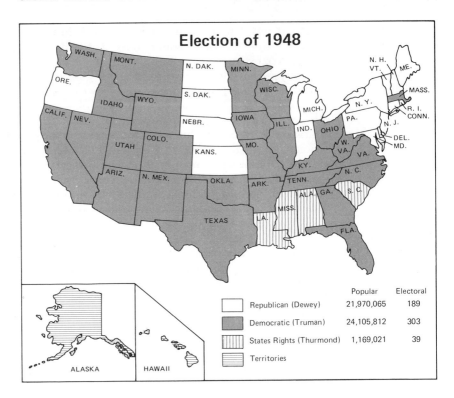

Election of 1948

	Popular	Electoral
Republican (Dewey)	21,970,065	189
Democratic (Truman)	24,105,812	303
States Rights (Thurmond)	1,169,021	39
Territories		

ALASKA   HAWAII

didacy had not made the predictably large inroads into northern urban
and industrial support for the Democratic ticket. He polled but 1,157,326
popular votes. The defection of southern conservatives and northern
liberals, then, had not cost Truman reelection. By invoking the legacy of
Roosevelt and the sins of the Republicans, Truman had secured the
support of many liberals, blacks, laborers, middle-income groups, small
businessmen, and farmers who feared that a Democratic defeat could
mean a reversal of the New Deal. This strategy also enabled the Democrats to gain control of Congress: 263–171 in the House and 54–42 in the
Senate.

The Truman victory, however, was no mandate for future reform.
The president had waged an effective negative campaign, appealing to
the fears of many Americans for whom the Great Depression was a recent
experience. This strategy succeeded owing to the intemperate anti-New
Dealism of leading elements of the 80th Congress and HUAC's crude
partisanship. In 1948, many Americans had voted to retain those benefits
they already enjoyed.

Nonetheless, Truman interpreted his 1948 victory as a mandate for a
legislative program that could both relieve economic inequalities and
restore the battered New Deal coalition. Responsive to the Cold War

liberalism symbolized by the Americans for Democratic Action, Truman described this program as a Fair Deal (seeking thereby to distinguish his objectives from those of the Roosevelt New Deal). His recommendations included repeal of the Taft-Hartley Act, a fairer and more progressive tax structure, a minimum wage base of seventy-five cents an hour, expansion of social security, civil rights legislation, resource development and public power legislation, national medical insurance, and federal aid to education. The president's proposed farm program, the Brannan Plan, symbolized this political effort (to forge a liberal-labor-farmer coalition) and the departure from New Deal policies. Truman proposed instead to abandon production controls in favor of a system basing government price supports on the size of the farmer's crop (with a maximum limit of $26,100 in support payments).

McCARTHYISM AND PARTISAN POLITICS

Truman's successful strategy of attacking Congress and accusing his Republican opponents of selfish motives exacerbated already tense executive-legislative relations. This conflict shaped the politics of the ensuing years. To Republican strategists, Truman's victory had demonstrated the popularity of New Deal principles and the need to adopt a different strategy. Thereafter, they sought to exploit "national security" concerns by a crude strategy. Beginning in 1949, moderate and conservative Republican congressmen rather than simply attacking the New Deal began to condemn sharply past administration foreign policy decisions, to question the adequacy of presidential internal security procedures, and to tar executive personnel with the brush of "appeasement" or "disloyalty." Conservative Republican Senator Robert Taft (known as Mr. Republican) advised his fellow Republicans that "We cannot possibly win the next election unless we point out the utter failure and incapacity of the Truman Administration to conduct foreign policy. . . . We cannot possibly win on domestic policy, because every domestic policy depends entirely on foreign policy." This failure, the Republican senator pointedly emphasized in another speech, was the result of internal subversion: "The greatest Kremlin asset in our history has been the pro-Communist group in the State Department who succumbed to every demand of Russia at Yalta and Potsdam and promoted at every opportunity the Communist cause in China until today [1950] Communism threatens to take over all of Asia."

The immediate setting for these charges were two events in 1949–1950: the Chinese Communist defeat of the Chinese Nationalists and the Soviet explosion of an atomic bomb. The loss of its atomic monopoly was especially galling to many Americans. The public rationale for the security procedures instituted under the Atomic Energy Act of 1946 had been to preserve the American atomic monopoly and key military officials had claimed that the United States could retain this monopoly for twenty years. President Truman's announcement thus elicited conservative accusations that this development owed less to Soviet science and technology than to Soviet subversion.

A number of events, which dominated the news in 1949 and 1950, seemingly confirmed both the existence of a major subversive threat and the inadequacy of administration internal security efforts in coping with this threat. On March 6, 1949, Judith Coplon, a Justice Department employee, was arrested and tried on the charge of having given departmental secrets to a Soviet UN employee. On July 20, 1948, the twelve leaders of the U. S. Communist party had been indicted under the Smith Act, and their trial lasted through 1949 and dominated news coverage. Simultaneously, on December 15, 1948, Alger Hiss was indicted and tried on two counts of perjury. His first trial in early 1949 ended in a hung jury; in the second trial, Hiss was found guilty and sentenced in January 1950. Then, on February 3, 1950, Klaus Fuchs was arrested in Great Britain and confessed that while employed at the Los Alamos, New Mexico, atomic bomb project during 1943–45 he had passed atomic secrets to Soviet agents. His confession soon led to the arrest of Julius and Ethel Rosenberg and to widely publicized FBI charges of an atomic espionage ring. These events combined to identify Communist party membership or popular front activities with disloyalty and treason. More important, the idea was fostered that subversion (and not Soviet power or resources) was the basis for the extension of Soviet international influence.

In the midst of this charged atmosphere Senator Joseph R. McCarthy burst onto the national scene. In a now-famous February 9, 1950, speech in Wheeling, West Virginia, launching a rancorous politics dubbed "McCarthyism," the Wisconsin senator attributed the extension of Soviet influence during the postwar years, and the origins of the Cold War, directly to Communist infiltration of the State Department. The specificity of McCarthy's citation of the number of "known Communists" in the State Department (the figure he cited was 205 in the Wheeling speech, 57 in February speeches in Reno, Nevada and Salt Lake City, Utah, 81 in a February 20 speech on the Senate floor) seemingly offered a definite explanation as to why the United States was enmeshed in a frustrating Cold War: Communist infiltration had resulted in the Roosevelt administration's "appeasement" policy and the Truman administration's unwillingness to reverse that policy. McCarthy's charges became the basis for a Republican strategy that capitalized on the popular conviction of American omnipotence and disaffection over the unilateralism by which presidents had conducted foreign and internal security policy.

Truman and the Democrats found it difficult to dismiss McCarthy's Communists in Government charges as simply partisan politics. To defuse McCarthy's appeal, Senate Democrats, led by Millard Tydings of Maryland, on February 22, 1950 introduced a resolution to establish a special subcommittee to investigate the senator's claim of evidence linking eighty-one State Department employees to communism. The so-called Tydings Committee, however, failed to discredit the Wisconsin Senator. A complex of factors insured this: including Truman's refusal to permit unlimited access by the committee to the loyalty files of the "eighty-one cases" enumerated on February 20 by Senator McCarthy, Republican support of McCarthy for reasons of partisan politics (supporters included Senators Robert Taft and Henry Cabot Lodge, Jr., and Republican National Committee Chairman Guy Gabrielson), and the outbreak of the Korean War in June, 1950.

In the Communist issue, the Republicans had uncovered a means of reaping political benefits. Following a Republican Senate Policy Committee meeting of March 22, 1950, indeed, Senator Taft privately advised McCarthy that he should "keep talking and if one case doesn't work out, proceed with another one." The Korean War, moreover, involved the nation in a frustrating, lengthy undeclared war, and one wherein the Truman Administration sought by a limited war strategy to avert intensification into a major military confrontation with the Soviet Union and the People's Republic of China. As one byproduct, the war increased popular frustration with Truman's leadership and with the policy of containment. The Korean War became Truman's war—it had not been declared by an act of Congress but through presidential initiative. Truman refused to utilize atomic weapons to achieve victory. In April 1951 he fired General Douglas MacArthur, then commander-in-chief of UN forces in Korea, because the General opposed the president's cautious military policy. Why, many Americans asked, were U.S. military resources not fully utilized? Why was General MacArthur shackled, thereby preventing the attainment of "victory over communism"? Responding to these doubts, Republicans offered the simple explanation: the influence of "Communists in government"!

This combination of popular frustration and Republican strategy also resulted in congressional passage, over Truman's veto, of the Internal Security Act of September 1950. The so-called McCarran Act provided for the forced detention of aliens liable for deportation who were denied admission to their native lands; it also barred Communists from employment in defense industries and from securing passports. Communist, Communist-front, and Communist-action groups were required to submit lists of their members and publications and to register as agents of a foreign power with a specially created Subversive Activities Control Board. Whenever the president declared a situation of national emergency, moreover, "dangerous radicals" could be rounded up and forcibly detained in special camps. (Ironically, Senate liberals had first proposed this concentration camp provision in a substitute internal security measure of August 1950.) In a companion legislative effort, Congress enacted Public Law 733 empowering Cabinet officials to dismiss summarily, without hearings or due process, federal employees deemed to be "security risks."

By late 1950, the debate over internal security policy had so narrowed that traditional defenders of civil liberties, whether the conservative Robert Taft or the liberal Hubert Humphrey, excluded Communists from the protection of established constitutional guarantees. In 1954, Humphrey urged passage of a proposed anti-Communist bill by admonishing his colleagues: "Either senators are for recognizing the Communist party for what it is or they will continue to trip over the niceties of legal technicalities and details." And, U.S. Attorney General J. Howard McGrath in speeches before law enforcement and fraternal organizations in 1949 and 1950 exaggerated the peril that Communists posed to American liberties and security. "There are today many Communists in America," he warned. "They are everywhere—in factories, offices, butcher stores, on street corners, in private business—and each carries in himself the germs of death for society." To meet this peril, the Department of Justice in 1951 introduced and lobbied for legislation to legalize wiretapping, to repeal the statute of limitations in espionage cases, to grant immunity for testimony involving national security before grand juries and congressional committees, and to expedite prosecution in perjury cases. Without seeking new legislation, the department drastically expanded FBI surveillance authority to focus on left-wing political activists.

Nor did the Supreme Court (reconstituted during the Truman years, as four new justices were appointed between 1945 and 1950) thwart federal challenges to first amendment guarantees. In two major decisions in *Bailey* v. *Richardson* (1951) and *Dennis* v. *U.S.* (1951), the Court imposed no constitutional restrictions over the procedures unilaterally established by the president in administering a federal employee loyalty program, upheld the constitutionality of the Smith Act, and extended the "clear and present danger" principle of the Schenck case (1919) to a new standard of "appreciable probability."

"National security" fears had moved American politics sharply to the right. The 1950 congressional elections returned conservative candidates of both parties to Congress, with the Republicans reducing Democratic majorities to 234–198 in the House and 49–47 in the Senate. Seeking to institutionalize this politics, in December 1950 the Senate established its own counterpart to HUAC, the internal security subcommittee of the Committee on the Judiciary. In an attempt to promote Senator McCarthy's campaign, in 1951 the Republican caucus appointed the Wisconsin senator to the powerful Appropriations Committee. And by exploiting the unpopularity of summit diplomacy to justify restrictions on executive authority, conservative senators in February 1952 proposed a constitutional amendment, the so-called Bricker Amendment, requiring congressional ratification of all executive agreements and treaties that affected domestic policy.

Cold War "national security" fears, by shifting politics rightward, also undermined Truman's Fair Deal legislative program of civil rights, housing reform, medical care, repeal of Taft-Hartley, Point IV aid to underdeveloped countries, and agricultural relief. The administration's

Joe McCarthy, the junior senator from Wisconsin, in
action at Senate hearing
(Wide World Photos)

proposal, the Brannan Plan, to resolve the perennial problem of farm
surpluses by imposing a maximum limit on production payments, never
came to a vote in Congress. Administration attempts to secure congressional approval for the establishment of a permanent Fair Employment
Practices Committee, national health insurance, federal aid to education,
and repeal of Taft-Hartley were all defeated. Critics of these measures
moreover couched their opposition in anti-Communist terms. Truman
succeeded only in extending social security coverage to ten million workers, in liberalizing social security and minimum wage provisions, and in
securing the Housing Act of 1949. This Act funded the construction of
810,000 low-income housing units and slum renewal and authorized
federal mortgage assistance to middle-income groups.

Consistent with the national security emphasis of the Cold War
years, Truman's most notable legislative achievements were not domestic
reforms but the Truman Doctrine, the Marshall Plan, NATO, the Na-

tional Security Act of 1947, the Atomic Energy Act of 1946, and the Selective Service Act of 1948 (the latter establishing a permanent peacetime draft).

By the 1950s anti-Communist politics narrowly restricted political debate, stifled dissent, and caused many Americans to question the loyalty of those advocating domestic reform. More important, by 1952, a confrontation situation existed between Congress and the president over the resort to executive secrecy and executive privilege and the president's unilateral conduct of foreign and internal security policy. Indeed, part of the appeal of Senator McCarthy and other conservative congressmen derived from their attack on secret conduct of foreign policy, and the removal of basic decisions from popular or congressional control. In this sense, the McCarthyite protest was democratic, and sought to insure presidential accountability. Established conservative leaders, such as Robert Taft and John Bricker, may have been disturbed over the crudity of McCarthy's tactics. Yet, they supported the Wisconsin senator to discredit New Deal principles as well as to reestablish a balance between Congress and the executive. Taft expressed these priorities when he claimed "whether McCarthy has legal evidence, whether he has overstated or understated his case, is of lesser importance. The question is whether the Communist influence in the State Department still exists."

Ironically, however, despite all the sound and fury of the postwar debate, Truman bequeathed a strengthened presidency to his successor. Decision making remained unilateral and secretive: despite the McCarthy assault, Truman extended security classification and claims to executive privilege. His successor, President Dwight D. Eisenhower, would be forced to confront this legacy and to decide whether or not to reverse Truman's transformation of the presidency.

SELECTED BIBLIOGRAPHY FOR SECTION VI

Two essential books on American foreign policy before World War II are WALTER JOHNSON, *The Battle Against Isolationism* (1944) and MARK L. CHADWIN, *The Warhawks: American Interventionists before Pearl Harbor* (1968).* In his *Wartime Journals* (1970), CHARLES LINDBERGH vigorously presents the isolationist case. Reinterpretations of American foreign policy are numerous. The "old isolationist school" is best represented by CHARLES A. BEARD's two books, *American Foreign Policy in the Making, 1932–1940* (1946) and *President Roosevelt and the Coming of the War, 1941* (1948). C. C. TANSILL's sharp criticism of Roosevelt, *Back Door to War: Roosevelt's Foreign Policy, 1933–1941* (1952) is answered, albeit indirectly, by HERBERT FEIS, *The Road to Pearl Harbor* (1950).* WILLIAM A. WILLIAMS, *The Tragedy of American Diplomacy* (1962) *

* Available in paperback.

ushered in a second wave of criticism of U.S. foreign policy. For a more recent economic analysis, see LLOYD C. GARDNER, *Economic Aspects of New Deal Diplomacy* (1964).*

HERBERT FEIS, in his three volumes, *The China Tangle* (1953),* *Churchill, Roosevelt, Stalin* (1957),* and *The Atomic Bomb and the End of World War II* (1966),* provides useful insights into wartime diplomacy. GABRIEL KOLKO, *The Politics of War: The World and United States Foreign Policy, 1943–1945* (1969)* presents a leftist analysis of the war years. Soviet-American wartime relations, especially the agreements reached at Yalta, are criticized from the right in WILLIAM H. CHAMBERLAIN, *America's Second Crusade* (1950).* These relations are defended by a Roosevelt administration member in E. R. STETTINIUS, *Roosevelt and the Russians: The Yalta Conference* (1949) and analyzed from the left in DIANE S. CLEMENS, *Yalta* (1970).*

The best general study of the war on the homefront is now JOHN MORTON BLUM, *V Was for Victory: Politics and American Culture during World War II* (1976). Also see RICHARD POLENBERG, *War and Society, 1941–1945* (1972)*; R. E. MERRILL, *Social Problems on the Home Front* (1948); and JACK GOODMAN, ed., *While You Were Gone: A Report on Wartime Life in the United States* (1946). On black Americans during the war, see GUNNAR MYRDAL, *An American Dilemma* (1944)*; LOUIS RUCHAMES, *Race, Jobs, and Politics: The Story of FEPC* (1953); and RICHARD M. DALFIUME, *Desegregation of the United States Armed Forces* (1969). Labor during the war is treated in SAUL D. ALINSKY, *John L. Lewis* (1970 ed.)*; MATTHEW JOSEPHSON, *Sidney Hillman: Statesman of American Labor* (1952); and IRVING HOWE and B. J. WIDICK, *The UAW and Walter Reuther* (1949).

Among the better general studies of the Cold War are LOUIS J. HALLE, *The Cold War as History* (1967)*; ANDRÉ FONTAINE, *History of the Cold War* (2 vols., 1968–69); LLOYD GARDNER, *Architects of Illusion* (1970)*; WALTER LAFEBER, *America, Russia, and the Cold War, 1945–1966* (1968)*; LYNN DAVIS, *The Cold War Begins* (1974); and JOHN L. GADDIS, *The United States and the Origins of the Cold War, 1941–1947* (1972).* Diplomacy as seen from the Russian side can be followed in M. D. SHULMAN, *Stalin's Foreign Policy Reappraised* (1963)* and ADAM ULAM, *Expansion and Coexistence* (1974).* Other important studies are HERBERT FEIS, *From Trust to Terror: The Onset of the Cold War, 1945–1970* (1970)*; DAVID HOROWITZ, *The Free World Colossus: A Critique of American Foreign Policy in the Cold War* (1965)*; STEPHEN A. AMBROSE, *Rise to Globalism: A Critique of American Foreign Policy* (1971)*; RICHARD J. BARNET, *Roots of War* (1972)*; GABRIEL and JOYCE KOLKO, *The Limits of Power* (1972)*; GAR ALPEROVITZ, *Atomic Diplomacy* (1965)*; and the best and most recent analysis of nuclear diplomacy, MARTIN J. SHERWIN, *A World Destroyed: The Atomic Bomb and the Grand Alliance* (1975).* The Cold War in Asia may be followed best in HERBERT FEIS, *Contest over Japan* (1967)*; JOHN K. FAIRBANKS, *The United States and China, 1941–1950* (1965)*; TANG TSOU, *America's*

Failure in China (1963) *; BARBARA TUCHMAN, *Stillwell and the American Experience in China, 1941–1945* (1970) *; DAVID REES, *Korea: The Limited War* (1964) ; and G. D. PAIGE, *The Korean Decision: June 24–30* (1950). For a sharp criticism of revisionist studies of the Cold War, see ROBERT W. TUCKER, *The Radical Left and the Origins of the Cold War* (1973).*

As with the literature on the Cold War, historical interpretations of the domestic policies of the Truman Administration have diverged sharply. There is no good historical study surveying the period as a whole. The most comprehensive surveys are ALONZO HAMBY, *Beyond the New Deal* (1973) ; LAWRENCE WITTNER, *Cold War America* (1974) *; and BERT COCHRAN, *Harry Truman and the Crisis Presidency* (1973). Most works have focused on specific issues, with the major focus on civil rights, McCarthyism, and internal security policy. The best books on these themes include ATHAN THEOHARIS, *Seeds of Repression* (1971) *; ROBERT GRIFFITH, *The Politics of Fear* (1970) *; RICHARD FREELAND, *The Truman Doctrine and the Origins of McCarthyism* (1972) *; RICHARD FRIED, *Men Against McCarthy* (1976) ; EARL LATHAM, *The Communist Controversy in Washington* (1966) ; ROBERT GRIFFITH and ATHAN THEOHARIS, eds., *The Specter* (1974) *; BARTON BERNSTEIN, ed., *Politics and Policies of the Truman Administration* (1970) *; MORTON HALPERIN et al., *The Lawless State* (1976) *; and WILLIAM BERMAN, *The Politics of Civil Rights in the Truman Administration* (1970). Economic policy and the major political issues are surveyed in STEPHEN BAILEY, *Congress Makes a Law* (1959) ; R. ALTON LEE, *Truman and Taft-Hartley* (1966) ; ALLEN MATUSOW, *Farm Politics and Policies of the Truman Administration* (1967) ; RICHARD DAVIES, *Housing Reform During the Truman Administration* (1966) ; JAMES PATTERSON, *Mr. Republican* (1972) ; SUSAN HARTMANN, *Truman and the 80th Congress* (1971) ; and NORMAN MARKOWITZ, *The Rise and Fall of the People's Century* (1973).

VII

The Eisenhower Decade
and After

In 1953 the Republicans returned to national political power for the first time in
two decades as General Dwight David Eisenhower became the new president.
Instead of reversing five terms of Democratic rule, President Eisenhower in effect
institutionalized the reforms of the New Deal and Fair Deal. He also pursued
the same foreign policies as his Democratic predecessors. Under Eisenhower both
the welfare-warfare state and the Cold War became the accepted modes of
domestic politics and diplomacy.

   If the Eisenhower Republicans wrought no great changes in either domestic
affairs or foreign policy, population shifts and economic changes did begin
to realign domestic politics. For the first time since the end of post–Civil War
Reconstruction, the Republican party during the Eisenhower years began to
make inroads in the hitherto one-party South. Increasingly losing its identification
as the party of civil rights and black Americans (a process begun during the
Roosevelt years), the Republican party now won support among affluent urban
and suburban white southern segregationists. And as population grew rapidly
in the South and Southwest and industry led and followed the movement
of peoples, what subsequently became characterized as the "southern rim"
or "sunbelt" gained greater importance in national politics.

For eight years the general as president presided over an apparently quiet and tranquil nation, one that had survived the storms of McCarthyism and succeeded in keeping a cold war from turning hot. It was a time noted for its conformity, domesticity, and conspicuous consumption, a time when Americans turned away from public affairs and concentrated on private satisfactions. Yet the placidity and conformity of the 1950s, rather than lulling citizens permanently to sleep, seemed to precipitate instead a new demand for political activism, which brought the youthful John F. Kennedy to the presidency. And the new president, unlike Eisenhower, promised Americans challenge, adventure, and action. During his all too brief and tragic presidency, Kennedy's twentieth-century American Camelot proved more image than reality, more showmanship than substance.

24

The General as President: The Politics of Stability and Tranquillity 1953-1960

As Franklin Delano Roosevelt personally dominated national politics from 1933 to 1945, so did Dwight David Eisenhower during the years 1953 to 1960. Eisenhower's dominance differed from Roosevelt's, however, in two important respects: he failed to transform national values, and he failed to extend his popularity and electoral appeal to his party. Throughout this period, the Republicans remained a minority party. The Republicans did capture control of Congress in 1952, but their margin was narrow (48–47, and 1 independent in the Senate and 221–213 in the House) and their triumph short-lived. The Democrats regained control of Congress in the 1954 congressional elections (48–47, and 1 independent in the Senate and 232–203 in the House), sustained this control despite Eisenhower's sweeping reelection victory of 1956 (49–47 in the Senate and 234–201 in the House), and in the 1958 congressional elections, increased their Senate majority to 64–34 and House majority to 282–154. National attitudes concerning the proper role of the federal government and presidential powers, however, were never altered—despite frequent Republican campaign pledges of 1952 and thereafter. New Deal programs were sustained and power remained centralized in the presidency.

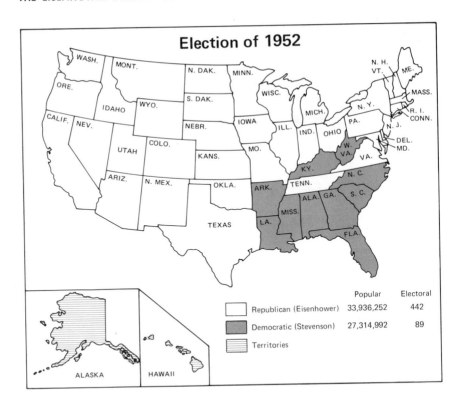

Election of 1952

	Popular	Electoral
Republican (Eisenhower)	33,936,252	442
Democratic (Stevenson)	27,314,992	89
Territories		

Although voters responded to the 1952 Republican campaign theme of "time for a change," they were not then committed to repudiating the New Deal. To be sure, the temper of the country was conservative. Nonetheless, the public still endorsed the principles of federal controls over the economy and federal responsibility to promote economic growth. Popular conservatism derived from a fear of threats to national security and, from this, of internal social and economic reform. Republican leaders had earlier ridden anti-Communist themes to political success, charging the Democratic administration of Harry S. Truman with "softness toward communism" and harboring "Communists in Government," and equating dissent and reform with disloyalty and treason. Their success, however, derived from public concern over international, not domestic, developments.

THE POLITICS OF IMAGE

The foremost practitioner of conservative anti-Communist politics had not been Dwight D. Eisenhower but the conservative Ohio senator, Robert Taft. The early favorite to win the Republican presidential nomination of 1952, Taft had then raised the traditional conservative complaint that New Deal–Fair Deal programs threatened individual liberties and private property. Moving beyond the politics of the 1930s, Taft criticized the Democrats for tolerating Communist subversion. Thus, he specifically supported as "fully justified" Senator McCarthy's demand for an investigation of the Department of State. The FBI, the Ohio Republican further charged, had been shackled: its investigative reports had been ignored by an administration viewing Communists as simply "just another form of Democrats."

The emotionalism of Taft's rhetoric, the partisanship of his attack on the Democrats, and his identification with opposition to New Deal and Fair Deal reforms had made him a controversial candidate. These positions, combined with his support for retrenchment in overseas commitments and resistance to the militarization of U.S. foreign policy, made his candidacy anathema to many eastern Republicans. In early 1952, some of these Republicans (notably Henry Cabot Lodge, Jr., Sherman Adams, and Thomas Dewey) sought to draft Eisenhower, then NATO commander, in an effort to stop Taft. In Eisenhower, these Republicans saw a candidate possessing numerous positive qualities: he was noncontroversial, not identified with the McCarthyite right, had a national reputation as a war hero, and unlike Taft, supported the general outlines of the Truman administration's bipartisan foreign policy.

Despite an image of moderation and nonpartisanship (at the time few really knew his party affiliation), Eisenhower was conservative in his political philosophy and identified with the corporate business community. His conservatism was reflected in his grave concern about the consequences of the previous Democratic administration's spending policies and in his belief that the budget must be balanced. An ardent anti-Communist, Eisenhower pointedly articulated his deep concern about the grave internal security threat confronting American society in a June 4, 1952, address in Abilene, Kansas. This address initiated a concerted campaign for delegate votes. Candidate Eisenhower demanded the elimination from government service of "any kind of Communist, subversive, or pinkish influence."

Unlike Taft or the McCarthyites, Eisenhower could effectively exploit popular aversion to politicians and fears of internal subversion. Not directly identified with the Republican party's conservative wing, he could raise the subversive issue without seeming to threaten the accomplishments of the New Deal. In addition, Eisenhower projected the images of the amateur in politics, of a disinterested public servant, and of an honest man of simple tastes and democratic principles. Yet beneath this mask lay a shrewd and at times ruthless politician.

Eisenhower was not simply a son of Abilene, Kansas. He had grown up there, to be sure, but had gone on to attend West Point and to embark on a career as a sophisticated organization and public relations man. His meteoric rise in the army during the 1930s and 1940s derived not from brilliance on the battlefield as a tactician or strategist but rather as a publicist and an organizer of men and supplies. During the 1930s, he wrote speeches for General Douglas MacArthur, demonstrating his abilities as press agent and editor. Subsequently, as commander of Allied forces during World War II, the general proved his organizational genius. His thirty-month return to civilian life as president of Columbia University (in 1948) involved him in fund-raising activities wherein he established close ties with leaders of the New York business and financial community. Thereafter, his closest friends and associates came from the corporate community and not West Point or Abilene. The image of simplicity and innocence masked a man of proven organizational abilities who had acquired cosmopolitan values far removed from those of rural Abilene.

Similarly, Eisenhower's literary work demonstrated a keen sense of the importance of precision and clarity. This work stood in stark contrast to his responses during presidential press conferences. Eisenhower press conferences were frequently characterized by mangled syntax and confused (and confusing) phrasings as well as by the president's frequently expressed ignorance about specific issues raised by the Washington press corps. Thus, when confronted by difficult or potentially compromising questions, the president oftentimes responded obtusely. Pressed during a May 22, 1957 press conference as to whether he "would be more disposed to support those [Republicans] who do back your program and less disposed to back those who do not, next year," Eisenhower replied: "I think it will be a pity if ever we tried to organize political parties that are based upon slavish adherence to every detail and concept of government that can be advanced. But, I do believe this: when a political party gets together and agrees upon a platform and that platform is presented to the American public as the political basis of which they are going to try to conduct the government if elected, they should remain true to it. So, I have no right and no desire to punish anybody. I just say this: I am committed to the support of the people who believe as I do, that the Republican platform of 1956 must be our political doctrine."

Cultivating his image as an amateur, of a man having limited interest in secondary issues Eisenhower delegated authority broadly through a hierarchical staff system. He successfully controlled the flow of information. His press conferences, held regularly, conveyed the image of accessibility and accountability and yet avoided the pitfalls of embarrassing disclosures. In contrast to his image as an amateur not fully knowledgeable about detail, Eisenhower was briefed by twenty to thirty aides before each press conference on matters that might come up. The decision to express ignorance was thus a political ploy to control what became public knowledge. So too was Eisenhower's resort to confusing phrasings. Indeed, during the crisis of 1955 precipitated by the Chinese Communists' shelling of the Nationalist-held islands of Quemoy and Matsu, James Haggerty urged the president to respond "no comment" to any question raised about this matter at a scheduled press conference.

Rejecting this advice, Eisenhower assured his press secretary: "Don't worry, Jim. If that question comes up I'll just confuse them."

Eisenhower's reputation as a conciliator and also a man who delegated authority further strengthened his control over national politics. Despite a contemporary reputation as a man who abjured responsibility, and who deferred to his expert advisers, in practice Eisenhower followed events closely and was a shrewd and perceptive questioner during Cabinet and National Security Council meetings. The president did not blindly accept the advice of others, knew how to delegate authority, distinguished between major and minor matters (delegating the latter to administrative assistant Sherman Adams or Vice President Richard Nixon), and used the White House staff system to insulate himself from unwanted pressures. Moreover, Eisenhower made all major policy decisions, whether to oppose the British-French military action in the Suez crisis of 1956 or to insure Senate rejection of the Bricker Amendment in 1954. Typically Secretary of State John Foster Dulles, or some other responsible official, would announce these decisions and bear the brunt of criticism. Eisenhower also cloaked his taste for political power by frequent golfing, hunting, and fishing excursions. This posturing, however, masked a hard-working and domineering president.

EXECUTIVE POWERS, CONGRESS, AND McCARTHYISM

An important theme of Republican protests since 1950 had been to condemn the abuses of power deriving from the Roosevelt and Truman administrations' secretive conduct of foreign policy. To redress this situation, the Republican congressional leadership had championed two measures: resolutions to repudiate the Yalta agreements and a proposed constitutional amendment restricting executive agreements and treaty-making authority. As a candidate first for the Republican presidential nomination and then for the presidency, Eisenhower seemingly shared these concerns, having pledged conciliation and cooperation with Congress. Candidate Eisenhower specifically promised to repudiate secret, unilateral diplomacy, as symbolized by the Yalta Conference of February 4–11, 1945, to consult with Congress prior to formulating foreign policy, and to purge "disloyal" individuals from the federal bureaucracy.

Inaugurated as president on January 20, 1953, Eisenhower did seek to harmonize relations between the executive and legislative branches. Nonetheless, his subsequent presidential actions for the most part amounted to a repudiation of his specific campaign pledges. In late February 1953, for example, the Eisenhower administration sought to avert congressional enactment of a resolution calling for the repudiation of Yalta agreements by introducing a resolution criticizing the Soviet

Union for violating those agreements. Because this resolution tacitly amounted to the repudiation of a central Republican charge, the Senate leadership under Robert Taft quietly had the administration's Yalta resolution killed in committee.

The proposed repudiation of Yalta was a symbolic act, involving as it did an oblique attack on the past conduct of diplomacy. A proposed constitutional amendment to restrict executive foreign policy authority, introduced in 1952 by Republican Senator John Bricker of Ohio and supported by sixty-five Senators (including forty-four of the forty-seven Republican senators) , was quite another matter. The Bricker Amendment involved an issue of substance: to preclude the repetition of the Yalta diplomacy, all treaties or executive agreements affecting domestic policy would require congressional approval. Powerful conservative groups such as the American Medical Association, which feared that socialized medicine might be introduced through the World Health Organization of the United Nations, and southern segregationists, who worried that ratification of the UN Covenant on Human Rights might undermine states' rights and the system of segregation in the South, actively promoted this amendment. Reversing themselves in 1953, Secretary of State John Foster Dulles and Republican Senator Alexander Wiley of Wisconsin (chairman of the Senate Foreign Relations Committee) publicly opposed the amendment. Eisenhower did not provide concerted public support for Dulles's and Wiley's effort to defeat the amendment. Adopting a low key approach which had Dulles assume leadership of opposition to the amendment, the president portrayed the issue as involving the effective conduct of foreign policy and not a presidential quest for power. This strategy succeeded. By one vote short of the needed two-thirds, in February 1954, the Senate narrowly rejected the Bricker Amendment.

The Bricker Amendment and the Yalta resolution had posed the issue of whether Congress should limit executive control over foreign policy and should act to avert the unilateralism that had characterized presidential actions since 1939. During Truman's presidency, moreover, conservative Republicans had assailed Truman's pointed claims in 1948 and thereafter to executive privilege when denying congressional requests for executive branch documents. Repeatedly, Senator McCarthy and other conservative Republicans (notably Taft and then Congressman Richard Nixon) charged that these claims to executive privilege were being used to frustrate the implementation of an effective internal security program, to cover up incompetence and disloyalty, and to prevent the creation of a resolute foreign policy that would insure victory in the Cold War. This effort had a narrow partisan purpose—to discredit the Democrats. Republican House majority leader, Joseph Martin, Jr., pointedly articulated this conviction: "My fellow Americans, the record of the last twenty years should convince everyone of us that we must clean house at Washington. The only way that we can get back on the road of real Americanism is to get rid of those responsible for this mess we are in and substitute bold, courageous, intelligent leadership." During his campaign for the presidency, candidate Eisenhower similarly denounced this resort to secrecy and the unfortunate policy consequences. Once elected, however, President Eisenhower did not allow policy to be determined by opposition politics.

The Eisenhower administration amended Truman's loyalty program, for example, by executive action and not through consultation with Congress. On April 27, 1953, President Eisenhower issued executive order 10450 revoking the Truman loyalty program and substituting an employee security program based on congressional legislation of September 1950 (Public Law 733), which had authorized cabinet officials to dismiss summarily individuals holding "sensitive" security positions. In effect, Eisenhower's order extended this dismissal authority to all federal departments. Instituted independently, the Eisenhower "security" program was far-reaching and repressive. The elaborate hearing and review procedures provided under President Truman's program—enabling accused employees to defend themselves before being dismissed—were scrapped. Under Eisenhower's program, dismissal was no longer based on the government's proving "reasonable doubt as to loyalty" but on whether the individual's employment was "clearly consistent with the interests of national security." To receive clearance, moreover, federal employees would have to be "reliable, trustworthy, of good conduct and character, and of complete and unswerving loyalty to the United States." Under this program the burden of proof shifted from the government to the accused employee who thereafter would have to prove that his/her continued employment was "clearly consistent" with security interests.

This more nebulous standard of suitability, which penalized individuals for unconventional political activities, does underscore Eisenhower's principal concerns and his extreme anticommunism. By moving quickly, moreover, the president had gained the initiative from Congress, but he had not settled the questions of whether Congress or the president should direct national policy or what voice the McCarthyites would have in developing national security policy. Having tasted victory, and firmly believing in the need for a strengthened congressional internal security role, congressional conservatives—particularly Congressman Harold Velde, chairman of HUAC; Senator William Jenner, chairman of the Internal Security Subcommittee; and Senator Joseph McCarthy, chairman of the Permanent Investigations Subcommittee of the Government Operations Committee—were not willing to follow blindly even a conservative Republican president. Whether a confrontation would ensue would depend on the Administration's subsequent actions.

Under McCarthy's leadership, the Permanent Investigations Subcommittee soon initiated an investigation of the International Information Agency (later renamed the USIA) to ascertain whether its overseas libraries carried "subversive" literature. Responding to this investigation, on March 18, 1953, the State Department banned from U.S. information centers "the works of all Communist authors," "any publication which continuously publishes Communist propaganda," and the works of art of "any Communists, fellow travelers, et cetera." Overreacting to this order, some frightened agency personnel burned the books of alleged left-wing authors carried by their libraries, an action denounced by many foreign and domestic observers. In a relatively unpublicized address at Dartmouth College, President Eisenhower obliquely condemned book-burning. When reporters at a subsequent press conference queried whether his Dartmouth remarks referred to Senator McCarthy, Eisenhower responded by stating that he refused to indulge in personalities.

In essence, the administration at first sought to avoid a direct confrontation with Senator McCarthy. As part of this effort Vice President Nixon, the White House's liaison with McCarthy, in 1953 urged the Wisconsin senator to explore other issues than the Republican administration's security procedures. This effort eventually failed; in the fall of 1953 McCarthy initiated an investigation of Army (i.e., Eisenhower administration) security procedures at Fort Monmouth, New Jersey (convicted atomic spy Julius Rosenberg had been employed there in 1944).

Senator McCarthy's harsh questioning of General Ralph Zwicker, the commanding officer at Fort Monmouth, during the initial stage of these hearings led to the intercession of Secretary of the Army Robert Stevens. To protect lower-echelon officers from Senator McCarthy's harassment, Stevens directed army officials not to testify before McCarthy's subcommittee. Instead, the army secretary stated, he would appear. Stevens's action thereby changed the focus of these hearings from the question of the adequacy of existing security procedures (the issue precipitating McCarthy's harsh treatment of General Zwicker had been why an obscure radical dentist draftee, Major Irving Peress, had been promoted and then given an honorary discharge) to an army-McCarthy confrontation.

Still intent on avoiding a confrontation with the Wisconsin senator, administration personnel quietly arranged a private conference between Secretary Stevens and Senator McCarthy. At first relenting, the secretary soon reconsidered and threatened to resign unless the army's position was supported. Stevens's threat forced a reluctant administration to support a public investigation of the army's complaint that Senator McCarthy and his staff had used improper influence to secure preferential treatment for a former consultant to the McCarthy subcommittee, then army private G. David Schine. This public confrontation, however, had been forced by McCarthy and not the president.

Ironically, McCarthy proved to be his own worst enemy. His conduct during the nationally televised Army-McCarthy hearings (held between April 17 and June 17) raised doubts about his methods and honesty. Appalled by McCarthy's performance, Republican Senator Ralph Flanders on June 11, 1954 introduced a resolution to censure McCarthy and led the Senate that month to establish a special committee to investigate his charges. Chaired by the conservative Utah Republican Arthur Watkins, this committee after a lengthy investigation in September recommended that the Senate censure McCarthy on two counts of conduct unbecoming a senator. Responding in turn, McCarthy accused the committee of aiding international communism. The vote on the committee's recommendations was delayed until after the November congressional elections. Even then, the administration did not support the pro-censure forces. Vainly, Vice President Nixon worked behind the scenes, attempting to convince McCarthy to apologize publicly and thereby possibly avert censure. McCarthy's refusal ended all efforts at compromise. On December 2, the Senate voted sixty-seven to twenty-two to condemn McCarthy; the Wisconsin senator's only support coming from conservative Republicans.

The Army-McCarthy hearings had brought to the surface yet another issue—the claim to executive privilege. On May 17, 1954, Eisenhower directed his staff not to comply with Senator McCarthy's request for information about January 1954 oral and telephone conversations between army counsel John Adams and White House personnel. The president's directive stipulated: "Because it is essential to efficient and effective administration that employees of the executive branch be in a position to be completely candid in advising with each other in official matters, and because it is not in the public interest that such advice be disclosed." Immediately challenging this claim, on May 27, the senator declared that all federal employees should recognize that "it is their duty to give us any information which they have about graft, corruption, communism, treason, and that there is no loyalty to a superior officer which can tower above and beyond their loyalty to their country."

The May 17 Eisenhower directive was but one of the administration's subsequent forty-four claims to executive privilege. Paradoxically, one legacy of McCarthy's tactics and censure had been an increased tolerance for such claims. These claims encompassed a wide variety of issues, some involving important questions of policy and others decisions that, if publicly revealed, could have been politically embarrassing. In 1957, for example, the administration turned down a request of a Senate committee, chaired by Missouri Democratic Senator Thomas Hennings, for government plans to maintain civil liberties in the event of a nuclear attack on the United States. In 1958, the administration refused to provide Texas Democratic Senator Lyndon Johnson with a copy of the Gaither Repotr. (The report was prepared by a special presidential committee studying Soviet military capabilities, U.S. national defense spending, and civil defense needs.)

THE ADMINISTRATION AND ANTI-COMMUNIST POLITICS

In part the Administration's refusal to lead the effort to curb McCarthy had been based on political expediency: a recognition of the Senator's value to the Republican party and an unwillingness to antagonize

McCarthy's principal supporters in the Republican party's right wing. The Republican right had grave suspicions of President Eisenhower, stemming from his defeat of Senator Taft at the 1952 Republican Convention. Subsequent administration actions—lobbying to defeat the Bricker Amendment, subverting congressional attempts to repudiate the Yalta agreements, nominating as U.S. ambassador to the Soviet Union the former interpreter at, and still defender of, the Yalta Conference, Charles Bohlen, and claiming executive privilege—led many conservatives to question the administration's Republicanism and Americanism. Disgruntled over the president's actions, in early 1954 a number of conservatives formed a new organization, the For America Committee, headed by former White House aide Clarence Manion. The committee offered two prospects. First, it could lobby for conservative principles outside the structure of the Republican party. Second, the committee could provide the basis for a permanent third party. Simultaneously, a number of conservative intellectuals led by William Buckley (a recent graduate of Yale University and coauthor of a sympathetic study of McCarthy) launched the *National Review,* a new periodical intended to be the organ of American political conservatism.

The Administration's hesitancy to confront McCarthy also derived from its shared commitment to an anti-Communist politics. During the 1952 campaign and as president, Eisenhower effectively resorted to a sophisticated form of red-baiting either to discredit the Democrats or to sustain a more conservative politics. To accomplish these objectives, the newly inaugurated administration quickly moved to institutionalize anticommunism. One impetus to this action was the desire to purge New Deal holdovers from the federal bureaucracy. Upon acceding to the presidency, Eisenhower inherited a bureaucracy staffed by individuals who had gained employment during the twenty-year period of Democratic control of the presidency, a time when liberals and even radicals were attracted to the federal government. Civil service appointees, moreover, had job tenure; they could not be dismissed on loyalty grounds without the government proving a case against them. It was not evidence of disloyalty but his own differing political philosophy that led Eisenhower, on March 18, 1953, to send a letter to Secretary of Commerce Sinclair Weeks. In it he condemned individuals who through "a process of selection based upon their devotion to socialistic doctrice and bureaucratic control practiced over the past two decades" had advanced to important policy-making posts.

To eliminate these "socialistic" or "bureaucratic" influences, Eisenhower resorted to two methods: (1) the nebulous "suitability" standard of his "security" program and (2) executive order 10440 of March 31, 1953, authorizing the Civil Service Commission to reclassify federal personnel either by phasing out positions or creating new job categories to be filled by his administration. The administration's Cold War conservatism thus led it to prefer conventional personalities unsympathetic to political reformism. In turn, this insured an atmosphere even more stifling of free inquiry than had been the case during the height of

Senator McCarthy's influence in the Truman years. The event best dramatizing this was the administration's decision to review atomic scientist J. Robert Oppenheimer's security clearance.

During World War II, Oppenheimer had played a major role recruiting scientists to the atomic bomb project. After the war, and until he dissented in 1950 from the decision to undertake a "crash program" to develop a thermonuclear bomb, Oppenheimer continued to exercise a major advisory role. Because of the sensitivity of his position, the scientist underwent numerous security investigations that focused on his earlier associations with, and tenuous involvement in, radical politics. Nonetheless, his security clearance had always been sustained. Because Oppenheimer's advisory role had virtually ended by 1954, the AEC could simply have terminated his consultative status. Instead, it created a special board to review the atomic scientist's security clearance, a decision with which President Eisenhower concurred. (Privately conceding that earlier loyalty-security investigation had clearly confirmed Oppenheimer's loyalty, the president added, "However, this does not mean that he might not be a security risk.") After a lengthy investigation, the board recommended against clearance, basing this decision not on grounds of Oppenheimer's disloyalty or commission of subversive acts but the scientist's politics. Justifying its conclusion, the board emphasized that national security "in times of peril must be absolute."

Oppenheimer's case was not atypical. Security officials depicted Soviet peace feelers of 1953 as a cloak for increased spy activities. Twenty-six states enacted legislation either barring Communists from running for public office or requiring teachers, paleontologists, even wrestlers, to sign loyalty oaths as condition for certification. The most extreme case of this obsession involved the 1953 denial of a security clearance to William L. Greene, the vice president and general manager of an engineering firm under contract to the Navy Department. Cleared four times in loyalty investigations of 1949–1952, Greene was denied clearance in 1953. The bulk of the charges against Greene centered on his associations with his former wife (an alleged Communist from whom he had been divorced in 1947).

Administration officials, moreover, attempted to exploit the subversive issue for partisan purposes. Thus, in his January 1954 State of the Union address, President Eisenhower claimed that 2,200 "security risks" had been dismissed from the federal government under his administration's security program. During the 1954 congressional campaign, Vice President Nixon accused the Democrats of earlier laxity toward and of positive affinity for communism. The Communist party, Nixon charged, was working against Republican congressional candidates in 1954 because "the candidates running on the Democratic ticket in the key states are almost without exception members of the Democratic party's left-wing clique which has been so blind to the Communist conspiracy and have tolerated it in the United States."

In April 1954, moreover, the administration sought additional internal security legislation to grant immunity from prosecution to individuals testifying on national security matters before congressional committees and grand juries and to authorize wiretapping in national security cases. In 1954 Congress approved the administration's proposed immunity bill but refused to enact wiretapping legislation. Lacking legislative authorization, the administration nonetheless continued to authorize wiretaps during so-called national security investigations. And in May 1954 Attorney General Brownell authorized FBI microphone surveillance (bugging), even when this required physical break-ins to install the bugs, for intelligence gathering involving the "national interest," "internal security and the national safety." Encouraged by this attitude, the FBI instituted in 1956 on its own authority what became a series of counterintelligence programs intended to "harass, discredit, and intimidate" extremist political activities. And the CIA would begin to open the mail of American citizens in 1955 and after 1958 forward information obtained through this program to the FBI. In a different vein, the administration supported passage of the National Defense Education Act of 1958. Providing federal aid to secondary and higher education to promote scientific development—including a program of graduate fellowships—this measure responded to a concern over the Soviet Union's successful orbiting of the first space satellite (Sputnik) in 1957.

The administration's legislative efforts strengthened an already strong anti-Communist obsession, and in particular a congressional effort of August 1954 to extend anti-Communist controls. An administration-sponsored bill to stamp out communism, the Communist Control Act of 1954, was broadened during congressional debate to impose far-reaching restrictions on individual liberties. "Communist-infiltrated" organizations were denied the right to obtain the privileges of the National Labor Relations Act of 1935, the Communist party was denied the right to appear on the ballot, and the registration requirement (of the 1950 McCarran Act) was extended to "Communist-infiltrated" organizations (a provision specifically directed at left-oriented groups, whether they were radical trade unions or peace movements). The framers of the act publicly rationalized that the Communist party, and similarly Communist-infiltrated organizations, were not entitled to the "rights, privileges, and immunities attendant upon legal bodies" because they were conspiracies to overthrow the United States government.

THE IMPACT OF THE WARREN COURT

The Eisenhower administration's cautious conservatism precluded a direct attempt to address two of the important social strains of the Cold War years—involving civil rights and civil liberties. These questions, however, could not be ignored, in part because the important constitutional issues they posed were confronted by the U.S. Supreme Court. Between 1954 and 1959, the Supreme Court, under the leadership of

Chief Justice Earl Warren (appointed by President Eisenhower in September, 1953 to succeed Fred Vinson), issued rulings that extended individual liberties either by restricting congressional, executive, and investigative powers or by striking down state-imposed segregation.

In *Yates* v. *U.S.* and *Jencks* v. *U.S.*, the Court in 1957 restored constitutional restrictions on governmental prosecution of domestic radicals. In *Yates,* the Court in effect revised the Vinson Court's 1951 ruling in *Dennis* v. *U.S.* upholding the conviction under the Smith Act of the eleven leaders of the U.S. Communist party. In that ruling, the Vinson Court seemingly had upheld the conviction of individuals who had merely advocated revolutionary change. Not directly overturning this ruling, the Warren Court modified its impact when reversing the conviction of second-echelon leaders of the Communist party under the Smith Act. *Dennis,* the Warren Court held, prohibited incitement to illegal action and not mere advocacy of revolutionary doctrine. In *Jencks,* the Court ruled that an accused defendant had the right to examine the statements made by prosecution witnesses to the FBI during pretrial investigations.

In *Cole* v. *Young* (1956), *Peters* v. *Hobby* (1954), *Service* v. *Dulles* (1957), and *Greene* v. *McElroy* (1959), the Court curtailed the arbitrariness of presidentially established loyalty programs. In sum, the Court affirmed the right of accused employees to due process during dismissal hearings and the right to challenge the veracity of individuals whose charges provided one basis for the denial of a security clearance. Without formally challenging the constitutionality of executive-initiated loyalty programs, the Court reversed the dismissal of Peters (a consultant to the Public Health Service) and Service (a Foreign Service Officer) on grounds that the Truman-established Loyalty Review Board had exceeded its authority. In *Cole,* the most significant of these decisions, the Court held that Eisenhower's security program exceeded the statutory authority on which it had been based—Public Law 733. That statute, the Court noted, authorized summary dismissals only for security positions, while the administration had extended this to nonsensitive positions.

The Supreme Court's civil liberties rulings were bitterly assailed. This assault paled in contrast to the reaction to the Court's unanimous decision of May 17, 1954 in *Brown* v. *Board of Education of Topeka.* Segregated school systems were unconstitutional, the Court ruled, "in the field of public education the doctrine of 'separate but equal' has no place. Separate educational facilities are inherently unequal." Clarifying this ruling in 1955, the Court required the abolition of segregated systems "with all deliberate speed."

Almost immediately, southern political leaders condemned the *Brown* decision and billboards sprang up on highways throughout the South demanding the chief justice's impeachment. Newly formed White Citizens Councils organized resistance to desegregation; a third party, the Independent States Rights party, was formed; and Democratic Senator J. Strom Thurmond of South Carolina conceived and helped draft the so-called Southern Manifesto. Signed by 101 of the 128 southern U.S. senators and representatives, the manifesto in essence declared "political war against the Court's decision" and made respectable defiance of that decision.

This defiance came to a head in September 1957 with the attempted desegregation of Little Rock, Arkansas, high schools. Opposed to court-ordered desegregation, Arkansas Governor Orval Faubus ordered National Guard units to surround Little Rock's Central High School, ostensibly to "maintain order." In effect, the troops prevented black students from entering the school. Eventually, Faubus agreed to withdraw the guard; however, local whites had become so inflamed by the governor's actions that they attacked black students seeking admission to the high school. Only then did President Eisenhower act to insure compliance with federal court orders. On September 23, he federalized the National Guard, dispatched federal troops to Little Rock, and ordered that obstruction of court orders cease.

Eisenhower's reluctant action reflected his views on desegregation. At no time did the President endorse the principle of desegregation or even assume moral responsibility to insure respect for desegregation decisions. Indeed, in his first press conference following the *Brown* decision, he lamely described the Court's ruling as the law of the land, which must be respected. For Eisenhower, segregation posed no moral or constitutional problem.

The civil rights issue would not be defused. The legitimacy accorded to integrationist principles by the Supreme Court emboldened the black community. Black Americans began to challenge long-established southern segregationist policies with such actions as the Montgomery, Alabama, bus boycott organized by the Reverend Martin Luther King, Jr., which began in December 1955, and the student-led sit-ins to integrate dime-store lunch counters which began in Greensboro, North Carolina, on February 1, 1960. Liberals and blacks particularly pressed for federal action to end southern restrictions on black voting. A 1959 study disclosed, for example, that while blacks comprised 30 percent of the voting age population of Alabama, only 8.1 percent were registered to vote. Mississippi statistics were even more stark: only 3.9 percent of the black population qualified to vote whereas blacks constituted 41 percent of the total population. No longer could federal action of some form be avoided. The issue of insuring elemental civil rights would have to be confronted. Pressured by the Eisenhower administration, liberal congressmen, and Democratic Senate majority leader Lyndon Johnson of Texas, in 1957 and again in 1960, Congress enacted legislation to insure suffrage rights for blacks.

The 1950s were characterized by neither passivity nor moderation nor was there an absence of major problems and deep divisions. The right-wing John Birch Society, for example, was formed (in 1958). Sharing that society's repudiation of the accommodationist philosphy underpinning the Eisenhower administration's foreign and domestic policies was Senator Barry Goldwater, who in 1960 published what soon became the political bible of American conservatism, *The Conscience of a Conservative*. Southern conservatives bitterly denounced and sought to prevent the desegregation of public schools and public facilities. Civil rights had surfaced as a national issue, though in the 1950s the predominant view was that race was a peculiarly southern problem. In addition, blacks had become more militant and were less willing to accept as victories the 1957 and 1960 civil rights legislation or the Supreme Court's desegregation decree. McCarthy might have been censured, but McCarthyism continued to flourish. Nor had power become decentralized; neither the federal bureaucracy nor the institutionalized presidency were dismantled.

The Eisenhower administration, moreover, had not ushered in a new politics; despite conservative denunciations of federal spending and controls, New Deal-Fair Deal policies had not been frontally attacked. The administration moved as far as it could in abandoning New Deal programs. Its nebulous "modern Republicanism," however, incorporated many New Deal spending and welfare policies in an effort to forge a more affluent society through reliance on military spending and tax allowances to stimulate the economy. Thus on the one hand, in 1953 and 1954, the Reconstruction Finance Corporation was liquidated, legislation was enacted granting title to offshore oil to the states (specifically Louisiana and Texas), businessmen received increased tax depletion allowances, and an unsuccessful attempt was made to reduce the Tennessee Valley Authority's electrical power activities by awarding a generating contract to a private utility group, Dixon-Yates (conflict of interest revelations would force the administration to rescind this contract). On the other hand, a Department of Health, Education and Welfare was established, social security and unemployment compensation benefits were extended, the minimum wage was raised, and support to agriculture was continued. Unbalanced budgets remained the norm. In fiscal 1959, in fact, the federal deficit reached $12.5 billion, the highest peacetime deficit ever, and the federal administrative budget reached $76.5 billion. Most important, the administration indirectly but massively subsidized the construction and automobile industries through the Federal Highway Act of 1956, which it backed strongly. This act financed, mostly through the federal treasury, the building of a vast interstate freeway system, which reshaped urban America and the geographical distribution of the American people. The new highways further undermined already decaying older central cities in favor of new suburbs and the South and Southwest at the expense of the Northeast and the North Central states.

In a sense, the Eisenhower administration sanctioned and even expanded welfare statism. "Modern Republicanism" was never more than an empty public relations slogan; the Eisenhower administration had merely legitimated the institutional realities of New Deal and Cold War America.

25

Harsh Words, Cautious Action: Eisenhower Diplomacy 1953-1960

Two themes characterized American foreign relations during the Eisenhower years. First, the Eisenhower administration continued the Truman containment policy but with greater emphasis on military aid and defensive alliances, less on foreign economic programs, and greater reliance on the CIA's "covert operations" capabilities. Containment thereby became more rigid as John Foster Dulles, Eisenhower's secretary of state, sought to erect a world-wide chain of alliances against Communist expansion and to prevent left-wing leaders from retaining power by subsidizing right-wing military coups. Second, an apparent diminution of American international influence occurred during Eisenhower's tenure in office. In part that reflected the rigidity of containment as practiced by Dulles and the failure of the secretary of state to respond effectively to crises in the Middle East and Latin America. The Suez War in 1956 particularly strained the North Atlantic Alliance and accelerated Western Europe's desire for greater independence from the United States. In part the decline in influence also reflected the world's growing fear of nuclear war and a natural tendency toward neutralism, especially among newly independent nations. Finally, Soviet Russia's rapidly growing economy as well as her military arsenal and technological advances seemed to suggest that the United States now had a powerful rival in science and technology. As Soviet military power grew, Western European nations recovered from the ravages of war, and former colonies asserted their nationhood, the United States inevitably lost some of its global power.

THE EISENHOWER-DULLES LEADERSHIP

One of General Eisenhower's strongest assets during the presidential campaign of 1952 had been his experience in foreign affairs. As wartime supreme commander in Western Europe, he had adroitly managed a difficult coalition war, a task that in many ways was more diplomatic than military. He had repeated that feat as the first supreme commander of the newly formed NATO. Large numbers of Americans, therefore, confidently expected the general to end the Korean War satisfactorily and to plot a course of peace and security abroad.

During his two terms in the presidency, Eisenhower became a respected symbol of peace throughout the world. His greatest contribution was precisely in foreign affairs, where he helped persuade the American people to accept the unpleasant consequences of stalemate in the Cold War. He ended the Korean War without full victory, avoided military involvement in Indochina, and inched East-West relations toward a measure of détente or reduction of tensions. Perhaps, as columnist Walter Lippmann commented, only an unimpeachable conservative Republican chief executive could have achieved that much. Certainly, keeping in mind the anti-Communist hysteria of the late Truman era, a liberal Democratic president undertaking Eisenhower's role might have faced shrill charges of softness on communism.

Yet some critics here and abroad concluded that Eisenhower failed the challenges of the 1950s. His conservatism, they asserted, precluded any bold new approaches to foreign problems. Containment was heavily military when the post-Stalin era seemed to call for greater flexibility and new policies. Eisenhower drew on conservative advisers with narrow views about atomic controls, foreign aid, and summit, or great power leader, conferences—such people as Dulles, Eisenhower's two treasury secretaries, George Humphrey and Robert Anderson, Admiral Arthur W. Radford, chairman of the Joint Chiefs of Staff, and Lewis Strauss, the head of the Atomic Energy Commission.

Another cause of complaint about Eisenhower arose from what appeared to be his limited information about public affairs. Ike by his own admission was not much of a reading man. Unlike other chief executives, Eisenhower did not pore over newspapers or care for long, detailed reports and memoranda. Instead, he relied upon his staff and his principal advisers to keep him informed. Unsurprisingly, he came to be regarded here and abroad, erroneously we now know, as a chief executive who reigned but did not rule. When illness caused Dulles to resign from the State Department in early 1959 and politics had forced out Sherman Adams, the chief controller of White House affairs, a British newspaper cartoon portrayed Ike as a sick and doddering old man leaning upon British Prime Minister Harold Macmillan for support and leadership. In fact, however, the departure of these chief lieutenants saw Eisenhower, beginning in 1958, to emerge publicly as a much more informed and active chief executive, especially in foreign affairs. Even before then, Eisenhower in reality was more informed about world events than he revealed publicly and more in command of the nation's foreign policy than his critics knew.

John Foster Dulles unquestionably ranks as one of America's most influential secretaries of state. The grandson of Secretary of State John W. Foster and the nephew by marriage of another, Robert Lansing, Dulles had been involved in foreign affairs in various capacities since World War I. He had advised Republican presidential nominees during the 1944, 1948, and 1952 campaigns, and had helped draft the Japanese peace treaty in 1951. As secretary of state, he worked closely with President Eisenhower. While other high officials often found it difficult to obtain direct access to the president, Dulles was in constant and close communication with him. It was a unique relationship. As one foreign diplomat expressed it, "We felt that Dulles was the United States and the United States was Dulles. He gave this feeling to the whole world."

Yet Dulles became the target of growing criticism from liberals in the United States and from European diplomats and observers. A principal cause lay in Dulles's moralizing. A man of deep religious faith and a prominent Presbyterian layman, Dulles spoke in simple moral terms and viewed the world in moral absolutes. Foreign officials and diplomats often reacted with bafflement to Dulles. To British diplomat Sir Oliver Franks, the American secretary of state was a "Reformation character" who regarded foreign affairs from a puritanical theological point of view.

Dulles at first treated even high officials in the State Department as if they could not be trusted fully. Moreover, he felt that he needed only information from them; he himself would supply the policy. From his own peculiar interpretation of Communist ideology he concluded that there must be no compromise with the godless Soviet leaders or with radical nationalists whether in Iran or Guatemala. He resolved to contain the Soviets by threats of war, to encourage European unity and greater responsibility for its own defense, to rely upon the CIA to overthrow radical political leaders, and to rely upon superior American moral and material force eventually to liberate countries under Soviet control.

At first, too, the new secretary allowed McCarthyism a rather free hand to terrorize the State Department. He permitted Scott McLeod, a close friend of Senator Styles Bridges, to serve as departmental security officer and to launch extensive loyalty investigations. Although over five hundred employees eventually were forced out, only eleven were "security risks" (and then because of excess drinking or other personal weaknesses that might invite blackmail) and none were proven disloyal or subversive. A number of able foreign service officers, such as John Paton Davies, who had written realistic appraisals about China during World War II, were forced out of the diplomatic service. In short, for the first two years of the new administration, as McCarthy continued his anti-Communist witch-hunt, the formulation of foreign policy was paralyzed by domestic politics as much as it had been during Truman's last few years in office.

CONSERVATIVE CONTAINMENT

Although Republican campaign promises in the 1952 election had frightened many by their calls for drastic changes in foreign policy, the Eisenhower administration, in the main, continued Truman's policies. During the 1952 presidential election year, Dulles in a *Life* magazine article and on the stump called for the liberation of the enslaved peoples behind the iron curtain. He implied that the immorality and internal weaknesses of the Soviet system doomed it to failure if the Western world remained firm. During the campaign Eisenhower himself declared that the people were right to distrust a Democratic leadership that had "allowed the godless Red Tide" to engulf millions and that failed to "see the Red stain seeping into . . . our Government." The gist of Republican promises, therefore, called for: a new dynamic policy to liberate the satellites and force Russia upon the defensive; a tougher approach in the Far East to end the Korean War and to "unleash" Chiang Kai-shek's forces on Taiwan to invade mainland China if the Nationalists chose; greater European efforts to rearm; a clean-up of the disloyal in the State Department; and adoption of the Bricker amendment to the Constitution to curtail such "unwise" or "evil" executive agreements as those made at Yalta.

In power, however, the Eisenhower administration failed to carry out these campaign promises. "Liberation," moreover, proved empty phrase-making. The West dared not risk a major war to force Soviet Russia out of central and Eastern Europe.

The tragic Hungarian Revolution of 1956 graphically demonstrated the American dilemma. Earlier, in October 1956, domestic unrest in Poland had brought the independent Communist Wladyslaw Gomulka to power. Gomulka eased Communist rule, restrained the secret police, widened Polish autonomy, and established better relations with the Catholic Church. The Gomulka government set the first example since Tito of "national communism," and it shook the other Soviet satellites, indirectly triggering a revolution in Hungary later that month. The Hungarian uprising brought to power Imre Nagy, a moderate Communist earlier imprisoned by the hard-liners. Nagy, however, lost control of the movement, which proclaimed a democracy and Hungary's neutrality in the Cold War. The Soviet Russian leadership could not tolerate such a direct challenge to its security and, after some hesitation, moved quickly to crush the uprising. Early in November 1956, Russian tanks fought their way into Budapest and brutally smashed the popular uprising. The United States and its allies did no more than express sympathy for the rebels and introduce empty UN resolutions condemning Russia. More direct intervention, they feared, would only have precipitated World War III.

As for other Republican promises in 1952, Chiang on Taiwan was "unleashed" as President Eisenhower announced in February 1953 that the U.S. Navy would "no longer be employed to shield Communist China." This "unleashing" did not result in the liberation of China, for without U.S. military assistance China's forces could do no more than launch an occasional raid on the mainland. Within a few years, in fact, the administration released China, when concluding a mutual defense treaty with the Nationalists requiring among other provisions mutual consultation prior to any ventures in Asia. And the administration fought congressional efforts to check executive power in foreign affairs.

The ending of the Korean War, moreover, legitimated Truman's limited war approach. Resorting to "brinkmanship," as Dulles later called it, Eisenhower upon his return from his Korean visit in December 1952 warned that unless the truce talks succeeded soon, the United States might retaliate in unspecified ways. Dulles subsequently hinted to the People's Republic of China that atomic bombs might even be used. New Soviet leaders—Stalin died early in 1953—also helped bring the war to an end. Consequently, on July 27, 1953, an armistice was signed. It was an armed truce only, for negotiaions on reunification failed and the United States concluded a security treaty with South Korea and stationed American troops indefinitely along the armistice line. Yet the outcome clearly accorded with Truman's decision to repudiate forcible reunification and to seek a compromise settlement.

Indochina policy also demonstrated Eisenhower's caution in foreign affairs. As World War II ended, Vietnamese nationalists opposed the reassertion of French control over a colony it had ruled since the mid-nineteenth century. Led by Ho Chi Minh, a Communist who founded the Vietnamese Communist party in 1930 and worked ceaselessly for independence from French rule, the Nationalists in 1946 established the independent Democratic Republic of Vietnam. France refused to grant Indochina its independence, and a civil war erupted in 1946 that was to last for eight years. French soldiers held the cities and most of the towns, while the rebels controlled most of the countryside. The United States in 1950 backed France and recognized the French puppet regime of Emperor Bao Dai as part of an effort to contain Communist expansion. Presumably China as part of the Soviet world empire controlled the Vietnamese rebels, though in fact the revolution was indigenous and basically anticolonial in origin though led by committed Communists.

The United States, however, financed France's effort to reassert imperialism and by 1954 underwrote about 70 percent of the costs of the war.

By 1954, France had become weary of an endless guerilla war in Indochina. The French army thus sought a decisive battle by luring the Vietminh into open combat at the remote fortress of Dien Bien Phu. The Vietminh responded by laying siege to the fortress, cutting it off from the outside world and bringing it under murderous bombardment. France appealed to the United States for direct intervention to support it in Indochina. The administration split on the issue, Dulles and Admiral Radford favoring naval air strikes to relieve Dien Bien Phu, Air Force Chief of Staff Nathan Twining even contemplating use of small tactical atomic bombs, while the army leaders opposed such intervention. Eisenhower though calling Indochina a domino whose fall could set off a chain-reaction of disintegration in Southeast Asia, refused to risk American ground forces to aid the French. Consequently Dien Bien Phu fell on May 7, 1954.

Meanwhile, an international assemblage of the interested powers, including the People's Republic of China, the Soviet Union, Britain, and France, gathered at Geneva in 1954 to negotiate a settlement for Indochina. A new French ministry was determined to conclude a peace and two pacts were signed in July 1954. The Geneva Armistice Agreement and the Final Declaration of Geneva instituted a truce between the French and the Vietminh; a temporary partition and demilitarized zone along the 17th parallel, with French troops withdrawing to the south of that line and Ho Chi Minh's to the north; free exchange of peoples desiring to leave either half of Vietnam; an armistice commission of India, Poland, and Canada; and supervised free elections by 1956 to reunify the country. Although Ho Chi Minh controlled an estimated two-thirds of Vietnam, he accepted this compromise, confident that he would win the proposed general election.

The American government refused to sign the Geneva agreements, which Dulles believed turned millions of people over to Communist rule. Instead, it tried to shore up Southeast Asia against further Communist gains. In South Vietnam, the United States helped bring Ngo Dinh Diem, an ardent anti-Communist nationalist, to power, and it gradually supplanted France as the principal western presence there. American military aid and advisers poured into South Vietnam.

THE "SPIRIT OF GENEVA"

In March 1953 Joseph Stalin died of a cerebral hemorrhage. His successors, among whom at first Georgi Malenkov and then Nikita Khrushchev stood to the fore, established an uneasy collective leadership and turned a more benign face toward the West. All issues, they declared, could be settled by peaceful negotiation. An era of peaceful coexistence and competition, as Khrushchev later phrased it, had dawned.

Instead of perceiving that new possibilities for flexibility and negotiations were opening, Dulles proclaimed that the Stalin era had ended and the Eisenhower era had begun and clung to his view that continued pressure would force the Soviets to retreat. Consequently both he and Eisenhower reacted coolly to the new Russian leaders and to European proposals for summit conferences to probe Soviet intentions. The Eisenhower administration preferred the sharper confrontations of the Cold War and found Soviet moderation difficult to accept.

But the pressures for détente ultimately triumphed. The new Soviet leaders in effect "bought" a summit conference by agreeing in 1955 to end the occupation of Austria. Under the treaty signed on May 15, Soviet and Western forces withdrew, and a reunified Austria pledged itself to strict neutrality. The Austrian treaty encouraged hopes for progress on a German settlement, while Eisenhower was eager to explore possibilities of mutual arms reductions. President Eisenhower joined British Prime Minister Anthony Eden, French Premier Edgar Faure, and the Soviet leaders, Nikolai Bulganin and Nikita Khrushchev, at Geneva for conferences in July 1955. Although little was achieved, the atmosphere was cordial and hinted that the Cold War had thawed. The Russians bargained over Germany, proposing a vague reunification that would have removed Western and Soviet troops and neutralized Germany, but the United States, determined to rearm West Germany, was uninterested. Instead, Eisenhower advanced an impractical if inspiring plan for "open skies" or Soviet-Western aerial surveillance of each other to prevent sudden attacks. The conferees, at most, loosened Soviet-Western relations through cultural exchange programs and established the friendlier "Spirit of Geneva."

The Geneva Conference convinced Secretary of State Dulles that the United States must remain firm. He saw the Austrian settlement as one proof that pressure on the Soviets would result in still greater concessions. The United States, Dulles believed, ultimately could dictate the terms of a general settlement.

Yet actual events weakened the dominant power of the United States. Shortly after the Eisenhower administration took office it had begun to develop a new defense strategy. Early in 1954, Dulles had proclaimed the policy of "massive retaliation." In the future, America would not be bled by local wars waged by Russia through proxies such as the North Koreans. Instead it would reserve the right to retaliate instantly and massively directly at the center of the enemy's power and rely on the CIA either to prevent radical nationalists from attaining power or to help overthrow such governments (the Iranian Mossadegh in 1953, the Guatemalan Arbenz in 1954, the Congolese Lumumba in 1960). Simultaneously, the administration's "new look" policy on defense emphasized saving money by reducing conventional armed forces while building up the Strategic Air Command's long-range bombers, equipped with atomic and hydrogen bombs. As the secretary of defense allegedly remarked, the United States intended to get "more bang for the buck." Yet Russia had sufficient nuclear weapons of its own to devastate the United States. Consequently the United States found itself prepared only to fight the kind of war with Russia that no sane person wanted.

THE TROUBLED MIDDLE EAST

This volatile area, at the minimum embracing the Arab-speaking lands of Asia and Egypt, and at the maximum also including Iran, Turkey, and North Africa, is "unified" by the Moslem religion. Oil also linked many of the region's states. Oil exports through the Suez Canal had increased from five million tons in 1938 to 68 million tons annually by 1955. According to estimates, the Middle East presently contains two-thirds of the world's proven reserves. As Western Europe became more and more dependent upon Middle Eastern oil, the Western powers clung to their role in the area more tenaciously than ever.

But World War II weakened the Western grasp in the Middle East as elsewhere in the colonial world. After the war, France found itself pushed out of Syria and Lebanon, leaving Britain alone to uphold the Western client-state system in the Middle East. Since the early postwar years were ones in which Britain reluctantly liquidated much of her empire elsewhere under nationalist pressures, she might have done so in the Middle East except for the crucial role played in her economy by oil. Consequently, ignoring the intensity of Arab nationalism, Britain struggled to retain influence in this vital area.

The emergence of Israel added the final explosive element to a treacherous situation. Israel constitutes one of the few examples of a state deliberately created in pursuit of an idea, a national Jewish home to replace the one destroyed by Roman dispersions of the population in the first century, A.D. Zionism emerged from European persecutions of Jews in the nineteenth century, influenced also by Western doctrines of liberal nationalism and self-determination of peoples. Dr. Theodore Herzl founded the Zionist movement in 1897, at a congress in Basle. In World War I, Dr. Chaim Weizmann obtained the Balfour Declaration in 1917 from the British government, promising Jews a "national home" in Palestine, subject to not harming the non-Jewish peoples already living there. By the end of World War I, only 55,000 Jews lived in Palestine but the establishment of a British mandate there opened the area to Jewish immigration. By 1944, the ratio of Jews to Arabs had increased from one to eight to one to two: 83,790 Jews to 600,000 Arabs in 1922, 528,000 Jews to one million Arabs by 1944.

Arabs resisted the Jewish immigration. Britain found herself caught between promises to the Zionists and need for Arab oil. Consequently, the British government responded to Arab pressures in 1939 by limiting Jewish immigration to 75,000 during the next five years and a complete cessation thereafter. Zionists responded to British restrictions in some cases through terrorist organizations such as the Stern gang that attacked British officials in Palestine. By 1948, as a civil war ensued between Arabs and Jews in Palestine, Britain withdrew from responsibility.

AMERICAN POLICY IN THE MIDDLE EAST

American policy toward the Middle East at first tended to drift with events. The State Department left Middle East responsibilities in British hands as long as the English exerted power there. Reflecting sympathy with Zionist nationalism, heightened by the recent publicity of Hitler's genocide policy toward European Jews, American public opinion overwhelmingly favored the Jews in Palestine. The Truman administration undoubtedly also respected the influence within the Democratic party of this voting bloc. By 1947 a weary Britain finally decided to yield the Palestine question to the United Nations for solution, surrendering its mandate over the area. That body, under American pressure, decided to divide Palestine into a Jewish and an Arab state.

War resulted when British forces withdrew in May 1948. Arab armies from surrounding countries promptly invaded Palestine to crush the newly-proclaimed Jewish state of Israel. The numerically inferior Jewish forces quickly smashed the invaders in battle. The Arabs signed a truce with Israel but refused to conclude a treaty recognizing the new state's existence. Some 700,000 Arabs fled Israel, or were encouraged to flee, and were settled by the Arab states in refugee camps along Israel's borders in the Gaza Strip and in Jordan. And many refugees, encouraged by Egypt and other Arab states, dreamed of a war of revenge to exterminate the hated Jewish state.

As British influence waned, the United States assumed the primary burden of keeping the Middle East and its vital oil in the western camp. In 1951, the American government backed creation of the Middle East Defense Organization to limit Communist penetration. Egypt and the other Arab countries declined to join this alliance, seeing it rightly as a device for continued western predominance and control. A revolution in Egypt in 1952 brought to power Colonel Gamal Abdel Nasser and overthrew the corrupt regime of King Farouk.

The first of a new generation of Arab nationalists, Nasser felt he had a mission to unify the Arab world, and he persuaded Britain, with American encouragement, to withdraw all its forces from Egypt in 1954. Nasser promised to maintain former British bases on a standby basis, and he reaffirmed the 1888 Convention of Constantinople that had called for unimpeded passage through the Suez Canal. With Britain's consent, the American government promised Egypt economic aid and eventually, in December 1955, offered some $270 million, including a World Bank loan, to help finance Nasser's pet project of constructing the Aswan High Dam on the Nile. American policy, heretofore pro-Israeli, now shifted toward a more pro-Arab tendency. President Eisenhower intended to show the Arabs that they had western friends and to let Israel know that the United States planned to pursue a more equal policy in the Middle East.

But United States policy, as practiced by Dulles, proved short-sighted. The Baghdad Pact of 1955 was intended to strengthen the area against Russian expansion and to fortify Britain's position in Iraq by linking Britain, Turkey, Iran, Iraq, and Pakistan. It disturbed the Arabic world and especially Nasser who regarded it as an undesirable extension of NATO to the Middle East and as a British device to build up Iraq as a rival to his leadership in the Arab world. Egypt managed to keep the rest of the area out of the new alliance. Russia, also alarmed by the pact, now began an active intervention in Middle Eastern politics.

The second blow to Western hopes resulted from Egyptian-Israeli hostilities. In February 1955, Israeli forces launched a large-scale raid in the Gaza Strip, in retaliation for numerous border clashes. Israeli forces caught the Egyptian army totally unprepared and inflicted a humiliating defeat. Enraged and abased by this defeat, Nasser intensified the border war and asked the West for arms. In accordance with the Tripartite Declaration of 1950, Britain and the United States refused. Therefore, Nasser turned to the Soviet bloc and in September 1955 made a deal with Czechoslovakia for $200 million in arms. The terms of the deal aroused Western fears that Nasser would become a Soviet puppet. And the more the Western powers distrusted Nasser, the more anti-West he grew.

As Nasser drew closer to Russia, both Britain and the United States began to reexamine their policies. Dulles reacted sharply against Nasser's hints that Russia had offered more generous aid for construction of the Aswan Dam, and he was particularly angered when Nasser recognized the People's Republic of China in May 1956. Hence, in a manner calculated to humiliate Nasser, on July 22, 1956, Dulles publicly withdrew the Aswan Dam aid offer on the grounds that the project was unsound. Nasser responded four days later by announcing the nationalization of the Anglo-French–owned Suez Canal and the use of its revenues to build the dam.

Britain and France then used force to topple Nasser. Prime Minister Eden, like many Britishers clinging to the shreds of empire, saw Nasser as a latter-day Hitler who must be topped, not appeased. Although Nasser had only broken a contract with the privately chartered Suez Canal Company, Britain maintained that he had violated international law, including the 1888 Convention for unimpeded use of the canal by all nations. To insure that canal transit was disrupted, Britain ordered all Western pilots off the job. Nasser managed to operate the canal nevertheless.

Eisenhower, then in the midst of the 1956 presidential election campaign, feared the outbreak of war. He and Dulles decided that force was unjustified and that Britain's case was weak. American leaders thus wisely rejected Anglo-French aggression. But Eden expected the Americans to restrain Russia while Anglo-French forces toppled Nasser. Dulles, however, first proposed a managerial board for the canal and then a Canal Users Association to negotiate terms with Nasser and to control shipping via London and Paris. Eden felt betrayed when Dulles publicly disavowed the use of force. Hence Eden finally agreed to act without consulting or informing Washington.

On October 29, Israeli forces, encouraged by France, struck the Sinai, taking 6,000 captives, subsequently exchanged for four captured Israelis. Then Britain and France sent Israel and Egypt an "impartial ultimatum" to withdraw from the area around the Suez Canal, to which Israel promptly agreed, but Egypt refused. On November 5, British and French forces landed to seize the Suez Canal and bombed targets along its course. Eisenhower and Dulles felt betrayed by America's allies. Hence, to forestall Russian action, and to teach Britain and France that they could not act independently of Washington, Dulles had a resolution introduced in the UN Assembly for a cease-fire and supported a plan for UN policing of the Suez Canal. The American government thereby condemned its two major European allies. Under American pressure and feeling the effects of an Arab oil embargo as well as Russian military intervention, Britain and France accepted a cease-fire and began to pull back their forces without seizing control of the canal. Israel also withdrew and a truce was instituted under UN supervision. But truly Israel emerged with clear gains, opening the port of Elath on the Gulf of Aqaba and capturing an ample supply of Czech-Egyptian war materials. Seeking to exploit this opportunity, the Soviet Union extended financial and technical assistance to Egypt for the Aswan Dam. The administration's diplomacy thus did not enhance its standing in the Arab world while contributing to a deterioration in U.S. relations with France.

To forestall aggressive Egyptian Pan Arabism and, in the American view, the extension of Russian influence in the Middle East, the Congress passed a joint resolution in early 1957, the so-called Eisenhower Doctrine, that authorized the chief executive to send aid or troops to any Near Eastern nation that requested it to resist Communist threats. Hailed as a bulwark against Communist expansion, this was another Dulles effort to extend the American security system around the entire globe and to encircle Russia. Eisenhower invoked the doctrine to bolster Jordan against Egyptian threats in the spring of 1957, and in 1958 American forces briefly were landed in Jordan and Lebanon to suppress another crisis instigated or exploited by Nasser. The United States thus tried to supplant Britain as the "stabilizer" of the Middle East.

In most cases, however, Eisenhower preferred to exercise American influence in the Middle East through arms sales and economic leverage rather than direct military intervention. Saudi Arabia and Lebanon, in effect, became American client states, dependent on American arms and support to protect their traditional leaders against more radical Arab nationalists. The State Department, moreover, consistently supported the interests of private American oil companies in Arabia and other mineral-rich Persian Gulf states. And when a reform administration in Iran threatened the holdings and profits of Anglo-American oil companies, in 1953 Eisenhower authorized the CIA to overthrow the Mossadegh government and replace it with one more friendly to Western oil companies. The CIA abetted a successful conservative coup that brought the Shah to power in Iran in 1953 and thereafter the largest of Persian Gulf states became a staunch defender of the West and a special recipient of American military and economic largesse.

One way or another, the United States under Eisenhower supplanted British influence in the Middle East. The United States replaced Britain as the protector of Western oil interests and the antagonist of Russia in the area. Eisenhower attempted to hold the oil-rich Arab states in the Western camp at the same time that he guaranteed Israel's independence and territorial integrity. This delicate diplomatic balancing act would persistently involve the United States in Middle East turmoil as Arab-Israeli conflict refused to abate.

The entire diplomatic pattern of the Eisenhower years revealed the president's virtuosity in balancing contradictory tendencies. On the one hand, Dulles promised to roll back the iron curtain, and on the other hand, Eisenhower recognized the legitimacy of Soviet interests in Eastern and central Europe. Dulles encircled Russia with hostile alliances and military bases, threatening the Communists everywhere, including Indochina, with massive retaliation; Eisenhower restrained the military and tolerated the use of force only where real conflict was unlikely, as in Lebanon in 1958. Dulles proclaimed a holy moral war against godless communism; Eisenhower sought to reduce tensions with the Soviets and became identified with the "Spirit of Geneva." Under Eisenhower the Cold War remained a rhetorical game not a military exercise.

Eisenhower also presided cautiously, albeit reluctantly, over the inevitable diminution of American global influence and power. As Western Europe and Japan prospered economically, Russia, China, and other socialist states grew more stable, and the anti-Western, anticolonial national liberation movements intensified, the United States experienced a sense of shock. If the United States in 1960 was economically wealthier and militarily more powerful than it had been in 1952, developments elsewhere in the world caused a relative loss in American power and influence. That loss of power would be used by Eisenhower's successors as a reason to increase American military strength and to heat up the Cold War.

26

A New Age Dawns: John F. Kennedy and the Promise of Camelot 1960-1963

An exciting personality, John Fitzgerald Kennedy is remembered nostalgically for having reoriented national politics during the 1960s. Yet, this positive image masks a politician who was as much a prince of ambiguity as he was a prince of Camelot, who both intensified and mitigated Cold War tensions, and who moved reluctantly to advance reformist programs. Kennedy, moreover, was mostly blind to what would dominate American life in the sixties—whether poverty or racial prejudice. His New Frontier programs were cautious and never ardently pressed.

This was not surprising. The image of bold reformist leadership emerged only after Kennedy's assassination on November 22, 1963. Kennedy's pre-presidential career, in fact, was strikingly conventional. As a U.S. Senator from 1952 to 1960, Kennedy sponsored no major legislative measure and his voting record was not consistently liberal. He supported social welfare legislation and was known as a friend of labor unions, but often voted with conservatives on financial and internal security policy matters.

Kennedy's emergence as a national political leader during the 1950s was the consequence more of image politics than principled leadership: it flowed from his wit and engaging personality, from the publicity he gained from writing a best-selling book, *Profiles in Courage* (published in 1956), and from his prominent role in investigations of labor racketeering. Undertaking an extensive speech-making effort between 1957 and 1959 crisscrossing the country to address a variety of organizations, the Massachusetts senator developed invaluable political contacts in all geographic regions and major urban centers while capitalizing on the potential political asset of his Catholicism (the Communist issue having led many Catholics to defect in 1952 and 1956 from their traditional support of Democratic candidates). At the same time, the Massachusetts senator grew increasingly more liberal on foreign and domestic policy.

As an aspirant for the Democratic nomination, Kennedy encountered two principal obstacles. First, he had to dispel the conventional wisdom that a Catholic could not be elected president. For him, the primaries were crucial to demonstrate the minimal handicap of his Catholicism. A second, and more formidable, obstacle derived from the candidacies of a number of powerful Democrats—Senate majority leader Lyndon Johnson of Texas, former Air Force Secretary and Missouri Senator Stuart Symington, leader of the Senate liberal bloc Hubert Humphrey, and the Democratic presidential candidate of 1952 and 1956, Adlai Stevenson. All these men had had longer, and more distinguished, careers in congressional and party politics.

Kennedy's decision to enter the primaries did not insure a head-on confrontation with these aspirants. Johnson and Symington did not enter the primaries, emphasizing their Senate responsibilities. Their strength, in any case, was organizational, not popular. After a resounding defeat in 1956, Stevenson's chances for attaining the nomination were slim, and he did not enter the primaries. The only major candidate Kennedy faced in the primaries, then, was Hubert Humphrey.

In 1960, Humphrey retained strong support from liberal Democrats, and to win the nomination Kennedy needed to control this segment of the party. Seeking to force the issue early, Humphrey invited Kennedy to enter the Wisconsin primary, an invitation posing grave risks to Kennedy given Humphrey's base in neighboring Minnesota and his positive reputation with Wisconsin farmers. In an extensively funded and efficiently organized campaign, Kennedy decisively defeated Humphrey. The Wisconsin results did not resolve whether Kennedy's Catholicism was a political liability. (The Catholic issue was clouded, as Humphrey did best in predominantly Protestant rural areas and Kennedy best in heavily Catholic urban areas, leaving unanswered whether agrarianism and Humphrey's solid agricultural record were more important than Kennedy's Catholicism.) As such, the next primary, in heavily Protestant West Virginia, assumed particular importance. There, the same tactics and organizational efforts resulted in an even more decisive Kennedy victory.

The West Virginia and Wisconsin primaries eliminated Humphrey as a serious contender, partially dispelled the Catholic issue, and enabled Kennedy to consolidate his political base. His demonstrated popularity and organizational efficiency led to a first ballot victory, as Kennedy received 806 votes (761 needed to nominate). To strengthen the Democratic ticket, Kennedy turned to Lyndon Johnson, his chief opponent for the nomination, for the vice-presidential post. Johnson's qualifications were his experience, solid support from the South and from important Democratic leaders in Congress and in state politics, religion (Protestant), and regional base (the Southwest). Unexpected, this announcement embittered many delegates who condemned it as a betrayal of liberalism and for its sheer political expediency.

Kennedy's Republican opponent was the incumbent vice president, Richard Nixon. Eisenhower's nonpartisan stance as president and foreign policy decisions had alienated the party's conservative leadership. Vice President Nixon since 1953 had acted as the administration's contact with the party leadership and Republican conservatives. These contacts consolidated Nixon's base, made him the acknowledged frontrunner for the Republican presidential nomination and insured his first ballot nomination. To balance the ticket and as a concession to liberal Republicans, candidate Nixon chose as his vice-presidential running mate the U.S. ambassador to the United Nations, Henry Cabot Lodge, Jr. (an important leader of the draft-Eisenhower movement in 1952).

The 1960 presidential campaign was marked by one novel development, the scheduling between September 26 and October 21 of a series of four nationally televised debates between the two candidates. Although the format for each session was precisely drawn, the debates did not serve to distinguish sharply the candidates' specific positions on the issues. The major differences that emerged during the debates and more generally during the campaign were those of style and personality. Kennedy stressed the need for more dynamic leadership to get the country moving again, extend the nation's international influence, and improve the quality of life in America. Nixon, in contrast, emphasized his experience and ability to stand up to the Russians, sought to make an issue of his opponent's youth and wealth, and blamed the Democrats for inflation. On internal and international security issues, moreover, both candidates adopted similar anti-Communist positions.

During the campaign, for example, candidate Kennedy intoned, "I run for the presidency because I do not want it said that in the years when our generation held political power America began to slip. I don't want historians writing in 1970 to say that the balance of power in the 1950s and the 1960s began to turn against the United States and against the cause of freedom." In the first televised debate, moreover, Kennedy deemed nonessential the defense of Quemoy and Matsu (islands that served as defense outposts for the Nationalist government then residing in Formosa). The Nationalists, he hoped, could be persuaded to abandon these "indefensible" islands to avoid an unnecessary war. Responding aggressively, Nixon charged that the issue was not territory: "I oppose handing over to the Communists one inch of free territory." Yet in a later debate Kennedy condemned the Eisenhower administration's

Cuban policy as "too little and too late" and specifically called for a four-point program including an "attempt to strengthen the non-Batista, democratic anti-Castro forces in exile, and in Cuba itself, who offer eventual hope of overthrowing Castro." But, condemning this stance as adventurist, Nixon now accused Kennedy of wanting to intervene illegally in Cuba and instead advocated nonintervention and self-government.

The television debates were not without significance. Television offered possibilities for a new political strategy. Brilliantly exploiting television's communication possibilities, Kennedy projected an image of efficiency, detailed knowledge, and vibrancy and recognized the distinction between scoring points and winning audiences (which Nixon did not because he was convinced of his superior debating skills). Not surprisingly, then, a Roper poll revealed that, of four million Americans who admitted having been influenced by the debates, three million voted for Kennedy. Television had made its mark and further transformed American politics by reducing the importance of issues and political philosophy and strengthening factors like personality, appearance, and projected image.

The absence of sharp policy differences between the candidates would indirectly accentuate Kennedy's Catholicism. Thus, public knowledge of Kennedy's religion increased from 47 percent in May 1959 to 87 percent in August 1960, rising slightly higher thereafter. Early in the campaign, prominent Protestant ministers had directly questioned whether Kennedy would subordinate his national responsibilities to church discipline. To dispel these and more scurrilous charges, Kennedy forcefully outlined his views on church-state relations in a speech on September 12 to the Greater Houston Ministerial Association. Declaring his belief in "an America where the separation of church and state is absolute," Kennedy added that he thought it no more proper for a Catholic prelate to tell a Catholic president how to act than for a Protestant minister to tell his parishioners how to vote. Fundamentalist Protestant ministers nonetheless continued to emphasize Kennedy's Catholicism. In addition, the frequency of Richard Nixon's denials that Kennedy's Catholicism was an issue, and those of Republican spokesmen, indirectly accentuated Kennedy's religion as an issue.

In some areas, particularly rural Indiana and Oklahoma, Kennedy lost votes because of his religion. But Kennedy's Catholicism was an asset in urban and ethnic areas. The final outcome was a razor-thin victory. Of a total 68,412,709 votes cast, Kennedy received 118,550 more votes than Nixon (34,227,096–34,108,546). Because he won the major industrial states (Nixon won more total states), Kennedy's electoral college margin was wider, 303–219. The closeness of the presidential race did affect congressional contests, with the Republicans recovering slightly from the devastating setback of the 1958 elections: they gained two seats in the Senate (64–36) and twenty-two seats in the House (263–174).

Kennedy had campaigned on the need to provide bold and resource-

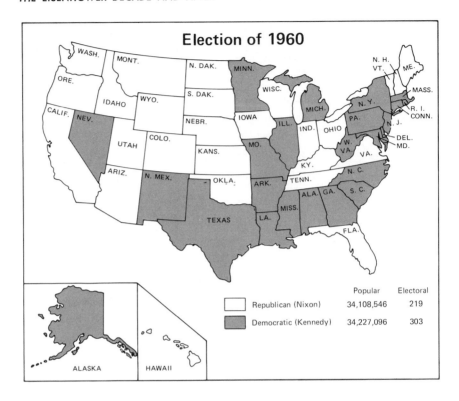

Election of 1960

		Popular	Electoral
☐	Republican (Nixon)	34,108,546	219
▨	Democratic (Kennedy)	34,227,096	303

ALASKA   HAWAII

ful leadership to "get the country moving again" and, through a dynamic anti-Communist foreign policy, to attain a peace based on strength. The Eisenhower administration's fiscal conservatism and attempt to reduce defense expenditures, the Democratic candidate charged, contributed to a "missile gap" that seriously affected the U.S. military position vis-à-vis the Soviet Union. Instead, he outlined what would become his administration's foreign policy, involving sharp increases in defense expenditures (conventional and nuclear) and the extension of economic and military assistance to anti-Communist governments in Latin America, Africa, and Asia.

Kennedy's inaugural address, outlining his so-called New Frontier, also expressed his administration's foreign and domestic policy priorities. In this address, the newly-inaugurated president affirmed that his administration would base its policies on the principle of "ask not what your country can do for you; ask what you can do for your country." In his acceptance speech at the Los Angeles convention, candidate Kennedy had sharply articulated this conception of responsibility: "All mankind awaits our decision. A whole world waits to see what we will do. We cannot fail their trust. We cannot fail to try." This responsibility, Kennedy believed, required expert leadership: "Most of the problems that we now face are technical problems, are administrative problems.

They are very sophisticated judgments which do not lend themselves to the great sort of 'passionate movements' which have stirred this country so often in the past."

A STRENGTHENED PRESIDENCY

Kennedy's speeches were not simply rhetorical flourishes, but reflected his elitist conception of the presidency. To Kennedy, the president was not simply coequal to the Congress or the repository of the public will. The president's function, Kennedy believed, was to "lead, inform, correct, and sometimes even ignore constituent opinion." In his view, the problems of a sluggish domestic economy, an inequitable social system, and current international crisis all resulted from the Eisenhower administration's failure to provide leadership. Intending to rectify this failure, Kennedy moved to centralize power in the presidency.

Although he held regular press conferences and enjoyed the give and take with the Washington press corps, Kennedy's attitude toward the media was often defensive and belligerent. The media was an instrument to be manipulated in order to shape public opinion, create a sense of the president's moral leadership, and retain control over events. Equating the national interest with his administration's policy objectives, Kennedy effectively exploited the media to reach the public through televised press conferences, periodic nationwide television and radio addresses, and personal television appearances such as Jacqueline Kennedy's tour of the White House and the president's informal discussions with selected television commentators.

The press remained nonetheless an unwieldy instrument because it also uncovered administration mistakes and the actual bases for policy decisions. Insofar as this independence intruded on the administration's penchant for secrecy in planning and executing foreign policy, a confrontation ensued. Following the Bay of Pigs debacle of April 17–19, 1961, the President lamented that press reports often presented "the nation's foes" with information otherwise obtainable only through espionage. Then, in the aftermath of the Cuban missile crisis of October 1962, Assistant Secretary of Defense for Public Affairs Arthur Sylvester spoke of news as "part of the weaponry" available to the government in the Cold War and affirmed the government's "right, if necessary, to lie to save itself" from nuclear war. President Kennedy also attempted to control his administration's press contacts. Tight restrictions were imposed during the Cuban missile crisis on Pentagon and State Department officials' contacts with the press. At the same time, White House aides were required to clear all communications with newsmen first with White House press secretary Pierre Salinger and to report back in writing the subject of these communications. Soon forced to abandon these procedures, the president nonetheless on two occasions in 1961 and 1962 directed the FBI to investigate the sources of leaks of "national security" information to the press.

This reliance on secrecy to sustain executive initiative in the formulation and enunciation of policy also diluted the cabinet's independent authority. The president accomplished this by two means. First, Kennedy appointed to the cabinet individuals of recognized administrative ability who lacked an independent political base. Kennedy appointed Robert McNamara of the Ford Motor Company secretary of defense and not Senator Henry Jackson or Senator Stuart Symington; he appointed Dean Rusk of the Rockefeller Foundation secretary of state and not Adlai Stevenson or Chester Bowles. Although able administrators, Rusk and McNamara lacked the nationwide constituency or political base of a Symington or a Stevenson. Kenndy's other cabinet appointments followed the same lines. The most controversial of these was his nomination of his brother, Robert Kennedy, as attorney general. Robert Kennedy's nomination raised questions of nepotism and competence—a lawyer, the attorney general-designate had had no prior legal experience, having served as counsel to various congressional committees after graduation from law school. No less important, Robert Kennedy had played a major role in his brother's campaigns for the Senate in 1952 and the presidency in 1960. This appointment, far more than those of J. Howard McGrath in 1949 or Herbert Brownell in 1953, threatened to politicize the Justice Department.

During Kennedy's tenure, the White House staff assumed many of the cabinet's advisory functions. Under the direction of McGeorge Bundy in foreign affairs and Theodore Sorenson in domestic affairs, an efficient staff was developed. The Kennedy White House staff, although primarily academics, were also an able group of technicians well versed in specific aspects of social, economic, or foreign policy. This staff included such men as Walt Rostow, William Bundy, Arthur Schlesinger, Jr., James Wiesner, Walter Heller. Kennedy's reliance on the White House staff strengthened his authority in two respects. The claim to executive privilege better enabled the president to conduct policy secretly. Unlike cabinet personnel, who were confirmed by the Senate and whose authority was created by congressional statute, White House aides were not liable to interrogation by congressional committees. Again, unlike cabinet officials, who were appointed either because of their political base or their association with powerful special interest groups (as the labor and commerce posts), the White House aides lacked an independent constituency. Their power and authority derived exclusively from their access and loyalty to the President.

THE NEW FRONTIER

These institutional changes did not insure congressional enactment of the president's New Frontier program of medical care for the aged, tax reform, elimination of regional poverty and technological unemployment, and aid to education. To enact these programs, the president would have to surmount the obstacle posed by conservative domination of the major committee posts dating from 1938. In his effort to do so, the president relied on Vice President Johnson's inside knowledge of the Senate. Moreover, in early 1961 the administration attempted to reduce the legislative roadblock that conservative control of the powerful Rules Committee posed by supporting Speaker Sam Rayburn's proposal to increase that committee's membership by three. Despite intensive lobbying, this effort barely succeeded—by a vote of 217–212.

Congress's mood remained conservative. Even though its proposals would have instituted only limited changes, the administration suffered a series of defeats. Its tax reform proposal was drastically amended, its public school aid bill was killed in committee, and its proposal to tighten production controls to reduce the size of the agriculture surplus was defeated in the House. Congress refused to enact the administration's Social Security reforms to enlarge payments, broaden coverage, and extend the number of weeks unemployed workers could collect. Moreover, on July 17, 1962, by a vote of 52–48, the Senate rejected the administration's most innovative recommendation—medical insurance to retired workers over sixty-five under the Social Security Act.

Having failed to move Congress, the president first attempted to develop popular support for his legislative program through televised press conferences and nationwide addresses. Then, the administration prepared to focus the 1962 congressional campaign on these issues. Before this could be fully attempted, the Cuban missile crisis of October 1962 intervened, compelling an abrupt termination of the planned extensive campaigning. The ensuing election thus provided no mandate for the New Frontier, as the composition of Congress was not significantly altered: a number of conservative congressmen were defeated (notably Walter Judd in the House and Homer Capehart in the Senate), and the Democrats sustained their dominant position in the Congress, losing only two seats in the reapportioned House (259–176) and gaining four seats in the Senate (68–32).

Never able to enact its broad program, the Kennedy Administration won only minor legislative victories. The Congress enacted the Area Development Act of 1961 to aid rural and economically depressed areas, the Higher Education Act of 1963 to aid colleges and community colleges to construct buildings and improve libraries (similar assistance was provided to medical and dental schools), and the Manpower Retraining Act of 1962 appropriating $435 million over three years to train the unemployed in new skills. Congress also ratified the president's executive order of March 1961 creating the Peace Corps. This dramatic program sent thousands of young men and women (and some middle-aged and retired persons) overseas to provide technical and educational assistance to underdeveloped countries. The Peace Corps exemplified the idealism of many young Americans: by March 1963, five thousand volunteers were serving overseas, by 1964 about ten thousand.

On the whole, however, Kennedy's legislative record was neither striking nor a bold contrast to that of the Eisenhower administration. Not that there were no economic problems at this time. In 1961, 6.7 percent of the labor force was unemployed; in 1960 the rate of national economic growth was less than 3 percent, and the nation's balance of payments deficit had increased from $1 billion in 1957 to nearly $4 billion in 1960.

The administration's cautious approach to economic reform limited its options. At no time during the 1960s did the Kennedy administration even attempt to develop popular support for a bold assault on poverty or social injustice. This can be explained in terms of its major priorities: to insure an activist foreign policy, balance the budget, and curb inflation. The appointment of the conservative Douglas Dillon as secretary of the treasury reflected the president's fear of an inflation stimulated by vast domestic spending programs.

The administration's desire to maximize U.S. international influence by sharply increasing defense spending further complicated this situation. Between 1961 and 1963, the development of solid-fuel intercontinental missiles, an accelerated submarine-launched Polaris missile program, and a commitment to stronger conventional forces including a counter-insurgency capability added roughly $17 billion to the defense budget. Because it was committed to controlling inflation and improving the U.S. trade position, the Kennedy administration could not advocate far-reaching domestic reform measures or counter the arguments of the fiscally conservative congressional leadership.

Rather than relying on public works spending to stimulate the domestic economy, the administration sought to increase business productivity and efficiency. Thus in 1962 it recommended a tax bill providing a 7 percent tax credit to business firms for investment either in new machinery or in plant modernization. Similarly, in 1962 the Internal Revenue Service liberalized depreciation-allowance rules, speeding up by more than one-third the rate at which machinery and equipment could be written off for tax purposes. The combination of tax credits and the liberalized IRS ruling reduced business taxes by $2.5 billion in 1962, and amounted to an 11 percent tax cut for corporations. President Kennedy did recommend personal income tax cuts of up to five percent to increase consumer purchasing power. Congress never seriously considered this measure. Never pressing the issue, in July 1962, Kennedy rejected the AFL–CIO's recommendation that he do so.

At the same time, the administration promoted the flow of American capital to Europe. A serious balance of payments problem existed and threatened to worsen. Between January 1960 and January 1969, for example, total U.S. foreign investment increased from $29.7 to $64.7 billion. By 1966, moreover, U.S. firms and individuals provided slightly more than 60 percent of all foreign capital investments in the world ($54.5 billion of $89.6 billion) . (In striking contast to this level of U.S. foreign investment, the Japanese component was only 1 percent; instead of investing overseas Japanese reinvested their earnings at home.) This capital outflow was not counterbalanced by an equally large increase in the export of manufactured and agricultural goods (which would produce jobs at home).

The Kennedy administration never developed policies effectively addressing these problems. On the one hand, it considered, but then rejected as unfair, curbs on foreign tourism. Capital investment overseas was not controlled or discouraged through higher taxes, restrictions were not imposed on dollar convertibility, and the dollar was not devalued to improve the U.S. trade position. The administration only sought to stimulate foreign trade. In 1962, the president urged another two-year extension of the Reciprocal Trade Agreements Act of 1934 and requested discretionary authority to reduce U.S. tariff rates by as much as 50 percent over a five-year period and to reduce to zero tariffs on those commodities traded primarily between the United States and the European Common Market. Congress approved these recommendations. Ensuing international negotiations to reduce European tariff barriers broke down, following France's 1963 veto of British admission to the Common Market. Farm exports rose by 70 percent, but much of this gain derived from the sale of U.S. surplus wheat to the Soviet Union. Capitalizing on the more relaxed atmosphere following Senate ratification in September 1963 of the Nuclear Test Ban Treaty, the Kennedy administration negotiated a Soviet purchase of 150 million bushels of U.S. surplus wheat at world commercial prices with one-half carried in U.S. merchant vessels.

ANTI-COMMUNIST POLITICS AND McCARTHYISM

In part, the Kennedy Administration could not develop broad support for its New Frontier reforms because of the persistence of Cold War anti-Communist fears. The administration never attempted to dispel these fears or even to curb the excesses of the programs instituted during the Truman and Eisenhower years ostensibly to protect the national security. The administration did not terminate the Eisenhower administration's rather repressive federal employee security program or institute more carefully defined procedures and norms. The president, for one, concurred that restrictions on individual liberties were needed to safeguard the nation at home and was unwilling to invest the political capital necessary to create a more restrained and liberal program (than one in which retention was based on the nebulous standard of "suitability"). Accordingly, Kennedy reaped the legacies of this nonpolicy. For, those individuals who had risen to the top security clearance posts during the Truman and Eisenhower years held distinctly alarmist views about disloyalty and subversion.

In Otto Otepka, the Department of State's top security official, the

Kennedy administration confronted one consequence of this passive policy. A conservative anti-Communist, Otepka refused to recommend security clearances for important Kennedy nominees to key policy positions (most notably Walt Whitman Rostow). Otepka based his refusal on the past political associations and views of these individuals. At first, the administration sought to bypass Otepka either by making temporary appointments or by appointing individuals to the National Security Council staff, neither of which required his clearance. Furthermore, by a November 1961 executive order, the president reduced the State Department's security staff by twenty-five, allegedly for economic reasons. One of the positions phased out was Otepka's post of deputy director of the Office of Security. Since he had civil service tenure and could not be fired, Otepka was promoted to head the Division of Evaluations, a post that was more honorific than substantive. Disturbed by this attempt to reduce Otepka's influence, conservatives on the Internal Security Subcommittee of the Senate Judiciary Committee initiated an investigaton into the adequacy of the State Department's security procedures. First, inviting the security officer to testify during its 1961 hearings, the subcommittee staff then retained covert contact with Otepka. When Otepka provided the subcommittee staff with classified documents in violation of a long-established executive order (of 1948), he was summarily dismissed from the State Department in 1963.

Ultimately, the Otepka affair resulted in a more restrained security program wherein merely holding controversial views or having had radical associations did not in themselves insure a denial of security clearance. The process by which Otepka's influence had been reduced, and the administration's hesitancy to challenge publicly either the unthinking anticommunism of the Cold War years or the belief that a serious internal security threat existed, minimized the political impact of this change. Despite this change in personnel, an elaborate security system was sustained, and a program based on extensive files detailing the dissident political activities of private citizens.

In 1961 and 1962 Attorney General Robert Kennedy actively lobbied for legislation authorizing wiretapping in national security cases and in criminal investigations involving extortion, kidnapping, murder, and narcotics. Failing in that legislative effort, the department nonetheless continued to authorize electronic surveillance. The attorney general made no attempt to restrain the FBI's use of this authority, acceding without question to all such FBI requests including (in October 1963) a wiretap on civil rights leader Martin Luther King, Jr. Nor did Attorney General Kennedy countermand former Attorney General Herbert Brownell's May 1954 directive authorizing wide-ranging microphone surveillance (bugging). During the Kennedy years, moreover, the FBI frequently installed bugs without securing the attorney general's prior approval on a case-by-case basis and in 1961 extended its so-called counterintelligence program to the Socialist Workers party, without having informed the attorney general of this action or even the 1956 program.

The fervid anti-Communist politics of the 1950s, however, would abate. There were two sides to the Kennedy administration's responses in the national security area: underlying these responses was a cautious liberalism but also a hesitancy to break from the anti-Communist norms of the 1950s. On the one hand, the administratiom heightened Cold War tensions by its July 1961 recommendation that Americans consider constructing family bomb shelters and its November 1961 announcement of federal aid for community shelters. The Bay of Pigs invasion, the administration's space and military defense recommendations, and the Cuban missile crisis further intensified anti-Communist politics. On the other hand, beginning in 1963 the administration sought to promote détente with the Soviets. In nationwide addresses, including a June 1963 commencement speech at American University and speeches urging ratification of the Nuclear Test Ban Treaty (approved by the Senate on September 24, 1963), President Kennedy emphasized the importance of co-existence and the shared interests of the United States and Soviet Union in reducing Cold War fears and tensions. Earlier, in March 1961, the Kennedy administration rescinded restrictions (of 1951 and 1956) on mail deliveries of pamphlets published in the Soviet Union or in Communist countries. (In 1962, Congress reestablished these restrictions, but the Supreme Court in *Lamont* v. *Postmaster General* (1965) declared this legislation unconstitutional.)

THE POLITICS OF CIVIL RIGHTS

Civil rights at first had not been a major priority of the Kennedy administration; it soon became the most explosive issue confronting the administration. From the first, the president and his attorney general expressed an interest in the plight of black Americans and condemned southern segregation practices. Yet the administration neither supported legislation to advance the civil rights of blacks nor exercised bold leadership to develop public understanding of such legislation as a moral issue. Instead in 1961 and 1962, the administration preferred the more time-consuming process of litigation.

This approach could not be sustained. In the aftermath of the *Brown* decision, black leaders aggressively challenged southern segregation practices by adopting tactics that insured confrontation. Leading this challenge were black college students. The example provided in February 1960 by students at North Carolina Agricultural and Technical State University, Greensboro, North Carolina, who staged a sit-in at chain store lunch counters, soon spread throughout the South (eventuating in the desegregation of lunch counters in over two thousand Southern cities by 1962). The Supreme Court's November 13, 1956, unanimous decision affirming a lower court ruling declaring an Alabama bus terminal segregation statute unconstitutional had a similar consequence.

In May 1961, to test compliance with this Court decision the Congress of Racial Equality (CORE), a black civil rights organization, organized the "freedom rides" from Washington, D.C., to New Orleans.

The well-publicized freedom rides encountered bitter white resistance in the South. Outside Anniston, Alabama, the Greyhound bus carrying the CORE freedom riders was incinerated by a white mob; continuing on another bus, the same freedom riders were mauled as they left a Trailways terminal in Birmingham, Alabama, and later were arrested and jailed in Jackson, Mississippi. CORE's intent to continue the rides posed the prospect of more threats to life and property. In response, the Justice Department pressured the ICC to issue rules banning segregation in carriers and terminals. At the same time, through quiet negotiations between civil rights leaders and liberal private foundations (the Ford Foundation and the Taconic Fund), an informal agreement was reached whereby civil rights groups shifted their energies from freedom rides to voter registration.

The voter registration drive did not reduce white or black militancy. The passivity of federal law enforcement officials—symbolized by FBI agents taking notes while blacks were arrested and at times beaten by local police officials during voter registration demonstrations—frustrated and increased the militancy of civil rights leaders. In contrast, diehard southern white leaders responded violently to black militancy by using terror and intimidation. The Kennedy administration responded cautiously to this potential confrontation; only when a major crisis emerged did the administration act to enforce federal law in the South.

Such a crisis erupted in the fall of 1962 when James Meredith, a black war veteran, attempted to enroll in the all-white University of Mississippi. Lengthy and involved negotiations between Attorney General Kennedy and Mississippi governor, Ross Barnett, to resolve this issue eventually broke down. Having exhausted all legal delays, Governor Barnett refused to allow Meredith to register at the university when he arrived with federal marshalls bearing a court order for his registration. Threatened with a contempt of court citation, Barnett backed down, and Meredith was allowed to register on September 30. In the interim, however, an angry mob had converged on the campus from all over the South, causing a riot that resulted in the deaths of a French journalist and a townsman who were merely observing the riot. Another 375 people were injured, including the shooting of 29 and the injuring of 166 federal marshals.

The Mississippi desegregation incident (though not the attendant violence) was repeated in May 1963, when Alabama Governor George Wallace sought to defy a court order to desegregate the University of Alabama. Less conciliatory and trusting this time, Attorney General Kennedy acted decisively, asking for definite assurance from Wallace that order would be preserved. Lacking this assurance, Kennedy federalized the Alabama National Guard and forcefully effected desegregation.

Black militancy was not confined to efforts to desegregate the universities. By 1963, young civil rights workers were risking harassment and terror to organize voter registration drives and test local segregation ordinances. Led by black civil rights leader Martin Luther King, Jr., in the spring of 1963 the black community of Birmingham, Alabama, staged repeated mass protest marches, which Police Chief Eugene ("Bull") Connor met with snarling police dogs, electric cattle prods, tear gas, and high-pressure water hoses. Thousands of school children were arrested as the violence of the police response was carried on national television. In September, four black children were killed as the result of a bombing of a Birmingham church—the twenty-first bombing involving blacks in that city during an eight-year period, all of which went unpunished.

Combined, these events created a moral issue compelling federal action. In response to the Meredith incident, the president went on national television to condemn senseless violence and to commend racial equality. Finally (having during the 1960 campaign criticized the Eisenhower administration's failure to end racial discrimination in federally assisted housing by executive order) Kennedy issued the appropriate executive order on November 22, 1962 banning segregation in new public housing. At the same time, the president created the President's Committee on Equal Employment Opportunity to combat discrimination in government agencies and among private contractors. Then, on June 19, 1963 the administration introduced a civil rights bill to implement desegregation in places of public accommodation, in publicly owned facilities, and in employment; and to extend the powers of the Department of Justice to enforce voting rights and expedite school desegregation. The administration's proposal encountered southern congressional opposition. By then, however, the civil rights movement had emerged as a powerful political force: on August 28, 1963, leaders organized a March on Washington of over 200,000 citizens to pressure Congress to enact the administration's civil rights bills.

Concurrent with this debate over civil rights and the attendant assault on segregation, the Supreme Court in *Baker* v. *Carr* (1962) introduced another thorny issue. In that decision, the Court enunciated the principle of "one man, one vote," ordering state legislatures to reapportion their lower houses on the basis of population. Until that decision, rural areas had greater representation than more densely populated urban areas, a system matching the "rotten boroughs" of nineteenth-century England. In Tennessee, the state that had been the subject of the 1962 Court decision, the state constitution specified that reapportionment be made every ten years. Since 1901, however, the state legislature had rejected all bills attempting to carry out that mandate. As a result, one-third of the electorate nominated two-thirds of the legislature.

In *Reynolds* v. *Sim* (1964) and *Wesberry* v. *Sanders* (1964) the Court extended its 1962 ruling to apply to both state legislative houses and to federal congressional districts. The Court's congressional district ruling had potentially large consequences for the House of Representatives. Until 1964, many rural– and small-town–dominated state legislatures had consciously gerrymandered congressional districts. Urban congressional districts, under this system, sometimes had 500,000 voters, while rural ones might have fewer than 100,000. In 1954, for example, Republican candidates for the House of Representatives from New York received 51 percent of the statewide vote but collected 61 percent of the seats.

All in all, having initially focused on foreign affairs, by 1963 the Kennedy administration had shifted to domestic affairs and politics. In the process, the Kennedy administration adopted more liberal positions on social and reform issues and moved haltingly to confront the challenges posed by southern segregation and an anti-Communist politics. Whether the administration would have adopted bolder positions cannot be known. On November 22, 1963, the young president was assassinated in Dallas, Texas, while on a trip seeking to repair the deep divisions within the Texas Democratic party and to mobilize support for his reelection. In death, Kennedy acquired the image of a romantic young president who had called the nation to greatness and who seemed on the verge of providing bold, moral leadership. Americans preferred to remember their fallen leader as a handsome, bold, Prince of Camelot rather than as a cool, calculating Machiavellian politician motivated as much by opportunism as principle.

SELECTED BIBLIOGRAPHY FOR SECTION VII

Because of their recency there is only a limited scholarship on the Eisenhower and Kennedy administrations. Most accounts are of the memoir or journalistic variety. The best historical surveys of the Eisenhower years include GARRY WILLS, *Nixon Agonistes* (1969) *; LAWRENCE WITTNER, *Cold War America* (1974) *; WILLIAM O'NEILL, *Coming Apart* (1971) *; HERBERT PARMET, *Eisenhower and the American Crusades* (1972) ; CHARLES ALEXANDER, *Holding the Line* (1975) ; JAMES SUNDQUIST, *Politics and Policy* (1968) ; SAMUEL LUBELL, *Revolt of the Moderates* (1956) *; GARY REICHARD, *The Reaffirmation of Republicanism* (1975) ; WALTER MURPHY, *Congress and the Court* (1962) ; ARCHIBALD COX, *The Warren Court* (1968) ; ARTHUR M. SCHLESINGER, JR., *The Imperial Presidency* (1973) *; H. L. NIEBURG, *In the Name of Science* (1966) ; RAOUL BERGER, *Executive Privilege* (1974) *; and NORMAN DORSEN and STEPHEN GILLERS, eds., *None of Your Business* (1975) .* Recommended for the Kennedy years are WILLIAM O'NEILL, *Coming Apart* (1971) *; JAMES SUNDQUIST, *Politics and Policy* (1968) ; ARTHUR SCHLESINGER, JR., *A Thousand Days* (1965) *; THEODORE SORENSON, *Kennedy* (1965) *; TOM WICKER, *JFK and LBJ* (1968) ; AUGUST MEIER and ELLIOTT RUDWICK,

* Available in paperback.

eds., *Black Protest in the Sixties* (1970) ; VICTOR NAVASKY, *Kennedy Justice* (1970) ; JIM HEATH, *John F. Kennedy and the Business Community* (1969) ; PAT WATTERS and STEPHEN GILLERS, eds., *Investigating the FBI* (1973) *; SANFORD UNGAR, *FBI* (1975) ; NELSON BLACKSTOCK, *COINTELPRO* (1976) *; and MORTON HALPERIN et al., *The Lawless State* (1976) .*

The standard works on the U.S. economy, society, and culture during the 1950s and early 1960s include JOHN K. GALBRAITH's two long essays, *American Capitalism* (1952) * and *The Affluent Society* (1958) *; C. WRIGHT MILLS, *White Collar* (1951) * and *The Power Elite* (1956) .* Other significant books are DANIEL BELL, *The End of Ideology* (1960) ,* SEYMOUR MARTIN LIPSET, *Political Man* (1962) .* For race relations and civil rights, see NUMAN V. BARTLEY, *The Rise of Massive Resistance: Race and Politics in the South during the 1950s* (1969) ; NEIL R. MC-MILLEN, *The Citizen's Council: Organized Resistance to the Second Reconstruction* (1971) ; DONALD R. MATTHEWS and JAMES W. PROTHRO, *Negroes and the New Southern Politics* (1966) ; CHARLES ABRAMS, *Forbidden Neighbors* (1955) ; and ELI GINZBERG, *The Negro Potential* (1956) .*

Among the books well worth consulting for the diplomacy of the 1950s and early 1960s, see NORMAN A. GRAEBNER, *The New Isolationism: A Study in Foreign Policy since 1950* (1956) ; HERMAN FINER, *Dulles Over Suez* (1964) ; MELVIN GURTOV, *The First Vietnam Crisis: Chinese Communist Strategy and United States Involvement, 1953–1954* (1967) *; GEORGE M. KAHIN and JOHN W. LEWIS, *The United States in Vietnam* (rev. ed., 1969) *; *The Pentagon Papers* (1971) *; JAMES L. RICHARDSON, *Germany and the Atlantic Alliance: The Interaction of Strategy and Politics* (1966) ; THEODORE DRAPER, *Castro's Revolution: Myths and Realities* (1962) ; DAVID WISE, and THOMAS ROSS, *The U-2 Affair* (1962) *; HERMAN KAHN, *On Thermonuclear War* (1960) *; and HENRY KISSINGER, *Nuclear Weapons and Foreign Policy* (1957) .* Two important works on Eisenhower's secretary of state are LOUIS GERSON, *John Foster Dulles* (1967) and TOWNSEND HOOPES, *The Devil and John Foster Dulles* (1973) .* For the military-industrial complex, read SEYMOUR MELMAN, *Pentagon Capitalism: The Political Economy of War* (1970) .* Among the better revisionist studies that criticize Kennedy's foreign policy are RICHARD WALTON, *Cold War and Counter-Revolution* (1972) *; LOUISE SIMMONS, *The Kennedy Doctrine* (1972) ; KARL MEYER and TAD SZULC, *The Cuban Invasion* (1962) ; cf ROBERT F. KENNEDY, *Thirteen Days* (1969) *; ELIE ABEL, *The Missile Crisis* (1966) ; and ROBERT A. DIVINE, ed., *The Cuban Missile Crisis* (1971) .* Two essential books concerning the early U.S. involvement in Vietnam are DAVID HALBERSTAM, *The Best and the Brightest* (1972) * and MALCOLM BROWNE, *The New Face of War* (1965) .

VIII

The Crack in the Picture Window: The Illusion of Affluence and the Crisis of the System

For almost three years the myth of John F. Kennedy's charisma cloaked the realities of American society. But as Camelot beckoned but never realized itself, Americans grew more aware that they lived in a class-ridden society. Since the Great Depression of the 1930s, many more citizens than ever before had achieved material affluence and government welfare programs protected millions of Americans. Yet the nation was still plagued by poverty amidst plenty, by a system that compelled anywhere from one-fifth to one-fourth of its people to live at or below the poverty level. It was a society also that still assigned its nonwhite citizens and most of its females to a form of second-class citizenship.

While poverty and discrimination remained the reward for millions of individual Americans, the nation's older cities and the industrial heartland of the Middle Atlantic, New England, and North Central states faced a crisis of their own. As population and industry moved to the south and west, the old, the nonwhite, and the poor filled the older industrial cities of the Northeast. Precisely at the moment that such metropolises as New York, Philadelphia, Cleveland, and Detroit were least able to offer their residents jobs, the demand for public service and social welfare increased. Deserted by the affluent white population and pockmarked by decayed and abandoned housing, the older central cities began to resemble devastated war zones. In New York City, for example, whole sections of the South Bronx and Brooklyn's Brownsville resembled the shattered Berlin of 1945. Ironically, the affluence of the 1950s and 1960s did more to damage urban America than World War II had.

The failure of the American promise of equality to realize itself for nonwhites, women, and the poor of all races and sexes finally caused a social upheaval. By the mid-1960s, domestic discontent exploded in protest and violence as nonwhites, the poor, and youths all demanded a new equality, sometimes separately and sometimes jointly. Blacks burned and looted their urban ghettoes, the poor overloaded the welfare system, students closed down college campuses and disrupted high schools, and women marched out of the kitchen.

Lyndon B. Johnson sought to contain domestic discontent and satisfy the new equality through his "Great Society" program. From 1963 through 1965 Johnson pushed through Congress all the social, economic, and civil rights reforms that Kennedy had promised but never delivered. Johnson promised equality for all, the elimination of want through a war on poverty, and a better, freer America. Compared to previous administrations, the Johnson administration proved innovative in the welfare area and spent federal dollars generously on domestic affairs. But Johnson's heart and mind were soon captured by a war more real than his figurative war on poverty.

By 1965, America's leaders had decided to wage a real, unrelenting, and ultimately unwinnable war abroad. Johnson and his advisers poured money, men, and materials into the Vietnamese quagmire. Before that war drew to its costly end almost a decade later in the administration of Gerald Ford, it destroyed Lyndon B. Johnson politically, divided the American nation as never before, and raised serious questions about much of the nation's Cold War diplomacy.

27

Economic Growth and Mass Society: The Realities of American Life 1950-1970

Throughout the 1950s the United States economy dominated much of the globe. Though less dependent on foreign trade for economic growth than most other industrial nations, the relatively small percentages of United States domestic production and capital that entered international trade had an enormous impact on the economies of smaller, less productive nations. Despite the fact that America's gross national product expanded relatively more slowly than in other rapidly industrializing societies, the United States' productive base was so immense that between 1949 and 1960 absolute real GNP increased from $206 billion to over $500 billion, a rise of nearly 51 percent. Such economic power, especially in relation to weaker, less industrialized societies, allowed the United States to set the terms of trade. Thus American corporations during the 1950s purchased raw materials cheaply and sold manufactured goods dearly. As America grew wealthier, raw material producing nations in Latin America, Africa, and Asia became relatively poorer.

At first during the 1960s the United States, as its pace of domestic economic growth accelerated, threw its weight around the globe with abandon. But, then, in the mid-1960s, especially as the war in Vietnam consumed considerable amounts of economic resources, the United States found itself at a disadvantage in a singularly competitive international market. More efficient and aggressive West German and Japanese industrialists seized overseas markets once the reserve of American businessmen. These nations, more dependent than the United States on external sources of raw materials, bid up the price of such goods as oil, copper, and rubber. Under the pressure of foreign competition and rising raw materials prices, the dollar gap of the 1950s (when foreign nations purchased more from the United States than they could afford) became the dollar shortage of the 1960s, (when our expenditures overseas exceeded earnings). America's trade surplus turned into a deficit, and the dollar was discarded in favor of the mark and the yen. The world's largest economy and most affluent society thus found itself by 1970 in an unexpected economic predicament.

How did the domestic economy change as the United States evolved from a position of global economic supremacy to one in which it faced stringent international competition? Which industries prospered, and which declined? Who prospered at home, and who suffered? Which individuals, groups, and institutions wielded economic power, and which did not?

THE NEW GROWTH INDUSTRIES

During the 1950s the old standbys of industrial America—railroads, coal mining, textiles, and shoe manufacturing—continued a decline that had begun in the 1920s. Railroad freight traffic fell steadily before the inroads of highway trucking, and passengers discarded long-distance trains in favor of more rapid air or cheaper bus transportation. Indeed by the end of the 1960s nearly the entire rail network in the Northeast, including the giant Penn-Central, had gone bankrupt. Coal found itself unable to compete with oil, natural gas, nuclear power, and water power; the nearly 600,000 miners employed at the end of World War II had fallen to about 100,000 by 1970. Cotton and woolen manufacture succumbed to synthetic fibers and domestic production to cheaper foreign manufactures. The shoe industry wrote an equally sorry chapter. Endicott-Johnson, the world's largest shoe manufacturer, had employed about 28,000 production workers in its New York "Southern Tier" factories in the late 1940s; by 1970 the production force had dipped below 4,000, the company began to dismantle its mills, and it even purchased shoes from Rumania for sale in its American retail outlets. Such instances of economic decline caused permanent depression in many New England towns and Appalachian coal patches. Again in the 1950s, as in the 1920s, economic sores festered on a generally healthy economic body.

If parts of New England and Appalachia declined economically, other regions of the nation prospered as never before. Wherever chemicals, business machines, electronics, and computers were manufactured the economy boomed, for these were the postwar growth industries *par excellence*. They were the new industries fit for survival in a "new society." Their economic growth based on technological and scientific advances, electronic-chemical firms stressed research and development programs (almost half of which were financed by the federal government), hired thousands of new graduates from the nation's universities, and served as the employers for a technocratic-scientific élite.

E. I. DuPont de Nemours & Co., Dow, and Monsanto prospered by manufacturing the synthetic goods that increasingly transformed the United States into a plastic society. Women wore their nylon stockings, people cooked on their Teflon pots and pans, men donned Dacron suits and Orlon shirts, and cars rolled on synthetic tires. Electronics, the child of wartime technological innovations, transistorized the postwar world. As tiny transistors replaced bulky tubes, teenagers walked everywhere holding the ubiquitous portable radio, and homebodies carried small TVs from room to room and house to patio. It was a society in which stereophonic sound replaced high fidelity phonographs only to be displaced in turn by quadraphonic sound. The electronics industry promised to turn every home into a private concert hall; indeed some new houses were built with sound systems wired into every room. And electric eyes now opened and shut garage doors.

Meantime, automation and its associated business machines produced still greater profits and affected the economy more substantially than plastics and electronics. What Ford and General Electric symbolized in the 1920s, IBM and Xerox personified in post–World War II America. Ever since the industrial revolution, machinery had been replacing human labor in manufacturing. But where humans once operated the new machines, in the postwar era of automation such companies as IBM produced machines that controlled themselves as well as other machines. Automation, based on the same simple feedback principle that operated home thermostats, controlled steel strip mills, auto assembly lines, and entire petro-chemical complexes. Computers, the next stage in the process of automation and first introduced commercially in 1950, had the ability to remember, sort materials, and make decisions; computers could also write poetry, compose music, play chess, and simulate strategy in a football game. So varied were the computer's uses that hotel chains, insurance companies, banks, airlines, and even universities (by the 1960s college students were identified by their IBM numbers) utilized them to simplify increasingly complex paper transactions. Where automation once threatened only blue-collar industrial workers, it now endangered the job security of millions of white-collar clerks. Even politicians, eager to predict beforehand the results of elections, worshiped at the shrine of IBM (known to its managerial employees as "I've been moved.").

While electronic data processing assisted businesses in coping with a mounting flood of paper, xerography multiplied endlessly the copies of vital, and not so vital, documents. Carbon copies became a relic, as Xerox machines copied documents in any form, fashion, or substance; copying machines could even produce documents indistinguishable from the original. Xerography eased the labors of research scholars, simplified the reproduction of business records, and ironically, in some cases under-mined secrecy in business and government. Without Xerox there might have been no *Pentagon Papers,* Jack Anderson and other muckrakers would have had far less grist for their journalistic mills, and Watergate's ramifications would have remained murkier still.

A primary reason for the success of the new growth industries was their close link to the Department of Defense, postwar America's largest single business contractor. The Pentagon supplied a lavish market for electronic and chemical manufacturers, as its deadly nuclear missiles with their elaborate guidance systems relied on synthetics, transistorized modules, and advanced computers. Even the more mundane hardware used by infantry, artillery, and nonnuclear aircraft depended heavily on electronic components and computerized guidance. NASA, too, provided an economic bonanza for the world of electronics. Without transistors, computers, and chemical fuels, there would have been no flight in space, nor man on the moon. Between government contracts and consumer demand for household appliances (household use of electricity tripled in the 1950s), the growth industries prospered enormously.

Even American agriculture changed in the postwar era. Farming became a big business. For most of the first two postwar decades, al-though agricultural productivity rose more rapidly than demand for foodstuffs, forcing millions of smaller farmers off the land, larger farmers prospered as a result of government subsidy programs and their own efficiency. Because production rose so rapidly, prices for agricultural goods declined, and profits could be made only by lowering unit costs of production through intensive application of fertilizers, use of costly new farm machinery, and introduction of sophisticated managerial tech-niques. Smaller farms simply lacked the resources and the capital to purchase fertilizer, acquire new machinery, and hire costly managerial experts. They also lacked enough land to make the use of expensive new machinery profitable or to join the soil bank. The latter was a program intended to promote soil conservation by paying farmers cash subsidies to let some of their land lie fallow. In other words, because most federal farm programs and subsidies were directly proportional to farm size and productivity, large farmers received proportionately more benefits than small farmers. The beneficiaries of federal largesse, the big farmers also possessed the land, capital, and knowledge necessary to grow food and fibers most efficiently. Consequently the percentage of owner-operated farms rose, and the size of the typical farm increased substantially. Cotton production shifted away from the old South, where it remained profitable only on the extremely large plantation, to the immense corpo-rate, irrigated, farms of Arizona and southern California. Farming in such prosperous agricultural states as California, Arizona, and Florida was justly labeled "agribusiness." In some cases industrial corporations, as Tenneco among others, purchased large farms. These corporate farmers were in an advantageous position to reap windfall profits after 1970 when the international terms of trade shifted in favor of agriculture.

THE NEW MERGER MOVEMENT

As old industries declined and new ones thrived, the concentration of economic power in fewer corporate hands accelerated again after World War II. (The trend toward concentration had first become apparent in the 1880s, reached epic proportions from 1897 to 1904, and seemed to culminate in the 1920s.) During the 1950s, despite a previous half-century of federal antitrust legislation aimed at preserving industrial competition, the fifty largest firms swallowed 471 competitors without government demurrer. And during the prosperity of the 1960s the corporate merger movement picked up added speed as it assumed new dimensions. Indeed, by the end of the 1960s the movement toward economic concentration appeared to consolidate power in banks and financial institutions more rapidly even than in manufacturing corporations. In an economic landscape marked by millions of competing firms, a single giant—American Telephone and Telegraph—controlled assets that equalled the combined holdings of one million smaller, typical business enterprises.

Not only did large businesses continue to merge and consolidate economic power; their share of business sales, income, and profits also rose. The top one hundred industrial corporations, which possessed 25 percent of all corporate wealth in 1929, owned 31 percent by 1960. In the auto industry, the remaining smaller, independent domestic auto manufacturers fell by the wayside in the 1950s. Only the big three—General Motors, Ford, and Chrysler—survived successfully (American Motors retained a minuscule share of the domestic market owing to fear of an antitrust suit on the part of its bigger competitors), and each of them was among the ten largest enterprises in the nation. General Motors, the world's largest industrial enterprise, had assets, expenditures, and revenues greater than any American state and many foreign nations. It made almost as much profit per car as it paid out in wages, and it raised car prices by $3.75 for every dollar added to its wage bill. Its very size and economic power enabled GM's managers to target (i.e., plan) a 20 percent profit on capital after taxes and to reach that goal by operating company plants at full capacity for only thirty-six out of fifty-two weeks. Such power and planning enabled it to achieve, by 1965, over $2 billion in annual profits.

In effect, then, by the 1960s the United States had a two-level economy. At one level, millions of small firms with minimal assets struggled to survive competitively. "Mom and Pop" stores, service stations, TV-appliance repair businesses, and small contractors worked long hours to turn a profit. More failed annually than succeeded. On the second level, meanwhile, .1 percent of the larger industrial corpora-tions—500 firms—accounted for one-third of all corporate activity. And within this group of 500, the top 50 industrials achieved aggregate sales equal to the total of the bottom 450, while the profits of the top 10 firms equalled nearly half the profits of the remaining 490. As the economist Robert Heilbroner has suggested, if some catastrophe obliterated the nation's 150 largest enterprises, society would come to a standstill and the American economy would be effectively destroyed. "A tiny group of immense corporations," writes Heilbroner, "constitutes a bastion of formidable economic strength within the sprawling expanse of the Amer-ican economy—indeed . . . it forms a virtual economic system within an economic system."

Corporate concentration had not brought pure economic monopoly. In fact, the share of the market controlled by the largest firms in their primary fields seemed to stabilize and in some cases shrink during the 1950s and 1960s. Expansion, however, carried many firms outside their customary markets into totally unfamiliar areas of enterprise. Interna-tional Telephone and Telegraph, the most notable exemplar of such new trends, acquired hotel chains, auto rental agencies, bakeries, insurance companies, and even book publishers. During the 1960s, conglomerate corporations proliferated. Once independent publishing firms of Alfred A. Knopf and Holt, Rinehart and Winston became respectively parts of the RCA and CBS empires. Oil companies purchased coal mines, and natural gas firms bought farms. Retail supermarket chains even offered vacation travel packages to their customers, and CBS, for a time, owned the New York Yankees.

Several factors induced the trend toward conglomerate enterprises. As had happened in previous decades, firms with surplus resources—whether capital, labor, or managerial—sought new and more profitable outlets in existing fields of economic activity. For some firms the op-portunity to acquire business enterprises in unrelated sectors of produc-tion or sales was a form of economic insurance. Losses in one area of the economy might be compensated by gains in another. Some acquisitions were rendered attractive by federal tax laws that practically underwrote the complete cost of corporate expansion. In other cases, mergers brought windfall profits to their promoters and to those who could benefit from the resulting rise or decline in stock prices. Finally, expansion being the central force behind corporate capitalism, many firms in saturated or fully developed sectors of the economy believed that they had to acquire assets in rising sectors or face company decline.

More disturbing to many observers of the economy than the trend to conglomerate corporations was the emergence during the 1960s of the multi-national enterprise. Not that corporations previously had lacked transnational ambitions; as early as the 1920s, the large oil companies had established a global economic empire in which oil executives wielded considerable diplomatic power. Beginning in the 1950s, however, and quickening rapidly in the following decade, numerous large American corporations built production facilities overseas. Instead of manufacturing their goods at home and exporting them abroad, multinational companies manufactured products overseas and sometimes imported them into the United States. The trend, of course, could work both ways, as evidenced by the decision of the French tire maker, Michelin, to open a factory in South Carolina and the Swedish automaker, Volvo, to consider building an assembly plant in Virginia.

The emergence of multinationals nevertheless posed a set of hard problems for American policymakers. Union officials had to consider how to bargain with corporations that threatened to shift work from more highly paid, unionized American workers to cheaper, nonunion foreign laborers. Government officials faced the problems of how to determine the multinational corporation's impact on international trade and tariff policies, how its foreign operations affected domestic tax liabilities, and how antitrust legislation applied to transnational enterprises. Trade union leaders and government officials, however, gave no sign of being able to shut the lid on the Pandora's box opened by the multinational corporation.

WHO HOLDS POWER?
MYTHS AND REALITIES

Several myths about the nature of the American economic system gained wide attention in the postwar era. First and foremost was the concept that the United States during the Eisenhower years had built a "people's capitalism." "People's capitalism" stood on two economic legs: (1) The reality of ever-rising real incomes and the effective abolition of poverty by the affluent society, and (2) the rapid spread of stock ownership among the mass of Americans, whether by direct purchase or through mutual funds. A grain of truth buttressed both myths, but economic realities hinted at a more complex and less sanguine situation.

Rising incomes during the 1940s and 1950s did lift many Americans above the poverty level and give them material comforts unimaginable during the Great Depression. The depression and the war in fact stimulated a marginal redistribution of income away from the top 20 percent of the population to the remainder. But such improvements cloaked substantial inequalities in income and wealth that grew again after the Korean War. By 1953 the share of income received by the top 20 percent of the population rose, as did the share of the top 5 percent of citizens. In 1957 the highest fifth earned 45.3 percent of all income, and the top 5 percent received more than the bottom 40 percent combined. By the end of the 1960s the top 2 percent of income receivers enjoyed annual incomes ten times greater than the nation's average.

This functional economic system, which protected privilege at the top, fostered poverty at the bottom. In 1959, at the end of the affluent

Eisenhower years, a Census Bureau statistician esimated that, depending on precisely where one drew the poverty line, between 20 percent and 40 percent of American families lived in poverty. Michael Harrington's *The Other America* (1962), the book that triggered the Kennedy-Johnson war on poverty, was remarkably reminiscent of Robert Hunter's *Poverty* (1904); yet the intervening sixty years had seen Progressivism, a New Era, the New Deal, the Fair Deal, the New Frontier, two world wars, and numerous smaller wars. After all this, the world's wealthiest nation remained haunted by the biblical prophesy that "the poor ye shall always have with you."

Just as poverty persisted, even in a "people's capitalism," actual ownership of capital and wealth remained concentrated among a small elite despite wider stock ownership. A study by a University of Wisconsin economist estimated that in 1954, 1.6 percent of the adult population held 90 percent of corporate bonds and nearly all state and municipal bonds. Careful students of the modern corporation have shown that among the 150 supercorporations as few as 200 to 300 families effectively possess stock control of these firms. Moreover, the top 2 percent income level of all American families own between two-thirds and three-quarters of all corporate stock, and the concentration of such ownership has persisted since 1922. By 1970 many more Americans may have owned a few shares of stock but the same small elite of wealthy individuals and families, labeled the "super rich" by Ferdinand Lundberg, exercised effective economic power.

Those defenders of the American economic system who never merchandized the goods associated with "people's capitalism" hawked another myth: the concept of altruistic management. Adolph A. Berle, Jr., who together with Gardiner Means, had warned Americans early in the 1930s about the dangers inherent in an economic system that separated business management from ownership and hence promoted corporate lassitude and irresponsibility, in the 1950s asserted that corporate executives had developed a conscience. In his *20th Century Capitalist Revolution* (1955), Berle proclaimed that corporate management, staffed largely by university graduates with intellectual and cultural pretensions, individuals who operated the firm but did not own it, preferred public service to classical profit making. The modern corporation with a conscience served the local community through United Fund contributions, supported local cultural and recreational programs, and sometimes even pampered its employees. The popular observer of American mores, John Brooks, noted: "The big, coldly menacing grizzlies of 1939 [are] the superbig, smiling, approval-seeking pandas of 1964." "The capitalist robber baron," added another commentator, "has turned out to be a love-starved aunt cramming cake into eager little mouths."

The concept of public-service, nonprofit-oriented managements with a conscience conflicted with several economic realities. First, many top executives not only managed their companies but also owned large shares of the stock, at least 10 percent in the one hundred largest industrials.

Second, the actual income and economic security of executives depended on the profit-making potentialities of their firms, and most high executives were not bashful about raising their own salaries. In 1964 the incomes of the key men in the ten largest corporations ranged from $300,000 to over $600,000, with most of that income dependent on bonuses and incentive payments related to corporate profits. These men also cherished the power that flowed from corporate growth, which in turn derived from earnings and profits. Perhaps the Marxist economist Paul Baran, essentially captured the difference between the late nineteenth-century robber baron and the modern manager. "The one stole from the company," he wrote, "the other steals for it."

Like most modern industrial economies, the United States by the 1960s operated an economic system based on planning by business and government elites. In the words of John Kenneth Galbraith, "the mature corporation is an arm of the state." It was a system in which private executives and public officials allied themselves to manage aggregate demand, induce price stability, insure corporate profits, and stimulate economic growth. Publicly financed secondary schools and universities provided corporations with trained manpower. Government, moreover, used its monetary and fiscal authority to sustain aggregate consumer demand and its coercive power to stabilize wages and prices. In return, corporate officials served the avowed public goal of an ever-rising GNP. While government and corporations bolstered each other, individual executives like Charles E. Wilson of General Motors (first secretary of defense in the Eisenhower administration), Neil McElroy of Proctor and Gamble (Wilson's successor as defense secretary), and Douglas Dillon and John J. McCloy of Wall Street (key members of the State Department–national security complex) regularly passed through a revolving door that carried them in and out of public service. The federal executive drew its cabinet officials from the leading corporations, in turn the corporations recruited new executives from the government, especially from among military men. Generals Omar N. Bradley, Douglas MacArthur, and Lucius Clay, became directors of leading industrial corporations, and scores of army colonels and navy captains became business directors and purchasing agents.

By the 1950s the federal government was far and away the largest single consumer in the economic marketplace. Federal expenditures for all goods and services, which had been only $3.5 billion in 1929, were $57 billion in 1965 and had increased from 1.7 percent of GNP in 1929 to 8.4 percent in 1965. Federal budget decisions determined the difference between economic recession and boom, between corporate retrenchment and expansion. The Kennedy administration publicly asserted the federal government's economic role by its adoption of Keynesian economics. The Keynesian theory calls for the government to regulate aggregate demand by stimulating consumption and inducing prosperity through tax cuts and federal deficits and retarding inflation and checking demand by tax increases and budget surpluses.

In practice, however, the new economics worked effectively in only one direction. The Kennedy administration could reduce taxes in order to stimulate demand and promote employment. But the Johnson, Nixon, and Ford administrations could not raise taxes is order to dampen demand and check inflation. Keynesian economics also produced warped results. Lower taxes and higher deficits benefited the privileged proportionately much more than the underprivileged. And when the government sought to dampen runaway prosperity, the poor, as usual, paid the price in terms of rising unemployment. Worse yet, the bulk of government expenditures, instead of being used for schools, hospitals, libraries, or low-cost housing, went to the creation of weapons of destruction, for military-related expenditures provided the fulcrum for the Keynesian system.

The Cold War admirably suited the needs of the domestic economy. Government expenditures for housing, health, education, or income maintenance threatened the existing structure of economic privilege, caused class and group conflict, and subverted the politics of consensus. But few dared to question the cost of defense, for, as the cliché puts it, the price of freedom is never too dear. A *New York Times* letter to the editor warned about a 1969 proposal to end hunger in the United States: "Does Senator McGovern seriously mean that he is willing to risk annihilation of the entire United States just to subsidize the cost of solving the hunger problem?" Such beliefs bolstered an economic system in which, during the 1960s, half the government's funds went for military purposes, and the Defense Department had accumulated assets greater than the nation's seventy-five largest industries and spent more than the whole federal government had before the Great Depression. Military expenditures, moreover, regularly surpassed the cash total of federal personal income taxes, accounted for one-quarter of federal public works and employed some 3.2 million workers in defense industries and another 1.1 million as civilian employees of the Defense Department and armed services. Defense spending in the mid-1960s financed 30 percent of all manufacturing jobs in Kansas, 28 percent in Washington state, and over 20 percent in five other states. And the military subsidized one-third of all American research. Defense Department-sponsored programs saved the Litton Industries nuclear shipbuilding venture from bankruptcy, kept Grumman Aircraft alive on Long Island, and financed the research and production programs of such other aeronautical firms as North American Aviation, McDonnell Douglas, and General Dynamics as well as their direct and indirect subcontractors.

By the 1960s, even workers and their unions had been integrated into the corporate warfare-welfare state. As blue-collar employment declined, the increasing number of white-collar managerial employees identified their economic futures with the corporations that they served. Generally high employment levels as well as relatively high wages lessened the importance of trade unions as instruments of economic power. A variety of government programs, from minimum wage legislation to social security, stabilized income and improved job security, further undermining the role of the traditional trade union. As a result, trade unions stopped growing after the Korean War and actually lost members in such basic industries as steel and autos. Trade unions, especially those situated in the dominant mass production sectors of the economy, increasingly sought to ease employee discontent and encourage workers to identify with their companies, enforce uniform wage rates among competitive firms, and negotiate long-term contracts with binding no-strike clauses that provided economic security for large enterprises as well as job security for workers.

American industrialists, workers, and consumers seemed caught in an insurmountable economic web. "The imperatives of organization, technology, and planning operate," wrote John Kenneth Galbraith, to make "much of what happens . . . inevitable and the same." As the 1960s drew to a close, however, many Americans began to rebel against the restraints of an apparently runaway economic machine.

However productive and finely integrated the American economic system appeared, it was not without its flaws, flaws that grew as the 1960s passed into the 1970s. Technology could send a rocket to the moon but it could not eradicate slum housing. It could put men in space yet not render work more humane and satisfying. The economy could produce unprecedented national wealth but not end poverty or reduce special privilege. Industry could manufacture the most sophisticated weapons of warfare and destruction but not produce consumer goods that would work well or last long. Keynesian economics, as practiced by federal officials, could stimulate demand but not erase unemployment or halt inflation. As the 1960s ended, the economy seemed mired at a high permanent level of unemployment (still the primary cause of poverty aside from old age and illness) yet faced with an escalating rate of inflation that seemed impermeable to cure. Thus, as the 1970s began, the economic system came under attack from dissatisfied consumers, discontented workers, inflation-ridden pensioners, and low-income citizens.

MASS SOCIETY

The affluence that the economic growth of the 1950s and the 1960s produced failed to satisfy many concerned citizens and also critics of United States society. New questions began to be raised about the quality of American life. Where once left-wing intellectuals had lamented the ubiquity of poverty and mass unemployment, they now castigated a supermarket society in which shoppers had become as indistinguishable from each other as the prepackaged merchandise that they purchased. William F. Whyte berated the "Organization Man" who molded his personality to suit the corporate committee; C. Wright Mills condemned the new class of white-collar men who became captives of their status;

and David Riesman, the leading sociological critic of the affluent era, described the mass of postwar Americans as members of a "lonely crowd," unable to establish values or make decisions apart from the group. Both liberal and conservative observers began to worry that Americans had lost their sense of moral purpose amidst a plethora of consumer goods. They, too, wondered if a mass society could rise above the level of a car dealer's showroom.

AFFLUENCE AND A CONSUMER PUBLIC

Mass consumption depended on constantly rising real wage levels, a condition the United States economy sustained between 1945 and 1960. By 1956 the real income of the average American was more than 50 percent greater than it had been in 1929, and by 1960 it was 35 percent higher than it had been in the last year of World War II.

How the typical American spent his increased earnings was determined as much by external factors as by intrinsic, real personal needs. Indeed, the larger the income an individual earned the more choice he had in its disposal. As growing numbers of citizens satisfied their need for food and shelter, the manufacturers of attractive but nonessential goods competed lustily for the consumer's dollar.

To sell the autos, refrigerators, dishwashers, stereo sets, and other appliances that rolled off production lines, manufacturers resorted to Madison Avenue and intensive advertising.* Between 1946 and 1957 expenditures on advertising increased by almost 300 percent, rising to over $10 billion annually. Not only did the money devoted to advertising rise significantly, but the lords of Madison Avenue also developed the most sophisticated selling tactics in history. Successful advertising was complicated when consumers had to select from among breakfast cereals and cars that differed neither in price nor utility and also had to be convinced to buy products never before manufactured. Employing all the tools of normal (and abnormal) psychology, advertisers alerted consumers to the psychic benefits of larger cars, sweeter-smelling underarms, striped toothpaste, and Marlboro—the man's cigarette. Brighter teeth, Madison Avenue implied, guaranteed every wallflower a desirable husband, and the cigarillo won every man a buxom and accommodating female. Able to allocate money and talent to the one-minute television spot, advertisers bombarded viewers with irresistible commercials. Madison Avenue sales campaigns got such good results in the marketplace that many candidates for public office in time substituted the one-minute television spot for the half-hour platform speech. By the 1960s, Madison

---

* The term "Madison Avenue" became a synonym for high-powered advertising created by advertising agencies, many of which had their offices on New York City's Madison Avenue.

Avenue sold presidents as well as Pontiacs, congressmen as well as Cadillacs.

More than advertising was required to create the postwar consumer society. Regardless of the reality of rising wages, millions of citizens still lacked income sufficient to satisfy their demand for goods. A 1950 Census Bureau survey of over seven thousand families, for example, showed that 60 percent of them with earnings of $4,000 or less spent more than they earned. Moreover, even those workers whose incomes exceeded their current expenses seldom had a margin of savings adequate to sustain the cash purchase of such costly durables as autos and large home appliances. Only by borrowing money on the assumption that higher future earnings would render repayment painless could most citizens satisfy their desire for cars and dishwashers.

As advertising stimulated the demand for consumer goods, the nation's financial institutions financed their purchase. Between 1946 and 1957, although total public debt rose by only 11 percent and the federal debt actually declined, private indebtedness increased by 360 percent. More remarkable still was the rise in consumer installment indebtedness; the estimated annual installment credit outstanding soared from just over $4 billion in 1946 to over $34 billion in 1957. Automobile installment credit alone rose from under $1 billion to in excess of $15 billion. The propensity to buy now and pay later made the cash registers ring. Detroit produced over five million new cars in 1949 and in the peak year of 1955 it sold nearly eight million autos, a record not surpassed until the late 1960s.

For those individuals whose earnings rose annually, consumer credit and installment buying provided a relatively easy means to achieve rapid material affluence. But for those Americans whose income failed to rise, or rose only haltingly, installment buying became more an economic trap than an avenue to comfort. Unable to save sufficient cash to underwrite their purchases, these unfortunate consumers frequently failed to earn enough income to pay the interest as well as the principal on their installment contract. Indeed, in many cases, credit costs effectively increased the original purchase price by one-third or more.

The consumption craze took many strange shapes in the 1950s. Such economists as Walt W. Rostow suggested that when men and women in America's "high mass consumption society" satisfied their desire for cars and appliances, they invested surplus income in babies. Whatever the precise cause, no one could doubt that a population explosion took place from 1945 through the 1950s. Not only did medical science and improved nutrition lengthen life spans but the multiple (three or more) child household became commonplace. The public philosophy of the 1950s, as proclaimed by psychologists, TV comedians, preachers, and politicians, sanctified the home and woman's place in it. The ideal female married young and well, bore a large brood, and remained home to create the perfect environment for keeping the American family together. The sanctification of the family and the idealization of the woman as mother and homemaker played its part in promoting the growth of a consumer society. Larger families required bigger houses with more appliances to simplify "mom's" work and increased purchases to provide for the children. Before long many one-car families would become two-, three-, and in rare instances even four-car households.

If affluence enabled many Americans to enjoy unsurpassed material comforts, millions of citizens still struggled to make ends meet. If new recruits joined the "jet set" and flew to vacations in Rio, Biarritz, and Monaco, many workers, like the Bronx couple that *New York Times* reporter A. H. Raskin investigated, who lived half an hour by subway from Times Square saw "less of the Great White Way than the average farmer from Pumpkin Corners." John K Galbraith lamented in *The Affluent Society* the ubiquity of public squalor amidst America's opulence and hinted at the persistence of poverty. Regardless of how unequally and inequitably the fruits of affluence were distributed, many of those Americans who did not share fully still felt themselves more comfortable in the 1950s than they had been in the 1930s and more fortunate than non-Americans. As Raskin's Bronx worker remarked: "We're a lot better off than we would be anywhere else in the world. We may not get everything we want, but at least we can choose what to do with our money. In other countries they don't even have a choice. No matter how bad things are, we're better off than they are."

THE TRIUMPH OF THE SUBURBS

The emergence of an affluent mass consumer society saw the reassertion of a pattern of residential mobility and settlement that had been retarded by depression and war. In the 1950s, as also had happened in the 1920s, millions of citizens deserted the cities for the suburbs. Except in the South and Southwest where urban population continued to grow as a result of the annexation of adjacent land, the bulk of metropolitan population growth occurred in the suburbs. By 1960 in most northern metropolises, suburban residents outnumbered central city occupants, and as people fled the urban core, so, too, did businesses, trades, and professions. The "Miracle Mile" in Manhasset on Long Island's North Shore brought Fifth Avenue to the suburbs, just as similar suburban shopping centers elsewhere attracted downtown's most prestigious retailers to new locations with ample parking space and affluent consumers.

Suburban development stimulated a housing boom of unprecedented dimensions. As of 1960, one-fourth of all the housing in the nation had been constructed in the previous decade, during which annual new housing starts regularly exceeded the growth of new households. In the 1950s, for the first time in history, more Americans owned their homes, albeit usually with heavy mortgages, than rented dwelling space.

The reasons for this exodus to suburbia might have remained constant from the 1920s to the 1950s; after 1945, however, the opportunity to flee the city had expanded significantly. The desire for a private home with a lawn and garden in a suburban arcadia had long been an integral aspect of popular culture. The economic costs and occupational impracticality of suburban life, however, had put it beyond the reach of most Americans. All this changed in the postwar world, as federal credit and highway policies, technological innovations, and a mass consumer society reshaped metropolitan America.

In the postwar world, as automobile ownership became general, Americans were liberated from dependence on mass public transit. The possession of a private car snapped the link that hitherto had connected the individual's home to his place of work via public transit. Through federal and state highway programs funded by fuel taxes, limited access highways were constructed that linked new suburbs and older central cities. The prospect of smooth, unimpeded traffic flow on safe, modern highways, in private cars led passengers to abandon subways, trolleys, and buses and to move from the city to the suburbs. Americans were now free to reside wherever their incomes allowed, and suburbia was also opening up to a wider range of incomes.

Federal policies enlarged the suburban housing market by providing generous mortgage loans to World War II veterans and by insuring the mortgages marketed by private lending agencies. The self-amortizing mortgage, whereby the homeowner paid back his original loan at a fixed monthly rate (comparable to rent) over a twenty-to-thirty-year term, became the common means to home ownership. Federal tax policy also stimulated suburban expansion, for citizens received a generous income tax deduction for the interest charges and real estate taxes paid on their homes. The availability of long-term credit and the inducement of tax advantages drew comfortable middle-class Americans to suburbia. Working-class citizens, however, needed a further inducement: the chance to purchase a home within their means. Here the firm of Arthur Levitt and Sons provided one solution, doing for the housing market what Ford had done for autos. Just as Ford offered a basic car in a single color at a low price, Levitt sold a standardized dwelling unit in one color—white—at a price within the reach of thousands of working-class Americans. His original "little boxes" constructed in the first Levittown in central Long Island soon had counterparts in New Jersey and Pennsylvania.

Suburbia, in general, and Levittown, in particular, occasioned a new image of American society, one consonant with the concept of a mass, consumer public. Suburbia, in the words of social critic and planner, Lewis Mumford, offered the prospect of

> a multitude of uniform, identifiable houses, lined up inflexibly, at uniform distances, on uniform roads, in a treeless communal waste, inhabited by people of the same class, the same income, the same age group, witnessing the same television performances, eating the same tasteless pre-fabricated foods, from the same freezers, conforming in every outward and inward respect to a common mold.

A new life style
(Shel Hershorn/ Black Star)

In the "little boxes made of ticky tacky," about which Pete Seeger sang, lived William F. Whyte's "organization men" who in their haste to adjust smoothly to their fellow junior executives became as undifferentiated as the houses in which they dwelled.

Critics of suburbia mounted a contradictory offensive against the emerging character of national life. On the one hand, they charged suburban residents with uniformity, dullness, and unthinking accommodation to neighborhood mores. On the other hand, they indicted suburbanites, as did John Keats in *The Crack in the Picture Window* for alcoholism, adultery (wife-swapping was said to be the favorite indoor suburban sport), and juvenile delinquency. Whatever the substance of the criticism, it seemed to miss the mark, for suburban growth proceeded unabated.

In fact most social criticism attacked fictional suburbia, not its reality. By the late 1950s American suburbia contained as many differences as similarities; indeed, there was no single ideal-type suburban community. Communities of upwardly mobile young executives who preferred accommodation to conflict, uniformity to individualism, such as William F. Whyte located in Chicago's environs, did, of course, exist. So, too, did communities of wealthy senior executives and rentiers, whose incomes and security enabled them to experiment with architecture and engage in eccentric behavior. At the other end of the suburban spectrum, one could find developments of working-class people whose residents had moved from the city but had scarcely altered their life style; they still voted Democratic, preferred baseball to ballet, and the company of relatives to that of neighbors. Even the allegedly undifferentiated, standardized world of Levittown contained, as the sociologist Herbert Gans discovered, a universe of strikingly individualized homes. Levittowners wasted no time in applying personal touches and preferences to the standardized homes and to creating a society in which, according to Gans, they felt very much at home and comfortable.

More disturbing for the future of American society than suburbia's alleged propensity to uniformity, alcoholism, and adultery was the impact of suburbia on racial divisions. The flight to suburbia was primarily a white phenomenon, a movement that transformed the typical American metropolis into a white cupcake with a black filling. Between 1950 and 1960, nonwhite population increases accounted for more than 30 percent of the urban growth in the nation's fifty leading metropolises, and by 1960 blacks formed nearly a fifth of the residents in 212 standard metropolitan statistical areas. By 1970 every city in the state of New York, except Rochester, had experienced decline in its total white population. In that same year, the population of Washington, D.C. was 71.1 percent black, and Newark, N.J., Gary, Ind., and Atlanta, Ga. had populations more than 50 percent black. Seven other major cities had black populations in excess of 40 percent. The suburbs, however, experienced an increase in nonwhite population of from only 4.2 percent to 4.5 percent. In suburban Washington, for example, only 7.9 percent of the total population was nonwhite. This residential transformation laid the foundation for the creation of the two nations—one white and one black—that the Kerner Commission warned against in its report on the ghetto riots of the 1960s.

DEMOGRAPHIC CHANGE

Just as population redistributed itself between city and suburbs. it shifted between rural and urban districts, east and west. Even during the peak agricultural prosperity of World War II, millions of Americans left the countryside for jobs in defense-related urban industries. In 1943 alone, three million people deserted farms; and in eight of the thirteen years between 1942 and 1954, more than a million Americans a year gave up farm life. After 1957 the drift from the countryside accelerated, depositing millions of former agrarians, white as well as black, on the American cities' doorsteps.

In another population shift, many midwesterners and easterners moved west. California alone accounted for one-fifth of the nation's population increase in the 1950s, and by 1963 surpassed New York as the most populous state. Oregon and Washington also received their share of migrants, as did even Alaska and Hawaii, both of which achieved statehood in 1959. Nothing so graphically revealed the westward drift than an event in 1958 that rendered the impossible possible: the Brooklyn Dodgers deserted their hallowed Ebbetts Field for sunny Los Angeles, where a new mass market promised greater riches for the team's management. That same year the New York baseball Giants left Manhattan for San Francisco, and soon major league baseball teams, once limited to an area north of the Ohio River and east of the Mississippi River (St. Louis excepted), had franchises in Kansas City, Atlanta, Houston, Dallas (its suburbs in fact), Oakland, San Diego, and Seattle. Other professional sports also drifted south and west to follow population, the lucrative television market, and the consumer dollar.

Population redistribution took several unexpected forms. The South, which for a century had exported its surplus population, began in the mid-1950s to attract newcomers. Population growth was most striking in the boom space-defense industries region along the Gulf Coast from Houston, Texas, to Mobile, Alabama, and the retirement-vacation haven, Florida. By the 1960s, even the interior South, from Virginia to Alabama, benefited from the migration of industries and people, with industry expanding more rapidly in the rural South than elsewhere in the nation. By the 1970s major European manufacturers were considering the construction of plants in South Carolina and Virginia.

Population figuratively exploded in the postwar world. By 1960 there were one-third again more Americans than in 1940. The birthrate, which had begun to increase markedly during the war, took off afterwards, rising steadily each year until by 1956 it approached the levels common before the 1920s and the introduction of modern contraceptive techniques. In the 1950s, however, none of the factors operated that had previously countervailed high birth rates and thus retarded population growth. Modern medicine continued to reduce the incidence of infant mortality; war-stimulated advances in antibiotics and surgical methods rendered infections less fatal; and medical breakthroughs such as an antipolio vaccine ended one of the last of the childhood epidemic diseases. For everyone—infant as well as adult, men and women, whites and nonwhites—life expectancies rose, until by 1960 the average life expectancy neared the allotted biblical three score and ten.

Millions of Americans in the postwar years also began to fill a changed working world. Blue-collar work remained the dominant form of employment for men, the largest number of whom earned their wages in manufacturing, mining, and construction. Almost 50 percent of the male labor force toiled at traditional blue-collar vocations, a percentage that scarcely shrank in the postwar decades, though the proportion of un-skilled manual laborers fell precipitously. Although blue-collar workers remained the core of the workworld, the outlines of what some observers considered a "new working class" became manifest in the 1950s. As the proportion of Americans engaged in agriculture and in self-employ-ment trades and professions declined further, the number of citizens filling salaried professional and technical positions rose from only 4.3 percent of the work force in 1900 to 14.4 percent in 1970; at the same time the proportion of workers employed in white-collar clerical and sales jobs soared by 1970 to 23.4 percent of the labor force. Service, clerical, and technical workers in the so-called white-collar trades by 1960 out-numbered blue-collar laborers. Particularly, as more and more women entered the labor force, they filtered into clerical, sales, and service occupations (in 1970 almost 80 percent of female workers fell in those three categories), a form of work that commentators suggested created a different ambience and consciousness from blue-collar labor.

The emergence of a "new working class" in the 1950s and its rapid growth thereafter raised significant questions about the future of Ameri-can society. By and large the new occupations required a longer formal education, if not more intelligence, than traditional blue-collar jobs. Indeed, a college degree rather than a union card often became the means to opportunity. The increasing importance of white-collar work-ers, especially in the professional and technical areas, led some sociolo-gists to conclude that the era of militant labor unionism and employee-employer confrontations was ending. Professional workers and their white-collar associates, it was said, identified with management, not with each other, and assumed that their future security was implicitly linked to the growth of the firm. Other commentators suggested that the edu-cated salariat in command of society's most vital resource—knowledge—would ultimately use their brainpower to seize economic and social control from the money managers and profitmakers. In time the new "meritocracy" would play the role once prophesied for it by Thorstein Veblen: the professional technocrats would manage an economy based on production for use, not profit, for creation, not destruction. Still other critics, however, thought such images of the "professional meritocracy" to be fairy tales. These critics elaborated a different scenario for the future in which the technocrats, aware that they had knowledge but not power, intelligence but not autonomy, joined forces with the blue-collar union-ists to struggle against corporate management for workers' control. Which vision of the role of the "new working class" would materialize only the future would tell.

If the social impact of the transformed occupational universe seemed unclear as the 1950s drew to a close, the importance of formal schooling for individual social and economic advancement had become self-evident. By the 1950s only a rare worker in the under-30 age group had less than a

The war on the campuses, Columbia Univ.,
May 22, 1968 2:30 a.m.

(Wide World Photos)

high school education, and increasing numbers had had some higher
education. By 1970, over 30 percent of American males and 20 percent of
females had gone to college, with almost 20 percent of blue-collar workers
and over 80 percent of the "new working class" also having attended
college (over 65 percent of the technocrats completed at least four years
of college). More young Californians attended college in the 1960s than
the entire French university population, and in some years new college
registrations in the U.S. exceeded Britain's total student body in higher
education.

During the 1950s the rising college enrollment induced social
optimism; it seemed to presage a social order in which once-excluded
individuals and classes would rise to positions of government, corporate,
and professional power. By the mid-1960s, however, when universities
had become as much a part of the mass society as other American
institutions, pessimism began to replace optimism, anxiety conquered
certainty. Indeed, by 1970, as riots, bombings, and deaths paralyzed the

nation's campuses, higher education was perceived by some citizens more as a threat to the social order than as a panacea for the nation's ills.

MASS CULTURE

As affluence gave Americans wider consumption choices and technological innovation brought varied forms of entertainment directly into the home, mass culture replaced high culture. Not only did television and the unbreakable long-playing record seem to dilute the culture once reserved for wealthy or high-brow Americans but they also homogenized the ethnic and regional cultures associated with working-class Americans. In critic Dwight MacDonald's acerbic phrase, the United States in the 1950s created a "mid-cult" (also a "mass cult") that standardized, homogenized, and bastardized the more vital and lively popular and high cultures.

Television was the spearhead for the standardization of culture. In 1946 only 17,000 homes had television sets, and they were in the few major metropolitan centers that had transmitting stations. By 1949 annual sales reached almost three million sets, and by 1954 two-thirds of American families possessed a TV set. A new symbol—the television antenna—dominated the American skyline, whether on a New York tenement roof, a Mississippi sharecropper's shack, or a California ranch-style house. By the 1960s the multiset family became more common than the multiple-car family, and by the 1970s color television surpassed black and white as the preferred type.

For adult entertainment Saturday night around the tube replaced Saturday night at the movies, and for children Saturday morning TV viewing replaced Saturday afternoon at the movies. Private and public television personalities emerged and disappeared with startling rapidity. Sergeant Bilko (Phil Silvers), who dominated the situation-comedy scene in the 1950s, as the con-man leader of a group of comic sad sacks in the pre-Vietnam peacetime army, was probably unknown two decades later to most admirers of "Archie Bunker"; Lucille Ball ("I Love Lucy"), the quintessential dumb, helpless, yet singularly superior, "little woman" gave way to Mary Tyler Moore, the cool, talented, and capable modern career woman; and Molly Goldberg, the first-generation Jewish immigrant tenement "yenta"* was replaced by "Maude," her affluent, suburban reincarnation. Charles Van Doren, a culture hero of the vastly popular quiz show, "The $64,000 Question," became the first of a long line of idealized Americans who were shown to lack integrity when it was revealed that the knowledge that won him a fortune derived from rehearsed answers to expected questons. Television also transported its viewers as easily from the staged drama of a national political convention

* A Yiddish slang expression describing a female gossiper or busybody.

to the unstaged assassination of a president on the streets of Dallas; from a view of the "flower children" of Haight-Ashbury to the politicized children of 1968 being clubbed by the Chicago police; from the naturally scarred landscape of the moon to the man-raped landscape of Vietnam. Nothing, high or low, comic or tragic, real or imagined, escaped the camera eye.

And only Marshal Dillon endured.

Teenage culture epitomized, or so it seemed, the postwar cultural void. Pampered, petted, and pandered to in a society in which to be young was to be beautiful, teenagers spent billions of consumer dollars. The 1950s witnessed the evolution of a singular teenage society with its own highly ritualized dress and grooming, behavioral, and sexual patterns. The cut of a boy's hair, the style of a girl's dress, the nature of a young couple's relationship placed them within a stylized social context. Most teenagers rocked around the clock with "Bill Haley and his Comets" and moved their bodies to the beat of Elvis Presley's diluted black rock music. The crew cut distinguished the "jock" from the long, slicked-down hair of the "greaser," while the neat trim bedecked the "square." If all teenagers watched the same television programs, purchased similar records, and adored cars, their sartorial styles suggested quite different social ambitions and futures.

A film of 1973—"American Graffiti"—distills graphically the teenage culture that emerged during the late 1950s. The movie's smalltown California teenagers (ca. 1962) occupy themselves endlessly cruising the town's main street in a weird, almost surrealistic, parade of cars; they drift in and out of the drive-in hamburger stand; and tune their car radios to an all-night disc jockey who serves as the resident divine. Despite the film's portrayal of an apparently monochromatic adolescent culture, it also captures the subtle individual differences latent among 1950 teenagers. The cultural milieu of the fifties created the "beats"— young poets and novelists, among whom the most notable were Jack Kerouac, Alan Ginsberg, and Lawrence Ferlinghetti, who rejected affluence, the consumer society, and the work ethic, and dropped out of society in order to pursue their own pleasures or Oriental mysticism.

In reality, the affluent mass culture of the 1950s that bred a quiet generation of organization men lost in the void of a "lonely crowd" was more ephemeral than it first appeared. Indeed it was shot through with unseen cracks and flaws. John Kenneth Galbraith may have bemoaned the widespread public squalor amidst the private affluence but for more than thirty million Americans even affluence was beyond reach. Rural life decayed apace, urban ghettoes spread and festered, nonwhite Americans remained at best second-class citizens and at worst the hapless victims of brutal social and economic exploitation, and most wage-workers, regardless of skin color, endured as objects of external authority. Wealth and poverty, the ideal of equality versus the reality of inequality, authority against freedom remained inextricably at war in affluent

America. During the 1960s, the social tinder represented by poverty, racialism, and oppression would eventually ignite in the form of urban race riots and the impassioned militancy of the New Left and the radical feminist movements.

28

The New Equality: The Revolt of Nonwhites, Youth, and Women

In 1945 and 1946, black veterans left a segregated army to resume civilian life in a segregated society—one in which they were denied equal public accommodations, where restrictive real-estate covenants closed most of the housing market to them, and in which a dual labor market confined them to the least secure and lowest-paid jobs. Almost a decade later, in 1953 and 1954, black veterans returned home from a newly integrated army and a war in Korea to a society that still treated nonwhites as second-class citizens. The black man in white America could still expect in 1954 what James Baldwin described as his fate:

> The rope, fire, torture, castration, infanticide, rape; death and humiliation; fear by day and night, fear as deep as the marrow of the bone; doubt that he was worthy of life, since everyone around him denied it; sorrow for his women, for his kinfolk, for his children, who needed his protection, and whom he could not protect; rage, hatred, and murder, hatred for white men so deep that it often turned against him and his own, and made all love, all trust, all joy impossible.*

* James Baldwin, *The Fire Next Time*. Copyright © 1970 by the Dial Press. Reprinted by permission.

Other domestic minorities suffered their own singular indignities. In the Southwest, stretching from Texas to southern California, Americans of Latin, mostly Mexican, origin—the Chicanos—occupied the lowest, most despised rungs of the social ladder. Marked as inferior by virtue of color, language, and culture, Chicanos existed to serve as field hands and domestics. The Indian tribes that had survived the late nineteenth-century frontier wars were for the most part on reservations, invisible subjects of a dominant society that denied them adequate shelter, food, education, and opportunity.

Nonracial groups, too, experienced oppression, sometimes without being aware of it. Women, society ordained, belonged in the home to raise children and consume industry's products. Men and women with socially "unacceptable" patterns of sexual behavior had to disguise themselves and live furtively in society's dark corners. And students, from the kindergartens to the graduate schools, marched to the beat of their teacher's drum.

Until 1954 the American social order in which nonwhites, women, students, and others occupied inferior positions seemed to hold. Nonwhites deferred to whites, women to men, and students to teachers. Then, with amazing rapidity, the old order cracked. Black Americans arose to demand the rights that had eluded them since the end of the First Reconstruction. Brown Americans, too, organized and struggled to gain equal civil, social, and economic rights. Betty Friedan resurrected the old feminist battlecries of the 1920s, calling on women to come out of the kitchen and do as men did. And students, who initially served as allies of rebellious blacks, carried the tactics of the civil rights revolution into the nation's classrooms and campuses.

What caused the old order to crack? Why did individuals and groups that traditionally accepted the roles society defined for them now rebel? What did the protesters seek and how did they plan to accomplish their aims?

THE CIVIL RIGHTS REVOLUTION

No simple answer suffices to explain the eruption in the 1950s of protest against racism and its spread to epidemic proportions in the 1960s. Demographic changes, political realignments, and exigent foreign policy needs coalesced to break the shackles of segregation and to spark militant protest. As blacks left the South for the North in an ever-swelling stream beginning with World War II, they became more influential politically. Because many were now settled in compact urban communities where no poll taxes, unfair registrars, or veiled threats denied them the right to vote, Afro-Americans developed the political muscle to influence state, local, and national elections. In 1948 Harry Truman risked a southern white separation from the Democratic party in order to endorse civil rights and to secure black votes. Black voters played a decisive role in Truman's upset victory, and he repaid them by desegregating the armed services and promising civil rights legislation.

But Truman's policies conflicted with the realities of congressional politics in which southern Democrats and northern Republicans joined forces to defeat administration civil rights bills. In 1954, however, the Supreme Court broke the political deadlock by declaring the principle of "separate but equal" facilities (in this case public schools) unconstitutional in the case of *Brown* vs. *the Board of Education of Topeka*. For Afro-Americans the promise exceeded the reward. The Eisenhower administration failed to endorse the court's decision, and southern whites organized a bitter resistance that used courts, politics, and violence to thwart school desegregation. But this time Afro-Americans demanded the reward as well as the promise, the substance as well as the shadow of change; they now had the leadership and the will to fight for the rights so often and brutally denied them in the past; and they were no longer willing to let things take care of themselves, nor for the law to wend its slow course.

A year after the Supreme Court condemned segregation, black Americans in Montgomery, Alabama, acted decisively to achieve their civil rights. When a Montgomery seamstress named Rosa Parks refused to surrender her seat in the front of a bus to a white man in December 1955, she ignited the modern civil rights revolution. Her subsequent arrest by local police, moreover, brought to prominence the man who for the next decade would symbolize the movement: Martin Luther King, Jr. The son of an Atlanta clergyman, he himself was trained for the pastorate at Boston University. King came to his first ministerial post in Montgomery, the right man at the right time in history. Under his leadership, Montgomery Negroes participated in a months-long boycott of the city's bus lines, which terminated in the first in a series of victories against Jim Crow.

Although the NAACP continued to adjudicate in its traditional manner and win numerous legal decisions outlawing segregation in the South, its tactics lacked the militancy, color, and impact of mass direct action. Newspapers, magazines, and TV cameras preferred the drama of action in the streets to more solitary courtroom struggles. King's tactics and ideas became contagious, spreading first throughout the South and later into northern ghettoes, though seldom achieving the success in the North that was obtained in the South.

The movement Rosa Parks sparked and Martin Luther King kindled into flame blazed more brightly in February 1960 when four black students from North Carolina Agricultural and Technical College sat down at a Woolworth's lunch counter in Greensboro, North Carolina, to demand equal service. Thereafter, despite being spat on, beaten, burned, and insulted, young black students continued to sit in and demand equal service, a goal that they won at the lunch counters of more than 126 Southern cities by the end of 1960. In April 1960 at a conference called by King, the black college students formed the Student Non-Violent Coordinating Committee (SNCC), which became the spearhead for the civil rights revolt.

At first, committed to the principles and tactics of King, SNCC united young whites and blacks in a militant but nonviolent direct action movement aimed at eradicating the last vestiges of segregation. After desegregating lunch counters, whites and blacks rode together on interstate buses, waded in at southern pools and beaches, and checked in at motels and hotels. Always a step ahead of the existing law, these young people typically met violent resistance until their courage caused legislators to enact new laws or courts to declare existing laws unconstitutional. In the face of ever-present violence, the protestors compiled an enviable record of nonviolent behavior reminiscent of an earlier generation of American radicals whom historian Howard Zinn called to mind when he titled his history of SNCC: *The New Abolitionists.*

"The New Abolitionists," like their antebellum predecessors, waged a reform crusade steeped in Christian theological principles. It was no accident that a minister, King, personified the movement and that its impact was greatest in the South where blacks remained most closely linked to the church. From the Christian precept of redemption through suffering and the Gandhian concept of passive resistance, King forged a nonviolent strategy directed toward convincing white Americans that the victims of segregation were more Christian and moral than their oppressors. Encouraging his followers to apply the principle of Christan love, King advised them never to stoop so low as to hate the enemy. "We must use the weapon of love," he implored. "We must have compassion and understanding for those who hate us."

Heeding King's singular synthesis of Christian and Gandhian ideals, his followers, black and white together, young and old, marched from victory to victory. King's army could not be halted, in spite of jail sentences for their leader in Birmingham and Atlanta, resistance to classroom integration by the governor of Alabama himself (George Wallace, white supremacist, who barred the way at the University of Alabama), Sheriff Bull Connor's police dogs in Birmingham, or the violence of Alabama state troopers at Selma. The more vicious and violent the opposition the more nonviolently the civil rights protesters behaved and the more aid and encouragement they received from much of northern white America. In the summer of 1963 over 200,000 blacks and whites gathered together on the mall in Washington, D.C., to sing of how they would overcome their oppression, and to listen to King's "I have a dream" of a day "when the sons of former slaves and the sons of former slave-owners will be able to sit together at the table of brotherhood."

In 1963 the day of King's dream did not seem far distant, for it was a time when President Kennedy issued executive orders desegregating interstate transport and federally-financed housing, a time when he sent to Congress the most advanced civil rights legislation in a century. The

Black and white together, acme of the Civil Rights
Movement at Washington Monument Reflection
Pool, c. 1963
(Wide World Photos)

assassination of Kennedy in November, instead of retarding the civil
rights movement, abetted it. The new president, Lyndon B. Johnson,
pushed through Congress the civil rights bill stalled in committee during
Kennedy's last months. And when Johnson in a 1965 speech on civil
rights pledged that "We Shall Overcome," his words carried concrete
meaning. By 1965 the legal Jim Crow system was a shambles. Thousands
of public schools had been desegregated or were under court orders to do
so; public facilities, theaters, restaurants, hotels, and transit lines, had
been desegregated either by mass action or law; a series of congressional
acts stretching from the Eisenhower years in 1957 to the Civil Rights Act
of 1965 had restored voting rights to southern blacks. In 1965 as in 1867,
national law guaranteed black men and women their full civil rights—

from the polling place to the toilet. On paper, at least, a revolution, a Second Reconstruction, had been consummated.

FROM CIVIL RIGHTS TO BLACK POWER

In a real sense, then, the United States stood in 1965 where it had in 1867; having once again decided to guarantee blacks their full civil rights, the nation had to decide whether to offer Afro-Americans the economic and social opportunities that alone would render legal rights meaningful.

The answer in 1965 appeared to be the same as it had been a century earlier: *No!* In 1966, the veteran black radical and civil rights crusader Bayard Rustin summed up the place of Negroes in society twelve years after the *Brown* vs. *Topeka* decision. "Negroes today," Rustin wrote, "are in worse economic shape, live in worse slums, and attend more highly segregated schools than in 1954." Statistics buttressed his indictment: Negro unemployment was double that of whites (almost 32 percent among black youths), and the gap between white and black wages had widened; ghetto housing deteriorated even in northern open occupancy cites and states, and the Health, Education and Welfare Department reported that 65 percent of first grade Negro pupils attended schools from 90 to 100 percent black. "The day-to-day lot of the ghetto Negro," concluded Rustin, "has not been improved by the various judicial and legislative measures of the past decade."

The economic record cited by Rustin caused frustration among northern blacks who realized that the great expectations aroused by the civil rights movement had brought so few material rewards. As America grew more affluent and the consumer society enveloped all, the gap widened between what blacks desired and obtained, what they expected and received. For the mass of ghetto Negroes reality remained dirty homes on filthy dope-ridden streets in noisome neighborhoods that offered only inferior schools and dead-end jobs for its youngsters. These realities gave new meaning to the warning novelist James Baldwin had hurled at white America in 1963: "God gave Noah the rainbow sign. No more water, the fire next time!"*

The year 1965, the apogee of the civil rights movement, saw the fire ignite. Los Angeles' black ghetto (Watts) exploded in a frenzy of rioting. Rioters looted and burned white-owned businesses, leaving much of Watts a smoldering ruin. From Los Angeles the fire spread the following summer to Chicago and to New York's Harlem, where rioters also looted and burned, again focusing on white-owned enterprises. But this was only a prelude to the summer of 1967 when Newark, New Jersey, and Detroit blew up. Rioters, police, and troops killed over twenty-six and wounded more than twelve hundred (mostly black) in Newark, while in

* *The Fire Next Time.*

Detroit forty-three died and two-thousand were wounded. Vast sections of both cities' black ghettoes burned to the ground, and both were occupied by troops armed with machine guns and tanks. Encircled by local police and well-armed soldiers as well as overhead helicopters, black rioters (and nonrioters) were tightly confined to their ghettoes as the fires of rage smoldered out. Surveying Detroit from the air, Michigan Governor George Romney observed: It looks like "a city that has been bombed."

The ghetto riots raised more questions than they answered. Why, for example, should violence erupt after a decade of progress for black Americans? Why begin in the tree-lined, single-family-home ghetto of Watts and then spread to Newark, which had received proportionately more antipoverty money than any other city, and Detroit, where Negroes had better jobs and higher wages than elsewhere? Why had black and

The fire next time, Brownsville

(Leo de Wys, Inc.)

white unity collapsed in the spectacle of blacks burning white property and attacking white persons? What explained black rage against white America?

The nation's leaders pursued a traditional course to answer those questions: the appointment of special commissions to investigate the violence. In California, the McCone Commission analyzed Watts, and three years later President Johnson created the Kerner Commission to investigate racial violence nationally. Both commissions discovered the same facts and reached similar conclusions. They saw a society in which racial divisions were widening and the threat of domestic turmoil rising. They agreed that the civil rights movement had stirred expectations among blacks that American society refused to satisfy, and the Kerner Commission appended a scathing indictment of what it labeled as "white racism." It was easier, however, to locate the roots of violence, to condemn white racism, and to prophesy the emergence of a dual society than to propose specific policies that would assuage black rage and satisfy frustrated expectations. Not unexpectedly, a year after the Kerner Commission reported, a black veteran returning to the United States from a tour of duty in Vietnam observed that: "The rights we fought [for] for somebody else just don't exist for us."

Even before blacks ignited their ghettoes in fire, veterans of the civil rights movement had begun to rethink their tactics and strategy. What, they asked, were the actual results of passive resistance and civil rights legislation? What had King's reliance on nonviolence, the white man's conscience, and Christian charity brought?—the bombing of a black church in Birmingham and the death of four young black girls; the brutal murders in Mississippi in the summer of 1964 of James Chaney, a Southern black, and Michael Schwerner and Andrew Goodman, white northern college student civil rights activists; the Orangeburg, South Carolina, massacre in which state police shot down unarmed black college students; and finally the April 4, 1968 assassination of Martin Luther King. The words of black writer Julius Lester, not Preacher King, now resonated among young blacks. "Love," asked Lester? "That's always better done in bed than on picket lines and marches." Civil rights marchers used to sing "I Love Everybody," Lester recalled. "Now they sing,

> "Too much love,
> "Too much love,
> "Nothing kills a nigger like
> "Too much love."

Shifting perceptions of the realities of American society led blacks to move from passivity to resistance, protest to politics, integration to cultural nationalism. Power, not prayer, brought change. And most blacks needed social and economic power, not civil rights laws. But how could society's mudsill gain economic improvements? Only political power seemed to promise betterment—the use of the vote to influence government to redistribute wealth to the advantage of poor blacks, especially through preferential employment practices.

Lacking a voting majority of their own, black leaders turned to the Democratic party as the vehicle for coalition politics. In the summer of 1964 SNCC workers labored in the rural regions of Mississippi and other Deep South states to register black voters. Rejected by the regular Democratic party in Mississippi, blacks organized the Freedom Democratic party and pleaded with the 1964 Democratic convention and with congressional Democrats to purge the remnants of "lily-white" organizations from the party and to replace them with the FDP. But blacks won only a minimal compromise that offered them recognition but not power. The rewards of coalition politics thus appeared illusory.

In this milieu "black power" emerged as a new slogan and program among militant blacks. In Alabama SNCC rejected coalition politics and formed the Black Panther party, a political organization totally independent of the regular Democratic party, which sought first to organize black voters in Alabama, then the South, and ultimately the nation. Simultaneously black SNCC leaders purged their white student allies who, it was alleged (rightly so in many cases), patronized rural blacks and undermined their independence and initiative. In the summer of 1966 a new young black leader captured the headlines as he shouted "black power." That man, Stokely Carmichael, a West Indian immigrant, exceptional student at Howard University, and an impassioned orator, personified the rising assertiveness of black Americans and their desire to control their own destiny. To rejected white liberals who charged Carmichael with "reverse racism" he responded: "Once again, responsibility is shifted from the oppressor to the oppressed."

Carmichael's assertion of black independence had many echoes in the Afro-American community. CORE, originally founded by idealistic white and black liberals and dedicated to racial harmony and integration, purged white members at the same time that SNCC did. And Bayard Rustin, long-time exponent of integration and coalition politics, replied to white critics of "black racism": "It is both absurd and immoral to equate the despairing response of the victim with the contemptuous assertion of the oppressor."

What, in fact, did "black power" mean and what were its aims? Obviously it was not a civil rights movement focused on legal change and the achievement of equality before the law. Nor was it a movement with which white liberals could easily identify. Instead it was a self-interest movement to serve black-defined concepts of their own welfare based on the belief that what is good for blacks is good for democracy. At the simplest level, black power meant black votes for black candidates serving black needs. In that sense it scarcely differed from the customary American practice of ethnic politics. At a deeper level, however, it contained an antiintegrationist, separatist core. "The white man," wrote Carmichael, "is irrelevant to blacks, except as an oppressive force." Integration, too, was a delusion, for no one urged whites to integrate black schools and neighborhoods; rather blacks were to integrate white institutions, implying black inferiority and white superiority. Integration, asserted militants, only has meaning when it works both ways. Experience had taught Carmichael and others that there was no existing political group with which "to form a coalition in which blacks will not be absorbed and betrayed." "Only black people," asserted Carmichael, "can convey the revolutionary idea that black people are able to help themselves." The advocates of black power further insisted that they sought not simply an equal place for the Afro-American in white society but also a totally noncapitalist national society. It would be a society, they said, "in which the spirit of community and humanistic love prevail."

By the late 1960s, "black power" assumed more impact as a cultural than a political movement. Young northern blacks, in particular, rejected the tradition of skin bleaches and hair straighteners, the custom of black men and women seeking to act white. They now wore their hair natural (the so-called Afro style), donned dashikis, praised soul food and soul talk, and proclaimed that to be black is to be beautiful. Among the poorest, most despised residents of northern ghettoes a new religious movement, the "Black Muslim" faith, spread. Founded by Elijah Muhammed of Detroit and Chicago, it preached that whites were devils and blacks were Allah's annointed. Whatever its theological deficiencies, the Black Muslim faith saved many Negroes from drugs, made them proud and self-sufficient, and gave them self-respect. It also gave northern black America its most representatve spokesman, Malcolm Little, better known as Malcolm X. Before his assassination in 1965, Malcolm X, who had broken with Elijah Muhammed, promised to link the black Muslims of the United States to traditional Islam and to make it more than a blacks-only movement.

Cultural nationalism manifested itself in a variety of ways. The successful black dramatist and poet, LeRoi Jones, discarded integrationist themes (as well as a white wife) for antiwhite ones and changed his name to Imamu Amiri Baraka. And the basketball star, Lew Alcindor, converted from Christianity to Islam, changing his name to Kareem Abdul-Jabbar. And most spectacularly the brilliant and iconoclastic young heavyweight boxing champion Cassius Clay joined the Black Muslim faith, rejected the draft (for that exercise of his conscience he was stripped of his title for three and a half years), and changed his name to Muhammed Ali.

Ironically, however, those black militants who sought to build a society based on community and love increasingly turned to the rhetoric of despair and violence. H. Rap Brown, who replaced Carmichael as chairman of SNCC in 1967, advised blacks to get guns and remember that "violence is as American as cherry pie." When black militants on the West Coast organized the Black Panther movement in Oakland, they carried rifles as a symbol of their manhood. Police became known as "pigs," and Panther newspapers suggested that the only good "pig" was a dead one. When Detroit and Newark burned in the wake of Carmichael's impassioned cry for black power and policemen were shot down in the aftermath of Rap Brown's fiery speeches and the creation of the Black Panthers, Carmichael's earlier observation that "to most whites, black power seems to mean that the Mau Mau are coming to the suburbs at night," assumed new meaning.

As the ghetto fires burned themselves out and the police and the courts undermined the Panthers, many black leaders questioned the rhetoric of violence. Rustin asserted that the speeches of Carmichael, Brown, and Bobby Seale "isolate the Negro community, and encourage the growth of anti-Negro forces." As a small minority of the larger society and a smaller minority of the voting population, how could Afro-Americans progress without white allies? Where blacks were a majority they could practice black power and elect sheriffs, school superintendents, and mayors. But even then, what good was a black mayor or a black community on the verge of bankruptcy, as seemed to be the case in Newark? The black community of Gary, Indiana, depended on U.S. Steel, and blacks in Detroit relied on white-owned auto companies and banks.

Afro-Americans at the end of the 1960s found themselves in an unenviable predicament. A decade and a half of civil rights protest had raised consciousness and stirred expectations. Leaders like Malcolm X had taught them that "black is beautiful," and they came to show open pride in their skin color, culture, and life style. Opportunities for individual blacks were never better. They dominated professional basketball, and coached as well as played; ever since Jackie Robinson had broken the color line in baseball in 1947 and Emlen Tunnell a few years later in football, black men had starred in professional sports in numbers out of all proportion to their percentage of the population. The movies and TV began to cater to black audiences to whom they offered cool, black versions of Superman, Batman, and James Bond. Ivy League colleges recruited black undergraduates; universities sought black professors; and corporations hired black executives. In short, in the 1960s more blacks than ever before broke into the American middle class. Yet, despite all the real economic progress of the 1960s, by the start of the 1970s the median black family income had slipped to 59 percent of that earned by whites, 33 percent of the total black population still lived in poverty, and black unemployment remained twice as great as for whites. Afro-Americans, in 1970 as in 1950, depended on white society for advancement, for it was whites who controlled the economy and the power that flowed from wealth. If whites refused to yield power or position, how could a group doomed to minority status by its dark skin itself alter the social and economic order?

POWER! POWER! POWER!

The demand for power and the resurgence of cultural nationalism initiated by blacks soon reverberated among other minority groups in American society. Brown and red Americans began to question the myths of pluralism and to suggest, as blacks had previously, that the concept of pluralism cloaked a society based on white, bourgeois dominance. Americans of Indian and Hispanic origins could succeed socially only by discarding the language and culture of their ancestors. Even then only a minuscule minority rose above society's doorsill. Most red men and brown men remained mired as deeply as blacks in poverty and despair. Once Afro-Americans challenged white dominance, however, other minorities inevitably followed suit.

Concentrated in the cities and farmlands of the Southwest, where they supplied most of the region's low-paid labor, Americans of Hispanic origin began to assert themselves in the 1960s. Segregated in slums, stripped of their language in school, dominated by Anglo public officials, and doomed to a life of ill-paid stoop labor in California's "factories in the fields," the Chicanos fought back. Led by Cesar Chavez, a disciple of professional radical Saul Alinsky, field workers in California formed a labor union in 1963. Chavez, however, transformed the farm workers' struggle into a cultural as well as a labor battle. With support from Catholic priests, student radicals, and even mainstream organized labor, Chavez led *La Causa* against California's powerful agricultural interests in a fight for union recognition and improved working conditions. Denied the right to picket en masse and unable to pursue traditional strike tactics, the agricultural workers took their crusade to the nation's supermarkets asking consumers not to purchase California grapes and lettuce. The boycott, endorsed by Walter Reuther, George Meany, and Robert F. Kennedy among others, worked. By 1966 Chavez's union had negotiated labor contracts with the largest grape growers in California, Chicano field workers for the first time had an effective organizational voice, and the union prepared to challenge lettuce growers as well as Arizona and Texas ranchers.

Whereas Chavez allied with white liberals, endorsed coalition politics, and practiced traditional trade unionism, other Chicano leaders argued for their version of black power and the Black Panthers: *La Raza*. Rejecting the Puritan ethic and other white American values, advocates of *La Raza* demanded Chicano-only political organizations, the teaching of Spanish and its southwestern American dialects in the public schools, Chicano studies in the universities, and a Latin cultural alternative to the dominant national culture. Pluralism had meaning, militant Chicanos asserted, only if brown Americans could freely and with pride respect and practice their own traditional culture.

Indians, too, began to remember and respect their past. They wrote books like Vine Deloria, Jr.'s *Custer Died for Your Sins* and were the subjects of bestsellers such as Dee Brown's *Bury My Heart at Wounded Knee*. No longer did young Indians reflexively accept assimilation into American society as the only path to follow. Militants revived tribal customs and asserted that Indians also had a right to traditional culture. By the late 1960s Indians took to a figurative warpath; they occupied Alcatraz Island in San Francisco Bay, which they offered to buy from the federal government for $24 (in beads and cloth); they invaded the

Indian Bureau offices in Washington, and challenged federal power in the village of Wounded Knee, South Dakota. They, too, demanded "native American" studies in the universities, preferential hiring, and government reimbursement for what white men had stolen from Indians in the course of three centuries.

The advocates of the various forms of "racial" and minority power confronted a dilemma that had puzzled generations of American radicals: whether to seek immediate reforms by accommodating to the prevailing power structure or to refuse concessions and seek a total revolution; whether to work through such existing institutions as trade unions and major political parties or to form pure, independent revolutionary organizations. Effective existence and action depended on delivering the goods, extracting substantial concessions for minorities from dominant groups. Such material gains flowed most readily from alliances with the labor movement and the Democratic party. But those radicals who practiced "coalition politics," such blacks as Bayard Rustin and Julian Bond and such white ex-Socialists as Tom Kahn and Albert Shanker, president of the American Federation of Teachers, became mere appendages to the Democratic party or to George Meany and the AFL–CIO. Coalition led to collaboration, which in turn weakened radicalism. Yet those radicals who remained true to a revolutionary commitment and refused to accommodate to the established order scarcely fared better. Some black revolutionaries, notably Stokely Carmichael and Eldridge Cleaver, fled into exile overseas; others, including Angela Davis, H. Rap Brown, and Huey Newton, experienced the full force of the law. Although Davis, after a long and harrowing legal trial, won an acquittal, Brown was convicted and sentenced to prison for armed robbery and, as of November 1976, Newton remained a fugitive from justice on a murder warrant. Many young white radicals like Mark Rudd and Bernadine Dohrn (so-called Weatherpeople), unable to bear the frustration of political impotency, minuscule followings, and constant government surveillance, resorted to random acts of violence and a furtive underground life. Most American radicals in the 1960s, regardless of their skin color, age, or sex, failed to devise a strategy that enabled them to participate effectively in society without sacrificing their commitment to a new society.

For "brown," "red," and "black" power advocates the dilemma of the typical American radical was compounded. Indians and Chicanos, like Afro-Americans, were a minority in an overwhelmingly white society, and they also lacked substantial wealth and capital. Political and economic realities caused some influential Indian and Latin spokesmen, especially among those who had made substantial progress in their own careers, to criticize cultural nationalism as "reverse racism" and to insist that assimilation and integration were the only answers to the dilemma of American racial minorities. As the 1960s ended, the meaning of pluralism remained problematic, and the future of nonwhite minorities in a white society seemed uncertain.

As the old order cracked and its leaders could not decide whether to exculpate or to repress the protesting minorities, further fissures rendered the American consensus. College students who had joined with southern blacks to challenge white supremacy returned to their campuses unwilling to tolerate what they now considered an equally outmoded and authoritarian academic order. Student publications began to refer to the student as "nigger," the impotent subject of academic masters. At the University of California at Berkeley in 1964, militant students under the leadership of Mario Savio confronted the nation's greatest multiversity, protesting that it treated its students as identical ciphers on a mass-production educational assembly line. The Berkeley Free Speech Movement demanded a university in which students had autonomy, in which faculty served students, not corporations and governments, and in which education questioned rather than buttressed the social order. At Berkeley and elsewhere where militant students failed to win all their demands, they moved off campus to create "free universities" and "alternative classrooms" in which they might toy with ideas alien to the traditional university.

The real external world also impinged on the students in hitherto cloistered universities as it had long since done on faculty who moved regularly between classrooms and corporate boardrooms and government agencies as highly paid consultants. Students questioned educational institutions whose representatives served military agencies and business corporations as much as the quest for knowledge. The civil rights, which once had taken idealistic students away from the campus, now hit home, as administrators recruited blacks for the formerly exclusively white university world. And most important, as the war in Vietnam intensified, making conscription an ever-present reality to the male student, campus life grew more embittered. Antiwar protest, which was primarily a white phenomenon though endorsed by such blacks as Martin Luther King and Julian Bond, distracted attention from the problems of black "liberation" and weakened the black-white alliance forged in the earlier civil rights movement.

To radical students in the late 1960s American universities seemed to be an integral part of an oppressive, imperialistic society. College ROTC programs trained the officers who staffed a global armed forces; social scientists advised the government on counter-insurgency techniques and wrote scenarios for counter-revolution; and scientists developed the sophisticated, deadly weapons of modern warfare. The violence that afflicted American ghettoes and led to assassinations did not leave the campus unscathed. Students burned ROTC facilities, and in some cases the more radical even armed themselves. In the spring of 1968 militant Columbia students shut the university down. By occupying buildings and ransacking the president's office, thus coming under police attack, they brought the academic year to a premature end. The following academic year armed black students split the Cornell University campus and pressured a shaky administration into concessions. Then, in the spring of 1970, the intensification of the Vietnam war as a result of the Cambodian invasion that May caused all hell to break loose. Students protested, marched, struck, and closed scores of campuses weeks before the term ended; and tragically, at Kent State in Ohio, National Guard troops killed four students and wounded more than a score during a protest against the invasion. "The Fire Next Time" seared the nation's campuses in 1970 as frustrated radicals resorted to the torch and the bomb in such places as Santa Barbara, California, and Madison, Wisconsin.

But on the campuses, too, the fires or radicalism burned themselves out, leaving behind a mixed prospect. In some ways the university in 1970 was not what it had been in 1960; in other ways it remained much the same. No longer did most college administrators sit *in loco parentis,* for their students had won the right to live where they desired, to be free of curfews, to have coed dormitories, in short to be treated as adults. Students also obtained experimental new courses as well as a voice in rating their teachers and, in some cases, seats on university policymaking committees. Nonwhites and females, both as students and instructors, became more visible on college campuses. While political radicalism abated, the counter-culture associated with hardrock music, hallucinogenic drugs, and proletarian-style dress continued to attract students and separate students and other youths from their more conventional elders. Still, on most campuses effective power still rested with faculty and administrators, who were overwhelmingly white and male. Moreover, the majority of students entered traditional academic programs in order to pursue customary careers.

THE WOMEN'S MOVEMENT

Of all the movements that rent American society none was as potentially threatening to the social fabric as women's liberation. Not only did females come to protest their exploitation at work, in bed, and even in radical movements (Stokely Carmichael once remarked: "The position of women in our movement should be prone.") but they also criticized marriage, the home, and the nuclear family.* More militant females, deeming man the primary enemy, extolled onanistic and homosexual sex. For some, masturbation became the means to female power.

While radical women labored to subvert the domestic sexual order, women won several quite modest feminist goals that had eluded them in previous decades. As blacks, browns, reds, and even students shed the bonds of subservience, many women too came to reject law and custom. Indeed the Civil Rights Act of 1964 forbade discrimination on the basis of sex as well as race. Moreover, women, unlike nonwhites and students, had real economic power. Not only did they control the bulk of the

* The nuclear family consists of the parents and their children occupying a household in which no other related or unrelated individual dwells and in which there are no boarders or other nonfamily residents.

nation's disposable income and real wealth; they were an exceedingly vital factor in the labor market, filling two-thirds of the new jobs in the 1960s. With 43 percent of adult females employed and their numbers rising, the House of Representatives in 1970 finally approved, thus submitting for state ratification, the long-stalled Equal Rights Amendment. In several states women won the right to abortion and to control over their own bodies, one of several factors explaining the steep decline in American birthrates at the beginning of the 1970s. Many women, it was now clear, realized that they existed as more than breeders or consumers, and that, in the words of feminist Betty Friedan, they no longer had to feel "like freaks for not having that orgiastic bliss while waxing the floor."

Yet women's liberation, like black protest, red power, and student radicalism, brought change without revolution. For every female who preferred lesbian relationships, scores still chose heterosexuality. For every woman who scorned marriage, many more aimed ultimately for matrimony, however many unsanctified relationships preceded. And for every woman who preferred communal life and extended families, scores freely chose the private residence and the nuclear family. But as more and more women entered the labor force, traditional sexual roles necessarily became less distinguishable. Men could no longer claim to be sole breadwinners or to wear the pants, and especially among the middle class, they had to share household duties from marketing to diapering.

Perhaps the most visual changes in American society during the 1960s were the sexual ones. If the counter-culture won any lasting triumphs, a dubious proposition, it was in the realm of sexual liberation. The contraceptive pill removed the remaining anxiety from premarital sex, and widely distributed manuals, books, and films tutored inexperienced lovers in the varieties of sex. Male and female homosexuals came out of hiding to proclaim their gayness and demand their rights, an event unthinkable a decade earlier. Everywhere surface sexual differences vanished, as men, including professional athletes, let their hair grow, donned gaily colored clothes, and wore rings and beads. Women, meantime, put on pants.

Although American society during the 1960s in the title of a popular history of the decade seemed to be *Coming Apart,* the various minority rebellions produced an equally powerful reaction by a diverse, conservative, and sometimes repressive majority. Those Richard M. Nixon would refer to as his "silent majority"—affluent middle-class homeowners, well-paid and unionized workers, insecure whites fearful of losing their privileges to nonwhites, and women who still preferred existence in a "doll's house"—coalesced to guard the American center. The white majority shared presidential adviser Daniel Patrick Moynihan's belief that it was time nonwhites received a little "benign neglect." Moynihan meant by that that blacks should no longer appear openly as the primary concern and beneficiaries of federal programs, and that minority groups would progress best in the future by disappearing from the headlines, contro-

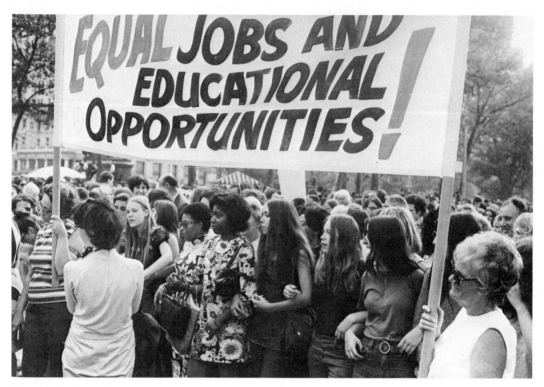

Out of the kitchen, 1970
(Richard Lawrence Stack/Black Star)

versy, and public view. The silent majority also seemed indifferent to the killing of four students at Kent State University, and it joined a rising chorus of criticism aimed at students and universities. And the silent majority had its sexual fears assuaged by the Burger Court in a 1973 decision which granted local majorities the right to define acceptable sexual mores on the stage, in films, and in books. How long the center would hold remained one question for future decision.

29

Camelot as the Great Society: Domestic Reform Politics 1963-1967

Suddenly elevated to the presidency with Kennedy's assassination, the ambitious and politically knowledgeable Vice President Lyndon Baines Johnson moved quickly to impose his stamp on national politics. When he accepted the vice-presidential nomination in 1960, Johnson surrendered a position commanding deference and power (as Democratic Senate majority leader) for the prestigious but largely honorific post of vice president. Vice president in the Kennedy administration, Johnson suffered the contempt that many Kennedy aides showed for his folksy manner and his political operator's style. Inevitably, then, personal considerations complicated his transition from functionary to policymaker. A far-reaching change in White House personnel was assured, though Johnson retained most of the Kennedy cabinet and expressed his commitment to the deceased president's general policies. From the start, however, the new president charted his own course in order to secure the Democratic presidential nomination in 1964 and to establish his own policy priorities.

THE GREAT SOCIETY

These priorities were incorporated in the phrase Great Society, which Lyndon Johnson adopted to describe his administration's basic purposes. The Great Society, the president stressed in his annual message of 1965, "asks not only how much, but how good; not only how to create wealth, but how to use it. It proposes as the first test for a nation: the quality of its people." Amounting basically to a reaffirmation of New Deal principles, the Johnson Great Society was less glamorous than the Kennedy New Frontier and focused on domestic reform, not an expansive and ambitious foreign policy. In addition, the theme Lyndon Johnson sounded during his successful campaign for the presidency in 1964 and reiterated throughout his tenure, was the "quest for union." He urged others to "come, let us reason together," implying that no differences were so fundamental they could not be reconciled. To Johnson, the president should be a harmonizer who insured the recognition of disadvantaged groups and reconciled often bitter divisions and competing claims. In this capacity, Johnson pointedly sought southern acceptance of civil rights. Indeed, he delivered his most eloquent campaign speech of the 1964 campaign in New Orleans where he counseled southerners to abandon the passions engendered by the Civil War and Reconstruction and to accept integration, adding that racism was the chief reason for the South's backwardness and the main obstacle to its advance. Johnson related an anecdote told to him by Speaker Sam Rayburn. The speaker had recalled an earlier conversation with a Mississippi-born Texas senator who added after recounting Mississippi's poverty and degradation, "Poor old state, they haven't heard a real Democratic speech in thirty years. All they ever hear at election time is nigra, nigra, nigra."

Johnson's legislative program included the advancement of civil rights, recognition of the arts, commendation of the contributions of intellectuals to society, resolution of urban and rural poverty (white and nonwhite), relief of the health problems of the aged, and aid for those who were poor because they lacked the necessary skills to secure employment in a complex industrial economy. Basic reforms, the President believed, could be attained without redistributing wealth or power.

Paradoxically, this president who sought to promote consensus, to establish a harmony of interests and shared values, and to concentrate on domestic reform became the focus of an increasingly more divisive and passionate politics. Johnson's administration ended on a discordant note and was enmeshed in foreign affairs. In part, the intensification of the Vietnam War had dissolved consensus; in part, the breakdown of consensus predated the war and was the product of deep racial and economic divisions. The contrasting record of executive purpose and policy results, and the accompanying social and political divisions marked the most crucial legacies of the Johnson presidency.

A MORE CENTRALIZED PRESIDENCY

Lyndon Johnson's legislative record had no parallel except the Franklin Roosevelt years of 1933–1935. And Johnson's record was even more notable: during the 100 Days Congress approved fifteen Roosevelt-proposed measures; in contrast, between January 4, 1965 and October 23, 1965, Congress approved eighty-five administration or administration-sponsored bills, many of which had been proposed earlier but had never been implemented.

To obtain his objectives, Johnson combined an inside knowledge of the congressional system and how power was wielded in Washington with a more centralized presidency. On the one hand, by cajolery, pressure, and limited congressional reform, he reduced legislative roadblocks to his programs. He lobbied to change House rules to permit the leadership to bring to the floor bills that the Rules Committee held for over twenty-one days, thereby eliminating what had been a major obstacle to enacting liberal proposals. The Johnson White House also assumed leadership of the liberal effort in 1964 to overcome a southern-led filibuster against civil rights legislation. Not only was the campaign more efficiently organized, with timely calls for quorums and for votes on key amendments, but the president expressed his willingness to sacrifice other administration programs in order to enact a civil rights bill. Johnson's tactics, the decision of the conservative Republican minority leader Everett Dirksen to support cloture, and the intensive lobbying by civil rights, labor union, and church groups combined to override the Southern filibuster— the first time that a filibuster had not been successful in a debate over civil rights legislation. On June 10, after seventy-four days of debate and fifty-seven days of filibuster, the Senate voted cloture by a margin of 71–29. On July 2, Johnson signed into law the Civil Rights Act of 1964 (discussed more fully later in this section).

Meantime, Lyndon Johnson further consolidated presidential powers. In essence, he continued Kennedy's dilution of the cabinet's functions and extended the powers of the White House staff. Johnson's presidential style alone differed from Kennedy's, particularly his domineering personality and his insistence on unquestioned loyalty and subservience by White House aides.

In early 1964, Johnson exploited the outpouring of emotion generated by his predecessor's assassination to pressure Congress to enact Kennedy's proposed tax cut and civil rights bills. In addition, Congress created the Office of Economic Opportunity and approved a $375 million measure for urban mass transit, a food stamp program, and acts providing for expansion of the National Defense Education Act and of hospital construction and legal aid to indigents.

Johnson then exploited the opportunities provided by the 1964 presidential campaign. In that campaign, conservative Republicans sought to challenge the changes wrought since 1932 by the Roosevelt New Deal. Convinced that the Republican Party had suffered defeat in presidential contests since 1936 for its adoption of "me-too" policies, conservatives believed that a candidate who forthrightly raised issues of principle and uncompromisingly attacked New Deal domestic and foreign policies could transform national politics and realign the Republican party in a more conservative direction. Such an effort seemed propitious. Richard Nixon's defeat during the 1960 presidential election, and subsequent defeat in his 1962 quest for the governorship of California, had left the party without strong national leadership.

In Arizona Senator Barry Goldwater, conservative Republicans had an attractive candidate: personable, with a rustic handsomeness, and an effective spokesman for an unabashedly anti-Communist foreign policy and anti-New Deal domestic policy. Moreover, because they controlled state and local party organizations, Republican conservatives in the nonprimary states were in a position to elect Goldwater delegations. Concentrating on these nonprimary states, they appealed to the conservatism of the Republican rank and file.

When he entered the presidential race, Goldwater was not assured that he would win. His candidacy, however, could insure conservative power within the Republican party and strengthen the party's base in the South and Southwest. Thus, the Goldwater campaign was not primarily concerned about popularity; not surprisingly, then, Goldwater suffered major defeats in the New Hampshire and Oregon primaries, among others. In addition, the divisions among moderate Republicans, the hesitancy of anyone besides the controversial Nelson Rockefeller (then governor of New York and recently divorced and remarried) to contest Goldwater for the nomination, and Richard Nixon's strategy of equivocation in order to emerge as the convention's compromise choice further enhanced Goldwater's chances. With his narrow defeat of Rockefeller in the California primary in June, Goldwater had literally won the Republican nomination: he had acquired sufficient delegate votes (883) to win a first-ballot victory at the San Francisco Convention.

Because their major goal had been to reshape the Republican party, the Goldwater Republicans made a number of seemingly inept political decisions. At the convention, they made no concessions to Republican moderates concerning the platform or even the selection of the vice-presidential nominee. An obscure, right-wing congressman, William Miller, was nominated vice president, and the tone of the platform was captured in the lines of Goldwater's acceptance speech: "extremism in the defense of liberty is no vice . . . moderation in the pursuit of justice is no virtue." The actual campaign was uncompromisingly conservative. Candidate Goldwater advocated the sale of TVA, assailed agricultural subsidies, denounced social security, supported right-to-work laws, opposed civil rights, and proposed giving local military commanders control over nuclear weapons.

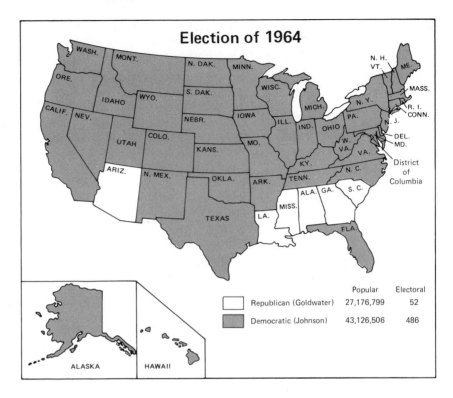

Election of 1964

	Popular	Electoral
Republican (Goldwater)	27,176,799	52
Democratic (Johnson)	43,126,506	486

The Goldwater delegates' open animosity toward "eastern Republicans" and also the news media led many moderate Republicans (notably Michigan Governor George Romney and New York Senator Kenneth Keating) to decide after the convention either to disavow Goldwater's candidacy or to concentrate on state and local politics. The Goldwater campaign did not, however, realign the Republican party nor national politics. Not only did Goldwater lose resoundingly, but conservative candidates in the Southwest, Far West, Middle West, and East went down to defeat at the same time as moderate Republicans had been able to trim their losses.

In 1964, the Democrats focused on the Johnson administration's legislative achievements and on the resentments and fears elicited by the Republican candidate's assault on New Deal programs. This strategy successfully averted the 1964 campaign from becoming a debate over principles, despite the profound philosophical differences between the two candidates. The character of the Democratic campaign was shaped by Goldwater's avowed antiwelfare state conservatism. Democratic vice-presidential nominee Hubert Humphrey's acceptance speech exemplified his party's approach. Citing the extensive and bipartisan support for administration-proposed measures such as the civil rights bill and the test ban treaty, Humphrey intoned after each citation "but not Senator Goldwater." The Democrats projected an image of Goldwater as an insensitive reactionary, whose politics and positions were irresponsible and foolhardy, and whose election would produce searing depression and nuclear war. One Democratic TV ad had a little girl picking petals from a daisy that dissolved into a mushroom-shaped cloud, while another commercial merely showed two hands tearing up a social security card.

This campaign strategy resulted in an overwhelming victory for Lyndon Johnson and the Democrats. Johnson won 61.1 percent of the popular vote (43,126,506) and 486 electoral votes (to Goldwater's 27,176,799 popular and 52 electoral votes) and carried all the states of the union but Louisiana, Mississippi, Alabama, South Carolina, Georgia, and Goldwater's home state of Arizona. In addition, Democratic majorities in the House increased to 295–140 and in the Senate to 68–32, and the Democrats picked up over 500 seats in the state legislatures.

The size of his popular mandate and the composition of the new Congress (owing to the defeat of conservative Republicans and the election of liberal Democrats) provided additional political leverage for President Johnson. In 1965, then, Congress responded almost slavishly to presidential legislative recommendations. In that year Congress repealed the national origins system for immigration quotas; enacted legislation on voting rights, pollution control, federal support for the arts, federal aid to education, including scholarships to the poor and aid to both public and private schools, and federal health insurance for the aged; extended Social Security coverage and benefits and federal assistance to develop the Appalachia region; raised and broadened minimum wage coverage; and created a Department of Housing and Urban Development and a manpower training program. In 1966, Johnson sought and obtained legislation aiding consumers (truth-in-packaging), establishing highway and safety standards, creating a department of transportation, providing rent subsidies for the poor, and funding a model (or demonstration) cities program.

Thereafter, the administration became bogged down in the Vietnam War. Its subsequent major legislative victories consisted of congressional enactment in 1968 of another civil rights act—barring discrimination in the selling, renting, financing, and advertising of 80 percent of the nation's housing units—and a 10 percent tax-surcharge to fight the inflation created by the intensification of the Vietnam War. To obtain congressional approval of these measures, the administration made major concessions to southern conservatives. The administration agreed not to oppose a rider to the housing bill making it a federal crime for individuals to cross state lines to participate in demonstrations to incite violence. To insure that the tax-surcharge bill would be reported out of the House Ways and Means Committee, the president publicly accepted the demand of the committee chairman, Congressman Wilbur Mills, to slash $6 billion in federal expenditures. Moreover, in 1968 (despite administration opposition), Congress passed an anticrime bill, the Safe Streets and Crime Control Act, that among other provisions authorized federal wiretapping for the first time.

In part, the steady decline in Johnson's legislative success revealed a change in the congressional mood. By 1968 the administration's relations with Congress were bitter, acrimonious, and stalemated, contrasting sharply with the relationship of 1964 and 1965 when Congress had without compromise or delay enacted the president's far-reaching legislative program. The Vietnam War had polarized the liberal community and at the same time had undermined the liberal climate of opinion that had been basic to the enactment of Great Society legislation. In addition, Republican candidates and political leaders capitalized on the war to challenge Great Society programs. On the one hand, the administration's rhetoric emphasizing the need to fight communism abroad and to still its antiwar critics strengthened a conservative anti-Communist politics. On the other hand, the inflationary impact of increased defense spending justified restricting domestic spending. The Republicans parlayed these domestic and foreign problems into a striking gain in the 1966 election, winning an additional 8 governorships, and 47 House, 3 Senate, and 540 state legislative seats.

ANTI-COMMUNISM, REFORM, AND THE GREAT SOCIETY

Lyndon Johnson came to the presidency intent on extending popular respect for liberal principles and, notably, respect for intellectual dissent and civil liberties. In one of his first acts as president, Johnson conferred the Fermi Prize on J. Robert Oppenheimer, emphasizing the atomic scientist's many contributions to science and society. Despite a distinguished record of public service and loyalty, Oppenheimer had in 1954 been denied a security clearance and had been portrayed thereafter as exemplifying the security problem posed by muddle-headed, idealistic scientists. Johnson's decision to honor a controversial scientist had symbolic significance: it indirectly challenged Cold War conformism.

To further respect for intellectuals, the Johnson administration scheduled a White House festival of the arts for June 1965. Intended as a testimony to American humanists and to commend the positive consequences of intellectual ferment and nonconformism, the festival almost immediately became intertwined with a sharp public challenge to the Johnson administration's Vietnam and Dominican Republic policies. Of those invited to the festival, some (including the poet Robert Lowell) publicly refused to attend for reasons of principle, others (the novelists Saul Bellow and John Hersey) attended but let it be known that they considered the festival simply a commendation of the arts (a purpose they thought commendable) and not that their presence did indicate acceptance of the administration's domestic or foreign policies, and still others (notably film critic Dwight Macdonald) attended in order to use the forum of the festival to criticize publicly the president's foreign policy.

The passions of these intellectuals, however, paled before those of the president. Informed of the prospect of public criticism, Johnson had the FBI conduct name checks on those artists who had been invited last. The FBI uncovered derogatory information on six (four of whom had art works on display). The president at first insisted that these six not be invited; he finally agreed to invite them to avoid being charged with establishing a political test for honoring artists based on the acceptability of their ideas or their support for his policies. Thereafter, the administration required prior FBI name checks on prospective guests to White House social functions.

This sensitivity to criticism negated the Johnson administration's other efforts to diminish Cold War conformism. Johnson's two attorneys general, Nicholas Katzenbach and Ramsey Clark, atypical postwar attorneys general because of their libertarian priorities, assumed leadership in this effort. Both were strongly committed to civil rights and civil liberties. Under their leadership, the Justice Department fully exploited civil rights legislation to extend the rights of blacks in the South. Never refusing a single FBI request to wiretap or bug in national security cases, Katzenbach did restrict FBI electronic surveillance of domestic political activities. In 1965, the attorney general rescinded the authorization to wiretap civil rights leader Martin Luther King, Jr. (instituted during Robert Kennedy's attorney generalship). Under Clark, even more stringent restrictions on FBI electronic surveillance were imposed. The FBI could wiretap only in investigations "directly affecting the national security." To insure that "national security" would not provide a cover for domestic political surveillance, Clark established stringent procedures, which the FBI was required to follow when requesting wiretapping and authorization. Each FBI request must describe the person to be tapped or bugged, detail the expected information to be gained, and explain the reasons for suspicions about the individual. During Clark's tenure as attorney general, accordingly, the number of "national security" wiretaps declined to 113 in 1967 and 82 in 1968 from highs of 519 in 1945, 322 in 1954, and 244 in 1963.

The heart of the attorney general's anticriminal program centered on special task forces and on improving the professionalism of local and federal police forces. These preferences made investigative work more difficult, at the same time insuring a minimum transgression on civil liberties. In contrast to his Cold War predecessors, moreover, Clark consistently opposed legislation to authorize electronic surveillance. Even following passage of the Omnibus Crime Control Act of 1968 legalizing wiretaps in domestic criminal and national security investigations, the attorney general refused to authorize taps except in national security cases.

This more libertarian Justice Department policy did not insure popular tolerance for dissent or eliminate antireformist Cold War politics. Clark's efforts were counterbalanced by the president's more general responses toward his antiwar critics. In 1965, Vice President Humphrey described antiwar demonstrations as "organized and masterminded" by "the international Communist movement," while President Johnson in a May 18, 1966 speech in Chicago accused "Nervous Nellies" of undermining his administration's conduct of foreign policy. Antiwar critics, the president charged, were ready to "turn on their own leaders, and on their own country, and on our fighting men." Implying that criticism was harmful if not actually subversive, the president offered a standard by which the critic should be judged: "Is he helping the cause of his country or is he advancing the cause of himself?" In private, Johnson was even less restrained when assessing his critic's motives. Former White House aide Eric Goldman recounts in his inside account *The Tragedy of Lyndon Johnson* that the president commended the FBI and CIA for keeping him informed of his critics' actions. (Beginning in 1967, the CIA and the National Security Agency expanded their investigative activities to include domestic organizations and individuals—even though this expansion was clearly illegal.) "Liberal critics! It's the Russians who are behind the whole thing," the president claimed. Antiwar senators, Johnson maintained, were in close contact with the Russians "who think up things for the senators to say. I often know before they do what their speeches are going to say." To obtain evidence for these suspicions, the president directed the FBI to investigate contacts between members of the Congress and certain foreign embassies.

The administration's assault on its antiwar critics benefited conservative politicians like Richard Nixon. The former Republican vice president exploited the deteriorating situation in Southeast Asia and the developing domestic antiwar criticism. Prior to the president's decision to increase U.S. involvement in Vietnam first by bombing North Vietnam and then by introducing U.S. ground troops, Nixon assailed the Kennedy-Johnson Vietnam policy for permitting "privileged sanctuaries" in North Vietnam and for its "Yalu River concept in South Vietnam" and denounced the concept of a negotiated settlement to the Vietnam War as "surrender on the installment plan." Following the Johnson Administration's decisions to increase gradually U.S. military involvement, Nixon decried each extension as inadequate. Throughout, the Republican politician echoed the president's assault on antiwar critics, condemning such criticism as only encouraging "the Communist leaders to prolong their resistance."

Unlike the Korean War period, these anti-Communist appeals did not silence dissent. During the early 1960s, a profound shift in the national mood had occurred, and specifically in the attitudes of college youth. In June, 1962, left-liberal and radical college students met in Port Huron, Michigan, to form the Students for a Democratic Society (SDS) to organize students around the principle that "the individual share in those social decisions determining the quality and direction of his life; that society be organized to encourage independence in men and provide the means for their common participation." The Vietnam War intensified student alienation. Increasingly after 1965 college campuses became centers of political and intellectual dissent. By 1968, demonstrations against the war and the Johnson administration became more belligerent, student dissent extended to a more general critique of American society, and the college unrest spilled over to the junior high and high schools. During the 1968 primaries, moreover, college students became actively involved in the campaigns of anti-Johnson presidential hopefuls Eugene McCarthy and Robert Kennedy.

THE POLITICS OF POVERTY AND OF CIVIL RIGHTS

One aftermath of Johnson's presidency then was a more divisive and strident politics, wherein tolerance and civility were readily sacrificed to the quest for order and discipline. This atmosphere undermined whatever chance might have existed to redress economic and racial inequities. Having pledged in May 1964 to wage an unconditional war on poverty, Lyndon Johnson had recommended a variety of legislative programs involving either federal funds to develop underdeveloped regions (Appalachia) and skills (the manpower development program) or to redress the deficiencies of the disadvantaged (the educational opportunities bill's assistance to primary and secondary schools to raise educational levels and improve the quality of teaching).

The programs themselves were innovative and promised an improvement in the lot of the neglected poor. A number of agencies to assist the poor were created under the Office of Economic Opportunity (OEO, the umbrella organization of the administration's war on poverty), to assist the poor, including Head Start, Upward Bound, VISTA, the Neighborhood Youth Corps, and Community Action. The act creating OEO defined its purpose: "To eliminate the paradox of poverty in the Nation by opening to everyone the opportunity to live in decency and dignity." Federal funding would relieve the technical and educational deficiencies presumably resulting in poverty. Thus, Head Start was designed to improve the learning skills of preschoolers, Upward Bound to motivate and assist disadvantaged students to attend college, and the Jobs Corps to provide skills for school dropouts. Essentially a domestic Peace Corps, VISTA would provide technical skills and resources to backward areas, while the Neighborhood Youth Corps and the Community Action program were based on the principle of using neighborhood centers to organize the resources of the community.

The promise of this "war on poverty," however, was not realized. In part, the limited appropriation of $1.6 billion for all these programs scarcely constituted a meaningful war on poverty. In addition, because they were administered by local and state officials and thus were often based on political considerations, the impact of federal spending programs was further reduced. A large percentage of the funds went for salaries and administrative expenses; few individual poor people actually benefited in the form of improved skills or increased opportunities.

The failure of these programs to realize their promise contributed to a dual response. On the one hand, many ghetto leaders assailed the antipoverty programs as irrelevant and paternalistic; on the other hand, many conservatives assailed them as inflationary programs that would lead to the unrealistic belief that poverty could be ended simply through federal funding, as well as to a loss of private initiative, to a disrespect for the work ethic, and to creation of an atmosphere of permissiveness. The Johnson administration's simultaneous bold assault on the twin problems of racial segregation and discrimination further contributed to domestic divisions.

By late 1963, the civil rights movement had emerged as a major force in national politics. Southern blacks were encouraged to register and to vote, often for the first time. In Selma, Alabama, for example, fully 97 percent of registered voters were white in a county where blacks outnumbered whites (15,000 to 14,000). In Lowndes and Wilcox counties, Alabama, not one black was registered to vote even though blacks outnumbered whites four to one. The violent reaction of white officials to peaceful black-led registration efforts (notably, the Mississippi voter registration project of the summer of 1964 and the March of Freedom from Selma to Montgomery, Alabama) strengthened the belief that even elemental rights such as voting were denied southern blacks and further that federal action was required to prevent southern violence.

Southern white resistance to black voting led the Congress to enact corrective legislation. In 1964, Congress approved the Civil Rights Act of 1964. That act outlawed racial, religious, and sex discrimination in employment and in places of public accommodation; authorized the attorney general to intercede in private suits for relief from discriminatory racial practices and to sue to desegregate public facilities and schools; terminated federal funding of local and state programs where discrimination was practiced; and extended the life of and granted new powers to the Civil Rights Commission. In 1965, Congress enacted the Voting Rights Act prohibiting counties from employing literacy or other tests for voter eligibility as means to discriminate racially. The act authorized the attorney general to appoint federal registrars when it could be proven that local officials discriminated against blacks and to assign election observers to insure fairness in voting. Both measures constituted major changes in federal policy toward the South, significantly extending federal assistance to blacks.

The striking civil rights gains of the Johnson years satisfied neither black nor white Americans. Many black ghetto leaders decried the Johnson programs as mere tokenism and as confirming the elitism of liberal politicians. At the same time, many whites who opposed civil rights contended that liberals had created an atmosphere insuring disrespect for the law, laziness, and criminality. This latter assault contributed to an anticivil-rights and antiliberal backlash, which had the further effect of shifting national politics to the right.

THE POLITICS OF 1968

Conservative in temperament, the politics of the late 1960s nonetheless focused principally on fears of disorder and on personality. Not coincidentally, then, the major theme of the 1968 presidential campaign—"law and order"—centered on Chief Justice Earl Warren and U.S. Attorney General Ramsey Clark. The assassination of civil rights leader, Martin Luther King, Jr., in Memphis had touched off deep anger in the black community, and the ensuing riots and systematic looting that broke out in many of the nation's cities expressed black rage. Typifying the attitudes of many local political leaders, Chicago's Mayor Richard Daley publicly suggested that future riots might be deterred if the police shot looters or others openly defying the law. Responding to Daley's statement, Attorney General Clark sharply rebuked "loose talk of shooting looters."

Clark's statement became a symbolic issue in the resultant campaign. Exploiting the law and order theme, both when campaigning for the Republican presidential nomination and later for the presidency, Richard Nixon specifically assailed Clark's attorney generalship. In his August 8, 1968 acceptance speech, candidate Nixon pledged "If we are to restore order and respect for law in this country, there's one place we're going to begin: We're going to have a new Attorney General of the United States of America." During the campaign, Nixon defined law and order as the "top [domestic] priority," and promised to appoint conservative jurists to the Supreme Court and to temper federal efforts at school integration. Appealing to the fears and prejudices of many dissatisfied Americans, candidate Nixon appealed to "the Forgotten Americans . . . those who do not break the law, who pay their taxes and go to work . . . people who love this country . . . cry out . . . 'that is enough, let's get some new leadership.' "

Alabama Governor George Wallace exploited similar popular fears and passions, if less subtly. In the aftermath of his 1963 attempt to prevent the desegregation of the University of Alabama, Wallace had emerged as a symbol of southern resistance to federal efforts to integrate southern schools. In 1964 Wallace carried his campaign to the North, entering the Democratic primaries of Wisconsin, Indiana, and Maryland, where he polled 34 percent, 30 percent, and 43 percent of the vote respectively. The outbreak of race riots and the demonstrations on the college campuses of 1965 through 1968 led Wallace to extend his appeal. As the 1968 presidential candidate of the American Independent Party,

Wallace assailed the elitism of liberals and the paternalism of Washington. "Liberals, intellectuals, and long hairs have run the country for too long," he charged. Wallace then pledged to throw out "all these phonies and their briefcases," to restore respect for law and order, and to deal forcefully with demonstrators: "If any demonstrator ever lays down in front of my car, it'll be the last car he'll ever lay down in front of."

In addition, the Democratic party was sharply divided over Lyndon Johnson's conduct of the Vietnam War. Announcing his candidacy for the Democratic presidential nomination on November 30, 1967, the relatively unknown liberal Democratic senator, Eugene McCarthy, exploited widespread resentment over the war and the centralized presidency to win significant delegate support, as did a belated entrant (March 16, 1968) into the race for the Democratic nomination, the then New York senator, Robert Kennedy.

Insofar as Robert Kennedy and Eugene McCarthy had based their campaigns on resentment over Johnson's presidency, their strategy required considerable reassessment following the president's surprise announcement of March 31 that he would neither seek nor accept the Democratic nomination. Then, on April 27, Vice President Hubert Humphrey appealed to the party's organizational leadership and centrist wing. The candidate of the middle, Humphrey also exemplified popular resentment over the life style and antiwar dissent of the college students, Senator McCarthy's principal source of support. Robert Kennedy's assassination on June 5, on the eve of his success in the California primary, moreover, removed Humphrey's major opponent for the nomination.

Radicalized by the Vietnam War, thousands of antiwar youths converged on Chicago in August to demonstrate their opposition to the war and to disrupt the Democratic National Convention. To insure that the convention would proceed with a minimum of disorder, the convention site area was turned into a fortress, federal troops were mobilized, and elaborate security plans were devised including electronic surveillance by the army's intelligence division. Under Mayor Daley's direction, the Chicago police adopted confrontation tactics to disperse the demonstrators that turned into what a subsequent commission study concluded was "a police riot."

These procedures were not confined to controlling dissenters outside the convention hall but were employed by the Democratic leadership at the convention to limit floor debate and insure Humphrey's nomination. These efforts insured a bitterly divided party and, ironically, one that many considered a symbol of the danger of permissiveness and still others the danger of repression.

The Wallace and Nixon campaigns were not simply appeals to racial prejudice. Both expressed the resentment of many middle and lower class Americans over the consequences of the liberal reforms and social controls of the 1960s. Both repudiated the liberal premise of a consensus of values and the attendant politics of ordered reason and deference to experts. In the final analysis, Nixon and Wallace appealed not to com-

The war hits home
(James Pickerell/Black Star)

mon purpose but to common resentment. Nixon's 1968 strategy might have sought to force a new alignment. Given its essentially negative character, this alignment could only be a fragile one insofar as its success was secured by the strong antipathy to the Johnson Presidency.

When he announced his decision not to seek reelection, Lyndon Johnson's popularity had declined to a new low. A Gallup poll revealed then that only 36 percent of the populace approved of his leadership, a level of unpopularity exceeded only by Harry Truman's 1951 low of 23 percent. Leaving office a repudiated president, his politics of consensus shattered, Johnson was nonetheless no weaker a president than had been the equally unpopular Truman. Under Lyndon Johnson, the power of the executive branch had been considerably extended, and an even more centralized presidency had been forged. Johnson's diminished popularity and reduced leverage after 1965 did not insure a decisive congressional or public role in the formation of national policy. The crucial decisions involving the determination of national priorities remained within the province of the executive branch.

30

The Tragedy of LBJ: The United States and Vietnam

Three conclusions can probably be drawn concerning the salient characteristics of the Kennedy-Johnson foreign policy of the 1960s. First, the Cold War abated in intensity. After the Cuban missile crisis of 1962, both great superpowers, the United States and Russia, realized that regardless of shifts in the balance of nuclear weapons, each possessed more than enough to destroy the other and much of the rest of the world as well. Since then, therefore, both powers have acted more cautiously, seeking to avoid direct confrontations and to achieve a degree of détente in their mutual relationship. Second, the strains associated with the costly involvement in the Vietnam War eroded domestic support for continued American attempts to act as global policeman. In addition, the multiplying signs that the Communist world was not monolithic but rather polycentric dispelled belief in the simplified Cold War dichotomy between "free" and "Communist" worlds. Third, and more speculative, was the return to a multipower world in which emergent and revived nationalisms dilute both NATO and the Soviet system, especially as new states in Africa and Asia exercised their independence.

And as China, Japan, and other nation-states influence global affairs more directly, a world dominated by two superpowers alone seems fated to vanish. Although Russia and the United States probably will long remain far more powerful than any other nation-state, they will experience sharper challenges from hitherto subservient nations.

THE KENNEDY ERA

In his three years in the White House, President John Fitzgerald Kennedy built up the United States nuclear and conventional weapons systems. He also tried to shift American policy toward a more dynamic course of foreign aid and the promotion of freer world trade. Ironically, despite his Cold War rhetoric, Kennedy sought a détente with Russia to defuse the threat of nuclear war.

His brief administration oscillated wildly between the harshest extremes of Truman-style anti-Communist containment and policies aimed at softening Soviet-American confrontations. Kennedy's foreign policy, on the one hand, brought the world to the brink of nuclear catastrophe during the Cuban missile crisis and precipitated the Vietnam tragedy; on the other hand, aspects of his policy indicated promise of statesmanship and greatness.

The last years of the Eisenhower administration had witnessed great progress by Russia in space technology and long-range rockets, leading Kennedy to conclude falsely that Russia had acquired a missile lead over the United States. Kennedy obtained from Congress approval of vastly increased defense expenditures and greatly enlarged the strength of American deterrent missiles and Polaris-type submarines armed with missiles. He also adopted General Maxwell Taylor's concept of military flexibility, or the preservation of defensive options, in case of an attack by strategic nuclear weapons, tactical A-bombs, or conventional arms. Presumably the United States would be able to fight on any scale from a direct clash with Russia to local "hot" wars and so-called wars of national liberation or insurgency. Thus by 1963, the United States had achieved an estimated nuclear superiority over Russia of three to one in ICBM missiles and an arsenal of 33,000 nuclear bombs or rocket payloads, with 15,000 more in preparation! By 1965, the United States possessed an estimated four-to-one margin in ICBMs. Gradually, as the pace of American procurement tapered off and Russia increased its production, the American lead narrowed. Kennedy also launched a crash space program to recover the initiative and regain prestige from Russia in exploring space and to place the first man on the moon. The United States scored great success by landing the first men upon the moon's surface in July 1969, and by the deep-space probes and televised fly-bys of Venus and Mars.

President Kennedy once remarked that "domestic policy can only defeat us; foreign policy can kill us." As Kennedy took office, Russia under Khrushchev appeared to threaten West Berlin. Kennedy journeyed to Vienna in June 1961 for an outwardly friendly two-power summit conference with the Russian leader. The Soviet leader avoided insults such as had disrupted the Paris conference in 1960, but made it clear that he was determined, in his words, to get the "bone" of West Berlin out of his throat. The American president, however, stood firm against Khrushchev's declaration of a six-month time limit for a German settlement. It was a grim confrontation that seemed to threaten nuclear war. According to one account, Khruschev told the American president that Russia had "grown up" and in fact that he felt it was militarily stronger than the United States. The results were that Kennedy upon his return to the United States alerted the American people to the new peril, called up reserve military units and strengthened American forces in Europe and West Berlin. The crisis saw the erection of the Berlin Wall in August 1961 and threatening tank maneuvers, but the Americans did not retreat. Once again Kennedy appeared to follow the Cold War precedents of the Truman era.

The Bay of Pigs fiasco in Cuba set the stage for the Vienna conference and Berlin confrontation. Since the American diplomatic break with Fidel Castro's Cuba, the Central Intelligence Agency had been training and equipping a Cuban refugee army to invade the island and topple Castro. Despite great doubts about the scheme, Kennedy shared his advisers' hopes that the planned invasion would touch off a popular uprising against the Cuban premier or at least would enable new forces to reach the Escambray Mountains for guerilla war. He refused, however, to give the invasion full American air support. Begun on April 17, 1961, the invasion failed miserably, as Castro's forces easily killed or captured the invaders.

Without question, the Bay of Pigs invasion was a grievous error. First, it is debatable that Castro's Cuba represented a serious threat to American security. Second, if Cuba did pose such a threat, the United States should have acted effectively and forcefully. At the Bay of Pigs the United States acted as an imperialist power but came away with none of the benefits and all of the costs of imperialism.

Although President Kennedy during the Bay of Pigs fiasco declared that not prestige but the substance of power counted most in international affairs, he himself practiced the politics of prestige. The Bay of Pigs invasion prompted Russia's leaders to arm the Cubans with intermediate range nuclear missiles that could reach the American mainland. In the summer and fall of 1962 Khrushchev established about forty missile sites in Cuba as a defense against future American attempts to topple Castro. Confronted for the first time with signs of direct Soviet military power in the American hemisphere, on October 17 Kennedy acted with unwarranted alarm. Russia, after all, had endured two decades of nuclear encirclement by American missile and bomber bases in Turkey and Western Europe.

As intelligence information arrived in Washington about Russian missiles in Cuba, the presence of which was blandly denied by the Soviet foreign minister, Gromyko, who visited the White House a week before the crisis broke, Kennedy decided upon forcible counter measures to avert the supposed peril. Ruling out a mere diplomatic protest or quick military air strikes to destroy the sites before Soviet missiles could be installed, on October 22 Kennedy ordered a naval blockade to halt future Soviet weapons deliveries while demanding withdrawal of those missiles that already had arrived. Khrushchev thus found himself in a delicate and difficult situation. By challenging the United States near the center of its power, he had placed himself in the dilemma of having to retreat or risk a major war. He chose to retreat and on October 28 agreed to withdraw the missiles in what Dean Rusk called an "eyeball-to-eyeball" confrontation. In order to improve Democratic chances in the November 1962 congressional elections more than to protect American security Kennedy played the old-fashioned Cold Warrior and risked a Soviet-American nuclear conflict.

After the missile crisis passed, however, Soviet-American relations began to improve greatly as both sides, having been sobered, sought a measure of détente. Hence they concluded the Nuclear Test Ban Treaty in July 1963.

The Alliance for Progress clearly represented Kennedy's second response to the Castro revolution and the threat it raised of future revolutions throughout Latin America. President Kennedy adopted the thesis put forth by his adviser and sometime economics professor Walt W. Rostow, that economic development could be spurred by a long-term assistance program and that cumulative economic growth would render left-wing revolutions unnecessary and unlikely. On March 13, 1961, Kennedy announced his new Latin America program, emphasizing as its goal the promotion of substantial economic development, social reforms, and political freedom.

Latin American leaders reacted warily to Kennedy's proposal for an "Allianza para el progreso." At a conference held at Punta del Este in Uruguay in August 1961, the United States promised to provide up to 55 percent or $1.1 billion each year for a ten-year, $20 billion program for rapid economic development. Of the remainder, the United States expected 15 percent each to come from private American investors, public and private sources in Western Europe and Japan, and international lending agencies. Kennedy envisioned the Alliance as not just another handout from Washington, but as an ambitious program to transform Latin American society and life. Latin American countries—Cuba was excluded—pledged appropriate tax and land reforms as well as housing, health, and educational programs. The United States hoped that steady economic growth and concomitant social reforms would forestall Communist penetration in the Western hemisphere.

In operation, the Alliance for Progress recorded some achievements but by and large fell lamentably short of its announced goals. The average economic growth rate rose to only 2 percent, which a rapidly growing population more than nullified; conservative ruling classes resisted yielding their entrenched privileges and condemned American pressure as "Yanqui" interventionism; and radicals accused an imperialistic United States of merely seeking to patch up a corrupt and moribund capitalism to cure a cancer with Band-aids. To have achieved substantial progress, Latin America would have had to undergo a veritable political and social revolution, and the last thing the United States wanted was leftist-inspired and led rebellions.

The Peace Corps, another Kennedy innovation, scored greater success. During the 1960 presidential campaign, Kennedy endorsed a program to send trained American men and women to help underdeveloped nations achieve modern skills and to demonstrate democracy at work. Until 1970, the Peace Corps aroused great support across the United States, especially from idealistic youths, and thousands of corpsmen were sent abroad to teach, to help build schools, roads, and sanitary systems, and to encourage farming reforms. It was welcomed by most underdeveloped nations and by 1969 over nine thousand Americans were serving abroad.

THE U.S. AND AFRICA

In the post–World War II era, over thirty newly-independent states have emerged in Africa as the old colonial empires disintegrated and nationalist currents swept the continent. Most of these new states achieved their independence without violent struggle and have preserved friendly relations with their former ruling countries in Europe. But radical Africans have vigorously denounced such relationships as a form of neocolonialism.

Because the United States in the past rarely acted as the imperialist in Africa, the relations between the United States and the new African states were at first peaceful and friendly. The United States' general lack of economic investments in black Africa reduced the possibility for friction. Similarly, the United States seldom interfered politically, with the exception of the Italo-Ethiopian War in the mid-1930s. The total amount of U.S. aid granted the African nations throughout these years remained modest and the United States tacitly allowed the former European colonial powers to uphold Western interests in Africa.

The Belgian Congo, however, provided one of the few trouble spots for the United States. Belgium unexpectedly and without prior planning granted independence to the Congo in June 1960. Only a few Congolese had received advanced education, and Belgium had traditionally encouraged tribalism and suppressed nationalism. With independence, the indigenous Congolese elite began a struggle for power and nationhood that resulted in violent disorders and substantial property and human losses. Belgium promptly sent troops back into the country, while Congolese Premier Patrice Lumumba appealed to the United Nations for help and threatened to turn to Russia for aid. The United States joined Russia in the UN by voting to require the departure of Belgian troops and the creation of a UN police force to restore order.

Only then did the United States intervene directly in African affairs and underwrote much of the cost of establishing a Congolese regime favorable to Western interests. The American effort, however, was complicated by the secession of mineral-rich Katanga province, led by Moise Tshombe, who in turn was backed by the Belgians. The American government distrusted Lumumba because of his alleged links to the Soviets, and the CIA actually plotted to assassinate the Congolese premier. Therefore, when Lumumba was slain in 1961, the United States was understandably blamed for his death and the triumph of Tshombe. The new Congolese regime expelled the alleged Russian agents, causing Russia to refuse to pay its share of the costs of maintaining the UN police force. Finally, by the end of 1963, the UN forces succeeded in crushing Tshombe's Katanganese rebellion and uniting the Congo under a regime acceptable to the Americans, who during the Kennedy-Johnson years turned the Congo into the primary seat of American influence in central Africa.

On the whole, the United States and Russia have treated Africa as peripheral to their primary global interests. But whenever it has served their purposes, both the United States and Russia have solicited allies among the new African states, a competition sometimes made tripartite by Chinese intervention. The United States treated the Congo as a client state and supported the white South African regime against black nationalists. Indeed, a secret State Department policy paper drafted by Henry Kissinger in 1974 suggested that the United States support the Portuguese colonies and the minority white regimes in southern Africa in order to resist Soviet penetration of the area. Russia thus found friends among the more radical North African states and among leftists in Mozambique and Angola when the latter two colonies in southern Africa were granted independence by Portugal in 1975–76. By the end of 1975, in fact, the Cold War promised to penetrate the heart of Africa, as President Gerald Ford asked Congress to provide funds to support American-backed anti-Soviet groups in Angola. Congress, however, rebuffed Ford, and the Soviet-backed anticolonialists, who were better organized and amassed greater popular support among the Angolans, triumphed. Nonetheless, as Kissinger's diplomatic efforts in 1976 to arrange for the peaceful transfer of political power to the black majority in Rhodesia and remain in the good graces of the white minority government in South Africa shows, southern Africa remains a global trouble spot and a potential area for Soviet-American conflict.

THE VIETNAM WAR

Lyndon Baines Johnson, Kennedy's successor, has been characterized by one biographer as a man of high intelligence, great ambitions, vast energy, and pride to the point of vanity. Until his landslide election victory over Barry Goldwater in 1964, Johnson acted cautiously in foreign affairs. After the election, however, Johnson revealed himself as an impetuous and strong-willed chief executive, so tough in foreign affairs that many advisers inherited from Kennedy grew dismayed. Johnson had concluded from the Bay of Pigs fiasco in 1961 and the 1962 Cuban missile crisis that American diplomatic indecisiveness threatened national security and that the decisive use of power could avert further Communist penetration of the Western Hemisphere and elsewhere. As he remarked to a newspaper columnist, "The real danger is that the other side is going to underestimate us—it's happened before. The danger is that they'll think we are fat and fifty—just the countryclub crowd."

If far from naïve, Lyndon Johnson brought to office a strong sense of patriotism inherited from his rural Texas background. Proud of the United States and of his high office as chief executive, he detested weakness. But, above all, the president was convinced that America's diplomatic course was morally right, and he passionately wanted to convince all his critics of that rightness. Indeed he tolerated neither foreign nor domestic criticism of his foreign policy, and his sense of righteousness would produce an American tragedy.

The background of the Vietnam War lay in a decades-old struggle by Indochinese nationalists to defeat French colonialism and the attempt by the Western powers, first France and then the United States, to reassert Western hegemony in Southeast Asia. The clash between the forces of colonialism and emergent nationalism, moreover, had been considerably influenced by the Cold War atmosphere of the 1950s and 1960s. American policymakers almost reflexively identified the Vietnamese nationalists with international communism, headquartered, in Dean Rusk's phrase, in Moscow and Peiping. By the same token, Americans identified Vietnamese clients of the West with the "free world." Thus the struggle in Southeast Asia between nationalism and colonialism became for American policymakers a battle between tyranny and freedom.

By 1954, after the battle of Dien Bien Phu, the Vietnamese nationalists, led by Ho Chi Minh, had practically compelled the French to sue for peace and seek a withdrawal from Vietnam. At a Big Four foreign ministers conference in Geneva in July 1954, the conferees settled the war in Vietnam and arranged for the withdrawal of French power.

During the Geneva conference, however, the United States began to plan for a new security alliance system to stabilize the area. And the United States soon thereafter engineered the creation of SEATO or the Southeast Asia Treaty Organization. In a sense, then, the United States in 1955 replaced France as the principal power in Southeast Asia.

President Ngo Dinh Diem of South Vietnam, the United States' preferred nationalist leader in the area, refused to recognize the Geneva settlement and ordered all flags flown at half-mast to mourn his nation's

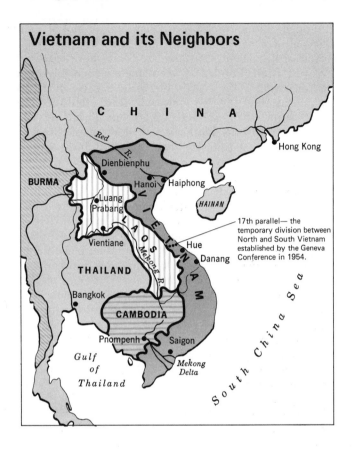

Vietnam and its Neighbors

17th parallel— the temporary division between North and South Vietnam established by the Geneva Conference in 1954.

partition. Diem refused to hold the elections on reunification scheduled for 1956 and despite American advice declined all consultation on the issue with the North. In fact, free elections in the American sense were scarcely possible in either North or South Vietnam. Men and women who had just shot at each other during a bitter war of national liberation were unlikely to accord each other full freedom or count each other's ballots. Moreover, North Vietnamese Premier Ho Chi Minh believed that he had liberated his nation on the field of battle and that Diem was simply a proxy for United States imperialism. If American-style elections had been possible and had been held, it is probably true, as President Eisenhower observed, that Ho Chi Minh would have won a substantial victory as a dedicated Vietnamese nationalist and the father of his country.

Although few observers thought that Diem's regime had any chance of survival in 1954, the United States backed him fully. In October 1954,

President Eisenhower wrote Diem and promised economic and military aid, subject to efficient use and the carrying out of promised social reforms. But Diem's promised reforms, more rhetorical than real, failed to avert a rebellion led by Vietnamese Communists (the Vietcong) in the South. In 1959 the North Vietnamese government in Hanoi called for reunification of the two Vietnams and abetted the rebellion in the South, establishing the National Liberation Front in 1960 to conduct the struggle within the southern half of Vietnam. Greatly disturbed over the Vietnamese situation, President Kennedy increased significantly the flow of American aid to Diem after 1961 and by mid-1963 would have sent about 16,500 American military "advisers" to South Vietnam. Nonetheless, Kennedy resisted the suggestion of many advisers for a more direct U.S. military role and instead emphasized counter-insurgency tactics. For a time, Diem's American-backed regime seemed in the ascendancy and Secretary of Defense Robert McNamara optimistically reported the imminent triumph of a "free" South Vietnam. But the Americans never understood the Vietnamese or what was happening in that tragic land, and the more light McNamara saw at the end of the tunnel, the darker grew the actual reality for Diem and his American supporters. When Diem's regime finally collapsed in 1963, an event President Kennedy in fact sought, Kennedy remarked, "for us to withdraw from that effort would mean a collapse not only of South Vietnam but of Southeast Asia. So we are going to stay there."

President Johnson adhered firmly to Kennedy's policy of intervention in Southeast Asia. At first opposed to any deeper involvement, he and his principal advisers soon became convinced that the United States should use more military power in South Vietnam. Johnson then consciously chose deeper involvement for the United States because he saw Asia as of prime importance to America, viewed South Vietnam as a victim of Communist aggression, and believed that the People's Republic of China sought a Communist-dominated Asia and manipulated the Vietcong rebellion. Himself familiar with foreign affairs, yet influenced by Secretary of State Dean Rusk and Walt W. Rostow who foolishly compared Ho to Hitler and South Vietnam to Czechoslovakia, Johnson by 1965 had decided that "international communism" could not be appeased and that the United States must act decisively to insure the continuance of an anti-Communist government in South Vietnam.

The president thus opted at first for a limited war in Vietnam and, especially during the 1964 election campaign, seemed to be an advocate of a reasonable, pacific foreign policy. But even during his campaign against Goldwater, Johnson intended to obtain American aims in Vietnam. Using as a pretext an alleged North Vietnamese attack on American warships patrolling in Vietnamese waters, Johnson in August obtained from a compliant Congress the so-called Gulf of Tonkin resolution that authorized the president to use force as he saw fit to retaliate against North Vietnamese attacks on American forces. The president, however, never informed Congress that the United States ships allegedly attacked had been involved in aggressive actions against North Vietnam or that the attacks had never been fully verified. This was to be only the first of many deceptions that Johnson and later Richard Nixon would use to garner congressional and popular support for an increasing level of American intervention in Southeast Asia.

After his reelection, President Johnson used his power under the Gulf of Tonkin resolution first to order U.S. bombing of North Vietnamese military targets, then to increase the number of American troops in South Vietnam, ostensibly to defend airstrips, and then to extend the U.S. role to active belligerency in the south. The fiction of an advisory, limited role was soon abandoned, and the U.S. became the major participant. By mid-1968, over 500,000 American troops were in South Vietnam. Johnson's use of U.S. military power had undoubtedly saved the South Vietnamese government from collapse, but only temporarily and at the cost of making the conflict largely an American war.

As American involvement in Vietnam increased after 1965, a "great debate" erupted in the United States about the morality and correctness of American foreign policy. Critics such as Senators Wayne Morse of Oregon and J. William Fulbright of Arkansas expressed mounting concern that the United States had overcommitted itself in a civil war in which no vital American interests were involved. Senator Morse, one of only two senators to vote against the Tonkin Gulf resolution, charged that Johnson's war, as it became known, was unconstitutional because congress had never formally declared war. College "teach-ins" also swept across America beginning in 1965 as college students and their teachers launched a campaign of opposition to the Vietnam involvement. And as American casualties soared and television newscasts brought home to American audiences the real costs of the Vietnamese war, domestic opposition to Johnson's foreign policy intensified. Many Americans also began to wonder about the morality of a war in which American officers explained that villages had to be destroyed in order to save them, in which more shells and bombs were dropped on Vietnam than on Germany and Japan combined during World War II, and in which American military power was employed against a helpless civilian population.

Yet until the surprising "Tet Offensive" launched by the Vietcong and the North Vietnamese against American bases and major cities in South Vietnam on January 30, 1968, LBJ remained firmly committed to his course. Although that attack was beaten back with heavy losses to the North Vietnamese and the Vietcong, President Johnson had reluctantly concluded that military victory was not attainable because the costs of such a victory were politically untenable. Accordingly, on March 31, 1968 the President announced that he would not run for reelection and proclaimed an unconditional partial bombing halt covering most of North Vietnam. In response, North Vietnamese Premier Ho Chi Minh agreed to peace negotiations that began in Paris in May 1968.

By the end of 1968, the Vietnamese War had caused tragedy for all involved. For Vietnamese, north and south, Cambodians, and Laotians, the use of American military power in small, simple, agricultural societies spelled disaster—countless villages had been destroyed, the land had been ravished, and countless lives (both civilian and military) had been lost. For Americans, the Vietnamese War meant domestic discord, civic disorders, and a loss of faith and trust in political parties and their leaders. For many young adult male Americans, it meant the loss of life, limb, or sanity on a Vietnamese battlefield, exile abroad as "draft-dodgers" or military deserters, and unease or exile at home in a society and state that had become foreign to them. Even many war veterans returned not as heroes but as forgotten soldiers; for them the costs and sacrifices seemed pointless, even frustrating. For Lyndon Johnson, Vietnam dissolved his dreams of being remembered as a great reform president, a true successor to Franklin D. Roosevelt. The war had driven Lyndon Johnson from office almost in disgrace, an incumbent president fearful of seeking another term lest he be repudiated either by his own party or the mass of voters. Thus the war in Vietnam had become a tragedy without end, and thus it would remain for four more years during the administration of Richard M. Nixon.

SELECTED BIBLIOGRAPHY FOR SECTION VIII

For the triumph of Keynesianism and corporatism in the American economy of the 1950s and 1960s, see HERBERT STEIN, *The Fiscal Revolution in America* (1969) * and JOHN K. GALBRAITH, *The New Industrial State* (1967).* On the maldistribution of wealth and income, read ROBERT LAMPMAN, *The Share of Top Wealth Holders* (1962); GABRIEL KOLKO, *Wealth and Power in America* (1962) *; and FERDINAND LUNDBERG, *The Rich and the Superrich* (1968).* The war on poverty was precipitated by MICHAEL HARRINGTON's *The Other America* (1960).* Many books with a similar theme followed, including HERMAN MILLER, *Rich Man, Poor Man* (1964) *; WILLIAM RYAN, *Blaming the Victim* (1971) *; and RICHARD PARKER, *The Myth of the Middle Class* (1972).* For a somewhat different slant on the problems of poverty, see DANIEL PATRICK MOYNIHAN, *Maximum Feasible Misunderstanding* (1968).* On American labor and working people's lives, examine ELI CHINOY, *Automobile Workers and the American Dream* (1955) *; STANLEY ARONOWITZ, *False Promises* (1973) *; STUDS TERKEL, *Working* (1972) *; FRANK CORMIER and WILLIAM J. EATON, *Reuther* (1970); JOSEPH C. GOULDEN, *Meany* (1972); JOHN HUTCHINSON, *The Imperfect Union: A History of Corruption in American Trade Unions* (1970); and WILLIAM SERRIN, *The Company and the Union* (1972), an analysis of collaboration between General Motors and the United Auto Workers.

The turbulent sixties saw the revolt of nonwhites, youth, and women.

* Available in paperback.

On the first topic see MARTIN LUTHER KING, JR., *Why We Can't Wait* (1964) *; LOUIS LOMAX, *The Negro Revolt* (1962) *; and HOWARD ZINN, *SNCC: The New Abolitionists* (1964).* The shift from civil rights to black power is examined in BENJAMIN MUSE, *The American Negro Revolution* (1969) *; HAROLD CRUSE, *The Crisis of the Negro Intellectual* (1967) *; DAVID L. LEWIS, *King: A Critical Biography* (1970); ALEX HALEY, ed., *The Autobiography of Malcolm X* (1964) *; and ELDRIDGE CLEAVER, *Soul on Ice* (1968).* Two important works dealing with black power organizations are AUGUST MEIER and ELLIOT RUDWICK, *CORE* (1973) * and PHILIP S. FONER, ed., *The Black Panthers Speak* (1970).* For important statistical data, see the *Report of the National Advisory Commission on Civil Disorders* (1968).

Other nonwhite Americans have become the subject of historical inquiry only recently. A standard study is NATHAN GLAZER and DANIEL PATRICK MOYNIHAN, *Beyond the Melting Pot: The Negroes, Puerto Ricans, Jews, Italians, and Irish of New York City* (1970).* Other important works include STAN STEINER, *The New Indians* (1968) * and also his *La Raza: The Mexican Americans* (1970),* and MATT S. MEIER and FELICIANO RIVERA, *The Chicanos: A History of Mexican Americans* (1972).* On white ethnics, see ARTHUR B. SHOSTAK, *Blue Collar Life* (1969) * and MICHAEL NOVAK, *The Rise of the Unmeltable Ethnics: Politics and Culture in the Seventies* (1972).

The revolt of the young is covered in a variety of books. KENNETH KENISTON has written two perceptive studies on the topic, *The Uncommitted* (1965) * and *Young Radicals* (1968).* Other important works are by THEODORE ROSZAK, *The Making of a Counterculture* (1969) *; CHARLES REICH, *The Greening of America* (1970) *; JACK NEWFIELD, *A Prophetic Minority* (1966) *; IRWIN UNGER, *The Movement: A History of the American New Left* (1972) *; and KIRKPATRICK SALE, *SDS* (1973).* Women as a subject of historical inquiry is yet another area on which there is much to be written. A good place to begin is with LOIS S. BANNER, *Women in Modern America* (1974) *; BETTY FRIEDAN, *The Feminine Mystique* (1975 ed.) *; CAROLINE BIRD, *Born Female: The High Cost of Keeping Women Down* (1974) *; ROBIN MORGAN, ed., *Sisterhood Is Powerful* (1970) *; WILLIAM CHAFE, *The American Woman* (1972) *; and JULIET MITCHELL, *Woman's Estate* (1971).*

The historical literature on the domestic politics of the Johnson years is necessarily limited since the more important papers remain closed. There are a number of journalistic accounts and memoirs, but they must be read with great caution. The best studies are those of JAMES SUNDQUIST, *Politics and Policy* (1968); HUGH SIDEY, *A Very Personal Presidency* (1968); ERIC GOLDMAN, *The Tragedy of Lyndon Johnson* (1969) *; WILLIAM L. O'NEILL, *Coming Apart* (1971) *; LAWRENCE WITTNER, *Cold War America* (1974) *; ALONZO HAMBY, *The Imperial Years* (1976); TOM WICKER, *JFK and LBJ* (1968) *; ARTHUR SCHLESINGER, JR., *The Imperial Presidency* (1973) *; JEROME SKOLNICK, *The Politics of Protest* (1969); ARCHIBALD COX, *The Warren Court* (1968); ALEXANDER BICKEL,

The Supreme Court and the Idea of Progress (1970); NELSON BLACK-
STOCK, *COINTELPRO* (1976) *; MORTON HALPERIN et al., *The Lawless
State* (1976) *; SANFORD UNGAR, *FBI* (1975); and NORMAN DORSEN and
STEPHEN GILLERS, eds., *None of Your Business* (1975) .*

Criticisms of Johnson's Vietnam policy are legion. One of the best is
DAVID HALBERSTAM, *The Best and the Brightest* (1973) .* Also see
RICHARD N. GOODWIN, *Triumph or Tragedy* (1966); TOWNSEND HOOPES,
The Limits of Intervention (rev. ed., 1973) *; MARVIN KALB and ELIE
ABEL, *Roots of Involvement* (1971); J. W. FULBRIGHT, *The Arrogance of
Power* (1972) *; EDWARD FRIEDMAN and MARK SELDEN, eds., *America's
Asia: Dissenting Essays on Asian-American Relations* (1971) *; and
FRANCES FITZGERALD, *Fire in the Lake* (1972) .* For a defense of U.S.
Vietnam policy, see JOHN W. SPANIER, *American Foreign Policy since
World War II* (1973 ed.) .*

IX
Facing the Future

In the mid-1970s, the American people, perhaps for the first time in their history, together had to face the shock of failure and defeat. However much politicians tried to disguise the meaning of the end of the war in Vietnam, it was in fact a defeat for the United States, made more bitter and frustrating because the globe's most powerful military state had been overcome by a poor, agricultural, Third-World society. The Vietnam war, which revealed to some degree the limits of American power, coincided with another event that revealed America's vulnerability. In 1973, in the aftermath of yet another open war between Israel and the Arab nations, the oil exporting countries combined into the Organization of Petroleum Exporting Countries (OPEC) and embargoed the shipment of oil to most western states, the United States included. With the bulk of its foreign oil supplies cut off, the United States found itself faced with an energy crisis. A nation whose entire existence had been based on material abundance suddenly had to come to grips with scarcity.

The adjustment to failure and defeat was made more difficult by the strange career of Richard M. Nixon. A politician who had made his way in the 1950s as the personification of Cold War values, Nixon, from 1969 to 1973, together with his foreign affairs adviser, Henry Kissinger, practiced the diplomacy of

483

détente. But détente as practiced by Nixon proved peculiar indeed. On the one hand, the president and Kissinger smiled at the Soviets and courted the Chinese, the world's two leading Communist powers. On the other hand, they rained death and destruction on Southeast Asia, sought to topple Salvador Allende's socialist government in Chile, and adopted a hard line toward non-Soviet and non-Chinese leftist movements. Under Nixon, American foreign policy was a strange compound of détente and destruction.

Domestically, the Nixon years also seem contradictory if not confusing, as this arrogant president sought to make illusion prevail over reality. He spoke in terms redolent of the Eisenhower years, calling on Americans to lower their voices and tame their anger; he promised, as had the war hero a decade earlier, to promote social harmony and ease the tensions that had torn the nation apart during the 1960s. Yet, while he sounded like Eisenhower, Nixon practiced a far different politics; it was a politics in which critics were perceived as enemies to be annihilated and power was increasingly centralized in the White House and in the hands of officials appointed by and solely responsible to the president—a politics that perhaps inclined toward an imperial presidency.

Richard Nixon's peculiar brand of politics led ultimately to the Watergate affair, an event which epitomized the triumph of illusion over reality. In an ironic way, Attorney General John Mitchell's words—"Watch what we do not what we say"—can be taken as a fitting epigraph for the Nixon presidency. Yet in a final irony of history, Nixon suffered and was forced from the presidency not so much for any of his administration's domestic and foreign abuses of power but for what he said. Not what he did in practice but what he said in the privacy of his own office and recorded on tape brought the downfall of Richard Milhous Nixon and created the most severe crisis in United States history since the Civil War and Reconstruction.

31

Richard M. Nixon and the Crisis of American Politics

During the Cold War years southern allegiance to the Democratic party shattered as many southerners found themselves at odds with the liberal policies of Democratic presidents and platforms. This disaffection partly shaped Richard Nixon's strategy first in his effort to win election to the presidency in 1968 and then reelection in 1972. By 1968, the South was no longer safely Democratic. Steadily, although varying depending on the exigencies of each particular contest, Democratic nominees found that their gains in Northern urban areas were counterbalanced by the defection of the once-solid Democratic South.

In 1968, only the candidacy of Alabama Governor George Wallace on the American Independence party ticket averted a Republican sweep of the South. Nixon's percentage of the southern vote reached 34.6 percent as he carried Florida, Tennessee, Virginia, South Carolina, and North Carolina. Wallace polled 34.4 percent of the southern vote winning the electoral votes of Louisiana, Alabama, Mississippi, Georgia, and Arkansas. In contrast, Humphrey trailed both candidates with 31 percent of the southern vote, winning only Texas. Moreover, Humphrey led in only 237 of the 1,105 southern counties (all but 83 of these counties being in Texas), and fully two-thirds of his percentage of the total southern vote came from blacks. By 1972, when Nixon won every state of the union except Massachusetts (and the District of Columbia), the South had virtually shifted to the national Republican party. In that election, Democratic presidential nominee George McGovern's southern vote was 10 percent less than his national average.

The issues of civil rights, internal security, and national defense became intertwined and made possible Republican gains in the South. An anti-Communist politics identifying dissent and reform with disloyalty commanded considerable southern support. No longer opposing civil rights merely on racial or states rights grounds, southerners condemned the role of "outside agitators" and the allegedly subversive character of the civil rights movement.

The increase in federal defense spending, from roughly $50 billion in 1951 to $85 billion by 1973, also fundamentally altered southern politics. The large numbers of army and navy bases located in the South helped stimulate the South's economy; firms receiving major defense contracts either located or established subsidiary plants in the South. Traditionally supportive of free trade and an active foreign policy, the South thereafter provided widespread support for a strong national defense. National security and economic advantage thus combined with unabashed patriotism to move southern politics to the right. By the 1960s and 1970s, then, southern political attitudes were aligned more closely with the militant anticommunism of the conservative wing of the Republican party than with the increasingly more liberal policy positions of the national Democratic party.

These Republican gains extended as well to the Congress. Between 1955 and 1970, the number of Democratic senators from southern and border states declined from 30 to 18, the number of Democratic congressmen from 130 to 98. By 1970, 6 of the 22 southern senators and 27 of the 109 southern representatives were Republicans. In 1972, Republicans won an additional two Senate and nine House seats. In addition, southern Democratic congressmen increasingly voted with the majority of Republicans on major foreign and domestic policy issues. Thus, whereas as recently as 1953–54 not a single House Democrat voted as often with Republican as with Democratic majorities, by 1967–68 no fewer than 53 did (all but one being from southern and border states).

A POLITICS OF RACE AND "NATIONAL SECURITY"

Independent of these Republican gains in the South, Richard Nixon recognized the anomalous character of his 1968 victory and the obstacles remaining to his reelection in 1972. The race riots of 1965–68 within northern black ghettoes, the sharp increase in violent crimes, and the Vietnam War and the accompanying shrill and often violent protests against that war organized on college campuses during 1967 and 1968, had precipitated the presidential candidacies of Eugene McCarthy and Robert Kennedy, shattered, at least temporarily, traditional Democratic allegiances, and polarized the American body politic. Having won the presidential nomination of a divided Democratic party, Hubert Humphrey could not readily insure party unity.

In his 1968 campaign, Nixon had capitalized on Democratic divisions. Using television with great sophistication, Nixon strategists prepared commercials that flashed pictures of rioting cities and campuses, assailed the "permissiveness" of federal authorities, and specifically condemned controversial decisions of the Supreme Court and of Lyndon Johnson's attorney general, Ramsey Clark. In this advertising effort, the Nixon campaign sought to exploit middle-class and middle-aged fears about crime (between the years 1960 and 1968 murders had increased by 36 percent, rapes by 65 percent, and assaults by 67 percent). He contrasted the shouting of the youthful protesters with ". . . . another voice, it is a quiet voice in the tumult and shouting. It is the voice of the great majority of Americans, the forgotten Americans, the nonshouters, the nondemonstrators." These "forgotten Americans," candidate Nixon argued, were the "good people" of America: "They're decent people. They work and they save and they pay their taxes and they care." In another speech, the Republican candidate emphasized that "when 43 percent of the American people are afraid to walk in the streets of their cities, it's time for a housecleaning, a new attorney general, and a new policy to establish freedom from fear in this country. Let me tell you: I am an expert in this field. I pledge to you I'll take personal charge." The Democrats, Nixon further charged, were responsible for: "The longest war in American history, the highest taxes in American history, the worst crime rate in American history, the highest increases in prices in a generation, the lowest respect for America we have ever had."

Candidate Nixon's appeals to the fears and concerns of many Americans produced his slim electoral victory of 1968: Nixon received 43.4 percent of the popular vote and 301 electoral college votes to Humphrey's 42.7 percent popular and 191 electoral votes and Wallace's 13.5 percent popular and 46 electoral votes. Significantly, Humphrey had been defeated by only 500,000 votes (31,275,165 to 31,785,480).* Moreover, the Democrats retained their control of Congress, 58–42 in the Senate and 246–189 in the House.

After the inaugural, Richard Nixon acted on his campaign pledges and almost immediately began plans to insure his reelection in 1972. In part, this effort was intended to appeal to the Wallace constituency and to consolidate the president's position in the South. Thus, southern conservatives were nominated to the Supreme Court, stringent anticrime politics were instituted, and the emotional school desegregation issue was fully exploited.

---

* But it must be remembered that Nixon and Wallace ran similar campaigns and together received 57 percent of the popular vote.

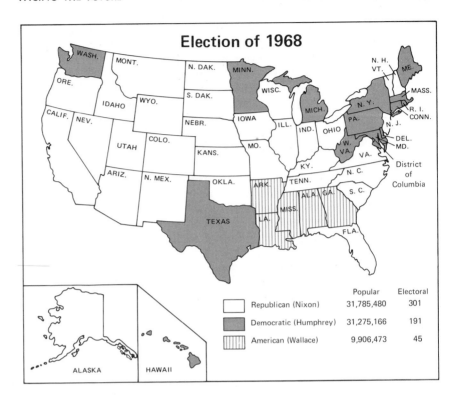

Election of 1968

	Popular	Electoral
Republican (Nixon)	31,785,480	301
Democratic (Humphrey)	31,275,166	191
American (Wallace)	9,906,473	45

To replace retiring Supreme Court Chief Justice Earl Warren, Nixon nominated a conventional conservative, Warren Burger, a Minnesota federal judge. Far more controversial was his August 1969 nomination of another conservative jurist, Clement Haynsworth, Jr., a South Carolina federal judge. Haynsworth's lower court civil rights and labor decisions led northern civil rights advocates and labor union officials to lobby against his confirmation. Because decisions he had made as a federal judge suggested conflict of interest improprieties, Haynsworth's nomination was rejected by the Senate on November 21, 1969 by a vote of 55–45. Following this defeat of the Haynsworth nomination, on January 19, 1970, Nixon submitted for Senate confirmation the name of G. Harrold Carswell, a Florida Court of Appeals judge. The Senate also rejected this nomination on April 8, 1970 by the closer vote of 51–45. Instrumental in this decision were Carswell's undistinguished legal record, questions raised about his competence, revelations detailing his earlier segregationist views, and the patent partisanship of Nixon's concession to the South.

At the same time, the administration publicly opposed extension of the Voting Rights Act of 1965, half-heartedly enforced recently enacted civil rights legislation (leading many career lawyers in the Department of Justice to resign), asked a federal court to postpone the scheduled date for desegregating Mississippi school districts, publicly opposed court orders for busing pupils to integrate northern and southern public school systems, supported "no-knock" and preventive detention legislation to curb crime in the District of Columbia, and announced its intention to wiretap radicals during "domestic security" investigations.

The 1970 congressional elections, however, demonstrated the administration's political vulnerability and the limited benefits it had reaped from its efforts to exploit the race and the "law and order" issues. In an extensive, well-publicized speaking campaign, President Nixon and Vice President Spiro Agnew hit hard on the themes of student protest and law and order; at the same time White House personnel funneled millions of dollars to key Republican Senate and House candidates. This effort to elect conservative candidates and secure Republican control of the Senate, however, failed. The Democrats increased their House majority by nine (255–180) but lost two Senate seats (56–44). Many vulnerable Democratic senators, however, who had won election in the atypical 1958 and 1964 contests were reelected. Furthermore, the Democrats gained eleven governorships, reversing the Republican margin of 32–18 to a Democratic majority of 29–21.

The closeness of the 1968 presidential contest and the demonstrated failure of the "law and order" strategy during the 1970 congressional elections influenced subsequent White House preparations for Richard Nixon's reelection campaign of 1972. Looming large in this effort (though inadvertently) was what became known as the Watergate Affair—the decision of security officials of the Committee to Re-elect the President (Nixon) to bug the Democratic National Committee headquarters housed in Washington's Watergate apartment complex and then the White House attempt to cover up the degree of these officials' and other White House aides' involvement.

The so-called Watergate Affair assumed two forms. The first involved the planning and funding leading to the actual break-in. The second involved the efforts of high-level personnel in the Committee to Re-elect the President (Nixon) and on the White House staff to limit the FBI investigation into this break-in and insure that the seven men who were indicted would remain silent. (The seven men indicted included the five who on June 17, 1972 had been caught in the Democratic headquarters and the subsequently arrested former White House aides, E. Howard Hunt and G. Gordon Liddy.) As part of this elaborate cover-up, large sums of money were paid to those arrested, documents were destroyed, and key White House aides either committed perjury, suborned perjury, or made false reports to the press, the FBI, and the CIA.

At first dismissed by White House press secretary Ron Zeigler as a "second-rate burglary," the Watergate break-in was much more than that. The involvement of Hunt and Liddy particularly threatened to disclose even seamier illegal surveillance activities conducted from 1969 through 1972 by White House aides. Part of a general use of "dirty tricks," Nixon campaign officials in early 1972 had authorized the break-in out of concern over the president's reelection prospects. A February 1971 Harris poll had shown the acknowledged Democratic front-runner, Senator Edmund Muskie of Maine, leading Nixon 43–40 in a trial Presidential heat; by May, Muskie's lead had widened to 47–39. A series of "dirty tricks" were then planned to disrupt the Muskie campaign. The target of the Watergate bugging operation, moreover, was the seasoned Democratic professional and then Democratic National Committee chairman, Lawrence O'Brien; one purpose had been to uncover possible derogatory information about O'Brien. Independent of the Watergate break-in, Nixon campaign officials had also been concerned about public opinion polls demonstrating George Wallace's continued appeal. Another Wallace third party candidacy could negate the impact of the president's Supreme Court nominations and soft-pedaling of civil rights enforcement. Political necessity and their conclusions about the 1968 campaign thus had led Nixon strategists during 1970–72 to employ practices intended to undermine the candidacies of the president's moderate and conservative opponents.

As part of this effort, the Nixon staff in 1970 secretly funneled over $400,000 of left-over 1968 campaign funds to former Alabama governor Albert Brewer, who was then challenging George Wallace for the Democratic gubernatorial nomination of Alabama. Wallace's defeat would have denied him a base for launching another third party presidential campaign. Failing in this 1970 effort, the Nixon strategists then shifted their attention to the American Independence party. During 1972, for example, Nixon aides secretly funded the American Nazi party's membership drive in California hoping thereby to reduce the American Independence party's membership and to deny that party a place on the California ballot in 1972. Amateurish at best, these efforts had no significant impact on the 1972 presidential race. Instead, the attempted assassination of Wallace by an unemployed, insecure youth, Arthur Bremer, during the May 1972 Maryland Democratic primary had far greater political consequences. Had Wallace intended to use the Democratic primaries to launch another third party effort, the attempted assassination stymied him. Bremer's action fortuitously rebounded to Nixon's advantage by removing a candidate who had more appeal to many frustrated Americans and further by permitting the Nixon strategists to wage an image-style media campaign. Wallace's absence meant that candidate Nixon did not need to state his position on issues but could campaign as the president.

In 1972, the White House succeeded in containing the Watergate investigation, by defusing Watergate as a campaign issue, and thus in implementing a campaign strategy depicting the Democratic candidate, Senator George McGovern of South Dakota, as inconsistent, incompetent, and a dangerous radical. On the one hand, Republican strategists capitalized on McGovern's controversial stands on the Vietnam War, welfare, and tax reform issues. On the other hand, they focused on McGovern's changing positions on his vice-presidential choice (dropping Senator

Thomas Eagleton from the ticket when it became known he had undergone psychiatric treatment), on his tax program, and on his postconvention efforts to repair relations with labor leaders and urban bosses. Nixon strategists also sought to maximize the president's appeal to independents and dissatisfied Democrats by creating an independent committee to promote his presidential candidacy, the Committee for the Reelection of the President. The very title of this committee confirmed their sense of Richard Nixon's vulnerabilities—there was no reference to the president's Republicanism, and support was solicited not for the man but for the officeholder. (Indeed, a poll taken in sixteen states the month before the 1972 election underscored the Republican candidate's lack of popular appeal: only 34 percent of the respondents thought Nixon the more attractive personality, 26 percent chose McGovern, and 32 percent responded "neither.")

Nixon overwhelmed McGovern, receiving 45,767,218 popular and 521 electoral votes to the Democratic candidate's 28,357,668 popular and 17 electoral votes (McGovern carried only Massachusetts and the District of Columbia). The decision to minimize Nixon's Republicanism and to conduct a campaign wholly independent of the Republican National Committee did result in one striking result: in contrast to comparable

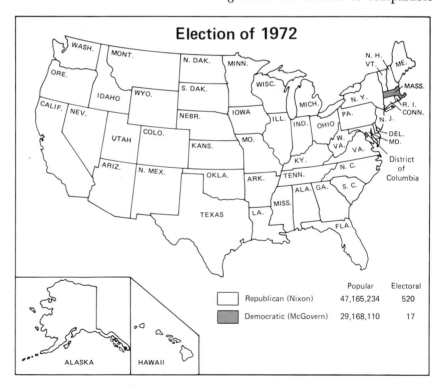

Election of 1972

	Popular	Electoral
Republican (Nixon)	47,165,234	520
Democratic (McGovern)	29,168,110	17

presidential contests (those of 1920, 1936, and 1964) where the victorious candidate had received over 60 percent of the popular vote, the Republicans failed to win control of the Congress. Indeed, the Democrats increased their congressional majorities by two seats in the Senate (58–42) and one in the House (256–179).

SURVEILLANCE AND WIRETAPPING

By 1972 an atmosphere of disrespect for constitutional and legal principles had been created within the Nixon White House. Scarcely normal procedures at any time, wiretapping and break-ins were not viewed by Nixon personnel as abhorrent practices but, rather, as essential to the fulfillment of noble goals. A disdain for constitutional prohibitions, moreover, had acquired legitimacy from the "national security" psychology of the Cold War years.

By 1969, an earlier popular aversion to wiretapping was changing. In 1934, reflecting this earlier aversion, the Congress through section 605 of the Federal Communications Act of 1934 had prohibited the interception and divulgence of the contents of any wire communication. Additionally, in 1937 and in 1939 (*Nardone* v. *U.S.*), the Supreme Court had ruled that this section's prohibition applied to federal agents and that information gained through illegal wiretapping was inadmissible as evidence in criminal proceedings.

Despite the statutory prohibition and the Court's rulings, the Department of Justice in private intraadministration memoranda of 1940 and 1941 interpreted the Court's decision as prohibiting only the divulgence of information gained through wiretapping and not the practice itself. In May 1940, moreover, President Roosevelt issued an executive order authorizing the FBI to wiretap in investigations involving espionage, sabotage, or violations of neutrality legislation.

This remained executive policy until July 1946 when Attorney General Tom Clark convinced President Truman to extend FBI wiretapping authority to include "cases vitally affecting the domestic security" and domestic crime. Then, in May 1954, President Eisenhower's attorney general, Herbert Brownell, authorized the FBI to resort to microphone surveillance (bugging) even when it involved trespass; moreover, Brownell did not require that the bureau secure the attorney general's prior authorization. Steadily, then, the FBI's authority to utilize wiretapping and bugging in internal security and gambling investigations had been expanded. Because it was illegally obtained, information obtained through these investigations could not be used for prosecutions. Not resigned to this legal limitation, the Justice Department at various times during the 1950s and 1960s (1951, 1953, 1959, 1961, 1962) unsuccessfully sought to exploit the heightened security atmosphere of the Cold War years to secure the enactment of legislation authorizing electronic surveillance in "national security" cases.

In *Berger* v. *New York* (1967), however, the Supreme Court ruled that, prior to installing taps, state and local officials must establish probable cause that a specific crime had been or was being committed. This decision implied that court-approved wiretapping was constitutional and, combined with the greater fears about domestic crime and unrest prevalent in the aftermath of the militant radicalism and urban riots of the late sixties, led Congress to enact the Omnibus Crime Control and Safe Streets Act of 1968. Title III of this act specifically authorized electronic surveillance without court order in "national security" cases and conceded that the president had undefined constitutional powers to authorize wiretapping "as he deems necessary."

The Nixon administration immediately exploited this legislative authority when acceding to power, but not to uncover and prosecute foreign agents. In a brief filed during the 1969 trial of the Chicago Eight (radical antiwar activists indicted for crossing state lines allegedly to incite a riot at the 1968 Democratic National Convention), Attorney General John Mitchell claimed that the president had an inherent right to authorize without court order wiretaps of those individuals and groups who threatened the "domestic security." This attempt to expand national security claims to incorporate domestic surveillance was eventually rejected by the U.S. Supreme Court in a unanimous ruling of June 19, 1972 (*U.S.* v. *U.S. District Court*). Then the Attorney General's broad claim to order wiretaps without prior court authorization during "domestic security" investigation was ruled unconstitutional; the Court, however, conceded that the president could authorize wiretaps in cases clearly involving national security (whether espionage or foreign intelligence).

Until this Supreme Court ruling, the Nixon administration operated without any constraints in an expansive effort to curb political dissent. Thus, in 1969 the Small Business Administration issued new rules for the granting of loans: loans were denied to individuals who were members of "subversive" organizations or who took the Fifth Amendment when declining to testify about "subversive" activities. That same year the Internal Revenue Service established a special staff to investigate individuals and organizations for tax violations, the basis for selection being involvement in liberal or radical political activities. Furthermore, Attorney General Mitchell urged the Supreme Court to reverse its ruling in *U.S.* v. *Alderman* (1969) requiring the Justice Department to turn over all illegal wiretap information to defense attorneys. In an unprecedented effort to influence the Court, the attorney general had wiretap logs delivered to the justices hoping that they would become convinced that the *Alderman* ruling would impair the government's national security functions by forcing the disclosure of foreign embassy wiretaps.

Conducting diplomacy secretly and alarmed by liberal and radical criticism of the administration's foreign policy, in 1969 the Nixon administration approved FBI electronic surveillance of seventeen individuals, allegedly to uncover the sources of unauthorized leaks of classified information to the press. Beginning in May 1969 and extending through

February 1971, the residences and offices of members of the White House staff, the National Security Council, and the Washington press corps were tapped. The taps were not instituted merely for national security reasons. For even after National Security Council aides Morton Halperin and Anthony Lake had left government service, taps on their phones continued. In addition, White House staffers John Sears and William Safire were tapped even though they had no access to classified documents.

The White House did not rely exclusively on the FBI for its political surveillance objectives. Using unexpended 1968 campaign funds, two former New York City policemen, John Caulfield and Anthony Ulasewicz, were hired in 1969 to conduct surveillance of certain citizens, including syndicated newspaper columnist Joseph Kraft, conservative Congressmen Richard Poff and Mario Biaggi, and the roommates of Mary Jo Kopechne (an aide to Senator Edward Kennedy who drowned in July 1969 when the car driven by the senator plunged off a bridge at Chappaquidick Island off Martha's Vineyard).

Consistently, the Nixon administration depicted criticism of its foreign policy decisions (whether by liberal congressmen or antiwar activists) as threatening the internal security. Speaking on national television on November 3, 1969, the president proclaimed that "North Vietnam cannot defeat or humiliate the United States. Only Americans can do that." This attempt to equate antiwar dissent with the objective interests of communism lacked a substantial basis—the administration did, however, pressure the CIA to ascertain whether domestic dissent was funded or influenced by foreign agents or states. Violating statutory prohibitions denying it any internal security authority, the CIA instituted an intensive investigation including the compiling of files on thousands of individuals and organizations. Despite this illegality, the CIA concluded in reports of 1969 and 1970 that it had uncovered no evidence of foreign funding and that student-led antiwar protests resulted from indigenous causes.

In 1971, in an attempt both to shape public opinion and to convict Daniel Ellsberg (a former Defense Department employee indicted for publicly releasing the still-classified multivolume Pentagon study of the origins of U.S. involvement in Vietnam) White House aides Hunt and Liddy, under explicit authority from high level White House officials, organized a break-in to the office of Dr. Lewis Fielding, Ellsberg's California psychiatrist. The purpose was to uncover potentially damaging evidence about Ellsberg's character. In addition, the White House ordered the Central Intelligence Agency to prepare a psychological profile on Ellsberg and to provide equipment to be used in the break-in—both requests violated the 1947 statute establishing the agency and specifically prohibiting its involvement in domestic surveillance. In 1970, moreover, the president approved a series of recommendations (known as the Huston Plan), which included authorization of "clearly illegal" activities. Because they were dissatisfied with current intelligence reports on domestic radical activities and with what they believed to be the hesitant FBI responses to their investigative demands, the president and key White House aides sought through this plan to expand domestic surveillance investigations. Approved by the president on July 14, 1970, this plan authorized the extensive use of electronic surveillance and mail covers, the recruitment of students to infiltrate campus radical organizations, and the establishment of a central interdepartmental agency under White House supervision to coordinate and evaluate information acquired by the various federal intelligence agencies.

Concerned over the impact of the new interagency on the bureau's independence and also that future disclosures of FBI involvement could tarnish the FBI's reputation (the plan was formally instituted by a July 23 memo and under the authority of White House aide Tom Charles Huston), FBI Director Hoover originally opposed this radical proposal. The director's continued opposition eventually led President Nixon on July 27 to rescind this order. Nonetheless, the administration remained committed to this objective of expanding surveillance activities. Later that year, accordingly, two of the Huston Plan's recommendations were implemented. In September, the FBI began recruiting college students to spy on campus and off-campus radical organizations. Then, in December, an Intelligence Evaluation Committee was created, to be housed within the Internal Security Division of the Department of Justice with the assigned task of coordinating and evaluating all information concerning domestic radicalism and foreign subversion gathered by the various federal intelligence agencies (FBI, CIA, NSA, DIA). Moreover, ongoing surveillance projects about which the president had not been briefed (a CIA mail intercept program, the FBI's COINTELPRO, and an NSA international electronic surveillance program) continued despite the president's rescission of the Huston Plan, which for the first time would have provided formal presidential authorization for such activities.

AN IMPERIAL PRESIDENCY

Wiretapping and surveillance proved essential to Richard Nixon's secretive style of operation and his elitist conception of presidential power. Having preferred secrecy to disclosure since his inaugural in 1969, President Nixon had not held regular press conferences, in part because he sought to avert potentially embarrassing revelations and in part so that he could time the release of important policy decisions. By direct and often dramatic television addresses (like his July 15, 1971 announcement of his proposed early 1972 visit to mainland China), the president sustained the initiative in foreign affairs and thereby indirectly reduced the leverage of the Congress. Morover, from 1969 to May 1970, when the U.S. military invaded Cambodia, the administration secretly authorized 3,630 bombing raids over Cambodia. To preserve the secrecy of these operations, reports on U.S. bombing missions in Southeast Asia were deliberately falsified; these raids were depicted as having occurred over South Vietnam. Even after the May 1970 invasion this falsification continued—until April 1971, in fact, the administration continued publicly to profess respect for Cambodian neutrality. Moreover, responsible administration officials (in State and Defense) affirmed this false information in testimony before and official reports to congressional committees. These actions provided the impetus for Congress to attempt to regain traditional prerogatives and to challenge directly executive conduct of foreign policy.

This confrontation extended into the domestic area. Fresh from his resounding reelection victory of 1972, wherein he had represented congressional spending policies as irresponsible and as the cause of a serious inflation, President Nixon claimed the right to impound congressionally appropriated funds in order to reduce federal spending. This presidential claim to authority was challenged both by Congress and federal jurists. In June 1973, one federal judge pointedly described the president's impoundment of $6 billion in water pollution control funds as a "flagrant abuse of executive discretion and in violation of the spirit, intent, and letter of the congressional act providing for the funding."

The Nixon White House also sought to make information held by the executive branch of government inaccessible to Congress and the public through the silence of White House aides and the secrecy insured by presidential claims to executive privilege. More specifically, until May 1973, Nixon claimed the unreviewable right to prevent any White House aide from testifying before congressional committees. In April 1973 congressional testimony, in fact, Attorney General Richard Kleindienst had argued that the president could claim executive privilege to prevent the testimony of any employee of the federal government (including, by this standard, even the custodial staff of federal agencies). Should it object to this expansive claim, the attorney general observed, Congress could either test this authority in the courts or attempt to impeach the president.

This claim encountered its first court test in a lower federal court ruling of August 1973 rejecting President Nixon's claimed right to an unreviewable executive privilege over important White House communications. On July 23, 1974, in a unanimous 8–0 ruling, the Supreme Court in *U.S.* v. *Nixon* upheld the lower court decision. In its ruling, the Court refrained from addressing directly the issue of the limits to presidential executive privilege claims, which had been enunciated with increased frequency and scope since Truman's presidency. The Court only rejected Nixon's sweeping claim to an absolute presidential authority to determine whether information should be made public. The Court based this ruling on the narrow premise of the specific requirements of ascertaining whether White House aides had engaged in illegal activities.

Publication of the Pentagon Papers in 1971 also precipitated a strong reaction to executive classification policies. That same year, moreover, a former military classification expert, in testimony before a congressional committee, claimed that over 90 percent of classified documents could be declassified without adversely affecting the national security and that classification only shielded high officials from political embarrassment.

The House Committee on Freedom of Information already had executive classification procedures under study. After a two-year study, the committee recommended that the existing classification system's basis of executive orders be replaced by one relying on statutory authority if stricter guidelines balancing the public's right to know with the administration's claim to secrecy on national defense grounds were to be insured. Publication in 1973 of a study confirming that the federal government had for seventeen years maintained a secret press censorship installation at Western Maryland College increased support for the committee's recommendations. (This installation had originally been established to censor the press during national emergencies; allegedly it had never operated and had been retained for contingency reasons.) The Nixon administration's attempts of 1973 to restrict the news broadcasting and political programming of the federally-funded Corporation for Public Broadcasting intensified these concerns. The administration had first recommended a reduction in the corporation's funding and then had appointed personnel less supportive of in-depth political analysis and reporting. Combined with the impact of the Watergate Affair, these developments led Congress in November 1974 to pass (over President Gerald Ford's veto) amendments to the Freedom of Information Act of 1966 stringently restricting executive branch classification powers.

THE ECONOMY

If a far less dramatic issue, the state of the economy nevertheless constituted one of the Nixon administration's principal problems. Between 1969 and 1973, the federal deficit increased by over $73 billion as the consequence of the cumulative impact of the Johnson administration's defense expenditures, the Nixon administration's reliance on more costly bombing during 1969–1972 to fight the Indochina War, and the steady rise in the nation's balance of payments deficit. To slow down this spiraling inflation, the Nixon administration after 1970 reduced federal nondefense expenditures, which resulted in turn in increased unemployment. Ironically, Nixonian economic policies proved unsuccessful: by 1971 the rate of unemployment reached 6 percent (up from 3.3 percent at the end of 1968), yet inflation remained high (5.5 percent in 1970, increasing to 14.5 percent between January 1969 and August 1971). The resultant loss of anticipated tax revenues insured a federal budget deficit of $23.2 billion in that year alone.

In August 1971, President Nixon responded to the failure of his economic policies by announcing a ninety-day freeze of wages, prices, and rents; tax cuts for business; and a 10 percent surcharge on imports. Then, in November the president introduced a new phase of his antiinflation program providing for the gradual removal of the August federal controls. For the rigid freeze the president substituted ceilings on wages (5.5 percent) and prices (2.5 percent); these ceilings were not extended, however, to profits or dividends. To improve the nation's foreign trade position, the administration devalued the dollar and floated U.S. currency in international markets. The administration shifted abruptly again and in late 1972 abandoned mandatory controls entirely for a program of recommended guidelines and of supervision of wages and prices.

This policy of selective controls, then abrupt reversal to a policy of voluntarism, proved bankrupt. The economy suffered a series of sharp crises including the steady decline of the dollar on the foreign monetary market, a worsened balance of trade deficit wherein for the first time since 1893 imports exceeded exports, a balance-of-payments deficit of $29.6 billion, an 8.8 percent rise in the Consumer Price Index, and a housewife-led consumer boycott against rising meat and food prices. By 1973, inflation was increasing at an annual rate of 9 percent, and prices for farm products and processed food and feed had reached what would have been an equivalent annual rate of 43 percent. Accordingly, in June 1973, the Nixon administration froze food prices for sixty days at the levels of the week of June 1–8 and announced that wage and price controls might be reinstituted. Inflation continued unabated and became an even more critical issue in 1974 when it was complicated by a developing economic recession.

President Nixon's policy decisions revealed how fundamentally American conservatism had changed in the aftermath of the Cold War. Significantly, between 1969 and 1974 this conservative president had conducted foreign policy through secret executive agreements and summit diplomacy, had resorted to New Deal-type controls over exports, prices, and wages, had sought to centralize power in the presidency, and had either countenanced or authorized illegal procedures that imposed far-reaching restrictions on individual liberties. These actions contradicted what had been traditional conservative principles opposing centralized power and emphasizing the right to privacy. Richard Nixon had not betrayed but loyally followed what had become the major priorities of Cold War conservatives—reflected in the personnel who staffed his administration and recommended these policies, whether John Mitchell, H. R. Haldeman, Pat Buchanan, or Tom Charles Huston.

Conversely, the Nixon years widened a developing chasm within American liberalism. The Vietnam War had revealed fundamental differences among liberals over foreign and internal security policies and over the powerful, bureaucratized presidency. These differences had surfaced first during the campaign of Eugene McCarthy and then of George McGovern.

In part, the McCarthy and McGovern campaigns indirectly challenged what had become liberal positions during the Cold War years: the desirability of the centralized presidency and an expansive, anti-Communist foreign policy. Not reconciled to these challenges, other liberals (whether Henry Jackson or Hubert Humphrey) continued to endorse an interventionist foreign policy, the need for continued federal surveillance of radical activists, and a strong presidency. These divisions were at heart a contest over the future character of liberalism. Disclosures publicized by the special congressional intelligence committees in 1975 and 1976 of abuses of power by presidents and internal security bureaucrats dating from Franklin Roosevelt's presidency further intensified these differing liberal positions.

EXPOSURE AND RESIGNATION

President Nixon's increasing assertion of executive prerogatives and authorization of illegal activities by White House aides inevitably produced congressional and journalistic opposition. So inquisitive did several journalists (especially Carl Bernstein and Bob Woodward of the *Washington Post*) and congressmen become about White House activities that Nixon's direct involvement in the attempts since June 1972, first to contain the investigation of the Watergate break-in and then to insure the silence of the Watergate defendants, could not long remain secret. Responding to unanswered questions about the break-in, in February 1973 the Senate created a Special Committee on Presidential Campaign Activities (the Ervin Committee), authorizing it to probe the Watergate break-in and any improprieties connected with the 1972 presidential campaign. After careful preparations, the Ervin Committee commenced nationally-televised public hearings, which lasted from May 17 through August 7, 1973 and which successfully transformed Watergate into an explosive political issue. The committee's findings conclusively established White House illegality and involvement in the Watergate cover-up; further, the investigation suggested the possibility of the president's complicity. These revelations, following President Nixon's decision to fire Special Prosecutor Archibald Cox in October 1973, in turn led the House Judiciary Committee to consider resolutions calling for the president's impeachment. In February 1974, the Judiciary Committee commenced hearings.

Attempting to be thorough and fair, the House Committee proceeded deliberately, and the evidence it gained was not publicly released until July 9; public debate on articles of impeachment through nationally-televised hearings did not commence until July 24. The evidence was overwhelming; by July 30 the committee had approved three articles of impeachment against President Nixon (for involvement in the Watergate cover-up, abuse of power in use of federal agencies, and defiance of Congress in withholding evidence).

Before the full House could even debate the proposed articles of impeachment, the president in a nationally-televised address on August 5 admitted having withheld relevant evidence from the Judiciary Committee and the special prosecutor (appointed in May 1973 to conduct a thorough investigation into the Watergate affair). Then he released the evidence (the precipitating factor being the Supreme Court's decision in *U.S.* v. *Nixon* concerning the president's refusal on grounds of executive privilege to turn over to the special prosecutor certain tapes of White House conversations). One of the released tapes of a June 23, 1972 White House meeting disclosed that the president had participated directly in the Watergate cover-up. This revelation (the latest in a series revealing the scope of the Nixon White House's abuse of power) led even diehard Nixon supporters and conservatives to demand that the president resign or be impeached. Protesting his innocence but claiming a desire to avert a lengthy confrontation and constitutional crisis, on August 8 Richard Nixon announced his decision to resign as the thirty-seventh president of the United States. On August 9, Gerald Ford (confirmed as vice president following Spiro Agnew's resignation on October 10, 1973 after he had pleaded no contest to an income tax evasion charge) was sworn in as the new president.

Ford's accession to the presidency ended the most serious constitutional crisis in the nation's history. Nixon's dramatic resignation culminated a developing crisis that dated from April 1973 and was intensified by a stream of revelations not only about his administration's abuses of power but about his deceit with the Congress and with the American people. If the resignation terminated the immediate constitutional crisis, it did not resolve the larger problem of abuse of power deriving from presidential willingness to exploit "national security" and "executive privilege" for political advantage. This broader issue constituted one basis for subsequent congressional efforts to curb presidential powers and for the congressional investigations of 1975 of federal intelligence agencies (FBI, CIA, IRS, NSA). And the clash between congressional and presidential prerogatives would persist during the brief presidency of Gerald Ford.

THE FORD INTERLUDE

Having acceded to the presidency through Richard Nixon's forced resignation, Gerald Ford inherited a serious national crisis. The unemployment rate hovered around 8 percent, while inflation reached 12 percent. More important, the revelations concerning Richard Nixon's abuse of presidential powers had shattered public confidence. Each succeeding revelation of 1973 and 1974 seemingly had further confirmed the extent of Nixon's abuse of power and personal dishonesty.

Thus, Gerald Ford's first responsibility as president was to restore public confidence in the national leadership. Having consistently defended Nixon's innocence, having earlier sought to discredit the congressional investigations into the Watergate Affair by charging that they were motivated by partisanship, and having won confirmation as vice president because he appeared to have neither the abilities nor the ambition to seek the presidency, Gerald Ford confronted an overwhelming political problem. His decision of September 8, 1974 to grant Richard Nixon a full pardon before judicial proceedings were even initiated—thereby suggesting yet another cover-up—compounded this problem.

Not surprisingly, then, the combination of a declining economy and the Republicans' identification with Nixon's abuses of power produced a sweeping Democratic victory in the 1974 congressional elections. The Democrats won virtually a two-thirds majority in the new Congress—61–38 (with one independent) in the Senate and 290–145 in the House (having gained an additional 43 seats).

The Watergate revelations produced a popular reaction against the "imperial presidency" and also undercut uncritical public deference to "national security" claims. These concerns were heightened by newspaper revelations in December 1974 that the Central Intelligence Agency (CIA) had compiled dossiers on thousands of American citizens and organizations engaged in dissident activities (in direct violation of the Agency's legislative charter, which specified that the CIA had no "internal security" authority). At the same time the press soon revealed in February 1975 that FBI Director J. Edgar Hoover had retained in his private office secret dossiers on hundreds of prominent personalities (including presidents and members of the Congress).

Responding to the furor precipitated by these revelations, President Ford, by executive order 11828 of January 4, 1975, appointed a presidential commission to investigate the CIA. Headed by Vice President Nelson Rockefeller and composed of conservative individuals unlikely to recommend far-reaching changes, the so-called Rockefeller Commission confined its investigation exclusively to the CIA's domestic surveillance activities. Not surprisingly, then, the Rockefeller Commission minimized the Agency's abuses and concluded that they were either atypical or derived from administrative errors. In its June 6, 1975 report to the president, the commission accordingly recommended instituting limited reforms through executive order.

If President Ford's purpose in establishing the Rockefeller Commission had been to restore public confidence in the intelligence community and to retain executive initiative, the continuing revelations of internal security abuses nonetheless led the Congress to initiate its own investigation. On January 21, 1975, Democratic Senator John Pastore introduced Senate Resolution 21 calling for the creation of a special Senate committee to investigate fully the intelligence agencies—the CIA's foreign operations as well as its domestic surveillance and the activities of such other federal agencies as the Federal Bureau of Investigation (FBI), the National Security Agency (NSA), and the Internal Revenue Service (IRS). Slightly amended, S. Res. 21 was approved by the Senate on January 27, 1975.

The newly created Senate Select Committee on Intelligence Activities (known as the Church Committee) secured access to the files of the intelligence agencies and initiated the first serious investigation ever of these agencies. The Committee's investigation uncovered a multitude of abuses—including the CIA's planning of assassinations of foreign political leaders and its extensive resort to covert operations, widespread FBI surveillance and wiretapping of American citizens and organizations, the political use of the FBI by presidents since Franklin Roosevelt's administration, and the ineffectiveness of presidential oversight of the intelligence community.

The series of revelations, however, only numbed the public and the Congress. Ironically, by the end of 1975 the congressional investigations had raised a far different concern: the desirability of publicity. The assassination of CIA official Richard Welch in Athens, Greece, on December 24, 1975 dramatically raised this issue.

Exploiting the concern over the release of sensitive intelligence data, the Ford White House, in conjunction with congressional conservatives, sought to limit the proposed reforms of the intelligence community. Thus, the House of Representatives on January 29, 1976 voted 246–124 not to release the report of the special House committee investigating the intelligence agencies (in 1975 the House had also created a special committee headed by Congressman Otis Pike)—a vote reflecting a greater concern for secrecy than for exposing abuses of power. Following quickly upon this vote, President Ford by executive order 11905 of February 18, 1976 announced proposed reforms of the intelligence community, which were limited in scope.

This strategy, however, did not wholly succeed. The Church Committee's release in April 1976 and in succeeding months of a series of reports raised anew the abuse of power issue and the wisdom of relying exclusively on executive reforms. Liberal Senators thereby moved to regain the initiative. In May 1976, the Senate voted to establish a new permanent intelligence committee with oversight and legislative authority over the intelligence community. The intrusion of the presidential election campaign, however, precluded congressional action on the Church Committee's other legislative recommendations.

If a legislative-executive confrontation over reform of the intelligence community had been postponed, this was not the case with economic policy. Committed to reducing inflation by reducing federal spending on social welfare programs, the Ford administration's fiscal conservatism conflicted with the priorities of the liberal Democratic Congress. During his limited tenure, President Ford accordingly vetoed sixty-six different congressional bills. Commanding the support of conservatives from both parties, Ford's vetoes were generally sustained.

Gerald Ford, an unelected, accidental president, however, had to fight hard for the Republican presidential nomination. As a member of Congress Ford had never demonstrated inspiring legislative leadership nor had he excited the public imagination. His bland presidential style and decision to pardon Richard Nixon did not then enhance his image. Questions about Ford's leadership abilities (which were indirectly popularized in the weekly television satirical program, *Saturday Night*) encouraged the conservative former California governor, Ronald Reagan, to challenge this accidental president for the Republican presidential nomination. Despite the advantage of incumbency and the absence of clear ideological differences with his conservative opponent, Gerald Ford only narrowly won the Republican presidential nomination at the August 1976 Republican National Convention by the vote of 1187 to 1070.

The Reagan-Ford contest suggested, moreover, that the mood of the country was conservative. For the Watergate Affair and the Vietnam War had not contributed to a reassessment of Cold War values or of the imperial presidency; instead they had seemingly raised a cry for more restrained, principled, and trustworthy leadership.

The popular mood was further confirmed in the Democratic primaries. Although numerous candidates with distinct political bases sought the Democratic presidential nomination (ranging from liberals such as Congressman Morris "Mo" Udall, former Oklahoma senator, Fred Harris, Senators Birch Bayh and Frank Church, and California governor, Jerry Brown, to conservatives such as Senator Henry Jackson and Alabama governor, George Wallace), a relatively unknown, one-term governor of Georgia, James Earl (Jimmy) Carter, emerged from the primaries as the clear front-runner. By the time the Democratic National Convention convened in New York City in July, Carter had secured the nomination. Unlike recent Democratic conventions, moreover, that of 1976 lacked bitter conflict over the platform or the nominee. Eager to maximize unity, the Carter forces avoided controversial or divisive issues and appealed to a broad range of groups. The Democratic platform, nonetheless, was decidedly liberal, and Carter selected the liberal Minnesota senator, Walter Mondale, as his running mate.

The presidential election confirmed once again the distinct advantage of incumbency. Republican strategists were able to regain the initiative and to focus the final campaign on the Democratic nominee's lack of political experience and of a national identity. The result was a tightly contested presidential race (atypical because of nationally televised debates between the major party candidates sponsored and organized by the League of Women Voters) and yet overwhelming Democratic congressional and gubernatorial victories. Carter narrowly outpolled Ford in the popular vote (40,827,394 to 39,145,977–49.98 percent to 47.92 percent), and barely won the electoral vote, 297–241. Reconstituting the former New Deal coalition (although it was seriously reduced in numbers and appeal), Jimmy Carter won the presidency by carrying all the southern states except Virginia, reversing thereby what had been a trend in the South toward the Republicans, most of the liberal Northeast, a smattering of midwestern states, plus Hawaii. Carter's narrow defeat in other states, however, demonstrated his broad national appeal. As well,

*Jimmy Carter announcing his candidacy,
Washington, D.C., Dec. 12, 1974*

(Official White House Photograph)

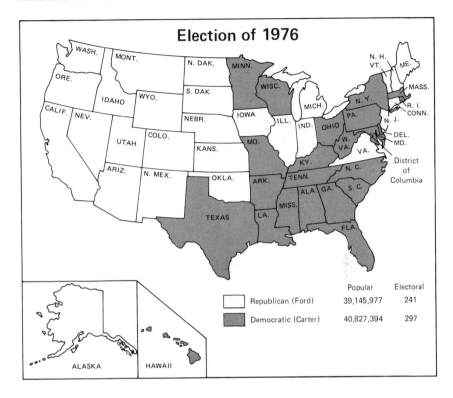

Election of 1976

		Popular	Electoral
☐	Republican (Ford)	39,145,977	241
■	Democratic (Carter)	40,827,394	297

the Democratic president would have a decidedly liberal Congress, one sympathetic to the activist thrust of his campaign to provide leadership to resolve the problems confronting American society. For the Democrats were able to sustain and build slightly upon the striking gains they had made in the 1974 congressional elections, winning an additional two seats in the House, 292–143, and preserving their 61–38 Senate majority (with one independent).

In his primary and final campaigns, candidate Carter had capitalized on deep popular concerns over the lack of personal integrity and moral principles in the national leadership. He promised no quick solutions to national problems but pledged to restore public trust in government and to be a principled and accessible president. Once inaugurated, Jimmy Carter (he preferred the informality and simplicity of the nickname) acted to implement this pledge by a series of admittedly symbolic actions. These included walking with his family down Pennsylvania Avenue to the White House after the inauguration, enrolling his eight-year-old daughter, Amy, in an inner-city Washington public school, answering questions from the public on a live, nationwide radio phone-in, wearing a cardigan instead of a business suit when he appeared on TV to urge the public to conserve energy, ordering that thermostats in the White House and federal buildings be turned down, and spending the night in the home of a middle-income family in Clinton, Massachusetts, when he visited that community to answer questions at a public meeting in the town hall. In addition, Carter insisted that his cabinet appointees (which included two women, Patricia Harris and Juanita Kreps, and black civil rights activist Andrew Young) publicly disclose their financial worth and investments. At the same time the president adopted a more forthright stand against human rights violations in other nations, to convey the impression that moral principle and not simply expediency would determine his administration's foreign policy.

President Carter's first months in office were not marked simply by symbolism. Having pledged to institute a new energy policy during the course of his campaign for the presidency, Carter was soon faced with an energy crisis, particularly in the Northeast, created in part by the severity of the winter of 1977. First he proposed certain temporary measures to alleviate the immediate crisis; then in April he recommended to Congress a comprehensive energy plan to reduce consumption and to shift from a dependence on oil and gas to other forms of energy. These proposals required economic sacrifice and a change in life style on the part of the public and also challenged the economic interests of powerful corporations; therefore they were not insured of passage. Carter, however, had succeeded in defining the direction of congressional deliberation on national energy policy.

Substantively, the Carter administration's record in its first months was neither dramatic nor innovative. His actions, however, were popular and symbolized new directions and procedures. Indirectly, this popularity confirmed the limited impact of the Vietnam War and the Watergate affair on national politics—personal failings of the presidents, and not institutional power, had been the source of these problems; what was needed was the restoration of morality in government and the elimination of excessive secrecy.

32

Global Policeman or Moral Preceptor: The United States and the World 1969-1976

Global events in the 1970s seem to have followed the basic patterns set by Kennedy and Johnson in the previous decade. The United States and Soviet Russia have continued to avoid military confrontations with each other. A nuclear stalemate and its attendant balance of terror persists. Because of the diplomatic and domestic costs of Vietnam, however, Washington policymakers have acted more cautiously before committing American military power abroad. Finally, the bipolar world that has existed since the end of World War II seems shakier than ever. Both great superpowers face challenges within their respective spheres of influence. For the foreseeable future, Russia must contend with rising nationalism in eastern Europe and the Chinese challenge in Asia; the United States must bargain with increasingly assertive allies in Western Europe, Japan, and Latin America; and both powers must deal with Third-World nation-states that play off against each other the United States and Russia, while asserting their own autonomy.

NIXON'S APPROACH TO FOREIGN AFFAIRS

President Richard Milhous Nixon, who built his political reputation as a cold warrior and Red hunter, paradoxically tempered America's post-World War II policy of containment and helped launch a new era of détente and balance of power with the Communist world. After his victory over Hubert Humphrey in 1968 and then his landslide triumph over George McGovern in 1972, Nixon revealed a remarkable flexibility in foreign affairs. Nixon's flexibility reflected his changed conception of national interest and the influence of his principal adviser for foreign policy, Professor Henry A. Kissinger of Harvard. A brilliant analyst of international affairs, Kissinger, with Nixon's authorization, built up a "little State Department" within the National Security Council, to serve the president. Thus, while William Rogers, the appointed secretary of state from 1969 until 1973 and one of Nixon's closest and oldest friends, headed the State Department, Washington seethed with rumors of his small role in shaping policy. Many critics undoubtedly agreed with Missouri Senator Stuart Symington in his comment that Rogers was "the laughing-stock of the cocktail circuit," because Kissinger "had become secretary of state in everything but title."

Kissinger's role in negotiating the Vietnam peace and his frequent "secret" missions abroad for the president contributed to an apparent decline of the State Department. But, in fact, the shift away from the State Department's role in formulating, as distinguished from administering, foreign policy began during the Second World War and after, when FDR and then Truman acted decisively to free the executive from bureaucratic and congressional restraints. After 1948 Truman relied on the National Security Council and the Central Intelligence Agency (established by an act of Congress in 1947) to gather information for the president and shape policy. In the Eisenhower era, the NSC retained this role, and executive office control of foreign affairs further expanded. As secretary of state, moreover, Dulles ordinarily neglected the advice of his department's career officers and implemented policy largely at presidential direction and discretion. After the Bay of Pigs incident, President Kennedy further centralized the flow of information about foreign policy through his White House assistant, McGeorge Bundy. Bundy and his successor, Walt W. Rostow, continued this process during the Johnson administration, often briefing the president upon various foreign policy issues.

Nixon continued this trend toward centralizing foreign policy information and decision making within the White House. He depended heavily on the National Security Council as the organizational pinnacle of the foreign policy process and on his presidential adviser Kissinger. Kissinger, in fact, not only continued Bundy's and Rostow's role in channeling the flow of information and memoranda about foreign policy,

Superstars of the early seventies, Joe Namath,
(left) and Henry Kissinger, (right)

(Leo de Wys, Inc.)

he also served as the chief executive's primary adviser for decision making. Thus, from 1969 through 1972 Kissinger was, next to the president, the most influential person in the making of foreign policy decisions.

After all wars and strong presidencies Congress has acted to reduce the power of the executive branch over foreign affairs. It was not surprising, therefore, that Nixon faced congressional resistance to his foreign policy, presiding as he did at the end of an era of hot wars and crises that had expanded presidential authority at the expense of Congress. The latest phase in this perennial battle between executive and legislative branches began during the Johnson era when Congress rebelled against strong presidential leadership and especially against the Vietnam War. Some congressmen charged that the executive waged an illegal and unconstitutional war in Vietnam. And when Nixon continued the war in Southeast Asia and intensified aerial bombing (secretly in Cambodia and in violation of treaties and congressional resolutions), he encountered growing opposition in Congress. Thus, although at Nixon's invitation,

Congress repealed the Tonkin Gulf resolution in early January 1971, the president persisted in acting unilaterally in Southeast Asia, using military force as he chose. Against critics of his continued use of armed power in Vietnam, the president maintained that he still retained ample constitutional powers as commander-in-chief and chief executive officer to conduct such operations as he deemed necessary.

Nixon began a process of issuing an annual report to Congress and the people on the state of foreign affairs. His first such report, on February 1970, called for a "lowered profile" for the United States henceforth in world affairs, with greater emphasis on self-help and partnership with other nations in coping with world crises. As he warned in an Air Force Academy address, on June 4, 1969, however, the American people must not permit themselves to relapse into isolationist sentiments or views. Such would "be disastrous for our nation and the world. . . . America has a vital interest in world stability and no other nation can uphold that interest for us." Thus at the same time that Nixon suggested the United States curtail its commitments overseas, he refused to repudiate the concept of globalism.

Subsequently, during his Asian tour in the summer of 1969, the president proclaimed a "Nixon Doctrine" for that area and presumably for the world. At Guam he reaffirmed that the United States stood ready to meet Communist threats or attacks on any area it deemed vital to American security. For other kinds of aggression, such as subversion or border clashes, the president emphasized, the United States would furnish aid and support but would leave the countries directly involved to bear the main responsibility for their own survival. In short, he implied no more Vietnams for the United States, unless, to be sure, such conflicts threatened national security as determined by the president.

Despite his reputation as a hardline anti-Communist, Nixon in office successfully pursued détente with the two great powers of the Communist world, the People's Republic of China and the Soviet Union. The famous "ping-pong gambit," in which the People's Republic of China invited an American table tennis team to visit China and subsequently received the group royally, opened the way for a rapprochement with the United States. Henry Kissinger secretly flew to Peking and announced in July 1971 that President Nixon would visit China in the spring of 1972. After this startling announcement, the United States openly advocated admission of the People's Republic of China to the United Nations, while retaining a seat for Taiwan. Despite a show of anger when the General Assembly in October 1971 expelled Taiwan and seated Peking, the United States reacted differently.

Unquestionably, Kissinger's balance-of-power theories explained the American move toward rapprochement with the People's Republic of China. Similar considerations, also undoubtedly, explained Peking's overtures to the United States. Apparently China's leaders continued to be fearful of the Soviet Union and its troops along Chinese borders. Consequently Peking consciously wooed the United States in an effort to

The great diplomatic turnaround, Nixon-Mao handshake
(Wide World Photos)

counterbalance Russia. The American government, moreover, viewed improved relations with China as offering a way out of Vietnam as well as a means of improving relations with the entire Communist world.

Nixon's trip to China took place in early March 1972. For the first time since ex-President Grant had been there in 1879, an American chief executive visited China, a country with which his government had had no official relations for a quarter of a century. The two governments released a fifteen hundred-word communiqué after Nixon had toured the Forbidden City in Peking, viewed the Great Wall, and held lengthy talks with Mao Tse-tung, Chou En-lai, and other Chinese leaders. In marked contrast to the usual diplomatic procedure, the communiqué presented each side's views frankly, the United States announcing that it desired to reduce world tensions and promote human freedom and China re-pledging its faith in the liberation of oppressed peoples and the "inevitable" proletarian revolution as the "irresistible trend of history." After such rhetorical flourishes, both powers pledged themselves to progress towards normalization of their relations with each other and reiterated that they would try to rescue the world from the dangers of international warfare and that neither would negotiate in behalf of any third party nor aid each other in any threatening moves aimed against a third party. The two governments also agreed to improve their relations through exchanges of scientists, artists, journalists, and sportsmen while working out future diplomatic contacts. As for Taiwan, the United States acknowledged the Chinese view that the island was part of China and eventually would be reunified with it. And in the spring of 1973 the two nations announced that there would be an "informal" exchange of diplomatic missions. Despite the improvement in Chinese-American relations, the United States commitment to the Nationalist Chinese of Taiwan served as a persistent sore point in dealings between the two powers.

President Nixon followed his triumphal visit to China with an equally satisfying tour of the Soviet Union in June 1972. Both well-publicized events thus signalled that the Cold War had eased and that continued progress was being made toward détente among the great powers. While in Moscow, Nixon signed the Anti-Ballistics Missiles Treaty, a five-year pact that had been worked out previously. The treaty froze at their existing level the number of intercontinental ballistics missiles possessed by each side. The United States thus retained a lead in total number of warheads, four thousand at the end of 1970 to eighteen-hundred for Russia, while the Russians kept a lead in the size of warheads—that is, in the total megatonnage of its missile warheads. Both powers continued to have enough nuclear weapons to destroy each other and the whole world many times over. The pact also included provisions for each side to build two "equal" defensive antiballistic missiles, a prerogative that the United States so far has not chosen to exercise. Nixon and Soviet Prime Minister Brezhnev also agreed on the necessity of avoiding armed confrontations in the future. Despite some conservative criticism within the United States Senate, that body approved the ABM Treaty in October 1972.

THE VIETNAM "PEACE"

Nothing better illustrated the priorities that underlay Nixon's foreign policy and his refusal to restrain the unilateral exercise of executive power than the war in Vietnam. While the president journeyed to Peking and Moscow in order to establish better relations with the two major Communist powers, during these same years he dispatched American bombers over Hanoi and Cambodia, blockaded Haiphong Harbor in 1972, and invaded Cambodia and Laos in 1970, all to contain the expansion of "international communism." While he promised Americans an era of peace and global goodwill, Nixon had expanded the war in Southeast Asia, deliberately misleading Congress and the American people about his administration's actions and intentions.

On becoming president, Richard Nixon had immediately found his administration burdened by the same bloody and apparently endless war in Vietnam that had destroyed Johnson politically. The Paris Peace talks, begun by President Johnson in 1968, dragged on in a welter of haggling, while Nixon steadily reduced American land forces in Vietnam. When the North Vietnamese and Vietcong undertook a major drive across the demilitarized zone and into Cambodia, Nixon retaliated by resuming and intensifying the bombing of the North in May 1972, unleashing America's strategic B-52 bombers on Guam in devastating raids upon Hanoi and the seaport of Haiphong. To cut off or reduce the steady flow of arms from China and the Soviet Union, he also had North Vietnamese ports and waterways mined. Despite criticism at home and intensified antiwar protests, the president continued unilateral use of air and naval power at the same time that he was pursuing détentes with China and the Soviet Union. Apparently, Russian and Chinese leaders were as callous about the treatment of small nations, including their own clients, as Americans.

On October 8, 1972, Henry A. Kissinger, the chief executive's foreign policy adviser, announced that he had achieved a breakthrough in the peace talks at Paris. His announcement apparently contributed to Nixon's smashing reelection victory over Senator George McGovern of South Dakota. When the Paris talks subsequently bogged down because of objections from South Vietnamese leaders, Nixon sought to assure them of continued American support and again unleashed bombers over North Vietnam. Once again his tactics appeared to succeed, for the deadlock in the Paris talks was broken and a truce was signed at last on January 27, 1973. Under its terms, Poland, Hungary, India, and Canada were to comprise a special truce force to supervise a cease-fire in South Vietnam. All American troops were to be withdrawn within sixty days and prisoners of war released by both sides, while the International Control Commission (the four countries listed above) was to oversee truce observance and the release of prisoners by both sides.

Thus ended the longest war in American history, after a loss of 49,433 Americans killed in action and another 303,616 wounded in twelve years of bloody conflict. South Vietnam lost an estimated 183,528 dead and perhaps as many as 415,000 civilian casualties, and North Vietnam-Vietcong an estimated casualty list of 924,048. No accurate count existed of civilian casualties in the North, where American bombing destroyed agricultural villages, industrial cities, highways, and bridges. Two peripheral areas of the Southeast Asian conflict, Laos and Cambodia, suffered equally severe human and material losses. Indeed before peace returned, Cambodia, once the most placid and prosperous of Southeast Asian lands, had been shattered beyond recognition.

The war in Vietnam ends, Saigon 1975
(Wide World Photos)

The Nixon-Kissinger peace did not finally resolve the Vietnam tragedy. Peace in Vietnam, Nixon and Kissinger assured the American people, satisfied United States objectives in Southeast Asia. American sacrifices had been worthwhile because the treaty checked Communist expansion, preserved American honor intact, and enabled South Vietnam to survive as a free nation. To a South Vietnamese government now bereft of the American military power that had stood between it and collapse for two decades, Nixon and Kissinger secretly promised American military support if North Vietnam violated the agreements and invaded the South. To the North Vietnamese, the Nixon-Kissinger peace agreement vindicated a cause they had been fighting for since 1946. With the removal of *all* American military forces, the Vietnamese could settle their own civil war, and the leaders in the North were certain it was only a matter of time before the American-supported government in the South collapsed and an independent united Vietnam emerged under Communist control. In short, the Nixon-Kissinger peace promised all things to all people. Only future events would establish the real victors in Southeast Asia.

Not until Nixon was forced from office in disgrace did Americans learn the fragility of their former President's proclaimed accomplishments in Southeast Asia. Less than a year after Nixon resigned as president, the American-supported South Vietnamese government fell at the first sign of northern strength. As North Vietnamese forces moved south in the late winter and early spring of 1975, South Vietnamese officers deserted their troops, who in turn pillaged and raped among their own people. By May Day 1975, Saigon fell to the "enemy," as America's Vietnamese allies hastily fled their own country. Almost simultaneously, leftist rebels took power in Cambodia, ousting an equally corrupt and incompetent American-supported government. Then, when Nixon's successor, Gerald R. Ford, asked Congress to authorize American aid for the "free" South Vietnamese and Cambodians, Congress said, "No!"

It had taken a quarter of a century before the American Congress refused to support a foreign policy based simply on the need to resist communism. Billions of American dollars and hundreds of thousands of lives had been squandered in the Southeast Asian quagmire, and the end result was probably worse than it would have been had the United States never intervened. Perhaps Congress realized that when Americans chose to save other people from themselves, all they in fact did was to achieve false salvation through real destruction.

OTHER TROUBLED AREAS

The Middle East continued to defy efforts at peacemaking and promotion of greater stability despite Henry Kissinger's often frantic but yet adroit "shuttle diplomacy." When Egypt's Gamal Abdel Nasser decided early in 1967 to force Israel's hand by compelling the UN police force to withdraw from the region, blockading the vital Israeli port of Elath, and moving Egyptian forces toward the Israeli frontier, he precipitated another round of war in the Middle East. On June 5, Israel decided to strike first, before the more populous Arab nations could move. Six days later, by June 10, Israeli armies had smashed both the Jordanian and Egyptian military. Israel occupied all of the Sinai desert right up to the banks of the Suez Canal, took control of the entire west bank of the Jordan River, and drove a salient force into Syrian and Lebanese territory with the seizure of the Golan Heights. It was an even more decisive victory and crushing humiliation to Israeli's Arab opponents than the 1956 war.

Though many Americans probably sympathized with Israel, the government pursued an "even-handed" policy, which in effect allowed the Israelis to enjoy the fruits of their military prowess. The Russians, who had been supplying the Arabs with arms ever since 1956 and advising the Egyptian military, also reacted cautiously. Indeed the Soviets made no real threats against Israel and did nothing tangible to assist the Arab states to regain the territory that they had lost on the battlefield. Hence when Nasser died in 1970, his successor, Anwar Sadat, maneuvered to reduce Egyptian reliance on Russia. In August 1972 Sadat expelled Russian forces and turned toward the United States for assistance. Simultaneously, Syria and Iraq also made friendly overtures to the United States. Although a pleased Kissinger strived to obtain concessions from Israel to reduce tensions in the region, the Israelis remained intransigent. Consequently, in October 1973, at the moment of the Jews' most sacred holy day, Yom Kippur, Arab armies struck against an unprepared Israeli military. After suffering initial setbacks, however, the Israeli armed forces regrouped and decisively halted the Arab penetration with heavy losses. Kissinger engaged in another round of shuttle diplomacy that produced yet another truce in the Arab-Israeli conflict, but again failed to bring an enduring peace to the region.

In late 1971, chronic Indian-Pakistani rivalry exploded into a short war. The immediate cause lay in mounting discontent within East Pakistan, inhabited largely by Bengalis who resented rule by the military dictatorship entrenched in West Pakistan. The Bengali rebels proclaimed an independent state of Bangladesh and appealed to India for aid when they faced a crushing defeat by West Pakistani armed forces. India responded with a short victorious war that defeated Pakistani armies in December 1971.

Seeing a chance to outflank China, the Soviet Union aided India by arms supplies and also cast a veto against a UN motion calling for a ceasefire and mutual withdrawal. Russia thereby gained immediate prestige and favor in India; the United States government meanwhile ordered the American fleet into the area as a gesture in behalf of Pakistan. The episode had the effect also of furthering Chinese-American relations, since China also felt threatened by events in India. Again as in Vietnam, America backed the losing side locally, as Kissinger, now secretary of state as well as presidential policy adviser, called for the United States in its south Asia policy to favor Pakistan.

A NEW LATIN AMERICAN POLICY

The Nixon administration followed a less ambitious policy toward Latin America than Kennedy and Johnson had. In his "low profile" address of October 31, 1971, President Nixon in effect told Latin America not to look to the United States for substantial governmental aid but instead to rely on increased private investments. Nixon and Kissinger preferred to manage Latin America through traditional dollar diplomacy and open-door policies as pursued by private American corporations. As might be expected, American corporations and financiers preferred to invest in those Latin countries, most notably Brazil, in which right-wing military governments guaranteed to protect foreign investments.

That the United States was more concerned with economic gain in Latin America than with promoting democracy and social reform was made clear by events in Chile. There a democratically elected left-wing government led by President Salvador Allende nationalized foreign holdings and instituted extensive economic and social reform. Before and after Allende came to power, Nixon and Kissinger secretly planned first to prevent his election and then to undermine his socialist government. These plans included providing aid to right-wing and liberal political parties and newspapers, considering assassination, and encouraging social and economic unrest. In September 1973, although independent of these efforts, right-wing army officers forcibly overthrew the Allende government (President Allende was murdered during the coup) and replaced it with a brutal right-wing dictatorship. The United States promptly supplied the new government in Chile with substantial government and private economic aid.

President Nixon's departure from office and his replacement by Ford scarcely altered the main lines of American foreign policy. Kissinger remained as secretary of state and promoted détente with Russia and China. Neither the president nor the secretary could do anything when in 1975 the United States-supported governments in Southeast Asia collapsed or when a year later pro-Western forces in Angola lost out to Soviet-supported Angolans. Despite Ford's and Kissinger's demands that Congress authorize economic and military assistance for the "free" South Vietnamese and Angolans, a majority of congressmen refused to plunge the country back into the Asian quagmire or enter a new one in Africa.

If Ford, like Nixon, could avoid confrontations with the Soviets and Chinese, he too could act precipitously in the style of an imperial president. For in May 1975, when the new Communist Cambodian government captured the American merchant ship *Mayaguez* off its shores, Ford responded with a show of American power. The president authorized an attack by marines on the Island of Koh Tang, where American intelligence mistakenly assumed the captured crewmen to be, and the bombing of the Cambodian mainland. The military action cost the United States fifteen dead, three missing, and fifty wounded to rescue a smaller number of merchant sailors already in the process of being returned together with their ship by the Cambodians. Despite Ford's costly blunder, Congress, the nation's press, and most of the public applauded their president's decisive action. Waving the flag and using military force against minor powers remained as popular a course of national action as it had been before the Vietnam debacle. Congress still seemed willing to tolerate chief executives who acted unilaterally and practiced a form of gunboat diplomacy that was almost a half century out of date.

As President-elect Jimmy Carter prepared to enter office in January

1977, decisions still had to be made about the United States role and aims in world affairs. Although Carter would obviously remove Henry Kissinger as secretary of state, the president certainly could ill afford to reverse détente with Russia or China. Whether Carter would consult the Congress before acting overseas remained more problematic. In the first months of his administration, President Carter demonstrated that his foreign policy at least would differ in style if not in substance from that of his predecessors. Speaking out critically of Soviet violations of human rights and reviewing U.S. economic assistance to Latin American governments that violated human rights, the new president placed a greater emphasis on morality and principle. At the same time, however, Carter expressed concern over revelations of earlier secret CIA economic assistance to foreign leaders (notably Jordanian King Hussein) and sought to reduce the number of individuals in the government having access to highly classified information in order to curb future leaks.

33

Whither the United States?
Americans Face the Future

In the 1970s the United States remained the world's most affluent and productive society. Ironically, however, the factors and resources that in the past had accounted for America's exceptional material wealth in the future threatened to undermine the United States global economic hegemony. Indeed, only a quarter of a century after Henry Luce had proclaimed "The American Century," a developing international scarcity of raw materials, especially energy resources, and intensified international economic competition had dealt severe blows to the United States economy. By the mid-1970s a transformed global economic milieu had set the preconditions for a domestic American crisis of unprecedented proportions.

A society that from its founding had flourished on the unfettered exploitation of nature's bounty had to come to grips in the last quarter of the twentieth century with limits imposed by nature on the availability of vital raw materials. A nation that customarily met the problems posed by social inequality through territorial expansion and economic growth rather than the redistribution of wealth and commodities no longer had land frontiers at home or abroad to exploit or the easy prospect of an economic pie that could be endlessly enlarged. Whether or not Ameri-

519

cans could adjust to a new international economy in which other industrial nations competed aggressively for ever scarcer resources and in
which less-developed societies used their natural resources to combat big-
power domination remained problematic. Future decades would tell
whether or not the United States could build a decent society for all its
citizens as well as a productive economy. Yet the prospects for the
American future would flow ineluctably from the heritage of the past.

THE PERSISTENCE OF CLASS

As the nation prepared to cope with the problems of the seventies, the
persistence of social class and the tensions it caused could not be evaded.
Indeed, class divisions would reveal themselves with a renewed tenacity.

The unequalled economic growth of the post-World War II decades
had failed to ameliorate two of the worst aspects of United States society:
enormous disparities in the possession of income and wealth; and the
persistence of mass poverty. The prosperity of the mid-1960s that had
pulled millions of Americans above the poverty line gave way at the end
of the decade to a more erratic pattern of economic growth. In 1973 the
Census Bureau estimated that 24.5 million Americans lived below the
officially designated poverty level, which it set at $4725 for a nonfarm
family of four. More citizens now escaped poverty as a result of congressional action increasing social security benefits 10 percent for the elderly
after January 1, 1972 than because of any basic improvement in economic
conditions or in the distribution of income. Indeed, the payroll taxes
required to finance the increases in social security payments served to
reduce the disposable income available to the needy. Moreover, many of
the fiscal and monetary policies implemented by federal, state, and local
governments benefited the wealthy at the expense of the poor. A variety
of tax advantages, such as capital gains write-offs, depreciation allowances, and tax and interest payment deductions gave well-to-do citizens a
government bounty that dwarfed the pittance expended on welfare for
the poor. The combination of a private market economy and government
economic policies that favored the affluent created a system in which the
rich grew richer more rapidly than the poor advanced and in which
disparities in wealth widened instead of narrowing. Such a system contained within itself the seeds of a future social explosion.

Ironically, also, the economic factors that had played the largest role
in reducing poverty during the mid-1960s in the 1970s further strained
the United States economy. The economic boom and prosperity fueled by
the war in Vietnam set in motion a wave of uncheckable price inflation.
Because, among other reasons, the federal government refused to raise
taxes yet continued to spend beyond its income, the value of the dollar
crumbled at home and abroad. By the early 1970s, despite a variety of

Nixonian economic "game plans" (which included direct price and wage controls), price rises, especially for foodstuffs, outran wage increases for millions of citizens. In 1972 and 1973, as prices soared and social security payroll taxes climbed, workers had to cover increased family expenses with reduced take-home wages. Within two years, the value of the dollar fell by as much as 40 percent in relation to the German mark and the French franc. American soldiers stationed in Germany either had to send their families home or their wives out to work in the German economy. The cost of French wine began to exceed the pocketbooks of even middle-class families and the price of the Volkswagen—for over two decades the chief low-price competition for the American auto industry—soared above that of its major United States competitors (the Pinto and the Vega).

In order to restrain inflation and protect the dollar's value in the international economy, the federal government pursued monetary policies designed to tighten the supply of money, raise interest rates, and cool off the economy. The effect of such policies was to make the poor shoulder the burden of fighting inflation, a battle that brought more defeats than triumphs. As Washington struggled to curb inflation by accepting a high level of unemployment and by keeping minimum wages from rising too high, the poor, especially if they were nonwhites or female, found themselves neglected—and not benignly. More significantly, by 1975 as "stagflation" took its toll through price inflation and unemployment that exceeded 8 percent of the labor force, for the first time since the Johnson years the number of families the Census Bureau classified as living in poverty actually increased statistically. And more surprisingly, the bulk of the increase came among white families with two-parent households whose principal breadwinner, usually the husband, had been victimized by long-term unemployment.

Just as poverty persisted in the 1970s, so, too, did racialism and discrimination against women. While the number of poor whites defined as poverty stricken continued to decline, the number of poor blacks increased in 1972 from 7.4 to 7.7 million. The Census Bureau estimated that in 1972 only 9 percent of all white people lived in poverty compared to 33 percent of all blacks. Poverty also hit hardest among female-headed households, which in 1972 formed 43 percent of all poor families compared to 23 percent in 1959. Indeed, the entire increase in nonwhite poverty occurred in families headed by women who were unemployed or restricted to the lowest paying jobs in the economy. Millions of women who worked fulltime could not earn wages sufficient to support a family. At all levels of the economy, moreover, from managerial to menial work, compensation for females lagged far behind that for men. White or black, college educated or not, talented or unskilled, women consistently earned considerably less than comparable men doing the same job.

Nonwhite Americans, who had made substantial economic progress from 1964 to 1969, began once again to slip down the economic ladder beginning in 1971. The gap in median income between whites and blacks, which had diminished in the 1960s, widened again in the seventies. In 1972 black median income stood at $6,864 compared to $11,549 for whites, a cash difference of $4,685 contrasted to the differential of $3,577 that existed in 1968. Black unemployment rose to 10 percent, or double the 5 percent rate of white unemployment, and in 1972 black teenage unemployment soared to 33 percent and more. One-quarter of all black families contrasted to 5 percent of white families, received public assistance. The nonwhite infant mortality rate was still at least twice that of the white rate. An old American story repeated itself: blacks shared in the general economic growth, as did poorer whites, but at a consistently slower pace than whites. Neither a decade of civil rights protest and legislation nor half a decade of unequaled prosperity could alter persistent black-white economic disparities and the legacy of racialism.

Indeed, the racial confrontations that had plagued the South in the aftermath of the Supreme Court's 1954 *Brown* decision spread to the North during the 1970s. By 1974, in fact, southern schools were considerably more integrated than many northern institutions. Segregation persisted in the North in cities where racially-restricted neighborhoods and carefully drawn school attendance zones created all-black and all-white classrooms and in suburbs in which the cost of housing and restrictive real estate practices excluded most nonwhites. When in the late 1960s, federal courts began to rule that northern urban school districts were required under law to integrate their classrooms, white resistance mounted. Candidates ran for public office on platforms that stressed the neighborhood school and opposed the busing of children for the purpose of integration. Many northern congressman endorsed legislation, including in some cases a constitutional amendment, to outlaw "forced busing," and their proposals won the endorsements of Presidents Nixon and Ford. In Pontiac, Michigan, where a court order compelled the local school board to integrate classrooms, white parents kept their children home and some travelled to Washington to demonstrate against busing. A few fanatics among them even dynamited the city's school buses. And in Boston in the fall of 1974 white parents and their children also resisted a court-ordered school integration plan that necessitated busing. When whites and blacks subsequently fought violently in South Boston, Mayor Kevin White dispatched riot police, asked for federal marshals, and received from Massachusetts Governor Francis Sargeant unwanted state troops. Passions became so inflamed that Senator Edward Kennedy, a political idol among the state's Irish, was booed and pelted with tomatoes by a white, antibusing crowd in Boston. Ironically, as the South integrated with "all deliberate speed" after 1955, the North segregated its schools in haste. By 1977, two decades after the *Brown* decision, northern urban schools had become increasingly nonwhite in most large cities, while the suburbs with practically all-white schools rejected suggestions that attendance zones cross juridical boundaries in order to foster integration.

ECOLOGY AND SOCIAL CLASS

Questions about the quality of life came to the forefront in the 1970s. "Ecology" became the watchword of the affluent. Those citizens with inherited wealth anxiously observed the new middle class invade once reserved domains. Hitherto private baronial estates were subdivided into vacation and year-round resorts where middle-class neighborliness replaced upper-class solitude. Isolated stretches of ocean beach, secluded mountain lakes, and forest wilderness areas crumbled before the real-estate developer's bulldozers. As the "recreational vehicle" industry expanded, national parks and forests became as crowded in midsummer as Coney Island had once been. Some citizens began to wonder how much longer the United States could preserve its wilderness areas when hundreds of thousands of weekly visitors camped in those parks and forests amidst sanitary bathroom facilities, electric appliances, TV antennas, and overflowing garbage cans.

Consequently, during the 1970s the traditionally wealthy and the newly affluent both evinced exceptional interest in preserving and restoring the quality of American life. In order to enjoy their large boats, costly fishing gear, and lakeside cottages, they demanded cleaner water. Having purchased annually the millions of oversized automobiles that guzzled gas and poisoned the atmosphere, wealthy Americans called for cleaner air. Secure in their professions, wealth, and status, affluent citizens insisted that industry cease polluting streams, lakes, and the atmosphere, that the quality of life take precedence over economic growth.

The ecology movement, in short, beckoned Americans to look at the world around them in a new way. They were cautioned to think in terms of conservation, not exploitation; existence in harmony, not in conflict, with nature. Land was to be regulated and preserved by public authorities for posterity and not carelessly developed for the profit of real-estate speculators and building contractors. People were counseled to walk or bicycle, not to spew car fumes into the air. Ecology advocates suggested that industries that caused pollution should be shut down or compelled to invest in costly antipollution devices. It was suddenly realized that clean air and pure water, resources that had customarily been considered cost-free, came at a considerable social cost. In fact, the whole program of the ecologists carried a high price tag, in some cases so high that sharp conflict ensued concerning who should pay the price for a purified environment.

Those who already owned suburban or exurban homes on large lots could quite comfortably demand land control and zoning codes in order to restrain future real-estate development. And those who already possessed summer homes in the wilderness, mountains, or oceanfront might well struggle to preserve what remained of nature's original domain. Two-and three-car families might easily resort to the bicycle for exercise, and doctors, lawyers, and dentists might struggle to close industrial plants that polluted their communities.

But individuals who had struggled and scrimped to buy a home had substantial reservations about zoning regulations that put the cost of land beyond their means. Those workers, who in the past had been forced to rely on mass public transit or walk to work, did not believe that they should now be denied the private cars their labor and improved wages made possible. And those citizens who for the first time could afford summer vacations away from home preferred not to vacation at Coney Island for the sake of nature and posterity. Industrial workers, moreover, looked unkindly on suggestions that their employers close their businesses in order to clean the air and water for other citizens. Even if factory owners chose to invest in pollution-control devices rather than close down, workers wondered about who would ultimately pay the costs.

If high-paid workers saw in the ecology movement an effort to deny them the pleasures hitherto tasted by the wealthy, the poor perceived an even greater threat. If economic growth were restrained, resource exploitation limited, the prices of scarce items raised to conserve them, how would the poor escape their poverty? The crusade to improve the quality of American society, as personified by the Nixonian suburban middle and upper classes, implied the creation of a good life for those able to purchase it. For the poor, however, it suggested persistent unemployment and the pricing of many commodities, necessities as well as luxuries, beyond their pocketbooks.

"Ecology," in reality, as distinguished from the illusion, was a movement of, by, and for the affluent in which the economically less fortunate would receive only incidental benefits. Unless the United States redistributed income and wealth, ecological considerations necessarily would price the material aspects of the "American Dream" beyond the reach of millions of citizens.

THE "ENERGY CRISIS" AND A SOCIETY OF SCARCITY

Not only the poor, the nonwhite, and the female suffered economically from the inflation of the seventies. What came to be known as the "energy crisis" threatened the material comforts of even affluent citizens. The declining international value of the dollar and domestic ecological pressures precipitated in the winter of 1973–1974 a shortage of the fuels needed to run the economy, heat our homes, and propel our automobiles. As Western Europe and Japan prospered, international demand for oil and natural gas outran supply. The United States could no longer provide for its energy needs from domestic production (over 30 percent of all fuel oil had to be imported) and had to compete against stronger currencies in the international market—an economic reality that by 1973 caused shortages in heating oil, natural gas, and motor fuel, steeply rising domestic prices for the scarce resources, and the prospect of a more serious, permanent long-term fuel shortage. The outbreak of a fourth Arab-Israeli war in the Mideast in the fall of 1973 and a subsequent reduction in the amounts of oil the Arab nations supplied to the Western world exacerbated the "energy crisis."

In the aftermath of the war, the major Mideast producers as well as their associates in the Organization of Petroleum Exporting Countries (OPEC) more than quadrupled the price of crude oil. And again in 1975 and in December 1976 OPEC nations increased oil prices, although by the latter date fissures began to appear in the hitherto solid bloc of oil-producing nations. Some economists suggested that by 1980 the Arab oil states, as a result of higher prices for their primary product and the fuel's essential role in industrial development, would command the vast bulk of the nonsocialist world's currency reserves.

In other times coal might have provided an economic, feasible alternative source of energy. But in the 1970s the United States' superabundant domestic supply of coal (three to four centuries' amount of reserves) conflicted with national concern about ecology. The cheapest, most productive means of obtaining coal—strip mining—was also ecologically the most destructive, turning parts of the country where it was used extensively into a lunar landscape. (Furthermore, only about 3 percent of the nation's coal reserves were located in areas that could be stripped.) Not only did increased coal mining threaten to damage the landscape but the type of coal most readily available, high in sulphur content, polluted the atmosphere when burned. The United States in 1977 was decades behind England, West Germany, and other European nations in the application of efficient coalmining and coal-burning technology.

If the "energy crisis" of the 1970s proved real and permanent, Americans would have to learn to tolerate homes that would be cooler in winter and warmer in summer, to drive smaller cars less frequently or use mass public transit more often, and to pay much more for the scarce fuels they still consumed.

In almost all aspects of American life the 1970s raised the specter of abundance giving way to scarcity. Just as Americans faced the ultimate prospect of fewer, smaller cars, they had to consider the possibility of less commodious and fewer private homes. America's lumber industry simply could not satisfy the needs of the domestic home-building industry and the demands of the insatiable Japanese lumber market without denuding the national forests. Considering ecological pressures, lumber, like fuel, seemed a resource destined to be in short supply.

Most unexpectedly in the 1970s, foodstuffs, whose abundance and cheapness were long taken for granted by Americans, became a scarce and costly commodity. Again, prosperity in other nations (as well as global population growth) increased the international demand for foodstuffs, and stronger currencies enabled foreign buyers to outbid Americans for our own farm produce. As Russians purchased American wheat, Japanese consumed American soybeans, and all industrial societies demanded more American beef, supermarket prices in the United States soared, and many Americans, especially the elderly and the poor, could no longer afford beef in their regular diets.

Here, too, concern for ecology conflicted potentially with the need for an adequate supply of foodstuffs. Chemical fertilizers, which were responsible for a considerable share of the post-World War II growth in agricultural productivity, in many cases polluted our water supply, threatening the health of wildlife and human life. If ecological factors restricted the use of fertilizers and pesticides, agricultural productivity might be cut back at precisely the moment that global demand for foodstuffs reached unprecedented levels. In that case the result could be a food shortage as perilous as the fuel shortage—and the prospect of hungry stomachs was much more serious than empty oil furnaces and gas tanks. Moreover, the fuel shortage itself threatened to burden American agriculture, which was an energy-intensive enterprise dependent on gas and oil to run its cultivating and processing machines as well as on fertilizers that were petroleum-based products. Such were the unexpected interrelationships of a complex modern economy.

THE METROPOLITAN PARADOX

Paradox enveloped all aspects of society in the 1970s. As dissatisfaction with cities and industrial life grew apace, the United States became more urbanized and industrialized than ever. Over 75 percent of Americans resided in metropolitan areas, and despite considerable rhetoric extolling the advantages of nature, rural society continued its inexorable decline. That last stronghold of American agrarianism—the Old South—collapsed before the inroads of industry. Between 1950 and 1972, agricultural employment in the eleven former Confederate states declined from 3.8 million to 2.4 million, and factory employment rose from 1.5 million to 4.4 million. Factories invaded a once totally rural landscape, as industrialists sought cheaper labor, less expensive land, and lower taxes. The Old South raced to catch up with the remainder of the nation and voluntarily sacrificed its slower, more natural rural pace of life to the insistent time pressures of modern industrial technology. Southerners, much as other Americans had done in the past, chose money before leisure, factory discipline over rural rhythms.

During the 1970s, after more than a decade of controversy about the urban crisis and a plethora of experiments in urban renewal, American cities appeared less habitable than ever. The white middle class kept up its headlong flight to suburbia, and in the 1970s "swinging singles" joined the more respectable family-style suburbanites. Some New York City neighborhoods, once culturally rich and vital ethnic communities, resembled targets of a saturation air raid.

Worse than the physical decay that infected poorer neighborhoods was the contagious fear that stalked city streets. The poor, and the nonwhite among them in particular, had always lived with the reality of random violence—whiskey-induced Saturday night brawls, teenage gang fights, and endemic crime traditionally had figured prominently in working-class ethnic neighborhoods. In this respect black ghettoes scarcely differed from the white immigrant communities that preceded them. By the 1970s, however, past traditions of lower-class crime seemed pale in comparison to the new techniques of violence. Modern technology rendered criminals more mobile and violence more deadly. The ready availability of weapons—from the crudest handgun to the most complex automatic rifle—produced a surfeit of potential killers. In a single year more homicides occurred in New York City than in all of Great Britain, and New York, in proportion to its total population, was scarcely the most homicidal community in the United States (Detroit, the leader, had a homicide rate more than double that of New York in a population less than one-third the size of New York City's) .

Life in the American city became a real as well as a metaphorical war for many citizens. Television news programs brought domestic and foreign violence into the living room; the most popular weekly video series featured private eyes and public cops chasing criminals and themselves causing mayhem; and movies offered superscreen images of the most technologically advanced and brutal forms of murder. At night, in the typical urban resident's mind, if not in statistical fact, city streets seemed safer for muggers than for ordinary pedestrians, and criminals lurked in apartment house vestibules, stairways, and elevators. "I'm not exaggerating when I say that tenants are living under conditions of virtual house arrest," commented one resident of a New York City luxury apartment complex "We are afraid to walk around after daylight has dimmed. No one feels completely safe."

Those who felt least safe in the cities or lacked intrinsic economic and cultural links to urban life fled to the suburbs. But the more people moved to suburbia, the more it resembled the central city in significant aspects. Apartment houses, including high rises, office buildings, and factories appeared in the suburbs. Suburban traffic jams became as ghastly as city ones and sometimes worse, for the suburbs lacked even the rudimentary and rundown mass transit systems that most large cities still operated. In many instances, moreover, crime joined the suburban flight, as criminals (burglars if not muggers) pursued their affluent prey.

In the long run, migration to suburbia was not a true escape, for the city's problems derived from human, not locational factors. Thus, as the suburbs became the new population centers, they inherited many hitherto singularly urban problems. In the 1970s, then, one had to question whether the quality of suburban life could be preserved while the central cities were sacrificed. That seemed unlikely, for in a densely populated metropolitan society interdependence among the parts appeared the rule, and one unhealthy sector threatened to infect the remainder. Rather than facing the prospect of saving, or renewing, its cities alone, the United States instead had to tie cities, suburbs, exurbs, and rural countryside tightly together into a viable and satisfying system of human existence.

WORK AND ITS DISCONTENTS

Not only did Americans grow increasingly dissatisfied with the metropolitan existence the vast majority of them had chosen by the 1970s, but larger number of citizens began to question the traditional work ethic. Social analysts discovered what they labeled the "blue-collar blues," a mental condition that flowed directly from work and its discontents. Especially among younger workers, absenteeism, drugs, alcohol, and disobedience to rules became commonplace. For the first time since the labor upheaval of the 1930s, industrial workers openly rebelled against the pace and structure of work. In Lordstown, Ohio, young workers at the General Motors Vega assembly plant struck in 1972 to slow down the pace of the assembly line and to win more autonomy for workers within the factory. Union-management negotiations throughout the economy began to focus more on work rules, safety standards, and early retirement than on higher hourly wages. For those too young for even early retirement and unable to endure the insistent pressures of mass-production labor, drugs and alcohol provided the easiest escape. On many an auto assembly line only a "stoned" worker seemed able to confront the day's work.

White-collar workers and lesser professionals sang their own version of the work blues. They, too, felt discontented with vocations that offered little intrinsic satisfaction and that infringed on their personal autonomy. Like industrial workers, they rebelled against rules set by their superiors and demanded more freedom and variety in their work. So-called professionals—teachers, nurses, interns, residents, and a variety of public servants—acted like traditional trade union members, and in many cases transformed hitherto ineffective professional associations into potent labor unions. Indeed, white-collar workers and public employees became in the 1960s and 1970s the most rapidly expanding sector of the labor movement. The AFSCME (American Federation of State, County, and Municipal Employees) became one of the largest unions in the AFL–CIO, and the United Federation of Teachers (UFT) developed into one of the most powerful unions in New York City and State. As teachers, nurses, and civil servants unions (including police and fire-fighters) won higher wages and improved fringe benefits, they, too, moved on to demand more effective job control.

Employers, however, proved quite aware of the new consciousness that stirred American workers. Some companies responded to changed work-place attitudes by allowing their employees to rotate among different work assignments, encouraging them also to offer suggestions for improved efficiency, and in a few instances, even granting workers the right to complete the day's task or production quota in their own way. Other companies, rather than surrendering vital aspects of managerial authority, experimented with longer daily work shifts that promised those employees able to endure a twelve-hour day the prospect of a three- or four-day weekend.

Whether Americans had really turned away from the work ethic and preferred leisure to money, autonomy at work to additional consumer goods, remained debatable. It also seemed questionable whether workers could have complete control over their jobs in a society and an economy that remained capitalistic and hierarchical in structure. In other words, to grant workers full control over in-plant assignments, production methods, and rules would be to create a nonmanagerial, noncapitalist society. That, however, did not appear to be a high priority item on the American agenda for the 1970s.

THE GLOBAL MILIEU

Changes in the structure of the American society and economy in the 1970s, however, would necessarily be constrained by the realities of inter- national economic competition. In the 1970s, unlike in the 1950s, the United States economy no longer reigned supreme within the nonsocialist world. While the dollar might still speak loudly at home (especially during elections), it only whispered abroad. As the German, Japanese, French, and even some socialist economies proved more productive than that of the United States, American workers could not simply choose leisure in preference to higher wages. The American worker now had to work harder and longer to compete with foreign workers for bread, beef, poultry, fuel, and clothing. Indeed, a real possibility existed that the stringency of global economic competition would bring about an intensi- fication of work discipline in America, not the widening of workers' control or individual job autonomy.

The direction that the American society and economy would choose for the future, then, was by the 1970s inextricably linked to changes in the global economic environment. Our largest corporations, in fact, were already an integral part of multinational industrial empires whose domains transcended the authority of national states and national trade unions. In the 1970s corporation executives acted on an international economic stage, meeting and dealing regularly with their managerial counterparts in socialist and nonsocialist states. Could American workers learn to do the same with their foreign brothers and sisters? Only the future would tell.

As Americans looked ahead from the 1970s to the future, one had to wonder if the words of social commentator Herbert von Borch—that

"American society possesses virtually inexhaustible capacities for self-redress"—still rang true. In the past, Americans had proved heedless about exhausting land and natural resources. Now living on a globe in which land, water, fuel, and the air itself had become quite exhaustible, could the American spirit remain inexhaustible? Perhaps! But only, it might be argued, if the national spirit became less materialistic and more egalitarian.

The American spirit, as personified by Henry Luce, who gave us the "American Century," proved less than prophetic and an enormous burden as well. Compared to the British century, which stretched from 1815 to 1914, the "American Century" had a half life. By the 1970s, the United States' global dominance was a relic of the past and Americans had yet to show that a continental society could adjust as smoothly to loss of empire as an island-nation could—that improving the quality of life at home for all citizens could become as important as maintaining overseas hegemony. If Americans, individually and collectively, could make the choice to renounce empire and to distribute the fruits of labor more equally, then, perhaps, their society might indeed possess "virtually inexhaustible capacities for self-redress."

SELECTED BIBLIOGRAPHY FOR SECTION IX

Despite the recency of the Nixon administration, more is known about its domestic policies than for some previous administrations—the congressional investigations and judicial proceedings resulted in the publication of an extensive literature. At present, most published accounts are journalistic. The best include GARY WILLS, *Nixon Agonistes* (1969) *; ROWLAND EVANS and ROBERT D. NOVACK, *Nixon in the White House: The Frustration of Power* (1971) *; three books by JOHN OSBORNE, *The Nixon Watch* (1970), *The Second Year of the Nixon Watch* (1971), and *The Third Year of the Nixon Watch* (1972); KEVIN PHILLIPS, *The Emerging Republican Majority* (1969); BRUCE MAZLISH, *In Search of Nixon* (1972); and LEONARD SILK, *Nixonomics* (1972). For more serious studies of his presidency, see ALONZO HAMBY, *The Imperial Years* (1976); LAWRENCE WITTNER, *Cold War America* (1974) *; and DANIEL PATRICK MOYNIHAN, *The Politics of a Guaranteed Income* (1973). For suppression of domestic dissent and internal surveillance techniques, read MORTON HALPERIN et al., *The Lawless State* (1976)*; SANFORD UNGAR, *FBI* (1975)*; DAVID WISE, *The American Police State* (1976); NORMAN DORSEN and STEPHEN GILLERS, eds., *None of Your Business* (1975) *; and RAOUL BERGER, *Executive Privilege* (1974).* Watergate and the fall of Richard Nixon can best be followed in the work of two young reporters, BOB WOODWARD and CARL BERNSTEIN, who wrote *All the President's Men*

* Available in paperback.

(1974) * and *The Final Days* (1975) *, as well as in THEODORE H. WHITE, *Breach of Faith: The Fall of Richard Nixon* (1975),* *The Watergate Hearings* (1973),* *The White House Transcripts* (1974),* and *The End of a Presidency* (1974).* Gerald Ford's former press secretary has written a sympathetic but superficial account of Ford's political career that offers little sense of the Ford Administration's policies; see JERALD terHORST, *Gerald Ford and the Future of the Presidency* (1974).

For American foreign policy during the Nixon and Ford Years, see HARLAND B. MOULTON, *From Superiority to Parity: The United States and the Strategic Arms Race, 1961–1971* (1972); ROBERT E. OSGOOD et al., *Retreat from Empire? The First Nixon Administration* (1973) *; HENRY BRANDON, *The Retreat of American Power* (1973) *; DAVID LANDAU, *The Uses of Power* (1974) *; and LLOYD C. GARDNER, ed., *The Great Nixon Turnaround: America's New Foreign Policy in the Post-Liberal Era* (1973).*

For accounts of the problems of multinational corporations and of the raping of the earth's environment, read FRANK GRAHAM, JR., *Since Silent Spring* (1970) *; BARRY COMMONER, *The Closing Circle* (1971) *; EMMA ROTHSCHILD, *Paradise Lost: The Decline of the Auto-Industrial Age* (1973) *; and RICHARD J. BARNET and RONALD MULLER, *Global Reach: The Power of the Multinational Corporations* (1974).* On the future of America, see ALVIN TOFFLER, *Future Shock* (1971) *; ROBERT HEILBRONER, *An Inquiry into the Human Prospect* (1975) *; and two fictional jeremiads, RAY BRADBURY, *Farenheit 451* (1972) * and JOSEPH HELLER, *Something Happened* (1975).*

Appendix Tables

POPULATION: WHITE, NONWHITE, URBAN, AND RURAL
(in thousands)

	1900	1920	1930	1940	1960*	1970*
Total Population	76,094	106,461	123,077	132,122	180,671	204,879
White Population	66,900	95,510	110,559	118,629	160,023	179,491
Percent of Total	88	90	90	90	89	88
Nonwhite Population	9,194	10,951	12,518	13,494	20,648	25,387
Percent of Total	12	10	10	10	11	12
Urban Population	30,160	54,158	68,955	74,424	125,269	149,325
Percent of Total	40	51	56	57	70	74
Rural Population	45,835	51,553	53,820	57,246	54,054	53,887
Percent of Total	60	49	44	43	30	26

* Includes Alaska and Hawaii. All statistics are from: *Bicentennial Edition, Historical Statistics of the United States, Colonial Times to 1970* (Washington, D.C.: Government Printing Office, 1975).

PERCENT ILLITERATE IN POPULATION BY RACE*

	1900	1920	1930	1940	1959	1969
Total	10.7	6.0	4.3	2.9	2.2	1.0
White	6.2	4.0	3.0	2.0	1.6	0.7
Nonwhite (based only on Negro population)	44.5	23.0	16.4	11.5	7.5	3.6

* Figures for 1900 through 1940 are for population 10 years old and over; figures for 1959 and 1969 are for population 14 years old and over.

HIGH SCHOOL GRADUATES BY SEX
(in thousands, except % column)

	1900	1920	1930	1940	1960	1970
Total Number	95	312	667	1,222	1,864	2,906
Percent of Persons 17 Years Old	6.3	16.3	28.8	49.0	63.4	75.6
Male	38	124	300	579	898	1,439
Female	57	188	367	643	966	1,467

BIRTH RATE: Total for Women 15–44 Years Old By Race
(based on live births per 1000 population)

	1900	1920	1930	1940	1960	1970
Total	NA	117.9	89.2	79.9	118.0	87.9
White	130.0	115.4	87.1	77.1	113.2	84.1
Nonwhite	NA	137.5	105.9	102.4	153.6	113.0

LIFE EXPECTANCY (in Years) for White and Nonwhite
(prior to 1929, for death-registration area only)

	1900	1920	1930	1940	1960	1970
Total: Both Sexes	47.3	54.1	59.7	62.9	69.7	70.9
White	47.6	54.9	61.4	64.2	70.6	71.7
Nonwhite	33.0	45.3	48.1	53.1	63.6	65.3

TOTAL DEGREES CONFERRED

	1900	1920	1930	1940	1960*	1970*
Total Bachelor's or First Professional Degree	27,410	48,622	122,484	186,500	389,183	827,234

* Includes Alaska and Hawaii.

FEDERAL GOVERNMENT EXPENDITURES FOR NATIONAL DEFENSE AND INTERNATIONAL RELATIONS
(in millions of dollars)

	1902	1922	1932	1940	1960	1970
Total	165	875	721	1,590	48,922	84,253
Military Services only	162	864	702	1,567	41,340	76,550

TRADE UNION MEMBERSHIP
(in thousands)

	1900	1920	1930	1940	1960*	1970*
Union Membership	868	5,048	3,401	8,717	17,049	19,381
Percent of Total Labor Force	3	12	6.8	15.5	23.6	22.6
Total Nonagricultural Employment	18,691	30,948	29,424	32,376	54,234	70,644
Union Membership as Percent of Total Nonagricultural Employment	5	16	11.6	26.9	31.4	27.4

* Includes Alaska and Hawaii.

MOTOR VEHICLE REGISTRATION
(in thousands; includes military vehicles)

	1900	1920	1930	1940	1960	1970
Total	8.0	9,239.1	26,749.8	32,453.2	73,868.6	108,407.3
Automobiles	8.0	8,131.5	23,034.7	27,465.8	61,682.3	89,279.8
Buses	NA	NA	40.5	101.1	272.1	379.0
Trucks	NA	1,107.6	3,674.5	4.886.2	11,914.2	18,748.4

GROSS NATIONAL PRODUCT (GNP) IN CURRENT DOLLARS

	1900	1920	1930	1940	1960*	1970*
Total (Bil. Dol.)	18.7	91.5	90.4	99.7	503.7	977.1
Per Capita (Dollars)	246	860	734	754	2,788	4,808

* 1960 includes Alaska and Hawaii.

Index

Note: (T) following page reference denotes Table.